THE HANDBOOK OF PERSON-CENTRED PSYCHOTHERAPY AND COUNSELLING

To Miraj.

In solidarity

Maureen

The Handbook of Person-Centred Psychotherapy and Counselling

Edited by

Mick Cooper, Maureen O'Hara,
Peter F. Schmid and Gill Wyatt

First published 2007 by
PALGRAVE MACMILLAN
Houndmills, Basingstoke, Hampshire RG21 6XS and
175 Fifth Avenue, New York, N.Y. 10010
Companies and representatives throughout the world

PALGRAVE MACMILLAN is the global academic imprint of the Palgrave Macmillan division of St. Martin's Press, LLC and of Palgrave Macmillan Ltd. Macmillan® is a registered trademark in the United States, United Kingdom and other countries. Palgrave is a registered trademark in the European Union and other countries.

ISBN-13: 978-1-4039-4512-9 paperback
ISBN-10: 1-4039-4512-8 paperback
ISBN-13: 978-0-230-53526-8 hardback
ISBN-10: 0-230-53526-7 hardback

This book is printed on paper suitable for recycling and made from fully managed and sustained forest sources. Logging, pulping and manufacturing processes are expected to conform to the environmental regulations of the country of origin.

A catalogue record for this book is available from the British Library.

A catalog record for this book is available from the Library of Congress.

10 9 8 7 6 5 4 3 2 1
16 15 14 13 12 11 10 09 08 07

Printed in China

Contents

       Keith Tudor

       Freedom to learn   380
       Freedom to train   384

       Resources   390
       Roelf J. Takens

       National organizations   390
       International cooperation   390
       Training and accreditation in European countries   396
       Internet addresses   399

       Index of persons   401
       Subject index   407

Tables and Figures

Tables

Figures

Notes on Contributors

The editors

Mick Cooper, PhD, is a professor of counselling at the University of Strathclyde and a UKCP-registered existential psychotherapist, whose work is informed by person-centred, existential, interpersonal and postmodern modalities. He is co-author, with Dave Mearns, of *Working at Relational Depth in Counselling and Psychotherapy* (Sage, 2005), author of *Existential Therapies* (Sage, 2003), and has written numerous papers and book chapters on person-centred, existential and self-pluralistic approaches to counselling and psychotherapy. Mick lives in Glasgow with his partner and their children.

Maureen O'Hara, PhD, is Chair of the Department of Psychology at National University in La Jolla, California. She formerly served as President and Executive Vice President of Saybrook Graduate School in San Francisco, California and is a psychologist, organizational consultant and futurist. She has trained therapists and counsellors worldwide and worked for many years with Carl Rogers and others in developing large-group person-centred processes. Maureen is a 'big picture' observer. Her current preoccupations include the impact of cultural shifts on the evolution of consciousness, the emergence of a new post-enlightenment global worldview, and what psychotherapists can contribute. Maureen is a fellow of the World Academy of Arts and Sciences, and fellow of the American Psychological Association.

Peter F. Schmid, Univ.Doz. HSProf. Mag. Dr, works at the University of Graz, the Sigmund Freud University and the Institute for Person-Centred Studies in

Vienna, Austria. He is a part-time faculty member of Saybrook Graduate School, San Francisco, and founder of person-centred training in Austria and co-founder of the World Association (WAPCEPC) and the European Network (NEAPCEPC). Peter works as a psychotherapist and is author and co-editor of 14 books and numerous publications and co-editor of the international journals *Person-Centred and Experiential Psychotherapies* and *PERSON*. His main concern is with the anthropological and epistemological foundations of person-centred therapy and the development of psychotherapy towards a dialogical understanding.

Gill Wyatt works as a psychotherapist, supervisor, facilitator and consultant. She has managed, designed and tutored on training courses at postgraduate and undergraduate levels for 20 years and was the director of Person-centred Connections. She is the series editor of Rogers' *Therapeutic Conditions: Evolution, Theory and Practice* (PCCS Books). Her current research involves developing a participative/emergent perspective to person-centred theory and practice, the victim/oppressor dynamic, and the role of dialogue in facilitating new emerging levels of organization within groups.

The contributors

Gay (Swenson) Barfield, PhD, Lic. MFT, was a fellow of Centre for Studies of the Person for nearly 30 year where she created one of the first women's centres in San Diego and the Living Now Institute. With Carl R. Rogers she directed the Carl Rogers Institute for Peace, a project applying person-centred principles to real and potential crisis situations. Currently semi-retired, she continues to offer workshops internationally and mentor young therapists, and is writing about her experiences over the past 40 years as a 'gatherer', social activist and stubborn idealist.

Godfrey (Goff) Barrett-Lennard is Honourary Fellow in Psychology at Murdoch University in Perth, Australia. He studied with Carl Rogers at the University of Chicago (PhD, 1959) in a career that has combined academic affiliations and practice. His contribution includes original research and writing over a 50-year span. Author of *Carl Rogers' Helping System: journey and substance* (Sage, 1998), his present perspective is distilled in *Relationship at the Centre: healing in a troubled world* (Whurr/Wiley, 2005).

Arthur C. Bohart, PhD, is currently affiliated with Saybrook Graduate School and Research Centre in San Francisco, California. He is co-author of *How Clients Make Therapy Work: the process of active self-healing* (American Psychological Association, 1999), co-author of *Foundations of Clinical and Counselling Psychology* (Waveland Press, 2006), and co-editor of *Empathy Reconsidered* (American Psychological Association, 1997), as well as numerous articles.

Jerold D. Bozarth, PhD, learned client-centred therapy from working with chronic psychotic, hospitalized clients. He has published over 300 articles and book chapters and three books, and has consulted with person-centred training programmes in Austria, Brazil, Czech Republic, England, Portugal and Slovakia. He is Professor Emeritus of the University of Georgia and a member of the Golden Pantry Coffee Club.

Lorna Carrick is a lecturer at the University of Strathclyde. She is a UKRC-registered psychotherapist with more than 12 years experience working in the person-centred approach as a therapist, supervisor and developer. She is a founder member of one of the first free person-centred counselling services in Scotland and has a deep commitment to the development of person-centred working in a wide range of settings. Lorna is currently undertaking an MSc on counsellor's experiences of working with clients in crisis.

Jeffrey H.D. Cornelius-White, PsyD, is Assistant Professor of Counselling at Missouri State University, Editor of *The Person-Centred Journal* and Associate Editor of the *Journal for Border Educational Research*. Jeff values being a family member, and externed at the Chicago Counselling Centre and Pre-Therapy Clinic. He is a social justice advocate and the author of several works in person-centred education, including a meta-analysis. Jeff likes to bike, swim, play, read, write, listen, talk and be a part of nature.

Robert Elliott is Professor of Counselling at the University of Strathclyde. He has served as co-editor of *Psychotherapy Research* and *Person-Centred and Experiential Psychotherapies*, and also as President of the Society for Psychotherapy Research. He is co-author of *Facilitating Emotional Change* (1993), *Research Methods for Clinical Psychology* (1994; 2002), and *Learning Emotion-Focused Psychotherapy* (2004).

Jobst Finke is a specialist in psychiatry, neurology and psychotherapy, an instructor of GwG, ÄGG and at the psychiatric hospital of the University of Duisburg-Essen. His fields of work include empirical research in person-centred therapy, theory and practice of therapeutic methods of the person-centred approach. He also has an interest in the person-centred approach towards various disorders, and concepts of the relationship in different psychotherapeutic schools.

Elizabeth Schmitt Freire is a Brazilian psychologist with an MSc in clinical psychology and a PhD in developmental psychology at Universidade Federal do Rio Grande do Sul (Porto Alegre, Brazil). She is a person-centred therapist and supervisor, and has been the co-ordinator of the person-centred training programme of the Institute Delphos in Brazil. Currently she is residing in Scotland where she works as tutor and researcher at the University of Strathclyde.

Lila Z. Hakim, MA, is a doctoral candidate in clinical psychology at York University, Toronto, Canada. A member of the York Psychotherapy Research Group, her research focuses on therapists' personal and professional contributions to the therapeutic process. Ms Hakim is also a member of the Society for Psychotherapy Research and is involved in an international study of the development of psychotherapists. She currently practises as an experiential therapist at various rehabilitation and mental health centres.

Valerie Henderson was assistant to Carl Rogers for 14 years and is a former director of the Center for Studies of the Person (CSP). She co-edited (with Kirschenbaum) *The Carl Rogers Reader* and *Carl Rogers: Dialogues*, both published by Houghton Mifflin in 1989. She has served as facilitator of numerous cross-cultural workshops and training programmes in the person-centred approach throughout Europe and on the staff of CSP's peace project in Austria and Costa Rica. She served as director of adult services at the Center for Attitudinal Healing in California and is now semi-retired.

Martha Johns, MD, MPH, has practised and taught a person-centred approach to health care for more than 25 years. In addition to patient care, she teaches clinician–patient communication and has done extensive medical writing and editing. She is currently Director of Clinical and Outreach Services for Wardenburg Health Centre at the University of Colorado at Boulder.

Dr Martin van Kalmthout is a person-centred therapist in private practice. He has published widely on the history and foundations of psychotherapy in general and person-centred therapy in particular. His special interest is in person-centred therapy as a practical philosophy of living and the consequences of that view for the future of person-centred therapy.

Suzanne Keys works as a psychotherapist, supervisor and trainer in London, France and Martinique. She edited *Idiosyncratic Person-Centred Therapy: from the personal to the universal* (PCCS Books, 2003) and has written about her training, human rights, ethics, politics, love, prayer and therapy. She is currently interested in the interconnections between the political, spiritual, sexual and therapeutic. She is also curious about how becoming a mother for the first time affects it all.

Colin Lago was Director of the Counselling Service at the University of Sheffield from 1987 to 2003. He now works as an independent counsellor, trainer, supervisor and consultant. He is a fellow of BACP, an accredited counsellor and trainer and UKRC-registered practitioner. He is a visiting lecturer to the Universities of East Anglia and Strathclyde. Deeply committed to 'transcultural concerns' he has had articles, videos and books published on the subject. These publications include: *Race, Culture and Counselling* (2nd edition 2005), *Carl Rogers Counsels a Black Client* (with Roy Moodley and Anissa Talahite) and *Anti Discriminatory Counselling* (with Barbara Smith.)

Elke Lambers was trained in Holland as a clinical psychologist and client-centred therapist and has a private practice as a person-centred therapist, supervisor and trainer. She has written about 'Supervision in person-centred therapy' in *Person-Centred Therapy Today* (Mearns and Thorne, Sage, 2000). Her other main interest is in developing an understanding of psychopathology from a person-centred perspective. She is currently Chair of the Board of the World Association for Person-Centred and Experiential Psychotherapy and Counselling.

Charles J. O'Leary, PhD, LMFT, is the author of *Counselling Couples and Families: a person-centred approach.* He teaches graduate students and offers workshops throughout the United States, Great Britain, Ireland and Italy. Charles was a member of the Centre for Studies of the Person for 20 years, studying there with Carl Rogers. In addition to his couples and family therapy practice in Denver and Arvada, Colorado, he is working on his second book, *Finding A Better Way To Feel Sorry For Yourself.*

Gillian Proctor, DClin.Psych, is a clinical psychologist currently working in the mental health therapy team of North Bradford PCT and honorary research fellow with the Centre for Citizenship and Community Mental Health, Bradford University, UK. Gillian is author of *The Dynamics of Power in Counselling and Therapy: ethics, politics and practice* (PCCS 2002), co-editor of *Encountering Feminism* (PCCS, 2004) and co-editor of *Politicing the Person-centred Approach: an agenda for social change* (PCCS, 2006).

Dr Garry Prouty is Director of the Pre-Therapy International Network and a scientific associate of the American Academy of Psychoanalysis and Dynamic Psychiatry. He was trained in person-centred/experiential psychotherapy by Eugene Gendlin and developed his own therapeutic approach at clinics and hospitals dealing with psychotic and retarded clients. He is the author of *Theoretical Evolutions in Person-Centred/Experiential Therapy: applications to schizophrenic and retarded psychoses* as well as co-author of the German text *Prae-Therapie.*

Natalie Rogers, PhD, REAT, is an expressive arts therapy pioneer. She founded the Person-Centred Expressive Therapy Institute in California, leads training sessions in the Americas and abroad, and teaches an expressive arts certificate programme at Saybrook Graduate School. In 1998 she received the first Lifetime Achievement Award by the International Expressive Arts Therapy Association. Website: www.nrogers.com

Pete Sanders worked as a counsellor, trainer and supervisor for almost 30 years before eventually retiring in 2003 to concentrate on developing the list of person-centred books at PCCS Books, where he is co-director with his wife Maggie. He is interested in working with anyone who is committed to the demedicalization of distress, developing a psychosocial person-centred practice and the intersection between politics and therapy.

Roelf J. Takens, PhD, is Associate Professor in Clinical Psychology at the Vrije Universiteit in Amsterdam and Director of the Amsterdam Postgraduate

Programme in Clinical Psychology. He is co-author of *Klärungsprozesse in der Psychotherapie* (with Rainer Sachse, 2004), and past-president of the Network of European Associations for Person-Centred and Experiential Psychotherapy and Counselling. Alongside his academic work, Roelf is a person-centred psychotherapist in private practice.

Ludwig Teusch is a professor of psychiatry and psychotherapy at the University of Duisburg-Essen. He is Medical Director of the Protestant Hospital (Ev. Krankenhaus) Castrop-Rauxel. His empirical research on person-centred treatment includes the development of manuals and controlled clinical trials on anxiety disorders and depression in comparison with behaviour therapy and pharmacotherapy.

Shaké G. Toukmanian, PhD, is Senior Scholar and Professor Emerita of Psychology at York University, Toronto, Canada. She has extensive experience in teaching, supervision and research in person-centred and experiential psychotherapies. Her research focuses on using relevant concepts from cognitive science for the study of change processes in psychotherapy. She has authored/co-authored several book chapters and research articles, and is the co-editor of *Psychotherapy Process Research: Paradigmatic and Narrative Approaches* (Sage, 1992).

Keith Tudor is a registered psychotherapist, group psychotherapist and facilitator, and a director of Temenos, Sheffield, and its postgraduate/MSc course in person-centred psychotherapy and counselling. He is a widely published author with over 60 papers and seven books to his name. He is on the editorial advisory board of three international journals, including *Person-Centred and Experiential Psychotherapies*, is the series editor of *Advancing Theory in Therapy* (Routledge) and is an honorary fellow in the School of Health, Liverpool John Moores University.

Dion Van Werde has studied at the Catholic University of Leuven. He is ward psychologist on a person-centred ward for treating people suffering psychotic functioning, and practises there a multidisciplinary contact milieu along the lines of Prouty's Pre-Therapy. He is coordinator and trainer of the Pre-Therapy International Network and co-authored with Prouty and Pörtner *Prae-Therapie*, now translated into four languages. Dion serves on the editorial advisory board of the journal *Person-Centred and Experiential Psychotherapies*.

Margaret S. Warner, PhD, has written extensively on person-centred theory in relation to difficult client process. She is currently a professor at the Illinois School of Professional Psychology, where she helped develop a Minor and a Certificate in client-centred and experiential psychology in collaboration with other person-centred faculty members. She completed her doctorate at the University of Chicago and trained in client-centred therapy at the Chicago Counselling Centre.

Richard Worsley has worked as a priest, a counsellor trainer, and now as a university counsellor. He has published books and articles on process orientation, and on the philosophy and spirituality of therapy. Richard has an abiding interest in the work of Martin Buber and Emmanuel Levinas. Being with staff and students is crucial for him to reflect on practice and the therapeutic relationship.

Preface

*Mick Cooper, Maureen O'Hara,
Peter F. Schmid and Gill Wyatt*

These are exciting times for the field of person-centred psychotherapy and counselling. Over the last few years, we have witnessed major developments in our approach: an increasing in-depth exploration of its foundations and its underlying philosophy, a rapid diversification – with the emergence of such forms as 'classical', 'dialogical' and 'Pre-Therapy' – and cross-fertilization with related orientations like existential and experiential therapies. We are witnessing a growing intensity of international collaboration and networking through the establishment of the World Association for Person-Centred and Experiential Psychotherapy and Counseling (WAPCEPC) and its journal, *Person-Centred and Experiential Psychotherapies*. Moreover, where once the focus of person-centred writings was primarily on therapeutic practice, we are seeing a rapidly expanding interest in such fields as anthropology and epistemology, developmental psychology, organizational transformation, peace studies, political theory and psychotherapeutic research, with person-centred writers and therapists at the forefront of many of these fields.

The person-centred approach to psychotherapy and counselling, increasingly one of the best empirically supported approaches in the realm of therapy, today has a depth and enjoys a variety of theoretical explanatory models that would make it the envy of many other therapeutic disciplines. In fact, the paradigm-change provoked by person-centred thinkers, from the frame of 'treatment of patients' to the 'mutual encounter of persons', has influenced the orientation and the development of theory and practice in many other schools of therapy, with an increasing emphasis on the relational foundations of all counselling and psychotherapeutic practices and a growing respect for the rights, choices and potentialities of all clients.

In this *Handbook of Person-Centred Psychotherapy and Counselling*, we have aimed to capture this person-centred spirit, integrating it into a uniquely comprehensive, detailed and vibrant exploration of our field. With original contributions from many of the leading, avant-garde international figures in the person-centred field, we hope that the book will be a unique companion to students on all advanced-level person-centred courses, as well as to a wide range of professional practitioners: both those within the person-centred field and those outside who would like to learn more about our work at its cutting edge. Furthermore, the *Handbook* is an inclusive and state-of-the-art summary of the person-centred approach which will serve as a basis for many further explorations, developments, research and further academic engagement.

In capturing the spirit of the contemporary person-centred approach, contributors to this book come from a diversity of positions within the person-centred universe (see Chapter 9, this volume, for an overview of these positions). We have contributions, for instance, from those who are affiliated to a 'classical' model of client-centred therapy (e.g. Bozarth, Freire), those at the forefront of a newly emerging 'encounter', 'dialogical', or 'interpersonal' orientation (e.g. Barrett-Lennard, Cooper, O'Hara, Schmid), those who stress organismic and holistic thinking (Cornelius-White, Wyatt), those developing creative ways of clinical work and theory (e.g. Warner), those more closely aligned to a medical model of therapy (e.g. Finke, Teusch), and those leading the way in the development of 'Pre-Therapy' (e.g. Prouty, Van Werde). While contributors from each of these positions present somewhat different perspectives on the theory and practice of person-centred therapy, we see this diversity as a great strength of both the field and the book.

Having said that, as may have been noted above, the editors of this book are particularly aligned with a newly emerging relational approach to person-centred therapy, and this emphasis is evident in a number of the *Handbook*'s chapters. Here, influenced by the writings of dialogical and postmodern philosophers, there is a move away from the early one-sided emphasis on independence and autonomy, towards a balanced perspective with an appreciation of the inherently relational nature of human being, growth and therapy. In this respect, the book not only represents a consolidation of developments in the person-centred field, but also the foundations for a major new way of conceptualizing and practising person-centred therapy, which should be of interest to practitioners or students who wish to incorporate person-centred thinking into their work.

One of the most important dimensions of this *Handbook* is its internationality and interdisciplinarity. This follows from our understanding of the person-centred approach: that by embracing plurality and diversity we gain a much better picture of the human being and the therapeutic endeavour. Besides the United Kingdom, our authors come from a wide variety of countries, language groups and backgrounds. Their work represents diverse philosophical, psychological, scientific, medical, sociological, empirical and clinical perspectives.

With respect to the issue of diversity within person-centred therapy, we should also say something of what has not been included in this *Handbook*.

Within the field of humanistic therapy, one of the most exciting developments over the last few decades has been the 'experiential' therapies: in particular, 'focusing-oriented therapy' and 'process-experiential'/'emotion-focused' therapy (see Chapter 9, this volume). These therapies have emerged from, and are closely aligned with, the person-centred approach, even though there are differences regarding the foundations, the theory and the practice. A great deal of collaboration has taken place with these two fields, not least through the WAPCEPC and the *Journal of Person-Centred and Experiential Psychotherapies*, mentioned above. Nevertheless, for the purposes of this *Handbook*, we have not attempted to cover the field of experiential therapies in depth, though it is touched on in several places. This is primarily because it would be impossible to do it justice in the space; and also because an excellent handbook of experiential therapies already exists (Greenberg et al's *Handbook of Experiential Psychotherapy*, London: Guilford, 1998). As editors of this volume, however, we fully welcome dialogue with those who take a more 'process-guiding' approach to therapy, and look forward to extended discussion and exploration in years to come.

With respect to the format of the *Handbook* and its chapters, we have attempted to achieve a balance between the coherence of a consistently structured text and the creativity and individuality that a less formal structure allows. While in some parts of our book, then, each of the chapters contain common sections (such as 'core concepts', 'from theory to practice'), chapters in other parts of the book have a more flexible structure. Readers will also note some variations in the style and emphasis of our contributors, as well as the orientation of the authors, as highlighted above. Throughout each chapter in this book, however, readers will find a comprehensive and critical exploration of the aspect of person-centred therapy under discussion, and one that points readers to further sources through which to expand their knowledge and practice. Here, the core principles at the heart of this *Handbook* are those of critical openness and inclusivity: to the range of ideas and developments within the person-centred field, to the limitations and challenges of our approach, and to the potentialities that exist to help us take this field forward. For us as editors, such principles must be at the heart of this *Handbook*, for we see them as the very essence of the person-centred approach.

Throughout the chapters in this book, there is also an emphasis on illustrating theoretical or practical ideas with actual therapeutic dialogues or cases, to ensure that the real humanity and meaning of the writings is brought to life and to give an idea of the practice.

This book begins with a short introductory piece by Carl Rogers – previously unpublished in the English language – which is a condensed version of a talk given to psychotherapists at the Medical Faculty of the University of Vienna, Austria, on 2 April 1981. In this introductory piece, readers can learn how Carl Rogers introduced person-centred therapy to colleagues from other orientations. In unpretentious yet challenging language, he presents the actualizing tendency as the basic axiom, personal growth as the basis for a theory of personality and the fundamental importance of a facilitative relationship. To put this into practice he highlights three of his six necessary and sufficient conditions for constructive change in psychotherapy. It is astonishing how clearly and seeming simply the founder outlines what he considers to be the basic and distinguishing characteristics of his approach to psychotherapy.

The book is then divided into four parts, with a brief introduction at the beginning of each part to give an overview of its chapters. The first part of the book looks at the theoretical, philosophical and historical foundations of the person-centred approach. The second part builds on this by examining the fundamental principles of person-centred practice, critically examining all six of Rogers' 'conditions'. The third part of this book looks at how person-centred conceptualizations and practices can be applied to specific client groups in specific therapeutic settings. Finally, the book considers professional issues for person-centred therapists such as ethics, supervision and training.

As editors, we hope that this book will provide readers with an integrated, comprehensive understanding of the contemporary person-centred field, in all its creativity, diversity and depth. More than anything, though, we hope this book will motivate readers to develop and further their own theory and practice and, in doing so, to take the field forward in ever more innovative and exciting ways.

The editors are particularly grateful to Catherine Gray and the team at Palgrave for all their support and encouragement in the production of the book. Thanks also go to Pete Sanders and Lisbeth Sommerbeck for their earlier version of Chapter 11 on psychological contact. Chapter 1, Rogers' introduction to the basic conditions of the facilitative therapeutic relationship, was transcribed by Aglaja Przyborski and Peter Frenzel, and titled and abridged by Peter F. Schmid (first published in German translation in Frenzel, Schmid and Winkler *Handbuch der Personzentrierten Psychotherapie*, Cologne: Edition Humanistische Psychologie, 1992). Finally, the editors would like to thank all the contributors to this handbook for their enthusiasm, commitment and creativity in bringing this project to life.

CHAPTER 1

The Basic Conditions of the Facilitative Therapeutic Relationship

Carl R. Rogers[1]

The point of view that I represent has often been seriously misunderstood, and I hope to give you a clear view of what client-centred therapy or the person-centred approach really is. It is an experiential way of being. Let me indicate some of the distinctive features about client-centred therapy which perhaps sets it a little apart from some of the therapies you may be accustomed to. The client-centred point of view is distinctive because it starts from different premises than many other psychotherapies.

In the first place it relies on a constructive actualizing tendency of the human organism as the motivating force for psychotherapy. I don't find evidence of innate destructive tendencies nor a necessity of keeping human nature under control. We found instead that you can tap a positive force within the individual which is constructive and developmental in nature.

A second characteristic is that it definitely rejects the medical model which involves looking for pathology and developing a specific diagnosis, or thinking of treatment in terms of cure. That model seems to me quite inappropriate for dealing with most psychological problems. We prefer a model based on personal growth and development. In other words trying to release growth and development rather than thinking of it as a pathology to be cured – one of the distinctive features of the client-centred approach. Our theory develops

1. Condensed version of a talk, based on Rogers (1980), given to psychotherapists at the Medical Faculty of the University of Vienna, Austria, April 2nd 1981. Transcript by Aglaja Przyborski and Peter Frenzel; title and abridgement by Peter F. Schmid. First published in German translation in Frenzel, Schmid and Winkler, 1992.

on our experience with the clients, it is not an arbitrary theory which was developed and then we fit the clients to it.

Why am I talking about 'client', not 'patient'? For me that has a real significance. A patient means someone who is sick, who puts himself in the hands of the doctor, who feels that the doctor is probably the authority who will tell him what to do. A client, on the other hand, is a self-respecting person who comes to someone else for service: I go to a lawyer for help, what I want is expertise. But I am still the one in charge, I am the one to decide whether to take his advice or not, I am the one who is self-responsible. The use of the term client is to stress the fact that we regard the person coming for help as a self-responsible, autonomous individual who is seeking help, and we are trying to provide a climate from which he can find that help for himself. The use of the word client means a greater respect for the autonomy of this person.

The basic hypothesis is that if the therapist can provide a facilitative, growth-producing psychological climate the person himself can move toward greater self-understanding, toward more significant choices toward changing behaviour or a change in self-concept. All of the outcomes that we think of in regard to psychotherapy will gradually come about if the therapist can provide an affirmative facilitative climate which permits the actualizing tendency to take over and to begin to develop. One of the most important contributions we have made is trying to define what sort of a climate that is which enables the client to search within himself to develop better insight, to develop better understanding, to bring forth a constructive change in his way of coping with life.

There are three conditions which are essential: that the therapist is himself a real person, a congruent person; that the therapist cares for the client, prizes the client; and that the therapist exhibits a real empathy for what is going on in the client.

Empathy is perhaps most easily described and understood. I believe it to be a process rather than a state. The way of being with another person which is termed empathic has several facets. It means entering the private perceptual world of the other and becoming thoroughly at home in it. It involves being sensitive, moment to moment, to the changing felt meanings which flow in this other person, to the fear or rage or tenderness or confusion or whatever that he or she is experiencing. It means temporarily living in his or her life, moving about in it delicately without making judgements, sensing meanings of which he or she is scarcely aware, but not trying to uncover feelings of which the person is totally unaware, since this would be too threatening. It includes communicating your sensings of his or her world as you look with fresh and unfrightened eyes at elements of which the individual is fearful. It means frequently checking with him or her as to the accuracy of your sensing and being guided by the responses you receive. You are a confident companion to the person in his or her inner world. By pointing to the possible meanings in the flow of his or her experiencing, you help the person to focus on this useful type of referent, to experience the meanings more fully and to move forward in the experiencing.

To be with another in this way means for the time being you lay aside the views and values you hold for yourself in order to enter another's world without prejudice. In some sense it means that you lay aside your self and this can only be done by a person who is secure enough in himself that he knows he will not get lost in what may turn out to be the strange or bizarre world of the other, and can comfortably return to his own world when he wishes. This description makes clear that being empathic is a complex, demanding and gentle way of being.

Teaching this kind of therapy is by trying to teach people what it means to be empathic in that sense, to be non-judgemental and yet to very subtly understand all that is available in the consciousness of this other person, and perhaps just a little bit below the layer of consciousness. In being empathic, the therapist is not trying to go back into the past, it's not trying to leap ahead into the future; it's trying to catch the meaning that is real to the client at that moment. What the client is talking about might have reference to the past or reference to the future but the meaning he is talking about is an immediate meaning, is that meaning we would like to be sensitive to, enter into and be a companion to.

The second attitude that is important is an attitude of prizing the client or caring for the client and having an unconditional positive regard for the client. It is not always easy to care for the person who comes to you. The kind of caring I am talking about is at its best when it is a non-possessive, non-judgemental caring. It is perhaps most similar to the feeling that a parent feels toward a child, where a child may misbehave at times, may do things that are wrong in the parent's eyes, but overall the parent prizes that child, regards the child as someone of worth, someone to love and care for, regardless of specific behaviours. That type of caring is most effective in therapy. It is something that the therapist cannot order within himself. But the relationship is going to be more profitable if that kind of caring exists. A term I have sometimes used for caring is 'unconditional positive regard'. It is a positive caring which has no conditions attached. If I say, 'Well I like you when you do such and such, but not when you do this other thing', that is a conditional kind of caring and we often see parents to do that kind of caring. There is no doubt that has certain values, too. But for the emotional growth, for the development of the individual, the relationship is best in our experience when the care is really unconditional. When it is a caring for the person as the person is at that moment.

The third condition that we discovered to be important is that in our experience the therapeutic relationship is most likely to be effective when the therapist in a relationship is a real person. I mean that in every sense of the word. If I am in a relationship with another individual I would like to know what it is I am experiencing inside in my gut. I would like to be aware of what I am experiencing in relationship with the client; I would like to be able to express that to the client, if it seems appropriate. It means that the client is in relationship not with a person in a white coat, not with a professional, not with a facade but with a real honest-to-God person. That takes away from something that some therapists prize a great deal, namely the professional facade that they put on when they meet someone else. It is more effective when the therapist is himself or herself as he or she is at that moment. For that kind of genuineness we use the term 'congruence' to indicate a matching between what is being experienced inside and what is in awareness in the intellect and what is expressed verbally.

If all those three match in a therapist then I think the client is very fortunate, and constructive personal change is most likely to occur.

In talking about these three conditions sometimes people, in reading about them, have turned them about into shoulds: you *should* be empathic. That is not at all what I am talking about. It is that *if* in a relationship this kind of empathy or of caring exists, *then* the relationship will be constructive, but it is not as though you can tell yourself to be empathic and immediately be there. What I am saying is if these three conditions exist, then change is much more probable. But you cannot order yourself to do that.

You may ask how does change come about in a client in face of these facilitating conditions, how does this produce any effect at all. I would like to give a very simple explanation of it which may help to indicate why these attitudes seem to be effective in therapy. Let us assume for a moment that the client is a woman. If the client finds herself really listened to in this intense, sensitive and deep way, she begins to listen to herself more: 'What is going on in me?' In other words the empathic attitude on the part of the therapist encourages in the client a more sensitive listening to herself. As the therapist exhibits more of a positive and unconditional caring toward the client, the client begins to feel: 'Possibly I am worthwhile, possibly I can care for myself more, possibly I can regard myself with greater respect.' And there she begins to change the often very negative self-attitudes which are so common in clients. So it begins to develop a more positive self-concept in the client. In other words what happens in the client is a real reciprocal of what's occurring in the therapist. As the therapist listens to the client, the client comes more to listen to himself or herself; as the therapist cares with a more unconditional caring for the client, the client's self-worth begins to develop. As the client responds in herself in both those ways then the client is becoming more real, more congruent, more expressing of what is actually going on inside.

From the very first we have been concerned in framing our theory, which in turn is based on our practice, framing it in terms which make it possible to investigate it empirically. Back in 1957 I first began to enunciate some of these conditions of psychotherapy as necessary and sufficient conditions. That article (Rogers, 1957) has probably stimulated more research than anything I've ever written, and now there is a quite enormous body of research built on the effectiveness of these conditions on all different kinds of clients – so-called neurotic clients who come to a clinic, persons on the backward of the schizophrenia ward in the state hospital, normal people. These conditions describe some very important elements in therapy which have been confirmed by a great deal of research in many different countries.

REFERENCES

Frenzel, P., Schmid, P.F., Winkler, M. (eds) (1992). *Handbuch der Personzentrierten Psychotherapie*. Cologne: Edition Humanistische Psychotherapie.

Rogers, C.R. (1957). The necessary and sufficient conditions of therapeutic personality change. *Journal of Consulting Psychology*, 21(2), 95–103.

Rogers, C.R. (1980). Client-centered psychotherapy. In H.I. Kaplan, A.M. Freedman and B.J. Sadock (eds), *Comprehensive Textbook of Psychiatry, III, vol. 2*, 3rd ed. (pp. 2153–68). Baltimore: Williams and Wilkins.

PART
I
Theoretical, Historical and Philosophical Foundations

In Part I of the *Handbook*, nine chapters consider the philosophical, historical and theoretical foundations of the person-centred approach. In itself, this part constitutes one of the most in-depth and thorough explorations of the roots and foundational principles of person-centred therapy that has yet been undertaken.

This part begins with an accessible introduction to the theory of the person-centred approach by Pete Sanders, author of *The Person-Centred Counselling Primer* (2006: PCCS Books) and publisher. Sanders introduces key concepts of person-centred personality and development theory, which are explained in more detail later in this part of the book. The value of this overview lies in its systematic conceptualization, which also serves as a basic introduction to those unfamiliar with person-centred theory and practice so far. Sanders describes the original concepts of Carl Rogers and also points to current developments and publications.

This is followed by an in-depth introduction to the early history of Carl Rogers' work and the person-centred movement by Godfrey Barrett-Lennard from Australia, one of the foremost authorities on the history of the person-centred approach. His chapter – like his 1998 book: *Carl Rogers' Helping System: learning and substance* (London: Sage) – serves to locate the development of the person-centred movement within the historical context.

Austrian Peter F. Schmid, author of Chapter 4, has been described by Dave Mearns as the 'philosopher of the person-centred movement', spearheading an understanding of person-centred therapy as the art of encounter in numerous German books and English writings. His discussion of the anthropological and ethical foundations of the person-centred approach provides a unique insight into the person-centred understanding of what it means to be a person. Tracing the various influences on Carl Rogers' image of humankind, Schmid explores the two complementary conceptualizations that underpin a person-centred anthropology – the person-as-individual and the person-as-relational – and outlines a dialogical conception of human-being in which the 'Other' plays an essential and challenging role.

Following on from this, Chapters 5 and 6 examine two of the key principles underlying a person-centred understanding of human existence. In the first of these, Arthur (Art) Bohart from the United States, co-author of one of the most important person-centred texts of the last decade – *How Clients Make Therapy Work: the process of active self-healing* (1999, Washington: American Psychological Association) – presents an in-depth exploration of the concept of actualization, examining its relationship to associated concepts such as 'the fully functioning person'.

The following chapter, by Mick Cooper, co-author of the ground-breaking book *Working at Relational Depth in Counselling and Psychotherapy* (with Dave Mearns, 2005, Sage), examines the phenomenological and experiential roots of person-centred therapy. He describes how, in the person-centred approach, the person's lived experiences are taken as the starting point for both understanding the person and for the practice of psychotherapy and counselling.

Cooper's work is situated on the interface between person-centred and existential-phenomenological therapies, which he has brought into fruitful dialogue. He has also written extensively on person-centred developmental and personality theory, which is the subject of the subsequent chapter. Here, he outlines Rogers' model of human development and presents the most systematic and comprehensive analysis yet of attempts within the person-centred field to critique and develop this model.

Chapter 8 looks at another key foundation of person-centred theory and practice: group work. Although the primary focus of the *Handbook* is on one-to-one therapy, the authors of this chapter, Maureen O'Hara (a pioneer in work with large groups and in person-centred cultural philosophy) and Peter F. Schmid (author of the standard German three-volume *Handbook on Person-centred Group Therapy*, 1994–8), draw upon their experience as group-work facilitators to show the primary importance of group work and group theory to the development, practice and understanding of the whole approach.

The final chapter in Part I by Pete Sanders, editor of *The Tribes of the Person-Centered Nation* (2003, PCCS Books), maps out the different schools of thought within the person-centred field and the debates regarding the nature of person-centred therapy. This chapter serves as an invaluable overview of, and introduction to, the different orientations and positions within the 'family' of person-centred and experiential psychotherapies.

CHAPTER

2

Introduction to the Theory of Person-Centred Therapy

Pete Sanders

As a first theoretical overview, this chapter presents the essentials of person-centred personality and development theory. It includes a theory of change in psychotherapy, and introduces a person-centred understanding of such concepts as holism, distress, self, congruence/incongruence, process, motivation, actualizing tendency, self-actualization, the six necessary and sufficient conditions, encounter, non-directivity and power.

What are now known as client/person-centred therapies began with Rogers' work in the 1930s and 1940s (Rogers, 1939, 1942). We may trace his influences from his own writings and through others' readings of his work (e.g. Rogers, 1942, 1951, 1959, 1980; Kirschenbaum, in press; Barrett-Lennard, 1998; Sanders, 2004).

The importance of understanding the debates regarding the philosophical roots of a psychotherapy approach cannot be overstated, because it is the image of the human being on which the theory and practice of a therapeutic approach is based (see Chapter 4 by Schmid, this volume, and Tudor and Worrall, 2006). The person-centred image of the human evokes a theory of the personality, its development and change that, unlike other therapeutic approaches, sets off from health and wholeness, actualization and self-determination.

Personality, order and distress

The study of traditional human psychological structure tells us 'how people are put together, how they work and, of interest to [therapists] how they fall apart' (Sanders, 2006: 16). Person-centred psychology is a holistic, organismic theory that takes the organism as an integrated whole, and this pulls against the whole idea of dividing the organism into 'body' and 'mind' and further into elements of mind such as 'personality' and even 'self'.

Rogers' chapter 'A theory of personality and behaviour' (Rogers, 1951: 481–533) is arranged in 19 propositions dealing with: the nature of experience; the development and structure of personality; the nature of order, disorder and distress; and therapeutic change. He refined his ideas in 1959 in the seminal chapter 'A theory of therapy, personality and interpersonal relationships as developed in the client-centred framework' in Koch (1959).

Distress

Psychological distress has a single cause in classical client-centred theory. Whilst other person-centred therapies suggest different possibilities for a person-centred psychopathology, here we look at Rogers' original work to sketch the origin of psychological distress.

In précis, distress is caused by incongruence in the total personality between the self-structure (largely the self-image or the self as perceived, see below) and the lived experience of the person (Rogers, 1951: 481–533; 1959: 226–7). In classical theory there are likely to be only a few specific antecedents to this state of incongruence (see below) and an almost unlimited array of possible consequences. So person-centred theory posits a unitary cause of distress which finds an infinity of expressions according to the uniqueness of each individual. This trajectory of distress is, therefore, absolutely unpredictable in the individual case, and therefore at odds with any conventional model of diagnosis, including the traditional medical model. It means that person-centred literature is not overburdened with essays on how to treat this problem, or that diagnosis. For professionals who associate highly differentiated diagnostic categories with sophistication, this leaves person-centred theory simplistic and naïve. However, Mearns (1997: 146) explains, 'There is no attempt to use theory to predict the behaviour of the individual client. ... Theory will not give a detailed understanding – only empathy can do that.'

The human infant: development and needs

The infant experiences herself as the centre of 'reality', that is, the ever-changing world around her – for the infant, this experience is reality. The developing organism has an inherent tendency to actualize, maintain and enhance herself and responds to her world in an organized way as a whole organism, as a result of the needs she experiences in order to actualize.

The infant also has an inherent tendency to value experiences which maintain and enhance her organism positively. Experiences which work against actualization of the organism are valued negatively. 'Valuing' can mean something as simple as 'liking' or 'enjoying'. This is the organismic valuing process. As she develops, the infant is attracted towards, and accepts, positively valued experiences whilst avoiding and rejecting negatively valued experiences.

The development of self and personality

At some point the infant differentiates a part of her world-as-experienced as having a particular quality: being different and 'special'. This differentiated portion of experiences comes into awareness as the self. The infant then builds up a picture of herself as she experiences the world, particularly as a result of being with others and being evaluated by others. This picture is the 'self-concept'.

As the infant becomes aware of her self, her general need for satisfaction (originating in the acceptance of actualizing experiences) becomes a particular need for positive regard from others. Positive regard from others is so potent (because it is associated with enhancement of the actualizing organism) that it becomes more compelling than the 'organismic valuing process' in determining behaviour. Such evaluations from others are taken into the self-concept as though they had originated from the organismic valuing process and are called 'introjected values'.

When the infant accepts or avoids a self-experience as a result of positive regard from another, the infant has developed a 'condition of worth'. As the self-develops into a recognisable entity, it too has a tendency to actualize – to maintain and enhance itself (known as self-actualization) but because the self may contain material introjected directly from the evaluations of others, the self may actualize in a different direction from that of the organism. This is a state of disharmony between self and organism. The individual's awareness tends to be dominated by self-related experience. In other words, the self becomes the focus of attention, through which all experience is processed. So it is important that experiences can be recognized and handled by the 'self-structure'.

'Congruence/incongruence and psychological tension'

When the individual has an experience which fits with her 'self-concept', the experience is in harmony, or congruent with its self-structure and can be symbolized accurately. However, since the self-concept contains introjected material, the individual will have experiences which are not in harmony with her self-structure and may not be symbolized accurately. This is incongruence between self and experience, which leads to psychological tension. The more disharmony there is between self and the organism as a result of introjects, the greater is the likelihood of incongruence between self and experience, and a greater potential for psychological tension.

As there is incongruence between self and experience, so incongruence also develops between two sorts of behaviour: (i) *behaviours consistent with the 'self-concept'* (the individual is aware of this behaviour) and (ii) *behaviours consistent with the rest of the organism* (the individual may not recognize these behaviours as self-related: in other words, may not 'own' them).

Threat, defence, breakdown and therapeutic change

Experiences which are incongruent with the self-concept not only may not be symbolized accurately, but are also experienced as threatening to the integrity of the self-structure. The experiences would imply that the 'self-concept' was 'wrong', and since this is the effective centre of the self-structure, the whole of the self would be under threat.

Threatening experiences can be dealt with in two sorts of ways: (i) they can fail to come into full awareness – that is, they are 'denied' symbolization to experience – or (ii) they can be changed ('distorted') so that they fit into the self-concept without threat.

In a 'fully functioning' individual the self-concept is a changing, flexible collection of ideas about 'me' or 'I'. However, when it is under threat, the organism protects itself further by making the self-concept rigid and inflexible. As it becomes more rigid it relies more and more on past experiences. Therefore more and more current experiences will be distorted or denied. The processes of defence become entrenched and psychological tension builds up so that under certain circumstances (a particularly large threat to the self-concept, or the accumulation of threat), the self-concept effectively 'breaks' under the pressure. The resulting state of dis-organization will be experienced idiosyncratically by the individual as anxiety, depression, confusion or pain.

The organism will be restored by integration of all experiences into the self-concept. However, a flawed self-concept will continue to resist this by denial and distortion. Removing threat to the self-concept will result in a relaxation of its rigidity and its defences. Newer experiences, previously discrepant with the self-concept may be tentatively admitted and the process of integration begins. This is the process of therapeutic change.

Change and personality as processes

As a consequence of his work with Eugene Gendlin on the 'Wisconsin Project' (see Kirschenbaum, in press), Rogers further developed his interest in the process of therapy. Whereas some approaches propose a learning model for change, Rogers advanced an actualizing or growth model for change. The organism does not *specifically learn* to be different, it *generally grows* to be different; learning may or may not be a part of this process.

This actualizing change process has certain features (Rogers 1961: 125–59) denoted by movement from relative fixity to fluidity. Rogers uses a number of continua to illuminate the nature of the process, including fixity/fluidity of feelings, expressions, personal constructs, attitudes to change, and differentiation and elaboration of experience.

Rogers' interest in process did not stop with the process of change. He extended the idea, following Gendlin (1996), to include human personality itself. To Rogers, the personality was not a 'thing' (like a computer program or an energy-balancing system in the mind), but the very process of the experiencing human being. Personality was not a state or thing but a journey. So it would make no sense in person-centred terms to expect a distressed person to be 'restored' to a previously non-distressed, pre-morbid state, or 'repair' some faulty mental machinery. Instead, person-centred theory would have the person grow through and with their present moment of experiencing to a new, different one, embracing a host of other healing experiences, unique to the trajectory of the individual client's life along the way. (For more on the understanding of human development and personality see Chapter 7.)

Motivation

The actualizing tendency

Person-centred theory is organismic (see above), so human motivation cannot be reduced to primary drives of hunger, sex, pain avoidance and the like. Rogers proposed the single idea that an organism always strives to maintain and enhance itself in everything it does. This is what he called the 'actualizing tendency'. It is not so much a theory of motivation as a description of what living organisms do. Indeed it may not be helpful to differentiate at any level between 'the actualizing tendency' and 'the organism'.

The actualizing tendency has been criticized from all quarters. As Rogers wrote:

> I can sense the reactions of some of my readers. ... 'Do you mean that man [sic] [is] nothing but a human *organism* ...? Who will control him? Who will 'socialise' him? ... Have you merely released the id in man?' To which the most adequate reply seems to be ... 'He is realistically able to control himself and he is incorrigibly socialized in his desires. There is no beast in man. There is only man in man.'
>
> (Rogers, 1961: 105, original emphasis)

The actualizing tendency is inherent, a quality of life itself. It is active in that it does not wait for a deficit in something in order to maintain homoeostasis; it is present and operating continuously. The actualizing tendency is directional in that the organism inexorably moves towards development, enhancement, differentiation and increasing complexity. Moreover, contrary to homoeostatic drive-reduction mechanisms, the actualizing tendency increases tension in the organism, making it continually strive for new experiences. It can never be satisfied. This leads to an organism in continuous motion, a motion evident and integrated from its continuous flow of experience through to its complex social behaviour and creativity (see also Barrètt-Lennard, 1998: 74–6; Merry, 2003; Embleton Tudor et al, 2004: 26–31).

The fundamental position of person-centred psychology is that when the actualizing tendency is not fettered by restrictions, the organism flourishes and may realize its full potential. In the right conditions, the individual may become, in Rogers' terms, 'fully functioning' (Rogers, 1959), and be psychologically well adjusted. However, during development in infancy and childhood, the actualizing tendency is shaped by socialization.

If the tendency is for the organism to grow towards health, how does the organism come to grow towards maladjustment, anxiety, vulnerability and distress? The psychological and material environments in which the vast majority of the human race is reared are somewhat less than ideal (see Merry,

1995/2006). In general terms, Rogers' ideal psychological environment for therapeutic change translates into the ideal environment for child-rearing: namely an environment free from fear and judgement, one rich in understanding, and authentic unconditional love (see below). Such environments are not commonplace.

Self-actualization

Part of the natural developmental process of becoming a human adult involves the development of an idea of 'me' or 'I' that is separate from my experience of the rest of the world, and this is actualized along with everything else – our existence as thinking, feeling beings is maintained and developed as a part of living. The term 'self-actualization' refers to the actualization of this particular element of our experience. This presents a conundrum – it can be seen that on the one hand the organism itself can actualize as a whole entity in a positive, constructive way that fits a social species. On the other hand, we can also see that once the self emerges, it might actualize in the direction of survival and enhancement of the self-structure rather than the organism as a whole. Moreover, self-actualization might be in a different, possibly antagonistic direction from the pro-social organismic actualizing tendency of the whole organism.

Understanding this split between the actualizing tendency and self-actualization is one of the foundations of person-centred theory. If the material, social and psychological conditions during development are not favourable, then actualization of the self can be potentially set against the actualization of the organism as a whole. Rogers suggested that the psychological environment becomes unfavourable when the individual only feels loved when s/he conforms to certain expectations, and he called this effect 'conditions of worth'. (For discussion of the 'actualization conundrum' and related issues, see Merry, 2003; Mearns and Thorne, 2000; Tudor and Worrall, 2006. Chapters 5 and 7 explore actualization and development in more detail.)

Change theory and therapy practice

The necessary and sufficient conditions for therapeutic personality change

We have seen how Rogers explains the need for a threat-free, empathic relationship with an authentic person in terms of personality development and actualization. The conditions required for healthy growth are the basis for 'the necessary and sufficient conditions for therapeutic personality change' (Rogers, 1957, 1959), which themselves are the foundation of the practice of person-centred therapy (see Chapter 1). The essential features of these conditions are that they put the active interpersonal relationship at the heart of human growth and development. This 1950s 'necessary and sufficient conditions' statement is the starting point for Rogers' 'if–then' hypothesis building, which characterized the thrust of most research into client/person-centred therapy for the next two decades. If the necessary and sufficient conditions are present, then therapeutic change will result. No other elements or factors are necessary. Rogers presented these conditions in both his 1957 and 1959 writing. Here is the 1959 version (Rogers, 1959: 213) with differences in the 1957 version in italics:

1. That two persons are in (*psychological*) contact.
2. That the first person, whom we shall term the client, is in a state of incongruence, being vulnerable, or anxious.
3. That the second person, whom we shall term the therapist, is congruent (*or integrated*) in the relationship.
4. That the therapist is experiencing unconditional positive regard toward the client.
5. That the therapist is experiencing an empathic understanding of the client's internal frame of reference (*and endeavours to communicate this to the client*).
6. That the client perceives, at least to a minimal degree, conditions 4 and 5, the unconditional positive regard of the therapist, and the empathic understanding of the therapist. (*The communication to the client of the therapist's empathic understanding and unconditional positive regard is to a minimal degree achieved.*)

The substance of this helping system is covered in Chapter 1, and further detailed attention is paid to the conditions in Part II of this book (see also Wyatt and Sanders, 2002; Wyatt, 2001; Bozarth and Wilkins, 2001; Haugh and Merry, 2001). Joseph and Worsley (2005) edited a collection discussing psychopathology (Condition 2) and Tudor and Worrall (2006) present a recent cogent evaluation of the conditions.

Therapy as encounter

Rogers' work firmly established the relationship as an encounter between two persons which is the heart of the therapeutic process, not a formulaic 'treatment' or the expertise of the therapist or the pathology of the client in the form of a diagnosis. In the prevailing therapeutic culture of the 1950s this was one of Rogers' revolutionary contributions. (For the relational dimension of person-centred therapy see Chapters 4, 7, 8 and 10, this volume.)

Person-centred therapists press home the idea that the conditions must be considered as a piece, not one by one. The helping relationship, whilst dissectible in theory, in person-centred practice can only exist as an indivisible entity – with the commonalities and contradictions coexisting in the dynamic tension of the relationship. The conditions, then, are attitudes to be held, not skills to be assembled and practised. These distinctions further distinguish person-centred practitioners (and their training, see Chapter 28, this volume) from other therapeutic approaches.

Power, influence and non-directivity

The issue of power and influence is something of a conundrum in the social science of human relationships (see Proctor, 2002, for a discussion of the dynamics of power in therapy). Rogers wrote, to introduce 'non-directive' therapy,

> Unlike other therapies in which the skills of the therapist are to be exercised upon the client, in this approach the skills of the therapist are focused upon creating a psychological atmosphere in which the client can work. ... Client-centered counseling, if it is to be effective, cannot be a trick or a tool. It is not a subtle way of guiding the client while pretending to let him guide himself.
>
> (Rogers, 1942: 419–21).

> ... The non-directive approach places a high value on the right of every individual to be psychologically independent and to maintain his psychological integrity.
>
> (1942: 126–7)

Clearly therapists should not behave in a way that parades their expertise, or is intentionally coercive or influential. It should also be noted that Rogers' emphasis on non-directivity began at a time when psychological therapy was almost entirely a process of diagnosis, interpretation and psycho-education. The therapist was an expert and gave advice based on that expertise. It was the fallacy of therapist expertise in the relationship that Rogers was challenging. Nor did he renounce non-directivity as a key principle of his approach, since ten or so years before his death, he said in an interview:

> I still feel that the person who should guide the client's life is the client. My whole philosophy and whole approach is to strengthen him in that way of being, that he's in charge of his own life and nothing I say is intended to take that capacity or opportunity away from him.
>
> (in Evans, 1975: 26)

Grant (1990/2002) described two types or styles of non-directivity. First is *principled* non-directivity, which originates from the therapist's deeply held values. It is a spontaneous non-systematic attitude of non-interference and ethical respect. It is not a repertoire of 'hands off' behaviour, nor is it a technique for 'use' in the early stages of a therapeutic relationship to build trust or a therapeutic alliance. Second is *instrumental* non-directivity, which is seen as a set of behaviours to be applied in an interview with a particular end in mind. In other words, it is used like a tool or instrument for example, to foster a sense of trust in the client.

For readers unfamiliar with client/person-centred theory, this chapter has provided the most basic of introductions. From a set of fundamental universal principles proposed around 60 years ago has sprung one of the most influential psychologies in the world. It is now a family of therapies (see Chapter 9, this volume) which continues to develop theory and practice for the widest range of clients and applications. This book, a sampler in itself, is testimony to the depth, diversity and strength of the body of work now understood to be 'person-centred'.

REFERENCES

Barrett-Lennard, G.T. (1998). *Carl Rogers' Helping System: journey and substance*. London: Sage.

Bozarth, J. and Wilkins, P. (2001). *Rogers' Therapeutic Conditions*. Volume 2. *Unconditional Positive Regard*. Ross-on-Wye: PCCS Books.

Embleton Tudor, L., Keemar, K., Tudor, K., Valentine, J. and Worrall. M. (2004). *The Person-Centred Approach: a contemporary introduction*. Basingstoke: Palgrave MacMillan.

Evans, R. (1975). *Carl Rogers: the man and his ideas*. New York: Dutton.

Gendlin, E.T. (1996). *Focusing-Oriented Psychotherapy*. New York: Guilford.

Grant, B. (1990/2002). Principled and instrumental nondirectiveness in person-centered and client-centered therapy. *Person-Centered Review*, 5(1), 77–88. Reprinted in D. Cain (ed.) (2002). *Classics in the Person-Centered Approach*. Ross-on-Wye: PCCS Books: 371–6.

Haugh, S. and Merry, T. (eds) (2001). *Rogers' Therapeutic Conditions*. Volume 2. *Empathy*. Ross-on-Wye: PCCS Books.

Joseph, S. and Worsley, R. (eds) (2005). *Person-Centred Psychopathology: a positive psychology of mental health*. Ross-on-Wye: PCCS Books.

Kirschenbaum, H. (in press). *The Life and Work of Carl Rogers*. Ross-on-Wye: PCCS Books.

Koch, S. (ed.) (1959). *Psychology: a study of science*. Volume 3. *Formulations of the Person and the Social Context*. New York: McGraw-Hill.

Mearns, D. (1997). *Person-Centred Counselling Training*. London: Sage.

Mearns, D. and Thorne, B. (2000). *Person-Centred Therapy Today*. London: Sage.

Merry, T. (1995/2006). *Invitation to Person-Centred Psychology*. London: Whurr: 29–37.

Merry, T. (2003). The actualisation conundrum. *Person-Centred Practice*, 11(2): 83–91.

Proctor, G. (2002). *The Dynamics of Power in Counselling and Psychotherapy: ethics, politics and practice*. Ross-on-Wye: PCCS Books.

Rogers, C.R. (1939). *The Clinical Treatment of the Problem Child*. Boston: Houghton Mifflin.

Rogers, C.R. (1942). *Counseling and Psychotherapy*. Boston: Houghton Mifflin.

Rogers, C.R. (1951). *Client-Centered Therapy*. Boston: Houghton Mifflin.

Rogers, C.R. (1957). The necessary and sufficient conditions of therapeutic personality change. *Journal of Consulting Psychology*, 21, 95–103. Reprinted in H. Kirschenbaum and V.L. Henderson (eds) (1990). *The Carl Rogers Reader*. London: Constable: 219–35.

Rogers, C.R. (1959). A theory of therapy, personality and interpersonal relationships, as developed in the client-centered framework. In S. Koch (ed.), *Psychology: a study of science*. Volume 3. *Formulations of the person and the social context* (pp. 184–256). New York: McGraw-Hill.

Rogers, C.R. (1961). *On Becoming a Person: a therapist's view of psychotherapy*. Boston: Houghton Mifflin.

Rogers, C.R. (1980). Client-centered psychotherapy. In H.I. Kaplan, A.M. Freedman and B.J. Sadock (eds), *Comprehensive Textbook of Psychiatry, III*, Vol. 2 (pp. 2153–68). Baltimore, Md.: Williams and Wilkins.

Sanders, P. (ed.) (2004). *The Tribes of the Person-Centred Nation: an introduction to the schools of therapy associated with the person-centred approach*. Ross-on-Wye: PCCS Books.

Sanders, P. (2006). *The Person-Centred Counselling Primer*. Ross-on-Wye: PCCS Books.

Tudor, K. and Worrall, M. (2006). *Person-Centered Therapy: a clinical philosophy*. London: Routledge.

Wyatt, G. (2001). (ed.), *Rogers' Therapeutic Conditions. Volume 1. Congruence*. Ross-on-Wye: PCCS Books.

Wyatt, G. and Sanders, P. (eds) (2002). *Rogers' Therapeutic Conditions. Volume 4. Contact and Perception*. Ross-on-Wye: PCCS Books.

Origins and Unfolding of the Person-Centred Innovation

Godfrey T. Barrett-Lennard

This chapter traces Rogers' formative history in order to illuminate the origins and unfolding of his main ideas. His family, educational journey, early professional experience, and features of the wider cultural and socio-political context of his time, were all major influences on his path and outlook. Here, the focus is on Rogers' journey until his mid-fifties, culminating in the pivotal formulation in 1957 of his enduring theory of change.

Knowing how a major development began and unfolded creates the possibility of understanding it in depth. The context of time and circumstance are especially vital to consider in the case of an innovation in thought and practice. The fact that Carl Rogers was an American and that he grew up, lived and worked in particular historical times has great bearing on the nature and impact of his contribution. His family and educational experience were major factors in his positioning for the life that followed. Already an adolescent when the United States entered the First World War, Rogers' tertiary education and first professional steps occurred in the 1920s. He then worked full-time as a practitioner psychologist through the Great Depression and 1930s, and went on to launch into his academic career and ground-breaking contribution during the Second World War. This chapter works to trace both the contextual roots and the surging development of Rogers' thought and therapy through its most formative period.

Carl Rogers: personal origins and influences

Rogers was a middle child in a religiously strict, socially conservative and close-knit family. He grew up in Chicago and the country nearby, before and during the First World War. The family atmosphere was judgemental, not directly expressive of feeling yet also strongly valuing of its members. As a child, Carl's rich imaginative life existed side-by-side with a family emphasis on pursuits of a very practical nature. In school he was confident of his abilities and excelled in English and science (Rogers, 1967: 346–7).

Looking back, it seems that the stage was set either for Carl to pursue a bounded pathway that continued many of the family norms, or for a difficult, distinct breakout to a different balance of life meaning and purpose. Family-based assumptions about his abilities and potential, and about the importance of integrity, working hard and taking responsibility, no doubt stood him in good stead as he explored and found his way. That he would opt for tertiary studies in the University of Wisconsin was taken for granted. There, his inherited religious interest triggered involvement in a Sunday-morning discussion–exploration group, facilitated in non-directive style by one of his professors. The experience with this group of 'real closeness and intimacy' outside his family was new to him and became an extremely important developmental influence (Rogers, 1967: 349). The next year, participation in a form of religion-based 'Peace Corps' of student volunteers inspired Carl to the career goal of going into Christian work. He then switched his major studies from agricultural science to history, a significant shift reflecting his evolving ambition.

A further and profoundly influential episode began with his selection as one of ten students from the United States to take part (in 1922) in a World Student Christian Federation Conference, in Peking. The trip, beginning just after Carl's 20th birthday, was a six-months-long experience (travelling by sea) with a band of other bright, enquiring participants. Carl mailed his journal record and reflections to his family. By the time he got home, it was clear that his written accounts and 'radical' change in outlook had disturbed his parents and produced a new quality of mental-emotional separation from them (1967: 350–1). Concurrently, another primary attachment was developing in Rogers' life: a closely sharing love relationship. Carl and his sweetheart Helen married right after Rogers' graduation and headed for New York, to begin the next phase in Carl's educational journey.

Rogers intended to build on from his liberal arts studies and religious interest and devote himself to a Christian and pastoral ministry. His choice of the Union Theological Seminary, which was notably searching and liberal in its thrust, worked to facilitate discovery of his own path. One high point was a self-organized but approved credit seminar where there was no official instructor and the topical scope reflected the participants' own questions and searching. Most seminar members 'thought their way right out of religious work' (1967: 354). Carl had already sampled courses in Teachers College, Columbia University, and transferred into doctoral studies there, in clinical and educational psychology (1967: 355).

Training in accord with this new direction included a year-long fellowship in the recently formed Institute for Child Guidance in New York, where the ethos of 'eclectic Freudianism' counterbalanced the objective, measurement-oriented emphasis of the Teachers College programme (1967: 356–7). After this eventful scholarship year, and with his dissertation focused on child-adjustment and well on the way, Rogers secured (in 1928) his first regular job, as a psychologist in a monitoring and service agency for children and families established by the Rochester Society for the Prevention of Cruelty to Children (Rogers, 1967: 357). No academic connection accompanied this position, but what mattered to Rogers was the opportunity, realized over the 12 professionally formative years that followed, to do work that interested him with people.

The incubation phase of client-centred therapy

With a wealth of practical experience already under his belt, and a desire to advance and make a difference in his field, Rogers worked on his first book, published in 1939 as *The Clinical Treatment of the Problem Child*. The text reflects close study of pertinent literature, but its organization and described practice came largely from the author's own experience working with a young clientele who were usually referred by schools, courts and other community agencies. Parent participation was very uneven but sufficient for a valuable vein of experience that contributed to Carl's later direction in adult psychotherapy. The book was a success, a well-regarded, widely distributed and useful resource in its time.

Rogers uses the term 'treatment' frequently and with broad meaning in this work. Besides interview therapy, changing a child's environment by placement in a foster home, or by working to modify parent attitudes or a school's response, or using carefully chosen group and camp experiences, are all treatment responses to draw from after diagnostic appraisal. To readers conversant with Rogers' later view that external diagnosis in psychotherapy is mostly unhelpful (1951: 219–27), his emphasis on its crucial function in his earlier work may come as a surprise. Evidence from tests, interviews, referral reports and other sources were fitted within an original framework of eight 'component factors' that needed to be jointly weighed as a basis for decision on treatment. One large component was that of family influence, especially the attitudes and response of the parents to the child. The author's first discussion of personal psychotherapies (1939: 191–209) falls within his discussion of treatments that have potential to change parent attitudes.

Rogers' account here is that of a searching reporter and synthesizer of core ideas and procedures from two main approaches: 'interpretive therapy' (in particular, psychoanalysis) and 'relationship therapy', the latter flowing especially from the work of Otto Rank (1936/1945), Jessie Taft (1933) and Frederick Allen (1942/1947). Speaking of the second approach, he stressed that 'the relationship between the worker and the parent is the essential feature'; it was pivotal to help the parent 'freely to experience and realise his own attitude', and worker acceptance was a vital ingredient in this process. The viewpoint implied 'reliance on the parent himself to determine independently the manner of dealing with the child' (Rogers, 1939: 197). The primary value of this approach, Rogers suggested, lies 'in the fresh viewpoint of non-interference and reliance upon the individual's own tendency toward growth which it has emphasized' (1939: 200).

The Rochester years amounted to an advanced 'residency' for what was to come: a preparation that was unusually independent and that involved significant leadership experience (as director of the Child Study Department and appointed head of the more broad-ranging Rochester Guidance Center when it was later established (Rogers, 1967: 360; Rogers, 1961: 12)). Effectively, this positioned a person of Rogers' talent, interest and drive for another level of contribution. And, by the time his first book was completed, what was to become non-directive client-centred therapy was germinating strongly in the thought and practice of its founder. For its fruition, Rogers needed to place his own stamp on the direction he had found in the work of other pioneers (see, e.g. Kramer, 1995; Rogers and Russell, 2002: 11–12, 111–13; Thorne, 1992/2003: 58–60).

Rogers' trajectory of development was occurring within a larger context transforming American life and outlook, on the heels of the massive socio-economic dislocation and crisis of the Great Depression. The resulting new order of remedial structures and process significantly influenced the intellectual life of the nation and brought a revolution in the relation of ordinary people to the state and, in particular, to their president. By the time Franklin Roosevelt took office at the depth of the Depression, 15 million Americans, or about one-fourth of the US labour force, had lost their jobs (Leuchtenburg, 1963: 14). The nation itself was under acute stress and a 'societal crisis therapy' was called for.

The new president brought unique assets to his job, flowing in part from a huge crisis in his own life. He had contracted poliomyelitis some 15 years earlier, and had brought tremendous inner drive and focus to his rehabilitation over a period of several years. Wheelchair-bound – although able to stand upright with metal braces – he went on to live with full and extraordinary energy, further sensitized in his human awareness through the adversity of his disease and self-propelled recuperation. He re-entered politics as governor of New York, and presided and learned in that role through the worst period of the Depression.

In 1933–4, as president-elect and then in office, Roosevelt called on an array of key advisors and collaborators, drawn particularly from the academic and professional communities. These included people trained in the field of social work and experienced in innovative programmes for structurally disadvantaged groups, people who shared John Dewey's belief in social intelligence as a foundation in structuring society for human benefit (Leuchtenburg, 1963: 33). In an initial 100-day ferment of presidential initiatives and legislative and public response, Congress wrote into law 'the most extraordinary series of reforms in the nation's history' (Leuchtenburg, 1963: 61). Fifteen major laws opened the way to a vast net of economic and other protection and opportunity. Among the effects was a huge tidal change in public morale. Roosevelt contributed personally to this through his highly engaging 'fireside chats', beamed by radio directly to the American people.

Roosevelt's perceptive and highly communicative personal style no doubt contributed to his tremendous rapport with ordinary people (see Perkins, 1947: 124–5). The confidence they felt in him was further affirmed in his landslide re-election, in late 1936, to a second presidential term. A detailed study of his time, presidency and style seen in its relation to the philosophy and advance of Rogers' work (Barrett-Lennard, 1998: 34–55) reveals distinctly conducive features and some striking parallels. One feature was the 'priority ... to bring about practical improvement in the circumstances and life quality of ordinary people' (Barrett-Lennard, 1998: 40). A related element of convergence with Rogers' stance is that the New Deal was both visionary and highly pragmatic in character. Perkins notes that on programme and policy issues Roosevelt's question always was 'Will it work, will it do some good?' Carl Rogers' self-acknowledged pragmatism – 'Does it work? Is it effective?' (1967: 358) – echoes the same attitude.

The direction of Rogers' community-based work in Rochester was in keeping with the government concern to establish and support programmes on behalf of the more vulnerable and needy groups in society. A shift toward a more collectivist social vision and network of arrangements (with special support for those in difficulty) was reflected in the New Deal and implicit in Rogers' work. Citizen participation in decision making increased in a great variety of contexts (examples in Leuchtenburg, 1963: 85) and the new therapy was uniquely democratic. The president sought to inform, explain and influence, with concern for new awareness and change. He listened well and was unusually responsive as well as strongly initiating. Rogers became a responsive-initiator par excellence. Both men held an essentially optimistic view of human nature. People in all walks of life and in extraordinary measure felt themselves to be in relationship with Roosevelt. Engaging with Rogers personally, or even through his luminous writing, was a strongly relational experience.

From childhood, Carl was an avid reader. Later absorption in his work no doubt limited his lateral reading but did not block his interest in literature. Literary voices of the 1930s made a powerful contribution to visions of human nature and social need. William Faulkner's writing came to full flower and prominence then. In his later Nobel Prize acceptance speech – to give the briefest example – Faulkner referred to 'problems of the human heart in conflict with itself which alone can make good writing' (in Thorp, 1955: 759–60). John Steinbeck's socially oriented novels, which soared into prominence during the thirties, evoked images of suffering and strength in ordinary people in ways that were reminiscent of Rogers' emphases, for example, on inner frames of reference. So too in the cases of Ernest Hemingway and other notable writers, including Archibald MacLeish. Rogers later quoted the latter in expressing a viewpoint close to his own heart: 'We do not feel our knowledge. Nothing could better illustrate the flaw at the heart of our civilization. ... Knowledge without feeling is not knowledge and can lead only to public irresponsibility and indifference, and conceivably to ruin' (in Rogers, 1974: 105).

The interested reader will find a much fuller picture in my earlier book (Barrett-Lennard, 1998: 15–55) of the whole terrain of development, connection and confluence outlined here. That features of the times and context particularly encouraged, influenced and supported Rogers in his direction is, in my view, beyond reasonable doubt. I will come shortly to the cataclysm of the Second World War, with consequences at home that contributed to Rogers' speeding advance. First, more of the interior story of the settings and trajectory of the new school of therapy is called for.

The new therapy coming to fruition: steps writ large

Rogers' first book and already exceptional experience and record of leadership contributed to the new phase of his career that began with an appointment, in January 1940, as professor in the psychology department of Ohio State University. He was quickly in demand for the supervision of thesis studies, and the collection of interview records and other data for research started in short order. He was drawn to further formulate his ideas on the therapy process, notably in an address at the University of Minnesota in December 1940. Of the response to that episode, he later wrote, 'I began to believe that I might personally, out of my own experience, have some original contribution to make to the field of psychotherapy' (Rogers, 1974: 8). He did not look back, the gestation phase was over, and the offspring became non-directive client-centred therapy. The Minnesota address became the chapter titled 'Old and new viewpoints in counseling and psychotherapy' in his swiftly following second book (1942a: 19–47).

The 'newer therapy' Rogers described is an evolution of his earlier account of relationship therapy. The therapeutic relationship is seen as the crucial agent or vehicle for change; it is propelled, however, by the individual's own drive toward growth and health. Feeling aspects of the client's experience are emphasized, with the main attention given to the present situation rather than analysis of the past. The therapy is described as an orderly sequence, with the individual's decision to come for help as the first step. Free expression of feelings is visibly encouraged, and further process steps lead to instances of fresh insight and self-understanding and, in turn, to experienced choices and their testing. Finally, the client feels a diminished need for help and recognizes that the therapy relationship must end (1942a: 30–44).

There is no doubt now of Rogers' own advocacy of the newer approach he presents. The originality of his founding statement lay less in its theory than in the highly distinctive mode of documented practice. Rogers' consistent and versatile application of therapist reflection and clarification of feelings and personal meaning was without precedent. The generous illustrations from recorded therapy interviews include the famous verbatim record of an eight-interview therapy case (1942a: 261–437). Also, the author was able to draw on the first of the formal therapy research studies stimulated by his work, notably including Porter's doctoral dissertation (1941), which systematically compared the interview behaviour of counsellors independently classified as clearly directive or as non-directive in orientation. A study by Victor Raimy (1943/1948) helped to initiate the development of self-theory as a central axis in Rogers' forming theoretical system. Other studies broke new ground, and fresh papers flowed from Rogers' own pen: on learning from interview sound recordings (1942b), on a study of insight in the counselling process (1944a), and on adjustment difficulties and counselling with returning servicemen (Rogers, 1944b).

Following the rapid advance and swiftly growing visibility of his work, Rogers was offered a professorship at the University of Chicago. It was an irresistible opportunity to establish his own counselling and research centre in a top-flight university. But first he was committed to teach 'simple counselling methods' to the staff of the United Services Organization across the United States, who 'were being besieged by servicemen with personal problems' (Rogers, 1967: 363). To this end, a special-purpose book was prepared (Rogers and Wallen, 1946). The term 'client-centred', implying a new responsiveness to client agendas and meaning, does not appear in Rogers' 1942 book but, by 1946, is being used side-by-side with 'non-directive'. In a word, counselling is presented as 'a way of helping the individual to help himself' (1946: 5; Rogers, 1943: 284). Counsellor attitudes at the core of a non-directive helping stance included a belief in the person's (inherent) capacity for adjustment and growth, and true concern to facilitate self-understanding and acceptance. In a rare statement, Rogers (with Wallen, in this case) alludes to a likely relationship between his therapy and the societal context in which it was developing. One sentence explicitly suggests the link: '*It is perhaps no accident that this emphasis in counseling has reached its fruition in America*' (1946: 23. Italics added).

Near the start of his 1942 book *Counseling and Psychotherapy*, Rogers had related his counselling approach to wartime needs, and to the democratic vision and its preservation. He spoke also of the relevance of counselling in maintaining military morale and keeping men fit for their military roles (1942a: 9–10). For returning veterans there were difficulties of re-entry to a non-service world of much less regulation and unity of purpose, and of re-entry to relationships distanced by reshaping war experiences (1944b). Much later, when asked about the response to his 1942 book, Rogers spoke of 'the floods of veterans coming back with problems people hadn't anticipated', and the perception that he 'seemed to have something to say to people who were trying to help returning veterans adjust; so that meant the book skyrocketed and began to have enormous impact. If it had not been for the War I don't know' (Rogers and Russell, 2002: 136).

The president's longer-range and often-expressed concerns reached beyond the war to the quality of the peace that would follow. Words in his last prepared speech, which he did not live to deliver, might have come from within the helping field: 'Today we are faced with the pre-eminent fact that if civilization is to survive, we must cultivate the science of human relationships' (Zevin, 1946: 455).

The leadership qualities of statesman and psychologist had much in common. Perkins (1947) describes Roosevelt's qualitative influence in terms that are strikingly in keeping with Rogers' then-evolving views of leadership (see Gordon, 1955) and his own way of being a leader in the University of Chicago Counseling Center:

> To sum up Roosevelt's role in the War, I would say that he was the catalytic agent through whose efforts chaotic forces were brought to a point where they could be harnessed creatively. He was a creative and energizing agent rather than a careful, direct-line administrator.
>
> (Perkins, 1947: 308)

The wartime momentum of development around Rogers continued after the war in the Chicago setting. Extension of counselling-helping principles to the administration of the Counseling Center itself, to training and teaching, to group work and play therapy, all occurred. By the later 1940s Rogers was preparing another major book that brought each of these areas as well as adult psychotherapy into sustained focus. It was a work (Rogers, 1951) through which client-centred therapy came of age, as a well-tried, multi-sided field of practice and thought. And, the main author and founder of this widely influential school had not yet turned 50!

Unlike any other school of psychotherapy, non-directive client-centred counselling was continually under the microscope of research. A variety of studies, from the early to late 1940s provided evidence that the therapy discourse was a consistent, ordered phenomenon (see Barrett-Lennard, 1998: 232–9). Attention then focused on the effects of this known phenomenon. A sample of 29 clients (with 12 different therapists) provided the data for by far the most ambitious study of therapy outcome undertaken at that time, and a dozen interlocking studies were reported together in book form (Rogers and Dymond, 1954). This research and further studies of client-centred therapy outcome are closely reviewed in my 1998 book (240–58). Given evidence that the therapy has measurable effects, what is it exactly in the experience and process of therapy that enables these effects? Rogers was working on an answer to this question even before the main outcome of the research (see Chapter 24, this volume).

Honing in on a theory of the causal conditions for therapeutic change

As noted, the importance of therapist attitudes was stressed in Rogers' early writing. At first, the crucial attitudes (such as respect, a non-directive stance, and belief in inherent growth forces) and the working of change were rather broadly expressed. By 1946, however, Rogers was clearly on the track of a systematic formulation, as shown by an article in the first volume of the *American Psychologist*. There he distinguished six needed 'conditions' of therapist attitude and behaviour. These were: that therapists regard their clients, first, as self-responsible and, second, as inherently motivated toward development and health; that they create a warm, permissive, accepting atmosphere; that any limits set on behaviour *not* apply to attitudes and feelings; that they respond with 'deep understanding of the emotionalized attitudes expressed', especially through 'sensitive reflection and clarification of the client's attitudes'; and that they abstain from probing, blaming, interpreting, reassuring or persuading (Rogers, 1946: 416). 'If these conditions are met', he proposed, healing and growthful process will be reflected within therapy and in awareness and behaviour beyond therapy (1946: 416–17).

In an important subsequent paper Raskin argued that a genuinely non-directive attitude centred on the client's feelings and frame of reference was the central therapist quality that underpinned true acceptance and created the potential for understanding in depth (Raskin, 1948: 105–6). In close sequence Rogers distinguished empathic from emotional identification, and pointed out that empathic recognition and response does not involve self-entanglement in the other's feelings (Rogers, 1949: 86). He also acknowledged (as did Raskin) that the client's perception of the counsellor's response needed to be reckoned with (1949: 89–91). The term 'empathic understanding' is now mentioned although not yet defined (1951: 29). So too with the idea of genuineness of response.

Rogers spoke (1953) of the positive feelings that can naturally arise toward a client sharing his or her innermost consciousness in a sensitive difficult search for deeper connection and wholeness. Respect that ignites into spontaneous warmth, even affection, can be part of the human reality of a deepening helping relationship. Rogers was on the edge of suggesting that a client's growing regard for self flows in significant part from the therapist's respectful positive regard. Standal, working with Rogers, would have begun his thesis exploration (1954) of positive regard, viewed as a basic human need. His important contribution to client-centred theory fed into Rogers' further systematic thought on personality development (1959, 223–6). Standal's study also brought into view the idea of 'conditions of worth', referring to entrenched beliefs about acceptable and unacceptable personal qualities; beliefs acquired through the highly conditional reactions of others. Thus also the concept that the therapist's positive regard needs to be unconditional to help undo the client's self-devaluing or censoring conditions of worth.

In his mid-1950s 'current view' of client-centred therapy, Rogers gives primary importance to the therapist being 'genuine, whole, or congruent in the relationship' (1956: 199–200). If the client is to venture into the reality of self, the therapist needs to be real or transparent in this relation. Therapist (genuine) acceptance or unconditional positive regard (both terms are used) is a second vital factor, and the therapist's desire and ability to understand with sensitive empathy is the third ingredient of the relationship. By 1956, Rogers' sustained pondering and refinement of ideas on the therapist–client relation had moved him, step by incremental step, to a transformative articulation of the conditions for therapeutic change. This bold formulation, published the next year (Rogers, 1957), gave a new level of clarity and force to the cause–effect equation of therapy trialled a decade earlier.

Why did the new formulation have so much greater impact, even for his students (I was one) and others around Rogers? The clear logical form of his direct unqualified portrayal of the six crucial change-producing conditions made it arresting. The economy of the theory and the idea of sufficiency – that the equation was complete – added force for many readers. The boldness of Rogers' claim that these were the fundamental underlying conditions for healing and growthful change in any psychotherapy woke people up. By now, the author was a leading – even famous – figure in his field; his asserted 'general theory' could not simply be ignored: blood pressures rose in some quarters. Added to the conditions already mentioned, just one basic client quality was singled out as necessary, that of incongruence – implying inner division and conflict. For other conditions to be realized it was necessary that client and therapist be in 'psychological contact', that they be present in each other's experiential fields. Finally, the crucial features of therapist response needed to be perceived or have reality for the client. Under these conditions, constructive personal change would occur. That was the whole theory, in a nutshell.

I have traced the path to this newfound theory of change, which remains a central milestone in person-centred thought and of basic relevance to the history and practice of therapy and facilitation in this approach. Further illumination of the conditions themselves will be found, especially in Part II of this book. My chapter there will, in effect, take up the story where this one ends. This chapter moves from distilling the principal roots of the person-centred approach through to its 'mid-life' flowering. The period is a major formative part of an evolving journey, a part that shines light on the further course of this journey – now seen freshly in this volume.

Allen, F.H. (1942/1947). *Psychotherapy with Children.* New York: W.W. Norton (1942) and London: Kegan Paul, Trench, Trubner and Co. (1947).

REFERENCES

Barrett-Lennard, G.T. (1998). *Carl Rogers' Helping System: journey and substance.* London, Thousand Oaks, New Delhi: Sage.

Gordon, T. (1955). *Group-Centered Leadership.* Boston: Houghton Mifflin.

Kirschenbaum, H. (1979). *On Becoming Carl Rogers.* New York: Delacorte.

Kramer, R. (1995). The birth of client-centered therapy: Carl Rogers, Otto Rank, and 'the beyond'. *Journal of Humanistic Psychology,* 35(4), 54–110.

Leuchtenburg, W.E. (1963). *Franklin D. Roosevelt and the New Deal, 1932–1940.* New York: Harper and Row.

Perkins, F. (1947). *The Roosevelt I Knew.* London: Hammond, Hammond and Co.

Porter, E.H. (1941). The development and evaluation of a measure of counseling interview procedures. Doctoral thesis, Ohio State University. (Published in *Educational and Psychological Measurement,* 1943, 3, 105–26 and 215–38).

Raimy, V.C. (1943). The self-concept as a factor in counseling and personality organization. Doctoral dissertation, Ohio State University. (Core of thesis published in the *Journal of Consulting Psychology,* 1948, 12, 153–63.)

Rank, O. (1936). *Will Therapy: an analysis of the therapeutic process in terms of relationship.* New York: Knopf. Republished in 1945 with Rank's *Truth and Reality,* in one volume. (The 1945 Knopf edition is the source used here.)

Raskin, N.J. (1948). The development of non-directive psychotherapy. *Journal of Consulting Psychology,* 12, 92–110.

Rogers, C.R. (1939). *The Clinical Treatment of the Problem Child.* Boston: Houghton Mifflin.

Rogers, C.R. (1942a). *Counseling and Psychotherapy: newer concepts in practice.* Boston: Houghton Mifflin.

Rogers, C.R. (1942b). The use of electrically recorded interviews in improving psychotherapeutic techniques. *American Journal of Orthopsychiatry*, 12, 429–34.

Rogers, C.R. (1943). Therapy in guidance clinics. *Journal of Abnormal and Social Psychology*, 38, 284–89.

Rogers, C.R. (1944a). The development of insight in a counseling relationship. *Journal of Consulting Psychology*, 8, 331–41.

Rogers, C.R. (1944b). Psychological adjustments of discharged service personnel. *Psychological Bulletin*, 41, 689–96.

Rogers, C.R. (1946). Significant aspects of client-centered therapy. *American Psychologist*, 1, 415–22.

Rogers, C.R. (1949) The attitude and orientation of the counselor in client-centered therapy. *Journal of Consulting Psychology*, 13, 82–94.

Rogers, C.R. (1951). *Client-Centered Therapy: its current practice, implications and theory*. Boston: Houghton Mifflin.

Rogers (1953). Some directions and end points in therapy. In O.H. Mowrer (ed.), *Psychotherapy: theory and research* (pp. 44–68). New York: Ronald.

Rogers, C.R. (1956). Client-centered therapy: a current view. In F. Fromm-Reichmann and J.L. Moreno (eds), *Progress in Psychotherapy*, Vol. 1 (pp. 199–209). New York: Grune and Stratton.

Rogers, C.R. (1957). The necessary and sufficient conditions of therapeutic personality change, *Journal of Consulting Psychology*, 21, 95–103.

Rogers, C.R. (1959). A theory of therapy, personality, and interpersonal relationships as developed in the client-centered framework. In S. Koch (ed.), *Psychology: a study of a science. Vol. 3: Formulations of the persona and the social context* (pp. 184–256). New York: McGraw-Hill.

Rogers, C.R. (1961). *On Becoming a Person: a therapist's view of psychotherapy*. Boston: Houghton Mifflin.

Rogers, C.R. (1967). Autobiography. In E.G. Boring and G. Lindzey (eds), *A History of Psychology in Autobiography*, Vol. 5 (pp. 341–84). New York: Appleton-Century-Crofts.

Rogers, C.R. (1974). Remarks on the future of client-centered therapy. In D.A. Wexler and L.N. Rice (eds), *Innovations in Client-Centered Therapy* (pp. 7–13). New York: Wiley.

Rogers, C.R. and Dymond, R.F. (eds) (1954). *Psychotherapy and Behavior Change*. Chicago: University of Chicago Press.

Rogers, C.R. and Russell, D.E. (2002). *Carl Rogers: the quiet revolutionary – an oral history*. Roseville, Calif.: Penmarin Books.

Rogers, C.R. and Wallen, J.L. (1946). *Counseling with Returned Servicemen*. New York: McGraw-Hill.

Standal, S. (1954). The need for positive regard: a contribution to client-centered theory. Unpublished doctoral dissertation, University of Chicago.

Taft, J. (1933). *The Dynamics of Therapy in a Controlled Relationship*. New York: Macmillan.

Thorne, B. (1992/2003). *Carl Rogers*. London: Sage.

Thorp, W. (ed.) (1955). *A Southern Reader*. New York: Knopf.

Zevin, B.C. (ed.) (1946). *Nothing to Fear: the selected addresses of Franklin Delano Roosevelt, 1932–1945*. Boston: Houghton Mifflin.

The Anthropological and Ethical Foundations of Person-Centred Therapy

Peter F. Schmid

Person-centred practice and theory, like any form of action or thinking, is founded upon basic beliefs. For the person-centred approach, these assumptions are already expressed in its name: person-centred therapy is a special case of an 'approach' to encountering another human being as a 'person'. This chapter examines the influences of philosophical, theological and psychological strands of thinking that led to the person-centred paradigm shift and discusses further consequences and developments thereof. It explicates the image of the human being in Rogers' theory and practice, and explains central concepts like person, encounter, presence and dialogue. These considerations point to an understanding of person-centred therapy as a primarily ethical task.

The importance of the reflection on the image of the human being

All human beings base their acting and thinking – consciously or not, reflected or not, scientifically (i.e. systematically) investigated or not – on assumptions of what and how people are. We all have an image of ourselves and the human being in general that constitutes our 'anthropology': that is, our understanding of us as humans. We all have conceptions: why we act and think in one specific way and not in another (theory of motivation), how we develop and change (theory of personality), how we relate to others (theory of relationship), how and why processes occur that make us suffer or unhappy (theory of 'disorders') and how we can help each other, or generally influence each other (theory of therapy). (These are explored further in Chapters 2, 7 and 8 and, in general, in Part II, this volume.)

If for instance, one is going to help a friend because the friend is in need, one does so on the basis of a specific idea of what could be of help for the friend. And this requires an idea of how human beings 'function' and an understanding of the needs of the friend. Finally, or primarily, we have an underlying conception of what it means to be called to help a person in need. People may never have explicitly reflected on such questions, but their living their life is based on assumptions which are (in many cases, tentative) standpoints regarding these issues. In other words, their living is founded in basic beliefs, in a more or less consistent image of the human being as part of their world view (*Weltanschauung*) developed through experience and discussion.

Beliefs about the nature of human beings cannot be verified or falsified. Therefore, it does not make sense to argue about different images of the human being or to try to convince each other. However, it is of use to listen to each other and try to understand the other's beliefs – not in order to contradict but in order to further develop one's own beliefs (see Schmid, 2002a, 2002c).

What is true for one's private life is even more true for professional activities. Theories of psychotherapy are different because the underlying image of the human being, the anthropology, is different. Therefore there are different schools of therapy.

The humanistic paradigm: from natural science to human science

The so-called humanistic orientation in psychotherapy is the only one which has so far explicitly taken the image of the human being as a starting point for practice and theory building. Its anthropological, epistemological and ethical convictions were summarized in the form of theses by James Bugental (1964), in what is called the 'Magna Charta' of humanistic psychology. Among them are the statements that human beings supersede the sum of their parts (a holistic perspective including 'body', 'soul' and 'mind'), that they live consciously, have the free will to decide and live towards aims. An important conclusion of such assumptions is that a science adequate for the human being, namely a *human* as opposed to a *natural* science (hence named 'humanistic'), is still to be developed.

Humanistic psychotherapy is the practice resulting from this image of the human being. This marks a profound revolution in psychology and psychotherapy, a true change of paradigms, that has not yet been fully sounded out. The individual who has thought this through most fully, implemented it in practice, and is probably the most influential of the humanistic thinkers is Carl Rogers; and the philosophy, theory and practice that radically adheres to this image of the human being is that of person-centred therapy.

Sources of and influences on Carl Rogers' image of the human being

Rogers developed his anthropology mainly out of reflections on his practice, his origin and upbringing, and out of the confrontation with social, political, scientific, psychological, philosophical and religious trends and movements (Kirschenbaum, 1979; Barrett-Lennard, 1998; Korunka, 2001; see Chapter 3). (The vastness of this subject makes it necessary to refer readers to further studies in the references where appropriate.)

- Essential elements of Rogers' basic belief 'system' stem from Judeo-Christian theology – the bible, Martin Buber, Paul Tillich and others – due to his parental background, his study of theology and his pastoral practice. These elements include the notion of the person, the monocausal theory of motivation, trust in the nature of the human being, plurality, encounter orientation, unconditional positive regard as *agape* (i.e. love in the biblical sense), ethics, optimism, rejection of dogmatism, and spirituality – not to forget the socio-political dimension of the person-centred approach. Along with others, these elements were further developed by Bowen, Thorne, Schmid, van Kalmthout and Grant (see Schmid, 1998a, 2006a).
- Some aspects show far-Eastern influences, including Lao-tse and Zen Buddhism, due to Rogers' trip to China and the Zeitgeist in the second half of the twentieth century: for instance, the particular notion of power, unintentionality, spirituality.
- Some models and schemata of thinking have their origin in agriculture due to his family background and study of agriculture: amongst them are the orientation on experience and the organismic model.
- Concepts from classical ontology and philosophical anthropology (e.g. Aristotle and Thomas Aquinas) can be found throughout Rogers' thinking – due to his education and studies. For instance, the Aristotelian doctrine of act and potency can be found in the idea of resources to be developed by the actualizing tendency (Schmid, 2007), the teleological character of his anthropology (i.e. directed towards aims) and the thinking in 'if–then' categories. Further elaborations come from Brodley, Bohart, Ellingham, Schmid and many others (see Chapter 5, this volume).
- Individualism and subjectivism in Rogers' thinking are based on the culture of the contemporary Zeitgeist in the American Mid-West and his study of psychology (influenced by the 'American Dream', the 'New Deal', Emerson, Thoreau, Kilpatrick, Dewey etc.): individuality, growth orientation, pragmatism, optimism, experience orientation, epistemology, self-concept, 'what is most personal is most general' (Rogers, 1961: 26). Among others these were further developed by Brodley, Zimring, Gendlin and the experiential therapies. (See Chapter 3, this volume.)
- Phenomenology and a critical view of the underlying philosophy of science in psychology came in through experience, a critical view of traditional psychological concepts and reflection on his own research (influenced by Snygg, Combs, Polanyi, Tillich): rejection of logical positivism, primacy of experience and empirical knowledge, non-directiveness, therapist conditions, epistemology. Further developments came about through the work of Gendlin, Bozarth, Shlien, Pfeiffer, Zurhorst, Spielhofer, Pagès, Swildens, Lietaer, Mearns, Elliott, Brodley and Bohart (see Chapter 6, this volume).
- Conceptions of existential philosophy were triggered by students and Rogers'

reading of Kierkegaard and others, as well as face-to-face discussions (e.g. with Tillich): theory of personality, freedom of choice, conditions of worth. This strand was enlarged by Swildens, Cooper and others.

- Personalism and encounter philosophy came in by the same ways (e.g. study of and discussion with Buber). Central concepts like person, encounter, presence, dialogue and congruence grew out of these roots. These dimensions were further worked out mainly by Pfeiffer, Schmid, Binder, Thorne, Barrett-Lennard, Mearns and Cooper (see below).
- Precursors of constructivism and postmodernism (e.g. Bateson) can be found in the construction of reality, the self or the actualizing tendency. This was continued and connected with models of systems theory and narrative approaches by Holdstock, Land, Kriz, Stipsits, Fehringer, Frenzel, O'Hara and others (see Chapter 23, this volume).
- Traditional medical concepts and traditional psychiatry were rejected from early on in the conceptualization of the person-centred approach. This happened in academic discussions and was underlined later through Rogers' experiences in working with severely disturbed persons in Wisconsin. It furthered health-oriented (instead of disorder-oriented) conceptions as well as the refusal of conventional diagnostics and theories of mental illness. New concepts were later developed by Prouty (see Chapters 9 and 18, this volume), Swildens, J. and U. Binder, and others.
- Behaviourism can also be traced (Thorndike, empirical, quantitative studies), though the reaction against it left a stronger mark (e.g. through the dialogues with Skinner); self-determination, inner and outer freedom, phenomenological and qualitative research, rejection of natural scientific and reductionistic models derive from a clear counter-position. Temporarily a close relationship with behaviourism was picked up and continued by Martin in the United States and Tausch and other Germans in their early *Gesprächstherapie* concept.
- Psychoanalysis was influential, particularly through the work of Rank due to Rogers' work in the Child Guidance Clinic in early years and workshops, for example with Taft. It left its remnants in ideas of the non-conscious/unaware, therapy through relationship, insight, will. The counter-position to classic analysis generated the rejection of diagnostics, interpretation and orientation towards transference and brought the use of the term 'client' instead of 'patient' (as used already by Rank in the 1930s). This was more radically phrased by Shlien. Later psychodynamic concepts became influential for the theory of developmental psychology by Biermann-Ratjen (see Chapter 7, this volume) and integrative views (Finke; see Chapter 21, this volume).
- Rogers was strongly influenced by humanistic psychology, the 'third force' beyond psychoanalysis and behaviourism, represented by Allport, Goldstein, Maslow and May, as well as by gestalt psychology and the encounter movement. Their respective concepts are autonomy, freedom of choice, actualizing tendency, empathy, the humanistic ideal of 'a truly humane science' and new paradigms in research (see Chapter 24, this volume), the developments of encounter groups and large groups (see Chapter 8, this volume), and

conflict and peace work (see Chapter 23, this volume). The latter was significantly developed by Wood, O'Hara and Barrett-Lennard. Throughout this book numerous authors are mentioned who elaborated and extended the humanistic conception of person-centred therapy.

Person: the autonomy and interrelatedness of the human being

The approach is called after what in the history of occidental (Western) philosophy became *the* term for a view of the human being as described by the humanistic authors: the human being as a *person*. Even if the name of the approach may first have originated for pragmatic reasons (to find a comprehensive term for possible new fields of application beyond clients), Rogers deliberately chose it because of its essential meaning (Kirschenbaum, 1979: 424). This meaning, which has since been thoroughly analysed in dialogue with encounter and existential philosophy and phenomenology (see Schmid 1991, 1998a, 1998b, 2001/02 for details and references), has far reaching consequences for our understanding of ourselves and our fellow humans. And it is through the understanding of this term and those related to it, I believe, that the truly humanistic image of the human being underlying all of person-centred theory and practice can be profoundly understood.

The Greek word προσωπον (prósopon), from which the Latin word 'persona' comes, implies a twofold meaning: it originally meant 'face' (which usually is what you look at to find out who somebody is), and later, derived from it, the 'mask' of an actor who 'pulls a face' (but, unlike what we associate with a mask today, namely a concealment, the mask in ancient Greek drama served to disclose the embodied character, to reveal the god played by the actor and make him present). Deriving from the latter, 'persona' in Roman times meant the social role in society. Both notions are characteristic in their dialectical meaning: who somebody is for him/herself (the individual notion) and who somebody is in relationship to and through others (the relational notion).

Thus to view the human being as a person combines two inescapable dimensions of human existence: the substantial (or individual) aspect of being a person and the relational (or dialogic) aspect of becoming a person. These two strands can be found throughout the history of occidental philosophy.

Independence

The *substantial conception* was first defined by Boëthius: 'Persona est rationalis naturae individua substantia' (the person is the indivisible substance of a rational being). 'Substance' derives from 'sub-stare' which literally means 'remain standing on the basis of what is underneath' and therefore 'remaining present by being bolstered from underneath, in spite of external forces'. Hence it means 'achieving a standing position from below', standing by oneself, being based upon oneself and thus implies autonomy and independence.

Prominent thinkers contributing to the substantial dimension were Thomas Aquinas (autonomy), the philosophers of the Enlightenment like Locke and Leibniz (self-confidence), Immanuel Kant (dignity and freedom), Edmund Husserl (social environment), Dietrich von Hildebrand (development), Max Scheler (realization of values), Helmuth Plessner (self-reflection, corporality). The contemporary most influential philosophy in this regard is existentialism: Martin Heidegger (*Dasein* – being-here), Karl Jaspers (existential decision), Søren Kierkegaard (self-experience and responsibility), Romano Guardini (uniqueness and enigma) and others. Today, the human rights declared by the United Nations and the Charter of Basic Rights of the European Union reflect these values explicitly (references in Schmid, 1991, 1998b).

Therefore, everyone who associates person with independence and uniqueness, freedom and dignity, unity, sovereignty and self-determination, responsibility, human rights and so on sees him or herself in the tradition of such a substantial conception of the person. That is what is meant when the human being is defined as a person, starting from the moment of conception and regardless of the person's physical or mental health and development. Being a person therefore means being-from-oneself and being-for-oneself.

This conception of the person is especially influential in the (early) period in Rogers' thinking during which, based on the actualizing tendency, he mainly understands the human from the individualistic point of view. He consequently sees therapy as a process of the development of personality, with its emphasis on confidence in the organism, a realistic self and, above all, positive regard and empathy as beneficial conditions. As an ideal notion of the mature human being, Rogers coins the phrase 'fully functioning person'. Beyond this, the substantial dimension is mirrored in concepts like the person as self-determined (and thus responsible), individual, the actualizing tendency, trust in the organism, experience, self and self-actualization, symbolization, authenticity as congruence between experience and self, incongruence as central factor of 'dis-order', presence as awareness, the Other and so on.

Interdependence

The *relational notion* of the person was defined by Richard of St Victor in the tradition of patristic theology. He understood the person as 'naturae intellectualis eksistentia incommunicabilis' (incommunicable existence of an intellectual nature). Here, person is not conceived as a sub-sistence, but as an ek-sistence. Richard deliberately spelled 'eksistence' in order to stress the coming into being from outside ('ek, ex'), through others, by being put up. Therefore, a person is one who has become him/herself precisely through others, which implies interdependence, solidarity and responsibility.

From the Fathers of the Church such as Augustine ('esse ad', i.e. pure being related, self-knowledge through dialogue) to Duns Scotus (transcendental relationship), we find a continuous strand through phenomenology (the subject beyond any objectivation), the *Wertphilosophie* ('philosophy of values': authenticity versus alienation) and the precursors and proponents of encounter or dialogic philosophy (also called 'personalism'), the other contemporary philosophical orientation highly influential on the notion of person. These included Johann Gottlieb Fichte ('The human only becomes human among humans.'), Friedrich Heinrich Jacobi ('Without a Thou, the I is impossible'), Ferdinand Ebner ('In the beginning was the logos'), Martin Buber ('I–Thou-relationship') and Emmanuel Levinas ('Thou–I relationship', the Other and the Third One). Not to forget Teilhard de Chardin, well known by Rogers, with his understanding of personalization of the whole creation (references in Schmid 1991, 1998b).

So, those who understand the person through relationship, dialogue, partnership, connection with the world, through interconnectedness, who see themselves in the totality of the community, follow the tradition of the relational conception. Hence, being a person means being-from-and-in-relationship; that is, being through and towards others. In other words: we are not only *in* relationships; as persons we *are* relationships.

This conception of the human as a person particularly characterizes Rogers' later phases, where he understands people as being relational, in a group and in community, as 'person to person'. Consequently, mutual encounter is a decisive element in therapy and personal development, and Rogers now considers genuineness as a pre-eminent facilitative condition. The relational dimension is mirrored in concepts like the person as process ('becoming a person'), encounter, presence as openness to others, authenticity as congruence between experience and communication, unconditional acknowledgement, empathic understanding, immediacy, context, group, society: the person-centred approach as a 'way of being with'.

A substantial-relational being

These ways of understanding the human being are contrary, even conflicting, yet it is exactly this tension of self-reliance and commitment, sovereignty and solidarity, which uniquely characterizes being human. Both are radically taken seriously in the person-centred approach. It can clearly be shown that the meaning of 'person' in the original and genuine person-centred context precisely refers to these two dimensions, which may be characterized by the terms 'actualizing tendency' and 'fully functioning person' on the one hand (see Chapter 5, this volume), and 'encounter' and 'presence' on the other hand. Furthermore, this anthropological stance, well elaborated by phenomenology and personalistic philosophy, is the distinctive characteristic of person-centred understanding and action. Only in the dialectic of both interpretations, not in an 'either–or' but in a 'both–and', does the mystery of the person become accessible to whoever allows themselves to become involved in a relationship from person to person. A conception gained from these two perspectives of the person contrasts with a privatistic (seclusive, apolitical) conception of the human being, just as it does with a collectivistic one.

For many years Rogers himself dealt theoretically more with the individual aspect of the person, emphasizing the person as a unique and not-to-be-directed individual in therapy. It was only later that he concentrated more and more on the relational dimension. Furthermore, he did not document this in the structured way he wrote about the substantial aspect in his earlier writing. Nevertheless, contact and relationship were a central category of his anthropology from the very beginning (cf. Schmid, 2001/02), and the formulation of the 'necessary and sufficient conditions of therapeutic personality change' (Rogers, 1957) could never have taken place without it. Already, here the first condition refers to contact – a relational foundation (see Part II).

All in all, he combined both views in a unique way for psychotherapy when he built his theory and practice upon the actualizing tendency that works at its best in facilitative relationships of a certain kind (see below). Person-centred personality and relationship theory understands personalization as a process of becoming independent *and* of developing relationships.

It is certainly no coincidence that Rogers repeatedly referred explicitly (e.g. Rogers, 1961: 199) to two philosophers to whom the history of the conception of the person has always accorded a position of prime importance: Kierkegaard, who considers the misery of the individual, and Buber, who points out the opportunity implied by dialogue.

To sum it up: the basic dialectical axiom in person-centred anthropology is the actualizing tendency as the force of the individual embedded in the interconnectedness, the social nature, of the person. Both strands of the axiom form the foundations of the understanding of personalization – of authentically 'becoming a person' (Rogers, 1961). It is important to be aware that self-determination and interrelatedness refer essentially to one and the same human nature, although we may view and experience these as different dimensions. *To regard the human as a substantial-relational being is what is meant by designating him or her as a person.* Authenticity is the process of balancing individuality and interrelatedness. This includes becoming the author of one's own life in responsibility: responsibility understood as response-ability to oneself and the others.

Encounter: the acknowledgement of the otherness of the Other

As early as 1939, Rogers wrote in the context of child guidance that 'the relationship between the worker and the parent is the essential feature' (1939: 197). The six necessary and sufficient conditions start with contact and end with communication. Thus, although Rogers was convinced from the very beginning that 'the interpersonal relationship' is 'the core of guidance' (1962a), only later in the development of both Rogers and person-centred therapy was more emphasis laid on the relational dimension, until Rogers (1965: 20) clearly stated that the nature of the human itself is 'incurably social'. This led to a considerable development in the understanding of the therapeutic endeavour as far as the client–therapist relationship as a relationship of person-to-person is concerned. And it led to significant progress in the appreciation of group therapy and the social dimension of therapy and counselling (see Chapters 8 and 10, this volume).

Consequently, Rogers (1962b) finally came to explicitly understand therapy as *encounter*. With this term he characterized psychotherapy as a particular way of relating between human beings, namely from person to person – well known in encounter philosophy as the only adequate way of meeting, acknowledging and understanding a human being as a person. Again, to understand what this means for counselling it helps to become familiar with the anthropological implications and consequences (see Schmid, 1994, 1998a, 1998c, 2000, 2001/02, 2002a for details and further references).

Being with and being counter

One of the consequences of viewing the human being as a person is the realization that accepting another person means truly acknowledging him or her as an Other. He or she is no alter *ego*, no close friend a priori, no identifiable person, but rather an entirely different person. Only when this fact of fundamental difference is fully appreciated do encounter and community become possible. Etymologically the word 'encounter' comes from Latin 'contra' which is 'against' (see Schmid, 1998c: 75). To en-*counter* another person first of all means recognizing that the Other really 'stands counter', because he or she is essentially different from me.

The German philosopher and Catholic theologian Romano Guardini (1955) defined encounter as an amazing meeting with the reality of the Other: encounter means that one is touched by the essence of the opposite. In order for this to happen, there must be a non-purpose-oriented openness and a distance which leads to amazement. So, encounter is always a risk, an adventure which contains a creative seed, a breakthrough to something new. For an interpersonal encounter this means that both affinity and alienation can be experienced at the same time.

The Protestant theologian Paul Tillich, with whom Rogers entered into an open dialogue (Rogers and Tillich, 1966), pointed out that the person emerges from the resistance (i.e. the being-counter) in the encounter of the Other. If the person:

> were not to encounter the resistance of other selves, then every self would try to take itself as absolute. ... An individual can conquer the entire world of objects, but he cannot conquer another person without destroying him as a person. ... If he does not want to destroy the other person, then he has to enter into a community with him. It is through the resistance of the other person that the person is born.
>
> (Tillich, 1956: 208)

'Being counter', according to the Jewish theologian Martin Buber (1974), one of Rogers' favourite philosophers, is the foundation for meeting face to face. To be opposite to the Other offers the possibility to face and to acknowledge him or her. According to Buber, being a person consists in the event of encounter or dialogue, of communicating oneself. He defines encounter as the immediacy of the I–Thou relationship, an event in which one becomes present to the Other. The I is not constituted until such an encounter relationship: 'The I becomes through the Thou. Becoming an I, I say Thou. ... All real life is encounter.' (Buber, 1974: 18) Therefore encounter is where dialogue happens.

To stand counter also means to give room to each other and to express respect. In facing the Other, I can acknowledge the Other's uniqueness and qualities. *In facing Others I do not think what I could know about them, but I am ready to accept what they are going to disclose* – with far-reaching consequences for therapeutic epistemology (see below).

The priority of the Other

The French existential philosopher Gabriel Marcel (1935) emphasizes that the Other has always been there in advance. Similarly, but much more radically, the Lithuanian philosopher Emmanuel Levinas (1961, 1983) lays emphasis on the truth (both phenomenological and developmental) that the Other always comes first.

He points out that all of the occidental philosophy has remained 'egology'. (This also applies to psychology as philosophy's 'daughter' and to psychotherapy as its 'grand-daughter', including its so-called humanistic orientation in the twentieth century. This fixation on the 'I' is clearly predominant in the terminology of those forms of humanistic psychology that are only concerned with self-development.) Despite all positioning against objectivism and instrumentalism, such approaches end up reducing the Other to what the Other means to *me*. In this connection, even Buber's 'I become through the Thou' suddenly sounds quite different: even here, as is to be suspected, everything is still focused on me.

In his main work *Totality and Infinity* (1961), Levinas illustrates that to exist means to be entangled in oneself, caught in the totality of one's own world. Accordingly the first alienation of the human being is to be not unable to get rid of oneself. The awakening from the totality of the being-caught-in-oneself does not happen through 'being independent'. Rather, the Other is the power which liberates the I from oneself. The foundation of self-confidence is not reflection on oneself, but the relationship to the Other. This overcomes the limits of the self: the self is born in the relationship to another person.

In the same context Levinas uses the metaphor of 'visage' ('that which is seen', i.e. the face) to characterize the Other, which reminds us of the origin of the term 'person'. This face addresses us, speaks to us, even demands and challenges us. The Other – who is absolutely different, thus not to be seen from my perspective – is the one coming towards me, approaching me. The Other 'enters' the relationship – what Levinas calls a 'visitation' (i.e. 'going to "see" somebody'): my look is touched by the look of the visage. *The movement goes from the Thou to the I.* Also, from a developmental perspective, the movement always originates from the Thou: it is the call, the addressing of another human being, which evokes a response, confronts with freedom and risk. Encounter happens to a human long before he or she can aim at obtaining such an experience.

Thus, encounter in dialogue turns out to be a condition for self-consciousness, a common transcendence of the (totalitarian) status quo, a start without return (an 'in-finity'). In other words, encounter is always a challenge: 'Encountering a human being means being kept awake by an enigma,' states Levinas (1983: 120).

Therapy as dialogue

Among others, these explicit philosophical conceptions characterize the global philosophical background in which Rogers and other theorists and practitioners developed their ideas. In some cases Rogers described psychologically what philosophically was stressed by notable philosophers, and he only become aware of that afterwards. Some of the philosophical thoughts were explicitly adopted by Rogers (he entered into dialogues with Buber and Tillich, he read Kierkegaard), while he did not deal with others, who might nevertheless well serve as a basis to better understand and develop his theories of personality and relationship. Again, other conceptions contrast with those of Rogers. Trying to understand Levinas' ideas, for instance, can help to critically develop an understanding of person, self, encounter and therapeutic relationship.

It is important to be aware that Rogers himself developed his ideas throughout his life. He moved from a more individualistic position to a more relational one, yet always having both in mind and viewing their connection dialectically. After the dialogue between Buber and Rogers, for instance, both developed their own stances (Schmid, 1994); likewise such a confrontation of Rogers' ideas with contextual and contemporary thinking can have an enormous impact on a better understanding of the powerful and radical notion of Rogers' theories and their genuine development. Buber and Levinas, to name only these two, have been serving as a basis to further develop an image of the human being and an understanding of the therapeutic relationship. Therefore, a contemporary person-centred perspective favours a much more dialogical view (Schmid, 2006b; Schmid and Mearns, 2006).

On a closer examination it can be found that much of this was already implicit in Rogers' work, in many cases even from the very outset. To give some examples: the acknowledgement of Otherness that is crucial for a true encounter-oriented view of psychotherapy is already implicit in Rogers' basic concepts of the centrality of empathy, unconditional positive regard, active listening and non-directiveness. With these terms Rogers took a clear stance on how to approach another individual adequately as an Other. Another example is the discovery of the parallel of Rogers' individualistic-relational view of the person and the respective strands in philosophical anthropology. A third case is the understanding of the therapist conditions as dimensions of one central 'way of being with': that is, presence (see below).

To understand psychotherapy as an encounter and as a dialogue between persons is increasingly accepted within the contemporary person-centred field and in many other orientations. This is a consequence and genuine development (independently spearheaded by Schmid, 1994, 2002b, 2002c; Schmid and Mearns, 2006; Barrett-Lennard, 2005; Mearns and Cooper, 2005; and others) of the phenomenological and humanistic foundations of the person-centred approach – faithful to Rogers' anthropological and epistemological positions, which in many ways turned out to be more radical than he himself was aware of.

Thus, taking the person-centred image of the human being seriously, person-centred therapy must be seen as a *bi- (or multi-)polar model of psychotherapy*, where both (or all) persons involved are in the focus of reflection, forming a process of co-creating the therapeutic venture.

Accordingly, encounter is the core of an *intersubjective, co-creative process of personalization* (i.e. becoming a person) through meeting at relational depth or encounter (Mearns, 1996; Schmid and Mearns, 2006). Therapy therefore springs from a *fundamental We* (Schmid, 2001/02, 2003, 2006b); its nature is to co-respond to the situation the clients find themselves in. This also means therapist and client are co-responding to the relationship they find themselves in the very moment of their being together. So they are co-creating the relationship out of mutual encounter. The clients' contribution to this fundamentally dialogic process is to actively make use of their inherent capacity to make acknowledgement and empathy of the therapist work (as is explained by Bohart in Chapter 5, this volume and Bohart, 2004; Bohart and Tallman, 1999). The contribution on the therapist's part is to be present.

Presence instead of techniques

Presence – literally the underlying Latin word 'prae-esse' means 'to be fully there' – is the existential foundation and deeper meaning of the well-known, yet all too often superficially misunderstood, therapist conditions of authenticity, acknowledgement and comprehension (to use Buber's philosophical terms, which widely coincide with Rogers' basic attitudes). The therapist's task is to realize these continuously and in any given situation – thus responding to the challenge of the relationship in its concrete context (see Schmid, 1994, 1996, 2001/02, 2002a; cf. Geller and Greenberg, 2002).

Among other things, this implies a strict rejection of both an abstinent attitude and the use of preconceived techniques. It rules out the therapist considering himself or herself as an expert in the correct usage of methods and means, and even excludes any use of methods and techniques that is not rooted in the immediate experience of the relationship. The only 'means' or 'instrument' employed is the person of the therapist him- or herself. Only where 'every means has fallen apart' encounter takes place, as Buber (1974: 19) stated. (With this phrase he unsurpassably and precisely also grasped the process of such a relationship.) Therefore, '*im-media-cy*', a favourite term of encounter philosophers, is an important characteristic of person-centred therapy. Consequently, the therapist cannot claim to be the expert on the client's experience nor on the contents or means of the therapeutic process; on the contrary, the client is the expert – it is this emancipatory stance that holds the enormous subversive potential of person-centred therapy.

All in all, this is the foundation for an epistemology that is complete opposite of the traditional psychotherapeutic theory of knowledge: the movement does not go from me to the other individual – as is the case with traditional diagnosis where the therapist as the expert 'examines' the other to identify the frame in which what is observed can be fitted. Rather the question is what the other, as truly being an Other, shows, discloses, reveals. This means that I cannot simply extrapolate from myself and my experience to the self and experience of the other person. The attitude, rather, is to open up and genuinely accept and empathically try to comprehend what the partner in the relationship is going to disclose. In a nutshell: to understand is to listen, to realize is to appreciate, to become aware of is to follow (and not to direct – hence the 'non-directiveness', to be understood as facilitative responsiveness; see Chapter 2, this volume, and Schmid, 2005). Thus the relationship must correctly be named a *Thou–I relationship*, because it has its origin in the opening up of the 'Thou' (See Schmid, 2001/02, 2003, 2004 for references and details).

This is entirely compatible with a phenomenological and existential stance (see Chapter 6, this volume) and an ethical posture which can be seen as both the consequence and the foundation of person-centred anthropology.

Ethics: therapy as a Thou–I relationship

Rogers elaborated his approach out of his experiences in relationships. What Rogers observed in therapies and drew his hypotheses from were not indifferent data but personal experiences; they came out of being touched and moved personally. This means that they imply a distinct value judgement. The same applies to psychotherapy as such. By doing psychotherapy and by reflecting this theoretically, a decision is made to respond to the misery, to the grief, to the need, to the life of another person – to share that person's joys and sorrows. It derives from being addressed by the Other, from being touched, from being asked, being called, from being appealed to, from a demand. This means that the need of the Other is there first and that psychotherapy is responding, is answering to this demand. Thus all psychotherapy takes its origin at the Other. It sees him or her as a call and a provocation.

If the point is that the other is an Other on principle, this means that he or she is somebody who is strange to me, who surprises me and whom I have to meet with the respect of not-knowing and acceptance. The fellow being is the one with whom I am opposed, face to face, and whom I have to face – neither monopolizing nor rejecting him or her. Since the presence of the Other always 'comes first' and is seen as a call for a response, I cannot escape because nobody can respond in my place. We are obliged and responsible to the Other, to whom we owe an answer. As already shown, this causes the Other to become a 'priority'. The crucial point therefore is that, starting from a phenomenological, existential and dialogic consideration, *psychotherapy must be regarded as an ethical phenomenon and enterprise*. (This must not be misunderstood in a moralistic way. From a phenomenological and anthropological point of view, ethics denotes moral philosophy not casuistry or moralizing. Ethics means the philosophy of the challenge of living in terms of how to respond, to live response-ibly, to live one's response-ability. Details and references in Schmid, 1996, 2001/02, 2002b, 2000c; Grant, 2004.)

Ethically seen, therapists have to offer what they think to be the best they can offer. If psychotherapy is understood as an encounter relationship where clients are opening up and revealing themselves, the task of the therapist is not to try to get knowledge about them but to acknowledge the persons who are showing themselves. The therapist is the person responding to the needs of another person and therefore responsible in the communication. In a word: psychotherapy is ethically founded. Working as a therapist or counsellor means being asked to respond out of one's response-ability.

As with philosophy, essential ethical features are also implicit in Rogers' work. Taking a closer look at the core of person-centred theory, as expressed in Rogers' 1957 statement, one finds that the ethical foundation is already included here: according to Rogers, psychotherapy means responding to incongruence, to a vulnerable or anxious person. It follows that, if Rogers' conditions are regarded as necessary and sufficient for a constructive development of the person by means of psychotherapy, then it is an obligation for the therapist to take those conditions into account (contact, client's incongruence, communication of therapist's attitudes) or to offer them respectively (congruence, unconditional positive regard, empathy).

The basis for this understanding of psychotherapy can also be found in the thinking of Levinas (1983) who held the view that the fundament of self-consciousness is not the reflection of the I through the Thou, but the experience of relationship. This marks a shift from the 'I–Thou' relationship to a 'Thou–I' relationship (thus managing to get closer to the verge of the underlying 'We'). Therefore response-ability is the basic category of being a person: out of encounter arises the obligation to respond. Accordingly, psychotherapy means service to the fellow person out of engagement and solidarity. The commitment towards the Other means a responsibility that originates in the basic dependency of the human being on his or her fellow beings.

REFERENCES

Barrett-Lennard, G.T. (1998). *Carl Rogers' Helping System: journey and substance*. London: Sage.

Barrett-Lennard, G.T. (2005). *Relationship at the Centre: healing in a troubled world*. London: Whurr.

Bohart, A.C. (2004). How do clients make empathy work? *Person-Centered and Experiential Psychotherapies*, 3(2), 102–16.

Bohart, A.C. and Tallman, K. (1999). *How Clients Make Therapy Work*. Washington: APA.

Buber, M. (1974). *Ich und Du* [I and thou], 8th edn. Heidelberg: Lambert Schneider.

Bugental, J.F.T. (1964). The third force in psychology. *Journal of Humanistic Psychology*, 4(1), 19–26.

Geller, S. and Greenberg, L. (2002). Therapeutic presence: therapist's experience of presence in the psychotherapy encounter. *Person-Centred and Experiential Psychotherapies*, 1(1–2), 71–86.

Grant, B. (2004). The imperative of ethical justification in psychotherapy: the special case of Client-Centered Therapy. *Person-Centered and Experiential Psychotherapies*, 3(3) 152–65.

Guardini, R. (1955). Die Begegnung: ein Beitrag zur Struktur des Daseins [Encounter: a contribution on the structure of existence]. *Hochland*, 47(3), 224–34.

Kirschenbaum, H. (1979). *On Becoming Carl Rogers*. New York: Delacorte.

Korunka, C. (2001). Die philosophischen Grundlagen und das Menschenbild des Personzentrierten Ansatzes [The philosophical foundations and the image of the human body in the person-centred approach]. In P. Frenzel, W. Keil, P.F. Schmid and N. Stölzl (eds), *Klienten-/Personzentrierte Psychotherapie: Kontexte, Konzepte, Konkretisierungen* [Client/person-centred psychotherapy: contexts, conceptions, illustrations] (pp.33–56). Vienna: Facultas.

Levinas, E. (1961). *Totalité et infini: Essai sur l'extériorité* [Totality and infinity; essays about exteriority]. Den Haag: Nijhoff.

Levinas, E. (1983). *Die Spur des Anderen: Untersuchungen zur Phänomenologie und Sozialphilosophie* [The trace of the Other: investigations on phenomenology and social philosophy]. Freiburg i. Br.: Alber.

Marcel, G. (1935). *Être et avoir* [Being and having]. Paris: Aubier.

Mearns, D. (1996). Working at relational depth with clients in person-centred therapy. *Counselling*, 7(4), 306–11.

Mearns, D. and Cooper, M. (2005). *Working at Relational Depth in Counselling and Psychotherapy*. London: Sage.

Rogers, C.R. (1939). *The Clinical Treatment of the Problem Child*. Boston: Houghton Mifflin.

Rogers, C.R. (1957). The necessary and sufficient conditions of therapeutic personality change. *Journal of Consulting Psychology*, 21(2), 95–103.

Rogers, C.R. (1961). *On Becoming a Person: a therapist's view of psychotherapy*. Boston: Houghton Mifflin.

Rogers, C.R. (1962a). The interpersonal relationship: the core of guidance. In C.R. Rogers and B. Stevens, *Person to Person: the problem of being human* (pp.89–104). Moab: Real People.

Rogers, C.R. (1962b). Some learnings from a study of psychotherapy with schizophrenics. (Summer). *Pennsylvania Psychiatric Quarterly*, 3–15.

Rogers, C.R. (1965). 'A humanistic conception of man'. In R. Farson (ed.), *Science and Human Affairs* (pp.18–31). Palo Alto: Science and Behavior Books.

Rogers, C.R. and Tillich, P. (1966). *Dialogue between Paul Tillich and Carl Rogers*. San Diego: San Diego State College.

Schmid, P.F. (1991). Souveränität und Engagement: Zu einem personzentrierten Verständnis von 'Person' [Sovereignty and engagement: towards a person-centred understanding of 'person']. In C.R. Rogers and P.F. Schmid, *Person-zentriert: Grundlagen von Theorie und Praxis* [Person-centred: foundations of theory and practice] (6th edn. 2007; pp.15–164). Mainz: Grünewald.

Schmid, P.F. (1994). *Personzentrierte Gruppenpsychotherapie. Vol. I.: Solidarität und Autonomie* [Person-centred group psychotherapy. Volume 1. Solidarity and autonomy]. Cologne: EHP.

Schmid, P.F. (1996). *Personzentrierte Gruppenpsychotherapie in der Praxis. Vol. II.: Die Kunst der Begegnung* [Person-centred group psychotherapy in practice. Volume 2. The art of encounter]. Paderborn: Junfermann.

Schmid, P.F. (1998a). *Im Anfang ist Gemeinschaft. Vol. III.: Personzentrierte*

Gruppenarbeit in Seelsorge und Praktischer Theologie [In the beginning there is community. Volume 3. Person-centred group work in pastoral work and theology]. Stuttgart: Kohlhammer.

Schmid, P.F. (1998b). 'On becoming a Person-centered therapy': a person-centred understanding of the person. In B. Thorne and E. Lambers (eds), *Person-Centred Therapy: a European perspective* (pp.38–52). London: Sage.

Schmid, P.F. (1998c). 'Face to face': the art of encounter. In B. Thorne and E. Lambers (eds), *Person-Centred Therapy: a European perspective* (pp.74–90). London: Sage.

Schmid, P.F. (2000). 'Encountering a human being means being kept awake by an enigma': prospects on further developments in the person-centered therapy. In J. Marques-Teixeira and S. Antunes (eds), *Client-Centered and Experiential Psychotherapy* (pp.11–33). Linda a Velha: Vale and Vale.

Schmid, P.F. (2001/02). Chapters: Authenticity; Comprehension; Acknowledgement; Presence. In G. Wyatt (ed.), Series: *Rogers' Therapeutic Conditions: evolution, theory and practice* (Vol.1, pp.217–232; Vol.2,pp. 53–71; Vol.3, pp. 49–64; Vol.4: pp. 182–203). Ross-on-Wye: PCCS Books.

Schmid, P.F. (2002a). Knowledge or acknowledgement? Psychotherapy as 'the art of not-knowing': Prospects on further developments of a radical paradigm. *Person-Centred and Experiential Psychotherapies*, 1(1/2), 56–70.

Schmid, P.F. (2002b). 'The necessary and sufficient conditions of being person-centered': on identity, integrity, integration and differentiation of the paradigm. In J. Watson, R.N. Goldman and M.S. Warner (eds), *Client-Centred and Experiential Psychotherapy in the Twenty-first Century* (pp. 36–41). Ross-on-Wye: PCCS.

Schmid, P.F. (2002c). Anspruch und Antwort: Personzentrierte Psychotherapie als Begegnung von Person zu Person [Demand and response: person-centred psychotherapy as person to person encounter]. In W. Keil and G. Stumm (eds), *Die vielen Gesichter der Personzentrierten Psychotherapie* [The many faces of person-centred psychotherapy] (pp.75–105). Vienna: Springer.

Schmid, P.F. (2003). The characteristics of a person-centred approach to therapy and counseling: criteria for identity and coherence. *Person-Centered and Experiential Psychotherapies*, 2(2), 104–20.

Schmid, P.F. (2004). Back to the client: a phenomenological approach to the process of understanding and diagnosis. *Person-Centred and Experiential Psychotherapies*, 3(1), 36–51.

Schmid, P.F. (2005). Facilitative responsiveness: non-directiveness from an anthropological, epistemological and ethical perspective. In B. Levitt (ed.), *Embracing Non-directivity: reassessing person-centred theory and practice in the twenty-first century*, Ross-on-Wye: PCCS Books, 74–94.

Schmid, P.F. (2006a). *'In the Beginning there is Community': Implications and Challenges of the Belief in a Triune God and a Person-Centred Approach*. Norwich: Norwich Centre Occasional Publication Series.

Schmid, P.F. (2006b). The challenge of the Other: towards dialogical person-centered psychotherapy and counselling. *Person-centered and Experiential Psychotherapies*, 5(4), 241–54.

Schmid, P.F. (2007). The actualizing tendency: a dialogical perspective. In B. Levitt (ed.), *A Positive Psychology of Human Potential: the person-centred approach*. Ross-on-Wye: PCCS Books. In print.

Schmid, P.F. and Mearns, D. (2006). Being-with and being-counter: person-centered psychotherapy as an in-depth co-creative process of personalization. *Person-Centred and Experiential Psychotherapies*, 5(3), 174–90.

Tillich, P. (1956). *Systematische Theologie* [Systematic theology]. Volume 1. Berlin: De Gruyter.

5

The Actualizing Person

Arthur C. Bohart

This chapter presents an in-depth analysis of some of the key concepts in person-centred therapy, focused around the person-centred image of the human being as an actualizing organism. The actualizing person and associated concepts, among them the 'self' and the 'fully functioning person', are described in detail. The chapter also explores how far these person-centred concepts and assumptions are supported by research and what they contribute to an understanding of the psychotherapeutic process.

The concept of the actualizing person is one of a number of related concepts that appear in person-centred writing. Carl Rogers referred to: self-actualization, the actualizing tendency, the formative tendency and the fully functioning person (Bozarth and Brodley, 1991). He also wrote of 'becoming the self that one is'. In this chapter I will review this cluster. I will also evaluate actualization and self-actualization by considering criticisms. This will include whether the concept of self-actualization is culturally biased or not. Also, relational theories have emphasized the idea of the self as fundamentally relational or systemic in nature (Barrett-Lennard, 2005; O'Hara, 1992; Seeman, 2002; Schmid, 2003) in contrast to the individualistic emphasis found in Carl Rogers' writings. I will also consider whether people are basically good, and take a look at relevant research. Finally, I will consider implications for psychotherapy.

Actualization and self-actualization

My focus will primarily be on person-centred views of actualization. However there are precursors from outside the person-centred 'camp'.

Precursors

The concept of self-actualization goes back to Kurt Goldstein (1963). Goldstein, who worked with individuals struggling to overcome brain damage, believed in a holistic view of the person. The person could not meaningfully be separated into mind and body. The whole person interacts with the environment. Goldstein studied people's adaptation to brain damage, and believed that healing did not come through 'repair'. People do not return to states that existed before the traumatic experience took place, but rather adapt to the new conditions caused by the traumatic state. Holistic organisms cope with threats to their integrity, whether physical or psychological, by developing adaptational skills. This seems similar to Carl Rogers' views on actualization. It is also similar to a view of how clients 'self-heal' in psychotherapy (Bohart and Tallman, 1999, considered later in this chapter).

Abraham Maslow (1968, 1971) saw actualization as a state that could be attained. A person could 'be actualized'. Self-actualization is at the highest level of a pyramid of organismic needs. On the bottom of the pyramid are basic needs, such as those for food and water. Safety needs are at the next level up. Belonging needs come next. Above them are needs for self-esteem. All these are 'deficit' needs. That is, if a person doesn't have enough of them, he or she is motivated by the deficit to get more.

In this pyramid, each higher level defers to lower levels. Thus, if physiological needs for food and water are not satisfied, higher needs like belonging take second place. Above the deficit needs is the need for self-actualization. This has to do with fulfilling one's 'potential'. The qualities of self-actualized individuals include: being reality-centred, problem-centred, being comfortable being alone but also being able to enjoy deep personal relationships, autonomy, positive nonconformity, a sense of humour, humility, a strong sense of ethics, creativity, an ability to have peak experiences, and acceptance of self and others. Self-actualized people also exhibit certain values in their behaviour, such as a valuing of truth, goodness, beauty, transcendence, perfection and justice. According to Maslow, one will only focus on self-actualization when the deficit needs lower in the hierarchy are fulfilled. Thus, a poor farmer in a Third-World country scraping out an existence would not be able to self-actualize. Maslow (1971) believed that certain individuals could be identified as self-actualized. He did biographical analyses and identified examples such as Eleanor Roosevelt, Abraham Lincoln and Albert Einstein.

I have briefly mentioned these precursors to Rogers' ideas, particularly those views of Maslow, because Rogers' concept of self-actualization is different.

Carl Rogers' views

It is important to understand that for Carl Rogers self-actualization is a subset of the actualizing tendency, which is itself a subset of the formative tendency. Although historically the formative tendency was formulated later in Rogers' life, logically it is the core concept (see also Bozarth and Brodley, 1991).

The formative tendency

Rogers (1980; see also Ellingham, 2002) postulated that there was a tendency for things in the universe to move towards greater differentiation and integration. In opposition to the entropic principle, which says that the universe is gradually dissolving into random chaos, the formative tendency includes the development of greater complexity and inter-relatedness. Implied is the concept of emergence (Morowitz, 2004) which is that, under the right conditions, aspects of the universe have a tendency to jump to higher and more complex levels of organization. Key to the concept of emergence is the idea of creativity: when things jump to higher levels of organization new entities are created that are not merely the sum of the parts of the elements they are made out of (see also Mahoney, 1991).

The actualizing tendency

The actualizing tendency is the organismic embodiment of the formative tendency. Rogers (1959) postulated that living organisms are motivated by one overarching motive, which is to maintain and enhance themselves. He postulated this as a biological force. As the organism grows this includes a process of increasing differentiation, such as the differentiation of organs and of functions. It also includes the enhancement of effectiveness. Further, it includes a movement towards autonomy and away from external control. Finally, it is a movement towards wholeness and integration (Wilkins, 2003). The actualizing tendency, however, is not merely a motive to survive. Rather it is an organizational tendency to survive, cope and grow. By 'organizational tendency' I mean that it is a proactive tendency to organize the organism for optimal functioning given circumstances.

What about other motives? In order for an organism to maintain itself it must seek out what is needed for maintenance, such as food, water, shelter, safety and so on. Thus all other motives are implied by the actualizing tendency (Bozarth and Brodley, 1991).

It follows that the actualizing tendency is generative. It leads to growth and development, although the level of generativity would vary from species to species. However, Rogers notes that it can be found even in plants. One of his examples (1980) of the actualizing tendency is of potatoes growing toward the light in cellars. It certainly would be reflected in the learning capacity of organisms, which has been demonstrated even in lower organisms.

It is important to note that for Rogers, the existence of this tendency is biological. It is not fundamentally moral. Nor does it necessarily go in a morally positive direction. At the human level one could learn and become better and better at being a sadistic monster. All it postulates is a tendency to proactively grow and adapt. (Two basic texts from Rogers about his understanding of the actualizing tendency are 'The actualizing tendency in relation to "motives" and to consciousness' (1963), and Chapter 11 in *On Personal Power* (1977).)

Self-actualization

Self-actualization is a subset of the actualizing tendency (see Chapter 7, this volume). It refers to maintaining and enhancing that portion of the phenomenal field which is the 'self'. What is the self? It is not an internal agent, nor a particular psychic mechanism that 'drives' the organism. Rather, the self is a conceptual map that the organism develops in order to help it cope (Shlien and Levant, 1984; Wilkins, 2003). When they are fully functioning, people hold aspects of the self-concept tentatively (Rogers, 1961a). It is not healthy to have too firm a self-concept, as selves are growing and changing, and one must be able to modify one's self-concept to incorporate new experience just as one must revise other concepts to fit with experience.

The concept of self-actualization is one of the most misunderstood of Rogers' concepts. Rogers has been accused of representing the values of an individualistic society, and it is claimed that self-actualization is narcissistic – glorifying the actualization of individuals at the expense of others. These criticisms are not valid in terms of Rogers' concept. I consider these and related criticisms next.

Is the concept of self-actualization a Western, culturally specific notion?

It has been argued that Rogers' concept of self-actualization is culturally biased, reflecting a Western cultural emphasis on the separate, autonomous, individualistic self (the 'egocentric' self). In the critics' view of Rogers (Wilkins, 2003), self-actualization is presumably about actualizing the self, meaning that the individual focuses on personal development rather than on what is good for others. In contrast, many cultures in the world hold a 'socio-centric' view of the self. The self is seen in terms of its relationships to others, including even one's ancestors.

However, to perceive Rogers' concept of self as culture-specific is to misunderstand it. His concept is compatible with cultures which view the self in relational rather than individualistic terms, and even cultures that have no concept of self. First, it is not inevitable that a portion of the perceptual field will be differentiated out as 'self' if the culture does not have a concept of 'self'. Second, how the concept of self is differentiated out will crucially depend on how the culture defines that portion of the perceptual field. There is no reason Rogers' view of the self, as a conceptual map, could not include a map of the self as connected and socio-centric.

Self-actualization means enhancing or actualizing the self as the self is defined for that person and culture. In a socio-centric culture, self-actualization would be very different than in an individualistic culture, and might be family or group oriented.

Having said that, it is true that in many places Rogers promoted an individualistic concept of self that does reflect his cultural biases (see Chapter 7, this volume). I shall say more about this when I consider specific characteristics of the fully functioning person.

THE ACTUALIZING PERSON 51

Is self-actualization always positive?

Another criticism levelled at Rogers' view of self-actualization is that he is presumed to believe that self-actualization will always go in a positive, pro-social direction, when in fact actualizing the self might lead to narcissistic or self-centred behaviour. However, this criticism, too, is unjustified. Self-actualization is not postulated to inevitably move in a positive, pro-social direction. What is implied is that the organism will work to maintain and enhance what is defined as the self. This could lead to the enhancement of a negative and destructive development of the self. Along these lines, Wilkins (2003) has noted that self-actualization (and, I should note, actualization itself) is not a goal of therapy. Rather, it is the actualizing tendency which makes the growth that happens in therapy possible, but actualization per se is not a goal.

It is true that Maslow's concept of self-actualization is positive. For Maslow there are 'actualized people', who are creative, loving, prosocial, productively in charge of themselves and so on. Rogers' concept of self-actualization (and actualization in general) has relatively little in common with Maslow's. As we have seen, for Rogers self-actualization is the process of maintaining and enhancing the development of the self, and that may or may not be positive. Rogers did believe that the tendency of actualization was to go in a positive, prosocial, constructive direction. However he recognized that environmental factors could inhibit it or distort it so that it did not (Bozarth and Brodley, 1991). He would never have considered identifying individuals as 'self-actualized'. I shall have more to say on the contrast between Maslow and Rogers when I discuss Rogers' concept of the fully functioning person.

Related concepts

Above, I have considered the three concepts of Rogers that use the term 'actualization'. In other places he talks about 'being the self that one is' and 'the fully functioning person'.

To be the self that one is

In contrast to many theorists, Rogers never had a concept of the 'real self' as a separate and distinct entity that lay 'underneath' the overt self. To 'be the self that one is' does not mean to be something other than what one's normal 'operating personality' is. Rather it means to be congruent, to be in the process of continually integrating all aspects of oneself. This is also what 'authenticity' means in client-centred theory. To be the self that one is also means to be an organism that is in a constant process of growing and learning. As I have said elsewhere, one is always one's real self (Bohart, 2001). But one's real self may be more restricted than it could be if one were open to the process of learning and change.

To be the self that one is, then, is to be in a process, to be in touch with all aspects of oneself, and to have a trusting relationship towards oneself. These are all aspects of the 'fully functioning person'.

The fully functioning person

The concept of the 'fully functioning person' appears on the surface to be similar to Abraham Maslow's (1971) attempt to identify individuals who were self-actualized. For Maslow, self-actualization is a state of being that one can attain. In contrast, Rogers' concept of the fully functioning person is a process concept. There is no such thing as an 'actualized' person. Actualization is a process, not an outcome. Rather, the fully functioning person is someone who is open to information and is in the process of using that information to optimize growth. It is, essentially, someone who is open to learning (Bohart, 2003). A fully functioning person might be a person living in dire circumstances and poverty, who does not meet Maslow's 'actualization' needs, but who is doing the best for his or her family. Essentially it is someone who is not acting in incongruent ways that impede optimal growing and learning.

Understanding the fully functioning person may be easier if we consider Rogers' concept of the process scale (see Rogers, 1961b). Rogers says the scale:

> commences at one end with a rigid, static, undifferentiated, unfeeling, impersonal type of psychologic functioning. It evolves through various stages to, at the other end, a level of functioning marked by changingness, fluidity, richly differentiated reactions, by immediate experiencing of personal feelings, which are felt as deeply owned and accepted.
>
> (Rogers, 1961b: 33)

Rogers notes that this does not mean that the person is fulfilled, content, or even happy (1961a). He says that, 'life, at its best, is a flowing, changing process in which nothing is fixed' (1961a: 27). (See Chapter 17, this volume.)

Elsewhere, I have elaborated on what I believe it means to be fully functioning (Bohart, 1995, 2003). This is predicated on an underlying person-centred view of human personality and functioning. First, personality is a process. By this I mean that people are continually growing and changing. This does not mean that there is no continuity in personality. In fact, there may be considerable continuity. Just as Rogers and Freud held to the basic tenets of their theories throughout their lives, yet evolved and changed them as well, characteristics of personality exhibit both continuity and change. A personality is a 'structure in process'. Personality structures are continually evolving. People continuously change. Many changes consist of small, subtle modifications in how a personality characteristic may be expressed. I have used, as an analogy, viewing the coastlines of the continents from the standpoint of a space satellite. Although they may look the same over time, they are continuously changing. On the other hand, sometimes individuals experience major shifts in their personalities (Miller and C'de Baca, 2001). What is most important is to recognize that people are in the constant process of learning and modifying their ways of functioning.

Second, people live moment-by-moment. It has commonly been held that our behaviour in any given situation is determined by our past – by our beliefs and schemas which are imposed upon situations. However, both Neisser (1967), a cognitive scientist, and Epstein (1991), a radical behaviourist, have pointed out that we never really do the same thing twice. There is always variation in what we do from one time to the next. Our behaviour is a synthesis of past learning with the specifics of present circumstances. Behaviour is never an exact copy of the past. As I have written:

> general frames, personality traits, or rules that people use to help themselves cope in a given situation are never specific enough to concretely determine what the individual actually does. Behavior in any given situation is a creative application of the general structure to the specific circumstances in that particular situation, always resulting in something slightly new and different than before.
> (Bohart, 2003: 110)

Given these two aspects of human functioning, it follows that what most characterizes the fully functioning person is the potential for learning from experience. Included in this is a capacity for personal, everyday creativity. To be fully functioning, individuals will be creative in everyday life because each situation is a little different from the past and presents the challenge to creatively incorporate old learning into what is different and new about this particular situation. In the course of any given day, people are continually exploring and discovering new ways of being and behaving, even though many of these new ways represent relatively minor creative adjustments.

Referring to this creative tendency, Rogers has described it as the capacity 'to discover a new sense of meaning in the influences which he undergoes and in his early experiences, and to change consciously his behaviour in the light of this new meaning' (Rogers, 1946).

Implied in the idea of learning is openness to information. This involves both openness to internal information and to information from the external world. This suggests the importance of congruent self–self relationships as well as open, respectful dialogue with others.

Congruent self–self relationships consist of an open internal process of communication. One is able to listen to all aspects of oneself, including feelings, experiences and thoughts, in an open 'friendly' way, if they are needed for creative problem-solving. This includes listening to messages internalized from parents and society. Such listening allows one to mine the potential wisdom in all points of view, and allows the different internal perspectives to move toward creative synthesis. All internal perspectives may have something to contribute (Bohart, 2003).

To be congruent does not mean that one will always experience inner harmony. Sometimes one will be in a state of harmony; other times there will be inner conflict. Rather congruence, defined as an open receptivity to all inner voices, means the creative synthesizing process of the individual can move forward.

Of particular importance to being congruent is being open to experiencing. Both intellectual, rational thinking, and feelings and 'experiencing' are important sources of information about how to deal with the world. Experiencing, as defined by Gendlin, is the bodily felt, direct, non-verbal sensing of patterns and relationships in the world, between self and world, and within the self. It includes emotion but there is more to experiencing than emotion. Gendlin (1964) has called this a bodily felt sense. I would modify this and call it a 'bodily felt sensing'. People sense relationships that they cannot easily describe in words. For instance, people can sense when a human face is drawn out of proportion before they can identify what is wrong with it (Lewicki, 1986).

This bodily felt sensing is potentially a valuable source of information. When Rogers (1961) talked about the 'organismic valuing process', what he was referring to was the person's bodily ability to sense how interactions are going, and what is important. Experiencing can be more complex than verbal-conceptual thought, although verbal-conceptual thought can be contained within it. It is the source of creativity (Bohart et al, 1996).

Thus, 'being in touch with our experiencing process' is a way of enriching functioning. When Rogers talked about 'trusting our organisms' that is what he meant. He did not mean that these felt sensings were necessarily always accurate. Rather, fully functioning persons are open to both sources of information: bodily felt sensings and intellectual-conceptual thought. It is the person's creative capacity to learn through listening to both sources of information that enhances functioning. Cutting off either of these because one distrusts either one's thinking or one's experiencing robs one of the capacity to productively learn and grow.

I should particularly comment on the idea that full functioning includes 'trusting one's feelings'. For Gendlin, feelings are bodily felt sensings. They are not necessarily emotions like anger or fear or sadness. They are more like 'feeling that something is wrong in our relationship' or 'feeling like I don't know where I'm going'. Trusting feelings does not mean believing that a feeling such as 'there is something wrong with the relationship' is true. Rather, it means listening to it as a source of information. For instance, after exploration, it could turn out that there is nothing 'wrong' with one's relationship. Rather, one's partner has just been out of sorts for personal reasons, and that has generated the uneasy feeling. However, if one does not 'trust' the feeling enough to explore it, one may never clarify what is going on.

Agency and autonomy

In the list of characteristics of the fully functioning person given by Carl Rogers, there are several which emphasize the idea of the person as self-directed, independent and autonomous. For instance, Rogers (1961) lists: an internal locus of evaluation, moving away from meeting expectations and away from pleasing others, and moving towards self-direction (see Chapter 7, this volume).

Rather than focus on autonomy, I have suggested that we should more properly focus on human agency (Bohart, 2003). No matter in what culture they live, people have to be agentic in order to survive. That means they must take action and show initiative, although cultures may vary on when to show initiative and when to accept one's fate. If individuals feel paralyzed and helpless they will not be able to explore, learn and cope in productive ways (Dweck and Leggett, 1988; Tallman, 1996). A sense of ableness or effectance may be more important than a sense of autonomy (Bohart, 2003). The important thing is not personally chosen values versus societal values, but rather the degree to which the individual 'owns' and identifies with the values, and operates meaningfully from them (Sheldon and Houser-Marko, 2001). Individuals in socio-centric cultures may operate quite effectively from societally chosen values.

Respect for others

Although Rogers stressed autonomy, it is clear from his views on psychotherapy that he also highly valued an open, respectful stance towards others. He saw actualization as including a movement towards constructive social behaviour (Bozarth and Brodley, 1991). Part of this comes from his (1980) belief in multiple personal realities: that is, there are many different ways to construe reality, and individuals may live in different personal realities. Individuals and cultures find many different viable but workable ways of constructing personal realities. As O'Hara (1992) has put it, individuals live in different 'perceptual universes'. A key part of full functioning is the capacity to listen to and respect others' realities, as well as to dialogue productively with them. Another part is to prize and care for other people.

Peter F. Schmid's analysis of the authentic person

Schmid's (2003, 2004) philosophical analysis has led him to argue that the nature of the person is twofold (see Chapter 4, this volume, about encounter foundations). On the one hand is the person as an individual. When focusing on the person from this perspective, congruence between the experiencing organism and the self-concept becomes crucial for understanding effective functioning. However Rogers also emphasized the nature of the person as fundamentally social. Humans are not only in relationships, they are relationships. Thus Schmid argues for a synthesis of the individualistic view of the self (internal congruence between experiencing and self-concept), and the social view. He notes that self-determination and interrelatedness refer essentially to one and the same human nature, although we may view and experience these as different dimensions. Authenticity is the process of balancing individuality and interrelatedness. This includes becoming the author of one's own life, but also doing this in a context of responsible social relatedness.

Dysfunctionality

To understand the concept of the fully functioning individual, it may help to briefly describe dysfunctionality. From a client-centred point of view, dysfunctionality occurs when individuals are not congruent: when they are unable to listen productively to themselves and to others, or to explore the situations they are in in ways that would enable them to adaptively learn and cope. This is most likely to happen when they hold their self-concepts rigidly and/or are frightened and defensive. Then they may rely on old constructs and fail to examine the world afresh. Or, if they have never learned to listen to themselves, they cannot engage in the creative synthesis process that gives them the best chance to forge new relationships.

Put another way, dysfunctional behaviour arises from a failure to be open to corrective information. This particularly involves a failure to attend inwardly. This can occur because the person has rigid constructs that say that certain information should not be attended to. Or it may be because the individual is negatively judgemental towards the self. A lack of self-acceptance or self-trust could be said to be a core cause. Self-acceptance here means moving to a higher level of meta-cognitive functioning where one is able to accept both the conflicting feelings and action tendencies, the beliefs and constructs involved, and negative self-judgements, listen to all of them receptively, and find the wisest synthesis. This involves 'dis-identifying' with particular elements of consciousness and listening respectfully to all of them.

The major implication is that the biggest obstacle to enabling the actualizing process to operate optimally is defensiveness. Defensiveness gets in the way of the organism adopting an open, information-processing stance where the person can freely consider information and integrate it.

Does this imply that if defensiveness is reduced the person will move towards acting more prosocially? There are reasons why this might be so. Writers such as Seeman (2002) and Barrett-Lennard (2005) have argued that persons are parts of larger interpersonal systems. As such reduction of defensiveness and openness to information should move the persons towards valuing greater integration and congruence with others and with the outside world. If, as many have proposed, 'evil' behaviour comes out of a lack of empathy and egocentrism – an inability to de-centre and consider alternative points of view – then promoting openness may lead to a moving towards others in an integrative fashion. I do not have space to elaborate on this notion further here, but this is one way becoming more open might conceivably lead to more prosocial behaviour.

Relationship of actualization to the fully functioning person

Putting the concept of the fully functioning person together with the process of actualization, we can say that the actualizing process is the organismic process or tendency to productively cope and grow in relationship to life's stressors. It is what allows growth and adaptation. Fully functioning people are those who are operating in such a way (listening to feelings and so on) to allow the actualizing process to operate most effectively.

I want to comment on the phrase 'actualizing one's potential'. In Rogerian theory to actualize one's potential does not mean that one becomes wildly successful, incredibly creative, especially attractive to the opposite (or same) sex, rich, completely sure of oneself, or whatever. To the extent that the phrase 'to actualize one's potential' has merit, the phrase refers to using one's capacities for learning and problem solving in an optimal way. It means using one's full potential in the moment to solve problems and grow. Thus, one may continue to be conflicted, unsure of oneself, or depressed, and still be actualizing one's potential if one is coping with these things and with life in a productive learning-oriented way.

Are humans basically good?

Does Rogerian theory hold that human beings are basically good? The theory does not postulate that they are. I have noted that self-actualization, and actualization in general, do not necessarily go in a prosocial, positive direction. Shlien and Levant (1984: 3) have noted that: 'we are basically both good and bad. ... What is fundamentally assumed [by Rogerian theory] is the potential to change.'

On the other hand, many of Rogers' writings imply a positive view of human nature. For instance, Rogers describes individuals as having the potential to be positive, forward moving, constructive, realistic and trustworthy (Kirschenbaum and Henderson, 1990: 403). Rogers saw this as an empirical observation. However, he does not say they are basically good, but rather that they have this potential. He has also said:

> I am quite aware that out of defensiveness and inner fear individuals can and do behave in ways which are incredibly cruel, horribly destructive, immature, regressive, anti-social, hurtful. Yet one of the most refreshing and invigorating parts of my experience is to work with such individuals and to discover the strongly positive directional tendencies which exist in them, as in all of us, at the deepest levels.
>
> (Rogers, 1961a: 27)

For Rogers, the key is how people are treated. If they are responded to in fundamentally positive, respectful and empathic ways (as in psychotherapy), he observed that individuals grow in a positive, prosocial direction. The implication is that the actualizing tendency can go in a positive direction, given the right circumstances. What is different about this view compared to others is the implication that people can naturally and spontaneously grow in positive and prosocial directions given the proper supportive climate. They do not have to be 'taught' or 'programmed' to do so.

Research evidence

To what degree does research evidence support Rogers' view of actualization? I will briefly look at the following questions: does personality grow and change over the lifespan, or is it fixed? Is openness to experience associated with effective functioning? Do people actualize when confronted by psychological problems and/or trauma?

I do not have space to review the research on these three propositions extensively. Suffice it to say that there continues to be controversy over the fixity of personality. McCrae and Costa (2003) have argued that personality grows and develops into early adulthood, but is relatively fixed from there on. Feshbach et al (1996) and McAdams (1994) have argued that whether personality changes or not depends on what one means by personality. If one means only personality traits, then personality may appear to be relatively fixed from early adulthood on. However if one includes as parts of personality fundamental beliefs, values and goals, as well as over-arching self-organization, then there is evidence that personality continues to grow and change (Bohart, 2003; Feshbach et al 1996). Even at the level of personality trait, Srivastava et al (2003) found changes in personality traits over time.

Rogers hypothesized that openness to experience would be associated with more effective functioning. Evidence on this is contradictory. There is some evidence that 'tight' or rigid construing (Winter, 2003) is not beneficial. Seeman (2002) cites research that finds that openness does relate to higher levels of functioning. However, Gendlin and his colleagues (1968) found that focusing ability (openness to feelings) was not associated with better adaptation, although it was associated with a capacity to profit from psychotherapy. Other research has shown positive correlations between commitment to traditional religious values and positive mental health (Bergin and Richards, 2000). Yet, as Bergin (1980) has pointed out, traditional religious values do not necessarily stress the kinds of things that are associated with Rogers' view of openness, such as an emphasis on autonomy, not following authority, flexibility and self-actualization. Finally, McCrae and Costa (1997) have argued, on the basis of their research, that those high on the personality trait of openness are not necessarily more functional than those towards the 'closed' end of the spectrum.

Rogers came to his formulations from observing individuals in psychotherapy. Perhaps his observations on openness to experience have more to do with in-therapy behaviour than with functioning in everyday life. If this is so, then we must reconsider the idea of the process scale. Rather than see it as an ideal description of human functioning in general, it may be that it is more a description of the ideal processing mode in psychotherapy. It may well be that the conditions described by the process scale – fluidity, openness to experience and emotion, holding constructs tentatively and so on – are necessary for deep personal change and personal problem solving. They may describe optimal conditions for change, but not necessarily for everyday functioning.

Concerning the hypothesis that individuals exhibit a capacity for actualization, Bohart and Tallman (1999) have argued that there is considerable evidence that shows that individuals do indeed have a capacity for what we have called self-righting when confronted with problems and with adversity. Studies have shown that many individuals actually grow from trauma rather than be devastated by it (Tedeschi et al, 1998), that humans are generally resilient, that many people overcome problems without the aid of professionals, and that self-help activities often work as well or almost as well as professionally provided psychotherapy. Bohart and Tallman (1999) have further argued that the whole pattern of evidence concerning humans' capacities for self-righting and for getting better in psychotherapy supports the hypothesis that it is the client's capacity for self-healing and self-righting that makes therapy work, and that it is primarily the client who is the 'therapist'.

Of course individuals are not completely or perfectly self-healing and self-righting. Otherwise there would be no suicides, no deaths due to drugs and no need for psychotherapy. However, Bohart and Tallman would generally agree with Masten et al (1990: 438) that human development is 'highly buffered and self righting'.

Implications for psychotherapy

The major implication of the idea of actualization is that, given the right conditions, individuals will spontaneously move towards solving their problems and towards more adaptive personality and self-organization. These conditions are ones that support openness to information and reduction of fear and defensiveness. They consist of empathic listening, demonstrations of unconditional positive regard and therapeutic congruence. Therapy therefore does not need to guide clients towards positive, proactive choices. Rather, it can support their own actualizing process in such a way that it moves in a positive direction. As Carl Rogers (1974: 8) said, therapy 'relies much more heavily on the individual drive toward growth, health, and adjustment'. It 'is a matter of freeing (the client) for normal growth and development' (1974). And 'the confidence of the client-centred therapist is in the process by which truth is discovered, achieved, and approximated. It is not a confidence in truth already known or formulated' (1974: 9).

Similarly, Bohart and Tallman (1999) have argued that the research supports the view that it is clients who make therapy work. Clients do so by actively operating on whatever input therapists give and turning it into productive growth.

This view sees therapy more as self-healing, self-righting and actualization than as 'repair'. Growth occurs primarily (although perhaps not exclusively) through positive development of new and expanded capacities. As Peter F. Schmid (2004: 40) has said, 'The challenge is not so much what has gone wrong, but where the possibilities are to facilitate the process of life, i.e. the self-healing capacities.'

In conclusion, actualization is not the goal of psychotherapy. Rather it is the 'engine' which makes psychotherapy work. As clients are able to think and experience in open, supportive relationships, they are able to use their growth capacities to move forward in finding solutions to their problems.

REFERENCES

Barrett-Lennard, G.T. (1993). The phases and focus of empathy. *British Journal of Medical Psychology*, 66, 3–14.

Barrett-Lennard, G.T. (2005). *Relationship at the Centre*. Philadelphia, Pa: Whurr.

Bergin, A.E. (1980). Psychotherapy and religious values. *Journal of Consulting and Clinical Psychology*, 48, 75–105.

Bergin, A.E. and Richards, P.S. (2000). Religious values and mental health. In A. Kazdin (ed.), *Encyclopaedia of Psychology*, Vol. 7 (pp. 59–62). Washington, DC: American Psychological Association.

Bohart, A. (1993). Experiencing: the basis of psychotherapy. *Journal of Psychotherapy Integration*, 3, 51–67.

Bohart, A. (1995). The person-centered psychotherapies. In A.S. Gurman and S.B. Messer (eds), *Essential Psychotherapies* (pp.85–127). New York: Guilford.

Bohart, A. (2001). A meditation on the nature of self-healing and personality change in psychotherapy based on Gendlin's theory of experiencing. *The Humanistic Psychologist*, 29, 249–79.

Bohart, A. (2003). Person-Centered psychotherapy and related experiential approaches. In A.S. Gurman and S.B. Messer (eds), *Essential Psychotherapies*, 2nd edn (pp. 107–48). New York: Guilford.

Bohart, A. and Associates. (1996). Experiencing, knowing, and change. In R. Hutterer, G. Pawlowsky, P.F. Schmid and R. Stipsits (eds), *Client-Centred and Experiential Psychotherapy: a paradigm in motion* (pp.190–212). Vienna: Peter Lang.

Bohart, A. and Tallman, K. (1999). *How Clients Make Therapy Work: the process of active self-healing*. Washington, DC: American Psychological Association.

Bozarth, J.D. and Brodley, B.T. (1991). Actualisation: a functional concept in client-centered therapy. In A. Jones and R. Crandall (eds), *Handbook of Self-actualization* (Special issues of *The Journal of Social Behavior and Personality*, 6(5): 45–60).

Dweck, C.S. and Leggett, E.L. (1988). A social-cognitive approach to motivation and personality. *Psychological Review*, 95, 256–73.

Ellingham, I. (2002). Foundation for a person-centered, humanistic psychology and beyond: the nature and logic of Carl Rogers' 'formative tendency'. In J.C.Watson, R.N. Goldman and M.S. Warner (eds), *Client-centered and Experiential Psychotherapy in the Twenty-first Century: advances in theory, research, and practice* (pp.16–35). Ross-on-Wye: PCCS Books.

Epstein, R. (1991). Skinner, creativity, and the problem of spontaneous behavior. *Psychological Science*, 2, 362–70.

Feshbach, S., Weiner, B. and Bohart, A. (1996). *Personality* (4th ed.). Lexington, Mass.: D.C. Heath.

Gendlin, E.T. (1964). A theory of personality change. In P. Worchel and D. Byrne (eds), *Personality Change* (pp. 100–48. New York: Wiley.

Gendlin, E.T. (1990). The small steps of the therapy process: how they come and how to help them come. In G. Lietaer, J. Rombauts and R. Van Balen (eds), *Client-Centered and Experiential Psychotherapy in the Nineties* (pp.205–224). Leuven, Belgium: Leuven University Press.

Gendlin, E.T., Beebe, J., III, Cassens, J., Klein, M. and Oberlander, M. (1968). Focusing ability in psychotherapy, personality, and creativity. In J.M. Shlien (ed.), *Research in Psychotherapy* (Vol. III: 217–41). Washington, DC: American Psychological Association.

Goldstein, K. (1963). *The Organism: a holistic approach to biology derived from pathological data in man*. Boston: Beacon Press.

Greenberg, L.S. and Van Balen, R. (1998). The theory of experience-centered therapies. In L.S. Greenberg, J.C. Watson and G. Lietaer (eds), *Handbook of Experiential Psychotherapy* (pp.28–60). New York: Guilford.

Holdstock, T.L. (1990). Can client-centered therapy transcend its monocultural roots? In G. Lietaer, J. Rombauts and R. Van Balen (eds), *Client-Centered and Experiential Psychotherapy in the Nineties* (pp.109–121). Leuven, Belgium: Leuven University Press.

Holdstock, T.L. and Rogers, C.R. (1983). Person-centered theory. In R.J. Corsini and A J. Marsella (eds), *Personality Theories, Research, and Assessment* (pp. 189–28). Itasca, Il.: Peacock.

Kirschenbaum, H. and Henderson, V.L. (1990). *The Carl Rogers Reader*. London: Constable.

Lewicki, P. (1986). *Nonconscious Social Information-Processing*. New York: Academic Press.

Lewin, K. (1959). *A Dynamic Theory of Personality*. New York: McGraw Hill.

Linehan, M.M. (1997). Validation and psychotherapy. In A. Bohart and L.S. Greenberg (eds), *Empathy Reconsidered* (pp. 353–92). Washington, DC: American Psychological Association.

Mahoney, M. (1991). *Human Change Processes*. New York: Basic Books.

Maslow, A.H. (1968). *Toward a Psychology of Being*. New York: Van Nostrand.

Maslow, A.H. (1971). *The Farther Reaches of Human Nature*. New York: Viking.

Masten, A.S., Best, K.M. and Garmazy, N. (1990). Resilience and development: contributions from the study of children who overcome adversity. *Development and Psychopathology*, 2, 425–44.

McAdams, D.P. (1994). Can personality change? Levels of stability and growth in personality across the life span. In T.F. Heatherton and J.C. Weinberger (eds), *Can Personality Change?* (pp.299–314). Washington, DC: American Psychological Association.

McCrae, R.R. and Costa, Jr., P.T. (1997). Conceptions and correlates of openness to experience. In R. Hogan, J. Johnson and S. Briggs (eds), *Handbook of Personality Psychology* (pp. 826–48). New York: Academic Press.

McCrae, R.R. and Costa, P.T. (2003). *Personality in Adulthood* (2nd edn). New York: Guilford.

Miller, W. R. and C'de Baca, J. (2001). *Quantum Change: when epiphanies and sudden insights transform ordinary lives*. New York: Guilford.

Morowitz, H.J. (2004). *The Emergence of Everything*. New York: Oxford University Press

Neisser, U. (1967). *Cognitive Psychology*. New York: Appleton-Century-Crofts.

O'Hara, M.M. (1992, April). Selves-in-context: the challenge for psychotherapy in a postmodern world. Invited address at the Conference of the Society for the Exploration of Psychotherapy Integration, San Diego, Calif.

O'Hara, M.M. and Wood, J.K. (1983). Patterns of awareness: consciousness and the group mind. *The Gestalt Journal*, 6, 103–16.

Rogers, C.R. (1946). Significant aspects of Client-Centered Therapy. *American Psychologist*, 1, 415–22.

Rogers, C.R. (1959). A theory of therapy, personality, and interpersonal relationships, as developed in the client-centered framework. In S. Koch (ed.), *Psychology: a study of a science* (Vol. III). New York: McGraw-Hill.

Rogers, C.R. (1961a). *On Becoming a Person: a therapist's view of psychotherapy*. Boston: Houghton Mifflin.

Rogers, C.R. (1961b). The process equation of psychotherapy. *American Journal of Psychotherapy*, 15, 27–45.

Rogers, C.R. (1963). The actualizing tendency in relation to 'motives' and to consciousness (pp. 1–24). In M.R. Jones (ed.), *Nebraska Symposium on Motivation*. Lincoln, Nebr.: University of Nebraska Press.

Rogers, C.R. (1974). Remarks on the future of client-centered therapy. In D.A. Wexler and L.N. Rice (eds), *Innovations in Client-centered Therapy* (pp.7–13). New York: Wiley.

Rogers, C.R. (1977). *On Personal Power: inner strength and its revolutionary impact*. New York: Delacorte.

Rogers, C.R. (1980). *A Way of Being*. New York: Houghton Mifflin.

Schmid, P.F. (2003). The characteristics of a person-centred approach to therapy and counseling: criteria for identity and coherence. *Person-centered and Experiential Psychotherapies*, 2, 104–21.

Schmid, P.F. (2004). Back to the client: a phenomenological approach to the process of understanding and diagnosis. *Person-centered and Experiential Psychotherapies*, 3, 36–51.

Seeman, J. (2002). Looking back, looking ahead: a synthesis. In D.J. Cain and J. Seeman (ed.), *Humanistic Psychotherapies: handbook of research and practice* (pp.617–36). Washington, DC: American Psychological Association.

Sheldon, K. M. and Houser-Marko, L. (2001). Self-concordance, goal attainment, and the pursuit of happiness: can there be an upward spiral? *Journal of Personality and Social Psychology*, 80, 152–65.

Shlien, J.M. (1970). Phenomenology and personality. In J.T. Hart and T.M. Tomlinson (eds), *New Directions in Client-centered Therapy* (pp.95–128). Boston: Houghton Mifflin.

Shlien, J.M. and Levant, R.F. (1984). Introduction. In R.F. Levant and J.M. Shlien (eds), *Client-centered Therapy and the Person-centered Approach: new directions in theory, research, and practice* (pp.1–16). New York: Praeger.

Srivastava, S., John, O.P., Gosling, S.D. and Potter, J. (2003). Development of personality in early and middle adulthood: set like plaster or persistent change? *Journal of Personality and Social Psychology*, 84, 1041–1053.

Tallman, K. (1996). The state of mind theory: goal orientation concepts applied to clinical psychology. Unpublished Master's Thesis, California State University Dominguez Hills, Carson, Calif..

Tedeschi, R.G., Park, C.L. and Calhoun, L.G. (eds), (1998). *Posttraumatic Growth*. Mahwah, N.J.: Erlbaum.

Wexler, D.A. (1974). A cognitive theory of experiencing, self-actualization, and therapeutic process. In Wexler, D.A. and Rice, L.N. (eds), *Innovations in Client-centered Therapy* (pp.49–116). New York: Wiley.

Wilkins, P. (2003). *Person-Centred Therapy in Focus*. Thousand Oaks, Calif.: Sage.

Winter, D.A. (2003). Repertory grid technique as a psychotherapy research measure. *Psychotherapy Research*, 13, 25–42.

CHAPTER 6

Experiential and Phenomenological Foundations

Mick Cooper

Understanding human being in terms of how people experience their world is one of the cornerstones of person-centred epistemology and therapeutic practice. This chapter critically examines the experiential and phenomenological roots of the person-centred approach, in which lived experiences are taken as the starting point both for understanding the person and for therapeutic practice. It begins by looking at the prominence that Rogers and other person-centred writers have given to this experiential dimension. It then looks at how the experiential emphasis has evolved and discusses the relationship between person-centred thinking and the related field of 'phenomenology'. The chapter then explores the question 'What is experience?' drawing on both Rogers' writings and the works of some of his colleagues, most notably Eugene Gendlin. Finally, the chapter looks at some of the difficulties and limitations of founding a therapeutic approach on experiential principles.

What are you experiencing as you read this? Perhaps there is a feeling of interest at what you are about to read, or perhaps you are thinking 'I'll give this chapter a go and see if it's worth carrying on with.' Maybe, as you are reading this, you are aware of sounds around you, and perhaps there are other distractions: a child pulling on your sleeve or a partner wondering when you are going to turn the light off. Almost certainly, your experiencing will have a bodily dimension to it: a slight aching in your arms, perhaps, or tiredness behind the eyes, or the feel of the outside air on your skin.

Within many psychological and psychotherapeutic fields, such experiences are considered relatively superficial: 'epiphenomena' that mask the more fundamental laws and dynamics that constitute us. From a person-centred standpoint, however, our subjective experiencing is far more than that: not just an important part of who we are, but a fundamental aspect of our existence. Such a 'radical theory of knowledge' (Worsley, 2001: 59) has fundamental implications for the theory and practice of counselling and psychotherapy.

The primacy of experience

For Rogers, an understanding of human beings needs to start with an understanding of how they experience their world. For him, human beings live their lives as subjects, not as objects, so that any attempts to fully understand them must start in the realm of subjective experiences. He writes:

> If we could empathically experience all the sensory and visceral sensations of the individual, could experience his whole phenomenal field including both the conscious elements and also those elements not brought to the conscious level, we should have the perfect basis for understanding the meaningfulness of his behavior and for predicting his future behavior.
>
> (Rogers, 1951: 494–5)

Such was Rogers' belief in the 'fundamental predominance of the subjective' (1959: 191) that the first two of his 19 classic propositions (Rogers, 1951), in which he developed a theory of personality and behaviour, emphasize the experiential nature of human beings. In his first proposition, he states that 'Every individual exists in a continually changing world of experience of which he is the center' (1951: 483); and in his second proposition he adds: 'The organism reacts to the field as it is experienced and perceived. This perceptual field is, for the individual, "reality"' (1951: 484).

Such propositions make most sense when viewed against the psychological backdrop of their time. In the 1940s, behaviourism continued to dominate psychology – particularly in the United States – a school of thought that attempted to make psychology a 'proper' science by excluding from its realms of investigation and conceptualization anything that could not be objectively measured or observed (Gross, 1996). Behaviours and external reinforcers thus came to be seen as the appropriate subjects for psychological inquiry, whilst private experiences came to be seen as superfluous to both psychological research and theory: at best, sequelae to action and behaviours without any causal status of their own (see Skinner in Rogers, 1990). As a direct descendant of positivist thinking (a philosophical position contending that the only admissible basis of human knowledge is what we experience through our senses), behaviourists also held a firm belief in the existence of an external, 'objective' reality: one that functioned according to determined, unchanging laws, and which acted utterly independently of any human experiences or perceptions.

Rogers' (1951) first two propositions in his theory of personality and behaviour, then, are a direct challenge to the dominant psychological ideology of his day. In contrast to the 'empty organism' school of thought (Rogers, 1959), Rogers states that our experiencing of the world is an undeniable part of who we are: that to be human is to experience the world in ever-changing ways. More controversially, from a behavioural perspective, Rogers argues in his second proposition that human behaviour cannot be understood without reference to this experiencing. In other words, he suggests that there is no direct link between external 'stimuli' and human 'responses'; rather, our responses to the world are wholly mediated by the way in which we perceive and experience it, *because this is what we take reality to be*.

An example may help to illustrate this. Some time ago, my five-year-old daughter, Maya, who was just learning to spell, was 'typing' on our computer. I was working nearby, and after a few minutes she asked me how to spell the names of her two younger sisters, Ruby and Shula, as well as 'mummy' and 'daddy'. Maya said she was going to do something very special for us. A few minutes later, Maya showed me what she had typed onto the computer. It read 'daddyamummyamayaarubyashula'. I told her how lovely it was, and when she went to the bathroom, I decided to 'help' her by taking out all the 'a's that she seemed to have mistakenly inserted in between each name. When she got back, she looked at me slightly bemused, and asked me why I had done that. I explained that I was trying to tidy her typing up. She then told me that she had written the 'a's in between the words because she wanted to say 'and' between each of our names, but did not know how to spell it, so had just put an 'a' instead! Here, what is evident is that Maya and myself had reacted in entirely different ways to the same stimulus – the 'a's in between the words – because we had viewed them as part of two very different 'realities'. From my adult 'reality', the 'a's were errors to be erased; from her learning-to-spell reality, the 'a's were a meaningful symbol of a word she couldn't quite spell. Hence, how we acted towards the world was entirely dependent on what we took it to be: there were no fixed truths that caused us to act in any one particular way.

This second part of the second proposition – that the perceptual field is, for the individual, 'reality' – also challenges behaviourist thinking because it questions the idea of a fixed, universal 'truth'. While Rogers (1951), in his 19 propositions, does not claim that an individual's 'reality' is the '"true" reality', his assertion that our perceptions are our 'reality' fundamentally challenges the idea that human behaviour and experiences are determined by some external, trans-personal 'truth'. This is illustrated in Figure 6.1, where a behaviourist/ positivist model of one objective truth acting on multiple individuals is contrasted with a person-centred model of multiple individuals perceiving and acting according to multiple realities. For Rogers, then, 'There are as many "real worlds" as there are people!' (1980: 102): each of us inhabits our own personal and subjective sphere through which we act towards others.

This rejection of ultimate, universal laws (or, at least, the suggestion that they are irrelevant because we can never know them) means that, for Rogers (1959), 'truth' is not something that can be found outside an individual. Rather, for Rogers, truth lies within us. He writes:

> *Experience is, for me, the highest authority*. The touchstone of validity is my own experience. No other person's ideas, and none of my own ideas, are as authoritative as my experience. It is to experience that I must return again and again, to discover a closer approximation to truth as it is in the process of becoming in me.
>
> Neither the bible nor the prophets – neither Freud nor research – neither the revelations of God nor man – can take precedence over my own direct experience.
>
> (Rogers, 1961: 24)

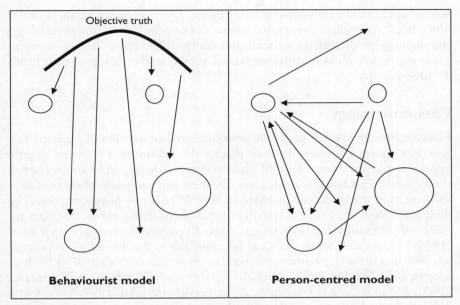

Figure 6.1 Behaviourist and person-centred models of truth

Later on in this chapter we will explore a third possibility: that 'truth' is neither inside nor outside, but co-constructed in the relationship between two persons.

The emergence of an experiential perspective

How did Rogers come to develop such an emphasis on the experiential, subjective dimension of human existence? Tracing his work back to 1942, one finds in *Counseling and Psychotherapy* no mention of 'experience', 'experiencing' or the 'subjective' realms of human existence. What one does find, however, is an assertion that clients are the 'best guides' to the issues which are of most importance to them, and an aversion to therapeutic techniques that attempt to direct, guide or reassure clients from a position of external authority. What one also finds in this book is the presentation of reflective therapeutic techniques which show 'unmistakable signs of intention to comprehend the inner world of the client' (Shlien, 1970: 102). To a great extent, then, Rogers' assertion of the 'fundamental predominance of the subjective' would seem to be rooted in his belief that the primary locus of change is in individuals themselves, rather than those around them, and that the role of the therapist is to help the client develop a deeper insight into his or her own feelings and attitudes.

By the time *Client-Centered Therapy* was published in 1951, however, Rogers' approach had taken on a much more experiential tone. To a great extent, this was probably due to his engagement with the work of Donald Snygg and Arthur Combs, two leading exponents of 'phenomenology' (see below) in the field of psychology (see Rogers, 1959: 197). Snygg and Combs' 1949 book *Individual Behaviour: a new frame of reference for psychology*, the manuscript of which was read and commented on by Rogers, contains many of the key ideas that Rogers would subsequently publish as part of his 19 propositions.

Phenomenology

Before exploring in more detail the person-centred conception of experience, it is worth taking a few moments to discuss the relationship between Rogers' approach and the related field of phenomenology. Snygg and Combs (1949), throughout *Individual Behaviour*, describe their approach as a 'phenomenological' one, and the book itself is based on a 1941 paper by Snygg, entitled 'The need for a phenomenological system of psychology'. Rogers, too, describes his theory of personality and behaviour as 'basically phenomenological in character' (1951: 532; see also 1964: 129) and his approach to theory as well as practice has been described as 'phenomenological' by numerous authors both within (e.g. Lietaer, 2002; Schmid, 2004; Shlien, 1970; Thorne, 1992; Embleton Tudor et al, 2002), and outside (e.g. Glassman, 2000; Pervin and John, 1997; Spiegelberg, 1972; Spinelli, 2005) the person-centred approach.

A brief description of the phenomenological movement will make it readily apparent why Rogers' theory and practice has been so frequently characterized in this way. Developed by the German philosopher Edmund Husserl (1960) around the turn of the twentieth century, phenomenology argued that the starting point for all knowledge must be our lived experiences: 'the "inner evidence" that is given to us intuitively in our conscious experiencing of things' (Cooper, 2003b: 10; see Moran, 2000, for an excellent overview of the phenomenological field). In other words, to truly understand ourselves – as well as the world around us – we must turn our attention to our conscious lived experiences, and Husserl outlined a range of strategies by which this can be achieved (see Ihde, 1986; Spinelli, 2005). These can be summarized as follows:

1. Put to one side ('bracket') prejudices, biases, expectations and assumptions, and focus on experiences as actually experienced.
2. Explore experiences descriptively rather than trying to explain or analyse them.
3. Treat all experiences as being of equal significance ('horizontalization').

In many respects, then, person-centred therapy can be seen as a form of 'applied phenomenology'. Not only is it orientated around an 'intensive and continuing focus on the phenomenological world of the client' (Rogers, 1980: 2153); but the practices of bracketing assumptions, remaining at a descriptive level, and treating all experiences as being of equal worth can all be considered integral elements of person-centred therapy (see Worsley, 2001). At the same time, it would be wrong to assume that Rogers was strongly influenced by Husserl and the post-Husserlian phenomenologists. There are no records of Rogers studying any of these authors' writings (Spiegelberg, 1972), and even Donald Snygg, from whom much of Rogers' phenomenology seems to have been derived, 'had no direct knowledge of their works and was certainly not influenced by them in formulating his phenomenological program' (Spiegelberg, 1972: 147). Moreover, there are some significant contrasts between a traditionally phenomenological perspective and a person-centred one (see Spiegelberg, 1972; Spinelli, 2005). For instance, in contrast to a person-centred standpoint, Husserlian phenomenologists were primarily interested in identifying the 'essential' structures of experiencing (they proposed, for instance, that consciousness is always consciousness of something ('intentionality') and that it consists of an act of experiencing ('noesis') and an object that is experienced ('noema')). Similarly, while Husserlian phenomenologists emphasized the importance of putting to one side all beliefs, person-centred therapists have embraced a number of metaphysical assumptions, in particular the notion of an actualizing tendency. What is probably most accurate to say, then, is that a number of significant parallels exist between a person-centred stand-point and a Husserlian, phenomenological one, but that the former emerged relatively independently of the latter. At the same time, it is worth noting that the phenomenological tradition provides a strong ally – both philo-sophically and psychologically – to a person-centred one, and provides a diverse range of tools by which its understanding, and conceptualization, of experience may be enhanced.

The nature of experience

Up to this point, we have explored how Rogers, like the phenomenologists, emphasized the experiential nature of human being. What we have yet to explore, however, is what Rogers and other person-centred theorists actually meant by 'experience'.

Used as a noun, Rogers defines it in his classic 1959 chapter in Koch's book on the science of psychology as follows: 'all that is going on within the enve-lope of the organism at any given moment which is potentially available to awareness' (p.197). He goes on to state:

> It includes events of which the individual is unaware, as well as all the phenomena which are in consciousness. Thus it includes the psychological aspects of hunger, even though the individual may be so fascinated by his work or play that he is completely unaware of the hunger; it includes the impact of sights and sounds and smells on the organism, even though these are not in the focus of attention. It includes the influence of memory and past experience, as these are active in the moment, in restricting or broadening the meaning given to various stimuli. It also includes all that is present in immediate awareness or consciousness. It does not include such events as neuron discharges or changes in blood sugar, because these are not directly available to awareness. It is thus a psychological, not a physiological definition.
>
> (Rogers 1959: 197)

Here, and in Rogers' other writings on experience and experiencing, we can see a number of key aspects of this phenomenon.

Potentially available to awareness

First, our experiences are all that, at any given moment, are potentially available to awareness. This use of the term 'potentially' is of critical significance, for Rogers (1951), drawing on the work of Angyal (1941) as well as Snygg and Combs (1949), is not suggesting that experience is only that which we are aware of. Rather, what we are aware, or conscious, of is just one part of our experiential field – that part which comes to be symbolized – and there may be many other parts of our experiential field that do not come to be symbolized in our consciousness. Rogers gives the example above of experiencing hunger but being so caught up in work or play that one is not actually conscious of feeling it as such. Another example might be of having a vague sense of dissatisfaction with a meal at a restaurant, but only becoming aware of it once someone else has expressed his or her own discontent. This distinction between what is experienced and what is symbolized in awareness is critical to the person-centred theory of personality and development, because it leads to the possibility that certain experiences can be 'subceived': that is, discriminated without awareness because they do not fit in with a person's concept of self (Rogers, 1959). This process will be explored much more fully in Chapter 7, this volume.

At the same time, Rogers' (1959) emphasis on phenomena that are potentially available to awareness means that his model of psychological functioning is quite different to a Freudian, psychodynamic one, with its tendency to emphasize psychological processes that are *inaccessible* to consciousness. Shlien (1970) makes the distinction here between a model of psychological functioning in which people *will not* express or acknowledge certain things, and one in which they *cannot* do so. For Rogers, 'a large proportion of this world of experience is *available* to consciousness' (1951: 483) and this belief – that people can become aware of the most significant determinants of their lives if they are provided with an environment in which they feel safe enough to do so – is at the heart of a non-directive, non-interpretative approach to therapy.

In the moment

Second, for Rogers experience is something that exists in the moment: at the 'instant of action' (Snygg and Combs, 1949: 15). Our experience is what is immediately present to us: past or future events can be part of our experience, but only inasmuch as they are manifested in the here-and-now: for instance, as memories or as deliberations on future choices.

Private

Third, experience is private. It has an 'inward' (Gendlin, 1970b: 138) or 'inner' (Lietaer, 2002: 8) quality. John Shlien writes: 'Experience is subjective, i.e., it takes place within the opaque organism of the experiencer, and may not be public or even repeatable' (1970: 99).

Bodily

Fourth, experience has a bodily dimension to it. It is sensory, visceral and affective, a 'psycho-physiological' flow (Rogers, 1980: 141). Experience is what we receive 'within' us through all our sense modalities (Rogers, 1951): what we feel, smell, hear, see and taste in the immediate moment that is potentially available to awareness. This bodily dimension of experiencing was particularly emphasized by Eugene Gendlin, one of Carl Rogers' key progeny, and someone who had a significant influence on Rogers' own understanding of experience and experiencing (see Rogers, 1980; Spiegelberg, 1972). Unlike Rogers and Snygg, Gendlin had immersed himself in the works of Husserl and the phenomenological school, and he was particularly influenced by the writings of Maurice Merleau-Ponty (Gendlin, 1962; Purton, 2004), a French existential-phenomenological philosopher who had emphasized the embodied nature of human existence (Cooper, 2003b). For Gendlin (1962), experiencing had a powerful pre-logical, *felt* dimension to it – what he termed the 'felt-sense' – and he argued that this dimension preceded, and would always exceed, the concepts that were used to symbolize it.

Process-like

Fifth, Rogers (1951), like Snygg and Combs (1949), emphasized the fluid and non-static nature of experience. It is an ever-changing gestalt, and if people are understood primarily in terms of their subjective experiencing, then the very nature of human being is to be a 'living, breathing, feeling, fluctuating process' (Rogers, 1961: 114) rather than an object-like 'self'. Gendlin too, with his roots in phenomenological and existential philosophy (a school of thought that emerged in the mid-nineteenth century and focused on the question of what it means to exist, see Cooper (2003a, 2003b, 2004)), put particular emphasis on this aspect of experience. He describes experiencing as a *flow* of sentient living, an *event* (Gendlin, 1970a) and writes, 'It is a process, an activity, a functioning, not a bag of static things' (Gendlin, 1962: 30). Indeed, in contrast to Rogers' earlier writings, Gendlin focuses on *experiencing* as a process rather than *experience* as a noun, and Rogers himself adopts this re-orientation in some of his later thinking (see Rogers, 1980; Spiegelberg, 1972).

Additional facets

Within the person-centred and experiential fields, several other authors have highlighted further aspects of experience and experiencing. Bohart (1993), for instance, emphasizes the way that experience is always holistic – our experiential field is an irreducible whole – and that it is always located within a particular context. Greenberg and Van Balen (1998), along related lines, emphasize the way that our experiences tend to be organized into coherent forms, such that experiencing has a purposive, meaning-creating quality. Cooper (2003a, 2003b, 2004), drawing on existential philosophy, has suggested that experiencing is characterized by both a sense of freedom and a sense of limitations, as well as having a basic orientation towards the future. Finally, authors in both the person-centred and experiential (e.g. Wolfe and Sigl, 1998) and existential-phenomenological (e.g. Sartre, 1958; Spinelli, 2005) fields have differentiated between 'immediate', 'primary' or 'pre-reflective' experiences, and those that are 'reflective' or 'secondary': that is, experiences about experiences. Such a distinction is useful when considering how some experiences may come to be symbolized and incorporated into the self-concept, whilst others may be experienced but never fully acknowledged or 'owned'.

Limitations

The concept of experience, then, lies at the heart of a person-centred approach to therapy, but such an orientation is not without its difficulties and challenges.

First, there is an issue of whether there are more determinants to behaviour than those that can be perceived or experienced. From a psychodynamic perspective, for instance, human behaviour is driven by libidinal and aggressive drives that lie far below the threshold of experiencing (Wolitzky, 2003). It is not just that we choose not to become aware of such 'unconscious' forces, it is that we cannot, just as we cannot become aware of such biological processes as how our muscles generate lactic acid. Jungian psychotherapists would argue much the same thing: that the archetypal forces which structure our thoughts, feelings and behaviour cannot be accessed by awareness. Rather, they are 'blueprints' for action that lie behind everyday experiencing (see Samuels, 1986). From these perspectives, then, the person-centred orientation around experiencing not only disregards many key determinants of behaviour, but also fails to explain why people experience their world in the way that they do.

Paradoxically, some of the most forceful challenges to this phenomenological orientation are the experiential therapists themselves (see Chapter 9, this volume), in particular Les Greenberg, who proposes that 'experiencing can be understood as the synthesized product of a variety of sensorimotor responses and emotion schemes, tinged with conceptual memories, all activated in a situation' (Greenberg and Van Balen, 1998: 45). Here, then, is a tendency to return to the notion of experiencing as an epiphenomenon: a product of deeper, non-experienceable forces – with a 'self' that serves to organize these experiences into a coherent whole – rather than a primary phenomenon in its own right.

A second critique of a classical person-centred perspective on experiencing comes from a very different angle. For Rogers (1951, 1959), as we have seen, experience is something 'subjective', 'private' and 'within' the individual. In recent years, however, many philosophers, psychotherapists and psychologists, both within the person-centred field (e.g. Barrett-Lennard, 2005; Mearns and Cooper, 2005; Schmid, 2004) and outside of it (e.g. Crossley, 1996; Merleau-Ponty, 1962; Spinelli, 2005), have argued that experience is not located 'inside' people, but rather on an 'inter-subjective' (i.e. between people) plane. Whilst we might assume, for instance, that our thoughts take place wholly inside our heads, the fact that we think with language – which is derived from a socio-cultural context – means that our very experiencing is infused with the ideas and communications of others. This does not discount the importance of experiencing, but it does suggest that we need to be wary of conceptualizing it in 'private' or 'subjective' terms. It also suggests that we may need to find new ways of thinking about experiencing which locates it in a more inter-personal context, as some person-centred writers are now beginning to do (Cooper, 2005; Mearns and Cooper, 2005; Schmid, 2003) (see Chapters 4 and 7, this volume).

Implications for practice

Although the experiential orientation of Rogers' (1951, 1959) theory of personality and behaviour was a sequela to, rather than an antecedent of, his non-directive approach to therapy, it has important resonances with the development of his practice. In particular, the introduction of empathy as a key variable in therapeutic personality change (Rogers, 1957) – in which the therapist enters into the client's 'internal frame of reference' (Rogers, 1959: 210) – would seem to necessitate, and closely parallel, a phenomenological approach to human beings. Indeed, Embleton Tudor et al suggest that empathy is essentially: 'a process of attending phenomenologically to the phenomenological world of another' (2002: 18). Congruence, too, would seem to have a close fit with experiential concepts: in this instance, a phenomenological attunement to one's own phenomenological world.

An understanding of human beings as *experiencing* organisms would also seem central to the person-centred model of therapeutic change, where 'full functioning' is described in terms of an increasing openness to experience, a willingness to be a 'process' rather than a 'product', and the ability to live fully in each moment (Rogers, 1959, 1961). As Embleton Tudor et al put it, from a Rogerian standpoint, the person who emerges from a long-enough experience of effective therapy can essentially be described as 'living phenomenologically' (2002: 19).

It is important to note, however, that not all person-centred therapists would consider experience and experiencing so central to the person-centred approach. Indeed, as with many other issues in the field, there is a wide spectrum of opinion as to how 'experiential' the person-centred approach to therapy is, or should be. Whilst Lietaer, for instance, writes that 'the focus on the experiencing process constitutes ... the deepest core of our paradigm' (2002: 8); others, like Sanders (2004), consider it neither a primary nor a secondary principle of person-centred therapy. There are also those, like Prouty, who warn of the dangers of 'phenomenological reductionism', whereby 'The process of experiencing rather than the existential *whole being* of the self is related to by the therapist' (1999: 9). To a great extent, these differences fall along the major cleft in the person-centred and experiential movement. At one end are those experiential therapists, like Lietaer (2002) and Gendlin (1996), who put the experiencing process at the heart of their understanding of human existence, and thereby see the therapist's role as primarily one of facilitating experiential awareness. At the other end of the spectrum there are those classical client-centred therapists, like Sanders (2004) and Brodley (1990), who primarily conceptualize the person as an *actualizing* organism, and thereby put more emphasis on adopting a non-directive stance. It should be noted, however, that charges of 'phenomenological reductionism' may come about because of the tendency of experiential therapists such as Gendlin (1962) to equate experiencing with the felt-sense, such that less embodied aspects of the experiential field – for instance, cognitions – become marginalized. This is clearly inconsistent, however, with Rogers' (1959) understanding of the experiential field, as '*all* that is going on within the envelope of the organism at any given moment' (p.197, italics added). An 'experience-centred' therapeutic approach, therefore, is by no means the same as an 'emotion-focused' approach to therapy (e.g. Elliott et al, 2004); and if a focus on experiencing is understood in its traditional phenomenological sense – as a commitment to bracketing and staying at the level of description – then it would seem much more consistent with the spectrum of person-centred therapies as a whole.

REFERENCES

Angyal, A. (1941). *Foundations for a Science of Personality*. New York: Commonwealth Fund.

Barrett-Lennard, G.T. (2005). *Relationship at the Centre: healing in a troubled world*. London: Whurr.

Bohart, A.C. (1993). Experiencing: the basis of psychotherapy. *Journal of Psychotherapy Integration*, 3, 51–67.

Brodley, B.T. (1990). Client-centered and experiential: two different therapies. In G. Lietaer, J. Rombauts and R. Van Balen (eds), *Client Centred and Experiential Psychotherapies in the Nineties* (pp. 87–107). Leuven: Leuven University Press.

Cooper, M. (2003a). Between freedom and despair: existential challenges and contributions to person-centred and experiential therapy. *Person-Centered and Experiential Psychotherapies*, 2(1), 43–56.

Cooper, M. (2003b). *Existential Therapies*. London: Sage.

Cooper, M. (2004). Existential approaches to therapy. In P. Sanders (ed.), *The Tribes of the Person-Centred Nation: an introduction to the schools of therapy related to the person-centred approach* (pp. 95–124). Ross-on-Wye: PCCS Books.

Cooper, M. (2005). The inter-experiential field: perceptions and metaperceptions in person-centered and experiential psychotherapy and counseling. *Person-Centered and Experiential Psychotherapies*, 4(1), 54–68.

Crossley, N. (1996). *Intersubjectivity: the fabric of social becoming*. London: Sage.

Elliott, R., Watson, J.C., Goldman, R. and Greenberg, L.S. (2004). *Learning*

Emotion-Focused Therapy: the process-experiential approach to change. Washington DC: American Psychological Association.

Embleton Tudor, L.E., Keemar, K., Tudor, K., Valentine, J. and Worrall, M. (2002). *The Person-Centred Approach: a contemporary introduction.* Houndsmill: Palgrave MacMillan.

Gendlin, E.T. (1962). *Experiencing and the Creation of Meaning: a philosophical and psychological approach to the subjective.* Evanston, Il.: Northwestern University.

Gendlin, E.T. (1970a). Existentialism and experiential psychotherapy. In J.T. Hart and T.M. Tomlinson (eds), *New Directions in Client-Centered Therapy* (pp. 70–93). Boston: Houghton Mifflin.

Gendlin, E.T. (1970b). A theory of personality change. In J.T. Hart and T.T. M (eds), *New Directions in Client-Centered Therapy* (pp. 129–73). Boston: Houghton Mifflin.

Gendlin, E.T. (1996). *Focusing-Oriented Psychotherapy: a manual of the experiential method.* New York: Guilford Press.

Glassman, W.E. (2000). *Approaches to Psychology.* Buckingham: Open University Press.

Greenberg, L.S. and Van Balen, R. (1998). The theory of experience-centered therapies. In L.S. Greenberg, J.C. Watson and G. Lietaer (eds), *Handbook of Experiential Psychotherapy* (pp. 28–57). New York: Guilford Press.

Gross, R. (1996). *Psychology: the science of mind and behaviour* (3rd edn). London: Hodder and Stoughton.

Husserl, E. (1960). *Cartesian Meditations: an introduction to phenomenology.* The Hague: Martinus Nijhoff.

Ihde, D. (1986). *Experimental Phenomenology: an introduction.* Albany, N.Y.: State University of New York Press.

Lietaer, G. (2002). The united colors of person-centred and experiential psychotherapies. *Person-Centred and Experiential Psychotherapies,* 1(1–2), 4–13.

Mearns, D. and Cooper, M. (2005). *Working at Relational Depth in Counselling and Psychotherapy.* London: Sage.

Merleau-Ponty, M. (1962). *The Phenomenology of Perception* (C. Smith, Trans.). London: Routledge.

Moran, D. (2000). *Introduction to Phenomenology.* London: Routledge.

Pervin, L.A. and John, O.P. (1997). *Personality: theory and research.* New York: Wiley.

Prouty, G. (1999). Carl Rogers and experiential therapies: a dissonance? *Person-Centred Practice,* 7(1), 11.

Purton, C. (2004). *Person-Centred Therapy: the focussing-oriented approach.* London: Palgrave MacMillan.

Rogers, C.R. (1942). *Counseling and Psychotherapy: newer concepts in practice.* Boston: Houghton Mifflin.

Rogers, C.R. (1951). *Client-Centered Therapy.* Boston: Houghton Mifflin.

Rogers, C.R. (1957). The necessary and sufficient conditions of therapeutic personality change. *Journal of Consulting Psychology,* 21(2), 95–103.

Rogers, C.R. (1959). A theory of therapy, personality and interpersonal relationships as developed in the client-centered framework. In S. Koch (ed.), *Psychology: a study of science*. Volume 3. *Formulations of the person and the social context* (pp.184–256). New York: McGraw-Hill.

Rogers, C.R. (1961). *On Becoming a Person: a therapist's view of psychotherapy*. London: Constable.

Rogers, C.R. (1964). Towards a science of the person. In T.W. Wann (ed.), *Behaviorism and Phenomenology: contrasting bases for modern psychology* (pp. 109–40). Chicago, Il.: University of Chicago Press.

Rogers, C.R. (1980). *A Way of Being*. Boston: Houghton Mifflin.

Rogers, C.R. (1990). B.F. Skinner. In H. Kirschenbaum and V. Henderson (eds), *Carl Rogers: dialogues* (pp. 79–152). London: Constable.

Samuels, A. (1986). *Jung and the Post-Jungians*. London: Routledge.

Sanders, P. (2004). Mapping person-centred approaches to counselling and psychotherapy. In P. Sanders (ed.), *The Tribes of the Person-Centred Nation: an introduction to the schools of therapy related to the person-centred approach* (pp. 149–63). Ross-on-Wye: PCCS Books.

Sartre, J.-P. (1958). *Being and Nothingness: an essay on phenomenological ontology* (H. Barnes, Trans.). London: Routledge.

Schmid, P.F. (2003). The characteristics of a person-centred approach to therapy and counseling: critiera for identity and coherence. *Person-Centered and Experiential Psychotherapies*, 2(2), 104–20.

Schmid, P.F. (2004). Back to the client: a phenomenological approach to the process of understanding and diagnosis. *Person-Centred and Experiential Psychotherapies*, 3(1), 36–51.

Shlien, J.M. (1970). Phenomenology and personality. In J.T. Hart and T.M. Tomlinson (eds), *New Directions in Client-centered Therapy* (pp. 95–128). Boston: Houghton Mifflin.

Snygg, D. (1941). The need for a phenomenological system of psychology. *Psychological Review*, 48, 404–24.

Snygg, D. and Combs, A.W. (1949). *Individual Behavior: a new frame of reference for psychology*. New York: Harper and Brothers.

Spiegelberg, H. (1972). *Phenomenology in Psychology and Psychiatry: a historical introduction*. Evanston, Il.: Northwestern University Press.

Spinelli, E. (2005). *The Interpreted World: an introduction to phenomenological psychology* (2nd edn). London: Sage.

Thorne, B. (1992). *Carl Rogers*. London: Sage.

Wolfe, B.E. and Sigl, P. (1998). Experiential psychotherapy of anxiety disorders. In L.S. Greenberg, J.C. Watson and G. Lietaer (eds), *Handbook of Experiential Psychotherapy* (pp. 272–94). New York: Guilford Press.

Wolitzky, D. (2003). The theory and practice of traditional psychoanalytic treatment. In A.S. Gurman and S.B. Messer (eds), *Essential Psychotherapies: theory and practice* (2nd edn: 69–106). New York: Guilford.

Worsley, R. (2001). *Process Work in Person-Centred Therapy: phenomenological and existential perspectives*. Basingstoke: Palgrave MacMillan.

Developmental and Personality Theory

Mick Cooper

How do human beings come to be the people they are? More specifically, why do some people come to experience the psychological difficulties that they do? These are the questions that developmental and personality theorists in the counselling and psychotherapy field have asked, and this chapter looks at person-centred attempts to answer these questions. The chapter begins with a historical overview of theories of personality and development in the person-centred field and then goes on to present a detailed summary of Rogers' (1951, 1959) original formulation. This is followed by a presentation of three key areas in which Rogers' work has been critiqued and developed by contemporary scholars in the person-centred field: relational theories of personality, self and development; pluralistic theories; and ones which attempt to broaden out Rogers' original model.

An important question to ask before undertaking a review of personality and developmental theory is that of its role in the person-centred field. Given the emphasis within this approach on adopting a phenomenological, non-interpretative stance towards our clients (see Chapter 6, this volume), it could be argued that pre-defined theories of why clients are the way they are will serve to undermine, rather than facilitate, therapeutic work. Certainly, some authors within the person-centred field have emphasized this danger (e.g. Rogers, 2001; Wilkins, 2003). As Carl Rogers (1964: 133) himself writes, however, it is simply not possible to engage with clients in an unbiased, a-theoretical way: we will always have theories and assumptions about how our clients come to be the way they are. The issue, then, is not whether or not person-centred therapists have theoretical assumptions; but whether or not they are aware of their assumptions and are able to put them to one side as fully as possible. In this respect, the role of theories of personality and development within the person-centred field is not to tell us – or our clients – why they are the way they are. Rather, it is a field of enquiry that can help us to reflect on, and challenge, our pre-existing assumptions, and that can provide us with possibilities that may help us be more open to the totality of our clients. By providing us with a theory of development and personality that is consistent with our theoretical practice, it can also serve to validate our work – both to ourselves and to the outside world – and act as the stimulus for further developments in our theories of practice.

Historical development

According to Barrett-Lennard (1998), Rogers' interest in personality-related issues, such as the self-concept, can be traced back to the beginnings of his career in 1931 and his development of a 'personality adjustment' measure. It was not until 1947, however, that he discussed these issues more publicly and systematically, presenting 'Some observations on the organization of personality' in his address as retiring president of the American Psychological Association. This was followed in 1951 by his publication of 'A theory of personality and behavior' in *Client-Centered Therapy*: a series of 19 propositions which together constituted a systematic conceptual framework for understanding human personality and development. This framework was extended and refined in Rogers' 1959 'theory of therapy, personality, and interpersonal relationships, as developed in the client-centred framework', published in Koch's *Psychology: a study of science*. This chapter is less well-known than his 1951 propositions, but it is generally regarded – by Rogers and others – as his most definitive, rigorous and systematic statement of theory (e.g. Barrett-Lennard, 1998). In 1963, Rogers published some further thoughts on the 'actualizing tendency', but after that date he made no further significant contributions to developmental and personality theory (Mearns, 2002). Indeed, from the 1960s to around the early 1990s, person-centred thinking in the field of human development and personality could be considered to have almost entirely stagnated, although the last decade or so has seen a significant re-emergence of interest in this domain (e.g. Biermann-Ratjen, 1998b; Cooper, 2000; Mearns, 2002; Warner, 2005).

In examining the emergence of theories of personality and development in the person-centred field, it is important to note that these theories have always tended to follow on from, rather than precede, theories of therapeutic practice and change. Rogers' (1942) first major publication on the practice of therapy with adults, for instance, *Counseling and Psychotherapy*, appeared almost ten years before his 1951 propositions, and contained virtually no mention of developmental or personality processes. Whilst in such therapeutic fields as the psychodynamic approach, then, theories of human development and theories of therapeutic practice have tended to grow up side-by-side, the same could not be said within the person-centred approach.

Rogers' original model

In developing a theory of personality and human development, Rogers (1951, 1959) drew from a wide variety of sources – including his own students (e.g. Standal, 1954). Two areas of thinking, however, can be considered of particular importance to his work, both of which have been examined in earlier chapters of this handbook. The first of these is the field of phenomenology (Snygg and Combs, 1949), which starts from the assumption that human existence can be best understood in terms of how people experience their world (see Chapter 6, this volume), rather than in such non-experiential terms as 'unconscious' processes, behavioural stimuli and responses, or an 'object-like' Self. The second assumption, coming from the field of humanistic psychology (e.g. Maslow, 1943), is that individuals are propelled forward in the direction of 'growth' or 'actualization' (see Chapter 5, this volume). Rogers defines this actualizing tendency as 'the inherent tendency of the organism to develop all its capacities in ways which serve to maintain or enhance the organism' (1959: 196) and identifies it particularly in the 'organismic valuing process'. This is described as the organism's innate tendency to positively value (as manifested in feelings of satisfaction) those experiences that are self-enhancing and self-maintaining, and to negatively value (as manifested in feelings of dissatisfaction) those experiences that are not self-enhancing or self-maintaining. Note that, in contrast to Maslow (1968), Rogers specifically uses the term 'actualizing tendency' to refer to this growth-motivating force, as opposed to 'self-actualizing' tendency. Indeed, for Rogers, as we shall shortly see, the tendency to actualize the 'self' – or, more accurately, what is conceptualized as the self – is the primary fount of psychological distress.

Rogers' model of human development, as outlined in his 1959 'Koch' chapter, is presented in Figure 7.1. It is summarized in the remainder of this section.

In the first stages of life, the child's experience of the world is an integrated, undifferentiated whole, in which there is no differentiation between 'me' and 'not-me' experiences. As children develop, however, a portion of their experiential field becomes differentiated as 'self-experiences': those experiences which the individual associates with their own being: for instance 'I am brushing my teeth'.

Ideally, the child's self-concept exactly matches their actual experiencing. A young girl, for instance, gets bored with feeding her baby sister bottles of milk, and thereby come to see herself as someone who sometimes gets bored with caring for others. The spanner in the works, however, is the infant's emerging need for positive regard: the desire to 'experience oneself as making a positive difference in the experiential field of another' (Rogers, 1959: 208). Because of this need, the child increasingly turns her attention to the positive regard she evokes in others, and begins to associate her self-experiences with certain levels of acceptance from others. In some very rare cases, a child will experience positive regard in relation to all her self-experiences – what Rogers refers to as 'unconditional positive regard'. More likely, however, the child

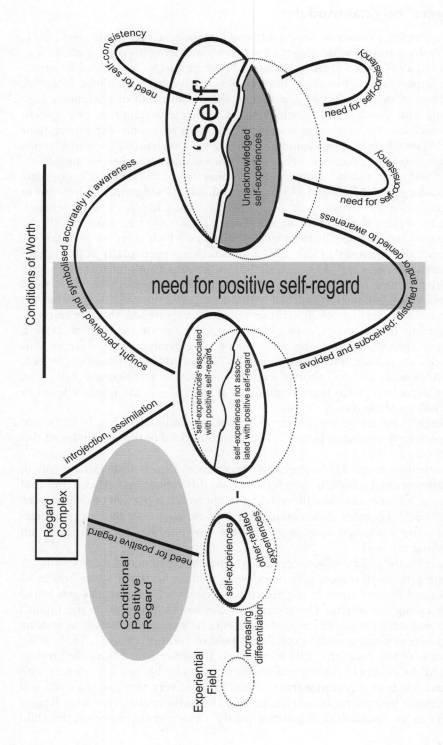

Figure 7.1 Rogers' (1959) model of human development

will begin to discover that certain of her self-experiences are associated with positive regard whilst others are not. She may experience, for instance, that people like her when she feels affectionately towards her younger sister, but not when she feels resentful towards her. Hence, the child develops a 'regard complex': 'all those self-experiences, together with their interrelationships, which the individual discriminates as being related to the positive regard of a particular social other' (Rogers, 1959: 209).

As the child develops, the associations between self-experiences and positive regard then come to be internalized, so that the child comes to experience 'positive self-regard' independently of the positive regard transactions from external others. Hence, for instance, the child no longer needs others to 'reward' her for experiencing affection towards her sister; now she rewards herself through the medium of the total 'self-regard complex'. The child has come to selectively view her self-experiences as more or less worthy of self-regard: she has acquired 'conditions of worth' (Rogers, 1959). And because, as an internalization of the need for positive regard, the child has a need for positive self-regard, she comes to selectively seek those self-experiences which are associated with positive self-regard and avoid those self-experiences which are not. So, for example, she spends more time feeding her baby sister milk than her organismic valuing process might otherwise indicate, because it evokes in her good feelings about herself. In other words, she has *introjected* a set of values that may not actually be consistent with her own organismic valuing process (Rogers, 1951).

Concomitant with these behavioural changes, the child's need for positive self-regard also means that she may begin to *perceive* her self-experiences selectively. Self-experiences consistent with her conditions of worth will evoke feelings of positive self-regard. Hence, the child should feel quite comfortable with reflecting on these self-experiences, symbolizing them accurately at the level of conscious awareness and integrating them into her overall concept of self. But those self-experiences that are inconsistent with the child's conditions of worth are likely to bring up more negative feelings, so that the child is less likely to feel comfortable with reflecting on them. Hence, she may be more likely to leave these self-experiences at a 'pre-reflective' level: refraining from symbolizing them accurately at the level of conscious awareness and failing to integrate them into her overall concept of self. Rogers (1951, 1959) refers to this process of discrimination without reflective awareness as 'subception', and suggests that it can be achieved by two strategies: 'denial' or 'distortion'. So for example, the young girl may simply deny that she feels bored feeding her baby sister, or she may distort the felt sense of boredom by telling herself that she is tired or worn-out. Hence, she can maintain her concept of herself as a caring person.

As well as denying some of her actual experiences, the child may also introject experiences associated with positive self-regard which lie entirely outside the realms of her own self-experiencing. For instance, a young boy may come to believe that he enjoys playing with guns because, when he plays with them, other people seem to take pleasure in his 'enjoyment' of them. The consequence of this selective perception, then, is that:

[a discrepancy] develops between the self as perceived, and the actual experience of the organism. Thus the individual may perceive himself as having characteristics *a, b, c,* and experiencing feelings *x, y, z.* An accurate symbolization of his experience, however, indicate characteristics *c, d, e* and feelings *v, w, x.*

(Rogers, 1959: 203)

This discrepancy is then reified as a consequence of the organism's need for self-consistency – a concept developed by Lecky (1945). Thus organisms further deny to awareness those experiences that are inconsistent with their sense of who they are, while further acknowledging and incorporating self-consistent self-experiences into their sense of self.

By the time most people have reached adulthood, therefore, Rogers' (1959) model of human development suggests that they are estranged from themselves to varying degrees, with levels of self-estrangement closely corresponding to levels of psychological disturbance. This association can be posited to exist for a number of reasons. First, if individuals are denying their experiences – or introjecting 'experiences' that are not their own – then their inherent, organismic ability to evaluate whether an experience is self-enhancing or self-maintaining is likely to be overridden. Hence, estranged individuals are less likely to engage in organismically satisfying and self-enriching activities, and more likely to engage in the kind of self-stagnating or self-destructive activities that can lead to feelings of boredom, hopelessness and depression. Second, the organism's attempt to maintain and enhance all of its capacities means that, even if certain experiences are distorted or denied, they will continue to be generated by the organism as a whole in its attempts to actualize. Consequently, the individual is likely to experience frequent feelings of anxiety: a sense that some unacceptable self-experience is lurking on the edges of awareness, threatening to disrupt the consistency of the self and undermine feelings of positive self-regard. Furthermore, where subceived needs or feelings are so strong that they become expressed overtly, then the person may experience a highly disconcerting sense of 'I am doing things which are not myself, which I cannot control' (Rogers, 1951: 514): perhaps even of being taken over by something 'alien'.

Critiques and developments of the original model

Within the wider psychological and psychotherapeutic field, a range of criticisms have been levelled at Rogers' model of human personality and development. Perhaps the most pervasive charge, related to the concept of the actualizing tendency, is that Rogers starts from an over-optimistic and naïve viewpoint and underestimates the human potential for destructive and anti-social behaviours. (This is discussed in Chapter 5, this volume.) A second common criticism is that Rogers' model excludes from investigation those variables that lie outside human awareness: in particular, 'unconscious' forces and dynamics (see Pervin and John, 1997, and Chapter 6, this volume). A third potential criticism of Rogers' model is that, despite its foundations in clinical observations, it lacks any contemporary, empirical evidence – particularly in the field of developmental psychology – to support its hypotheses. An excellent summary of such criticisms and an informed rebuttal can be found in Paul Wilkins' (2003) *Person-Centred Therapy in Focus*. This chapter, however, will focus more specifically on criticisms of Rogers' original model that have emerged from within the person-centred field and contemporary attempts to develop models of personality and human development that can address these concerns. Note, here, that we will also not be looking at models of personality and development that have emerged within the wider field of experiential psychotherapy (see Greenberg and Van Balen, 1998, for a highly sophisticated post-Rogerian model of being).

Intersubjective and relational perspectives

From both within the person-centred field (e.g. Barrett-Lennard, 2005; Bohart, 2003; Holdstock, 1993; Mearns and Cooper, 2005; O'Hara, 1992; Schmid, 1998; Stinckens et al, 2002) and outside it (Geller, 1982), one of the most common criticism of Rogers' (1951, 1959) original theory of personality and human development is that it is overly individualistic (see also Chapters 4, 5 and 6, this volume). As we have seen, Rogers' developmental model begins with an organism that is essentially separate from its world – a self-contained, self-regulating, discrete entity – that has the potential to achieve an independent and autonomous existence. For many contemporary 'intersubjective' theorists, however, this idea is highly problematic (e.g. Barrett-Lennard, 2005; Mearns and Cooper, 2005). They challenge the assumption that 'human beings are little self-encapsulated "shells" or monads' (Bohart, 2003: 112), and argue, instead, that we are 'fundamentally and inextricably intertwined with others' (Mearns and Cooper, 2005: 5).

Development as relational

Drawing on recent developments in the field of relational psychodynamics (e.g. Bowlby, 1979; Stern, 2003), several contemporary authors within the person-centred field (Biermann-Ratjen, 1998b; Mearns and Cooper, 2005; Schmid, 1998; Warner, 2000, 2001, 2002, 2005) have outlined a model of child development that puts another human being at its very core. These approaches differ from Rogers' (1951, 1959) original formulation in that, long before infants are considered capable of discriminating self-experiences, they are seen as being powerfully influenced by the existence of others. Moreover, in contrast to Rogers' original model, relationships with others are not just seen in a negative sense – in terms of the inhibiting impact of conditional positive regard – but also in terms of their importance in facilitating positive growth and development.

In terms of what infants might need from early relationships and what might happen if these needs are not met, contemporary developmental theorists have suggested a range of possibilities. For Biermann-Ratjen (1998a, 1998b), infants require much the same conditions for healthy psychological development as clients do for constructive personality change in therapy: unconditional positive regard and empathy from a congruent other. Note, here, Biermann-Ratjen is suggesting that infants have a 'need for positive regard from the first days of life onwards' (1998b: 120) – a position which is somewhat different from Rogers' (1959) assertion that the need for positive regard is a secondary or learnt need. Through being parented in this way, argues Biermann-Ratjen, infants can come to integrate all of their self-experiences into their sense of self and thereby develop as integrated, well-functioning adults.

Starting from this basis, Biermann-Ratjen (1998b) suggests three phases of human development, each of which she associates with particular forms of psychological distress. In her first phase of development, experiences associated with unconditional positive regard and empathy are incorporated into a very early sense of self. Stagnation at this phase, suggests Biermann-Ratjen, can lead to a fundamental incapacity to integrate emotional experiences into the self-concept, leading to such severe psychological difficulties as psychotic disintegration and a feeling of losing self-control. Biermann-Ratjen's second phase, however, is marked by the formation of a rudimentary self-concept, into which the infant can begin to integrate experiences. Now the issue is less one of the establishment of the self-concept and more one of whether or not an experience confirms or threatens the pre-existing sense of self. Biermann-Ratjen suggests that stagnation at this stage can lead to a feared collapse of self-concept or feelings of being worthless. A third phase is where the individual, having established some sense of self, begins to develop a psychosexual identity; stagnation at this stage, according to Biermann-Ratjen, is more associated with the fear of being inadequate and guilty.

Like Biermann-Ratjen (1998b), Warner (2000, 2005, 2001, 2002) also emphasizes the infants' need for a benign care-giving environment. In her writings, however, she puts particular emphasis on the young infants' need to be empathically understood, such that they can learn to effectively process – that is, make sense of – their life experiences. 'Infants are initially almost totally dependent on adults to hold experiences in any sort of sustained attention, to modulate the intensity of experience, and to name experience,' states Warner (2005: 93); and if adults 'scaffold' this processing in an adequate way, then Warner suggests that infants can begin to take over this processing activity for themselves. When this does not happen, however, Warner suggests that the infant may develop a 'fragile' processing style, in which they are not fully able to 'hold' their own experiences in attention. Consequently, they may easily feel violated, threatened and misunderstood by others, which may lead to feelings of defensiveness and rage towards others, in Warner's view. If they are not able to hold their own experiences in attention, Warner also suggests that they may experience feelings of emptiness inside.

A third contemporary person-centred perspective on early relational needs and the problems that may emerge if these are not met is outlined by Mearns and Cooper (2005). While Biermann-Ratjen (1998b) and Warner (2005) – alongside Rogers (1951, 1959) and most attachment theorists (e.g. Bowlby, 1979) – place an emphasis on what young infants need to receive from relationships, Mearns and Cooper argue that infants also have a basic need to give and to be involved in a bi-directional meeting: 'They want to be loved, but they want to interact with that other and that love, to give as well as to receive, and to experience an immediate and engaged contact' (2005: 8). On the basis of this hypothesis, Mearns and Cooper (2005) suggest that difficulties in adulthood may be linked to a person's failure to experience in-depth relational encounters with others, such that they cannot engage with others in in-depth and satisfying ways, and in ways that can buffer them against crises in their life-world.

The person in context

Moving beyond a focus on dyadic relationships, other authors within the person-centred field (e.g. Barrett-Lennard, 2005; Bohart, 2003; Cooper, 2003a; Embleton Tudor et al, 2002; Mearns, 2002; O'Hara, 1992; Schmid, 2003) have emphasized the importance of understanding human beings within their life-world: of seeing human beings as fundamentally woven into their social, cultural, political and historical context rather than separable from it. Perhaps the most ambitious framework developed here is that of Barrett-Lennard (2005), who suggests nine different systems of relation within which human existence is embedded, each with the potential for multiple sub-systems and complex, interdependent connections between them:

1. The individual.
2. The person's primary two-person relationships (e.g. spouse/partner).
3. The family system.
4. Small groups (e.g. a child's class).
5. Large groups/organizations (e.g. a child's school).
6. Communities of association and belonging.
7. States and nations.
8. The human race.
9. Planetary life systems.

In Barrett-Lennard's (2005) framework, then, to fully understand our clients, we must understand them in terms of the multiple social systems in which they are embedded. To understand them solely at the individual, intrapersonal level will only ever give us a partial understanding.

As well as being criticized for its individualistic understanding of human being, Rogers' (1951, 1959) theory of personality and development has also been criticized for its implicitly individualistic *values* (Bohart, 2003; Mearns and Cooper, 2005; Mearns and Thorne, 2000; O'Hara, 1992): that 'maturity' and psychological well-being involve a movement towards greater independence, self-regulation and autonomy. In other words, Rogers' model has been criticized for implicitly valuing independence over interdependence, and for promoting the values of a very particular, dominant socio-economic group – white, Western, liberal males (Bohart, 2003; Holdstock, 1993) – in a way that mistakenly assumes these are universal human motives and needs.

In contrast to Rogers' (1951, 1959) original theory, then, several contemporary authors have argued that optimal psychological development is not simply a matter of moving towards autonomy. Rather, it also involves the capacity to develop a 'relational self' (O'Hara, 1992), and to effectively mediate the psychological 'push–pull' (Embleton Tudor et al, 2002) between the desire for independence and the desire for relationship. Along these lines, Mearns (2002; Mearns and Thorne, 2000) suggests that the individual's 'actualizing tendency' (i.e. the desire to actualize his or her personal potential) will inevitably come up against the forces of 'social mediation' (derived from the action of the actualizing tendency on the social life space), and that both of these forces have an intrinsic validity. In other words, for Mearns (2002), it is not the case that the 'positive' drive of the actualizing tendency is 'cruelly' inhibited by the constrictions of society. Rather, social restraints have an important role to play, and the 'actualizing process', as Mearns defines it, is the configuring and reconfiguring of this balance between the actualizing tendency and the forces of social relationships.

Self-pluralistic perspectives

Like the intersubjective and relational theorists above, 'self-plurality' theorists have also moved away from Rogers' (1951, 1959) tendency to conceptualize personality and human development at the level of the unitary individual. In this case, however, it is from the entirely opposite direction. Here, several contemporary person-centred authors (Barrett-Lennard, 2005; Cooper, 1999; Cooper et al, 2004; Keil, 1996; Mearns, 2002; Mearns and Thorne, 2000; Warner, 2000, 2005) as well as those in the related fields of experiential therapy (Elliott and Greenberg, 1997; Greenberg et al, 1993; Stinckens et al, 2002) and assimilation theory (Stiles et al, 1990; Stiles and Glick, 2002) have argued that a focus on the individual not only overlooks the multiplicity of which the individual is a part, but also the *multiplicity by which the individual is constituted*. In other words, what these authors have suggested is that human beings are made up of multiple elements – or 'configurations of self' (Mearns, 2002; Mearns and Thorne, 2000), 'modes of being' (Cooper, 1999), 'inner persons' (Keil, 1996), 'subselves' (Barrett-Lennard, 2005), 'voices' (Stiles et al, 1990) or 'parts' (Warner, 2000) – and that an understanding of human beings as such can play a valuable part in the theory and practice of person-centred therapy.

As with other aspects of person-centred theorizing, much of this analysis is directly derived from clinical observations. Mearns (in Cooper et al, 2004), for instance, describes how, as he began to work with clients at 'relational depth', he noticed that they would begin to talk about different 'parts' of themselves. Similarly, Cooper (1999) gives the example of clients who spontaneously describe themselves as 'like Jekyll and Hyde' or 'schizophrenic'.

In attempting to incorporate self-pluralism into a person-centred understanding of human development and personality, self-pluralistic theorists have suggested a number of revisions or additions to Rogers' (1951, 1959) original model (though it is interesting to note that Rogers (1959) himself was in no way adverse to the idea of self-plurality). Barrett-Lennard (2005), Cooper (1999) and Keil (1996), for instance, have all pointed to the fact that different social environments or relationships are likely to confer positive regard onto a person for very different behaviours and experiences. A young man, for instance, may experience a great deal of positive regard from his peer group for enjoying alcohol, while his parents may be horrified by this behaviour. Hence, extending Rogers' original theory, these authors have suggested that people may develop a multiplicity of self-concepts to accrue positive regard – and hence positive self-regard – in a range of different social contexts.

Cooper (1999) has proposed another modification of Rogers' (1951, 1959) original model that can allow for the development of multiple 'selves'. Cooper suggests that, when people are faced with experiences that are dissonant from their self-concepts, denying or distorting the experiences may not be their only means of maintaining a consistency between self-concept and experience. Rather, he argues, what they may do is to develop a *new*, 'alter' self-concept that is consistent with the current experience. For example, if people who usually see themselves as measured and calm start to experience anger, they might temporarily develop a new concept of themselves as a 'rageful person'.

Mearns (2002; Mearns and Thorne, 2000) proposes a further means for understanding how multiple selves may develop. He suggests that they may start off as introjections – for instance, 'I am a failure' – around which the person may then constellate various cognitive, affective and behavioural elements. This, Mearns suggest, is a way that the person can give the introjection more of an 'established and functional' status, but it is also a way of compartmentalizing the introjection so that the person can concurrently hold different views of him or herself. Mearns (like Warner, in Cooper et al, 2004) goes on to suggest, however, that under situations of extreme stress – such as trauma or abuse – the various configurations of self may not be able to deal with the incongruities between them, leading to further separation and a state of dissociation (in Cooper et al, 2004).

In contrast to these developmental models, Barrett-Lennard (2005) suggests that the existence of multiple selves may also be a consequence of the inherently pluralistic nature of human beings. As he points out, we have a biological nature, a social nature, a psychological nature, and a huge array of specialized subsystems within our body and mind. Hence, there is no reason to assume that the self should have a 'single constant or master pattern' (2005: 6). Along similar lines, Warner (in Cooper et al, 2004) argues that one of the most basic tendencies of human beings is to 'self' – to create coherent narratives about who they are – but that the corollary of any such 'self-ing' is a tendency to identify experiences that do not completely fit into one's pre-existing sense of self. She gives the example:

> No sooner do you get yourself clear – 'That I realize now that I am an orthodox Catholic, I always have been and I always will be' – than a little part of you the next day says something different: maybe, 'Some part of me has always hated being told what to do and wants to do things that I think are really sinful.'
> (in Cooper et al, 2004: 180–1)

As can be seen, a number of similarities exist in how contemporary person-centred theorists conceptualize self-plurality, but there are also a number of significant differences. Cooper's (1999) model, for instance, comes from a strictly phenomenological standpoint (see Chapter 6, this volume), and thereby conceptualizes self-plurality in terms of the multiple self-concepts through which a person may *experience* their world. Other authors (e.g. Keil, 1996), however, have taken a more structural position, envisaging the different 'parts' as actual person-like entities inhabiting an 'inner world'. Closely related to this, while Cooper (1999) sees the person as moving from one 'mode of being' to another over time ('diachronous plurality'), theorists such as Keil (1996) tend to see the different 'persons' as existing concurrently ('synchronous plurality'). Another debate emerging within the self-pluralistic field is the issue of whether there is a 'deeper', 'truer' self, or whether all the different 'parts' can be considered equally authentic (see Cooper et al, 2004).

Despite these differences, what all these self-pluralistic theorists agree on is that it is not the existence of different 'parts', per se, that is associated with psychological distress. Rather, what is seen as being psychologically problematic is when these different 'parts' of the person relate to each other in conflictual, critical or abusive ways, as opposed to having harmonious, empathic and open relationships between them. From a developmental standpoint, then, the question is not so much 'How do these different "parts" develop?' as 'How do conflictual relationships between the different "parts" develop?' Here, little work has been done, though Cooper (2003b, 2004, 2005), drawing on the work of the Soviet developmental psychologist Vygotsky (1962), has suggested that the way people relate to themselves may be an internalization of the way others have related to them. Hence, for example, people who have been heavily criticized by their parents may come to develop a powerful 'inner critic', just as clients who experience the core conditions from their therapists may come to develop a more accepting, empathic way of relating to themselves.

Broadening person-centred theory of personality and development

Like the contemporary theorists discussed above, other critics of the original person-centred theory of personality and development (e.g. Cain, 1993; Pervin and John, 1997; Wilkins, 2003) have argued that Rogers' approach is not wrong, just overly limited. In other words, while it is accepted that Rogers' model of how people develop and come to experience psychological difficulties may explain some developmental processes and experiences, it is insufficiently broad or complex to explain them all – and particularly the development of the many different forms of psychological disturbance (Cain, 1993).

One attempt to broaden the person-centred developmental framework is proposed by Cooper (1999). He argues that the conflict between the actualizing tendency and the self-actualizing tendency, as outlined in the original model of development (Rogers, 1951, 1959), can be read as just one example of a wider range of conflicts that may emerge between different aspects of the actualizing tendency – conflicts which emerge, he suggests, because an environment may only allow the actualization of one potentiality at the expense of another. So, for example, while a young man may inhibit his desire to be a rock musician because his parents disapprove of such behaviour, it may also be that he suppresses this desire because he wants to spend more time developing his academic potentiality. Hence, in this model, psychological conflicts are not always reducible to the need to be approved of. Closely related to this, Cooper goes on to suggest that people may deny or distort experiences for a whole range of reasons alongside the need for self-consistency and the need for positive regard; and that, even when people are attempting to maintain their self-concept, this image of themselves may not necessarily have emerged to maximize positive (self-)regard (it may, for instance, simply have emerged from the reflective appraisal of others). Hence, while Cooper's model does not deny the significance or pervasiveness of the developmental process outlined by Rogers, it suggests that this is just one instance of a wider set of developmental possibilities.

CONCLUSION

Despite being developed over 50 years ago, there is an elegance and a succinctness to Rogers' (1951, 1959) theory of personality and development that makes it one of the most persuasive accounts available, as evidenced in its continued inclusion in major textbooks on personality and psychology (e.g. Glassman, 2000; Pervin and John, 1997). Today, increasing numbers of scholars within the person-centred field are reflecting on Rogers' original formulation, and devising accounts of human personality and development that are more consistent with contemporary developments in the philosophical, psychological and psychotherapeutic domains. Theories of personality and development may never be as central to the person-centred approach as they are to more diagnostic and analytical psychotherapies, but they have enormous potential to stimulate our questioning and understanding about the nature of our clients' lives – helping us to engage with our clients in a way that is open, non-dogmatic and deeply respectful of the paths by which they have come to be who they are.

REFERENCES

Barrett-Lennard, G.T. (1998). *Carl Rogers' Helping System: journey and substance*. London: Sage.

Barrett-Lennard, G.T. (2005). *Relationship at the Centre: healing in a troubled world*. London: Whurr.

Biermann-Ratjen, E.-M. (1998a). Incongruence and psychopathology. In B. Thorne and E. Lambers (eds), *Person-Centred Therapy: a European perspective* (pp. 119–30). London: Sage.

Biermann-Ratjen, E.-M. (1998b). On the development of persons in relationships. In B. Thorne and E. Lambers (eds), *Person-Centred Therapy: a European perspective* (pp. 106–18). London: Sage.

Bohart, A.C. (2003). Person-centered psychotherapy and related experiential approaches. In A.S. Gurman and S.B. Messer (eds), *Essential

Psychotherapies: theory and practice (2nd edn: 107–48). New York: Guilford.

Bowlby, J. (1979). The making and breaking of affectional bonds. In *The Making and Breaking of Affectional Bonds* (pp. 150–201). London: Routledge.

Cain, D.J. (1993). The uncertain future of client-centered counselling. *Journal of Humanistic Education and Development*, 31, 133–38.

Cooper, M. (1999). If you can't be Jekyll be Hyde: an existential-phenomeno-logical exploration on lived-plurality. In J. Rowan and M. Cooper (eds), *The Plural Self: multiplicty in everyday life* (pp. 51–70). London: Sage.

Cooper, M. (2000). Person-centred developmental theory: reflections and revisions. *Person-Centred Practice*, 8(2), 87–94.

Cooper, M. (2003a). Between freedom and despair: existential challenges and contributions to person-centred and experiential therapy. *Person-Centered and Experiential Psychotherapies*, 2(1), 43–56.

Cooper, M. (2003b). 'I-I' and 'I-Me': transposing Buber's interpersonal atti-tudes to the intrapersonal plane. *Journal of Constructivist Psychology*, 16(2), 131–53.

Cooper, M. (2004). Encountering self-otherness: 'I-I' and 'I-Me' modes of self-relating. In H.J.M. Hermans and G. Dimaggio (eds), *Dialogical Self in Psychotherapy* (pp. 60–73). Hove: Brunner-Routledge.

Cooper, M. (2005). From self-objectification to self-affirmation: the 'I-Me' and 'I-I' self-relational stances. In S. Joseph and R. Worsley (eds), *Psychopathol-ogy and the Person-Centred Approach* (pp. 60–74). Ross-on-Wye: PCCS Books.

Cooper, M., Mearns, D., Stiles, W.B., Warner, M.S. and Elliott, R. (2004). Developing self-pluralistic perspectives within the person-centered and experiential approaches: a round table dialogue. *Person-Centred and Experiential Psychotherapies*, 3(3), 176–91.

Elliott, R. and Greenberg, L.S. (1997). Multiple voices in process-experiential therapy: dialogue between aspects of the self. *Journal of Psychotherapy Integration*, 7(3), 225–39.

Embleton Tudor, L., Keemar, K., Tudor, K., Valentine, J. and Worrall, M. (2002). *The Person-Centred Approach: a contemporary introduction*. Houndsmill: Palgrave MacMillan.

Geller, L. (1982). The failure of self-actualization theory: a critique of Carl Rogers and Abraham Maslow. *Journal of Humanistic Psychology*, 22(2), 56–73.

Glassman, W.E. (2000). *Approaches to Psychology*. Buckingham: Open University Press.

Greenberg, L.S., Rice, L.N. and Elliott, R. (1993). *Facilitating Emotional Change: the moment-by-moment process*. New York: Guilford.

Greenberg, L.S. and Van Balen, R. (1998). The theory of experience-centered therapies. In L.S. Greenberg, J.C. Watson and G. Lietaer (eds), *Handbook of Experiential Psychotherapy* (pp. 28–57). New York: Guilford Press.

Holdstock, L. (1993). Can we afford not to revision the person-centred concept of self? In D. Brazier (ed.), *Beyond Carl Rogers*. London: Constable.

Keil, S. (1996). The self as a systematic process of interactions of 'inner persons'. In R. Hutterer, G. Pawlowsky, P. Schmid and R. Stipsits (eds), *Client-Centred and Experiential Psychotherapy: a paradigm in motion* (pp. 53–66). Frankfurt am Main: Peter Lang.

Lecky, P. (1945). *Self-consistency: a theory of personality*. New York: Island Press.

Maslow, A.H. (1943). A theory of human motivation. *Psychological Review*, 50, 370–96.

Maslow, A.H. (1968). *Towards a Psychology of Being* (2nd edn). New York: Van Nostrand Co., Inc.

Mearns, D. (2002). Further theoretical propositions in regard to self theory within person-centered therapy. *Person-Centered and Experiential Psychotherapies*, 1(1and2), 14–27.

Mearns, D. and Cooper, M. (2005). *Working at Relational Depth in Counselling and Psychotherapy*. London: Sage.

Mearns, D. and Thorne, B. (2000). *Person-Centred Therapy Today: new frontiers in theory and practice*. London: Sage.

O'Hara, M. (1992). Relational humanism: a psychology for a pluralistic world. *The Humanistic Psychologist*, 20(2and3), 439–46.

Pervin, L.A. and John, O.P. (1997). *Personality: theory and research*. New York: Wiley.

Rogers, A. (2001). Do we need 'a' theory of personality? *Person-Centred Practice*, 9(1), 37–42.

Rogers, C.R. (1942). *Counseling and Psychotherapy: newer concepts in practice*. Boston: Houghton Mifflin.

Rogers, C.R. (1947). Some observations on the organization of personality. *American Psychologist*, 2, 358–68.

Rogers, C.R. (1951). *Client-Centered Therapy*. Boston: Houghton Mifflin.

Rogers, C.R. (1959). A theory of therapy, personality and interpersonal relationships as developed in the client-centered framework. In S. Koch (ed.), *Psychology: a study of science*. Volume 3. *Formulations of the person and the social context* (pp. 184–256). New York: McGraw-Hill.

Rogers, C.R. (1964). Towards a science of the person. In T.W. Wann (ed.), *Behaviourism and Phenomenology: contrasting bases for modern psychology* (pp. 109–40). Chicago, Il.: University of Chicago Press.

Schmid, P. (1998). 'On becoming a person-centered approach': a person-centered understanding of the person. In B. Thorne and E. Lambers (eds), *Person-Centred Therapy: a European perspective* (pp. 38–52). London: Sage.

Schmid, P.F. (2003). The characteristics of a person-centred approach to therapy and counseling: criteria for identity and coherence. *Person-Centered and Experiential Psychotherapies*, 2(2), 104–20.

Snygg, D. and Combs, A.W. (1949). *Individual Behavior: a new frame of reference for psychology*. New York: Harper and Brothers.

Standal, Stanley W. (1954). The need for positive regard: a contribution to client-centered theory. Chicago, Il.: unpublished dissertation.

Stern, D.N. (2003). *The Interpersonal World of the Infant: a view from psychoanalysis and developmental theory*. London: Karnac.

Stiles, W.B., Elliott, R., Firthcozens, J.A., Llewelyn, S.P., Margison, F.R., Shapiro, D.A. et al (1990). Assimilation of problematic experiences by clients in psychotherapy. *Psychotherapy*, 27(3), 411–20.

Stiles, W.B. and Glick, M.J. (2002). Client-centered therapy with multi-voiced clients: empathy with whom? In J.C. Watson, R. Goldman and M.S. Warner (eds), *Client-centered and Experiential Psychotherapy in the Twenty-first Century*. Ross-on-Wye: PCCS Books.

Stinckens, N., Lietaer, G. and Leijssen, M. (2002). The valuing process and the inner critic in the classic and current client-centered/experiential literature. *Person-Centred and Experiential Psychotherapies*, 1(1–2), 41–55.

Vygotsky, L.S. (1962). *Thought and Language*. Cambridge, Mass.: MIT Press.

Warner, M.S. (2000). Person-centred therapy at the difficult edge: a developmetally based model of fragile and dissociated process. In D. Mearns and B. Thorne (eds), *Person-Centred Therapy Today: new frontiers in theory and practice* (pp. 144–71). London: Sage.

Warner, M.S. (2001). Empathy, relational depth and difficult client process. In S. Haugh and T. Merry (eds), *Empathy* (pp. 181–91). Ross-on-Wye: PCCS Books.

Warner, M.S. (2002). Psychological contact, meaningful process and human nature: a reformulation of person-centred theory. In G. Wyatt and P. Sanders (eds), *Contact and Perception* (pp. 76–95). Ross-on-Wye: PCCS Books.

Warner, M.S. (2005). A person-centred view of human nature, wellness and psychopathology. In S. Joseph and R. Worsley (eds), *Psychopathology and the Person-Centred Approach* (pp. 91–109). Ross-on-Wye: PCCS Books.

Wilkins, P. (2003). *Person-Centred Therapy in Focus*. London: Sage.

Group Therapy and Encounter Groups

Peter F. Schmid and Maureen O'Hara

Thinking about therapy does not mean about only one-to-one relationships – on the contrary: the foundations of person-centred therapy would be incomplete without considering the importance of group processes, in both everyday life and therapy. From the beginning and in much of life, human life takes place in groups. The group is the primary social fact, and because it is the interface of person and society this also suggests a 'therapeutic primacy' of the group. This chapter investigates the nature of the group and the centrality of group work for psychotherapy and counselling from a person-centred perspective, and discusses the person-centred group process and facilitation and the need for a perspective of change beyond the individual.

'In the beginning there was the group, in the end the individual.' This statement by Jacob Levi Moreno (1959: 9), the founder of psychodrama, is also true for the person-centred approach. In terms of both content and history it can be shown (Schmid, 1994, 1996b) that – although developed as a procedure for counselling individuals – the person-centred approach came into being in groups.

At least as early as the Hawthorne studies in the 1920s we have known that groups have enormous power to change human behaviour (Roethlisberger and Dickson, 1939). These studies and the work on field theory by Kurt Lewin in the 1940s (which Rogers encountered mostly through contact with Lewin's graduate students through their work at the National Training Labs) had great influence on Carl Rogers' thinking. For Rogers (1970: 9), the group was 'probably the most potent social invention of the century'. And indeed, the person-centred approach has, from the very outset, been a social approach, a group approach. 'Since its beginnings, client-centred therapy has also sought wider spheres of influence, beyond the individual, both in attempting to explore the relevance of its ideas in contexts broader than traditional dyadic therapy and in seeking to apply its approach to wider social milieus' (Wexler and Rice, 1974: 313).

Personality and group theory: the group as a primary social fact and as the interface of person and society

What is a group? Does a gathering of individuals form a group, making it a secondary, dependent variable; or is the group there first and the individuals second, formed by and developed from the group they live in? For many people, the question of which is primary, the group or the individual, may seem a bit like the chicken and the egg debate. But for the understanding of the person and his or her problems as well as for therapy it has deep theoretical and practical implications, offering as it does a way of viewing human existence that transcends the dualism of Western thought while maintaining a sense of a sovereign personhood (see Chapter 4, this volume).

Human beings generally live in groups; the 'natural' and, in this sense, original living arrangement of human beings is the group. In terms of developmental psychology, the group provides the context in which human beings experience life, whether in a family, at school, at work, in social interest associations or other form. In all those contexts, one-to-one situations are the exception, groups are the rule. Even pair relationships usually exist as part of a group, embedded within it. Human beings are born into groups – at least as a rule. It is within groups that we discover our identity. Through them, we know who we are and where we belong (O'Hara, 1997: 314; Schmid, 1996a: 57–76).

The primary manifestation of humanness, then, is not the individual, but the human being together with other human beings. The human being is a social being and, from the very beginning, is predisposed by his or her very corporeity to communicate with the world and with human beings. On a purely biological level, the human being originates in a human relationship. That humans are primarily social beings is not just true in their needs but in their very essence. This is also true for epistemology: human knowledge is not possible without human society. Body, awareness, sociality, values, language, communication – none of these would exist without community. The human world is always a world of interactions. Human existence is coexistence.

From this relational, socio-centric or holistic perspective, which as anthropologists point out is the most common view in most of the world's cultures (Geertz, 1979), the group is far from being merely a gathering of individuals or an extension of the 'one-to-one relationship'; it is rather a primary social fact. It is both a place where persons experience their selves-in-relationship (i.e. themselves in their social and individual qualities) and it is their connection to larger social communities and to society and humankind as such. A group both constitutes the persons belonging to and participating in it and has its own autonomous existence as a social entity, which in turn is connected to and participates in other groups within the broad social context. In this fashion these interconnected groups are contributing parts of the greater whole that constitutes the totality of society. The group exists at the interface of individual and society; therefore it is *the* field for both personal encounter and mutual exchange within society. Thus a group is neither a mere collective nor is it the sum total of its members, but a complex social system, an entity of its own, existing in a state of tension between person and society, a process in which individual and collective realities become clear and subsequently influence each other in many different ways (Schmid, 1996b: 72). In other words: 'The individual creates the group which creates the individual' (Wood, 1988: 245, authors' translation).

The most cogent substantive argument in support of the group as a primary reality comes from the person-centred approach itself. As already outlined in Chapter 4 of this volume, human beings are and become persons within their interpersonal relationships where they actualize their personhood, more exactly: it is within groups that a human being becomes a person. Carl Rogers (1965: 19f) stated that 'human beings are incurably social', 'social animals' (Rogers, 1961: 103). In overcoming the isolated I–Thou relationship the person-centred approach regards interpersonality to be founded in a fundamental 'We' (Schmid, 1996a: 521–40; 2003). The group is the arena for personal encounters in the context of the bigger community or society. (For more details see Schmid, 1996a: 19–112; 1996b: 616–20; 2001: 294–9; O'Hara, 1997.)

History: the group as an essential factor of the person-centred approach

Historically, client-centred therapy may have been described and developed, at least theoretically, for use largely in individual therapy, but, in actual practice and from the very beginning, it incorporated ideas that originated in group experiences, ideas which in turn influenced theory. On a closer examination of the history of person-centred therapy, a history inseparable from Carl Rogers' personal stages of learning, it is Rogers' own learning experiences in his relational groups – family, church and university – and his references to his own experiences in these groups which are of initial significance. He lived, learned, taught and worked in groups. Even in his first publication, an article on the World Student Christian Federation Conference in Beijing, Rogers (1922) voiced his fascination with the group experience.

By his own account, he had already begun in 1945 to work with students in groups as a professor at the University of Chicago. His staff groups played an increasingly important role. It was in these staff groups that the theoretical ideas were discussed and further developed on the basis of actual experiences. Furthermore, the approaches that were developed for person-centred training were set in groups from the very beginning. In 1947, Rogers had already developed a group-centred model to train counsellors for war veterans. Much later, he said about this period: 'They have all been encounter groups, long before the term was coined' (Rogers, 1973: 39).

In 1947, Rogers published his first article devoted, even in its title, to the group: 'Effective principles for dealing with individual and group tensions and dissatisfactions'. In a 1948 article entitled 'Some implications of client-centered counseling for college personnel work', Rogers also wrote extensively about group work and group therapy, touching on many of what later became his key principles, such as trust in the group, which he sees as an organism in its own right. In his 1951 book, Rogers included a chapter by Hobbs (1951) about 'group-centered psychotherapy' and Gordon's research in the same book focused on 'group-centered leadership' (Gordon, 1951; Bowen et al, 1979).

From 1964 onwards, after his university career and at the time of the encounter group movement in the 1960s and 1970s, Rogers got heavily involved in group work. His Academy Award winning film *Journey into Self* (Rogers and McGaw, 1968) and his book *On Encounter Groups* (Rogers, 1970) played an important part in the recognition of group work as an important factor in self-development, counselling and psychotherapy. From 1973 on he worked, together with his daughter Natalie, Maureen O'Hara and John Wood among others, in large group workshops and got engaged in intercultural and peace work (Rogers, 1977, 1980, 1983; Rogers and Rosenberg, 1977; Bowen et al, 1979; O'Hara and Wood, 1984; Wood, 1988; see Chapter 23, this volume). The 'La Jolla Program', a programme characterized by its alternation of large and small group experience (from 1967 on), became *the* model of person-centred facilitator training (Coulson et al, 1977). Although those workshops and programmes were not explicitly therapy, they contributed enormously to the growing political self-understanding of person-centred therapy. Quite early, small and large group workshops were held all over the world and further theory was developed. (Major contributions to theory stem from Pagès, 1968; Bowen et al, 1979; O'Hara and Wood, 1984, 2004; Wood, 1988; O'Hara 1997; Schmid, 1994, 1996a, 1996b, 1998, 2000; the latest reader was published by Lago and MacMillan, 1999.)

The work with 'intensive groups', as Rogers liked to call the encounter groups, contributed significantly to the development of the person-centred approach as such. The reciprocity of help Rogers often experienced in these groups exceeded such experiences in individual therapy. The conception of the group 'leader' as a facilitator affected the conception of the person-centred therapist in one-to-one therapy. The work with, and within, groups was instrumental in helping to understand human beings within relationships and interpersonal relationships as such. The definition of the 'fully functioning person', not simply as an individualistic self, but as a self within society, and the social and, by extension, political dimension of the person-centred approach, also originate largely in experiences from small and large groups. Finally, the highly democratic, egalitarian valuing of each person's contribution as equal to that of the facilitator (contrasting with other more expert-centred orientations) affirms the personal power of each participant. These points justify Raskin's (1986a: 281) comment that 'the encounter group was and remains one of the most outstanding forms of expression for the person-centred approach' (for more details see Schmid, 1994: 65–94; 1996b: 613–16; overviews of the history can be found in Raskin, 1986a, 1986b; Schmid, 1996a: 27–64; Barrett-Lennard, 1998: 145–76, 199–231).

Therapy theory: the 'therapeutic primacy' of the group

One of the consequences of the above outlined understanding of the group as a primary fact in the life of people and the essential contribution to the development of person-centred therapy is to understand that essentially the person-centred approach is fundamentally a group approach and person-centred therapy is fundamentally group therapy (Schmid, 1994). We suggest putting it even more pointedly: person-centred therapy is by its very nature not a process of individual therapy which just happens to be applicable to groups. Rather, it is, in its essence, a social approach, an approach relating to groups, and thus a 'group approach' which also happens to be applicable to relationships between two people (dyads, pairs), as special types of groups. This turns the traditional view upside down: person-centred therapy involving two people, so-called 'individual therapy', can be defined as a special type of group event, a 'group of two'.

This implies that the group should be considered the initial point of entry into therapy. In other words, unless other reasons make another decision obviously preferable, the group is the setting of choice for the human being to come to terms with him- or herself. Problems stemming from interpersonal relationships can be understood relationally and dealt with in interpersonal relationships. Once such a relational view is grasped, it follows that by recreating the context from which many psychological problems originate, the group provides the richest environment for addressing them successfully. Group psychotherapy brings the problems back to the point where they belong.

The relational perspective advanced in this chapter, where the notion of 'individual counselling' becomes reframed as counselling within a group of two, opens up the question as to whether the current focus on so-called individual counselling might be reconsidered as the entry point for most people seeking counselling, and the group reclaimed as a rich and potent setting for transformational growth. Following this perspective a therapist recommending somebody to psychotherapy should first consider the advantages of a group (for a discussion of the pair as a special form of group and the implications for therapy see Schmid, 1996a: 58–60).

One of the principal advantages of a group is that it permits a lived experience of the plurality and complexity of life. The rich diversity that is human existence comes alive in the group. In individual therapy, the client's multiple relationships (beyond the one to the therapist) can be addressed only indirectly, the actual experience (and attempts to try something new) happens outside, in between the meetings. In group therapy this is possible in the group itself: the relationships among the group members offer a broad field of experience and the possibility to try something new and receive immediate feedback and reflect upon it in real time. Often these learning experiences can be transferred immediately to other groups and relationships in the client's life.

In group work the whole group is 'the therapist'. Each member can be a facilitator for another member, which increases the possibilities of receiving feedback and learning from each other. The clients encounter multiple viewpoints and multiple values systems (unlike in individual therapy where they encounter only that of the therapist), thereby facilitating their discovery of their own values and perspectives. Self-development 'in the company of others' (Merry, 1988: 22) enriches empathy. To find 'fellow sufferers' and to find oneself 'not alone' can be an enormous relief, and greatly help to accept oneself. There are also 'spectator' effects as people witness others profiting from openness and risk taking. But more than this, it usually encourages people to similarly dare to open up and take a risk. That everybody can be therapeutic for somebody else brings home the fact that we are all fundamentally of value and capable – the realization of which is of enormous potential for therapy and personality development. Being able to help another intensifies self-esteem and can be therapeutic in itself. Furthermore, peer-to-peer interaction has a different quality than the client–therapist interactions. Being understood by a non-professional feels different from being understood by somebody whose job it is to do so. Also, confrontation, even by the therapist, is somehow easier to accept and process because there are probably other members who support the views or behaviours of a member.

Beyond this, group therapy has an anticipatory function. Representing society in microcosm, the group is the arena where current and even future developments, problems and trends in society can be observed, investigated and understood. New ways of dealing with them can be tested. Thus, the group is not only of psychological and therapeutic value, but has an enormous impact on societal changes.

The shift of perspective from 'therapy of an individual by an individual' to 'therapy of the person in a group' (to really be person-centred means to address somebody in their substantial and their relational dimension: see Chapter 4, this volume) opens up the possibility of seeing person-centred groups as a locus of healing within the larger society. (For further discussion of the implications of this for sociotherapy, see Schmid, 1996a: 511–32; 2002.)

Finally, there is a dimension of group experience that, when it is present, offers access to expanded levels of awareness. O'Hara and Wood (1984, 2004) have described the extraordinary moments in group life when the 'group mind' or the collective consciousness of the group as an entity becomes accessible to its members. In these moments people are often capable of reconciling complexities that had seemed intractable just minutes before – when we recognize that what we usually see as fragmented is really whole. Towards the end of his life, Rogers was becoming interested in the work of physicist David Bohm, acknowledging the similarities between person-centred approach experiences in large groups and Bohm's discussions of 'implicate order' (Bohm, 1983; Bohm and Edwards, 1991).

Group process: the participants are the process

To understand what goes on in a person-centred group, several distinct levels of process must be kept in mind at the same time.

- What is going on within the subjective experience of each individual?
- What is going on between individuals on the interpersonal level?

- What is going on at the level of the group as an entity?
- What are the externalities that provide the context?

In Chapter 6 of this volume, the subjective and interpersonal processes have been discussed in detail. Here we wish to consider the 'higher order' processes and how they express themselves in the lives of group participants.

As discussed throughout this volume, central to the person-centred approach is a basic trust in what Rogers thought of as a 'formative tendency' in nature, of which the 'actualizing tendency' in human beings is a manifestation (see Chapter 5, this volume). He observed that when core relational conditions of genuineness, unconditional regard and empathy (discussed in more detail in Chapter 1 and Part II, this volume) characterize person-to-person interactions, whether in a dyadic group or a group of up to a thousand, this actualizing tendency can be counted on to move both individuals and groups in the direction of growth and healing (Rogers, 1986). In individual therapy, it is the therapist who is primarily responsible for creating these conditions; in a group the facilitator is responsible for setting up important boundary conditions such as time of meeting, place, duration and membership, and makes other important contributions which we discuss below. The responsibility for the process of the group, however, is distributed among all the members who jointly contribute to the creation of an enabling climate of trust, acceptance and caring. In later years, Rogers also described the concept of 'presence' as a basic facilitative condition (see Chapter 4, this volume).

Rogers and others (Bowen et al, 1979; O'Hara and Wood, 1984, 2004; Wood, 1984; Natiello, 1987; Schmid, 1996a) have described the process of person-centred group development. Rogers (1970) identified 15 patterns in the group process. These do not necessarily occur exactly in sequence, but some version of this unfolding process is visible in most person-centred groups. A detailed description of these phases of the group's life can be found in Rogers' *On Encounter Groups* (1970) and they correspond closely to the stages of group development described in the group-dynamics literature (Bradford et al, 1964; for an overview of person-centred analyses on group stages see Schmid, 1996a: 181–92).

As the group unfolds over a day, an intensive weekend or over several weeks, in principle the same shifts occur. In the early stages of a group there is often a period of chaotic, incoherent and disconnected communications. Distrust and reticence are high. At the beginning, for most people, the sense of 'we' exists only as a theoretical potentiality – a hoped-for reality, perhaps to be realized, perhaps not. For some, the idea of 'we' is quite threatening as they fear the individual 'self' might not have a place in a collective 'we'. They are more concerned with their sense of individual reality and their place in the on-going events. In a group made up of warring factions in Northern Ireland, recorded in the film *The Steel Shutter*, for instance, members' mutual animosity made them at first closed to the idea of a 'we' with people from the other side (McGaw and McGaw, 1973). In recent work in South Africa and Guatemala, Adam Kahane (2004) has observed the same initial reluctance.

As the first tentative communications are heard, accepted and responded to, there is a deepening of expression of feelings and self-disclosure, which in turn provokes even more open sharing. Early on, most communications are directed to the facilitators but as the facilitators make it clear that they are not there to direct or fix anything, but to participate, gradually people begin to take risks, to test out their freedom and to allow themselves to be authentic with each other. They may express anger at another member, sadness about a loss, or irritation at the process. There is less talking 'about' the past or abstractions and more direct experience of immediate, here and now experience. At the same time people begin to attune to each other in deeply empathic ways. They listen more deeply and allow themselves to be moved by each others' humanity. They find themselves moved in powerful ways by the stories of the others and, as this happens, experience becomes more vivid and more intense. As Natalie Rogers has said, the group comes to 'listen to the music, not just the words' (2005, personal communication). Gradually, as people express more and more of their individual experience the essential 'we' – the sense of a greater entity to which the individual participants are contributing – emerges and begins to make its presence felt in the consciousness of everyone. In the immediacy of the present experience, a sense of what Levi (2005) has called 'group magic' becomes palpable to almost all. It is in this state where the truly transformative work occurs.

The shift to a transformative state is often sudden. It cannot be produced, hurried, engineered. It is a shift that happens in the group field beyond the direct manipulation by any individual. Often these expansive moments occur in the silence following some expressed deep feeling or compelling story.

To give a case example: in one group, after a period of chaotic, awkward and inauthentic conversation, an interaction between an African-American man and a white South African man became heated. They were (like many people who had talked before them) talking past each other, not listening, and expressing themselves in indirect, sarcastic jibes. Suddenly the African-American man exploded with frustration. He poured out his pain about the policy of apartheid and expressed his rage and distrust of the white South African man. The group listened in stunned silence. After he had finished, the South African member responded, just as forcefully and with equal frustration. He was an anti-apartheid activist who had left South Africa in fear for his life. He was terrified his family was in danger from both black and white South Africans. The two men looked silently into each other's eyes for a long time. As they did so the climate of the group shifted and a new state of being together emerged. Where there had been separateness there was now sense of alignment and attunement, where there had been a sense of despair there was now hope, and where there had been opponents there was now solidarity. As one member observed afterwards: 'At that moment I could see that we are all really one – there is no separation or disconnections except those we construct. When we meet in this way, I can see my way through. I can know universes.'

It is not always conflict that marks the phase shifts in a group. It might just as well be a moment of selfless giving, deep empathy, uncontrolled laughter of the kind that make ones sides ache, or a simple silence at the right time. Whether in a group billed as a person-centred approach group, or some other dialogical group process, what these moments have in common is that members surrender to the moment – fully aware of themselves as unique individuals, but fully engaged and attuned to the present moment. It is a point beyond dualism and what appear intractable contradictions at one moment seem solvable the next. O'Hara and Wood (2004: 65) have called these groups 'conscious groups'. John Wood (1988: 42) put it in a nutshell: the members 'are not "material" for the therapeutic process; they are the process.'

Group facilitation: the art of being co-player *and* counterpart

Understanding person-centred group facilitation presents us with a paradox. The most generative aspects of group processes occur among the members of the group and are not produced by the facilitators. Thus we do not talk about 'group leaders' or 'trainers'. but 'group facilitators' who foster the therapeutic, growth-promoting process of the group. The group itself takes the function of 'leading', and different participants take a leading role at different stages or for different tasks in the interaction of the evolving group process. As opposed to other conceptions, like guiding, steering, interpreting, inducing exercises and group games, staying absent or taking the role of an agent provocateur, the person-centred approach emphasizes the personal qualities of the facilitator – his or her ways of being – over the use of technical expertise. The primary task of group facilitators is – according to the image of the human being as a person (see Chapter 4, this volume) – to be an active, involved, committed participant in the group who trusts the actualizing tendency, the process and the persons, and can be more and more experienced as a person. Nevertheless, in our experience, at the same time, person-centred facilitation is a highly complex and multi-layered responsibility, and requires a level of self-mastery and personal and technical expertise not easily achieved. (For details on group facilitation see Rogers, 1970; Schmid, 1996a: 219–319.)

Facilitators must be able to express the core conditions in their interactions with individual participants in ways that are appropriate to the group setting – which are different from the individual counselling session – and in their interactions with the whole group. They must know, for instance, how to listen empathically to an individual who is speaking, but also to listen empathically to the group as an entity. For example, if one person is talking a great deal and others in the group are becoming bored or even hostile, it is sometimes the case that the facilitator has to make a choice between continuing to attend deeply to one individual in favour of making a comment about the obvious discomfort of someone else. In a group the timing of such a choice is very important. Too much self-expression by the facilitator too early can have an inhibitory effect on a group; too much too late, and it can shift the focus of attention back to the facilitator and away from the emerging group consciousness. Facilitators need to be co-players, inter-actors, co-participants and they need to be counterparts, persons to 'en-counter', 'Others' for the participants (see Chapter 4, this volume). They see their task as using their power to empower the group and the participants. Coghlan and

McIlduff (1990) have pointed to the importance of facilitators learning how to use their personal power effectively. Making assessments moment by moment as to when and how to intervene requires understanding of the dynamics operational at all four levels (see page 98–9), and above all, it requires preparation.

Rogers and both of the present authors have stressed the importance for facilitators co-leading person-centred group encounters to prepare psychologically as a team and reflect carefully upon the on-going process together. It has been our observation that groups have a remarkable capacity to pick up what is going on in the sub-group that is the 'staff'. If there is friction among facilitators, for instance, this will be noticed and reacted to by group members and if an individual leader is troubled in some way, this can have significant effects on group members, even if the facilitators do not disclose it. Such phenomena should not surprise us when we consider that the group is the site of human evolution. Before we had verbal language, as a matter of survival we knew how to read the signs expressed in the non-linguistic patterns of group life. In particular all group primates know that they need to stay very aware of what the dominant members are doing, or risk losing their place in the group (Waal, 1986). The more the facilitators can become open to and congruent with each other, achieve a high level of group attunement and alignment, the more their presence will be experienced as providing basic safety for participants and provide a model for group participation. (For more detailed discussion see Bowen et al, 1979; Rogers, 1980; O'Hara and Wood, 1984, 2004.)

The success of the person-centred group should not blind us to the potential negative outcomes. As Rogers (1970) has described, the group can be a frightening place. The unstructured group provides a setting where anxiety is generated and the various responses to that can be distressing to participants. Anger, rejection, ongoing self-defence, scapegoating, boredom, blaming, shaming, putting pressure on others can all go on in a group, especially with a poorly trained facilitator. It is the responsibility of all participants, the facilitators included, to meet these challenges and, particularly, to carefully deal with power issues. The negative aspects of groups in the early unstructured group experiments resulted in their falling into disfavour within the business setting and propelled innovations in the direction of more structuring by facilitators, which provided greater psychological security, more reliable task oriented outcomes and less distress (Alban and Scherer, 2005).

The chance for change beyond individual change

In the ongoing development of person-centred therapy as a dialogic therapy (see Chapter 4, this volume), the group plays a vital role in changing the perspective from the individual to the person in context, and contributes to recognizing the necessity for change beyond individual change. In broadening the view in this way, it may lead to an awareness of the social and political dimensions of psychotherapy.

From the beginning the group has played a central role in person-centred therapy training (see Chapter 28, this volume). Training groups not only provide a context for learning skills but also provide a chance and challenge to experience the group's potential, and potency for the trainee's personality development and self-understanding as a therapist. In our view the group provides the trainee an unequalled experiential base within which to learn to trust the group as a therapeutic option for both individual and social issues.

It is more than 60 years since Rogers' earliest exploration of the group as a site for psychological growth. Since then he and others have developed a diverse range of applications for person-centred groups, many of which are discussed in more detail in Part III.

REFERENCES

Alban, B.T. and Scherer, J.J. (2005). On the shoulders of giants: the origins of OD. In W.J. Rothwell and R. Sullivan (eds), *Practicing Organization Development*, 2nd edn (pp.81–105). San Francisco: Wiley.

Barrett-Lennard, G.T. (1998). *Carl Rogers' Helping System: journey and Substance*. London: Sage.

Bohm, D. (1983). *Wholeness and the Implicate Order*. New York: Ark Paperbacks.

Bohm, D. and Edwards, M. (1991). *Changing Consciousness*. San Francisco: Harper Books.

Bowen, M., O'Hara, M. et al (1979). Learning in large groups: implications for the future. *Education*, 100, 108–17.

Bradford, L., Gibb, J.R. et al (1964). *T-group Theory and Laboratory Method*. New York: Wiley.

Coghlan, D. and E. McIlduff (1990). Structuring and non-directiveness in group facilitation. *Person-Centered Review*, 5(1), 13–29.

Coulson, W.R., Land, D., Meador, B. (eds) (1977). *The La Jolla Program: eight personal views*. La Jolla: the La Jolla Program.

Geertz, C. (1979). From the native's point of view: on the nature of anthropological understanding. In P. Rabinow and W.M. Sullivan (eds), *Interpretive Social Psychology* (pp. 225–41). Berkeley: University of California Press.

Gordon, T. (1951). Group-centered leadership and administration. In C.R. Rogers, *Client-Centered Therapy* (pp.320–83). Boston: Houghton Mifflin.

Hobbs, N. (1951). Group-centered psychotherapy. In C.R. Rogers, *Client-Centered therapy: its current practice, implications, and theory* (pp.278–319). Boston: Houghton Mifflin.

Kahane, A. (2004). *Solving Tough Problems: an open way of talking, listening and creating new realities*. San Francisco: Berrett-Koehler.

Lago, C. and MacMillan, M. (eds) (1999). *Experiences in Relatedness: groupwork and the person-centred approach*. Ross-on-Wye: PCCS Books.

Levi, R.A. (2005). Group magic: an inquiry into experiences of collective resonance. *Reflections: The Society for Organizational Learning Journal*, 6(2–3), 20–27.

McGaw, W.H. and McGaw, A.P. (1973). *The Steel Shutter* (Motion picture). University of California-Santa Barbara Davidson, Library Dept. of Special Collections.

Merry, T. (1988). *A Guide to the Person-Centred Approach*. London: Association for Humanistic Psychology in Britain.

Moreno, J.L. (1959). *Gruppenpsychotherapie und Psychodrama: Einleitung in die Theorie und Praxis*. Stuttgart: Thieme. 3rd edn. 1988.

Natiello, P. (1987). The person-centered approach: from theory to practice. *Person-Centered Review*, 2(2), 203–16.

O'Hara, M. (1997). Relational empathy: from egocentric modernism to socio-centric postmodernism. In A.C. Bohart and L.S. Greenberg (eds), *Empathy Reconsidered: new directions in psychotherapy* (pp.295–320). Washington D.C.: American Psychological Association.

O'Hara, M. and J.K. Wood (1984). Patterns of awareness: consciousness and the group mind. *The Gestalt Journal*, 6(2), 103–16.

O'Hara, M. and J.K. Wood (2004). Transforming communities: person-centered encounters and the creation of integral conscious groups. In B.A. Banathy and J.P. Jenlink (eds), *Dialogue as a Means of Collective Communication* (pp. 95–126). New York: Kluwer Academic Plenum.

Pagès, M. (1968). *La vie affective des groupes, esquisses d'une théorie de la relation humaine*. Paris: Dunod.

Pfeiffer, W.M. (1993). Die Bedeutung der Beziehung bei der Entstehung und der Therapie psychischer Störungen [The significance of relationships for the development and therapy of psychological disorders]. In L. Teusch and J. Finke (eds), *Die Krankheitslehre der Gesprächspsychotherapie: Neue Beiträge zur theoretischen Fundierung* (pp.19–40). Heidelberg: Asanger.

Raskin, N.J. (1986a), Client-centered group psychotherapy: i. Development of client-centered groups. *Person-Centered Review*, 1(3), 272–90.

Raskin, N.J. (1986b). Client-centered group psychotherapy: ii. Research on client-centered groups. *Person-Centered Review*, 1(4), 389–408.

Roethlisberger, F.J. and Dickson, W.J. (1939). *Management and the Worker*. Cambridge, Mass.: Harvard University Press.

Rogers, C.R. (1922). An experiment in Christian internationalism. *The Intercollegian* (YMCA), 39,9.

Rogers, C.R. (1947). Effective principles for dealing with individuals and group tensions and dissatisfactions. *Executive Seminar Series in Industrial Relations* (Session 10). Chicago: University of Chicago Press.

Rogers, C.R. (1948). Some implications of client-centered counseling for college personnel work. *Educational and Psychological Measurement*, 8(3), 540–9.

Rogers, C.R. (1961). *On Becoming a Person: a therapist's view of psychotherapy*. Boston: Houghton Mifflin.

Rogers, C.R. (1965). A humanistic conception of man. In R. Farson (ed.), *Science and Human Affairs* (pp.18–31). Palo Alto: Science and Behavior Books.

Rogers, C.R. (1970). *On Encounter Groups*. New York: Harper and Row.

Rogers, C.R. (1973). My philosophy of interpersonal relationships and how it grew. *Journal of Humanistic Psychology*, 13(2), 3–15.

Rogers, C.R. (1977). *On Personal Power: inner strength and its revolutionary impact*. New York: Delacorte.

Rogers, C.R. (1980). *A Way of Being*. Boston: Houghton Mifflin.

Rogers, C.R. (1983). *Freedom to Learn for the 80s*. Columbus, Ohio: Charles E. Merrill.

Rogers, C.R. (1986). Client-centered therapy. In I.L. Kutash and A. Wolf (eds), *Psychotherapist's Case-book* (pp.197–208). San Francisco: Jossey Bass

Rogers, C.R. and McGaw, W.H., Jr. (1968). *Journey into Self*. UCLA Extension Media Center (Motion picture).

Rogers, C.R. and Rosenberg, R.L. (1977). *A pessoa como centro* [The person in the centre]. São Paulo: Editora Pedagógica e Universitária.

Schmid, P.F. (1994). *Personzentrierte Gruppenpsychotherapie*: Vol. I. *Solidarität und Autonomie: Ein Handbuch* [Person-centred group pychotherapy. Volume 1. Solidarity and autonomy]. Cologne: Edition Humanistische Psychologie.

Schmid, P.F. (1996a). *Personzentrierte Gruppenpsychotherapie in der Praxis*: Vol. II: *Die Kunst der Begegnung. Ein Handbuch* [Person-centred group psychotherapy in practice. Volume 2. The art of encounter. A handbook]. Paderborn: Junfermann.

Schmid, P.F. (1996b). 'Probably the most potent social invention of the century': person-centered therapy is fundamentally group therapy. In R. Hutterer, G. Pawlowsky, P.F. Schmid and R. Stipsits (eds), *Client-centered and Experiential Psychotherapy: a paradigm in motion* (pp.611–25). Frankfurt: Peter Lang.

Schmid, P.F. (1998). *Im Anfang ist Gemeinschaft*: Vol. III: *Personzentrierte Gruppenarbeit in Seelsorge und Praktischer Theologie: Beitrag zu einer Theologie der Gruppe* [In the beginning there is community. Volume 3. Person-centred group work in pastoral work and theology]. Stuttgart: Kohlhammer.

Schmid, P.F. (2000). Encounter-Gruppe [Encounter groups]. In A. Pritz and G. Stumm (eds), *Wörterbuch der Psychotherapie* [Dictionary of psychotherapy] (p.277). Vienna: Springer.

Schmid, P.F. (2001). Personzentrierte Gruppentherapie [Person-centred group therapy]. In P. Frenzel, W. Keil, P.F. Schmid and N. Stölzl (eds), *Klienten-/Personzentrierte Psychotherapie: Kontexte, Konzepte, Konkretisierungen* [Client/person-centred psychotherapy: contexts, conceptions, illustrations] (pp.294–323). Vienna: Facultas.

Schmid, P.F. (2002). Knowledge or acknowledgement? Psychotherapy as 'the art of not-knowing': prospects on further developments of a radical paradigm. *Person-Centred and Experiential Psychotherapies*, 1, 56–70.

Schmid, P.F. (2003). The characteristics of a person-centred approach to therapy and counseling: criteria for identity and coherence. *Person-Centered and Experiential Psychotherapies*, 2, 104–20.

Waal, D. (1986). Dominance 'style' and primate social organization. In V. Standen and R.A. Foley (eds), *Comparative Socioecology: the behavioral ecology of humans and other mammals* (pp.243–64). Oxford, Blackwell.

Wexler, D.A. and Rice, L.N. (eds) (1974). *Innovations in Client-centered Therapy*. New York: Wiley.

Wood, J.K. (1984). Communities for learning: a person-centered approach. In J.M. Shlien and R.F. Levant (eds), *Client-centered Therapy and the Person-Centered Approach: new directions in theory and practice*. (pp.297–316). New York: Praeger.

Wood, J.K. (1988). *Menschliches Dasein als Miteinandersein: Gruppenarbeit nach personenzentrierten Ansätzen* [Human existence as being-together: groupwork according to person-centred approaches]. Cologne: Edition Humanistische Psychologie.

CHAPTER 9

The 'Family' of Person-Centred and Experiential Therapies

Pete Sanders

As the final contribution to this first part of the handbook, exploring the foundations of the person-centred approach, this chapter provides an overview of the current strands of person-centred and experiential psychotherapies, in particular: classic client/person-centred, dialogic, focusing-oriented, process-experiential therapies and Pre-Therapy. It maps out the different schools of thought and discusses their commonalities and differences. This chapter provides an introduction to the various orientations and positions that are discussed throughout the *Handbook* – and it is an invitation to dialogue.

Carl Rogers' presentation at the University of Minnesota on 11 December 1940 is widely acknowledged as the birth of client-centred therapy (Kirschenbaum, 1979: 112) and he made his most complete theoretical statement in 1959 (Rogers, 1959). However, theories are like genies: they have the tendency of changing shape as soon as they are released. Rogers was at the epicentre of change in client-centred theory during his lifetime; he disliked dogma and rigidity, describing many of his most durable writings as 'tentative' and in his 1970 conversation with Joseph Hart he spoke of 'the value of presenting something before you are entirely sure of it' (Rogers and Hart, 1970: 520). In this conversation, Rogers was speaking about nothing less important than his 'necessary and sufficient conditions' (Rogers, 1957) and 'process conception of psychotherapy' (Rogers, 1958).

Not only did Rogers enjoy developing his own thinking, he positively encouraged it in his students and associates. The early years of client-centred therapy at the University of Chicago saw only a brief period as a 'unified school' (Barrett-Lennard, 1998: 58) and new developments in theory, research and practice were soon in full flow at an astonishing pace. It is not surprising then, that it very quickly became difficult to tell where 'client-centred therapy' ended and something qualitatively different began. Two ways of thinking emerged to cope with this. One held true to the fundamental principles outlined by Rogers in 1959; another favoured developing newer ideas at varying tangents to, yet wholly informed by, Rogers' original work. Hutterer (1993) identified these as two poles of a crisis of identity for the approach: one pole being the commitment to a set of core person-centred values, the other 'the attempt to free theoretical thinking of rigid concepts' (1993: 275). Or, put another way these represent the tension between the pure form and new ideas. They also provide the axes of the map for developments in the theory and practice of client-centred/person-centred and experiential therapies since 1959. Different developments can be located according to the coordinates of non-directivity, the necessity and sufficiency of the therapeutic conditions, and an understanding of the actualizing tendency (see Chapters 1, 2, 5 and 7, this volume).

In order to fully apprehend the details of the positions and arguments summarized in this chapter, serious students of contemporary person-centred and experiential therapies can look forward to an exploration of the extensive contemporary literature. Such exploration is not only generally informative, but also increasingly necessary in order that practitioners might accurately position themselves in the 'family' of these therapies.

Readers are first directed to a stream of papers and chapters complaining about, documenting or attempting to resolve a perceived threat of imminent fragmentation of the approach, starting with the prescient 'Roundtable discussion' in the August edition of the *Person-Centered Review*, 1986 (1(3): 334–52), 'What is most essential to the continued development of the theory and application of the person-centred approach'. Other notable contributions include Hutterer (1993), Lietaer (2000, 2002), Sanders (2000, 2004), Schmid (2002b, 2003) and Warner (2000). All are caught on the horns of the dilemma: freedom from rigid theory versus definition of core values. However, there has been movement in the 20 years since the inconclusive roundtable discussion. The later contributions all attempt to present ways of defining core values which place a premium on inclusivity and the embracing of difference, rather than excluding deviation from the pure form. Most also suggest a framework or system (different in each case) for judging the degree of person-centredness based in whole or in part on non-directivity, the necessity and sufficiency of the conditions and the actualizing tendency.

Core values as seen by different authors

A brief summary of Lietaer (2000, 2002), Sanders (2000, 2004), Schmid (2003) and Warner (2000) follows in order that readers might judge each approach catalogued in this chapter according to criteria presented in the respective papers.

Germain Lietaer: first and second-order factors

Lietaer in 2002, building on his 2000 paper, described 'first and second-order factors of theory and practice in the client-centred/experiential paradigm'. His first-order factors (central to the 'family') are:

- focus on the experiencing self
- moment-by-moment empathy
- a high level of personal presence
- an egalitarian, dialogical stance
- a belief that the Rogerian therapist conditions are crucial.

His second order factors (peripheral to, but particularly characteristic of, the 'family') are:

- holistic person-centredness
- emphasis on self-agency and actualizing process
- self-determination and free choice as human possibilities
- the pro-social nature of the human being
- autonomy and solidarity as existential tasks.

Lietaer's formulation is clearly influenced by his 'experiential' psychotherapy leanings (see below). The terms 'experiencing self' and 'moment-by-moment empathy' are redolent of the experiential thread. Further, he uses experiential therapy vocabulary as his benchmarks, which could be seen to imply that a nascent unified paradigm is defined by emerging experiential concepts rather than established client-centred ones.

Pete Sanders: principles based on the therapeutic conditions and non-directiveness

Sanders (2000) introduced the idea of primary and secondary principles based on Rogers' therapeutic conditions and non-directivity. His primary principles (essential to be included in the person-centred and experiential 'family') are:

- the primacy of the actualizing tendency
- assertion of the necessity and centrality of Rogers' (1959) therapeutic conditions
- the primacy of the non-directive attitude at least at the level of the content of the therapeutic encounter, but not necessarily at the level of process.

His secondary principles (optional, but particularly characteristic of the person-centred and experiential 'family') are:

- autonomy and the client's right to self-determination
- equality or the non-expertness of the therapist
- the primacy of the non-directive attitude and intention in its absolute, pure and principled (Grant, 1990) form
- the sufficiency of Rogers' (1959) therapeutic conditions
- holism: encountering the client as an organized whole entity.

To be included in the person-centred and experiential family on Sanders' terms means accepting the necessity (but not the sufficiency) of Rogers's (1957) therapeutic conditions and delineating the difference between directing the content of the therapy and directing its process. For him, espousal of the sufficiency of Rogers' conditions and non-directivity in both content and process of therapy would define the practice of the classic client-centred therapist (see below).

Peter F. Schmid: criteria for identity and coherence

Schmid (2003) took a comprehensive look at the characteristics that bring together the '"family" of person-centred therapies' and the criteria by which contenders can be evaluated. There is insufficient space to adequately précis all the aspects of his careful analysis here, but for the purposes of comparison, Schmid characterizes person-centred therapies as:

- founded upon an image of the person as inseparably individual and relational
- relationship and resource-oriented (as opposed to goal and solution-oriented)
- dialogical (see below)
- putting the client first: meaning not simply that the client is at the centre of the relationship, but that the client is the expert, emphasizing the phenomenological nature of the approach
- consisting in the presence of the therapist as non-directive, immediate, open and embodying Rogers' therapeutic conditions.

Schmid is concerned that the public face of person-centred therapy (PCT) is clearly stated, identifiable and congruent through its practice, theory and principles to its philosophy. This is no small task, but his endeavour along with the others here, is concerned with developing negotiated boundaries between PCT and other approaches and cohesion within those boundaries.

Margaret Warner: levels of therapist interventiveness

Warner (2000) differentiated approaches on the basis of five levels of therapist 'interventiveness', whilst taking Rogers' therapeutic conditions as the baseline, the minimum qualification for inclusion in the person-centred and experiential 'family'. Interventiveness is clearly derived from non-directivity, and is defined as the 'degree to which the therapist brings in material from outside the client's frame of reference and the degree to which this is done from a stance of authority or expertise' (Warner, 2000: 31).

- *Level 1*: the therapist brings nothing from outside the client's frame of reference.
- *Level 2*: the therapist uses personal experiences and theories in order better to understand (but not influence) the client's experience.
- *Level 3*: the therapist brings material into the relationship in ways that foster the client's choice as to whether and how to use such material.

- *Level 4*: the therapist brings material into the relationship from his or her own frame of reference from a position of authority or expertise.
- *Level 5*: the therapist brings material from outside the client's frame of reference so that the client is unaware of the intervention, its nature or the therapist's purpose in making the intervention.

Warner asserts that client-directed therapies would be found at levels 1–3, whilst therapies using interpretations, suggestions and techniques would be found at levels 4–5. She also suggests that the attitudes implicit in levels 1–3 would be more indicative of therapists who understood the actualizing tendency to be central to the change process. In short, she concludes that whilst some person-centred and experiential therapists might make a few interventions at level 4, her scale places person-centred therapies in levels 1–3.

Person-centred/client-centred therapy

Classic non-directive client-centred therapy: the pure form

The appellation 'classic' or 'classical' related to client-centred therapy, is a somewhat recent development, possibly used first by Lietaer (1990: 11) in the form 'classic Rogerians'. As new approaches and integrative variants sprang from the work of Rogers, those theorists and practitioners whose practice was defined by Rogers' early work in Chicago (see Chapter 3, this volume) struggled to identify themselves as different from what had become a general mêlée of generic person-centred therapists. Some preferred to identify themselves as 'non-directive' and others as 'client-centred' therapists (to set their work apart from what they see as the more inclusive term 'person-centred therapists'). Although far from universally accepted, the term classic client-centered therapy is becoming more frequently used as a descriptor of Rogers' founding formulations (e.g. Rogers, 1959), with a distinct emphasis on non-directive intent. Those most associated with this original form are Barbara Brodley (1996), Jerold Bozarth (1998) and most recently Tony Merry (2002), who gives a comprehensive account of the theory of motivation (actualization), personality (19 propositions, Rogers, 1951) and therapy (Rogers, 1959), and in summary form two years later (Merry, 2004).

The salient distinguishing features of the classic form are understanding and accepting:

- the actualizing tendency as the unitary motivation for human beings
- the need for positive regard and ensuing conditions of worth as the fundamental origin of psychopathology
- the necessity and sufficiency of Rogers' therapeutic conditions for personality change (driven and directed by the actualizing tendency)
- the inviolable sovereignty of the client and the client-centred location of the therapeutic process represented by principled non-directivity.

Although referred to as classic, original and pure, it cannot be said that this founding formulation does not itself continue to develop. Many practitioners have elaborated, extended and added to Rogers' original concepts and practice without violating the principles outlined above. An incomplete and contestable list of developments includes Barbara Brodley's refining and elevation of the concept of empathy, and origination of 'empathy-only' practice (Brodley, 1996, 2001); Dave Mearns' (Mearns, 1996; Mearns and Cooper, 2005) broadening the possibilities by developing the thesis of working at relational depth; Barry Grant's elaboration of principled and instrumental non-directivity (Grant, 1990/2002), and Jerold Bozarth's identification of unconditional positive regard as the 'curative factor' (Bozarth, 1998: 83) in personality change.

Encounter-oriented (dialogical) approaches

Originating in the work of philosopher Martin Buber, the idea that the human change process consists entirely in the co-created inter-subjective relationship between helper and person helped is widely acknowledged in the person-centred 'family' of therapies and is emerging as a sub-orientation in its own right. Such an approach is a tacit critique of the subjective, individual self-psychology at the centre of most interpretations of Rogers' work, and it is this strong theme that demands consideration as an approach in its own right. A dialogical approach is implicit in the recent work of Godfrey Barrett-Lennard (2004) and Dave Mearns (Mearns 1996; Mearns and Cooper, 2005), but Peter F. Schmid (1998, 2001a, 2001b, 2001c, 2002a, 2006) has been foremost in elaborating dialogical therapy through the work of philosopher Emmanuel Levinas. Schmid positions himself close to classic client-centred therapy, non-directive and espousing the sufficiency of Rogers' therapeutic conditions, but makes the encounter between the helper and helped much more than a mere conduit for helping ('encounter' being different from 'relationship'). In a sophisticated series of propositions, encounter-oriented dialogical therapy plays on moment-to-moment interdependent meanings of 'self', 'other' and 'meeting' in the encounter. It is very difficult to summarize these given the space allocated here, but they could be understood as appreciating all of the potentials made possible in the separateness of the Other anew in every moment of meeting. This acknowledgement of the Other means that the therapist approaches the client as a naïve seeker, open to whatever the Other has to offer (see Chapter 4, this volume).

It may be the case that, in practice, an encounter-oriented therapist might look very much like a classical client-centred therapist, but brings a very different repertoire of sensibilities. Of the many consequences of such an ethos is appreciation of human beings as necessarily social and creative. The individual, understood as 'self-first', is no longer centre stage. The Other and the co-created moment between Thou and I is at the core. A further consequence is that this approach emphasizes the social context of therapy and thus emphasizes the value and rich possibilities of group therapy (see Chapter 8, this volume).

How do dialogical approaches to psychotherapy fit into the person-centred and experiential 'family'?

Setting aside the historical emphasis on individual, subjective self-psychology, there are no differences of any substance between classical client-centred therapy

and the emerging dialogical therapy. Only through facing the Others and appreciating their uniqueness can therapists free them to actualize their potential.
Anything else would effectively constitute a limiting condition of worth, either
acted out, or implied by our personal philosophy. Such implications are powerful precursors to real behaviour and lead dialogical therapists to pay particular
attention to their deep understanding of what it is to be human.

The meta-perspective of integration

It is important to immediately distinguish between eclecticism and integration. Eclecticism – sometimes referred to as 'technical eclecticism', a term
coined by Dryden (1984) – denotes assembling a collection of techniques on
an ad hoc basis according to the requirements of the situation as seen by the
therapist. It mimics the medical approach to treating somatic disease by
affecting a 'diagnosis-and-application-of-appropriate treatment' method. The
many flaws with this type of approach include that there is no scientific basis
for such 'diagnoses' and there is scant evidence for the appropriateness of the
'treatments' which might be applied (Sanders, 2005).

The United Kingdom Council for Psychotherapy (UKCP) in its section on
'Humanistic and Integrative Psychotherapies' defines integrative therapy as
follows:

> Integrative therapy can be distinguished from eclecticism by its determination to
> show there are significant connections between different therapies, which may
> be unrecognized by their exclusive proponents. While remaining respectful to
> each approach, integrative psychotherapy draws from many sources in the belief
> that no one approach has all the truth.
>   (http://82.219.38.131/ukcp.org.uk/home.asp?p=sections_hips.asp)

Rather than react to the client in an entirely ad hoc way, then, integrative
models attempt to develop an effective prospectus for treatment by one or
more of the following methods:

- identifying and bringing together common theoretical components
- identifying and bringing together common techniques and methods
- development of a meta-theory (possibly derived from the first two points
  above, or by extending an existing theory).

Readers will probably be aware that this will give rise to numerous definitions
of integrative therapy – too many even to mention here. Also it may have
occurred to readers that the idea of integrative models is predicated on the idea
of 'pure forms', and so it may in fact be better to speak in terms of an integrative approach to therapy rather than integrative models. And finally all of this
reproduces the tensions in the 'family' of person-centred and experiential therapies already described – between the 'pure form' and the 'new developments'.

So rather than catalogue integrative models, I will direct readers to an
approach to integrating material into person-centred and experiential practice
whilst testing the process against person-centred core theory and exploring

the consequences, described by Richard Worsley. Worsley summarizes this approach thus 'What is to be integrated is life's experience as a whole!' and he continues: 'If the practitioner of the classical, client-centred model protests that they also do this, then I am delighted' (2004: 128). I wonder if this approach to therapy is what Rogers had in mind when he explained that he didn't want anyone to mimic him, but to find their own way? Worsley advocates continuous reflexive practice informed and directed by the central philosophical tenets of: collaborative practice; putting the client at the centre of the activity; respect for the sovereignty of the person; attention to the moment-by-moment experiencing of client (and therapist) and the necessity of the authentic open presence of the therapist.

Experiential therapies

Focusing-oriented psychotherapy

Eugene Gendlin, a student and later colleague of Rogers, was the first to develop theory and practice springing from, yet at a tangent to, Rogers' work (see Hendricks, 2001; Purton, 2004a, 2004b). The genesis of Gendlin's approach was the ill-fated research project at Mendota State Hospital (Rogers et al, 1967), directed from the University of Wisconsin, into the effects of psychotherapy with people diagnosed with schizophrenia. The work with the clients and the results of the study, together with earlier work of Kirtner and Cartwright (1958), all pointed to the importance of the nature of the client's experiencing as a crucial factor in the outcome of therapy. Whilst Rogers acknowledged the importance of this, he moved from Wisconsin to California in the early 1960s and to all intents and purposes withdrew from the development of one-to-one therapy theory.

Gendlin on the other hand continued to pursue the importance of the client's level of experiencing to the process of change. He concluded that clients who were not engaged with their experiencing (a low experiencing level) were less likely to change than those who could apprehend their moment-by-moment experiencing (a high experiencing level). Gendlin turned his attention to developing methods to help clients attend to their experiencing process, to pay more attention to their moment-by-moment experience. This is the essence of focusing-oriented psychotherapy.

Gendlin (1978) described a series of simple steps to help everyone learn how to focus on their experiencing process. It was *not* written as a guide for therapists, but a guide for every man and woman:

1. Clearing a space.
2. Identifying a 'felt sense' in relation to a problem or an issue.
3. Capturing the quality of the felt sense in a word, phrase or image.
4. 'Resonating' between the word or image and the felt sense.
5. Inquiring what it is all about, its context and meaning.
6. Receiving the understanding that comes.

Focusing-oriented psychotherapy sets out first to help the client better to engage with his or her experiencing. The therapist helps the client become aware of any blocks to the flow of experiencing, and this particularly involves the therapist being with the client in a way which does not hinder the natural process of healing. This way of being present corresponds with Rogers' therapeutic conditions. It also involves looking at the possibility that the client may suffer from any number of well-known (to focusing-oriented therapists) difficulties in accessing his or her experiencing, and inviting the client to work in particular ways to dissolve them.

How does focusing-oriented psychotherapy fit into the person-centred and experiential 'family'?

Purton (2004a, 2004b) asserts that focusing-oriented therapy takes Rogers' therapeutic conditions as its starting point for practice that does not block the clients' access to their experiencing, and he asserts that it is essentially non-directive. (Readers must remember that the focusing six-step procedure is not a method for therapists.) Differences arise between the pure form and focusing-oriented therapy in both personality theory and the theory of therapy or change.

It is clear, however, that there are potential differences in practice between classical client-centred therapy and focusing-oriented therapy. Individual classical client-centred therapy practitioners are obliged to be principled in their non-directivity (Grant, 1990), or work at Warner's levels 1 and 2 of interventiveness, since as I note elsewhere (Sanders, 2005: 34), classical client-centred therapy is the only approach which enshrines the clients' right to access healing without sacrificing their personal power. On the other hand, individual focusing-oriented therapy practitioners may operate at levels 4 and 5 if it will facilitate the clients' engagement with their experiencing and moving forward.

So by all the criteria described above, focusing-oriented therapy is certainly included in the person-centred and experiential 'family' of therapies, but we find that individual practitioners have licence to operate outside the boundaries of the family, if they so choose.

Process-experiential psychotherapy

The key figures in the development of process-experiential psychotherapy are Laura North Rice, Leslie Greenberg and their associates in North America. We find the origins of the approach in the work of Rice when she asks the question: 'What are the mechanisms of change?' (1974: 294). Rice set the tone of the process-experiential project in the same chapter, an ethos evident today in the latest work (Elliott et al, 2004b), when she declared: 'Spinning theories is not simply a luxury to be indulged in during the intervals of doing therapy by the seat of one's pants' (1974: 290). Inspired by Rogers' early emphasis on research (see, e.g. Raskin, 1948/2004; Rogers and Dymond, 1954), process-experiential theorists have also led a wide range of innovative research initiatives in the last 30 years (Elliott et al, 2004a).

Originally strongly influenced by Gendlin's discoveries concerning the importance of experience as a process, process-experiential therapy quickly broadened its horizons to integrate influences from a wide variety of sources from gestalt therapy to cognitive/information-processing psychology. Close observation and innovative research led to the building of theory which Elliott and Greenberg (2001: 279–81) summarized as being built on:

- the humanistic values of self-determination, the primacy of experiencing, lifelong psychological development, pluralism, egalitarianism, holism and authentic person-to-person relationships
- Greenberg's emotion theory (Greenberg and Paivio, 1997)
- a dialectical constructivist theory of self and change
- empirically supported methods
- a process orientation: that is, an emphasis on the unfolding of moment-to-moment process within the client's and therapist's experience and within their relationship.

The treatment principles and methods (explained at two levels of therapist responses and tasks) distilled through research, are described by Elliott and Greenberg (2001: 281–91):

- *Empathic attunement*: actively entering the client's world anew, resonating with the client's experience as it evolves from moment to moment, not as a technique to evaluate or diagnose the client.
- *Therapeutic bond*: the expression of non-judgemental, genuine prizing of the client.
- *Task collaboration*: build a relationship on mutual involvement in the goals and tasks of therapy (accepting the client-generated tasks and goals and describing the emotional processes involved).
- *Experiential processing*: facilitating optimal client engagement with moment-to-moment experiencing (helping the client work in appropriately different ways with different tasks to maximize effectiveness).
- *Task completion*: facilitate the client to complete the key therapeutic tasks identified (persisting in helping the client to stay on task).
- *Growth/choice*: emphasis on client agency by fostering client growth and self-determination (encouraging the client to make in-session decisions about goals, tasks and activities).

Within this protocol, the therapist might make use of specific interventions prescribed by process experiential therapy, including two-chair and empty-chair dialogue, focusing and meaning creation. Readers should be aware, however, that this is a snapshot of a therapeutic theory in progress, since process-experiential therapy is a developing approach that is a result of a continuous research programme.

How does process-experiential psychotherapy fit into the person-centred and experiential 'family'?

Process-experiential therapy has a clear agenda in terms of how the relationship is to be configured, the expert role of the therapist with regard to the therapeutic process, the direction and progression of interventions and the goals and tasks of the client. Whilst process-experiential therapy revolves around a therapeutic relationship founded on Rogers' therapeutic conditions, it extends considerably beyond the sufficiency 'rule'. It actively integrates relationship elements and techniques validated by process-experiential research, and in Warner's terms, process-experiential therapy is self-consciously interventive at level 4. A theory and practice edifice so constructed sparks fierce debate in person-centred and experiential circles, and by any measure it challenges definitions of what might be reasonably considered to be person-centred. But is this a bad thing? Its proponents, however, frequently reassert the links with Rogers' work and continually refer to the humanistic underpinnings, the centrality of Rogers' conditions to the therapeutic process, the right of the client to self-determination, and collaboration.

Pre-Therapy

Although Garry Prouty himself specifically referred to his work as being not a therapeutic approach per se, but pre- (coming before) therapy, it deserves a brief introduction in this review (Prouty, 1994; Prouty et al, 2002) (see Chapter 18, this volume, for a more comprehensive and detailed presentation). Prouty was the first person to make a serious study of psychological contact. His work confirmed Rogers' early hypothesis that therapeutic change cannot take place without psychological contact, and developed a conceptual and practical system for understanding and establishing contact with people whose ability to make contact had been impaired by illness or injury, organic or psychological. The range of applications (still growing) includes clients who are contact-impaired as a result of age-related and other forms of dementia, brain injury, terminal illness, 'psychosis', dissociation, severe learning disability or autism.

Prouty describes Pre-Therapy as 'applied phenomenology' and explains its action as 'pointing at the concrete'. Through irreducible 'contact reflections' (extremely simple reflections regarding verbal and facial expressions and the shared reality of the environment), the client is brought back into contact with his or her experience, other people and the world. When contact and everyday functioning is restored, psychotherapy is then possible. The 'pre-expressive' self (the person previously trapped inside) is now able to choose to take part in everyday human relationships and some of the secondary symptoms of chronic isolation dissolve.

Although it might appear simple to describe, Pre-Therapy is not easy to do. Most trained therapists have great difficulty in stripping away the finer aspects of therapeutic communication to get to the bare bones of applied phenomenology required for successful contact work.

How does Pre-Therapy fit into the person-centred and experiential 'family'?

There can be no doubt that Pre-Therapy is closest to the core of classic client-centred therapy in practical terms. It is vital to remember, however, that it is not a 'normal' human relationship in the strict sense. It is a way of being for special occasions. Its essential protocols are derived from the need to make the most basic of relationship moments with another human being and so are incomparable with other applications of Rogers' work. Yet Pre-Therapy is without doubt one of the purest incarnations of person-centred communication.

Modalities

There is no space to do more than list the various therapeutic applications of classical client-centred, person-centred, focusing-oriented and process-experiential therapies. It is important that readers realize that there are no theoretical or practical limits (save the imagination of the therapist) that would limit the application of this 'family' of therapies. Readers are directed to other chapters in this book and, among others, the work of the following innovators in their respective fields: Moon (2002) in child psychotherapy; O'Leary (1999) in couple therapy (see Chapter 20, this volume); Gaylin (2001) in family therapy; N. Rogers (1993) in expressive arts therapies (see Chapter 23, this volume); Hobbs (1951), Raskin (1986a, 1986b) and Shlien (2003) in group therapy (see Chapter 8, this volume).

CONCLUSION

If the terms 'person-centred' and 'client-centred' have become too general and lacking in discrimination, then new descriptors are necessary. And it is possible that this list of new names continues to grow even as I write, and certainly more variations will have been added by the time this book is published. So, reconciled to be forever one or two steps behind, I hope I leave readers better able to make decisions about the newest types of therapy that claim to be inside, or just outside, the big tent of the person-centred and experiential approaches.

It is clear that person-centred psychotherapies have developed and diversified considerably since 1960. Today the fashion elsewhere in psychotherapy is to be 'beyond schoolism', so readers might well ask why the client-centred community seems hell-bent on diversification, rather than unification? In addition, they might despair that such divergence might lead to conflict. It is my view, however, that the apparent proliferation of 'brands' is not competitive in nature; rather it is descriptive.

Better understanding of what therapists do is an ongoing process of description, refinement and development of ideas in which all therapists should engage for the sake of their prospective clients, for fellow professionals and for themselves. No therapists are beyond refining their understanding and description of their own practice, and we all have much to learn from the work of others.

REFERENCES

Barrett-Lennard, G.T. (1998). *Carl Rogers' Helping System: journey and substance*. London: Sage.

Barrett-Lennard, G.T. (2004). *Relationship at the Centre: healing in a troubled world*. London: Whurr.

Bozarth, J.D. (1998). *Person-Centered Therapy: a revolutionary paradigm*. Ross-on-Wye: PCCS Books.

Brodley, B.T. (1996). Empathic understanding and feelings in client-centered therapy. *Person-Centered Journal*, 3, 1, 22–30.

Brodley, B.T. (2001). Observations of empathic understanding in a client-centered practice. In S. Haugh and T. Merry (eds), *Rogers' Therapeutic Conditions* (pp. 16–38). Volume 2. *Empathy*. Ross-on-Wye: PCCS Books.

Dryden, W. (1984). *Individual Therapy in Britain*. London: Harper and Row.

Elliott, R.F. and Greenberg, L.S. (2001). Process-experiential psychotherapy. In D.J. Cain and J. Seeman (eds), *Humanistic Psychotherapies: handbook of research and practice* (pp. 279–306). Washington DC: American Psychological Association.

Elliott, R., Greenberg, L. and Lietaer, G. (2004a). Research on experiential psychotherapies. In M.J. Lambert, A.E. Bergin, and S.L. Garfield (eds), *Handbook of Psychotherapy and Behavior Change* (pp. 493–539). 5th edn. Washington DC: American Psychological Association.

Elliott, R., Watson, J.C., Goldman, R.N. and Greenberg, L. (2004b). *Learning Emotion Focused Therapy: the process experiential approach to change*. Washington DC: American Psychological Association.

Gaylin, N.L. (2001). *Family, Self and Psychotherapy: a person-centred perspective*. Ross-on-Wye: PCCS Books.

Gendlin, E.T. (1978). *Focusing*. New York: Everest House.

Greenberg, L.S. and Paivio, S. (1997). *Working with emotions in psychotherapy*. New York: Guilford.

Grant, B. (1990/2002). Principled and instrumental non-directiveness in the person-centred approach. *Person-Centered Review*, 5, 1, 77–88. Reprinted in D.J. Cain (ed.) (2002), *Classics in the Person-Centered Approach* (pp. 371–7). Ross-on-Wye: PCCS Books.

Hendricks, M.N. (2001). Focusing oriented/experiential psychotherapy. In D.J. Cain and J. Seeman (eds), *Humanistic Psychotherapies: handbook of research and practice* (pp. 221–52). Washington DC: American Psychological Association.

Hobbs, N. (1951). Group-centered psychotherapy. In C.R. Rogers. *Client-centered Therapy* (pp. 278–319). Boston: Houghton Mifflin.

Hutterer, R. (1993). Eclecticism: an identity crisis for person-centred therapists. In D. Brazier, *Beyond Carl Rogers* (pp. 274–84). London: Constable.

Kirschenbaum, H. (1979). *On Becoming Carl Rogers*. New York: Delacorte.

Kirtner W.L. and Cartwright D.S. (1958). Success and failure in client-centered therapy as a function of initial in-therapy behavior. *Journal of Consulting Psychology*, 22(5): 329–33.

Lietaer (1990). Preface. In *Client-Centered and Experiential Psychotherapy in the Nineties,* (pp. 11–13). Leuven: University of Leuven Press.

Lietaer, G. (2000). The client-centered/experiential paradigm in psychotherapy: development and identity. In J.C. Watson, R.N. Goldman and M.S. Warner (eds), *Client-centered and Experiential Psychotherapy in the Twenty-first Century: advances in theory, research and practice* (pp. 1–15). Ross-on-Wye: PCCS Books.

Lietaer, G. (2002). The united colors of person-centered and experiential psychotherapies. *Person-Centred and Experiential Psychotherapies,* 1(1–2), 4–13.

Mearns, D. (1996). Working at relational depth with clients in person-centred therapy. *Counselling,* 7(4): 306–11.

Mearns, D. and Cooper, M. (2005). *Working at Relational Depth in Counselling and Psychotherapy.* London: Sage.

Merry, T. (2002). *Learning and Being in Person-Centred Counselling,* 2nd edn. Ross-on-Wye: PCCS Books.

Merry, T. (2004). Classical client-centred therapy. In P. Sanders (ed.), *The Tribes of the Person-Centred Nation* (pp. 21–44). Ross-on-Wye: PCCS Books.

Moon, K. (2002). Non-directive client-centered work with children. In J.C. Watson, R.N. Goldman and M.S. Warner (eds), *Client-centered and Experiential Psychotherapy in the Twenty-first Century: advances in theory, research and practice* (pp. 485–92). Ross-on-Wye: PCCS Books.

O'Leary, C. (1999). *Couple and Family Counseling: a person-centered approach.* London: Sage.

Prouty, G. (1994). *Theoretical Evolutions in Person-Centered/Experiential Therapy: applications to schizophrenic and retarded psychoses.* Westport, CT: Praeger.

Prouty, G., Van Werde, D. and Pörtner, M. (2002). *Pre-Therapy: reaching contact-impaired clients.* Ross-on-Wye: PCCS Books.

Purton, C. (2004a). Focusing-oriented therapy. In P. Sanders (ed.), *The Tribes of the Person-Centred Nation: an introduction to the schools of therapy related to the person-centred approach* (pp. 45–67). Ross-on-Wye: PCCS Books.

Purton, C. (2004b). *Person-Centred Therapy: the focusing-oriented approach.* Basingstoke: Palgrave MacMillan.

Raskin, N.J. (1948/2004). The development of nondirective therapy. *Journal of Consulting Psychology,* 12, 92–110. Reprinted in N.J. Raskin (2004) *Contributions to Client-Centered Therapy and the Person-Centered Approach* (pp. 1–27). Ross-on-Wye: PCCS Books.

Raskin, N.J. (1986a). Client-centered group psychotherapy. Part I. Development of client-centered groups. *Person-Centered Review,* 1(3), 272–90. Reprinted in N.J. Raskin (2004), *Contributions to Client-centered Therapy and the Person-Centered Approach* (pp. 131–44). Ross-on-Wye: PCCS Books.

Raskin, N.J. (1986b). Client-centered group psychotherapy. Part II. Research on client-centered groups. *Person-Centered Review,* 1(4): 389–408.

Reprinted in N.J. Raskin (2004), *Contributions to Client-centered Therapy and the Person-Centered Approach* (pp. 145–59). Ross-on-Wye: PCCS Books.

Rice, L.N. (1974). The evocative function of the therapist. In D.A. Wexler and L.N. Rice (eds), *Innovations in Client-centered Therapy* (pp. 289–312). New York: Wiley.

Rogers, C.R. (1951). *Client-Centered Therapy*. Boston: Houghton Mifflin.

Rogers, C.R. (1957). The necessary and sufficient conditions of therapeutic personality change. *Journal of Consulting Psychology*, 21(2), 95–103.

Rogers, C.R. (1958). A process conception of psychotherapy. *American Psychologist*, 13, 142–9.

Rogers, C.R. (1959). A theory of therapy, personality, and interpersonal relationships as developed in the client-centered framework. In S. Koch (ed.), *Psychology: a study of a science*. Volume 3. *Formulations of the Person and the Social Context* (pp. 184–256). New York: McGraw-Hill.

Rogers, C.R. and Dymond, R.F. (1954). *Psychotherapy and Personality Change*. Chicago: University of Chicago Press.

Rogers, C.R., Gendlin, E.T., Kiesler, D.J. and Truax, C.B. (1967). *The Therapeutic Relationship and its Impact: a study of psychotherapy with schizophrenics*. Madison: University of Wisconsin Press.

Rogers, C.R. and Hart, J.T. (1970). Looking back and looking ahead: a conversation with Carl Rogers. In J.T. Hart and T.M. Tomlinson (eds), *New Directions in Client-Centered Therapy* (pp. 499–534). Boston: Houghton Mifflin.

Rogers, N. (1993). *The Creative Connection: expressive arts as healing*. Palo Alto, Calif.: Science and Behavior Books. Published in the UK in 2000 by PCCS Books.

Sanders, P. (2000). Mapping person-centred approaches to counselling and psychotherapy. *Person-Centred Practice*, 8(2): 62–74. Adapted and reprinted in P. Sanders (2004)(ed.), *The Tribes of the Person-Centred Nation: an introduction to the schools of therapy related to the person-centred approach* (pp. 149–64). Ross-on-Wye: PCCS Books.

Sanders, P. (2004). History of CCT and the PCA: events, dates and ideas. In P. Sanders (ed.), *The Tribes of the Person-Centred Nation: an introduction to the schools of therapy related to the person-centred approach* (pp. 1–20). Ross-on-Wye: PCCS Books.

Sanders, P. (2005). Principled and strategic opposition to the medicalization of distress and all of its apparatus. In S. Joseph and R. Worsley (eds), *Person-Centred Psychopathology: a positive psychology of mental health* (pp. 21–43). Ross-on-Wye: PCCS Books.

Schmid, P.F. (1998). 'Face to face': the art of encounter. In B. Thorne and E. Lambers (eds), *Person-Centred Therapy: a European perspective* (pp. 74–90). London: Sage.

Schmid, P.F. (2001a). Authenticity: the person as his or her own author. Dialogical and ethical perspectives on therapy as an encounter relationship. And beyond. In G. Wyatt (ed.), *Rogers' Therapeutic Conditions:*

evolution, theory and practice. Volume 1. *Congruence* (pp. 217–32). Ross-on-Wye: PCCS Books.

Schmid, P.F. (2001b). Comprehension: the art of not-knowing. Dialogical and ethical perspectives on empathy as dialogue in personal and person-centred relationships. In S. Haugh and T. Merry (eds), *Rogers' Therapeutic Series: evolution, theory and practice.* Volume 2. *Empathy* (pp. 53–71). Ross-on-Wye: PCCS Books.

Schmid, P.F. (2001c). Acknowledgement: the art of responding. Dialogical and ethical perspectives on the challenge of unconditional personal relationships in therapy and beyond. In J. Bozarth and P. Wilkins (eds), *Rogers' Therapeutic Series: evolution, theory and practice.* Volume 3. *Unconditional Positive Regard* (pp. 49–64). Ross-on-Wye: PCCS Books.

Schmid, PF (2002a). Presence: im-media-te co-experiencing and co-responding: phenomenological, dialogical and ethical perspectives on contact and perception in person-centred therapy and beyond. In G. Wyatt and P. Sanders (eds), *Rogers' Therapeutic Series: evolution, theory and practice.* Volume 4. *Contact and Perception* (pp. 182–203). Ross-on-Wye: PCCS Books.

Schmid, P.F. (2002b). Knowledge or acknowledgement: psychotherapy as the art of 'not-knowing' – Prospects on further developments of a radical paradigm. *Person-Centred and Experiential Psychotherapies*, 1(1–2): 56–70.

Schmid, P.F. (2003). The characteristics of a person-centred approach to therapy and counseling: criteria for identity and coherence. *Person-Centered and Experiential Psychotherapies*, 2(2): 104–20.

Schmid, P.F. (2006). The challenge of the Other: towards dialogical person-centered psychotherapy and counselling. *Person-Centered and Experiential Psychotherapies,* 5(4): 241–54.

Shlien, J.M. (2003). Basic concepts in group psychotherapy: a client-centered point of view. In J.M. Shlien, *To Live an Honorable Life: invitations to think about client-centered therapy and the person-centered approach* (pp. 131–7). Ross-on-Wye: PCCS Books. Original written in 1957.

Warner, M. S. (2000). Person-centered psychotherapy: one nation many tribes. *Person Centered Journal* 7(1): 28–39.

Worsley, R. (2004). Integrating with integrity. In P. Sanders (ed.), *The Tribes of the Person-Centred Nation* (pp. 125–48). Ross-on-Wye: PCCS Books.

PART
II
Therapeutic Practice

In the second part of the *Handbook*, we turn our attention to how the philosophical and theoretical person-centred foundations, focused on in Part I, inform our psychotherapy and counselling practice. The relationship between therapist and client is the foundation of person-centred practice. Carl Rogers recognized the significance of the qualitative nature of relationships, and in his seminal papers of 1957 and 1959 delineated these qualities as 'conditions' that were necessary and sufficient for a relationship to be therapeutic. The aim of person-centred practice is to establish and maintain a relationship characterized by Rogers' six conditions within which clients, due to the actualizing tendency, will find their own way, their own development, their own change. This is the unique nature of person-centred practice – the meeting of Rogers' six conditions with the actualizing tendency within what becomes the therapeutic relationship.

Our aim is to highlight and explore the central importance of relationship in person-centred practice by providing a comprehensive, succinct and accessible overview of the relational foundations to the practice of person-centred therapy, the qualitative nature of the therapeutic relationship as described by Rogers' six conditions, and the relational processes that occur and affect therapist and client.

Each author was asked to address the core concepts, to discuss and illustrate the therapeutic practice that emerges from these concepts, to look at any relevant research and to reflect on issues for the future.

The first chapter in this section, by Godfrey Barrett-Lennard, is in part a continuation of his historical review started in Chapter 3. Here he traces the development of relational thinking and its importance for therapy practice and provides a rich and formative introduction to the evolution of relational foundations of person-centred practice. He locates relationship as a fundamental way of being that reflects our interconnectedness.

The next six chapters each take one of Rogers' six conditions. Each condition describes an aspect of the therapeutic relationship that is highly significant for practice. It has sometimes been assumed that Rogers' proposed just three conditions for therapeutic personality change: the so-called 'core conditions' of empathy, congruence and unconditional positive regard. One aim here is to re-locate the 'core conditions' within the context of the three other 'lost' conditions of contact, client incongruence, and the client's perception of the therapist's empathy and acceptance. In order to understand the significance of the therapeutic relationship and be able to develop the relevant aspects in our person-centred practice, we need to study each different condition or quality and the whole that emerges when all six conditions are present. This idea of differentiation and integration runs through several of the chapters.

The first of these chapters focuses on Rogers' first condition 'psychological contact', and is authored by Gill Wyatt, editor of the series, *Rogers' Therapeutic Conditions: evolution, theory and practice* (2001, PCCS Books). This chapter presents Rogers' and three further conceptualizations – a Pre-Therapy, a relational and a holistic/emergent conceptualization of contact – in order to demonstrate the significance of psychological contact in developing our person-centred practice.

This chapter is followed by an examination of the second of Rogers' conditions, 'client incongruence'. Here, Margaret Warner reviews the original Rogers' model of incongruence as the fundamental source of psychological distress, along with other contemporary person-centred models of 'psychopathology', and then proposes a 'process-sensitive' model of psychopathology, a further development to her important work on 'fragile' and 'difficult' process.

The subsequent three chapters look at the more familiar 'core conditions' of congruence, unconditional positive regard and empathy. The chapter on congruence is written by Jeffrey Cornelius-White from the United States, one of the new generation of person-centred writers. He discusses Rogers' theory of congruence and Seeman's organismic integration and presence, arriving at a reformulation of congruence as an internal, relational and ecological construct which is closely related to the formative tendency.

Elizabeth Freire, from Brazil, another contemporary person-centred writer, authors the chapter on empathy. She presents a classical client-centred perspective, highlighting the shift of power that arises from empathy where the client becomes the expert and the therapist's non-directivity becomes central. This theme is continued in the next chapter on unconditional positive regard, contributed by the renowned scholar Jerold Bozarth from the United States. He contrasts the classical with the 'post-classical person-centred' perspective, and advocates that unconditional positive regard is the 'curative factor' in person-centred therapy.

Chapter 16 discusses the role of perception in Rogers' sixth condition. It is written by Canadian psychologist Shaké Toukmanian, who has founded her own 'perceptual-processing' approach to person-centred therapy, and her colleague Lila Hakim. They examine the role of perception in person-centred therapy and practice and in particular the importance of the client's perceptions of the therapist's empathy and unconditional positive regard as a relational process.

Part II concludes with a chapter that provides an overview of the therapeutic process, as understood within the person-centred field. It is written by Martin van Kalmthout from the Netherlands, an advocate of 'systems of meaning' in person-centred therapy, and it outlines the journey that many clients experience through the process of person-centred therapy: from fixity to fluidity, isolation to connectedness and from incongruence to congruence.

The Relational Foundations of Person-Centred Practice

Godfrey T. Barrett-Lennard

An emphasis on qualities of attitude and relationship, especially between therapist and client, has always been a feature of client/person-centred thought. This focus is linked to major innovations in practice and a generous associated literature. Recently it has led on to the broader question of what the phenomenon of human relationship is, an issue I will come to later in this chapter. No other therapy system has devoted such pivotal attention to the therapist–client relationship, with its long-considered theory of the critical ingredients of this relationship – a theory built largely from experience of practice and feeding back into practice and research. Some core principles have had great 'staying power' but there have also been evolutionary steps in thinking and application. This chapter tracks such principles and steps, albeit rather briefly and at some points in glimpsing view.

Core concepts

Otto Rank (1936/1945) believed that people have an inherent tendency to be active self-directing agents. Furthermore, just 'as the therapist can only heal in his own way, the patient also can only become well in his own way; that is, whenever and however he wills' (Rank, 1945: 99). Rogers' first book includes generous illustration of this broad approach (1939: 197–209 and 340–8). Especially in the case of child therapy it seemed to him that 'In no other type of treatment effort does the emotional situation between therapist and child occupy such a place of prominence' (1939: 343). Encouraged especially by the *practice* of Rankian relationship therapy, Rogers' basic direction was established and the advancement of his own thought and therapy accelerated through the next decade.

Client-Centered Therapy (Rogers, 1951) notably includes a long chapter (pp. 65–130) on 'the therapeutic relationship as experienced by the client', containing numerous and vivid illustrations of practice. Early empirical studies of the therapist–client relationship had by then been completed or were in progress (see Barrett-Lennard, 1998: 261–3). This research, including a study that emphasized personal feeling aspects of the relation between therapist and client (Bown, 1954), fed into Rogers' thought regarding the causal conditions for therapeutic change. Studies such as that of Fiedler (1950), suggesting that expert therapists of differing orientation tended to relate similarly, also encouraged Rogers to articulate his thought as a theory of change in psychotherapy generally, not only in client-centred therapy (1957, 1959).

Chapter 3 in Part I of this volume traces the build up to the pivotal crystallization of Rogers' thought that he first published in 1957. The (six) conditions for therapeutic change that he advanced (1957 and 1959) include the baseline feature that client and therapist must be in 'psychological contact', each one present in the experiential field of the other. This 'precondition' for the development of relationship had an importance beyond Rogers' own expectation, as elucidated in the next chapter of this book. The broad quality of client emotional vulnerability and incongruence is singled out as a second necessary condition. This can trigger painful anxiety and works as a motivation for change. The incongruence centres on the discrepancy between the person's primary experience and his/her acquired image of self (Rogers 1959: 203–4). Even if discrepancy is avoided in consciousness, its effects are likely to 'leak out' in behaviour and leave the person vulnerable to breakdown of his or her guarded idea of self.

Complementing this client quality, the therapist needs to be inwardly at ease and congruent at least *within the relation with the client*. This congruence permits a genuine quality of presence and full availability for experiential connection. A helper absorbed in the client Other, in the client's world of experience and meaning, is naturally sharing on a different level than the self-exploring client, and the congruent therapist's own experience is neither hidden nor a primary focus of expression in the helping context (Rogers, 1959: 214–15; Lietaer, 1993). There is a transparent quality to *the way the therapist responds* as s/he attends to and relates to the client's experience and issues (see later illustration and further chapters).

The language of the further pivotal condition of therapist unconditional positive regard is well known, but what exactly does it mean in practice? Certainly it implies that the therapist's warmth and regardful acceptance of the experiencing self of the client are vitally relevant. No conditions are placed on this quality of response, ideally; there are no messages of judging the other for the way *s/he feels and thinks*. Thus the client's self-judging 'conditions of worth' (Rogers, 1959: 209–10) are not reinforced, and this and other qualities of the helping encounter flow into a process of increasing and more relaxed openness to self-related experience. Within the meaning of the 'UPR' condition (and in keeping with affirming invitational responsiveness), the therapist is not *approving* of certain client feelings and not of others and, still less, is s/he approving of particular, possibly damaging, overt behaviours. Being deeply receptive to the other's felt experience without evaluating that person for *having those feelings* also fits with the therapist's focus on understanding the other in an empathic sense.

Empathy was not an explicit concept in Rogers' original writing on therapy (1939; 1942). He moved step by incremental step to his 1957 highlighting of empathic understanding as a necessary condition of therapy: not a technique but, foremost, a deep connective awareness of felt qualities and content of the other person's experiencing. It involves, first, an inner process of experiential recognition or 'resonation' in the empathic listener to what the other is feeling, meaning and going through (Barrett-Lennard, 1993; Schmid and Mearns, 2006). A necessary further step is to convey this empathic awareness in such a way that the client can become aware of its presence. The process is subtle, not simply a method or portrayal of something (Mearns, 1997) but the communication of an inner responsive arousal of empathic knowing (Barrett-Lennard, 1993; 2003: 39).

The crucial importance of client perception of the therapist's unconditional regard and empathy led to the listing of this as a separate, sixth condition of therapy (Rogers, 1957, 1959). Later work has principally focused on the primary relational variables in conditions theory (often called the 'core conditions'), including experienced therapist congruence as well as unconditional (and) positive regard and empathic understanding. Rogers' breakthrough theoretical encapsulation immediately triggered new lines of research to test its main hypotheses. One approach, initiated by Halkides (1958), used judges to rate the therapist's empathy, congruence and unconditional positive regard as heard in short audiotape interview excerpts. This method at best infers client experience from therapist verbal behaviour. It implies a transactional view of the therapeutic relationship and tends also to reinforce the idea of the therapist as literally the instrumental party, with the client as recipient.

The other line of research directly taps into the experience-based perceptions of the participants in the therapy encounter. It entailed development by this author of the Relationship Inventory, containing tested statements reflective of empathic understanding, regard and unconditionality (as two variables) and congruence (Barrett-Lennard, 1962; 2003: 93–112). This method treats relationship as a between-person encounter process with linked but distinctive reality for each participant. The resulting (second) line of research, considered closest to the theory, has largely supported it, and the trend of results using judge-rating of conditions lends some support along with method limitations (see, e.g., Barrett-Lennard, 1998: 26: 4–8, 281–5; Mitchell et al, 1977; Bozarth et al, 2002).

Conceptually, Rogers' work grew out of the individualist orientation of his time and place, which treated relationship as a crucial traffic bridge between individuals with their own separate lives and identity. The idea that human life is an inherently relational process was not contained in any formal way in Rogers' perspective. Later advances in this direction have been made by Schmid (1998, 2002) and others, although the shift in thinking remains a work in progress. The emphasis on 'relational depth' in therapy introduced by Mearns

(1996) and further developed by Mearns and Cooper (2005) embodies valuable exploration and moves toward greater mutuality within therapy. From his search through pertinent philosophical and developmental literature, as well as his experience of practice, Cooper notes that 'it is the encounter between the therapist and client, rather than the provision of a particular set of conditions for the client, that is conceptualized as being the key to psychotherapy' (Mearns and Cooper, 2005: 9; see also Schmid, 2002). In practice, the authors support the 'core conditions' principles when expressed in seamless combination in a therapist's whole, empathically attuned, openly present absorption in the helping engagement. The process they describe has a quality that permits more spontaneous expression by both partners than in earlier therapeutic work (Mearns and Cooper, 2005, middle chapters). This emphasis connects also with explorations of 'presence' in therapy.

A meeting in depth implies presence. Rogers himself introduced this term late in his life, in speaking of a special quality of expanded intuitive consciousness in the therapy relation when 'whatever I do seems to be full of healing' and in which 'simply my presence is releasing and helpful' (Rogers, 1986: 198). While not formally defined, presence is evocative of meaning. It implies 'being all there', absorbed in the immediate relation with one's whole, deeply attentive and connecting self. It goes beyond self-congruence in being centred on a quality of being in immediate relation (see McLeod, 2003, 174–77). New search extending to spiritual life, into 'presence and the core conditions', is highlighted in the volume by Moore and Purton (2006, pp. 116–68). In the same book, Thorne reflects from personal experience and his view of Rogers, on 'the gift and cost of being fully present' (pp. 35–47). Geller and Greenberg (2002) have delineated process features of therapist presence from a data-based study. Their model highlights therapist 'immersion' in the relational-experiential process, including the aspects of open inward attention and an altered or 'extrasensory' quality of communication. Schmid also has searched into presence in therapy, first building from Rogers' account with a focus primarily on the therapist's presence but then moving beyond this to an implied focus on mutual presence (Schmid, 2002: 190–2). His advanced thought on encounter implies two (or more) participants, but also a conjoining 'we' process.

It is not a big further step to the view that relationship is an emergent whole with its own life and influence, and thus not something that is individually generated, not basically a transaction or exchange, nor best construed as an intersubjective process. My latest thinking about the nature and pervasive working of relationship in human life (Barrett-Lennard, 2005; in press – 2007) has implications beyond those so far directly addressed in person-centred work – a topic I will eagerly, albeit briefly, return to in the final 'looking ahead' section of this chapter.

From concepts to practice

William Snyder's early *Casebook of Non-directive Counseling* (1947) was devoted to extensive records of interviews with several Rogerian therapists. Scrutiny of this work reveals that instances of client reference to feelings within and about the therapy relation were, at that stage, almost non-existent. Therapist congruence or transparency had not yet emerged in therapy discourse. The counsellors rarely used I-statements and clients hardly ever mentioned feelings they may have had toward the therapist.

Change toward a more person-to-person quality is very evident in illustrations in *Client-Centered Therapy* (Rogers, 1951). Perhaps the most striking material from clients appears in the third chapter (1951: 65–130). The vehicle of therapy is a distinctive conversation, at once with self and other. Some clients wrote down their afterthoughts between sessions and then shared these reflections with their therapist: reflections that eloquently express the relational impact of the therapy experience and how it seemed to clients to work (1951: 84–116). As an instance of reference to feelings toward the therapist, a client wrote: 'I remember how keenly I felt my own pleasure reflected in the eyes of the counselor whom I was looking at directly for the first time in any interview' (1951: 84).

As for how therapy worked, another client wrote that her counsellor 'would say to me things which I had stated but he would clear them for me, bring me back to earth, help me to see what I had said and what it meant to me', and he 'was almost part of me working on my problem as I wanted to work on it' (1951: 36–7). Rogers' comment and other illustrations suggest the intricate connection of awareness between the participants, but always with a focus on the client and his or her separate self. The therapy partners touch in their consciousness in such a way that the client hears him/herself freshly through another voice, not an echo but a voice with its own closely attuned reflective words. Looking back, the process seems quite often to have been potent and empowering, even implying 'relational depth', but it is unlikely to have worked this way all the time. Some of the 'necessary conditions' were yet to be identified.

Rogers believed that the core of human personality is 'both self-preserving and social' (1961: 92). A detailed example is his therapy with a client who moved from a position of bitter hatred and vengeful, almost murderous feelings through awareness of an underlying crushing hurt and, finally, on to the freedom of a largely hate-free, regardful caring outlook (1961: 92–103). Person-centred therapy provides the opportunity for deeply negative or despairing experience to be expressed, fully felt and received empathically as a reality of experience. This does not reinforce bad feelings, but defuses them. The therapist's way of being in the relationship is of a kind to bring out the more socially and emotionally positive potentialities that also are within the other's total make-up. It is in this sense selective in the direction of its influence, and the earlier designation 'non-directive' is partially true but also misleading – as dramatically illustrated in some of Rogers' own later work (see Bowen, 1996).

The further context of therapy with hospitalized schizophrenic clients poses great challenges, but ones that are due, in Rogers' view (1967: 183–4), less to psychotic symptoms and more to low motivation for change. Psychotic or not, a person may be fearful of any engagement of their inner self in a relationship that implicitly calls into question their 'retreat' into the best or only way of coping they know. As for symptoms, these are sensitive to context as dramatically illustrated in the case of 'Loretta' – interviewed in hospital by three therapists of diverse approach.

With Rogers, who responded in warmly personal vein and with acute empathic perception of her immediate issues and feelings, Loretta's delusional symptoms largely disappeared and her communication was clear (transcript and commentary in Farber et al, 1996: 33–56). Albert Ellis, on the other hand, tried to help Loretta see the irrationality of her thought and how she could modify her constructions and needed to do so (I have the full interview transcript). His cognitive-analytic efforts did not bring any diminution of delusional elements and the interview became an argument in which the client was a moving target who sought to turn the tables on Ellis. With Richard Felder, who reported a dream and other subjective experience with her, she became somewhat confused. The contrasts in therapist response and client process are striking.

Long after Wisconsin, Prouty brought related work back into original strong view. Especially for regressed schizophrenic persons who are seriously impaired in their capacity for relationship and associated experiential processing, a helping process concerned with rebuilding the person's capacity for contact was developed (Prouty, 1994 and Chapter 18 on Pre-Therapy, this volume). Prouty implies that the capacity for relationship is itself a variable: a property that can be almost non-existent or be adequate or, perhaps, highly developed. A more general proposition is that there are basic qualitative differences in the ways people relate. As I would put it, people are always living in relation but have diverse coping strategies; strategies that in some cases work as barriers to communication and engagement or, from the inside, as 'shields' against the uncontrollable and disturbing flow of open contact.

Sensitive empathic perception and an honouring of the client's agenda remain vitally relevant in contemporary practice. These agendas, however, nearly always encompass troubling experience and unresolved issues in the client's life within the relationship. Thus the therapist's empathic awareness is not just responsive to self-feelings (and the immediate therapy relation) but also to felt experience and struggle anywhere in the client's theatre of relational life. This awareness does not derive only from the immediate moment but is also a cumulative and partly intuitive process. The client's passage may be lonely but always entails involvement in relationship. Close attention and attunement to experience in this encompassing domain of life is a shifting emphasis in person-centred work.

An interview of my own, with 'Lucia', helps to illustrate the mentioned relational emphasis. Lucia was a volunteer client in a half-hour demonstration/real interview that she wanted to make the most of. In mid-session she is speaking of feeling driven to put the needs and feelings of others first. Her mother is one significant instance. She is very critical of herself for this, but explains 'that I feel selfish when I give the same importance to my feelings than [as] to the other's,' and mentions also that doing this is out of character as other people experience her:

Th 54 (GBL): So when you try to assert yourself, and consider yourself, other people get confused. And they feel you are behaving strangely and being selfish. So it's hard to break out of that pattern?

Cl 55 (Lucia): Yes, yes. It's hard because I know that I try to give all this importance to the other's feelings – because I need people. I need people now, too, so if people tell me that I'm wrong that blocks me (Th: yes) even if I know it's not wrong.

Th 55: Okay. (Softly) Even if you know you're not wrong it still throws you off.

Cl 56: It's like a choice I have: sometimes it seems to me that if I do what I want I will be alone (pause). Because sometimes I like to be alone but not always.

The complications and pain around relationship and separation seemed to be most acute in Lucia's home environment. She said she loved to travel to a far-distant region, with a different climate and kind of people – where 'I feel much more respected, and I feel I respect them more than here. (Th: mmm). I don't know why, but I notice that it's much easier for me to live there.' By this time the therapist, listening both through and 'between' her words, increasingly sensed unexpressed but implied connections in her world of relationship. Th. 67 expresses one such connection:

Th 67: And so when you go [names region] – you leave – you are far away from your family aren't you?

Cl 67: That's very beautiful for me!

Th 68: Is that right! (Cl and Th: Yes)

Cl 68: I know that if I would move there my family wouldn't approve that, but they don't approve anything I do, so …

Th 69: Oh, I see, so that would not be different.

Cl 69: Yes.

Th 70: They would not approve of you doing that, but they don't approve of things anyway, that you do.

Cl 71: Yes. (Pause)

Th 71: Yes … So is there anyone in your life who really does approve of what you do?

Cl 72: No.

Th 72: No.

Cl 73: I mean … (mentions her therapist – brief pause)

Th 73: That would be – that must be sometimes hard for you, to be on your own in knowing what fits you, what's good for you (Cl tearful; blows her nose).

Th. 71 is certainly a leading question, but not a probe. By that point the likely answer seemed already to be 'hanging in the air', an imminent shape in her acutely felt world. I felt that Lucia was a strong person, vulnerable but not fragile, and that she wanted to see more clearly into and beyond painful realities of her feeling-relational life. And our time was short. Soon, she returned (Cl 81) to mention her parents and to express a very poignant self/relational confrontation:

'And, so I think this is the most difficult thing: to accept that people that I love don't accept me.' At this point, she begins visibly to relax, our time is nearly up, and she remarks (Cl 89) 'What happens now is that I recognize that if I feel hurt [it] is because I have an expectation that is impossible.' Shortly, she says (Cl 91) 'It's okay for me [to stop]. I feel much quieter now.'

Lucia and I corresponded afterwards; she had been seeing a therapist but said that this brief session between us somehow marked a turning point for her. I was able to feel for and with her in her immediate world of relationship – oppressively present, dearly wanted and only found during travel – a world that mattered so much to her, outside and beyond our brief contact. She and I began (at least for me) as strangers. Yet, despite a 'careful' start, with observers surrounding us, we were drawn into not just a meaningful exchange but a quickly developing relationship and dialogical 'we', one that lasted inwardly and via occasional letters. Two or three years later Lucia turned up in my far-distant home town, on a long travel journey, not alone but accompanied in a relationship that had eluded her before – with a husband-partner, with whom she later started a family of her own.

Relationships are the central focus within family therapy, both as brought into and further discovered in the helping context. Prominent person-centred contributors to this sphere include Gaylin (2001) and O'Leary (1999). Both authors struggle, overtly (Gaylin) or by implication (O'Leary), with the ideas of personal independence or autonomy versus an emphasis on interdepend- ence and a view that relationships are emergent living systems with properties beyond those of component members. Rogers' helping conditions remain highlighted by each author though in slightly awkward application to the family therapy context. One supplemental feature in Gaylin's work, which he calls 'interspace reflection', occurs when the therapist moves from an empathic response to each person to acknowledge a dynamic of their twosome. As example, 'Danny' and 'Joan' each feel that the other fails to understand their reaction in a third-person relationship. The therapist puts their experience together, saying: 'Whenever you two try to talk about Danny's mom's relationship with Joan there seems to be some kind of barrier between you' (Gaylin, 2001: 119). In related vein, O'Leary (1999: 36–42) discusses counsellor 'reframing' that, for example, might bring out the way that each partner is both powering and suffering from an inter-reactive process that seems to have a life of its own.

Rogers did not practise couple and family therapy, but his later documented work includes an interview with 'Sylvia', published with critiques by both Cain and O'Hara (in Farber et al, 1996: 261–300). O'Hara's analysis is distinctive in her strongly argued presentation of an alternative to the individualist stance of both therapist and client. The client experiences inner conflict and external disapproval over her strong attraction to black men and features of their subcul- ture. Both therapy partners respond to this as a personal or intrapsychic prob- lem from which the client could free herself by working through felt issues to the point of self-acceptance. O'Hara points out that the client's unease and conflict over her attraction rests on a particular socially determined construc- tion of reality from which she could, with help, insightfully free herself. The contrasting analyses, by O'Hara and Cain, are a robust example of the diversity of perspective to be found within the person-centred movement (see also Hawtin and Moore, 1998).

The emerging future: person-sensitivity within an evolving consciousness of relationship

The one-to-one therapy relationship is a special case within a much larger orbit of relationships that potentially are open to facilitation and development. One-to-one relations and process form one crucial region or node within a much larger spectrum (Barrett-Lennard, 2002, 2005). Since arriving at this view in a progression of thought over time, it is not possible for me to treat what I see as one level and kind of relationship (for example, between therapist and client) as though it was a self-contained whole with an independent existence. In ecological perspective, anything in nature, especially any living being, exists in and through relation. In person-centred therapy, the influential context includes other pivotal relationships in the lives of each participant, the institutional or other setting and climate in which the therapy takes place, and the wider culture that is host to the whole enterprise of therapy.

In a similar way, due to the great complexity in structure and process of a conscious human person, many interactive-relational processes are occurring internally. An idea that has recently become familiar in the person-centred movement is to regard the self as a plurality or 'many in one' (Rowan and Cooper, 1999). It is, therefore, meaningful to speak of relations within the self, a context-sensitive self with distinctive configurations (Mearns and Thorne, 2000: 101–43) or subselves that come into play in different major relationships (Barrett-Lennard, 2005, Ch. 1). One way of studying configured subselves is by use of a self-descriptive inventory structured to tap the respondent's sense and pictures of self within the context of different relationships: relationships with an intimate partner, an own child or parent, a special friend (or enemy), with a boss or workmates or a close group or team (2005: 13–14).

Linked to this thought is a broader observation: the human self is formed in the crucible of relationship, especially during the path to adulthood, but continuing throughout life. It is only a modest further leap to the view that humans live always in and through relation, on many levels (Barrett-Lennard, 2002, 2005; Holdstock, 1993). Persons are distinct, each of us is a whole life, but we also are interwoven with others in our consciousness, inherently interdependent, and not by nature autonomous beings. Person-centred thought is transcending the philosophy of individualism in which it was rooted, while preserving its belief in the worth and dignity of each person. Given that living means living in relation, how can we best think of the underlying or basic meaning of relationship?

First, relationship cannot credibly denote a transaction between fundamentally separated beings. It is not primarily a 'passing across' or exchange process, however elaborate. It necessarily refers to an inherent and primary modality of human life that reflects our connective nature. Thus, human problems (that are not organically based) are not literally individual but problems in and of relation.

As well, such understanding lends itself to a systemic way of thinking, a non-linear and truly interactive view of influence among persons, families and groups. The broader epistemology is that lives and phenomena of almost any kind have their central meaning not one by one, as separated entities, but in the ways they connect, combine and give rise to emergents with fresh qualities.

Effective person-centred therapy is a process of developmental healing through relationship. Historically, the relationship conditions of therapy are conceived as providing the safety and support for people under inner tension or torment to be able to face and inquire into their deepest disharmony, reduce involuntary conditions of worth and achieve greater inner congruency. A person-sensitive ecological stance centres on the healing of relationship in the person's life, ranging from an ease and openness of relation within the plural or multi-configured self through qualitative enhancement of bonding in close personal relationships, a recovery or deepening of relation in group and communal life, and an active engagement in larger human and natural systems. To adopt this view is to imply that health of being is not located in a bounded self but pivots on health in relationship.

Advances have been made, but the last-mentioned emerging shift in thought is awaiting full translation into practice. It is related in concept to the crucial wider sphere of potential healing of relations between groups and larger systems, especially as explored in my latest book (Barrett-Lennard, 2005). Person-centred thought and practice has always been on the move, in a generally cumulative pattern with some periodic leaps. A principal direction is that of qualitative development of the long-standing emphasis on relationship, as will be evident also in further chapters. I have spoken here to the overall path and some of the main strands and contributors to this development. I take heart from the thought that the reader, too, will sense the wide challenging potential to build on fresh envisioning, to the further enhancement of helping practice within and beyond psychotherapy.

REFERENCES

Barrett-Lennard, G.T. (1962). Dimensions of therapist response as causal factors in therapeutic change. *Psychological Monographs*, 76 (43, Whole No. 562).

Barrett-Lennard, G.T. (1993). The phases and focus of empathy. *British Journal of Medical Psychology*, 66, 3–14.

Barrett-Lennard, G.T. (1998). *Carl Rogers' Helping System: journey and Substance*. London, Thousand Oaks, New Delhi: Sage.

Barrett-Lennard, G.T. (2002). The helping conditions in *their* context: expanding change theory and practice. *Person-Centred and Experiential Psychotherapies*. 1, 144–55.

Barrett-Lennard, G.T. (2003). *Steps on a Mindful Journey: person-centred expressions*. Ross-on-Wye: PCCS Books.

Barrett-Lennard, G.T. (2005). *Relationship at the Centre: healing in a troubled world*. London: Whurr/Wiley.

Barrett-Lennard, G.T. (in press, 2007). Human relationship: linkage or life form. *Person-Centred and Experiential Psychotherapies*.

Bowen, M. V-B. (1996). The myth of nondirectiveness: the case of Jill. In B.A. Farber, D.C. Brink and P.M. Raskin, P.M. (eds), *The Psychotherapy of Carl Rogers: cases and commentary* (pp. 84–94). New York and London: Guilford.

Bown, O.H. (1954). An investigation of therapeutic relationship in client-centered psychotherapy. Unpublished doctoral dissertation. Chicago: University of Chicago library.

Bozarth, J.D., Zimring, F.M. and Tausch, R. (2002). Client-centered therapy: the evolution of a revolution. In Cain, D. and Seeman, *Journal of Humanistic Psychotherapies: handbook of research and practice* (pp. 147–88). Washington, DC: American Psychological Association.

Farber, B.A., Brink, D.C. and Raskin, P.M. (1996). *The Psychotherapy of Carl Rogers: cases and commentary*. New York and London: Guilford.

Fiedler, F.E. (1950). A comparison of therapeutic relationships in psychoanalytic, non-directive and Adlerian therapy. *Journal of Consulting Psychology*, 14, 436–45.

Gaylin, N.L. (2001). *Family, Self and Psychotherapy: a person-centred perspective*. Ross-on-Wye: PCCS Books.

Geller, S. and Greenberg, L. (2002). Therapeutic presence: therapists' experience of presence in the psychotherapy encounter. *Person-Centered and Experiential Psychotherapies, 1* (1&2), 71-86.

Halkides, G. (1958). An experimental study of four conditions necessary for therapeutic change. Unpublished doctoral dissertation, University of Chicago.

Hawtin, S. and Moore, J. (1998). Empowerment or collusion: the social context of person-centred therapy. In B. Thorne and E. Lambers (eds), *Person-Centred Therapy: a European perspective* (pp. 91–105). London: Sage.

Holdstock, L. (1993). Can we afford not to revision the person-centred concept of self? In D. Brazier (ed.), *Beyond Carl Rogers* (pp. 229–52). London: Constable.

Lietaer, G. (1993). Authenticity, congruence and transparency. In D. Brazier (ed.), *Beyond Carl Rogers* (pp. 17–46). London: Constable.

McLeod, J. (2003). *An Introduction to Counselling* (3rd edn). Maidenhead, UK: Open University Press.

Mearns, D. (1996). Working at relational depth with clients in person-centred therapy. *Counselling*, 7, 306–11.

Mearns, D. (1997). Achieving the personal development dimension in professional counsellor training. *Counselling*, 8 (2), 113–20.

Mearns, D. and Cooper M. (2005). *Working at Relational Depth in Counselling and Psychotherapy*. London/Thousand Oaks/New Delhi: Sage.

Mearns, D. and Thorne, B. (2000). *Person-Centred Therapy Today: new frontiers in theory and practice*. London/Thousand Oaks/New Delhi: Sage.

Mitchell, K.M., Bozarth, J.D. and Krauft, C.C. (1977). A reappraisal of the therapeutic effectiveness of accurate empathy, non-possessive warmth, and genuineness. In A.S. Gurman and A.M. Razin (eds), *Effective Psychotherapy: a handbook of research* (482–502). Oxford: Pergamon.

Moore, J. and Purton, C. (2006). *Spirituality and Counselling: experiential and theoretical perspectives*. Ross-on-Wye, UK: PCCS Books.

O'Leary, C.J. (1999). *Counselling Couples and Families: a person-centred approach*. London: Sage.

Prouty, G. F. (1994). *Theoretical Evolutions in Person-Centered/Experiential Therapy: applications to schizophrenic and retarded psychoses*. Westport, Connecticut: Praeger.

Rank, O. (1936/1945). *Will Therapy: an analysis of the therapeutic process in terms of relationship*. Translated by Jessie Taft and published by Knopf in 1936. Republished in one volume with Rank's *Truth and Reality*, in 1945.

Rogers, C.R. (1939). *The Clinical Treatment of the Problem Child*. Boston: Houghton Mifflin.

Rogers, C.R. (1942). *Counseling and Psychotherapy: newer concepts in practice*. Boston: Houghton Mifflin.

Rogers, C.R. (1951). *Client-Centered Therapy: its current practice, implications and theory*. Boston: Houghton Mifflin.

Rogers, C.R. (1957). The necessary and sufficient conditions of therapeutic personality change, *Journal of Consulting Psychology*, 21, 95–103.

Rogers, C.R. (1959). A theory of therapy, personality, and interpersonal relationships as developed in the client-centered framework. In S. Koch (ed.), *Psychology: a study of a science*. Volume 3. *Formulations of the Person and the Social Context* (pp. 184–256). New York: McGraw-Hill.

Rogers, C.R. (1961). *On Becoming a Person: a therapist's view of psychotherapy*. Boston: Houghton Mifflin.

Rogers, C.R. (1967). Some learnings from a study of psychotherapy with schizophrenics. In C.R. Rogers and B. Stevens, *Person to Person: the problem of being human* (pp. 181–92). Lafayette, Calif.: Real People Press.

Rogers, C.R. (1986). A client-centered/person-centered approach to therapy. In I. L. Kutash, and A. Wolf, (eds), *Psychotherapist's Casebook* (pp. 197-208). San Francisco: Jossey-Bass. (Whole book republished, 1993, in Northvale, New Jersey and London, by Jason Aronson. Article republished in Kirschenbaum, H. and Henderson, V. L. (eds), 1989, *The Carl Rogers Reader* (pp. 135-152). Boston: Houghton Mifflin.)

Rogers, C.R., with Gendlin, E.T., Kiesler, D.J. and Truax, C.B. (eds) (1967). *The Therapeutic Relationship and its Impact: a study of psychotherapy with schizophrenics*. Madison, Wisconsin: University of Wisconsin Press.

Rowan, J. and Cooper, M. (1999). *The plural self. Multiplicity in everyday life*. London; Thousand Oaks; New Delhi: Sage.

Schmid, P.F. (1998). 'On becoming a person-centred approach': a person-centred understanding of the person. In B. Thorne and E. Lambers (eds), *Person-Centred Therapy: a European perspective* (pp. 38–52). London: Sage.

Schmid, P.F. (2002). Presence: immediate co-experiencing and co-responding. Phenomenological, dialogical and ethical perspectives on contact and perception in person-centred therapy and beyond. In G. Wyatt and P. Sanders (eds), *Contact and Perception* (pp. 182–203). Ross-on-Wye: PCCS Books.

Schmid, P.F. and Mearns, D. (2006). Being-with and being-counter: person-centred psychotherapy as an in-depth co-creative process of personalization. *Person-Centred and Experiential Psychotherapies*, 5, 174–90

Snyder, W.U. (1947). *Casebook of Non-Directive Counseling*. Boston: Houghton Mifflin.

Standal, S. (1954). The need for positive regard: a contribution to client-centred theory. Unpublished doctoral dissertation, University of Chicago.

Thorne, B. (2006). The gift and cost of being fully present. In J. Moore and C. Purton (eds) (2006). *Spirituality and Counselling: experiential and theoretical perspectives* (pp. 35–47). Ross-on-Wye, UK: PCCS Books.

11

Psychological Contact

Gill Wyatt

I looked forward to seeing her; there was an ease and flow between us, even when exploring a difficulty between us. I always felt more alive at the end of our session.

The client was silent for 20 minutes, staring at the ground, she seemed to not hear the occasional comment I made about her silence, our situation or what I was experiencing.

The way she looked at me did something to my innards. It was as if her need was so great that she would be able to suck the life out of me.

In these vignettes therapists describe experiences of their contact with clients. The everyday understanding of contact is 'to touch', 'to meet' and 'to communicate'. Do these vignettes describe psychological contact? In this chapter the evolving nature of psychological contact and its central concepts are explored in order to discover what significance psychological contact has for person-centred practice. This exploration includes Rogers' original conceptualization and three further conceptualizations – Gary Prouty's psychological contact and Pre-Therapy; a relational conceptualization; and a holistic/emergent conceptualization. A multiple perspective view of psychological contact results, where each conceptualization has a part to play in developing our person-centred practice.

The central concepts

Rogers' psychological contact

Rogers, in his 1957 and 1959 statements described the critical elements of a therapeutic relationship (see Chapter 1, this volume). The first of these necessary and sufficient conditions for therapeutic personality change he calls 'contact' and 'psychological contact', using these two terms interchangeably. Rogers states that 'two persons are in psychological contact, or have the minimum essential relationship when each makes a perceived or subceived difference in the experiential field of the other' (Rogers, 1959: 207). Psychological contact is therefore synonymous with 'a minimum essential relationship' where each person makes a difference to the experience of the other. Rogers highlights the extremity of the 'minimality' of relationship and clarifies the role of 'subceived differences' where 'the individual may not be consciously aware of the impact' (1957: 96) by referring to a 'catatonic' patient as being able to perceive or subceive the presence of the therapist at 'some organic level' (1957: 96).

Rogers reveals that at first, the term 'relationship' was used. This however, led to the construct being misunderstood and taken to mean 'the depth and quality of a good relationship' (1959: 207). Rogers clarifies 'the present term [contact] has been chosen to signify more clearly that this is the least or minimum experience which could be called a relationship' (1959: 207).

For Rogers, the central concepts in psychological contact are relationship, experience and perception. Rogers' meaning of psychological contact involves two people making some difference to each other whether they are aware of it or not. He concluded: 'this first condition ... is such a simple one that perhaps it should be labelled an assumption or a precondition.' He explained that it should be considered as 'an assumption or a precondition *in order to set it apart from those that follow*' (1957: 96, italics added). It is perhaps surprising that Rogers did not focus on psychological contact again, considering he also said that without psychological contact the other five conditions 'would have no meaning' (1957: 96).

A further differentiation was made within Rogers's six conditions that have affected the significance of contact in person-centred theory, practice and research. Initially three of Rogers's conditions – empathy, congruence and unconditional positive regard (UPR) were considered as the 'therapist provided conditions' (Watson, 1984: 21–4), and then later referred to as the 'core conditions' (Mearns and Thorne, 1988: 15). The majority of attention has been given to an examination of these conditions. In contrast, the remaining conditions were called the 'implied conditions' by Raskin and Rogers (2000/1989: 263) where they described conditions one (contact) and two (client incongruence) as the 'preconditions for therapy' (2000/1989: 264). Tudor (2000) has referred to these 'implied conditions' as the 'lost conditions'. Not surprisingly, the trend in person-centred research regarding psychological contact has been to assume psychological contact at best and ignore it at worst (Barrett-Lennard, 1962, 2002; Watson, 1984).

The evolving nature of psychological contact

This trend of paying little attention to contact continued until the renewed interest in psychological contact that emerged in the 1990s with Gary Prouty's work on Pre-Therapy and a more recent shift in interest to all of the six conditions from the 'core conditions'. Psychological contact received further attention as a result of this shift (see Wyatt and Sanders, 2002).

Psychological contact and Pre-Therapy

Garry Prouty developed his theory of psychological contact and Pre-Therapy as a result of his experiences with clients who seemed to be unreceptive to Rogers' client-centred therapy (2002/1994: 55). These clients were unable to establish the minimum relationship required for Rogers' condition of contact to be met. Prouty coined the terms 'pre-relationship' and 'pre-experiencing' and 'pre-expressive' to describe an individual who has no coherent 'self' to process experience, acknowledge the other and communicate with reality (See Chapter 18, this volume). Drawing from Gendlin's concept of 'experiencing' (1962) and gestalt psychotherapy, he extended Rogers' singular concept of contact to encompass three aspects: contact functions, contact behaviours and contact reflections. Psychological contact then is defined as '[T]he concrete awareness of reality (people, places, events and things), of affective states and the ability to communicate about this in a congruent and under-standable way' (Van Werde, 1998: 199). The goal of Pre-Therapy is therefore to help clients become able to process experience, become 'expressive', and develop or restore the ability to be in psychological contact.

Garry Prouty and his associates in the Pre-Therapy International Network have carried out numerous successful research projects demonstrating Pre-Therapy's effectiveness in establishing or improving psychological contact (see Chapter 18, this volume).

Discussion and two further conceptualizations

The Pre-Therapy definition of contact involves 'concrete awareness' of reality and affective states and communication. Rogers' approach involved a mini-mal relationship where each person made some 'perceived' or 'subceived' difference to the other. Margaret Warner points out how more 'elaborated', 'reality orientated' and 'process-rich' the Pre-Therapy definition is (2002: 79). The difference between these two conceptualizations is profound. Pre-Therapy's contact emphasizes concrete awareness, whereas Rogers' nearly minimizes awareness by introducing the concept 'subception' as this is discrimination without awareness (Rogers, 1959: 199–200). This means Pre-Therapy's contact has a higher threshold than Rogers' original conceptualiza-tion. With Rogers' definition, contact was 'always present' at the minimal level he referred to, as suggested by Dion Van Werde: 'the Rogerian thinking … almost presupposes contact *as continuously present*' (2002: 172, author's original italics).

Embleton Tudor et al arrive at a different position, asserting 'psychological contact is a digital or binary phenomenon. Two people are either in
psychological contact or they are not. It is not a matter of degree' (2005: 39).
This suggests that with contact present, therapists will be able to provide the
'therapist conditions' and clients will be able to perceive them, whereas when
contact is absent, the 'therapist conditions' become ineffective. The significance of Pre-Therapy is that it provides a theory and specific practice for
when psychological contact is impaired.

In considering the nature of contact, Rogers's conceptualization has some
ambiguity. If contact is a precondition necessary for the other five conditions
to be effective, this could support a view of contact as a binary event. This is
the psychological contact of Pre-Therapy and Embleton Tudor's interpretation, where psychological contact is made or not made. However if contact is
an assumption or continually present, then it becomes a minimal event that
describes the relational nature of our existence where people make perceived
or 'subceived' differences to each other all of the time.

A further suggestion from Whelton and Greenberg, and from Warner, is
that contact is a continuum. Whelton and Greenberg (2002) point out that
Rogers saw all his other conditions as a continuum (1959: 215). Neither
Whelton and Greenberg nor Warner describe the detail of the continuum, but
when Margaret Warner suggests minimal levels of psychological contact
would be sufficient for Rogers' therapist conditions to work to some degree
(2002), she might be implying that this would be towards one end of the
continuum. Beyond this might be the relationship between the 'contact-
impaired', 'pre-expressive' client and therapist undertaking Pre-Therapy, and
perhaps the other end might be the psychological contact of 'presence'
(Rogers, 1980), 'depth of contact' (Cameron, 2003) and 'relational depth'
(Mearns and Cooper, 2005).

This exploration of psychological contact being 'continually present', a
binary phenomenon or a continuum, can be understood in relation to different ontological (nature of reality) and epistemological (knowledge system)
frames. Ivan Ellingham has stated that Rogers' theory is critically flawed
because the theory belongs to the emerging organismic and holistic scientific
paradigm but its foundational concepts 'are not congruent representations of
this emerging paradigm but of the Cartesian–Newtonian paradigm that it
supersedes' (2002: 234). Ellingham elucidates that in Rogers' theory, experience, awareness and perception are given a quasi-Cartesian–Newtonian
'thing-like' quality as a 'pre-existing label' is attached via symbolization 'to
an already existing feeling, experience or perception' (2002: 242).

The nature of psychological contact changes according to whichever
ontological/epistemological frame it is experienced and viewed through.
Within the Cartesian–Newtonian frame, psychological contact will
involve two separate and bounded selves situated in a 'one-reality' and
'one-truth' universe. Here the effect of one person on another involves
uni-directional causality, as in one person doing something to the other
person to get a specific effect. For example, making a diagnosis and deliv-
ering a specific treatment. However as well as Rogers' concepts having

this 'thing-like' quality, a more organismic/holistic frame is also demonstrated when Rogers' psychological contact involves mutual perceived or subceived 'difference in the experiential field' (1957: 96). This describes the relational nature of an interconnected existence. His conceptualization of psychological contact therefore straddles the Cartesian–Newtonian and organismic/holistic frames.

Warner and Ellingham both present Gendlin's 'bodily felt sense' to replace the 'thing-like' 'pre-existing phenomena', as this offers a more process-based foundation to perception and experience. The 'bodily felt sense' is a 'holistic, unclear sense ... of a whole situation' at the edge of our awareness (Gendlin, 1984, quoted in Ellingham, 2002: 241).

Drawing from Gendlin and evolutionary psychology Warner offers an 'expanded definition of 'psychological contact':

> [It] is a fundamental adaptation of the human organism that allows human beings to feel that they are meaningfully present both verbally and non-verbally to themselves and each other.
>
> (Warner, 2002: 80)

Warner's 'adaptation' means a process that fits with the environment in which it is located. The nature of psychological contact is now *relational, contextual* and a *process* characterized by the 'meaningful presence' of the self, meeting with another's 'meaningful presence'. Meaning acts as the interface between individuals and culture. Warner's conceptualization offers more cultural sensitivity than others'. This is significant when considering cultural differences and how these differences affect the way psychological contact is made and is experienced (see Davies and Aykroyd, 2002).

With this shift away from the Cartesian–Newtonian frame, the world extends to become qualitative as well as quantitative (Reason and Goodwin, 1999). Whelton and Greenberg emphasize this qualitative nature of psychological contact when they state that it is the 'degree or quality of contact that is important' (2002: 97). Rose Cameron agrees when she suggests it is the degree of psychological contact that determines the depth of the relationship: 'The depth of contact is what makes the difference between a rather mechanical and lifeless therapeutic relationship and one that shimmers with energy and involvement' (2003: 87).

This more relational conceptualization of psychological contact, which emphasizes the qualitative nature of contact, involves multiple dimensions and processes. Maureen O'Hara describes psychological contact as a 'dynamical process, which is contextual, relational and emergent' (2006). This more emergent, qualitative nature of contact requires a radical reformulation of concepts. Ellingham provides a step in this direction when, in discussing perception, he refers to organisms as being 'fields of activity' that are also part of larger fields. Perceptions, experiences and feelings now, rather than having a 'thing-like' existence are 'felt aspects of the field of activity' (2002: 244).

The nature of psychological contact now becomes a changing qualitative felt sense that results from any activity within the field of the client influenced by any activity within the field of the therapist influenced by any other fields of which they are a part. The atomism of the boundaried self is replaced by a self open to the interpenetrative fields of influence from self, others, culture, and the organic world. This is akin to the 'inter-being' of Thich Nhat Than (1998). Contact then becomes a 'site of emer-gence' (O'Hara, 2006), which would have infinite qualities, and the image of a spiral now replaces the linear continuum. Psychological contact now has a *'co-experienced'*, *'co-created'* (Schmid, 2002: 196) *participative*, emergent nature arising from the interpenetrative fields of influences.

There has been little psychotherapy research yet carried out to support these recent hypotheses. Mick Cooper's research into relational depth supports Mearns and Cooper's exploration of 'working at relational depth' which they describe as 'intense relational contact and enduring experiences of connectedness' reporting of the 'striking' significance for the clients involved (2005: 1). Shari Geller's research on presence used qualitative research to explore the therapist's reflective experience of presence. She concluded that therapist's presence is both a necessary precondition for the other conditions and also 'a larger whole, an overarching condition by which empathy, congruence and unconditional regard can be expressed' (in Geller and Greenberg, 2002: 84).

From theory to practice

The significance of psychological contact for our person-centred practice depends on its nature, and its nature has evolved with each conceptualiza-tion. What I am proposing is a multiple perspective view where each concep-tualization of psychological contact plays a crucial role in developing our person-centred practice.

Rogers' conceptualization acts like a baseline, applicable in all of our prac-tice. Prouty's psychological contact and Pre-Therapy become invaluable in the close focus needed with 'contact-impaired' relationships. The relational conceptualizations of Warner, Whelton and Greenberg, and Cameron have relevance in person-centred relationships, including those with clients having fragile and dissociative process. The holistic/emergent view of psychological contact becomes invaluable, acting rather like a wide-angle lens, when the wider web of influence is significant and with encounter relationships or rela-tionships at depth. The task for therapists becomes to know or sense which conceptualization will inform their practice and when, whilst not losing the centrality of the client's self-directivity.

Psychological contact with contact-impaired relationships

Psychological contact in 'contact-impaired' relationships will meet Rogers' minimum relationship; however, therapists often experience person-centred therapy as ineffective, as the congruent therapist's empathy and UPR does not seem to reach, touch or be perceived by the client. The significance of Prouty's psychological contact and Pre-Therapy is that it provides a theory and specific practice for when person-centred therapists find contact 'problematic' or when the therapist feels 'out of contact' with the 'pre-expressive' or 'contact-impaired' client; this happens, for instance, with diagnoses of schizophrenia, dementia or mental retardation. The therapist has little idea of the clients' experiencing and of their frame of reference. The clients' pre-expressive, psychotic-charged communication does not use 'significant symbols that presupposes the other' (Shlien, 2003/1961); the other is not acknowledged. It is precisely this non-acknowledgement of the other that is the central feature of clients who are 'contact impaired' and experienced by others as 'out of contact'. This in part defines the quality of the psychological contact, which might be described as 'vacant' or 'bizarre'. The therapist can feel disturbed and this can affect his/her UPR and capacity to be empathic.

Pre-Therapy contact reflections provide the therapist with concrete empathic responses that facilitate the therapist in maintaining his/her availability for contact when usual empathic understanding responses create no bridge of contact between therapist and client. Sommerbeck calls this 'empathic participation', and likens it to 'empathic attunement' or 'empathic mirroring' (2006). The therapist uses contact reflections with the pre-expressive client until 'contact' occurs, by the client acknowledging the therapist in some way. This allows the therapist to shift to empathic understanding (Sommerbeck, 2003).

The following dialogue is with a client with 'grey-zone functioning' (Van Werde, 2002, 2005). This 'is a conceptual category between "healthy" and "severely contact-impaired" functioning' (2002: 171). Initially the client's functioning is psychotically charged and the therapist (Sommerbeck, 2005) experiences no basis for ordinary empathic understanding of the client's internal frame of reference. The dialogue demonstrates a shift in the quality of the psychological contact as the client's contact behaviours improve as a result of the therapist's contact reflections (CR). The therapist senses that she has 'reached' the client and as a result can empathize with the client's internal frame of reference through empathic understanding responses (EUR). The excerpt is from the sixth session.

(C moves her head around in abrupt jerks, staring at different spots.)
T: You turn your head this way and that way and look around (CR).
C: (Grinding her teeth) My father is Satan.
T: You grind your teeth and say 'My father is Satan' (CR).
C: He has slaughtered my mother, he is the real Satan, and the Danes are his devils and devils' brood.
T: He is the real Satan, because he has slaughtered your mother, and the Danes are his devils and devils' brood. (CR, apart from the 'because'; that is a causality assumption from the therapist's frame.)
C: Not all Danes, people here are nice to me, but he has slaughtered my mother and if he does it again I'll slaughter him.
T: You feel you'll slaughter him if ... (A mixture of CR ('slaughter him') and EUR ('you feel you'll').)
C: (Interrupts eagerly) Yes, he has terrorized my mother all her life,

psychological terror. ... Her name is Maria, if Satan harmed Maria ... Joanna would slaughter him, I'm Joanna.

T: You say 'I'm Joanna' (CR) and you feel like you think Joanna would feel if Satan harmed Maria, is that it? (An effort at EUR, but with too much inference from the therapist's frame of reference ('you feel like you think'.)

C: (Nodding her head and smiling) Yes, and I'm not afraid of Satan, I'm not afraid of anything.

T: You smile at the thought that you are not afraid of Satan or ... (EUR since an empathic inference is made about the smile and the thought. A CR would have been 'You smile and you say you are not afraid of Satan'.)

C: (Interrupting) Yes, I'm not afraid, I'm glad of that, but why does he always have to be so rotten, last time he visited he brought some fruit from his back garden; it smelled awful and then I took a bite and it tasted hellish ... I threw it all away.

T: You think that everything he brings ... (Start of an EUR.)

C: (Interrupting) Yes, why does he have to be so provocative?

T: Like 'Why the hell can't you buy me some good fruit that I like, instead of bringing me the rotten leftovers from your back garden?' (A full blown EUR – here the richness of the therapist's understanding of the client's frame of reference is considerably enlarged. This happens as the client turns to the therapist with a clear wish to understand and be understood ('Why does he ...').)

C: Yes, I think he never spreads anything but shit around him – I can't bear being near him.

(Sommerbeck 2005: 323–5)

The client spends the rest of the session exploring her relationship with her father in a way that seems more coherent and less infiltrated with psychotic ideation than earlier. The pre-expressive psychotic expression 'My father is Satan' initially has no reality sense or contact but gradually, through the therapist's contact reflections, the context and referent for the psychotic expression is provided by the client. The client's level of functioning shifts, as does the psychological contact, and as this happens the therapist shifts from using Pre-Therapy contact reflections to regular person-centred therapy. The implication for the therapist is to develop sensitivity to these shifts in psychological contact and be able to move from Pre-Therapy contact reflections to person-centred therapy.

Psychological contact in person-centred relationships

For the majority of person-centred therapists, most sessions will be with clients where psychological contact exists between client and therapist in relation to both Rogers' and Prouty's conceptualizations. Rogers' baseline is maintained, and psychological contact could be seen as simply the container for the congruent therapist's empathy and UPR.

Warner (2002), Cameron (2002) and Whelton and Greenberg's (2002) explorations mean there will be varying degrees and qualities of psychological contact, such as 'hesitant', 'intense', 'prickly', 'collaborative', 'uneasy'. These different qualities of psychological contact emerge from the meeting between:

- the 'self-organization' of the therapist (congruence)
- the 'self-organization' of the client (client incongruence)
- the cultural context.

Some client-centred therapists (Bozarth, 2006) would say that the quality of psychological contact is created by the therapist's congruent empathy and UPR. This is true. However it is not the whole picture. The therapist and client's availability and receptivity to meet, touch, know the other will influence the contact between them. This influences the therapist's congruence and ability to be empathic and have UPR, and the client's perception of the therapist's empathy and UPR. The degree and quality of the therapist's psychological contact will also ebb and flow in relation to the client's process, the nature of material being presented and any cultural difference. The client responds to the way the therapist responds, and then the therapist responds to how the client responds.

Embracing a relational view of psychological contact will mean that paying attention to the changing quality of psychological contact becomes central in person-centred practice as it influences our congruent empathy and UPR and how these are perceived by the client. How we respond to our clients now shifts from very sensitive empathic following, as with a client in fragile process (see Chapter 12, this volume), to empathic understanding or to a more dialogic encounter, as determined by the quality of contact.

A hypothetical example may illustrate what I mean. The session is difficult. The therapist has struggled to communicate her UPR through her empathic understanding and the client, even though she usually experiences her therapist's genuine empathy and UPR, feels both lost and irritated. Twenty minutes into the session, she says 'I don't know ...' hesitantly and then pauses. If the quality of the psychological contact is 'fragile' the therapist might respond with sensitivity saying: 'You don't know, and then you've paused.' If the quality of the relationship is more characteristic of 'ordinary' person-centred relationships, the therapist might say: 'You seem hesitant and I think irritated, although I am not sure what the focus of your irritation is.' If the contact has a feeling of relational depth or 'presence' despite the difficulties experienced, the therapist might say nothing, letting her own presence simply touch the presence of the client ... or say something like: 'There's an edge between us, I don't understand what's happening. Being empathic was so easy but it's not now.' The focus is the changing quality of psychological contact. The centrality of being congruent, empathic and unconditional is already known; what is new is acknowledging and making explicit this shifting qualitative sense of relationship as psychological contact.

Cameron notes: 'We are not all indiscriminately available for psychological contact' (2003: 88). We place limits and conditions on both our availability and on our receptivity of the other. She discusses how we extend, contract and block psychological contact towards one another in relation to:

- Cultural norms of what is socially appropriate within a specific culture.
- Our own needs and mood.
- Who the other person is and how that person behaves.
- Our response to the other person, for example if we feel apprehensive or irritated, we may block, withdraw and contract, rather than feeling interested and caring, and then extending and opening towards him or her.

The client can 'turn towards' (or 'away from') the therapist, and the therapist can 'turn towards' (or 'away from') the client. Davies and Aykroyd point out that we are more aware of psychological contact when there is an impediment as the flow of experiencing between therapist and client 'informs our felt sense of the quality of the meeting' (2002: 221).

Davies and Aykroyd (2002) highlight the problems of making psychological contact across a cultural divide, and assert that people in oppressed minorities are sensitive to others who demonstrate their non-availability for contact. Therapists may be aware of how homophobia, racism, nationalism, sexism and ageism are blocks to empathy, but may not have considered how (possibly out of awareness) they might affect availability for contact with another. Cameron elucidates the role of language in this process 'information is encoded by using language in a way that indicates our ethnicity, class, religion, politics etc' (2002: 95), and she highlights the point that shared meanings cannot be assumed. Therapists need to develop cultural sensitivity to recognize the different perceptions, values and beliefs underlying their and the clients' meanings, which are encoded in language. They will then be available and able to receive the clients' encoded messages and communicate their availability, their receptivity and their understanding of the encoded messages. As Cameron says 'What matters is whether the meaning we intend matches the meaning that is taken' (2002: 97). Supervision, additional training, dialogue with colleagues and personal therapy may all help the therapist in these areas, but perhaps living a multi-dimensional cultural life will have the deepest impact.

Psychological contact in holistic/emergent relationships

Ellingham (2002), Schmid (2002), O'Hara (2006), and my own explorations (Wyatt, 2004) accentuate the holistic/emergent nature of psychological contact. Here the relationality discussed in 'ordinary' person-centred relationships is extended. Our person-centred practice now changes and evolves to account for the interpenetrative fields of influence from self, others, culture and the organic-world: for instance, phases of the moon, the Tsunami, the 'fight against terrorism', the weight of patriarchy through the ages.

Encounter (Schmid, 1998, 2002) and relational depth (Mearns and Cooper, 2005) could be considered aspects of this holistic/emergent view of psychological contact. Therapist and client participate in the relationship and the degree of their availability and receptivity to each other influence the quality of psychological contact and the 'encounter' that emerges. The other, with all of his/her cultural and personal differences, is acknowledged as a person having an 'open future' (Schmid, 2002: 193). This means dropping all assumptions, expectations and aims we may have for the client. The therapist is available and receptive to contact with another, and this openness creates the possibility of being changed by the encounter. A 'special dance' is required by the therapist: a slowness to allow the client's story to unfold, a sensitive, accepting empathy or 'holistic listening' (Mearns and Cooper, 2005), a spontaneity and authenticity, a willingness to 'not-know' and be vulnerable, and perhaps most importantly a capacity for the client to matter and to affect the therapist. Sometimes this 'relational depth' will arise from very sensitive empathic responding, sometimes by silence and sometimes by being 'interactive, bi-directional and mutual', as described by Mearns and Cooper (2005: 9).

At times, an 'extra dimension' is accessed and a 'non-cognitive' intelligence is realized. Rogers described this as a knowing that is 'wiser than the intellect' (Rogers, 1963: 18), 'something around the edges of these conditions that is really the most important element of therapy' (Baldwin, 1987: 45). The quality of this psychological contact might be described as 'electric', 'intense', 'vital', 'oneness', 'transformative'. This is the 'presence' that Rogers wrote about (Rogers, 1980) and at these times all of Rogers' conditions are simultaneously present. Perhaps this extra dimension emerges from the wider web of influence.

The therapist also has awareness of the interpenetrative influences and how they may impinge on the therapeutic relationship. These might include: the increasingly frenetic pace of life; increasing ecological pressures such as climate change, pollution and decreasing bio-diversity; the bombings in London; bombardment by the media. The emphasis still remains with the client but there is also an availability of and receptiveness to these interpenetrative influences. The therapist is congruent with this wider web of influence and extends his/her empathy and UPR to this wider field. The encounter thus occurs within this wider field. This shifts the balance from an individualistic focused psychotherapy to a holistic psychotherapy where the individual is both a whole and a part of a society. Psychotherapy, in this way, can function as socio-therapy (Schmid, 2001) and eco-therapy (Roszak, 1993).

CONCLUSION

Each conceptualization of psychological contact examined here has, I believe, relevance for our practice. The implication is for therapists to develop ability to sense and move their way of contacting and relating in response to their clients, the evolving therapeutic relationship, the cultural context and wider web of influence. This could be seen as an extension of Margaret Warner's 'process-sensitive' therapy (see Chapter 12, this volume). With disturbed clients in pre-expressive or fragile process, Pre-Therapy's contact reflections may help, as may sensitive empathic responses. For clients in grey-zone functioning, the therapist would responsively shift from contact reflections to empathic understanding as the client moves from pre-expressive to 'expressive'. Many clients will respond to the contact characterized by the congruent acceptant empathic understanding of person-centred therapy whilst other clients draw a more 'interactive, bi-directional and mutual' encounter. The client as global citizen calls for an extended contact, which acknowledges mutual causality, inter-subjectivity and the interpenetrative fields of influence of an interconnected universe.

REFERENCES

Baldwin, M. (1987). Interview with Carl Rogers on the use of the self in therapy. In M. Baldwin and V. Satir (eds), *The Use of Self in Therapy* (pp. 45–52). New York: Haworth.

Barrett-Lennard, G.T. (1962). Dimensions of therapist response as causal factors in therapist change. *Psychological Monographs*, 76 (43, Whole No. 562).

Barrett-Lennard, G.T. (2002). Perceptual variables of the helping relationship: a measuring system and its fruits. In G. Wyatt and P. Sanders (eds), *Rogers' Therapeutic Conditions: evolution, theory and practice*. Volume 4. *Contact and Perception* (pp. 25–50). Ross-on-Wye: PCCS Books.

Barret-Lennard, G.T. (2005). *Relationship at the Core: healing in a troubled world*. London: Wiley.

Bozarth, J.D. (2006). Personal communication.

Cameron, R. (2002). In the space between. In G. Wyatt and P. Sanders (eds), *Rogers' Therapeutic Conditions: evolution, theory and practice*. Volume 4. *Contact and Perception* (pp. 259–73). Ross-on-Wye: PCCS Books.

Cameron, R. (2003). In J. Tolan and J. Skills (eds), *PC Counselling and Psychotherapy*. London: Sage.

Cooper, M. (2005). Therapists' experiences of relational depth: a qualitative interview study. *Counselling and Psychotherapy Research*, 5(2): 87–95.

Davies, N. and Aykroyd, M. (2002). Sexual orientation and psychological contact. In G. Wyatt and P. Sanders (eds), *Rogers' Therapeutic Conditions: evolution, theory and practice*. Volume 4. *Contact and Perception* (pp. 221–33). Ross-on-Wye: PCCS Books.

Ellingham, I. (1999). Carl Rogers' congruence as an organismic not a Freudian concept. *Person-Centered Journal*, 6(2), 121–40.

Ellingham, I. (2002). Madness and mysticism in perceiving the other: towards a radical organismic, person-centred interpretation. In G. Wyatt and P. Sanders (eds), *Rogers' Therapeutic Conditions: evolution, theory and practice* (pp. 234–58). Volume 4. *Contact and Perception* . Ross-on-Wye: PCCS Books.

Embleton Tudor, L., Keemar, K., Tudor, K. Valentine, J. and Worrall, M. (2005). *The Person-Centred Approach: a contemporary introduction*. Basingstoke: Palgrave MacMillan.

Geller, S. and Greenberg, L. (2002). Therapeutic presence: therapist's experience of presence in the psychotherapy encounter. *Person-Centred and Experiential Psychotherapies*, 1(1 and 2), 71–86.

Gendlin, E.T. (1962). *Experiencing and the Creation of Meaning*. New York: the Free Press.

Mearns, D. and Thorne, B. (1988). *Person-Centred Counselling in Action*. London: Sage.

Mearns, D. and Cooper, M. (2005). *Working at Relational Depth*. London: Sage.

O'Hara, M. (2006). Personal communication.

Prouty, G.F. (2002/1994). Pre-Therapy as a theoretical system. In G. Wyatt and P. Sanders (eds), *Rogers' Therapeutic Conditions: evolution, theory and practice*. Volume 4. *Contact and Perception* (pp. 54–62). Ross-on-Wye: PCCS Books.

Raskin, N.J. and Rogers, C.R. (2000/1989). Person-centered therapy. In N.J. Raskin *Contributions to Client-centered Therapy and the Person-Centered Approach* (pp. 245–89). Ross-on-Wye: PCCS Books.

Reason, P. and Goodwin, B.C. (1999). Toward a science of qualities in organizations: lessons from complexity theory and postmodern biology. *Concepts and Transformations*, 4(3), 281–317.

Rogers, C.R. (1957). The necessary and sufficient conditions of therapeutic personality change. *Journal of Consulting Psychology*, 21, 95–103. In H. Kirscenbaum and V. Henderson (eds) (1990). *The Carl Rogers Reader* (pp. 219–35). London: Constable.

Rogers, C.R. (1959). A theory of therapy, personality and interpersonal relationships, as developed in the client-centered framework. In S. Koch (ed.), *Psychology: a study of a science*. Volume 3. *Formulations of the Person and the Social Context* (pp. 184–256). New York: McGraw Hill.

Rogers, C.R. (1963). The actualizing tendency in relation to 'motives' and to consciousness. In M. Jones (ed.), *Nebraska Symposium on Motivation* (pp. 1–24). Lincoln: University of Nebraska Press.

Rogers, C.R. (1980). *A Way of Being*. Boston: Houghton Mifflin.

Roszak, T. (1993). *The Voice of the Earth: an exploration of ecopsychology*. New York: Touchstone.

Schmid, P. (1998). 'Face to face': the art of encounter. In B. Thorne and E. Lambers (eds), *Person-Centred Therapy: a European perspective* (pp. 74–90). London: Sage.

Schmid, P.F. (2001). Authenticity: the person as his or her own author. Dialogical and ethical perspectives on therapy as an encounter relationship. And beyond. In G. Wyatt (ed.), *Rogers' Therapeutic Conditions: evolution, theory, and practice*. Volume 1. *Congruence* (pp. 213–28). Ross-on-Wye: PCCS Books.

Schmid, P. (2002). Presence: im-media-te co-experiencing and co-responding. Phenomenological, dialogical and ethical perspectives on contact and perception in person-centre therapy and beyond. In G. Wyatt and P. Sanders (eds), *Rogers' Therapeutic Conditions: evolution, theory and practice*. Volume 4. *Contact and Perception* (pp. 182–203). Ross-on-Wye: PCCS Books.

Shlien, J.M. (2003/1961). A client-centered approach to schizophrenia: first approximation. In A. Burton, (ed.) (1961) *Psychotherapy of the Psychoses*. New York: Basic Books: 285–317. Reprinted in Shlien, J.M. (2003) *To Live an Honorable Life* (pp. 30–59). Ross-on-Wye: PCCS Books.

Sommerbeck, L. (2003). *The Client-Centred Therapist in Psychiatric Contexts: a therapists' guide to the psychiatric landscape and its inhabitants*. Ross-on-Wye: PCCS Books.

Sommerbeck, L. (2005). An evaluation of research, concepts and experiences pertaining to the universality of CCT and its application in psychiatric settings. In S. Joseph and R. Worsley (eds), *Person-Centred Psychopathology* (pp. 323–5). Ross-on-Wye: PCCS Books.

Sommerbeck, L. (2006). Personal communication.

Thich Nhat Than (1998). *Interbeing*. Berkeley: Parallax Press.

Tudor, K. (2000). The Case of the Lost Conditions. *Counselling*, 11(1): 33–7.

Van Werde, D. (1998). Anchorage as a core concept in working with psychotic people. In B. Thorne and E. Lambers (eds), *Person-Centred Therapy: a European perspective* (pp. 195–205). London: Sage.

Van Werde, D. (2002). Pre-Therapy applied on a psychiatric ward. In G. Prouty, D. Van Werde and M. Pörtner (eds), *Pre-Therapy: reaching contact-impaired clients* (pp. 61–120). Ross-on-Wye: PCCS Books.

Van Werde, D. (2005). Facing psychotic functioning: person-centred contact work in residential psychiatric care. In Joseph, S. and Worsley, R. (eds), *Person-Centred Psychopathology: a positive psychology of mental health* (pp. 158–68). Ross-on-Wye: PCCS Books.

Warner, M. (2002). Psychological contact, meaningful process and human nature: a reformulation of person-centered theory. In G. Wyatt and P. Sanders (eds), *Rogers' Therapeutic Conditions: evolution, theory and practice*. Volume 4. *Contact and Perception* (pp. 76–95). Ross-on-Wye: PCCS Books.

Watson, N. (1984). The empirical status of Rogers' hypotheses of the necessary and sufficient conditions for effective psychotherapy. In J.M. Shlien and R.F. Levant (eds), *Client-centered Therapy and the Person-Centered Approach: new directions in theory, research and practice* (pp. 17–40). New York: Praeger.

Whelton, W.J. and Greenberg, L.S. (2002). Psychological contact as dialectical construction. In G. Wyatt and P. Sanders (eds), *Rogers' Therapeutic Conditions: evolution, theory and practice*. Volume 4. *Contact and Perception* (pp. 96–114). Ross-on-Wye: PCCS Books.

Wyatt, G. (2001). Congruence: a synthesis and implications. In G. Wyatt (ed.), *Rogers' Therapeutic Conditions: evolution, theory and practice*. Volume 1. *Congruence* (pp. 229–37). Ross-on-Wye: PCCS Books.

Wyatt, G. (2004). Widening circles: an exploration of congruence, identity and diversity. Keynote lecture. British Association for the person-centred approach Conference, Loughborough University, UK.

Wyatt, G. and Sanders, P. (2002). *Rogers' Therapeutic Conditions: evolution, theory and practice*. Volume 4. *Contact and Perception*. Ross-on-Wye: PCCS Books.

Client Incongruence and Psychopathology

Margaret S. Warner

Person-centred therapies have been found to be effective with a broad range of kinds and intensities of psychological disturbance usually diagnosed as psychopathology (Elliott, 2002; Elliott et al, 2004). Yet classically oriented person-centred therapy is radically different from other orientations in its way of construing 'psychopathology', proposing that there is a single, fundamental source of psychologically based difficulties – incongruence – and a single set of relationship conditions that have the capacity to generate positive change.

Person-centred theory does not deny the enormous range of kinds and intensities of human distress. In fact, person-centred practitioners have been particularly effective in working with clients experiencing severe levels of disturbance. But, it does posit deep capacities for self-healing inherent within the human organism that apply across human experiences that seem very different on the surface.

This core position has led person-centred practitioners to take a range of positions in relation to psychopathology, ranging from avoidance of any categorization of clients to explications or translations of person-centred principles as they relate to traditional diagnostic categories. The author proposes a process-sensitive model of psychopathology, arguing that this model keeps the integrity of Rogers' original theory while adding depth of explanation in relation to clients experiencing 'difficult' forms of process.

Core concepts

Client 'incongruence' is presented in the second of the six conditions which Rogers (1957) proposes as 'necessary and sufficient' to therapeutic success (see Chapter 1, this volume). Rogers defines 'incongruence' as a 'discrepancy between the actual experience of the organism and the self picture of the individual's experience insofar as it represents that experience' (1957: 222) (see Chapter 7, this volume). Rogers' (1957, 1959) model of actualization proposes that human beings have inherent capacities and tendencies to resolve such incongruence between the self-concept and the organism in ways that take into account their social and cultural circumstances and the constraints of reality.

Rogers proposes one key way that natural human tendencies to process experience are often inhibited. He suggests that the human wish for social acceptance is so strong that individuals often 'introject' values from parents and significant others that create 'conditions of worth'. Perhaps a male client has grown up in a family that only values him when he is an 'aggressive go-getter'. If he then finds himself drawn to being sensitive and artistic at some point in his life, these experiences can feel exceedingly threatening to his whole sense of who he is and how he is to live in the world. Under these circumstances, clients' attempts to actualize 'self' may contradict or exist in tension with their attempts to actualize the totality of their organismic experience.

Rogers notes that experiences that threaten the self-concept create anxiety, with the degree of anxiety dependent on the degree to which the self-structure is threatened. Such experiences may be denied or distorted as a way to maintain the coherence of the self-structure. If a person isn't able to resolve incongruence (and protect the coherence of his or her self-concept) by denial or distortion, incongruent experiences may break through creating an overall state of disorganization in the person's experience.

In Condition 2 of his 'necessary and sufficient' conditions, Rogers suggests that the client needs to be 'in a state of incongruence, being vulnerable or anxious' for therapy to be successful. Pearson (1974) notes that this condition has created some confusion, since the relationship between incongruence and felt anxiety or vulnerability is complex. All people are incongruent to some degree all of the time (since human beings can never fully symbolize their experience), and some sorts of incongruence may actually lower anxiety. Perhaps in Condition 2 Rogers is simply saying that clients must, at least to a subliminal degree, sense themselves as having issues that cause them problems or discomfort in order to be motivated to engage in productive psychotherapy.

Reformulations of Rogers' theory of incongruence

Some later theorists have suggested reformulations of particular elements of Rogers' conceptualization of self and of incongruence. Ellingham (2001) and Warner (2005, 2006) have noted that Rogers' language sometimes implies a pre-existing reality under the surface, which is inconsistent with the phenomenological nature of the rest of his theory. For example, when Rogers says that: 'we protect ourselves from having to recognize attitudes or experiences which have been denied to awareness because they are threatening to the self' (Rogers 1951/1965 edition: 100), he is speaking as if fully formed attitudes and experiences already exist somewhere outside consciousness. This wording contradicts the creativity and existential freedom that are very deeply a part of the rest of Rogers' theory and practice.

Gendlin (1968) offers a way of addressing this issue, noting that making sense is a whole body process in which experiences which have been 'implicit' are carried forward into meaning. One metaphor for this carrying forward into meaning is the completion of a poem (Gendlin, 1995). If a poet has written nine lines and is looking for a final tenth line, he or she may try any number of lines before finding one that 'works'. Once the poet has written the final line, it may well feel like the only line that could have been written. Meaning, in Gendlin's philosophy, is like the last line of the poem in that it is neither totally constrained nor is it totally arbitrary.

Warner (2005, 2006) suggests ways of building on Rogers' and Gendlin's theories to generate a more consistently phenomenological and process-oriented understanding of the congruence between self and experience. She notes that human beings organize themselves in terms of 'soft phenomena' – notably, personal qualities such as emotions and intention, and social qualities such as responsibility or oppression – that do not stay constant across observers or across time. Following Gendlin (1968), she proposes that it is an essential and intrinsic aspect of human nature to take clusters of experiences that are not yet clear – perhaps stomach pains and vague feelings of dread and some puzzling actions – and to let those experiences go through changes until they form themselves into soft meanings that offer a sensible, coherent and personally satisfying version of what is happening. Once such soft meanings form within individuals, they are often experienced subjectively as if they had the solidness and stability of objects.

Experiences of 'self' are soft phenomena in this sense, rather than object-like phenomena that exist in a pre-formed way either on or below the surface of consciousness. Human beings are 'congruent' when their symbolized versions of soft aspects of their experience come together in experiences of self that genuinely carry forward the totality of the lived experience of the body. While only a few versions of self will fit with the totality of a person's experience, there is no single 'accurate' version of self that could be 'denied' or 'distorted'.

In a related train of thought, Cooper et al (2004), Cooper (2000), Mearns and Thorne (2000), Greenberg and Van Balen (1998) and Speierer (1998) have all noted that people often have a variety of constellations of self that may or may not be congruent with each other. Speierer (1998) proposes that most people experience incongruence, but that incongruence only becomes pathological when it surmounts an individually tolerable critical level.

A number of theorists offer plausible sources of incongruence other than 'conditions of worth'. Speierer observes that clients may suffer from 'dispositional incongruence' which 'results from inherited or constitutional biological deficits of congruence ability' (1998: 417). Greenberg and Van Balen (1998) and Speierer (1998) observe that incongruence may result from the sheer intensity of life events without particular 'conditions of worth' being involved. For example, a soldier who has a strong sense of self may still experience intrusive flashbacks of traumatic battle scenes. Warner (2000) proposes that, in addition to particular subjects of incongruence, early developmental or biological difficulties may thwart the full development of general processing capacities, leading to a variety of forms of 'difficult' client process.

From theory to practice: person-centred models of psychopathology

The model of no model

The first, and historically oldest, model of psychopathology within the person-centred approach might be called the 'model of no model'. Rogers notes that:

> The client is the only one who has the potentiality of knowing fully the dynamics of his perceptions and his behaviours. ... In a very meaningful and accurate sense therapy is diagnosis, and this diagnosis is a process which goes on in the experience of the client, rather than in the intellect of the clinician.
>
> (1951/1965 edition: 221, 223)

Following Rogers, many non-directive client-centred therapists consider all attempts at diagnostic categorization to be poorly grounded scientifically and potentially destructive to clients (Boy, 1989; Schlein, 1989; Schmid, 2004; Sanders, 2005). Seeman (1989) suggests that, at best, diagnosis is a tool that is valuable for discerning when clients might have issues relevant to different system levels (such as the body) which need to be addressed by avenues other than psychotherapy (such as medical doctors).

Problem-related descriptions of person-centred work

Alternately, a number of writers have made a case for the strength of the person-centred approach with particular disorders. In a recent book on *Person-Centred Psychopathology* (Joseph and Worsley, 2005), Leslie McCulloch addresses antisocial personality disorder, Stephen Joseph post-traumatic stress, Elaine Catterall maternal depression, Jan Hawkins early childhood abuse and dissociation, and Marlis Pörtner clients with special needs. Each author combines information from the literature on general issues these clients tend to face with person-centred theory, research and practice indicating the way that person-centred therapy tends to be particularly effective in helping clients resolve incongruence and handle these issues.

Richard Bryant-Jeffries has written a series of books giving in-depth fictionalized accounts of person-centred work with a number of particular client issues, including alcohol problems, obesity and gambling, as well as work with victims of warfare and of child sexual abuse (Bryant-Jeffries, 2001, 2003a, 2003b, 2005a, 2005b, 2005c). Nat Raskin (1996) describes work with 'very disturbed' clients. Lisbeth Sommerbeck (2003) offers in-depth descriptions of person-centred work with mentally ill, hospitalized clients.

Attempted translations using Rogers' personality theory

A number of practitioners have attempted to explicate traditional categories of psychopathology using Rogers' theory of personality change, sometimes in combination with other theories. E. Biermann-Ratjen (1998) cites two over-all models, one by Hans Swilden and another by Gert-Walt Speierer. Elke Lambers (1994a, 1994b, 1994c, 1994d) considers applications of the person-centred approach to neurotic, borderline and psychotic disorders as well as with clients diagnosed with personality disorders. She suggests that a delicate balance is needed between authentic expression of therapist reactions (Condition 3 – congruence) and unconditional acceptance of the sorts of client behaviours that are difficult for the therapist (Condition 4) in work with the vulnerabilities typical of personality disorders. In particular, she notes that therapists need to be wary of the opposite risks of becoming over or under-involved in client issues, repeating patterns in the client's life of being either a victim or a victimizer.

Eckert and Biermann-Ratjen (1998) advocate a client-centred approach to volatile, 'borderline' clients, using a combination of person-centred and object-relations conceptualizations of client relationship issues. They note that a number of qualities that are seen as typical of such clients – such as idealizing therapists at one moment and denigrating them at another – may pose challenges to the therapeutic relationship.

> So, here is a rule to stick to: as a client-centred psychotherapist treating a border-line patient, hang on to your unconditional positive regard for all you are worth. It is not just endangered by the patients' direct attacks or idealizations but also by the fact that they often seem to ignore you ... or perceive you in a way that has nothing to do with your own personality.
>
> (Eckert and Biermann-Ratjen, 1998: 357)

They note that relationship challenges are particularly severe as these clients form and end therapeutic relationships, both of which risk intense distress and disappointment. Eckert and Biermann-Ratjen observe that the non-directive attitudes implicit in client-centred therapy are helpful with clients diagnosed as 'borderline', since such clients are particularly likely to feel terrorized by the idea of being pressured or manipulated.

Rainer Sachse (1998) proposes that a strong advocacy of processing is needed to work with clients experiencing psychosomatic disorders, since he finds that these clients systematically avoid attention to or exploration of their own experience. For example, Sachse believes that therapists should ask these clients to talk about what they are feeling and wanting and, if they say that they 'don't know', continue to inquire quite persistently. Under these circumstances, Sachse suggests that a therapist might say something like: 'All we need now is a hint, traces on which we can base further work. Therefore I would like you to stay on this point and take a closer look' (1998: 310).

Gert-Walter Speierer (1998) suggests that psychosomatic disorders can be treated effectively with person-centred therapy, while clients with somato-form disorders, which result from clients' marked attention to and perception of their own bodies, are unlikely to benefit. He suggests that person-centred therapy may be actively harmful for some clients suffering from acute delusional schizophrenic psychoses, depressive disorders with psychotic symptoms and acute reactions to severe stress or adjustment disorders, since he believes that empathic responding may simply intensify dangerous beliefs.

Evolutions of theory relating to psychological contact and process sensitivity

Prouty (1994, 2001) and Warner (2000) suggest that, in addition to conditions of worth, some kinds of variation from normative ways of processing experience may affect clients' abilities to stay in psychological contact and to resolve incongruence. Therapist awareness of client ways of processing experience can allow a deepening of contact (Rogers' Condition 1), empathic understanding (Rogers' Condition 5) and/or a better ability to communicate empathy in ways that clients can understand (Rogers' Condition 6). It is important to note that in these models, the therapist is still simply trying to connect with and to understand the client rather than to change the client's experience in any way.

In Pre-Therapy, Prouty (1994, 2001) builds on Rogers' premise that the necessary and sufficient conditions for effective psychotherapy require that clients be in 'psychological contact'. He observes that when clients are out of psychological contact with 'self', 'world' or 'other', therapists can understand the surface of client communications but tend to be cut off from the client's broader meaning or frame of reference (see Chapters 18 and 11, this volume). For example, a client might be rocking and pointing to the corner of the room saying 'round and purple' over and over again, while not seeming aware that the therapist is present. Prouty suggests that 'contact reflections', a very close and concrete form of empathic responding, help restore clients' psychological contact.

Warner (1991) suggests that some clients experience forms of process that are 'difficult' for the client, the therapist or both. In addition to the psychotic process described by Prouty, Warner adds 'fragile process' (Warner, 1991, 2000, 2001) and 'dissociated process' (Warner, 1998, 2000). Warner emphasizes that these are forms of process diagnosis rather than person diagnosis, since clients may experience one or more forms of 'difficult process' at the same time.

Clients who are experiencing 'fragile process' have difficulty holding particular experiences in attention at moderate levels of intensity, and are often diagnosed as borderline or narcissistic (Warner, 2000). Given this difficulty of holding onto their own experience, they often have difficulty taking in the point of view of another person without feeling that their own experience has been annihilated. For example, one therapist suggested to a client that he thought that she should do more for herself and not feel that she needed to do so much for others. The client – who describes herself as having fragile process – felt that a whole way of being in the world that she valued was demolished with that one therapist comment and that she had no way of retrieving it. She also found herself unable to restore a sense of trust with the therapist or tell him the impact that his comment had on her.

Clients seem most likely to develop a fragile style of processing experience when the sort of empathic care-giving needed to develop processing capacities in early childhood has been lacking (see Chapter 7, this volume). Or clients may experience fragile process around newer edges of their experience that have not previously been received by themselves or others. Warner (2000) suggests that clients experiencing fragile process are often very sensitive to the way empathic responses are framed, needing therapists to stay very close to their actual words, or to be responsive to client directives as to what exact sorts of therapist responses work for them

Clients who experience 'dissociated process' (Warner 1998, 2000) quite convincingly experience themselves as having selves that are not integrated with each other for periods of time. This sort of client experience has been described at length in the literature on 'multiple personality' and 'dissociative identity disorder', and virtually always results from severe early childhood trauma (Putnam, 1989; Ross, 1989).

Since dissociative experiences are often foreign to the therapists, Warner (2000) notes that practitioners may often normalize the client's experiences without realizing it. Clients often initially experience or express this radical split in their subjective sense of self in somewhat indirect ways, such as:

- Actions without a sense of the client being the author. For example, a client might say, 'My hand wants to pick up the knife.'
- Feelings without context, as when a client says 'I was walking down the street and suddenly started sobbing for no reason.'
- Vagueness about what happened for periods of time. For example: 'I guess I must have been really out of line. That whole afternoon isn't too clear in my memory, but everyone seemed angry with me afterward.'
- Voices. For some clients these are experienced clearly and for others they are blurred together, sounding somewhat like a radio in the background.

Any of these sorts of experiences could be aspects of non-dissociative processes or just said in a metaphoric or joking way. Yet, if the therapist is able to respond in an accepting and accurate way – often needing to stay very close to the client's exact words – alternative personas or 'parts' which do exist will tend to emerge more clearly. For example, if a woman client said 'I feel like those last words just came out of my mouth. I don't know where they came from,' a therapist could easily respond 'You're surprised to find yourself saying that.' Staying closer, a therapist might say 'You really feel that those words just came out of your mouth, somehow. You don't know where they came from.'

This sort of difference in wording may seem subtle. But, if the client is experiencing dissociated parts, the first response is likely to convince her that the therapist is unwilling or unable to understand the degree to which dissociated experiences coming from one part are experienced as out of the control of another part. The second response provides an opening for her to say more if she wants to. The client may then say things that more clearly indicate the degree of autonomy such personas have. For example, she might then say something like, 'I have this strange feeling that there's a part of me that knows more than I'm ready to know about what happened with my stepfather. I'm afraid that she'll take the session over and I'm not ready to handle what she has to say.' Richard Bryant-Jeffries (2003a) has written a fictionalized account of work with a client in the midst of dissociative process that captures a great deal of the way such work feels in actual person-centred practice.

A process-sensitive model of psychopathology

Drawing together the variety of theoretical work in the person-centred approach, Warner (2005 and 2006) suggests a three-sided model of process vulnerability that considers various sources of psychological distress (see Figure 12.1). This model retains Rogers' emphasis on incongruence, while suggesting that clients' ability to resolve such incongruence is influenced by the difficulty of life experiences that they face at any given moment and by the degree to which they have well-developed processing capacities.

Press of life (unresolved by pre-existing understandings and strategies)	Processing capacities (grounded in early childhood physical and psychological development of the organism)

Relational support of processing (via empathy, genuineness, unconditional positive regard)

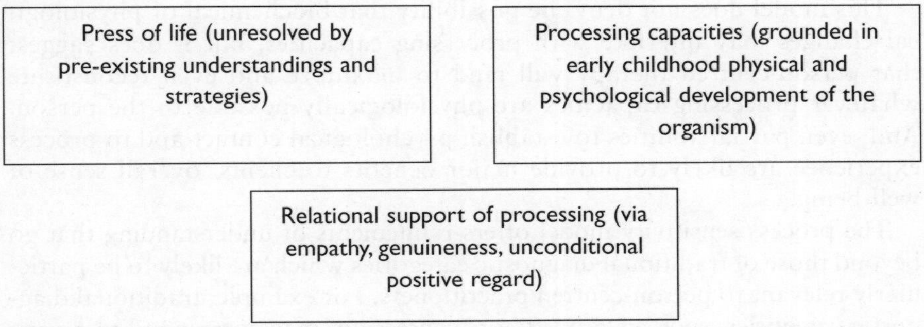

Figure 12.1 Warner's three-sided model of process vulnerability

Using this three-sided model, a continuum of psychological wellness and dysfunction can be developed.

1. *Well-developed processing capacities used effectively to process issues of low to moderate intensity*
   Suppose a client, who has had a generally nurturing childhood that allowed him to develop solid capacities to process experience, nevertheless has a 'condition of worth' that requires that he be accommodating and nice. He then faces a work situation that requires him to be assertive. He may begin to experience stomach-aches and to assume that his colleagues are feeling very judgemental toward him, even though they feel fine about his new behaviour.
2. *Well-developed processing capacities temporarily overwhelmed by moderate to extreme press of life*
   Suppose, for example, all of the client's family members were killed in a car accident. The person may experience incongruence related to 'conditions of worth', or incongruence that simply relates to the degree to which the press of life is overwhelming to the person.

3. *Difficult process, which can leave the person feeling overwhelmed by even low or moderate press of life*
At certain times, the experience of fragile process, dissociated process or psychotic process (or, perhaps, some other, not-yet-identified form of difficult process) can make it difficult for clients to handle very ordinary life challenges or to tolerate even minimal levels of directivity within therapy. For example, suppose a schizophrenic client begins hallucinating that people are threatening monsters whenever he sees police or medical personnel, because he can't tell if they are coming to take him away. The resulting incongruence is likely to be extremely difficult for him to process alone and is very likely to impede his day-to-day functioning.

Warner (2005a, 2005b) proposes that Rogers 'core conditions' are effective at all levels of this process vulnerability model. Yet, while more traditional ways of expressing empathy, congruence and unconditional positive regard are likely to be effective in work with the first two levels, higher levels of relational and process sensitivity are often required in relation to the third level.

This model does not deny the possibility that biochemical or physiological changes may interfere with processing capacities, but it does suggest that person-centred therapy will tend to maximize and even reconstitute whatever processing capacities are physiologically possible to the person. And, even partial abilities to establish psychological contact and to process experience are likely to provide major benefits to clients' overall sense of well-being.

The process sensitivity model offers refinements of understanding that go beyond those of traditional diagnostic categories which are likely to be particularly relevant to person-centred practitioners. For example, traditional diagnostic categories, such as 'anxiety' or 'depression' may correspond to a variety of different levels in the process vulnerability model. A client who shows signs of being clinically depressed might have strong processing capacities, but have a body that easily falls into physiological states of depression (Level 1), or may process well, but be experiencing overwhelming life events (Level 2). Yet another clinically depressed client may be experiencing fragile or dissociated or psychotic process – each of which can make it exceedingly difficult to process life changes that might be relatively insignificant for another person (Level 3).

Psychiatry, medication and person-centred practice

Person-centred practitioners vary in their views as to whether and under what circumstances psychotropic medication is helpful in relation to depression, bipolar disorder, obsessive-compulsive disorder, schizophrenia and other disorders that may have significant physiological components. When medications are used, person-centred practitioners focus on enhancing clients' processing capacities rather than merely eliminating non-normative ways of acting. And, they try to make decisions as collaboratively as possible with clients and their families.

Research

Client incongruence is difficult, and perhaps impossible, to research directly, since it involves aspects of experience that have not been fully symbolized by the client, to which others have no direct access. In the research project described in Rogers and Dymond (1954), researchers operationalize related phenomena in a variety of ways. John Butler and Gerard Haigh compare clients' actual sense of self with their ideal selves as measured by Q sorts, finding that the two scores tend to become closer as therapy progresses. In this Q sort research, subjects are offered sets of cards, with each card having a personal quality (such as 'responsible') on it. Subjects rank order the cards as to which qualities they believe represent themselves now, and again as to which qualities represent the way that they would like to be.

The Rogers and Dymond research finds that the strongest convergence between current 'self' and 'ideal self' is found with clients who are seen as 'definitely improved' by other measures. In a separate analysis, Rogers finds that when counsellors regard therapy as having shown little or no movement, there is often a marked discrepancy between the client's own view of the maturity of his or her behaviour and that of the counsellor and of close friends of the client (1954: 215–37). Rogers proposes this as 'a clear-cut and measured instance of the operation of defensiveness' (1954: 232). By defensiveness, Rogers seems to mean that a client denies or distorts experience to an extent that results in severe incongruence.

Chodoroff (1954) attempts to operationalize client incongruence by comparing client Q sorts of a list of self-referent items with therapist and expert ratings of the client's personality. He finds significant correlations between this sort of incongruence or 'defensiveness' and low ratings on scales of personal adjustment and with higher scores on tests of perceptual defence. This method, of course, has the considerable limitation of relying on the therapist as the expert on the client's 'real' experience.

Over time, the focus of research shifted from attempting to operationalize the amount of incongruence or vulnerability to considering the ways that clients relate to such felt vulnerability – in other words, defensiveness vs. openness to experience. In particular, a considerable body of research has been conducted on the 'experiencing scale', which measures clients' attention to the immediacy of bodily felt experience (which presumably manifests vulnerability related to incongruence) in ways that bring shifts in felt meaning (Hendricks, 2002). While some therapists doubt the conclusiveness of this research (Brodley, 1988), a considerable body of findings suggests that, overall, clients' attention to immediate felt experience correlates with success in psychotherapy (Hendricks, 2002).

While incongruence per se is difficult to measure, Rogers and Dymond do find client-centred therapy to be effective with clients experiencing a full range of disturbance or psychopathology, noting that: 'we find nothing in our data to indicate that the initial diagnostic status of the individual has any marked relationship to the therapeutic outcome' (1954: 427).

At the same time, they find that clients who are 'better adjusted and less aware of internal tension, who are ethnocentric in their attitudes and extra punitive in their personality characteristics' are somewhat more likely to drop out of therapy and less likely to profit from therapy if they remain (1954: 427). This finding seems to confirm Rogers' hypothesis in Condition 2 that clients need to feel a certain level of personal vulnerability in relation to their issues in order to profit from therapy.

In more recent work, Elliott (2002) and Elliott et al (2004) report that meta-analyses of research results support client-centred and experiential psychotherapies as effective in general and with a broad range of kinds and levels of severity of psychopathology in particular (see Chapter 24, this volume).

Reflections for the future

Both clinical experience and research find person-centred therapies to be effective across the broad spectrum of diagnostic disorders traditionally labelled as neurotic, characterological and psychotic. Person-centred therapies may have particular advantages in working with clients who are diagnosed with severe disorders since such clients tend to be experientially sensitive and often react very badly to interpretations and interventions.

Many therapeutic approaches view clients with serious disorders as unable to process experience, to make decisions on their own behalf, or even to participate in psychotherapy. The overall effectiveness of person-centred therapies offers support for the proposition that human beings have exceedingly strong inclinations and capacities to process experience, however much they may have suffered life challenges.

Given these various considerations, person-centred practitioners should become involved in promoting the person-centred approach in work with clients of all levels of severity of symptoms. They should be particularly active challenging the two-tiered structure of many mental health systems, which certify more directively trained psychiatrists and psychologists to work with more severely disturbed clients, while restricting person-centred 'counsellors' to work with less severe levels of psychopathology.

REFERENCES

Biermann-Ratjen, E. (1998). Incongruence and psychopathology. In B. Thorne and E. Lambers (eds), *Person-Centred Therapy: a European perspective* (pp. 119–30). London: Sage.

Boy, A.V. (1989). Psychodiagnosis: a person-centred perspective. *Person-Centered Review*, 4(2) 132–51.

Brodley, B. (1988). Does early-in-therapy level predict outcome. Paper presented at the Second Annual Meeting of the Association for the Development of the Person-Centred Approach, New York City.

Bryant-Jeffries, R. (2001). *Counselling the Person beyond the Alcohol Problem*. London: Jessica Kingsley.

Bryant-Jeffries, R. (2003a). *Counselling a Survivor of Child Sexual Abuse.* London: Jessica Kingsley

Bryant-Jeffries, R. (2003b). *Problem Drinking: a person centred dialogue.* London: Jessica Kingsley.

Bryant-Jeffries, R. (2005a). *Counselling Victims of Warfare.* London: Jessica Kingsley.

Bryant-Jeffries, R. (2005b). *Counselling for Obesity: person-centred dialogues.* London: Jessica Kingsley.

Bryant-Jeffries, R. (2005c). *Counselling for Problem Gambling.* London: Jessica Kingsley.

Chodoroff, B. (1954). Self-perception, perceptual defense, and adjustment. *Journal of Abnormal Social Psychology.* 49, 508–12.

Cooper, M. (2000). Person-centred developmental theory: reflections and revisions. *Person-Centred Practice,* 8(2), 87–94.

Cooper, M., Mearns, D., Stiles, W., Warner, M. and Elliott, R. (2004, Autumn). Developing self-pluralistic perspectives within the person-centred and experiential approaches: a round-table dialogue. *Person-Centred and Experiential Psychotherapies,* 3(3), 176–91.

Eckert, J. and Biermann-Ratjen, E. (1998). The treatment of borderline personality disorder. In L. Greenberg, J. Watson, and G. Lietaer (eds), *Handbook of Experiential Psychology* (pp. 349–67). New York: Guilford.

Elliott, R. (2002). The effectiveness of humanistic therapies: a meta-analysis. In D. Cain and J. Seeman (eds), *Humanistic Psychotherapies: handbook of research and practice* (pp. 57–81). Washington, D.C.: American Psychological Association.

Elliott, R., Greenberg, L.S. and Lietaer, G. (2004). Research on experiential psychotherapies. In Michael J. Lambert (ed.), *Bergin and Garfield's Handbook of Psychotherapy and Change* (pp. 493–539) (Fifth edition). New York: Wiley.

Ellingham, I. (2001). Carl Rogers 'congruence' as an organismic not a Freudian concept. In G. Wyatt (ed.), *Congruence* (pp. 96–115). Ross-on-Wye: PCCS Books.

Gendlin, E.T. (1968). The experiential response. In E. Hammer (ed.), *The Use of Interpretation in Treatment* (pp. 200–27). New York: Grune and Stratton.

Gendlin, E.T. (1995). Crossing and dipping: some terms for approaching the interface between natural understanding and logical formulation. *Minds and Machines,* 5(4), 547–60.

Gendlin, E.T. (1996). *Focusing-oriented Psychotherapy.* New York: Guilford.

Greenberg, L.S. Watson J.C. and Lietaer, G. (eds) (1998). *Handbook of Experiential Psychotherapy.* New York: Guilford Press.

Greenberg, L.S. and Van Balen, R. (1998). The theory of experience-centered therapies. In L.S. Greenberg, J.C. Watson and G. Lietaer (eds), *Handbook of Experiential Psychotherapy* (pp. 28–57). New York: Guilford Press.

Hendricks, M.N. (2002). Focusing-oriented/experiential psychotherapy. In D. Cain and J. Seeman (eds), *Humanistic Psychotherapies* (pp. 221–51). Washington, D.C.: American Psychological Association.

Joseph, S. and Worsley, R. (eds) (2005). *Person-Centred Psychopathology: a positive psychology of mental health*. Ross-on-Wye: PCCS Books.

Lambers, E. (1994a). The person-centred perspective on psychopathology: the neurotic client. In D. Mearns (ed.), *Developing Person-Centred Counselling* (pp. 103–9). London: Sage (2003 edition).

Lambers, E. (1994b). Borderline personality disorder. In D. Mearns (ed.), *Developing Person-Centred Counselling* (pp. 109–12). London: Sage (2003 edition).

Lambers, E. (1994c). Psychosis. In D. Mearns (ed.), *Developing Person-Centred Counselling* (pp. 113–16). London: Sage (2003 edition).

Lambers, E (1994d). Personality Disorder. In D. Mearns (ed.), *Developing Person-Centred Counselling* (pp. 116–20). London: Sage (2003 edition).

Mearns, D. and Thorne, B. (eds) (2000). *Person-Centred Therapy Today: new frontiers in theory and practice*. Thousand Oaks: Sage.

Pearson, P.H. (1974). Conceptualizing and measuring openness to experience in the context of psychotherapy. In D. Wexler and L.N. Rice (eds), *Innovations in Client-Centered Therapy* (pp,139–70). New York: Wiley.

Prouty, G. (1994). *Theoretical Evolutions in Person-Centred/Experiential Psychotherapy: applications to schizophrenic and retarded psychoses*. Westport: Praeger.

Prouty, G. (2001). A new mode of empathy: empathic contact. In S. Haugh and T. Merry (eds), *Empathy* (pp. 155–62). Ross-on-Wye: PCCS Books.

Putnam, F.W. (1989). *Diagnosis and Treatment of Multiple Personality Disorder*. New York: Guilford Press.

Raskin, N.J. (1996). Client-centered therapy with very disturbed clients. In R. Hutterer, G. Pawlowsky, P.F. Schmid and R. Stipsits (eds), *Client-Centred and Experiential Psychotherapy: a paradigm in motion* (pp. 529–31). Frankfurt am Main: Peter Lang.

Rogers, C.R. (1951/1965 paper edition). *Client-Centered Therapy*. Boston: Houghton Mifflin.

Rogers, C.R. (1957/1989). The necessary and sufficient conditions of personality change. In H. Kirschenbaum and K. Henderson (eds), *The Carl Rogers Reader* (pp. 219–35). New York: Houghton Mifflin, 1989.

Rogers, C.R. (1959). A theory of therapy, personality and interpersonal relationships, as developed in the client-centered framework. In S. Koch (ed.). *Psychology: a study of science*. Volume 3. *Formulations of the person and the social context* (pp. 184–256). New York: McGraw-Hill.

Rogers, C.R. and Dymond, R.F. (eds) (1954). *Psychotherapy and Personality Change*. Chicago: University of Chicago Press.

Ross, C. (1989). *Multiple Personality Disorder*. New York: Wiley.

Sachse, R. (1998). Goal-oriented client-centered therapy of psychosomatic disorders. In L.S. Greenberg, J.C. Watson and G. Lietaer (eds), *Handbook of Experiential Psychotherapy* (pp. 295–327). New York: Guilford Press.

Sanders, P. (2005). Principled and strategic opposition to the medicalization of distress and all of its apparatus. In S. Joseph and R. Worsley (eds), *Person-Centred Psychopathology: a positive psychology of mental health* (pp. 21–42). Ross-on-Wye: PCCS Books.

Schmid, P. (2004). Back to the client: a phenomenological approach to the process of understanding and diagnosis. *Person-Centered and Experiential Psychotherapies*, 3(1), 36–51.

Schlein, J. (1989). Boy's person-centred perspective on psychodiagnosis: a response. *Person-Centered Review*, 4(2), 157–62.

Seeman, J. (1989). A reaction to psychodiagnosis: a person-centred perspective. *Person-Centered Review*, 4(2), 152–6.

Sommerbeck, L. (2003). *The Client-Centered Therapist in Psychiatric Contexts: a therapist's guide to the psychiatric landscape and its inhabitants*. Ross-on-Wye: PCCS Books.

Speierer, G.W. (1998). Psychopathology according to the differential incongruence model. In L.S. Greenberg, J.C. Watson and G. Lietaer (eds), *Handbook of Experiential Psychotherapy* (pp. 410–27). New York: Guilford Press.

Warner, M.S. (1991). Fragile process. In L. Fusek (ed.), *New Directions in Client-Centered Therapy: practice with difficult client populations* (pp. 41–58). Chicago: Chicago Counseling and Psychotherapy Center, Monograph I.

Warner, M.S. (1998). A client-centered approach to therapeutic work with dissociated and fragile process. In L.S. Greenberg, J.C. Watson and G. Lietaer (eds), *Handbook of Experiential Psychotherapy*. New York: Guilford Press: 368–87.

Warner, M.S. (2000). Client-centered therapy at the difficult edge: work with fragile and dissociated process. In D. Mearns and B. Thorne (eds), *Person-Centred Therapy Today: new frontiers in theory and practice* (pp. 144–71). Thousand Oaks: Sage.

Warner, M.S. (2001). Empathy, relational depth and difficult client process. In S. Haugh and T. Merry (eds), *Empathy* (pp. 181–91). Ross-on-Wye: PCCS Books.

Warner, M.S. (2002). Psychological contact, meaningful process and human nature: a reformulation of person-centred theory. In G. Wyatt and P. Sanders (eds), *Contact and Perception* (pp. 76–95). Ross-on-Wye: PCCS Books.

Warner, M.S. (2005). A person-centred view of human nature, wellness, and psychopathology. In S. Joseph and R. Worsley (eds), *Person-Centred Psychopathology: a positive psychology of mental health* (pp. 91–109). Ross-on-Wye: PCCS Books.

Warner, M.S. (2006). Toward an integrated person-centred theory of wellness and psychopathology. *Person-Centered and Experiential Psychotherapies*, 5(1), 4–20.

CHAPTER

13

Congruence

Jeffrey Cornelius-White

You must be the change you want to see in the world.
(Mahatma Gandhi)

Congruence is perhaps the most difficult concept to understand, facilitate, develop, measure and agree upon within the person-centred approach. Rogers' explanations of congruence are rich, and many recent writings offer clarifications and developments (e.g. Bozarth, 1998; Brodley, 1998/2001; Ellingham, 2001; Haugh, 2001; Seeman, 2001; Schmid, 2001; Wyatt, 2001). Congruence refers to the internal, relational and ecological integration of persons. It is a 'broad-based construct that describes who we are and who we may become' (Seeman, 2001: 211).

This chapter examines congruence in terms of its central concepts of experience, awareness and communication, as well as organismic integration, presence and interconnectedness. The practice of congruence is explored in terms of internal and body awareness, communication, flow, spontaneity and encounter. The author concludes with cultural and ecological reflections for the future.

Central concepts

Rogers' congruence

Rogers uses congruence interchangeably with several other terms (e.g. real, genuine, transparent). He first mentioned congruence in 1951, but precursors are to be found as early as 1939 with an understanding of self as a necessary qualification of the therapist. He wrote about the therapist's 'genuine interest in the client' and how 'the counsellor is deeply and genuinely able to adopt these attitudes' (1946: 421). In 1951, Rogers first introduced congruence in his personality theory, referring to the consistency between the ideal self and the self (Rogers, 1951: 142, see also 525–32), and in 1954 he advocated therapists finding 'their genuine reality' (Rogers, 1961: 33).

By the late 1950s Rogers had drawn from the earlier work of Seeman (2001) in promoting the significance of the 'degree of integration' of the therapist, placing congruence as one of the core conditions of therapeutic change (1959: 201). He saw this condition as the 'growing edge' of the theory (1959: 214). Rogers' (1957, 1959) third condition for therapeutic personality change is: 'That the second person, whom we shall term the therapist, is *congruent* in the *relationship*' (Rogers, 1959: 213, author's italics). He writes, 'This means that the therapist's symbolization of his own experience in the relationship must be accurate, if therapy is to be most effective. ... He should accurately "be himself" [sic] in the relationship whatever the self of that moment may be' (1959: 214).

Thus a person is called congruent when the self allows experiences to be accurately symbolized, a matching between self and experience. Rogers used symbolization synonymously with awareness: 'Awareness is thus seen as the symbolic representation ... of some portion of our experience' (1959: 198). He goes on to say that the symbols we use may not accurately 'constitute our awareness' and may not accurately 'match ... the "real" experience' (1959: 198). If this is the case there would be a state of incongruence. He recognized that the way a person makes sense of experience is shaped by 'past experiences', which shape our awareness of our future experiences (1959: 198–9).

To illustrate: as I greet my client, I notice she doesn't make eye contact with me as she normally does. I feel a chill inside me, some apprehension; and I wonder what this means. Here I am accurately symbolizing 'apprehension' and 'wondering what this means' and I have an openness to what might unfold. I am in a state of congruence. However if when experiencing the chill and apprehension I make sense of this from my past experiences of feeling a failure when people withdraw and reject me by symbolizing, 'She's cross with me, she thinks I am no good, and she's going to leave,' this may be a state of incongruence. It would only be congruent if my client actually was angry with me and did want to leave, and I had been inadequate! Such incongruence could well restrict and influence how a therapist behaves with a client.

In his theoretical statements of congruence, Rogers (1957, 1959) names experience and awareness as the two processes that may or may not be congruent. However in some discussions he adds a third process arising out of 'freely' being the feelings that emerge (1957: 97) and 'accurately being himself in the relationship, whatever the self of that moment may be' (1959: 214). Here congruence becomes a matching between experience, awareness and the therapist's expression or communication. The following two quotes illustrate this 'three process' model of congruence.

I have found that the more I can be genuine in the relationship the more helpful it will be. This means that I need to be aware of my own feelings, insofar as possible, rather than presenting an outward facade of one attitude. ... Being genuine also involves the willingness to be and express, in my words and behavior, the various feelings and attitudes which exist in me. It is only in this way that the relationship can have reality, and reality seems deeply important as a first condition. It is only by providing the genuine reality which is in me, that the other person can successfully seek for the reality in him.

(Rogers, 1954, in Rogers, 1961: 33).

Thus there is a close matching, or congruence, between what is being experienced at the gut level, what is present in awareness, and what is expressed to the client.

(Rogers, 1980: 116).

Using the case example above, the therapist who was aware of 'being apprehensive' and 'wondering what was going on' may behave warmly and openly. She might have a look that conveys a little curiosity. She might express her experience directly with the client. For example, if the client was talking about a friend who had told her about how distant and rejecting the client had been, the therapist might make a statement of understanding and disclose how she experienced the client. She might share, 'When you arrived today I felt apprehensive and chilled. I noticed that you didn't look at me as you usually did, and I wondered what was happening for you.' As a result the client may feel understood and explore in depth how she disconnects from people and the results for herself and others. In this example, the therapist's experience, awareness and expression are congruent.

However the incongruent therapist, operating not from congruent experience of empathy and awareness but interpreting 'She's cross with me, she's going to leave because I'm not a good therapist,' may have conveyed withdrawal and defensiveness. She might have turned away from her client. When the therapist spoke, her voice might have been a little hesitant and cold while her eyes portrayed a distant look as if she had lost some of her 'aliveness'. The client during the session might have spoken less, staring down at the floor. The therapist's experience, awareness and expression could be said to be incongruent as she inaccurately symbolized the experience of feeling 'chilled' and 'apprehensive' from her past experiences. She interpreted her experiences in a way where she felt a failure and thought she was about to be rejected.

There has been much debate within the person-centred community regarding when it is appropriate for therapists to communicate their own thoughts and feelings to clients. Rogers suggests it is when therapists lose empathic understanding and unconditional positive regard as a result of their preoccupation with their own feelings. He cautions, 'Certainly the aim is not for the therapist to express or talk out his own feelings, but primarily that he should not be deceiving the client as to himself' (1957: 98). Another aspect within Rogers' writings on congruence that is particularly relevant here is the 'integration', 'realness' or 'wholeness' of the therapist, as this will influence the relationship between the therapist's experience, awareness and expression. The more actualized the therapist, the more experiences that will be accurately symbolized into awareness. Rogers speaks about being an 'integrated person', to 'be himself' (1957: 97), and 'that for therapy to occur the wholeness of the therapist in the relationship is primary' (1959: 215). He used phrases like to be 'freely and deeply' (1957: 97), 'endeavouring, to the best of his [sic] ability' (1959: 214) and to become 'completely and fully' his or her unique organism (1959: 215) to convey this broader and more holistic aspect of congruence. Congruence is a work in progress where an 'individual appears to be revising' himself through 'openness to experience' (Rogers, 1959: 206) in a 'fluid and changing gestalt, a process' (1959: 200).

Rogers states, 'The wholeness of the therapist in the relationship is primary, but a part of the congruence of the therapist must be the experience of unconditional positive regard and the experience of empathic understanding' (1959: 215). This meta-condition idea has been developed recently by others in that empathy, unconditionality and congruence are 'functionally one condition' (Bozarth, 1998: 80), 'one fundamental way of being, relating and acting' or 'the encounter condition' (Schmid, 2001: 220–1). This is supported by Sherer and Rogers' (1980) study finding that at the measured non-verbal level, the three conditions were highly interrelated.

Aside from two and three-level matching and integration, Rogers describes different dimensions of congruence and clarifies their relationships:

> Congruence is the term which defines the state. Openness to experience is the way an internally congruent individual meets new experience. Psychological adjustment is congruence viewed from a social point of view. Extensional is the term which describes the specific types behaviour of a congruent individual. Maturity is a broader term describing the personality characteristics and behavior of a person who is, in general, congruent.
>
> (Rogers, 1959: 207).

He elaborates upon the technical term 'extensionality' to convey how the open, mature, adjusted person interacts with not just his or her self or others, but the world. This way of being and doing has important implications for understanding congruence as complex and pluralistic. The extensional person tends 'to be aware of the space-time anchorage of facts ... to evaluate in multiple ways ... [and] to test his [or her] inferences and abstractions against the world' (1959: 206–7). Extensional behaviour interacts with reality and personal perceptions rather than denying or distorting interpretations or belief systems. More importantly, it attempts to engage the complexity of life (like Rogers' attempts to explore the complexity of congruence itself) through multiple vantage points and empirical and phenomenological methods. There is no one right way to be congruent. There is only a fluid process that appreciates one's self, others and the world as it is in that moment-to-moment encounter.

Seeman's organismic integration

Seeman's human systems approach to congruence (2001) developed Rogers' broader construct. This was more frequently termed 'organismic integration'. Whereas Rogers referred to experience, awareness and communication,

Seeman's system's approach extended this to multiple levels and processes: the biochemical, physiological, perceptual, precognitive, cognitive, interpersonal and ecological. These multiple levels and processes are linked through 'connection and communication'; the connection between the multiple levels and processes is the 'structure' whilst the 'communication' or 'resulting flow of information' between the different dimensions is the function. As a result multiple levels of the system mutually influence each other (2001: 204–6). Seeman conducted 25 studies, finding that organismic integration is characterized by a 'horizontal equalitarian style in contrast to a vertical status-oriented style of interpersonal behavior' (2001: 208–9). Similar to Rogers' extensionality, Seeman describes an important aspect of congruence as being 'to receive and process the reality data of [the person's] world'. Congruent people fully engage and extensionally respond to the world at every level of being and becoming.

Wyatt (2001, 2004), Haugh (2001), and Ellingham (2001) offer further elaborations of a holistic conception of congruence, where the process of connection and communication occurs across multiple levels. They each critique Rogers' less process-oriented conceptualization of congruence, which involves uncovering experience of which the person was unaware. Rather than involving pre-existing experience, Haugh clarifies that in congruence a process that is 'completely new has been created, not that something new (but already existing) has been perceived' (2001: 127). Congruence as this sort of emergence has clear roots in Rogers' process descriptions and Seeman's human systems conceptualizations beginning in the 1940s (Seeman, 2001). However, it is particularly difficult to articulate and maintain, given the prevailing cultural, linear paradigm grounded in our language. Presence offers a possibly useful construct beyond our usual linear paradigmatic language that expresses the 'multi-faceted nature of congruence' (Wyatt, 2001: 79).

Congruence and presence

Congruence is sometimes believed to have evolved into (Adomaitis, 1992) or been consumed by (Greenberg and Geller, 2001) the concept of presence. In an interview with Baldwin (1987) at the end of his life, Rogers stated, 'Perhaps I have stressed too much the three basic conditions (congruence, unconditional positive regard and empathic understanding). Perhaps it is something around the edges of those conditions that is really the most important element of therapy – when my self is clearly, obviously present' (in Baldwin, 1987: 45).

Rogers also stated:

> I find that when I am closest to my inner, intuitive self, when I am somehow in touch with the unknown in me, when perhaps I am in a slightly altered state of consciousness, then whatever I do seems to be full of healing. Then, simply my presence ... [or the] transcendental core of me [in which] our relationship transcends itself and becomes a part of something larger ... [is where] profound growth and healing are present.
>
> (1980: 129)

Hence, a presence conceptualization of congruence refers to an authentic, empathic and unconditional integration involving both the intuitive and the transcendent. When this is truly present, spontaneous expressions of one's own transcendent person in connection with others are poignantly facilitative.

Autonomy-interconnectedness

The foundation of Rogers (1959) theory is the actualizing tendency, the inherent inclination 'to maintain and enhance the organism' (1959: 196). At one level, congruence is the process of actualization, or a person's 'development toward autonomy' (1959: 196). When internally integrated, a person moves away from being controlled by or controlling others. However, Rogers' later discussion of presence as transcendental implies moving beyond the limits of the individual. He introduced the formative tendency to explain this motivation beyond the individual toward interconnection. The formative tendency applies to both people and non-people and is a general inclination for things to develop and become more complicated and interactive. Rogers elucidates 'a formative directional tendency in the universe' (1978: 26) that 'exhibits itself as the individual moves from ... knowing and sensing below the level of consciousness, to a conscious awareness of the organism and the external world, to a transcendent awareness of the harmony and unity of the cosmic system, including humankind' (1980: 133). He also clarifies the motivational structure of the person-centred approach as 'an evolutionary tendency toward greater order, greater complexity, greater interrelatedness' (1980: 133).

Rogers did not see this change from an actualizing approach within therapy to a formative approach within the world as a shift, but instead as a deepening and extending, stating about client-centred therapy and the person-centred approach that they are not 'different in me' (Rogers et al, 2005: 394). Hence, the actualizing and formative tendencies taken together indicate that to be congruent means not only to be aware and integrated in autonomy but also in an ecological connection (Cornelius-White, in press). Similarly, Schmid summarizes congruence as the 'two unrenounceable dimensions of [authentic] human existence: the substantial or individual aspect of being a person and the relational or dialogical aspect of becoming a person' (2001: 214).

From theory to practice

Lietaer writes, 'Personal maturity, together with the basic clinical aptitudes related to it, can ... be considered as the therapist's main instrument in client-centred therapy' (2001: 41). When reduced to a simple construct in quantitative outcome studies, congruence appears 'probably effective' and has a more modest impact than empathy, respect or overall relationship (Cornelius-White, 2007; Klein et al, 2001). However, when viewed within the relationship from the client's perception of realness rather than an observer's, congruence is 'demonstrably effective' (Cornelius-White, 2002). Also, the outcome research suggests that 'it is the absence of incongruence and phoniness that contributes to good therapy' (Grafanaki, 2001: 20). Hence, at the most basic level, the practice of congruence is the practice of realness. Therapists aim to be real by first just not faking or playing a role. However, they develop personal maturity through practising and becoming a way of being that facilitates both themselves and others to live in a fully engaged process. This involves internal congruence, communication, a sense of flow, disciplined spontaneity, body awareness and an encounter stance to the world.

Internal congruence and communication

Rogers' internal congruence is based upon self-awareness, or accurate symbolization of experience. A congruent person is in a process of understanding and accepting each of his or her perceptions and reactions as they occur. In other words, a therapist has empathy and unconditional regard for his or her own experiencing. Therapist self-acceptance is hypothesized to lead to unconditional empathy towards others, and helps others to realize it within themselves.

At the most important level, congruence, like unconditional regard, is rarely communicated deliberately in words (Brodley, 1998/2001). People pick up on levels of congruence through body language far more than through words. In a contest of the 'do' vs. 'say' to figure out if someone is real or not, the 'do' almost always wins. Tepper and Haase (1978) found that empathy is twice as strongly communicated, respect is five times more communicated and congruence is 23 times more communicated by non-verbal cues than verbal ones. Hence, communicating congruence is primarily a non-verbal by-product of being internally congruent. Non-verbal communication is largely unconscious. Nevertheless, people are interpreted differently from the ways they intend, even when congruent, which is where live and videotaped supervision and encounter groups become helpful. Therapists can learn how they are perceived and become better at allowing their non-verbal communication to be accurately received.

However, there may be times when therapists more deliberately communicate their congruence verbally. Rogers writes that if a therapist is 'persistently focused on his [sic] own feelings rather than those of the client, thus greatly reducing or eliminating any experience of empathic understanding, or ... unconditional positive regard', the therapist should express his/her own feelings (1959: 214). Hence, if being distracted by one's own process is inhibiting empathy and understanding for another, it may be practical to express an aspect of one's own process.

Likewise, Rogers (1959) wrote that verbal communication of congruence occurs in such as way as to 'never contain an expression of an external fact ... [and is spoken] in a context of personal perception' (Rogers, 1961: 341). Therefore, deliberate communicative congruence often takes the form of an 'I statement' in which an internally accepted personal feeling or reaction is offered about an event that is consensually agreed to have happened (factual). A statement such as, 'I feel you are being unfair' does not include a personal perception or potentially factual explicit or implicit referent and is not likely to be an expression of congruence. The statement, 'I feel sad when I hear you speak about your mother' appears to be accepted by the therapist as an experience, does include a personal feeling (sadness), and a referent that the listener is likely to understand (speaking about mother). Practice in groups where encounter is possible and discussion in supervision are ways to develop the ability to express congruence through self-disclosures, which often take the form of 'I-statements.'

Congruence and flow

Being and becoming the process of congruence is sometimes described in practice as an experience of flow. Counsellors often describe 'their experience in relational terms, and placed particular emphasis on the therapeutic value of achieving a state of "flow", in which counsellor and client were congruent and co-present with [or encountering] each other' (Grafanaki, 2001: 30–1). Rogers stated that to be authentic, 'you have to feel entirely secure as a person ... [and] surrender yourself to a process' (in Baldwin, 1987: 50). Feeling 'secure as a person' means learning to accept both your own vulnerability and personal power. Through studies of peak and fulfilling experiences, Csikszentmihalyi (1998) described the concept of flow, and is responsible for popularising it. Csikszentmihalyi's flow has several characteristics that are similar to how the experience of congruence is sometimes described. Flow is characterized by clear preparation of goals. Greenberg and Geller (2001) term this aspect of congruence 'preparing the ground' or bracketing irrelevant experiences. If a therapist notices her hand twitching before a session and begins to reflect, thinking that she is usually quite comfortable with this particular client, she may realize that she is nervous about a presentation she will be giving later in the day. In this situation, she can recognize and hold this part of her experience in a way that removes it from the immediate situation and allows more of her to be present in the actual encounter she is about to enter.

Flow also includes a sense of concentration. Grafanaki (2001) describes the practice of congruence as being entirely focused upon the shared relational experience. Flow involves a loss of self-consciousness. Wyatt (2001: 92) discusses how self-consciousness fades in the transcendent congruent encounter experience. Bozarth (2001) terms the lack of self-consciousness of congruence as unconditional positive self-regard. Flow is feeling alive and feeling that experience as intrinsically rewarding. Greenberg and Geller (2001) portray the practice of congruence as being attuned to the experiences and meanings which are most poignant to the client.

Disciplined spontaneity

Another way to realize congruence is through the practice of 'disciplined spontaneity' (Lietaer, 2001). Rogers wrote, 'I believe it is the realness ... when the therapist is natural and *spontaneous* that he [sic] seems to be the most effective' (1967: 185, italics added). Hence, the realness aspect of congruence is not only the fundamental process of not being phoney, but also just being who one is. This is a matter not only of accurate symbolization but also of organismic integration, presence and flow. Rogers continues, 'The person who is able to openly be himself [sic] at that moment, as he [or she] is at the deepest levels he [or she] is able to be, is the effective therapist. Perhaps nothing else is of any importance' (1967: 186). Here, he suggests that congruence is a quality of free intuitive interaction of the psychologically mature. Hence, congruence evolved to include self-disclosure (Lietaer, 2001). Nevertheless, communication of congruence is also a 'trained humanness' (Rogers, 1967: 185). Expressing a 'natural reaction' to a client is fostered from empathy and unconditionality (1967: 185–6) and is 'embedded in a fundamental attitude of openness' (Lietaer, 2001: 47). Brodley clarifies: 'Communications of one's self ... takes care and discipline and self-control' (1998/2001: 74–5).

While disciplined spontaneity results in idiosyncratic, emergent styles unique to each practitioner (Bozarth, 1998; Keys, 2003), they most frequently emerge in situations where clients ask implicit or explicit questions or relate emotionally unusual or intense experiences (Brodley, 1998/2001). Brodley offers this example of a disciplined spontaneous response to an explicit client question:

C: What do you feel about what I have said?
T: You want to know my personal reaction about what you told me or about my reaction towards you?
C: Both, I guess. I'm afraid your feelings about me will be different now you know I do that. I'm afraid you're disgusted by me.
T: I don't feel disgusted at all. My feelings aren't changed. I do feel a deep sadness that you want to hurt yourself.
C: Don't you feel it's sick?
T: I don't feel that. My thought about it is it's something that has come out of your suffering. Although it hurts you, it also relieves you.

(Brodley, 1998/2001: 70–1)

In this example, three elements are present. The therapist offers personal perceptions that directly address the question, 'I don't feel disgusted' and 'My feelings are not changed', but also offers a spontaneous disclosure of her sadness and an empathic interpretation of dialectical aspects of the client's experience. It is also clear that an accepting, understanding, open attitude is present both in the attempt to first understand the request and in the tone of each therapist disclosure. The 'discipline', 'trained humanness', or integration of empathic acceptance and speaking from personal perception in congruent communications is present. Likewise present is the 'spontaneity' of an authentic self-disclosing affective (sadness) and cognitive (interpretation) response.

Bodily felt congruence

Another layer of the development and practice of congruence is bodily felt. Schmid asserts that counsellors need to 'pay attention to their clients' bodies, and their own bodies' and that congruence 'always includes the facilitation of their awareness of their body' (2001: 222–3). Mindful breathing is perhaps the oldest and most fundamental area of building mind–body awareness (breath is etymologically from the same root as spirit).

Hence, knowing and developing the therapist's person is a process of organismic, or mind–body–spirit integration. Furthermore, not only body awareness but body health is vital for the practice of congruence. Person-centred educational research has shown that aerobic health predicts a therapist's endurance in holding the conditions; those who are not physically fit often show a pattern of declining condition presence as the day and week progress (Rogers, 1983). Finally, as our body communicates congruence 23 times more strongly than our words, awareness of the communicative aspects of our non-verbal experience – particularly facial expression, vocal intonation, eye contact and body orientation – is salient for the practice and development of congruence (Grafanaki, 2001; Tepper and Haase, 1978).

In addition to the use of videotapes, live supervision or encounter groups described above, mindfulness meditation and training in basic non-verbal communication can be helpful. For example, these methods can foster an appreciation for what might be unintentionally communicated by the therapist who crosses her arms and tilts her head down when physically cold during a session:

C: I'm sorry I'm late.
T: That's ok. (Adjusts in seat, looks down while speaking, and crosses arms.)
C: (Goes quiet)
T: (Waits and wonders and then says) Are you ok?
C: Yes, I was going to ask the same about you. I thought you were angry with me for being late.
T: Why would you say that?
C: I don't know. I just thought you were. (Continues with her story but in a muted, hesitant way.)

Arms crossed is typically received by others as a defensive, closed, scared or angry position, while head tilted down is most often seen when people are absorbed in their own emotions, particularly of a sad tone. This short example illustrates how a therapist's unconscious non-verbal communication can influence the therapeutic relationship. The feedback process of reflecting in yoga as to how people feel in different positions, being told in an encounter group or advised in supervision – all could enhance their sense of how they and others experience them non-verbally.

The authentic encounter stance

Rogers writes that the practice of 'therapy has to do with the [authentic] relationship, and has relatively little to do with techniques or with the theory and ideology' (1967: 185). In other words, ultimately, therapy is a connection between persons, and congruence is an authentic encounter stance that allows this connection to unfold. Schmid declares, the 'only legitimate "techne" (the original Greek word which means "art") is im-mediacy, or im-media-te presence (presence without media), in other words, the encounter person to person' (2001: 224). This stance allows for therapist and client to be mutually vulnerable and influenced. Authenticity is not intentionally persuasive. Congruent therapists develop a tendency to calmly tolerate a degree of ambiguity and discomfort and do not 'ask anything more of the client than to also be present' (Greenberg and Geller, 2001: 148). In essence, 'therapy is a process to overcome preconceived techniques and methods (which always come in between humans) by making them superfluous' within the authentic encounter (Schmid, 2001: 224). In the end, the practice of congruence is the lived experience of the authentic relationship encounter.

Reflections for the future: becoming the change you want to see in the world

When congruence is understood as a multi-level construct of integration from the intrapersonal to the interconnected, this suggests that one must engage culture to develop congruence and become the change you want to see in the world. Schmid states that 'you cannot reflect on being congruent if you don't experience and consider diversity' (2001: 218). Grafanaki concurs that there is 'a need for greater understanding of the possible influence of culture on the experience, expression and reception of congruence' (2001: 33). Culture is a pervasive element of persons' experience shaping the very way they symbolize their experience. For example, Ellingham asserts that feelings and thoughts that comprise congruence are 'always a social construction, very much a product of our cultural values and language' (2001: 106). The author has discussed how multicultural issues impact on the approach, especially surrounding individualistic interpretations and implicit cultural conditioning (Cornelius-White, 2003, 2006c, in press; Cornelius-White and Godfrey, 2004).

Hence, understanding the pluralistic world is necessary to practise this broader construct of congruence. For example, Rogers (1977) begins his book on cultural politics by deconstructing the use of masculine pronouns to refer to people. In this way, he provides an example of increased cultural congruence. He also writes about 'subtle ways of communicating' 'contradictory messages' (1961: 51) belying a lack of congruence (Cornelius-White, 2006c). Merry offers a more clinical example: 'a therapist, whose self-picture incorporates the notion that he or she is entirely free of prejudice, would experience some level of anxiety when confronted by a client of a different ethnic group ... [and] would find difficulty in allowing prejudice feelings into awareness' (2001: 179). Wyatt offers a personal testimony, 'I know I have prejudices, I know I am privileged by being white, hetero-sexual, able-bodied and middle class' (2004: 8). In other words, the impact of a pluralistic world on understanding congruence is under-appreciated. Persons understand their seemingly autonomous experience through their implicit relationships and interconnectedness to culturally similar and different others. The future of congruence is tied to understanding, integrating and encountering culture

In conclusion, it is our 'response-ability' to respond and fully engage the world at every level of our being and becoming (Schmid, 2001: 217). The practice of congruence leads to a sense of acceptance, understanding and integration from the internal to the relational and ecological. In this way, congruence is the core condition of the person-centred approach, realized not only or most importantly in therapy, but in our every action. It is 'obvious that the approach needs further development towards a truly social approach' and to 'authentically implement the essence of it into all fields of life' (Schmid, 2001: 226; see also Proctor et al, 2006). Congruent people engage themselves in awareness, others in encounter, and the world with extensionality. As Rogers (1983: 104) and Cornelius-White (2006a, 2006b) have asserted, the approach will play 'a vital role in the survival of people and other organisms within the world' (Cornelius-White, 2006b: 15). Congruence is being and becoming the change you want to see in the world.

REFERENCES

Adomaitis, R. (1992). On being genuine: a phenomenologically grounded study of the experience of genuineness and its place in client-centered psychotherapy. Unpublished dissertation, Northwestern University, Evanston, Il.

Baldwin, M. (1987). Interview with Carl Rogers on the use of the self in therapy. In M. Baldwin and V. Satir (eds), *The Use of Self in Therapy* (pp. 45–52). New York: Haworth.

Bozarth, J.D. (1998). *Person-Centered Therapy: a revolutionary paradigm.* Ross-on-Wye: PCCS.

Bozarth, J.D. (2001). Congruence: a special way of being. In G. Wyatt (ed.), Rogers' *Therapeutic Conditions: evolution, theory, and practice.* Volume 1. *Congruence* (pp. 184–99). Ross-on-Wye: PCCS.

Brodley, B.T. (1998/2001). Congruence and its relationship to communication in client-centered therapy. *Person-Centered Journal*, 5(2), 83–116, and in G. Wyatt (ed.), Rogers' *Therapeutic Conditions: evolution, theory, and practice* (pp. 55–78). Volume 1. *Congruence*. Ross-on-Wye: PCCS.

Cornelius-White, J.H.D. (2002). The phoenix of empirically supported therapy relationships: the overlooked person-centered basis. *Psychotherapy*, 39, 219–22.

Cornelius-White, J.H.D. (2003) Person-centered multicultural counseling: rebutted critiques and revisited goals. *Person-Centered Practice*, 11(1), 3–11.

Cornelius-White, J.H.D. (2006a) *Environmental Responsibility: a social justice mandate for counselors.* Manuscript submitted for publication.

Cornelius-White, J.H.D. (2006b). *A Review and Evolution of Rogers' Theory of Education.* Manuscript submitted for publication.

Cornelius-White, J.H.D. (2006c). Cultural congruence: subtle veil of whiteness and patriarchy. *Person-Centred Quarterly*, May, 4–6.

Cornelius-White, J.H.D. (2007). Learner-centered teacher-student relationships are effective: a meta-analysis. *Review of Educational Research*, 77, 113–43.

Cornelius-White, J.H.D. (in press). The actualizing and formative tendencies: prioritizing the motivational constructs of the person-centered approach. *Person-Centered and Experiential Psychotherapies.*

Cornelius-White, J.H.D., and Cornelius-White, C.F. (2005). Trust builds learning: context and effectiveness of nondirectivity in education. In B. Levitt (ed.), *Embracing Nondirectivity: reassessing theory and practice in the twenty-first century* (pp. 314–23). Ross-on-Wye: PCCS.

Cornelius-White, J.H.D. and Godfrey, P. (2004). Pedagogical crossroads: integrating feminist critical pedagogies and the person-centred approach to education. In G. Proctor and M. Napier (eds), *Encountering Feminism: intersections between feminism and the person-centred approach* (pp. 166–78). Ross-on-Wye: PCCS.

Csikszentmihalyi, Mihaly (1998). *Finding Flow: the psychology of engagement with everyday life.* New York: Basic.

Ellingham, I. (2001). Carl Rogers' congruence as an organismic; not a Freudian concept. In G. Wyatt (ed.), *Rogers' Therapeutic Conditions: evolution, theory, and practice.* Volume 1. *Congruence* (pp. 96–115). Ross-on-Wye: PCCS.

Grafanaki, S. (2001). What counseling research has taught us about the concept of congruence: main discoveries and unresolved issues. In G. Wyatt (ed.), *Rogers' Therapeutic Conditions: evolution, theory, and practice.* Volume 1. *Congruence* (pp. 18–35). Ross-on-Wye: PCCS.

Greenberg, L.S. and Geller, S. (2001). Congruence and therapeutic presence. In G. Wyatt (ed.), *Rogers' Therapeutic Conditions: evolution, theory, and practice.* Volume 1. *Congruence* (pp. 131–49). Ross-on-Wye: PCCS.

Haugh, S. (2001). The difficulties in the conceptualization of congruence: a way forward with complexity theory? In G. Wyatt (ed.), *Rogers' Therapeutic Conditions: evolution, theory, and practice.* Volume 1. *Congruence* (pp. 116–49). Ross-on-Wye: PCCS.

Keys, S. (ed.) (2003). *Idiosyncratic Person-Centred Therapy.* Ross-on-Wye: PCCS.

Klein, M.H., Michels, J.L., Kolden, G.G. and Chrisolm-Stockard, S. (2001). Congruence or genuineness. *Psychotherapy*, 38, 396–400.

Lietaer, G. (2001). Being genuine as a therapist: congruence and transparency. In G. Wyatt (ed.), *Rogers' Therapeutic Conditions: evolution, theory, and practice.* Volume 1. *Congruence* (pp. 36–54). Ross-on-Wye: PCCS.

Merry, T. (2001). Congruence and the supervision of client-centered therapists. In G. Wyatt (ed.), *Rogers' Therapeutic Conditions: evolution, theory, and practice* (pp. 174–83). Volume 1. *Congruence.* Ross-on-Wye: PCCS.

Proctor, G., Cooper, M., Sanders, P. and Malcolm, B. (eds) (2006). *Politicizing the Person-Centred Approach: an agenda for social change.* Ross-on-Wye: PCCS.

Rogers, C.R. (1946). Significant aspects of client-centered therapy. *American Psychologist*, 10, 415–22.

Rogers, C.R. (1951). *Client-Centred Therapy.* London: Constable.

Rogers, C.R. (1957). The necessary and sufficient conditions of therapeutic personality change. *Journal of Consulting Psychology*, 21, 95–103.

Rogers, C.R. (1959). A theory of therapy, personality, and interpersonal relationship as developed in the client-centered framework. In S. Koch (ed.),

Psychology: a study of science. Volume 3. *Formulations of the person and the social context* (pp.184–256). New York: McGraw Hill.

Rogers, C.R. (1961). *On Becoming a Person: a therapist's view of psychotherapy*. London: Constable.

Rogers, C.R. (1967). Some learnings from a study of psychotherapy with schizophrenics. In C.R. Rogers and B. Stevens (eds), *Person to Person* (pp. 181–91). Lafayette, Calif.: real People.

Rogers, C.R. (1977). *Carl Rogers on Personal Power*. New York: Dell Publishing.

Rogers, C.R. (1978). The formative tendency. *Journal of Humanistic Psychology*, 18, 23–6.

Rogers, C.R. (1980). *A Way of Being*. Boston: Houghton Mifflin.

Rogers, C.R. (1983). *Freedom to learn for the 80s*. Columbus, Ohio: Charles E. Merrill Publishing.

Rogers, C.R., Cornelius-White, J. H.D. and Cornelius-White, C.F. (2005). Reminiscing and Predicting: Rogers's Beyond Words Speech and Commentary. *Journal of Humanistic Psychology*, 45, 383–96.

Schmid, P.F. (2001). Authenticity: the person as his or her own author: dialogical and ethical perspectives on therapy as an encounter relationship. And beyond. In G. Wyatt (ed.), *Rogers' Therapeutic Conditions: evolution, theory, and practice*. Volume 1. *Congruence* (pp. 213–28). Ross-on-Wye: PCCS.

Seeman, J. (2001). On congruence: a human system paradigm. In G. Wyatt (ed.), *Rogers' Therapeutic Conditions: evolution, Theory, and Practice* Volume 1. *Congruence* (pp. 200–12). Ross-on-Wye: PCCS.

Sherer, M. and Rogers, R. (1980). Effects of therapist's nonverbal communication on rated skill and effectiveness. *Journal of Clinical Psychology*, 36, 233–6.

Tepper, D. and Haase, R. (1978). Effects of non-verbal communication of facilitative conditions. *Journal of Counseling Psychology*, 25, 200–4.

Wyatt, G. (2001). The multifaceted nature of congruence within the therapeutic relationship. In G. Wyatt (ed.), *Rogers' Therapeutic Conditions: evolution, Theory, and Practice* Volume 1. *Congruence* (pp. 79–95). Ross-on-Wye: PCCS.

Wyatt, G. (2001). Congruence: a synthesis and implications. In G. Wyatt (ed.), *Rogers' Therapeutic Conditions: evolution, theory, and practice*. Volume 1. *Congruence* (pp. 229–40). Ross-on-Wye: PCCS.

Wyatt, G. (2004). Widening circles: an exploration of congruence, identity and diversity. Keynote address at BAPCA Conference, Loughborough University, UK.

Unconditional Positive Regard

14

Jerold Bozarth

A major tenet of Carl Rogers' theory of therapy is that individuals have a 'need for positive regard' (Rogers, 1959: 208). It is the congruent therapist's experiencing of unconditional positive regard (UPR) toward the client along with empathic understanding of the client's internal frame of reference that precipitates therapeutic personality change.

The core concepts

An examination of UPR must be considered within the context of the 'conditions of the therapeutic process' (Rogers, 1959: 213), also referred to as the 'necessary and sufficient conditions' (1957). These conditions guide therapeutic practice in Rogers' theory of therapy (see Chapter 1, this volume).

History

The therapist's attitude of acceptance and respect (Rogers, 1951: 41) was the forerunner of unconditional positive regard (Rogers, 1959: 208). The inclusion and operational definitions of the concepts – positive regard and unconditional positive regard – clarified and concretized the theory (Bozarth, 2001a: 5).

In his book *Client-Centered Therapy*, Rogers (1951) set forth the attitude and orientation of the client-centred therapist. He also set forth a theory of personality and behaviour that included the 19 propositions introduced in Chapter 2 of this volume. In 1951, the premise for UPR was set as the therapist's perception of the 'client's self as the client has known it, and accepts it', with the caveat that 'the therapist accepts the contradictory aspects as part of the client with the same warmth and respect' (1951: 41). Hence, the client is 'enabled to do this [integrate his self-concept] ... because another person has been able to adopt his frame of reference, to perceive with him, yet to perceive with acceptance and respect' (1951: 41). Acceptance and respect evolves to become UPR in 1959. Rogers' theory of personality describes the central role of UPR in the section on 'The process of reintegration' (Rogers, 1959). There must be a decrease in the conditions of worth and there must be an increase in unconditional self-regard in order for reintegration to be possible. Communicated UPR is 'one way of achieving these conditions' (1959: 230).

Client-centred theory was evolving even as the 1951 book was published. Standal was working on and in 1954 completed his dissertation that focused on positive regard and unconditional positive regard. Rogers (1959) delineated the core of Standal's postulates in the 1959 theory, and adopted Standal's term unconditional positive regard. The need for positive regard was considered as a basic learned secondary need of individuals, usually developed in infancy.

Prior to Standal's dissertation, Oliver Bown contended that 'love' was what the therapist offered to and received from clients. Bown argued that love was communicated 'primarily at subverbal, subliminal or subconscious levels' (Rogers, 1951: 161). Bown's belief about the communication of 'love' is referred to in the theory (Rogers, 1959: 213) but became less obvious than Standal's constructs, which were more explicitly incorporated into client-centred theory.

Unconditional positive regard became an identified and integral part of client-centred therapy in Rogers' (1959) self-proclaimed magnum opus. Rogers considered the term to be more precise than such terms as love and affection that were used by others who proposed such needs as inherent traits (Rogers, 1959: 208).

The need for positive regard became central to the theory. Rogers adopted Standal's literal definition of positive regard as stated below:

> If the perception by me of some self-experience in another makes a positive difference in my experiential field, then I am experiencing positive regard for that individual. In general, positive regard is defined as including such attitudes as warmth, liking, respect, sympathy, and acceptance. To perceive oneself as receiving positive regard is to experience oneself as making a difference in the experiential field of another.
>
> (Rogers, 1959: 206)

Thus, one major assumption in the theory of 'client-centred therapy' (classical person-centred therapy) was established. Unconditional positive regard is defined more generally as: 'a warm acceptance of each aspect of the client's experience' (Rogers, 1959). Theoretically, unconditional positive regard occurs when the client perceives that he or she is making a consistent positive difference in the experiential field of the therapist.

The theory statement

The explanation of 'pathology' in Rogers' theory is that the client becomes *incongruent*, being vulnerable or anxious, due to 'conditions of worth' or 'from introjections' by significant others. The individual's conditions of worth develop into conditional positive self-regard (see Chapter 7, this volume). It is when conditional positive regard conflicts with the individual's organismic experiences that the person becomes incongruent. The corrective factor for the development of conditional positive regard is that the client perceives the therapist's unconditional positive regard. It is the client's perception of that unconditional positive regard offered through empathic understanding that facilitates the client's unconditional positive *self*-regard.

Unconditional positive regard is the factor that frees the client from 'conditions of worth' (Rogers, 1959: 224). It is the facilitation of freedom from 'introjected values', resulting in the incorporation of organismic experiences into the self-structure, that promotes the client's congruence of self with his or her organismic experiences; subsequently, aligned with the actualizing tendency.

Divergence of views

There are differing views of UPR among advocates of person-centred therapies. These views are reflected, on one side, by the assertions that UPR is the 'curative' factor in person-centred therapy (Bozarth, 2001a) and 'the distinct feature of client-centred therapy' (Freire, 2001). On the other side, UPR has also been argued to be a 'crucial' but impossible task for the therapist (Lietaer, 1984, 2001). The 'classical' view holds closely to Rogers' theory (Rogers, 1959). The other 'person-centred therapies' (post-classical) adhere to more focused activity by the therapist in addition to valuing the conditions espoused by Rogers. This group offers different theoretical thrusts and places less importance on UPR as constructed in the theory. Among these person-centred therapies are focusing-experiential therapy (Gendlin, 1974; Hendricks, 2001; Iberg, 2001) or focusing-oriented therapy (Purton, 2004), eclectic/experiential therapy (Lietaer, 2001), process-experiential therapy (Elliott and Greenberg, 2002), and clarification-oriented psychotherapy (Sachse, 2004). The integrative and existential positions have more complex relationships to Rogers' theory.

Bozarth (1998, 2001a), a representative of the classical view, argues that UPR is the 'the curative variable', asserting it can be no other way, since Rogers' 'theory of pathology' points to 'conditional positive regard' as the condition that creates the client's incongruence. *Unconditional* positive regard communicated through empathic understanding is in and of itself the curative factor that frees the client to integrate with the experiences of the organism. Thus, organismic and self-experiences ultimately become integrally aligned with the actualizing tendency.

Bozarth (2001a) proposed that this is Rogers' (1959) theory and that to ignore this underlying assumption results in radical changes of Rogers' theory of therapy by the post-classical person-centred therapies. With emphasis on the nature of Rogers' theory, he offered the following reconceptualization of the three therapist conditions:

- congruence as the state of therapist readiness
- empathic understanding as the conveyor of unconditional positive regard
- unconditional positive regard as the 'curative factor'.

(Bozarth 1998: 47)

Freire captures the theoretical nature of UPR in relation to the foundation block of the classical view when she states: 'The greater the extent the therapist trusts the client's actualizing tendency, the greater her capacity to experience unconditional positive regard towards the client' (2001: 147).

The primary difference between Rogers' (1959) theory of therapy (the 'classical approach' in this chapter) and other person-centred therapies (PCT or postclassical) is that most of the post-classical PCTs do not accept the 'necessary and sufficient conditions' as 'sufficient'. In the post-classical PCTs, the therapist often becomes an agent who promotes additional activities and processes that are viewed as facilitating growth. Therapists have intentions to influence clients in a particular way, and are explicit about process directivity (Brodley, in press).

Lietaer (2001) presents a multi-dimensional concept comprised of

- *Positive regard*: the affective attitude of the therapist toward the client.
- *Non-directivity*: an attitude of non-manipulation of the client.
- *Unconditionality*: constancy in accepting the client.

Lietaer offers a more 'precise definition' of 'unconditionality' as the therapist 'valuing the deeper core of the person, what she potentially is and can become' (2001: 92–3). He concludes with a compatible conceptualization with the classical view by indicating that UPR 'helps the client to become more innerdirected, more trusting of his organismic experience as a compass for living and hence to become a better "therapist for himself"' (2001: 105). The two views differ as to just how this is to be accomplished. Lietaer differs from the classical view in his more explicit notion that the therapist's task is that of attempting to 'maximize the experiential process of the client' (2001: 99).

Lietaer summarizes the sentiments of many 'client-centred/experiential' adherents when he claims that 'confrontational interventions have increasingly obtained a place within client-centred therapy' (2001: 99). Even though Lietaer (2001) and other PCT authors (Hendricks, 2001; Iberg, 2001) advocate an instrumental use of UPR as a way of preparing clients for 'real' therapy, there is general compatibility with the classical approach in adherence to respect for the client's self-direction. However, the fact remains that there is a substantially different view of UPR by post-classical therapies in relation to Rogers' theory of therapy. These different views have implications for practice.

Research

Quantitative research on unconditional positive regard within the personcentred paradigm has generally been examined along with the other 'necessary and sufficient conditions'. Studies of unconditional positive regard as a separate variable are quite sparse. Research on unconditional positive regard has been considered to be: 'conceptually difficult to handle as a single variable' (Barrett-Lennard, 1998: 81).

In a critique of research reviews, Patterson (1984) re-evaluated and summarized the research studies on the core conditions, including those on UPR, to conclude that there is strong evidence for the therapist conditions as necessary and sufficient. Later reviews reiterate this conclusion (Bozarth et al, 2002; Page et al, 2002; Watson and Steckley, 2001).

Another examination of quantitative research reviews is moderately supportive. These authors conclude that there is 'considerable variance in the findings linking positive regard to outcome' (Farber and Lane, 2002: 192). Their assessment is that positive regard seems to be associated with therapeutic success; however, they find that the effect sizes are modest. Hence, they conclude that UPR 'is a significant but not exhaustive part of the process-outcome equation' (2002: 191). Their conclusions are somewhat clouded by the focus on positive regard rather than upon UPR, and by the insertion of research not associated with Rogers' theory. Constructs from other therapeutic premises include 'therapeutic support', 'therapeutic alliance', and 'client affirmation', resulting in a murky mixture of other theoretical stances in relation to Rogers' hypothesis.

Watson and Steckley conclude that there is 'a wealth of information that points to the potency of UPR as well as to other relationship conditions in promoting healthy development and growth' (2001: 193). This is an important conclusion, in that the authors consider some of the major problems of measuring and examining the concept. The quantitative research studies demonstrate the importance and validity of the concept. However, the authors also point out that such studies do not adequately allow study of the interactive influences between therapist and client or capture the essence of non-linear relationships. They suggest that qualitative research is also needed.

In general more systematic controlled designs, improved measurements and more consistent operational definitions are needed in quantitative and qualitative research designs. The many therapy transcripts examined by Rogers and colleagues since the beginning of client-centred therapy are actually qualitative examinations of what goes on in therapy (Farber et al, 1996). However, they generally do not refer to particular qualitative research designs.

Brodley and Schneider (2001) provide transcripts by Rogers to demonstrate UPR communicated through verbal behaviour. The power of the empathic understanding response (EUR) as acceptance of the client's frame of reference implies the total acceptance of the client. They also point out that 'acceptance' (or unconditional positive regard) is communicated indirectly through the therapist's impartial, whole expressions and through syntax, choice of words and general manner of communication, perhaps most easily understood as the non-verbal behaviour and the presence of the therapist. Tone of voice and body language are noted as conveyers in non-verbal behaviour. Unconditional acceptance is also communicated 'by the absence of certain kinds of communications from the therapist's frame of reference' (2001: 155), such as interpretations, leading questions, confrontations and suggestions.

Other qualitative studies often examine client perceptions. These generally suggest the positive effects of clients feeling understood, accepted, self-validated and feeling safe to self-disclose (Bachelor, 1988; Freire, 2001; Freire et al, 2005).

From theory to practice

The translation of the concept of unconditional positive regard into practice varies between, and among, the classical and the post-classical therapies. The person-centred therapies, including the classical approach, are all predicated on Rogers' theoretical assumption that it is the client who has the capacity and resources to resolve his or her own problems. The classical approach honours this assumption through emphasis on the 'qualities of the relationship between client and counsellor' (Merry, 2004: 30).

Post-classical person-centred therapies also honour the assumption of client self-direction through the qualities of the relationship, but there are also intentions to direct, guide and encourage clients toward particular experiences that are deemed therapeutic by the therapist (Brodley, in press). These differences have implications for the role of UPR in the person-centred therapies.

Rogers' 'instructions' to therapists in his 'Conditions of the Therapeutic Process' are that the therapist be congruent in the relationship and should not only be experiencing unconditional positive regard toward the client but also be experiencing empathic understanding (EU) of the client's inner frame of reference. To be accurate, therapist congruence includes the experiencing of UPR and EU. The delineation of the two conditions as separate variables implies that UPR and EU are compatible conditions that do not have to be integrated. However, Rogers seldom, if ever, discussed empathy (used interchangeably with empathic understanding) without referring to UPR or synonyms such as 'warmth', 'acceptance', or 'prizing' (Bozarth, 2001b: 145).

Rogers consistently offered high percentages of empathic understanding responses in his therapy sessions. The preponderance of empathic responses conveys acceptance of the person by operationally removing judgemental communications and efforts to influence the client's direction.

An example that might illustrate the sufficiency of unconditional positive regard is one that involved a woman who was a client with me nearly 25 years ago. I (Bozarth, 1984) wrote about our sessions over 20 years ago. She was a graduate student who asked to enter therapy with me because she 'wanted to be'. Generally, three scenarios of behaviour took place over the sessions. First, she often walked around the large office, walking on chairs and the table, expressing herself with statements such as 'I want to beeeeee [buzzing like a bumblebee]. I want to beeee freeee.' My *experiencing* was that of her being free during those moments. I could imagine myself saying something like: 'Free like a bumble bee', but I am not sure that I actually made that statement. Second, she would go into what can be described as a 'catatonic' state. She would sit motionlessly in silence for an hour or longer, then suddenly get up and leave saying, 'Thank you'. I would mumble something now and then, depending upon my anxiety level. Otherwise, I would sit in silence with her. Third, I found that I sometimes entered her fantasies. She once fantasized going around the building on a homicidal binge. She would use a bee-bee gun, a rifle and a shotgun to go from office to office. I joined her fantasy, imagined walking around the building with her, and even carrying one of her weapons. While I might say something like, 'blood all over THAT white shirt', I was experiencing her wish to rid herself of all critics.

She discontinued therapy when she graduated and moved to another city. We saw each other several years ago. She said that she was happy and successful. She was planning to return to graduate school to work on a doctorate and, concomitantly, to start her own counselling practice. Briefly, we discussed our therapy sessions. She said of her sessions with me that she had 'never felt so confirmed and unconditionally accepted before' and that made a difference in her life.

The following scenario emphasizes UPR as being 'sufficient' as an intrinsic attitude of the therapist in the interaction.

Freire (2001) discusses therapy interactions with 'Rita'. Rita was a 45-year-old Brazilian housewife who came to therapy because she had a fear of water. She would not drink or wash her head with it. She wanted the therapist to resolve her problem for her. The unique relationship of the therapist experiencing unconditional positive regard is explained:

> I only 'walked' with her, following her self-direction, going with her at her own pace. I trusted her self-determination. I did not try to diminish her desperation, fear or powerless feelings. To the extent that I was fully present with her as she experienced these feelings, I accepted the feelings. It was never my intention to change her or her feelings. ... To me, her panic; her desperation and depression were acceptable parts of her. ...
>
> Rita lost her fear of water after the first few weeks of therapy. Four months after coming to therapy, Rita decided to stop therapy. She had 'deeply changed her personality, opening herself to feelings of fear and vulnerability. She discontinued forcing herself to be so powerful and strong.' ... [Rita] was more open to others and improved the quality of her interpersonal relationships.
>
> (Freire, 2001: 146, 147)

Freire's sessions with Rita depict a classical therapist's effort to place no constraints upon the client. She maintains her presence as total receptivity of the client's frame of reference, never attempting to resolve the client's problem or counter her powerless feelings. She accepts the client at all levels while 'experiencing a warm acceptance of each aspect of the client's experience being a part of the client' (Rogers, 1957: 100). It was with UPR being the distinct feature of her therapy that Rita was able to reintegrate previously denied experiences into her way of being in the world.

Self-instructions for therapists interpreted directly from Rogers (1959) theory of therapy would be something like the following:

- Be congruent in the relationship. Maximize your own unconditional positive *self*-regard. It is ultimately the therapist's psychological development that enables the therapist to create an atmosphere of unconditional positive regard to be perceived by the client. This is accomplished through the relationship with others who provide unconditional positive regard.

- Maximize your attitude of UPR through your empathic experiencing of the client. Focus extensively on the frame of reference of the client. Keep asking yourself, 'What is it like for this person?' It is when the client realizes that the therapist thoroughly understands and accepts the 'good, bad and the ugly' of her frame of reference that the client is free to accept him/herself with unconditional positive self regard.
- Trust the client to develop her own direction at her own pace, and in her own way. This requires letting go of pre-suppositions of what might or should happen in any given session.

Critical reflections for the future

Critical reflections for the future lie in the differences between unconditional positive regard (as interrelated with Rogers other five conditions) being viewed as 'sufficient' or 'not sufficient'. When UPR is not considered sufficient, the thrust of therapy is shifted to 'something more' that consists of either specific techniques or some form of therapist guidance/direction/intervention that replaces UPR as the central therapeutic factor. A critical question for the theory and practice of Rogers' theory of therapy is raised: is unconditional positive regard the 'curative' factor in Rogers' theory? My contention is that UPR as the curative factor is the only valid conclusion if one accepts the theory of 'client-centred therapy', as expressed by Rogers (1959). Acceptance of this 'fact' leads to other considerations for the future. For example: 1) Is it unconditional positive *self*-regard of the therapist during the relationship that reflects unconditional positive regard toward the client and enables the client to develop unconditional positive self-regard? And 2) Is it, in fact, unconditional positive self-regard of the therapist that stimulates therapist congruence? Or, possibly, is unconditional positive self-regard synonymous with congruence?

One consideration for the future might lie in the definition of *positive regard* as making a difference in the experiential field of the therapist that is stimulated by the client's self-experiences. The unconditional positive regard of the therapist is not that of applying or offering or using UPR toward the client. The therapist is experiencing and receiving the client in a way that makes a positive difference to the therapist. This is more than the acceptance of the client's experience, feelings and cognition at any given time. It is more than the 'willingness for the client to be whatever immediate feeling is going on'. It means that the experiencing therapist is 'receiv[ing] in the organism the impact of the sensory or physiological events which are happening at the moment' (Rogers, 1959: 197) including 'more complete and accurate symbolization' (1959: 196). The therapist is more than a passive, interested and understanding individual. The experiential world of the client 'makes a positive difference' in the therapist's experiential field. The therapist is affected positively by the client's self experiences. Subsequently, the therapist does like, prize, respect 'all' aspects of the client. This reverberates with Bown's thesis that the process of therapy is 'synonymous with the experiential relationship between client and therapist' (Rogers, 1951). It may also be consistent with the view that the therapist should attend to his or her own experiences in the interaction with clients (Hendricks, 2001).

CONCLUSION

The client's perception of unconditional positive regard communicated through empathic understanding by a congruent therapist is the crux of Rogers' theory. These therapist conditions (along with the contact between therapist and client, the client's incongruence, and the client's perception of the therapist's attitudes) are 'necessary and sufficient' for therapeutic personality change. No other conditions are needed. It is clear from Rogers' (1959) theory of therapy that the thrust of the therapy is 'to create a climate where there are no constraints upon the client and therefore they are able to reintegrate previously denied experiences into their way of being in the world' (Baker, 2004). This climate is created by the client's perception of the congruent therapist's experiencing of unconditional positive regard and empathic understanding.

Generally, the role of UPR in the post-classical person-centred therapies is the following:

- First, it is considered preliminary in that it is 'a safety-inducing element of the relational context within which the real therapeutic work is then accomplished' (Lietaer, 2001: 104).
- Second, it is dependent, in large part, on the client's level of experiencing (Purton, 2004: 49). The post-classical therapies, although valuing the client's view of the world and the client's self-direction, do not consider the conditions to be sufficient. Thus, UPR has a different role in the therapeutic process.

Despite the significant commonalities that are present among the person-centred therapies, a tension exists in relation to whether the core conditions, especially unconditional positive regard, are necessary and sufficient. As noted, this has implications for therapeutic practice.

The critical reflections for the future that cut across all of the person-centred therapies are (1) the determination of whether or not unconditional positive regard is the 'curative factor'; and (2) the extent to which the client is able to pursue his or her own direction, pace and way.

REFERENCES

Bachelor, A. (1988). How clients perceive therapist empathy: a content analysis of perceived empathy. *Psychotherapy*, 26, 372–9.

Baker, N. (2004). Experiential person-centred therapy. In P. Sanders (ed.), *The Tribes of the Person-Centred Nation: an introduction to the schools of therapy related to the person-centred approach* (pp. 67–94).Ross-on-Wye: PCCS Books.

Barrett-Lennard, G.T. (1998). *Carl Roger' Helping System: journey and substance*. London: Sage.

Bozarth, J.D. (1984). Beyond reflection: emergent modes of empathy. In R. Levant and J. Shlein (eds), *Client-Centered Therapy and the Person-Centred Approach: new directions in theory, research, and practice*. New York: Praeger: 59–75.

Bozarth, J.D. (1998). *Person-Centered Therapy: a revolutionary paradigm*. Ross-on-Wye: PCCS Books.

Bozarth, J.D. (2001a). Client-centered unconditional positive regard: A historical perspective. In J. Bozarth and P. Wilkins (eds), *UPR: Unconditional Positive Regard* (pp. 5–18). Ross-on-Wye: PCCS Books.

Bozarth, J.D. (2001b). An addendum to beyond reflection: emergent modes of empathy. In S. Haugh and T. Merry (eds), *Empathy* (pp. 144–54). Ross-On Wye: PCCS Books.

Bozarth, J.D. (2005). Non-directive person-centred groups: facilitation of freedom and personal power. In B.E. Levitt (ed.), *Embracing Non-Directivity*. Ross-on-Wye: PCCS Books: 281–302.

Bozarth, J.D., Zimring, F., and Tausch, R. (2002). Client-centered therapy: evolution of a revolution. In D. Cain and J. Seeman (eds), *Handbook of Humanistic Psychotherapy: research and practice*. Washington, DC: American Psychological Association: 147–80

Brodley, B.T. (in press). Directive and non-directive therapies in the person-centred community. *Person-Centred and Experiential Psychotherapies*.

Brodley, B.T. and Schneider, C. (2001). Unconditional positive regard as communicated through verbal behaviour in client-centred therapy. In J. Bozarth and P. Wilkins (eds), *Unconditional Positive Regard* (pp. 5–18). Ross-on-Wye: PCCS Books.

Elliott, R. and Greenberg, S. (2002). Process-experiential psychotherapy. In D. Cain and J. Seeman (eds), *Humanistic Psychotherapies: handbook of research and practice*. Washington D.C.: American Psychological Association.

Farber, B.A., Brink, D.C. and Raskin, P.M. (1996). *The Psychology of Carl Rogers: cases and commentary*. New York: Guilford Press.

Farber, B.A. and Lane, J.S. (2002). Positive regard. In J.C. Norcross (ed.), *Psychotherapist Relationships that Work* (pp. 175–94). Oxford: Oxford University Press.

Freire, E. (2001). Unconditional positive regard: the distinctive feature of client-centred therapy. In J. Bozarth and P. Wilkins (eds), *UPR: Unconditional Positive Regard* (pp. 145–54). Ross-on-Wye: PCCS Books.

Freire, E.S., Koller, S.H., Piason, A. and Silva, R.B. (2005). Person-centred therapy with impoverished, maltreated, and neglected children and adolescents in Brazil. *Journal of Mental Health Counselling*, 27(3), 225–37.

Gendlin, E.T. (1974). Client-centred and experiential psychotherapy. In D.A. Wexler and L.N. Rice (eds), *Innovations in Client-Centered Therapy* (pp. 211–46). New York: Wiley.

Hendricks, M.N. (2001). An experiential version of unconditional positive regard. In J. Bozarth and P. Wilkins (eds), *UPR: Unconditional Positive Regard* (pp. 126–44). Ross-on-Wye: PCCS Books.

Iberg, J.R. (2001). Unconditional positive regard: constituent activities. In J. Bozarth and P. Wilkins (eds), *UPR: Unconditional Positive Regard* (pp. 109–25). Ross-on-Wye: PCCS Books.

Lietaer, G (1984). Unconditional positive regard: a controversial basic attitude in client-centered therapy. In R. Levant and J. Shlien (eds), *Client-Centered Therapy and the Person-Centred Approach: new directions in theory, research, and practice* (pp. 41–58). New York: Praeger.

Lietaer, G (2001). Unconditional acceptance and positive regard. In J. Bozarth and P. Wilkins (eds), *UPR: Unconditional Positive Regard* (pp. 88–108). Ross-on-Wye: PCCS Books.

Merry, T. (2004). Classical client-centred therapy. In P. Sanders (ed.), *The Tribes of the Person-Centred Nation: an introduction to the schools of therapy related to the person-centred approach* (pp. 21–44). Ross-on-Wye: PCCS Books.

Page, R.C., Weiss, J.F. and Lietaer, G. (2002). Humanistic group psychotherapy. In D. Cain and J. Seeman (eds), *Handbook of Humanistic Psychotherapy: research and practice* (pp. 339–68). Washington D.C.: American Psychological Association.

Patterson, C.H. (1984). Empathy, warmth, and genuineness in psychotherapy: a review of reviews. *Psychotherapy*, 21(4), 431–8.

Purton, C. (2004). Focusing-oriented therapy. In P. Sanders (ed.), *The Tribes of the Person-Centred Nation: an introduction to the schools of therapy related to the person-centred approach* (pp. 45–65). Ross-on-Wye: PCCS Books.

Rogers, C.R. (1951). *Client-Centered Therapy: its current practice, implications, and theory*. Boston: Houghton Mifflin.

Rogers, C.R. (1956). The essence of psychotherapy: moments of movement. Paper given at the first meeting of the American Academy of Psychotherapists, New York, 20 October.

Rogers, C.R. (1957). The necessary and sufficient conditions of therapeutic personality change. *Journal of Consulting Psychology*, 21(2), 95–103.

Rogers, C.R. (1959). A theory of therapy, personality, and interpersonal relationships as developed in the client-centred framework. In S. Koch (ed.), *Psychology: a study of science*. Volume 3. *Formulations of the person and the social context* (pp. 184–256). New York: McGraw Hill.

Rogers, C.R. (1961). *On Becoming a Person: a therapist's view of psychotherapy*. Boston: Houghton Mifflin.

Rogers, C.R. (1964). Toward a science of the person. In T.W. Wann (ed.), *Behaviorism and Phenomenology* (pp. 104–40). Chicago: University of Chicago Press, Phoenix Books.

Sachse, R. (2004). From client-centred to clarification-oriented psychotherapy. *Person-Centred and Experiential Psychotherapies*, 3(1), 19–35.

Sanders, P. (2004). *The Tribes of the Person-Centred Nation: an introduction to the schools of therapy related to the person-centred approach*. Ross-on-Wye: PCCS Books.

Standal, S. (1954). *The Need for Positive Regard: a contribution to client-centred theory*. New York: Harper and Brothers.

Watson, J.C. and Steckley, P. (2001). Potentiating growth: an examination of the research on unconditional positive regard. In J. Bozarth and P. Wilkins (eds), *UPR: Unconditional Positive Regard* (pp. 180–97). Ross-on-Wye: PCCS Books.

CHAPTER 15

Empathy

Elizabeth S. Freire

Empathy is a core concept in the theory and practice of person-centred therapy. Rogers discovered in his very early years as a therapist that a therapeutic relationship is more effective the more completely the therapist tries to understand the client as the client seems to him or herself (Rogers, 1946). In the field of psychotherapy, where diagnostic knowledge is considered essential for effective therapy, this statement sounds as much like a heresy today as it sounded in the 1940s. In fact, Rogers provoked a revolutionary impact on the field of psychotherapy by requiring the therapist to 'lay aside his preoccupation with diagnosis and his diagnostic shrewdness' and to concentrate on providing an empathic understanding of the client's frame of reference.

Core concepts

Although the essence of the concept had been present since his early writings, the word 'empathy' was first introduced by Rogers only in 1951, in his book *Client-Centered Therapy*. There he described the role of the client-centred therapist as that of assuming:

> in so far as he is able, the internal frame of reference of the client, to perceive the world as the client sees it, to perceive the client himself as he is seen by himself, to lay aside all perceptions from the external frame of reference while doing so, and to communicate something of this empathic understanding to the client
>
> (Rogers, 1951: 29)

Empathy is presented then as a particular type of understanding, clearly distinct from the types of understanding that come from external frames of reference, such as psychodiagnosis. In Proposition VII of his 1951 theory of personality, Rogers stated that 'the best vantage point for understanding behaviour is from the internal frame of reference of the individual himself' (1951: 494), thus asserting the superiority of empathy over diagnosis in understanding an individual's behaviour.

Empathy in person-centred theory is a concept deeply intertwined with the concept of the 'actualizing tendency'. The therapist's aim of entering the client's internal frame of reference and the therapist's reliance on this empathic understanding to achieve therapeutic outcome is, according to Rogers, 'the most complete implementation of the central hypothesis of respect for and reliance upon the capacity of the person' (1951: 35–6). In other words, it is the therapist's reliance upon and trust in the client's actualizing tendency which ultimately underpins and sustains his/her empathic attitude in the therapeutic relationship.

In Rogers' 1957 and 1959 papers, empathy became one of the six necessary and sufficient conditions of therapeutic personality change (see Chapters 2, 3, this volume). Empathy was then defined as the state of perceiving 'the internal frame of reference of another with accuracy, and with the emotional components and meanings which pertain thereto, as if one were the other person, and without ever losing the "as if" condition' (1959: 210).

Rogers' hypothesis inspired a large body of research on empathy and the other companion conditions. Accordingly, Truax and Carkhuff (1967) developed an operational and behavioural definition of empathy for research purposes, which was further applied to the training of therapists, fostering the development of skills-training models of empathy (e.g. Carkhuff, 1971; Egan, 1998). In these models, empathic reflections might be done in a mechanistic way, reducing the intersubjective experiences of empathy, unconditional positive regard and congruence to a response technique (Bohart and Greenberg, 1997; Bozarth, 1998). For example, Egan instructs his readers to express empathic understanding through the use of the following 'empathy formula':

> You feel … [here name the correct emotion expressed by the client] … because (or when) … [here indicate the correct experiences and behaviours that give rise to the feelings].
>
> (1998: 84)

As a reaction to these models, Rogers revised his previous definition of empathy, asserting that it is a process rather than a state, and also a 'complex, demanding and strong – yet also a subtle and gentle – way of being' (1980: 143). He then presented empathy as a holistic experience of the therapist encompassing several facets:

> It means entering the private perceptual world of the other and becoming thoroughly at home in it. It involves being sensitive, moment by moment, to the changing felt meanings which flow in this other person, to the fear or rage or tenderness or confusion or whatever that he or she is experiencing. It means

temporarily living in the other's life, moving about in it delicately without making judgements; it means sensing meanings of which he or she is scarcely aware, but not trying to uncover totally unconscious feelings, since this would be too threatening. It includes communicating your sensings of the person's world as you look with fresh and unfrightened eyes at elements of which he or she is fearful. It means frequently checking with the person as to the accuracy of your sensings, and being guided by the responses you receive. You are a confident companion to the person in his or her inner world. By pointing to the possible meanings in the flow of another person's experiencing, you help the other to focus on this useful type of referent, to experience the meanings more fully, and to move forward in the experiencing. To be with another in this way means that for the time being, you lay aside your own views and values in order to enter another's world without prejudice. In some sense it means that you lay aside your self; this can only be done by persons who are secure enough in themselves that they know they will not get lost in what may turn out to be the strange or bizarre world of the other, and that they can comfortably return to their own world when they wish.

(1980: 142–3)

More recently, Schmid (2001) brought the philosophical perspective of Buber and Levinas to enlighten the meaning of empathy on person-centred theory. Empathy, to Buber, is a way of relating, which exposes oneself to the presence of the other. 'It is a way of acceptance instead of knowledge' which acknowledges the person and confirms her (Schmid, 2001: 58). Through empathy, the person is perceived in her 'wholeness and individuality', without reduction or abstraction (2001: 58). Being open to the Other's unique way of being allows the possibility of the encounter. Schmid also emphasized that empathy means not only to accept the person in her actual reality but, moreover, in her possibilities, it is trying to enter the essence of the person, imagining her also as the person she can become. Inspired by Levinas's existential ideas, he concluded that 'empathy is the art of not-knowing. It is the art of being curious, being open to being surprised, being kept awake by an enigma' (2001: 61).

Schmid has also clarified the difference between empathy, identification and interpretation. Identification means ignoring the boundaries between oneself and the other person and dissolving oneself in another's emotions. Hence identification 'ignores the otherness of the Other' (2001: 55). Interpretation means to judge what the other person thinks, feels or expresses, and to form an evaluation. Schmid therefore considers it objectifies the person, closing one's eyes to her uniqueness. Empathy, unlike identification and interpretation, means 'to resonate to the melody the Other plays, an accurate vibrating and sensing with the Other without completely dissolving in it' (2001: 55). Empathy keeps a necessary distance between two persons 'as an astonishment, a respect and reverence towards the other person. ... It does not pretend identity of the two, nor does it give up at the sign of diversity' (2001: 59–62). In fact, empathy 'bridges the gap between differences, between persons – without removing the gap, without ignoring the differences' (2001: 62). Although we are all fellow humans and thus alike, empathy enables us to see the other person as actually 'an Other' (2001: 55).

Relationship of empathy with the other core conditions

According to Rogers, 'true empathy is always free of any evaluative or diag-nostic quality' and the 'highest expression of empathy is accepting and nonjudgemental' (1980: 151–5). Bozarth pointed out that because of this non-evaluative and acceptant quality Rogers ascribes to empathy, it is more accurate to identify Rogerian empathy as unconditional empathic reception (2001: 152). Bozarth also considered that empathy in client-centred therapy is a manifestation of, and the purest way of communicating, unconditional positive regard. He concluded that 'Rogerian empathy' is so intertwined with unconditional positive regard that empathic and unconditional acceptance are, in essence, the same experience (2001: 147). In relation to congruence, Bozarth asserts that there is no empathy without congruence since it is the therapist's congruence which affords the therapist the capacity to experience empathy towards the client (1998: 81). Many contemporary authors in the person-centred community (e.g. Bozarth, 1998; Freire, 2000; Wyatt, 2001; Mearns and Cooper, 2005) have emphasized that although the Rogerian core conditions are taught as separate variables, their interrelationship is so high that they are ultimately and functionally one sole condition, which Mearns termed 'genuine empathic acceptance' (see Mearns and Cooper, 2005: 17).

Effects of empathy

Rogers considered empathy to be a healing agent in itself and one of the most potent aspects of therapy. Empathy dissolves alienation: 'it releases, it confirms, it brings even the most frightened client into the human race. If a person is understood, he or she belongs' (1986: 129). Empathy leads to 'self-empathy' (Barrett-Lennard, 1997). Being listened to by someone who understands makes it possible for the person to listen more accurately to herself, with greater empa-thy toward her own visceral experiencing (Rogers, 1980). When the client sees her own attitudes, feelings and perceptions accurately expressed by the thera-pist, she can accept into her self all these elements, now more clearly perceived. Because the therapist has been able to adopt her frame of reference, and to perceive with her, with acceptance and respect, the client can own and assimi-late these experiences into a now altered self-concept. And 'once the self-concept changes, behaviour changes to match the freely perceived self' (Rogers, 1980: 155). Receiving empathy also facilitates the development of the client's ability to empathize with others (Barrett-Lennard, 1997; Jordan, 1997).

These healing and therapeutic effects of empathy are supported by the evidence accumulated in psychotherapy research which strongly suggests positive correlations between empathy and therapeutic outcome (e.g. Bohart et al, 2002; Orlinsky et al, 1994; Stubbs and Bozath, 1994).

Empathy across the psychotherapeutic orientations

Nowadays, most approaches in psychotherapy (if not all) acknowledge the pivotal importance of empathy in the therapeutic relationship. For instance, in a study by Raskin (1974), 83 therapists from many different orientations described their concept of the 'ideal therapist', and they gave empathy the highest ranking out of 12 variables. In the newer psychoanalytical approaches, such as Kohut's self-psychology (Kohut, 1980, 1984) and the intersubjective perspective (see Trop and Stolorow, 1997), empathy assumed central importance. Empathy within the intersubjective psychoanalytical framework is viewed as a mode of investigation. Trop and Stolorow (1997) emphasized that, within this framework, empathy is exclusively an 'investigatory' stance. Also for Kohut, empathy is a means of gathering information, which can then be integrated with theory to offer a 'dynamic or genetic interpretation' to the patient (1980: 484). Many cognitive and behaviourist therapists, such as Beck (Beck et al, 1979) and Linehan (1997), also emphasized the importance of the therapist's empathy as a variable to help relationship building.

Bozarth, however, asserts that Rogerian empathy is different from all other concepts of empathy: 'the actualizing tendency as the foundation block for the [person-centred] approach creates a context that places Rogerian empathy in a different frame than empathy in other theoretical orientations' (1998: 146). In the classical perspective of person-centred therapy, the therapist does not intend any specific outcome from being empathic but only to communicate unconditional positive regard, whereas in other therapeutic approaches empathy is viewed as a means either to gather data for later interpretation or to bond the therapeutic alliance in order to prepare the client for receiving the therapist's other interventions.

From theory to practice

In 1951, Rogers considered the role of the therapist to be to put her self aside – 'the self of ordinary interaction' – and to enter into the perceptual world of the client as completely as she is capable of, becoming, in a sense, an alter ego of the client's feelings and attitudes. This would provide a safe opportunity for the client to experience himself more truly and deeply, to discern himself more clearly and to choose more significantly (Rogers, 1951: 35). Raskin (cited by Rogers, 1951) also emphasized that when the therapist is striving to experience empathy towards the client, she absorbs herself completely in trying to get within and 'in struggling to do this, there is simply no room' for any other type of activity or attitude. The therapist cannot be diagnosing the client, 'cannot be thinking of making the process go faster' (1951: 29). The empathic understanding must be acquired 'through the most intense, continuous and active attention to the feelings of the other, to the exclusion of any other type of attention' (1951: 29).

Rogers realized that in trying to understand the client empathically in that way, laying aside her own judgements and values 'in order to grasp, with delicate accuracy, the exact meaning the client is experiencing', the therapist's responses serve as a mirror (Rogers, 2002: 13). From the client's point of view, the therapist would be perceived as holding up a mirror, reflecting a clear image of the meanings and perceptions as experienced by him which would be clarifying and insight-producing. One of Rogers' clients (Slack,

1985) expressed her experience of being understood in this way like being reflected by a 'magical mirror'.

> It was like Dr. Rogers was a magical mirror. ... I looked into the mirror to get a glimpse of the reality that I am. ... This experience allowed me an opportunity to get a view of myself that was untainted by the perceptions of outside viewers. This inner knowledge of myself enabled me to make choices more suited to the person who lives within me.
>
> (Slack, 1985: 41–2)

For that reason, Rogers' typical way of communicating empathic understanding was initially described as a 'reflection of feelings'. However, this term has often been misunderstood and trivialized, and has become a caricature of person-centred therapy. Rogers became concerned with the use of 'reflection of feelings' as a 'wooden technique' (2002: 13), but Shlien (cited by Rogers, 2002), pointed out that the term 'reflection of feelings' was unfairly damned since 'it is an instrument of artistic virtuosity in the hands of a sincere, intelligent, empathic listener. It made possible the development of person-centred therapy, when the philosophy alone could not have.'

Given the common misunderstanding that the target of empathic understanding would be narrowly client's *feelings*, Brodley changed the name of 'reflection of feelings' to *empathic understanding response process* (EURP) (see Temaner, 1977). Brodley (2001) also stressed that EURP is not a technique, but rather a process and an attitude. It is a close following of the client, in which the therapist is not focused only on the client's feelings or the client's literal words, but instead 'is trying to grasp the meanings that the client seems to intend to be understood by the listener' (2001: 17). Also, in the EURP, all therapists' responses are inherently tentative, as if the therapist were asking the client: 'Is this accurate?' Hence, the EURP enables the therapist to correct misunderstanding and to access deeper levels of meaning. Brodley (2001) renamed this process as '*acceptant* empathic understanding', emphasizing that the primary intention of the therapist is to continuously experience an acceptant, empathic attitude in relation to the client. Brodley emphasized that the therapist's sole goal is 'to understand the client in a manner that is likely to result in the client's having the experience of being understood' (2001: 17–18). The therapist's empathic responses are not intended to deepen the client's experiential focus (in contrast to a process-experiential or focusing approach, see below) although this is a frequent consequence of acceptant empathic understanding and often plays a role in therapeutic change (Brodley, 1990; Prouty, 1999).

The excerpt below of the first session of one of my clients, a 23-year-old female, illustrates how this acceptant empathic understanding response process can result in the client focusing in her experiential flow and getting in touch with very deep and painful feelings:

C1:   I see that I am delaying things, delaying ... at the same time I think: 'am I not wasting this time', you know? Then, I am letting it pass, at the same time I think ... you know ... I do not have the courage to ... to ...

T1:   You feel you are putting it off ...

C2:   [Together with therapist] Putting it off ...

T2:   You are not wanting to see the problem ... but you know that it is there ...

C3:   Yes, exactly ...

T3:   Deceiving yourself, like that ...

C4:   Exactly ... my life is so mixed up, it is that ... gee! I am 23, I will be 24 next month ... I don't know, I have not got anything of substance for myself yet, you know? I imagined that at this age I would already have a career, that I would be fine, you know, all that ... to have made plans before, that is the problem, I think ... we come short ... we do all that planning, planning, and when you look at it, it is nothing like that ... this is so much more frustrating ...

T4:   The plans that you made for yourself, not ...

C5:   Yes, I think it is very frustrating ... Oh! I don't know! It is very complicated! I think that everyone must go through this crisis when ... thinking about life ...

T5:   Like you reached a moment when you started to question: 'where am I going in life?'

The therapist's empathic understanding responses above (T1 to T5) comprised not only client's feelings ('You feel ...') but also cognitive ('You started to question ...') and volitional ('You are not wanting ...') aspects of the client's narrative.

C6:   Yes, where am I going ... I know it only depends on me ... ok, I have my family, but there is a moment when pride is more important ... I like to pay for all my own stuff because I know that later I will not have my parents there to pay ... so I like doing this now already ...

T6:   It is a personal demand to be able to have this independence as soon as possible ...

The therapist tried to grasp the 'key' meaning of what the client was intending to communicate and 'reflected' it back to the client.

C7:   Yes ... like, an apartment for me, my own house, a place where I can ... that I leave my parents' house and have total independence ...

T7:   You are in a hurry for this ...

The therapist sensed the client's 'hurry' from her empathic attunement even though the client had not used the word 'hurry'.

C8:   I am, I am in a big hurry for this ... and ... this was one of the arguments that I had with my father, for me, if I could leave their house, not because of my mother, or my brothers, but because of my independence that I want and because of him, because he has the wrong idea about me ... my father thinks that I am manipulative, then I told him: 'Well, if you think I am manipulative, it is because you are, because you are seeing this in me, but you are not accepting this about me, and because this is what you are.' So, it was a confrontation like that ... horrible, isn't it. ... We had a serious argument about this, then I said: 'Well, if you do not trust your daughter, if you do not trust your family, then you do not trust anybody in this world ... and I am sad for you ... so I want to leave this house today' [with a choking voice], that is how I spoke to him: 'I would leave your house as soon as possible, because you do not trust me, because you do not know, because you have hurt me with this', that is how I spoke to him, then he said: 'Oh! You want to leave my house?' Then I said: 'Because of you', then he said: 'Oh, ok then, as from today I'm breaking all relations with you' ... of course it was much bigger than this, it was an argument that lasted about two hours, but, this willingness that I have to leave home is because of this also ...

T8: Because you felt very hurt by him ...

From the long client's narrative, the therapist chose to empathically 'reflect' to the client the deep feeling of being hurt that the client was communicating and expressing along her narrative. The therapist was so immersed in the client's phenomenological world, that she was able to 'feel' the hurt as if it was hers, and that experience was communicated to the client in the form of an empathic understanding response.

C9: [Crying] This ... has hurt me very deeply ...
T9: It is difficult to live with him after what has happened ...
C10: Yes, we do not even speak ... he keeps to himself and I keep to myself ... a few days ago he even said 'hi' to me, but I do not want a 'hi' from him, I want him to apologize to me, that is what I want ... just that he will never apologize ...

During this excerpt, the therapist's empathic understanding responses facilitated the client's process of symbolization and integration into awareness of the hurt that she had been feeling towards her father.

Although this acceptant empathic understanding response process is the landmark of the classical perspective on person-centred therapy (together with the emphasis on the therapist's non-directivity), what is typical for all other person-centred and experiential orientations – e.g. focusing (Gendlin, 1996) and process-experiential (Elliott et al, 2003) – is the belief that the core conditions of empathy, unconditional positive regard and congruence are 'crucial', in the sense that they are more important than the technical aspects of the therapeutic work (Lietaer, 2002). It was explicitly stated by Rogers in his 1957 hypothesis of therapeutic change that the techniques are 'relatively unimportant except to the extent that they serve as channels for fulfilling one of the conditions' (Rogers, 1990: 233). Although the focus on the phenomenological world of the client is a common ground for all person-centred orientations, there are differences among them in relation to how the therapist should communicate empathy and the associated conditions of unconditional positive regard and congruence.

For the classical perspective, the six conditions are 'necessary and sufficient', but in the view of the other orientations they are 'necessary but not sufficient' and should be supplemented with other procedures. Warner identified distinct 'levels of interventiveness', which she defined as 'the degree on which a therapist brings in material from outside the client's frame of reference, and the degree to which this is done from a stance of authority or expertise' (2000: 31) (see Chapter 9, this volume). There are significant differences among person-centred therapists of different orientations according to these levels of interventiveness: from almost exclusively empathic understanding responses to responding more from the therapist's frame of reference and giving process directives (Lietaer, 2002).

Accordingly, in the process-directive perspective, empathic understanding is conceived as conveying not only reflection but also 'selection' of client experience. The therapist should be selective in her response and focus on the client's current feelings and strong attitudes, particularly 'what is live and most poignant' in the client's message, and also focus on the 'the client's growth possibilities' (Greenberg and Elliott, 1997: 173). Process-directive empathic responses are based on this type of selection and they are intended not only to convey understanding but also to promote exploration of the client's experience. Greenberg and Elliott delineated five different forms of empathic responses: understanding, evocation, exploration, conjecture and interpretation. These forms vary according to whose frame of reference is being used in making the response – on a continuum from the client's frame of reference, through a shared frame of reference to the therapist's frame of reference – and on the degree of new information that is added – from reflective empathic understanding, where 'no new information is added', to empathic interpretation, where the highest degree of information is added (Greenberg and Elliott, 1997: 175). Rice (1974), inspired by the information-processing theory, developed the method of evocative reflection which aimed 'to open up the experience and provide the client with a process whereby he can form successively more accurate constructions of his own experience' (Rice, 2001: 290). Evocative reflections would allow the therapist to take initiative action, to be more active and to respond with personal reaction.

Lietaer (2001) considered that during the last 30 years the new branches that grew out of the person-centred approach realized a shift from the original Rogers' conceptualization of the therapist's role of putting her self aside and becoming an 'alter-ego' for the client to an 'I–thou' encounter characterized by a therapist's freer use of self, with more self-disclosure and self-expressiveness. This perspective has been further explored within the model of *Working at Relational Depth*, developed by Mearns and Cooper (2005).

In this debate concerning the role of the therapist's self in the therapeutic interaction, Warner (2001) emphasized the necessity for therapists to keep their frame of reference aside when working with clients engaged with difficult process (i.e. fragile process, dissociated process or psychotic process). She pointed out that it is paramount for the therapists to stay quite close to the clients' exact words and expressions when they are in 'difficult process', since 'even small increases in the complexity of the therapist's response can leave clients feeling violated and confused, and make it difficult for them to stay connected to their experience' (2001: 187). Warner asserted that clients, at such times, can be easily 'thrown off' by therapist communications that are too distant from the immediacy of their experience, such as paraphrasing, questions or comments. She found that the most helpful thing a therapist can do is 'to just stay present and maintain very close empathic connection' (2001: 186). When this happens, emotions shift and release and clients return to contact with reality.

Another recent development of empathy is the method of empathic contact, developed by Prouty (2001) in his theory of 'Pre-Therapy' (see Prouty et al, 2001) (see Chapter 18, this volume). Empathic contact is conceived as an expansion of the empathic method with the aim of reaching out to clients who are 'contact impaired': that is, who are psychologically withdrawn, isolated, and present autistic features. Therapists who work with retarded, schizophrenic, brain-damaged or demented clients often do not have access to the client's frame of reference. Prouty says that 'the therapist is handicapped empathically because of his–her limits in "resonating" with psychotic experience which curtail the ability to "feel into" them.' Empathic contact is then a literal and concrete form of empathic response, which allows the therapist to relate to the regressed aspects of psychosis or psychotic-like states.

Although there is no consensus in the person-centred community about the methods of conveying and communicating empathy, there is no dispute about the healing and powerful dimensions of the experience of being empathically understood.

Reflections for the future

The person-centred approach has been a revolutionary paradigm in the field of psychotherapy and helping relationships since its origins in the 1940s. When Rogers replaced diagnosis with empathic understanding, he dramatically reversed the power dynamics in the client–therapist relationship. Through empathy, the expert in the therapeutic relationship became the client and no longer the therapist. When therapists rely on the clients' frame of reference as the 'best vantage point for understanding' them, they depart radically from the medical paradigm and its model of power and control over the individual (see Proctor, 2005). This revolutionary aspect of empathy in psychotherapy has been difficult for other approaches to assimilate. Sometimes empathy has been 'absorbed' as merely a technique, a means of improving the ability of the therapist in making an 'effect' in the client's therapeutic process. However, dialogues between the person-centred community and other psychotherapeutic orientations are called for in order to unfold new perspectives on empathy, particularly the developmental and intersubjective perspectives, which illuminate the relationship between empathy and the experience of 'we-ness': that is, the transcendence of the separate and disconnected self (Jordan, 1991).

Person-centred therapy is nowadays one 'nation' with many distinct 'tribes', reflecting distinct understandings of person-centred theory and distinct ways of applying it to practice (Sanders, 2004; Warner, 2000). Notwithstanding the fact that empathy has been translated into practice in so many distinct ways, it is important for the future development of the person-centred approach that

'Rogerian' empathy, or 'genuine empathic acceptance' might stand as the very landmark of the approach, and that its unique and distinct feature as an approach which subverts the dynamics of power and control in the therapeutic relationship might be held as its ultimate identity.

REFERENCES

Barrett-Lennard, G. (1997). The recovery of empathy: toward others and self. In A.C. Bohart and L.S. Greenburg (eds), *Empathy Reconsidered: new directions in psychotherapy*. Washington: APA: 103–21.

Beck, A.T., Rush, A.J., Shaw, B.F. and Emery, G. (1979). *Cognitive Therapy of Depression*. New York: Guilford.

Bohart, A.C. and Greenberg, E.D. (1997). Empathy and psychotherapy: an introductory overview. In A.C. Bohart and L.S. Greenburg (eds), *Empathy Reconsidered: new directions in psychotherapy*. Washington: APA: 3–31.

Bohart, A.C., Elliott, R., Greenberg, L.S. and Watson, J.C. (2002). Empathy. In J.C. Norcross (ed.), *Psychotherapy Relationships that Work: therapist contributions and responsiveness to patients* (pp. 89–108). Oxford: Oxford University Press.

Bozarth, J.D. (1998) *Person-Centered Therapy: a revolutionary paradigm*. Ross-on-Wye: PCCS Books.

Bozarth, J.D. (2001). An addendum to beyond reflection: emergent modes of empathy. In S. Haugh and T. Merry (eds), *Rogers' Therapeutic Conditions: evolution, theory and practice*. Volume 2. *Empathy*. Ross-on-Wye: PCCS Books: 144–54.

Brodley, B.T. (1990). Client-centered and experiential: two different therapies. In G. Lietaer, J. Rombauts and R. Van Balen (eds), *Client-Centered and Experiential Psychotherapies in the Nineties*. Leuven: Leuven University Press: 87–108.

Brodley, B.T. (2001). Observations of empathic understanding in a client-centered practice. In S. Haugh and T. Merry (eds), *Rogers' Therapeutic Conditions: evolution, theory and practice*. Volume 2. *Empathy*. Ross-on-Wye: PCCS Books: 16–37.

Carkhuff, R.R. (1971). *The Development of Human Resources*. New York: Holt, Rinehart and Winston.

Cooper, M. (2005). Working at relational depth. *Therapy Today*, 16(8), 16–20.

Egan, G. (1998). *The Skilled Helper: a problem-management approach to helping* (6th edn). Pacific Grove: Brooks/Cole.

Elliott, R., Watson, J.C., Goldman, R.N. and Greenberg, L. (2003). *Learning Emotion-Focused Therapy: the process-experiential approach to change*. Washington: American Psychological Association.

Freire, E. (2000). The implementation of the core conditions on the client-centered therapeutic relationship. Unpublished masters dissertation. Universidade de Campinas.

Gendlin, E.T. (1996). *Focusing-Oriented Psychotherapy: a manual of the experiential method*. New York: Guilford.

Greenberg, L.S. and Elliott, R. (1997). Varieties of empathy responding. In A.C.

Bohart and L.S. Greenburg (eds), *Empathy Reconsidered: new directions in psychotherapy*. Washington: APA: 167–86.

Jordan, J.V. (1991). Empathy and self boundaries. In J.V. Jordan, A.G. Kaplan, J.B. Miller, I.P. Stiver and J.L. Surrey (eds), *Women's Growth in Connection* (pp. 67–80). New York: Guilford.

Jordan, J.V. (1997). Relational development through mutual empathy. In A.C. Bohart and L.S. Greenburg (eds), *Empathy Reconsidered: new directions in psychotherapy* (pp. 343–51). Washington: APA.

Kohut, H. (1980). Reflections on advances in self-psychology. In A. Goldberg (ed.), *Advances in Self-psychology*. New York: international Universities Press.

Kohut, H. (1984). *How Does Analysis Cure?* Chicago: University of Chicago Press.

Lietaer, G. (2001). Unconditional acceptance and positive regard. In J. Bozarth and P. Wilkins (eds), *Rogers' Therapeutic Conditions: evolution, theory and practice*. Volume 3. *Unconditional Positive Regard*. Ross-on-Wye: PCCS Books: 88–108.

Lietaer, G. (2002). The united colors of person-centered and experiential psychotherapies. *Person-Centred and Experiential Psychotherapies*, 1(1–2), 4–13.

Linehan, M.M. (1997). Validation and psychotherapy. In A.C. Bohart and L.S. Greenburg (eds), *Empathy Reconsidered: new directions in psychotherapy*. Washington: APA: 353–92.

Mearns, D. and Cooper, M. (2005). *Working at Relational Depth in Counselling and Psychotherapy*. London: Sage.

Orlinsky, D.E., Grawe, K. and Parks, B.K. (1994). Process and outcome in psychotherapy – noch einmal. In A.E Bergin and S.L. Garfield (eds), *Handbook of Psychotherapy and Behavior Change* (4th ed.). New York: Wiley: 270–378.

Proctor, G. (2005). Clinical psychology and the person-centred approach: an uncomfortable fit? In S. Joseph and R. Worsley (eds), *Person-Centred Psychopathology: a positive psychology of mental health* (pp. 276–92). Ross-on-Wye: PCCS Books.

Prouty, G. (1999). Carl Rogers and experiential therapies: a dissonance? *Person-Centred Practice*, 7, 4–11.

Prouty, G. (2001). A new mode of empathy: empathic contact. In S. Haugh and T. Merry (eds), *Rogers' Therapeutic Conditions: evolution, theory and practice*. Volume 2. *Empathy* (pp. 155–62). Ross-on-Wye: PCCS Books.

Prouty, G., Van Werde, D. and Pörtner, M. (2001). *Pre-Therapy*. Ross-on-Wye: PCCS Books.

Raskin, N.J. (1974). Studies of psychotherapeutic orientation, ideology and practice. Research Monograph No. 1 of the American Academy of Psychotherapists. Orlando, Florida (now New Bern, North Carolina).

Rice, L.N. (1974). The evocative function of the therapist. In D.A. Wexler and L.N. Rice (eds), *Innovations in Client-centered Therapy* (pp. 289–312). New York: Wiley-Interscience.

Rice, L.N. (2001). The evocative function of the therapist. In S. Haugh and T. Merry (eds), *Rogers' Therapeutic Conditions: evolution, theory and practice*. Volume 2. *Empathy* (pp. 112–31). Ross-on-Wye: PCCS Books.

Rogers, C.R. (1946). Significant aspects of client-centered therapy. *American Psychologist*, 1, 415–22.

Rogers, C.R. (1951) *Client-Centered Therapy*. Boston: Houghton Mifflin.

Rogers, C.R. (1957). The necessary and sufficient conditions of therapeutic personality change. *Journal of Consulting Psychology*, 21, 95–103.

Rogers, C.R. (1959). A theory of therapy, personality, and interpersonal relationships as developed in the client-centered framework. In S. Koch (ed.), *Psychology: a study of science*. Volume 3. *Formulations of the person and the social context* (pp. 184–256). New York: McGraw Hill.

Rogers, C.R. (1980). *A Way of Being*. Boston: Houghton Mifflin.

Rogers, C.R. (1986). Rogers, Kohut, and Erickson. *Person-Centered Review*, 1, 125–40.

Rogers, C.R. (1990). The necessary and sufficient conditions of therapeutic personality change. In H. Kirschenbaum and V.L. Henderson (eds), *The Carl Rogers Reader*. London: Constable: 219–35.

Rogers, C.R. (2002). Reflection of feelings. In D.J. Cain (ed.), *Classics in the Person-Centered Approach* (pp. 13–14). Ross-on-Wye: PCCS Books.

Sanders, P. (ed.) (2004). *The Tribes of the Person-Centred Nation: an introduction to the schools of therapy related to the person-centred approach*. Ross-on-Wye: PCCS Books.

Schmid, P.F. (2001). Comprehension: the art of not knowing. Dialogical and ethical perspectives on empathy as dialogue in personal and person-centered relationships. In S. Haugh and T. Merry (eds), *Rogers' Therapeutic Conditions: evolution, theory and practice*. Volume 2. *Empathy* (pp. 53–71). Ross-on-Wye: PCCS Books.

Slack, S. (1985). Reflections on a workshop with Carl Rogers. *Journal of Humanistic Psychology*, 25, 35–42.

Stubbs, J.P. and Bozarth, J.D. (1994). The dodo bird revisited: a qualitative study of psychotherapy efficacy research. *Journal of Applied and Preventive Psychology*, 3(2), 109–20.

Temaner B.S. (1977). The empathic understanding response process. Chicago Counseling and Psychotherapy Center Discussion Papers, Chicago, Il.

Trop, J.L. and Stolorow, R.D. (1997). Therapeutic empathy: an intersubjective perspective. In A.C. Bohart and L.S. Greenburg (eds), *Empathy Reconsidered: new directions in psychotherapy* (pp. 279–91). Washington: APA.

Truax, C.B. and Carkhuff, R.R. (1967). *Toward Effective Counseling and Psychotherapy: training and practice*. Chicago: Aldine.

Warner, M.S. (2000). Person-centered psychotherapy: one nation, many tribes. *Person-Centered Journal*, 7(1), 28–39.

Warner, M.S. (2001). Empathy, relational depth and difficult client process. In S. Haugh and T. Merry (eds), *Rogers' Therapeutic Conditions: evolution, theory and practice*. Volume 2. *Empathy* (pp. 181–91). Ross-on-Wye: PCCS Books.

Wyatt, G. (2001). Congruence: a synthesis and implications. In G. Wyatt (ed.), *Rogers' Therapeutic Conditions: evolution, theory and practice*. Volume 1. *Congruence* (pp. 229–37). Ross-on-Wye: PCCS Books.

16

Client Perception

Shaké G. Toukmanian and Lila Z. Hakim

Perception is at the heart of Rogers' person-centred theory of psychotherapy. Although often not readily apparent, it is the central and most pervasive concept that runs through and links the humanistic foundations of the theory to many of its basic propositions, including Rogers' unique conceptualization of the process of therapy and the nature of the therapeutic relationship.

Conceptually, Rogers' (1959) approach rests on 40 carefully defined constructs that are used to elaborate the theory's six hypothesized 'necessary and sufficient conditions' of therapeutic change. The focus of this chapter is on Condition 6 in which Rogers stipulates that the client must, at least to some degree, *perceive* the therapist as being empathically understanding and unconditionally accepting for therapy to be effective (Rogers, 1957, 1959). This condition is Rogers' only formal statement that addresses the client's perception directly. Furthermore, it is the only condition that captures the essence of the relational foundations of the theory in that, while emphasizing the importance of the therapist's contribution to the relationship, it recognizes also that the client is an active participant and an important player in determining the potential course of therapy. Beyond this assertion, however, there is relatively little in Rogers' writings about the impact of clients' perceptions of the attitudinal qualities of the therapist on the *process* of therapy. Most of our knowledge in this area comes from the vast body of theoretical and empirical work that has since emerged in the literature on person-centred and other humanistic psychotherapies.

Central concepts

Historical overview

Perception is one of the oldest and the most extensively studied concepts in the history of psychology. From early experimental work on sensory, pain and time perception, to attempts at studying how people perceive one another, and to the more recent constructivist formulations of the nature of human experience, perception has been a key element in understanding the role of subjectivity, awareness and meaning in how people function in everyday life.

By the mid-twentieth century, early social psychologists came to recognize that unlike the perception of objects, there is an inherent self-reflective process and a reciprocal element involved in the act of perceiving other people. This view suggested that social behaviour could best be understood as a function of people's perceptions of their world and not a function of objective descriptions of stimuli in their environment. For example, in his 'field theory', Kurt Lewin (1951) saw people in social contexts as being in a dynamic interaction with their environment, and argued that an understanding of the effect of the social context on the individual can be achieved only by adopting a *holistic* approach and by focusing on the *person's own perception or subjective view* of the situation.

Concurrent with the developments in social psychology during this period, perception also came to be recognized as an important phenomenon in psychotherapy. Most of the early writings in this area, however, failed to take into account the complex interplay among the clients' inner dynamics, their perception of self and the therapist, as well as how self-perceptions and environmental perceptions altered in relation to one another in the process of therapy. Rogers' 1947 article, entitled 'Some observations on the organization of personality', was one of the first attempts to address this complexity by focusing explicitly on the importance of self-perception as a basic factor influencing people's psychological adjustment. Eventually, Rogers' focus shifted to an emphasis on perception in the therapeutic interaction, particularly to the client's perception of the therapist's relational attitudes, as it came to be stated in his Condition 6 (Rogers, 1957, 1959).

Another profound influence on the development of the concept of perception in psychotherapy during the 1950s and 1960s came from the work of European philosophers (e.g. Buber, 1957; Kierkegaard, 1843/1954; Merleau-Ponty, 1962) who introduced phenomenological/existential views on the nature of human existence and methods for studying consciously experienced phenomena. The bedrock of these approaches, which have since become known as humanistic (e.g. May, 1961; Perls, 1969; Rogers, 1951, 1959), is the basic premise that people's perceptions play a significant role in how they act and interact with their environment and that the experiential world of the person can be understood only from the vantage point of the person's own view of reality (see Chapter 6, this volume). Accordingly, all humanistic approaches emphasize the uniqueness of human experience and, to the extent that all share the view that people have the capacity for awareness and creation of meaning, all rest on a shared but implicit assumption that the fundamental process that gives meaning, coherence and continuity to human functioning is *perception*.

This integrative view of perception became firmly established in the decades following the rise of the information-processing paradigm in psychology in the 1970s. For example, during this period, the focus in social cognition turned increasingly away from examining the characteristic properties of the perceiver, the perceived, and the context in which observations occurred and onto efforts at addressing the conceptual basis of *how* people make sense of themselves, others, and events in ordinary social and interpersonal situations. Initially, this area focused on expectancies, stereotypes, and the judgemental accuracy of social events, although more recent focus has been on the role of self-perception in the processes by which people make judgements about self and others and as it relates to the process of adaptation (e.g. Kihlstrom and Cantor, 1984; Linville, 1987; Stein and Markus, 1996).

Overall, this emphasis on the importance of perception in human functioning that has emerged across different fields in psychology is compatible with the basic tenets of humanistic psychotherapies. It also underscores the view that (1) perception is an inferential, meaning-making process that is centrally involved in the *construction and representation of one's own view of reality* and that (2) the way in which people organize and give meaning to information in the immediate present is based on their past *transactions* with the world. Taken together, these developments have had two important implications for psychotherapy theory and practice. First, they shifted attention away from earlier attempts at studying perception solely as the characteristic property of the individual participants of the therapy dyad and toward treating it as an interactive, transactional phenomenon occurring between the client and the therapist within the context of the therapeutic relationship. Second, they created a rapprochement between cognitive science and psychotherapy and in so doing set the stage for the development of more fine-grained conceptualizations of the role of perception in the therapeutic change process.

Perception in person-centred therapy

Although perception is inherent to the structure of all forms of psychotherapy, Rogers (1951, 1959) was the first to *explicitly* recognize its centrality in therapeutic work by giving it a prominent place as one of his hypothesized 'necessary and sufficient conditions' of therapeutic change. Rogers maintained all along that the therapist's congruence in the relationship (Condition 3), experience of unconditional positive regard for the client (Condition 4), and empathic understanding of the client's internal frame of reference (Condition 5) are critical therapist attitudes for successful therapy. He further asserted that it is only when the client *perceives* the therapist's empathic understanding and unconditional acceptance that positive therapeutic change can occur (Condition 6). This assertion reflects the theory's humanistic position that reality resides within a person's phenomenology or subjective experience of the world and that people have the inherent capacity to choose, make decisions, act, and alter their self-concept, behaviour, perceptions and attitudes toward others (e.g. May, 1961; Perls, 1969; Rogers, 1942, 1961). Rogers believed that this capacity becomes operative in a safe, supportive and facilitative therapeutic environment with a psychotherapist who is empathic, genuine and unconditionally accepting of the client.

Summary of relevant research findings

Rogers' views on what makes or fails to make psychotherapy therapeutic have been studied extensively with different populations and in a variety of contexts. The focus of much of this research has been on the Rogerian concept of the therapeutic relationship, the three therapist attitudinal conditions, and on various client and therapist attributes and factors hypothesized to be sources of influence on psychotherapy practice, such as client perceptions of therapist personality, perceptions of the therapist role, and client–therapist perceived similarity. The following are a few general conclusions, from among several pertaining to factors in Condition 6, that have emerged from various reviews of this vast literature.

With regards to empathy and unconditional positive regard (UPR):

- There is now considerable evidence to suggest that therapist empathy is the most potent predictor of client progress in therapy and therapy outcome (e.g. Bohart et al, 2002; Orlinsky et al, 2004; Watson, 2002). This evidence is stronger in studies that have examined the relationship between *client-perceived* ratings of therapist empathy and outcome (e.g. Barrett-Lennard, 1962; Lambert et al, 1978).
- Support for the hypothesis that UPR plays an important role in client change is inconclusive (e.g. Asay and Lambert, 2002; Sachse and Elliott, 2002), possibly because this attitude is integral to and essential for the provision of empathy.

With regards to client and therapist variables and perception:

- There is no consistent evidence to indicate that specific client and therapist attributes and global personality dimensions influence clients' perceptions of the therapist, and no evidence that such variables predict therapy outcome (e.g. Beutler et al, 2004; Clarkin and Levy, 2004).
- Results from a number of studies in psychotherapy and social cognition indicate that individual differences in perception are probably due more to factors internal to the perceiver (e.g. view of self, nature and intensity of inner psychological states, degree of differentiation and complexity of cognitive structures, inferential processes and strategies used in making sense of people) than to the characteristics of the perceived person (e.g. Linville, 1987; Moskowitz, 2005; Stein and Markus, 1996; Thagard and Kunda, 1998; Thompson and Hill, 1991).
- A number of qualitative studies (e.g. Rennie, 1994a, 1994b; Hill et al, 1992; Thompson and Hill, 1991) indicate that clients are active, self-aware

and agential participants in the therapy process, and that clients' ongoing perceptions of the therapist and the therapeutic relationship exert a powerful influence on how the therapy is construed and experienced in the moment.

With regards to therapist manner of communicating:

- Evidence shows that there is considerable variability in the effectiveness of different therapists practising within a given approach, and in the effectiveness of the same therapist working with different clients (e.g. Beutler et al, 1994; Elkin, 1999; Lambert and Okiishi, 1997). This suggests that the way in which therapists *interact with individual clients* is as important, if not more important a factor in successful therapy, as the therapy itself.
- Research indicates that therapist statements that express understanding, attentive listening and openness to the client's perspective are associated with successful therapy outcome (e.g. Henry et al, 1986; Watson et al, 1998).
- Studies also show that therapist interventions that are attuned to clients' manner of processing, are tentative in delivery, and engage in meaning explorations are associated with greater complexity and depth in clients' in-therapy process, and that attunement is a strong predictor of expressed empathy (Gordon and Toukmanian, 2002; Macaulay, 2005).

From theory to practice

Condition 6 and person-centred practice

How are the therapist's empathic understanding and unconditional acceptance of the client *transmitted* in therapy for the client to perceive them in a way that will promote the progress of therapy?

Although this question may appear to be relatively straightforward at first glance, in reality it is not. The difficulty, as we see it, is due mostly to the fact that, although Rogers' phenomenological approach put perception at the centre of his theory, the client's perception of the therapist-offered relational conditions was not adequately developed and fully integrated into his theory of psychotherapy in any of his writings (Sanders and Wyatt, 2002). Rogers, it would seem, assumed that when the therapist is congruent, empathic and accepting of the client in the relationship, then Condition 6 will occur automatically. There is no recognition in his approach of any necessary client characteristic, other than for the requirement that the client be 'vulnerable or anxious' (Rogers, 1959: 79), nor of factors that may impinge on the client's perceptions of what is being heard and experienced in the moment in therapy (Barrett-Lennard, 1998; Toukmanian, 2002). Also, his descriptions of the core relational conditions have remained 'broad and general with little, if any, consideration given to how they are manifested in the therapeutic relationship' (Patterson and Watkins, 1996: 417). As a result, what is practised in therapy is often guided by the individual therapist's understanding of the nature of these concepts, which is likely to be the product of his or her training.

Rogers is equally unclear in his treatment of the concept of perception (Toukmanian, 2002). As was noted earlier, the consensus in the current psychological literature is that perception is a dynamic meaning-making process that is centrally involved in the construction and interpretation of information in the immediate present on the basis of past transactions with the world (e.g. Moskowitz, 2005; Neisser, 1976). This view implies that, in any human encounter, there is a complex interplay between two unique perceptions or ways of construing the situation, and that the perception of each participant has the potential of affecting and being affected by that of the other. It is, therefore, crucial to acknowledge that there always is a reciprocal influence on how client and therapist perceive and experience one another in the moment and that the phenomenon is an *inevitable* component of all forms of psychotherapy.

This understanding, however, is implied and not explicitly articulated in Rogers' writings. As a result, person-centred therapists are often faced with the dilemma of how to translate theory into practice, when they are guided by a phenomenological approach that emphasizes the importance of the therapeutic relationship but fails to elaborate on how client's and therapist's perceptions play out during the course of therapy. Thus, trying to modulate the theory's assertions of what needs to happen and what is actually experienced in the moment with individual clients has been a challenge and a constant source of tension for therapists. And it was because of this tension that interest in understanding client's internal processes and experiencing in therapy emerged as an important focus in subsequent developments of person-centred and experiential theory and practice (see Cain and Seeman, 2002; Greenberg et al, 1998).

Translating Condition 6 into practice

Although Condition 6 is about the client's perception of the therapist, it should be noted that the therapist's perceptions of the client are as critical, if not more critical, than those of the client in the implementation of this condition. This is because of the transactional nature of therapy, which implies that without the therapist's awareness of and sensitivity to the client's subjective world it will be virtually impossible to convey empathy and UPR for the client to receive.

To elaborate, in his early writings, Rogers (1959) maintained that to be empathic is to accurately perceive the internal frames of reference of clients in terms of their emotional components and meanings. This, he believed, was made possible through the reflection of feelings and a non-directive manner of interacting with clients. In his later formulations, however, Rogers (1975, 1980) came to see empathy as a process rather than as a state of being. Accordingly, he emphasized the importance for therapists of understanding the changes in clients' 'felt meanings' and of checking the accuracy of their empathic 'sensing' of their clients' subjective world continually with them. This portrayal suggests that empathic understanding is the process of trying to grasp how clients are processing or construing and making sense of experiences. And, in terms of

Condition 6, it means that the therapist must be attuned to what the client is attempting to convey in any given moment as fully and as accurately as possible and must be able to translate what is actually being heard into words that capture the meaning of what lies behind the client's communications. It is also this process that serves to facilitate the expression of UPR.

There are thus two questions of central importance to our understanding of Condition 6:

- How do therapists come to recognize clients' implied meanings, or what is it that helps them 'sense' the changing 'felt meanings', in clients' narratives?
- How do clients come to perceive therapists' responses as being empathically understanding and accepting?

As Condition 6 does not play out directly or visibly in therapy, we have found that one way of addressing these questions is to use a conceptual framework that would help delineate the nature of clients' inferential processes as they occur during the course of therapy.

As we have indicated elsewhere (Toukmanian, 1990, 1992, 1996), our conceptual framework is based on two fundamental propositions: that (a) psychological dysfunctions are, by and large, difficulties associated with people's failure to perceive or to adequately process and 'make sense' of certain aspects of experiences in everyday life; and (b) that these dysfunctional ways of perceiving are developed through people's continuous transactions with the world. It is contended, therefore, that whether or not, and the extent to which, clients perceive the attitudinal qualities of the therapist will depend on their level of perceptual functioning at any given moment in therapy (Toukmanian, 2002). This perspective further maintains that, since perceptions are constructions involving different kinds of processing strategies, then the dysfunctional strategies with which clients construe their experiences at any given moment can serve to *inform* the therapist of the 'targets' (Zimring, 2000) of their empathic responding. In this sense, the therapeutic value of Condition 6 can be determined only when viewed in terms of therapists' communications that are guided by and are specific to clients' dysfunctional ways of perceiving.

Furthermore, one cannot know whether clients have experienced therapist empathy and unconditional acceptance unless the question is presented to them directly. This typically is done, if at all, through post-therapy evaluations attained from the client. Another way of evaluating the client's perception of the therapist, however, is to see whether or not Rogers' hypothesis of a causal relationship between the client's perception of therapist attitudinal qualities and positive therapeutic change exists. This question was addressed in relation to empathy in a recent study (Macaulay, 2005) that was conducted within a perception-focused experiential therapy framework (for a detailed description of this approach see Toukmanian, 1990, 1996). In this study, therapist-expressed empathy was examined in relation to three qualities of therapist interventions and tested for its relationship to client in-therapy perceptual process and outcome. It was found that, not only were therapist interventions high in attunement to clients' manner of processing predictive of therapist empathy, but also that there was a significant, positive relationship between therapist empathy and client process. The following excerpt was drawn from this study. It came from a segment that was rated high in terms of clients' internally-focused explorations of meaning. The segment was also rated high on therapist empathy as well as on attunement, tentativeness and meaning exploration qualities of therapist responding.

C: ... like in my last relationship, I flipped into a therapist mode ... I was there for him ... servicing his emotional needs ... and the thing that scares me is that when I look back at my past relationships ... I wonder if I wasn't doing exactly the same thing ... and *that really scares me*.

T: What's it like for you ... how do you see yourself in these 'scary' situations?

C: Just ... playing the rock of Gibraltar ... I see myself doing that in my relationships with friends too ... and that bothers me ... because I feel I am not allowing people to get to know the real me ... I feel isolated ... there are fewer and fewer people that really know the *real* me ... what I am really thinking ... feeling ...

T: Just like the rock of Gibraltar ... strong but somewhat aloof and distant ... I am not sure but ... there seems to be something in you that kind of doesn't allow you to be you ...

C: Yeah ... I guess I really hate hurting people ... I have difficulty pulling out of relationships ... I stay in them far too long ... to be nice, caring sort of a person ... I suppose ...

T: Ready to do anything for anybody (C: That's right) who needs anything in this world!! (C: Yeah ... that's right).

C: Yeah ... but when I look at all those positive characteristics in myself ... there's almost a point where ... 'too much giving and you're gone' ... and that's why I sort of pull myself into a hole and ... lose myself ...

T: Too much giving and I'll lose myself ... I'll have no boundaries for myself ... (C: Yeah ... yeah) ... and ... I kind of get the feeling that in your relationships the scariness relates to 'I'm going to lose myself again and become whoever the person wants me to be' ... Does this sound accurate?

C: Yeah ... yeah ... and I think I almost kid myself into believing that I'm not compromising in my relationships ... when I guess I am ... because I give so much in relationships emotionally that ... I come away with a sense of 'what will they do without me?' ... and I keep going on giving ...

T: ... and I guess that's when you cannot be sure of your boundaries ... and keep going on giving ... until the barrel is empty ... but somehow you seem to manage to pull out ... something in you tells you 'you've got to get out'

C: Yeah ... yeah ... [long pause] ... it's like I have an emotional cut off point ... I'm not sure where it comes from... maybe it's because I feel ... I don't deserve this ... I want to protect the *real me*.

Although brief, the above transaction demonstrates the importance of therapists being constantly aware of their client's inferential processes and able to respond accordingly. Coming back to our earlier questions regarding how Condition 6 plays out in therapy, this example illustrates that when the therapist attends to the client's difficulties in making sense of experiences and is responsive to the client's felt but unarticulated meanings, then two things happen: the client experiences the therapist as being empathic and accepting and, in this relational context, the client is gradually ushered into developing new and more personally meaningful perspectives. A major advantage of this process-oriented way of interacting with clients is that it requires therapists to develop discerning habits of listening to the ambiguities of meaning in clients' expressions and maintain a focus on clients' inner experience. For as Toukmanian asserts, 'when therapists are attuned to the client's manner of processing moment-by-moment, they are likely to rely less on their own subjectivity of what is or what is not salient to the client' (2002: 128). And, with this focus, therapists are more able to respond in ways that convey their openness and empathic understanding to the client, which, after all, is the main intent of Condition 6.

Future directions

Although we have gained some insight into the role of perception in Condition 6 as stated in Rogers' person-centred theory of therapy, we still have a number of challenges to face in both research and practice. With regards to research, there is now considerable evidence supporting the importance of the therapeutic relationship. However, questions still remain with regard to the relative contribution of the client and the therapist to the core Rogerian facilitative attitudes. If, as Toukmanian (2002) argues, the therapeutic relationship is a co-constructive process, then we need to examine the extent of the client's and therapist's contribution to this process and how the relationship is mediated by each participant's perception of the encounter. Furthermore, research is also needed to see whether the relationship in itself is therapeutic or if it functions to provide the necessary interpersonal context for other healing elements to emerge.

One way of exploring this area is through discovery-oriented, qualitative research into both therapy participants' perceptions of the encounter. Another possibility is to investigate the *quality* of therapist responses in relation to client in-therapy process and outcome. Currently, there is some evidence suggesting that therapist responses that are *tentatively* formulated and *attuned* to the client's experience in the moment are associated with greater complexity in the client's manner of processing. Therapist responses that engage clients in the exploration of *meaning*, on the other hand, are associated with deeper experiential involvement (Gordon and Toukmanian, 2002). It would also be informative to explore whether the quality of therapists' responses changes, and whether clients' responses to these qualities vary at different points in therapy. Also, there is now substantial evidence that the client is a major contributor to therapy outcome (Lambert and Hill, 1994). It is therefore crucial to know how clients' perceptions of the attitudinal qualities of the therapist, as well as their readiness for change and openness to establishing a therapeutic relationship, affect the process of therapy.

In terms of practice, we believe that a critical direction for future work is the education and training of person-centred psychotherapists. There continues to be a need for training programmes that, while maintaining an -

emphasis on facilitating the development of trainee relational attitudes, also recognize the importance of the more 'technical' aspects of psychotherapy practice. As it has been suggested by Toukmanian (1996), this balance, in any form of therapy, may best be achieved by conceptualizing training as a process consisting of two components: (a) the development of the personal/attitudinal qualities of the trainee, and (b) the acquisition and honing of theoretically relevant conceptual/procedural knowledge and skills for managing the moment-to-moment transactions in therapy.

Every trainee enters the field with a set of different beliefs, values and conceptions about human interactions and psychotherapy practice. Given the trainees' unique experiential histories, they perceive and respond to the exigencies of the profession differently. Thus, in order for trainees to truly embody the relational attitudes put forth by Rogers, they must initially work on developing an increased awareness of not only their needs, values and beliefs, but also of how their background and experiences play into their perception of the client and the therapeutic encounter (Toukmanian, 1996).

Once the overall attitude embedded in the person-centred framework is experienced and owned by the therapist, conceptual/procedural knowledge can take form. The imparting of the relational conditions in therapy requires that therapists first develop an ability to *listen* for ambiguities of meaning in the client's discourse and to follow-up with these in order to understand the client from the vantage point of his/her unique experiential frame of reference. Following this, they need to develop an ability to communicate in the framework of an interpersonal exchange, all the while being aware of how the client receives each communication. For example, empathy is both an intrapersonal phenomenon in how it is experienced by the therapist, and a relational phenomenon in how it is articulated. As was indicated earlier, being empathically attuned to the client implies that the therapist has an understanding of how the client is processing and what they are attempting to convey at any given moment in the encounter. Beyond this, the therapist must translate what is being heard into words that capture the meaning of the client's expression in a tentative, concise and easy to follow manner.

Rogers has offered a unique and compelling perceptually based perspective on the process of therapy. However, until recently, perception has remained a 'neglected' dimension in our understanding of the person-centred approach. The importance of perception is now recognized in the context of current developments in experiential psychotherapies and in emerging new perspectives in different fields of psychology. We are optimistic that these advances will give Condition 6 its true significance and allow for the development of a more complex person-centred theory and hence, more informed practice.

REFERENCES

Asay, T.P. and Lambert, M.J. (2002). Therapist relational variables. In D.J. Cain and J. Seeman (eds), *Humanistic Psychotherapies: handbook of research and practice* (pp. 531–57). Washington, DC: APA.

Barrett-Lennard, G.T. (1962). Dimensions of therapist response as causal factors in therapeutic change. *Psychological Monographs*, 76 (43, Whole No. 562).

Barrett-Lennard, G.T. (1998). *Carl Rogers' Helping System: journey and substance*. London: Sage.

Beutler, L.E., Machado, P.P.P. and Neufeldt, S.A. (1994). Therapist variables. In S.L. Garfield and A.E Bergin (eds), *Handbook of Psychotherapy and Behavior Change* (4th edn) (pp. 229–69). New York: Wiley.

Beutler, L.E., Malik, M., Alimohamed, S., Harwood, T.M., Talebi, H., Noble, S. and Wong, E. (2004). Therapist variables. In M.J. Lambert (ed.), *Bergin and Garfield's Handbook of Psychotherapy and Behavior Change* (5th edn) (pp. 227–306). New York: Wiley.

Bohart, A.C., Elliott, R., Greenberg, L.S. and Watson, J.C. (2002). Empathy redux: the efficacy of therapist empathy. In J. Norcross (ed.), *Psychotherapy Relationships that Work: therapist contributions and responsiveness to patients*. New York: Oxford University Press: 89–108.

Buber, M. (1957). The William Alanson White memorial lectures. *Psychiatry: Journal for the Study of Interpersonal Processes*, 20, 95–129.

Cain, D.J. and Seeman, J. (eds) (2002). *Humanistic Psychotherapies: handbook of research and practice*. Washington, DC: APA.

Clarkin, J.F. and Levy, K.N. (2004). The influence of client variables on psychotherapy. In M.J. Lambert (ed.), *Bergin and Garfield's Handbook of Psychotherapy and Behavior Change* (5th edn) (pp.194–226). New York: Wiley.

Elkin, I. (1999). A major dilemma in psychotherapy outcome research: disentangling therapists from therapies. *Clinical Psychology: Science and Practice*, 6, 10–32.

Gordon, K. and Toukmanian, S.G. (2002). Is how it is said important? The association between quality of therapist interventions and client processing. *Counselling and Psychotherapy Research*, 2, 88–98.

Greenberg, L.S., Watson, J.C. and Lietaer, G. (1998). *Handbook of Experiential Psychotherapy*. New York: Guilford.

Henry, W.P., Schacht, T.E. and Strupp, H. (1986). Structural analysis of social behavior: application to a study of interpersonal process in differential psychotherapeutic outcome. *Journal of Consulting and Clinical Psychology*, 54, 27–31.

Hill, C.E., Thompson, B.J. and Corbett, M.M. (1992). The impact of therapist ability to perceive displayed and hidden client reactions on immediate outcome in first sessions of brief therapy. *Psychotherapy Research*, 2(2), 143–55.

Hill, C.E., Thompson, B.J., Cogar, M.C. and Denman, D.W. (1993). Beneath the surface of long-term therapy. *Journal of Counselling Psychology*, 40(3), 278–87.

Kierkegaard, S. (1954). *Fear and Trembling and the Sickness unto Death*. (W. Lowrie, Trans.) Garden City, New York: Doubleday Anchor. (Originally published 1843).

Kihlstrom, J.F. and Cantor, M. (1984). Mental representations of the self. In

L. Berkowitz (ed.), *Advances in Experimental Social Psychology*, Volume 17 (pp. 1–47). New York: Academic Press.

Lambert, M.J., De Julio, S.S. and Stein, D.M. (1978). Therapist interpersonal skills: process, outcome, methodological considerations, and recommendations for future research. *Psychological Bulletin*, 85, 467–89.

Lambert, M. and Hill, C. (1994). Assessing psychotherapy outcomes and processes. In A.E Bergin and S.L. Garfield (eds), *Handbook of Psychotherapy and Behavior Change* (4th edn) (pp. 72–113). New York: Wiley.

Lambert, M.J. and Okiishi, J.C. (1997). The effects of the individual psychotherapist and implications for future research. *Clinical Psychology: Science and Practice*, 4(1), 66–75.

Lewin, K. (1951). *Field Theory in Social Science*. New York: Harper.

Linville, P.W. (1987). Self-complexity as a cognitive buffer against stress-related illness and depression. *Journal of Personality and Social Psychology*, 52(4), 663–76.

Macaulay, H. (2005). What are the qualities of therapists' empathic responses? Unpublished Master's thesis, York University, Toronto, Ontario.

May, R. (1961). *Existential Psychology*. New York: Random House.

Merleau-Ponty, M. (1962). *Phenomenology of Perception* (Colin Smith, Trans.). New York: Routledge.

Moskowitz, G.B. (2005). *Social Cognition: understanding self and others*. New York: Guildford.

Neisser, U. (1976). *Cognition and Reality: principles and implications of cognitive psychology*. New York: W.H. Freeman, Times Books, Henry Holt and Company.

Orlinsky, D.E., Ronnestad, M.H. and Willutzki, U. (2004). Fifty years of psychotherapy process-outcome research: continuity and change. In M. Lambert (ed.), *Bergin and Garfield's Handbook of Psychotherapy and Behavior Change* (5th edn) (pp. 307–90). New York: Wiley.

Patterson, C.H., and Watkins, C.E. (1996). *Theories of Psychotherapy* (5th edn). New York: HarperCollins.

Perls, F.S. (1969). *Ego, Hunger and Aggression: the beginning of Gestalt therapy*. NY: Random House.

Rennie, D.L. (1994a). Clients' deference in psychotherapy. *Journal of Counselling Psychology*, 41, 427–37.

Rennie, D.L. (1994b). Clients' accounts of resistance in counselling: a qualitative analysis. *Canadian Journal of Counselling*, 28, 43–57.

Rogers, C.R. (1942). *Counseling and Psychotherapy*. Boston: Houghton Mifflin.

Rogers, C.R. (1947). Some observations on the organization of personality. *American Psychologist*, 2, 358–68.

Rogers, C.R. (1951). Perceptual reorganization in client-centered therapy. In

R.R. Black and G.V. Ramsey (eds), *Perception: an approach to personality*. Oxford, UK: Ronald: 307–27.

Rogers, C.R. (1957). The necessary and sufficient conditions of therapeutic personality change. *Journal of Consulting Psychology*, 21, 95–103.

Rogers, C.R. (1959). A theory of therapy, personality, and interpersonal relationships as developed in the client-centered framework. In S. Koch (ed.), *Psychology: a study of a science*. Volume 3. *Formulations of the Person and the Social Context* (pp. 184–256). New York: McGraw Hill.

Rogers, C.R. (1961). The process equation of psychotherapy. *American Journal of Psychotherapy*, 15, 27–45.

Rogers, C.R. (1975). Empathic: an unappreciated way of being. *Counselling Psychologist* 5(2), 2–10.

Rogers, C.R. (1980). *A Way of Being*. Boston, Mass.: Houghton Mifflin.

Sachse, R. and Elliott, R. (2002). Process-outcome research on humanistic therapy variables. In D.J. Cain (ed.), *Humanistic Psychotherapies: handbook of research and practice* (pp. 83–115). Washington, DC: APA.

Sanders, P. and Wyatt, G. (2002). Introduction to Volume 4: contact and perception. In G. Wyatt and P. Sanders (eds), *Rogers' Therapeutic Conditions: evolution, theory, and practice*. Ross-on-Wye: PCCS Books: vii-xiii.

Stein, K.F. and Markus, H.R. (1996). The role of the self in behavioral change. *Journal of Psychotherapy Integration*, 6(4), 349–84.

Thagard, P. and Kunda, Z. (1998). Making sense of people. In S.J. Read and L.C. Miller (eds), *Connectivist Models of Social Reasoning and Social Behavior* (pp. 3–26). Mahwah, N.J.: Lawrence Erlbaum.

Thompson, B.J. and Hill, C.E. (1991). Therapist perceptions of client reactions. *Journal of Counselling and Development*, 69(3), 261–5.

Toukmanian, S.G. (1990). A schema-based information processing perspective on client change in experiential psychotherapy. In G. Lietaer, J. Rombauts and R. van Balen (eds), *Client-Centered and Experiential Psychotherapy Towards the Nineties* (pp. 304–26). Leuven, Belgium: Leuven University Press.

Toukmanian, S.G. (1992). Studying the client's perceptual processes and their outcomes in psychotherapy. In S.G. Toukmanian and D.L. Rennie (eds), *Psychotherapy Process Research: paradigmatic and narrative approaches* (pp. 77–107). London: Sage.

Toukmanian, S.G. (1996). Clients' perceptual processing: an integration of research and practice. In W. Dryden (ed.), *Research in Counselling and Psychotherapy: practical applications* (pp. 184–210). London: Sage.

Toukmanian, S.G. (2002). Perception: the core element in person-centered and experiential psychotherapies. In G. Wyatt and P. Sanders (eds), *Rogers' Therapeutic Conditions*. Volume 4. *Contact and Perception* (pp. 115–32). Ross-on-Wye: PCCS Books.

Watson, J.C. (2002). Re-visioning empathy. In D.J. Cain and J. Seeman (eds),

Humanistic Psychotherapies: handbook of research and practice (pp. 445–71). Washington, DC: APA.

Watson, J.C., Enright, C. and Kalogerakos, F. (1998). The impact of therapist variables in facilitating change. Paper presented at the Society for Psychotherapy Research, Snowbird, Utah, June.

Zimring, F. (2000). Empathic understanding grows the person. The *Person-Centered Journal*, 7, 101–13.

17

The Process of Person-Centred Therapy

Martin van Kalmthout

The 'psychotherapeutic process' refers to the process of change on the part of the client and can therefore be distinguished from the fundamental attitudes of the therapist or the so-called core conditions of empathy, respect and authenticity. The assumption is nevertheless that the aforementioned fundamental attitudes create a climate in which the process of client change can develop. In this chapter, I will concern myself only with the change process on the part of the client: what, from a person-centred perspective, does the change process involve and how can it be described and explained?

In the traditional psychotherapeutic literature, the process of client change was generally referred to as 'personality change' (Rogers, 1957; van Kalmthout, 1998). Personality change is considered a complex phenomenon. And in the contemporary world of therapy, many people, including person-centred therapists, think that personality change is too high a goal and far too idealistic an objective for therapy. According to these people, personality change simply does not fit into these modern times (Sachse, 2004). In my view the concept of personality change as developed by Rogers (1957, 1959) is essential to person-centred therapy, whether it takes the form of so-called classical, experiential, process-experiential or a more generalized form of person-centred therapy (see Chapter 9, this volume).

Core concepts

The central notions underlying the person-centred approach to personality change were developed and refined by Rogers during the course of his life. He also made considerable use of the work of his student, Gendlin, who later made Rogers' ideas more explicit and concrete. In order to do justice to the development of the relevant concepts, it is useful to distinguish a number of levels that are otherwise indistinguishable: the individual, the interpersonal and the existential.

The individual level

Rogers' ideas with regard to change follow directly from his theory about the origins of psychological difficulties. According to Rogers, psychological difficulties are the consequence of a discrepancy or incongruency between what he calls the organismic valuing process and the self-concept (see Chapter 7, this volume). The internal tension between the organismic experiencing and the self-concept leads to anxiety and depression or other psychological complaints (Rogers, 1959). The aim of therapy, according to Rogers, is then to bring the self-concept and organismic experiences of the person closer together. The person-centred description of this change is to say that the client has shifted from a state of incongruency to a state of congruency or, in more popular terms, becoming him or herself. Rogers (1961: 163) described the result of change process in the following famous terms: 'To be that self which one truly is'.

In Rogers' theory of change, the actualizing tendency of the individual also constitutes a central notion (see Chapter 6 in Rogers, 1980, and Chapter 5, this volume). The actualizing tendency is a tendency towards growth and development that Rogers argues is present in all living beings. When people change, they participate in this universal energy, which Rogers also refers to as the formative tendency (1980).

Crucial to the entire change process is that the person becomes increasingly aware of physical and visceral sensations in addition to cognitive perceptions. In ordinary language, this means that one comes into greater contact with one's own feelings and emotions, which are thus not denied or avoided. Gendlin used the term 'bodily felt sense' to refer to the physical experiences, and the term 'focusing' to refer to a special method intended to help clients consider their emotions and feelings (1996). Gendlin's approach is therefore referred to as experiential therapy precisely because the emphasis lies on the experiencing of emotions and feelings, becoming aware of them, and acting in accordance with them.

Rogers tried to describe the change process in terms of a number of successive stages. In his famous book that first appeared in 1961, *On Becoming a Person*, Rogers describes no less than seven stages or phases in the change process, with detailed specification of which criteria should be used to determine whether or not the change process is becoming more profound or being carried forward using Gendlin's terminology (see Rogers, 1961, Chapter 7, 'A process conception of psychotherapy'). The proposed criteria were originally supposed to make it possible to measure the level of experiencing along the so-called process scale. The principal line underlying the successive phases of change proceeds from fixation to fluidity, from a state of externalization to a state of being in contact with one's feelings and giving expression to these, and thus from incongruence to congruence. Also essential to the change process is the shift from detachment in relationships to intimacy. At the one end of the continuum, clients have no contact with their feelings; at the other end, they *are* their feelings and clearly communicate these to others. Experiencing is no longer structure bound, which means: 'the situation is experienced and interpreted in its newness, not as the past' (Rogers, 1961: 152). This boils down to the freedom to experience everything that we encounter, and to live without clinging to old structures that constrain our experiencing. This is clearly a very radical view of the process of change, which we call personality change.

The interpersonal level

Rogers assumed that, as clients progressed along the aforementioned continuum, their interpersonal relations would also improve as a matter of course. Change at the individual level was assumed to lead automatically to changes in interpersonal relationships and a shift from distance to intimacy. Although this may often be the case, the so-called interpersonal or interactionist branch of the person-centred approach to therapy has pointed out that explicit attention to the specific *interpersonal patterns* of clients may be of use and sometimes necessary (van Kessel and Lietaer, 1998; van Kalmthout, 2002a).

When viewed from this perspective, Rogers' theory can indeed be seen to constitute a distinctly relational theory with respect to not only the emergence of psychological problems but also the change process itself. That is, psychological problems emerge within the field of tension created by our universal longing for autonomy and our universal longing for connectedness. Speaking globally, two 'survival' strategies can then emerge in our youth to help us deal with this universal conflict: the first is isolation; the second is fusion. Both strategies are actually derailments in our attempt to develop autonomy, on the one hand, and connectedness, on the other. A healthy solution thus consists of a good balance between autonomy and connectedness as opposed to a one-sided 'preference' for isolation or fusion.

From this interpersonal perspective, for personality change to occur it is important that clients recognize their specific relational patterns and alter these. Many clients, for example, show a tendency to 'solve' their problems via isolation or avoidance. Others do this by making themselves completely dependent, or fighting others in such a manner that they always end up losing. Given that the patterns often involve deeply rooted survival strategies and are therefore difficult to change, it is necessary to tackle them as concretely as possible and to help the client change them at the level of overt behaviour. The therapeutic relationship provides an excellent opportunity to do this because it allows the client to experience actual contact with the therapist and thereby realize that a relational pattern other than the one that has been unconsciously developed during the course of his or her life is possible. Within the safe confines of the therapeutic situation, thus, an alternative relational pattern can be experimented with and practised for later application in daily life.

The existential level

According to Rogers (1951: x), 'therapy is of the essence of life, and is to be so understood.' In such a manner, he indicates that person-centred therapy is aimed at encouraging the individual to live all aspects of life with all its possibilities. Within this context, Rogers (1967) speaks of 'the fully functioning person' and does not mean a fixed end state such as enlightenment but a process or way of being. Personality change thus goes further than simply the treatment of symptoms. Personality change concerns life itself and how we can best live it. In the same article Rogers writes about the 'good life'. This is characterized by increased openness to experiencing, an increased degree of existential living, and increased trust in the organismic valuing process. This leads to not only greater creativity but also a richer and more meaningful existence. And it is this type of change that person-centred therapy is aimed at. The following extensive quotation demonstrates succinctly his person-centred vision of personality change and existential living, as exemplified by the concept of the fully functioning person.

> They [fully functioning persons] tend to move away from façades. Pretence, defensiveness, putting up a front, tend to be negatively valued.
> They tend to move away from 'oughts'. The compelling feeling of 'I ought to do or be thus and so' is negatively valued. The client moves away from being what he 'ought to be', no matter who has set that imperative.
> They tend to move away from meeting the expectations of others. Pleasing others, as a goal in itself, is negatively valued.
> Being real is positively valued. The client tends to move toward being himself, being his real feelings, being what he is. This seems to be a very deep preference.
> Self-direction is positively valued. The client discovers an increasing pride and confidence in making his own choices, guiding his own life.
> One's self, one's own feelings come to be positively valued. From a point where he looks upon himself with contempt and despair, the client comes to value himself and his reactions as being of worth.
> Being a process is positively valued. From desiring some fixed goal, clients come to prefer the excitement of being a process of potentialities being born.
> Perhaps more than all else, the client comes to value an openness to all of his inner and outer experience. To be open to and sensitive to all of his inner and outer experience. To be open to and sensitive to his inner reactions and feelings, the reactions and feelings of others, and the realities of the objective world – this is a direction which he clearly prefers. This openness becomes the client's most valued resource.
> Sensitivity to others and acceptance of others is positively valued. The client comes to appreciate others for what they are, just as he has to come to appreciate himself for what he is.
> Finally, deep relationships are positively valued. To achieve a close, intimate, real, fully communicative relationship with another person seems to meet a deep need in every individual, and is very highly valued.
>
> (Carl Rogers, in Kirschenbaum and Henderson, 1990: 182)

From theory to practice

In the following, I will present two case examples and one session transcript to illustrate the process of person-centred therapy and the resultant personality change, as described above. Although these refer to three different clients, the process they went through is essentially the same. In the non-judgemental therapeutic climate created by the core conditions, these clients explore the discrepancy or incongruency between their organismic self and their conditioned self or façade. They struggle to free themselves from the grip of their past by breaking through their old intrapersonal (the self concept) and interpersonal patterns.

Example I

This client is a woman of about 50 years of age. She is unmarried, has few friends and no contact with her family. She has a history of being the victim of physical, emotional and sexual violence. Despite all this, she has gone far with her education, work and hobbies. In this respect she is 'talented' – as in her daily social interactions. She nevertheless prefers to be alone and has a tendency to avoid intimate relationships or end them. In her work, she also usually leaves after some time and takes on a new job. Personal relationships appear to be threatening and therefore something that she flees from.

The client seeks help because she is totally burned out, is worried about her aggressiveness, and also concerned about her increased isolation. She has already made a link to her past, has a need to pursue the link further, and thus no longer denies the past. The client reports seeking help on multiple occasions in the past, for the same problems.

During therapy, a number of different patterns become apparent that can be clearly characterized as survival strategies. Her most important survival strategy is to withdraw and thus avoid becoming dependent on others. The pattern of withdrawal emerged under the horrible circumstances of the client's youth, but the price in her present life is that she has become not so much autonomous as isolated. The old survival strategy was very important earlier but now impedes her from successfully entering into an intimate relationship. A second survival strategy is always being as helpful as possible in order to be appreciated by others. This is a classic example of the operation of what Rogers (1959) calls 'conditions of worth'. The client has replaced an extremely negative self-image, developed as a consequence of sexual abuse, physical assault, and emotional neglect, with a positive self-image based on the helping of others. The price of such a survival strategy in adulthood, however, is that the client experiences fits of anger and can become very aggressive towards colleagues and clients at times. The individuals involved always bear a resemblance to people from earlier and thereby trigger her rage. Swallowing the pain and hurt incurred earlier, and hiding behind a friendly and helpful pattern of behaviour, has allowed a split between the external pattern and the internal emotions and feelings of the person to arise. Using Rogers' terminology, we can say that the client has not allowed her feelings of pain and rage to enter into consciousness and has denied these feelings with the development of a self-concept based on only being friendly and helpful.

Personality change for this client boiled down to breaking through the survival strategies that had developed and establishing a realistic and congruent self-image. The change process began with the insight that the old survival strategies had seen better days. This did not imply that the strategies had to be eradicated altogether; rather, the strategies had to be transformed as each pattern contains a healthy core. Change for this client meant that she had to do away with the lopsided growth that constitutes extreme derailment. Taken together, this means that the client became autonomous as opposed to isolated, and that she transformed her fear of fusion or being swallowed up by the other into a healthy connectedness by, for example, setting boundaries, learning to say 'no' and being more assertive. In such a manner, she learnt to enter into relationships without sacrificing her autonomy and swinging to the fusion that previously characterized her life. In the security of the therapeutic relationship, this client underwent a *corrective emotional experience*. She experienced that it is possible for someone (i.e. the therapist) to respect her unconditionally and to be sincerely concerned about her while also confronting her with certain patterns of behaviour and interaction that were tangible in the relationship with the therapist. On the basis of this, the client applied the new experiences and interpersonal patterns of behaviour to daily life.

This profound process of change took years and was a difficult battle involving considerable trial and error. The battle demanded a great deal from the client and the therapist. But when headway was made, the reward was large. The person was freed from the prison of the past, from the suffocating bonds of once successful survival strategies, and from a negative self-image. The client could now live her life instead of just surviving and start to enjoy the good life as described by Rogers (1967).

Example 2

This client is a man of almost 60. His wife has forced him to get psychotherapeutic treatment as she is otherwise going to divorce him. The reason is that there has been no personal or sexual contact between them for years. This client has no contact with his feelings whatsoever, avoids all responsibility, is not capable of reacting empathically to someone, and is locked into his own – often bizarre – cognitive constructions; for example, he cannot do anything until he has got a perfect plan. He is not in contact with himself and there is no contact with others. The reach of the client is no further than his own 'self'.

At the start of therapy, incidentally, the client was not at all aware of any of this. He was very obstinate in the face of any form of feedback or critique from his wife, his children or the therapist. The fact that the duration of the therapy was long also indicates just how difficult it was for this client to realize even a small change in his behaviour, not to mention his personality. And this raises the question of whether personality change was a legitimate objective for this client who, rather than having a negative self-image, lacked any self-image. This meant that when he looked at himself, a big black hole appeared and he experienced considerable anxiety. He did not experience an autonomous entity within himself and thus there was no entity that allowed him to take responsibility for his own life.

The change process for this client consisted of the following. First of all I helped him to take responsibility for his life and did not fall for his appeals to say what he should or should not do. Another important part of the change process was to have the client continually focus on his feelings and emotions. Finally, in relational therapy the client was confronted with the damage that he did to others by not only doing but also not doing certain things.

For this client every occasion on which neurotic structures were abandoned for even a moment constituted progress or so-called 'moments of movement', as fixedness lies at the core of this client's problems. Letting go, movement and change are big words, but the underlying processes manifest themselves in the apparently smallest everyday things. For the process of this client, this meant wrestling with repeated instances of falling and having to pick himself up again. The word 'discipline' appears to apply here. The client had to come into increased contact with his feelings and acknowledge both his fears and his longings. On the basis of this, he could then take increased responsibility for his own life and stop placing responsibility for his life beyond or outside himself. And this is what Rogers (1964) means by a more experience-oriented existential life.

Session transcript

To provide insight into the actual course of person-centred therapy, a transcript of a small part of a session of another client is presented below. It is a good example of a therapist who is active, engaged, congruent and at the same time respectful and empathic, and thus helps the client to experience a deeply felt insight into the core of his problems. Such an insight is one of the crucial aspects of the person-centred change process, wherein the client explores his inner world. The transcript concerns a client who begins the session with the announcement that things again went all wrong for him during the past week.

C: My mother was found in the gutter again, completely drunk, in really bad shape, one big mess. I really don't know what to do.

T: How did you react?

C: I ran home, crawled into bed, and didn't show myself for four days.

T: This incident appears to arouse a lot in you.

C: Yeah, all the feelings from earlier when things had again gone so far.

T: What kinds of feelings?

C: Utter despair.

T: I can imagine this after all you have told me about the situation. As a child, you could do absolutely nothing.

C: But I'm not a child anymore. I'd like to be rid of the bullshit once and for all.

T: Yeah and justifiably so. The problem is that it's like a button that gets pushed when you hear about your mother again: the old feelings send you completely out of bounds. You can only run away or get completely beside yourself in response to the helpless anger that you experience, just as in the past.

C: That's exactly it.

T: Such a reaction used to be completely functional. It's possible that you actually survived as a result of it. But now you'd like to get rid of it because it is only a burden.

C: Yes, that's right. I just don't know how.

T: Well, let's see if things can be done differently.

C: I have no idea.

T: I think you actually know as we have often discussed this in connection with other examples involving more or less the same problem. The problem is, of course, much worse in the case of your mother and also the hardest to get rid of.

C: What do you mean?

T: Because it all started there.

C: Oh, yeah.

T: The same pattern stands out in all the other examples though. If someone has problems, you quickly come to the rescue. But you do not know how to express your irritation or your rage at the same time. You're afraid to do so. You are afraid that you will fall apart, just as with your mother earlier.

C: That's right. That's why I usually avoid the contact, because I so quickly panic in such situations.

T: You've lost track of the limits. You think in two extremes: avoidance or complete devotion at the cost of yourself.

C: There's something in between. Helping people and expressing your irritation at the same time, if necessary.

T: Exactly, but then without tearing the other to pieces.

C: Strange that I still do not recognize that this is what is happening.

In this transcript the client clearly demonstrates a growing awareness of his relational patterns. His ability to contact his feelings and be open to hear the therapist show his openness to his experiencing. He is continuing the process of understanding his patterns of isolation and fusion and is beginning to find the middle ground where there is a balance between autonomy and connectedness. More concretely this implies that the client is expressing his feelings without being aggressive in a way which is out of proportion.

Research

Rogers and his colleagues were among the first psychotherapists to perform empirical scientific research on the results of psychotherapy and how the results can be explained. These two types of psychotherapy research are known, respectively, as *outcome research* and *process research*. From those days onwards, the conduct of process research has been a characteristic of the person-centred tradition (Elliott et al, 2004; Elliott et al, 2005). And for the present topic, this is also most relevant. In process research, there is an attempt to gain insight into that which actually occurs in psychotherapeutic sessions.

Rogers again provided the initial impetus by making the first audio recordings of therapy sessions and analysing these. In this way, he attempted to identify what made clients change and what the changes entailed. And also through this technique, he discovered the occurrence of so-called moments of movement or critical points in the change process (Rogers, 1961: 130). An example is the client coming into real contact with his or her feelings and subsequently giving expression to these instead of externalizing them. Another example is the client suddenly reaching a deeply felt insight. The experience scale described earlier can be used to measure the relevant change processes.

More recently this kind of 'process' research has been conducted and further developed extensively by two well-known person-centred researchers Les Greenberg and Robert Elliott. Elliott, for instance, undertook creative research on the process of the client's change, by asking him or her, after the session, what was really helpful. In this 'post-session process recall research' qualitative methods can play an important role (see Chapter 24, this volume).

Despite the importance of scientific research for the understanding of such complex phenomena as personality change, the limitations of traditional scientific methods should not be forgotten. In-depth insight into the process of change requires a fundamental attitude of enquiring on the part of both the client and the therapist; it is not only the power of reason but also that of the heart that are of greatest importance for this (van Kalmthout, 2005). In other words, the change process itself is a search in which nothing is fixed a priori and all external holds must be abandoned. And this requires a fundamental 'scientific' attitude in the deepest sense of the word. So, we should not limit the 'scientific' to the limited meaning of empirical research, but extend it to the enquiring attitude of both the therapist and the client in the process of change.

Critical reflections for the future

The process of person-centred therapy is a fundamental change process that imposes high demands on both the client and the therapist precisely because it is aimed at such fundamental change. Within the person-centred community itself, there are voices suggesting that person-centred psychotherapy has seen better days and should – in keeping with the times – set more modest objectives for itself, namely the treatment of complaints and symptoms instead of personality change (for example: Sachse, 2004). In my opinion, such a shift will mark the end of the person-centred tradition as it involves a clear loss of identity. The question, of course, is what exactly constitutes the identity of the person-centred approach. In the final phases of its development, Rogers considered his work to be more of a practical philosophy of living than a school of psychotherapy, and therefore started to speak of the person-centred approach rather than person-centred therapy (Rogers, 1980). Construed as a philosophy of life, the person-centred approach indeed starts to resemble such spiritual disciplines as Zen or Taoism (Purton, 2004). In the context of our topic, the process of change, this similarity receives further expression in the fact that Rogers increasingly speaks of becoming a process as opposed to a person in his later work and also speaks of a way of being as opposed to a therapeutic method. In this later phase of his development, the self-concept is viewed as more of an obstacle than a vehicle for the radical change that Rogers has in mind. And more than a specific personality change, the change process itself – which actually never ends – is the objective. Person-centred therapy has always been aimed at the person as opposed to the complaint or problem. In Rogers' later work, however, person-centred therapy definitely enters the domain of the spiritual or religious although in an extremely secular and modern form. Person-centred therapy can thus perhaps best be referred to as a modern system of meaning (van Kalmthout, 2004). And from such a perspective, it is not so strange that some people are of the opinion that the person-centred tradition is best conceptualized as a spiritual discipline with its future also thus in this direction (Thorne, 2002). In any case, the adoption of such a perspective sheds a completely new light on the person-centred school of thought and can certainly help us further develop our own identity in the future (van Kalmthout, 2006). In this conception of person-centred therapy, in contrast to the present fashion of a medical-like approach to therapy, the fundamental change process, as described in this chapter, is a central issue.

REFERENCES

Elliott, R., Greenberg, L. and Lietaer, G. (2004). Research on experiential psychotherapies. In M. Lambert (ed.), *Bergin and Garfield's Handbook of Psychotherapy and Behavior Change* (5th edn) (pp. 493–539). New York: Wiley.

Elliott, R., Watson, J., Goldman, R. and Greenberg, L. (2005). *Learning Emotion-Focused Therapy: the process-experiential approach to change.* Washington: APA.

Gendlin, E. (1996). *Focusing-Oriented Psychotherapy: a manual of the experiential method.* New York: Guilford.

Kirschenbaum, H. and Henderson, V. (eds) (1990). *The Carl Rogers Reader.* London: Constable.

Purton, C. (2004). *Person-Centred Therapy: the focusing-oriented approach.* Basingstoke: Palgrave MacMillan.

Rogers, C. (1951). *Client-Centered Therapy.* Boston: Houghton Mifflin.

Rogers, C. (1957). The necessary and sufficient conditions of therapeutic personality change. *Journal of Consulting Psychology,* 21, 95–103.

Rogers, C. (1959). A theory of therapy, personality, and interpersonal relationships, as developed in the client-centered framework. In S. Koch (ed.), *Psychology: a study of a science.* Vol. III (pp. 184–256). New York: McGraw-Hill.

Rogers, C. (1961). A process conception of psychotherapy. In *On Becoming a Person: a therapist's view of psychotherapy* (pp. 126–59). London: Constable.

Rogers, C. (1964). Towards a modern approach to values: the valuing process in the mature person. In H. Kirschenbaum and V. Land Henderson (eds) (1990), *The Carl Rogers Reader* (pp. 168–85). London: Constable.

Rogers, C. (1967). A therapist' s view of the good life: the fully functioning person. In H. Kirschenbaum, and V. Land Henderson (eds) (1990), *The Carl Rogers Reader* (pp. 409–20). London: Constable.

Rogers, C. (1980). *A Way of Being.* Boston: Houghton Mifflin.

Sachse, R. (2004). From client-centered to clarification-oriented psychotherapy. *Person-Centred and Experiential Psychotherapies*, 3(1), 19–35.

Thorne, B. (2002). *The Mystical Power of Person-Centred Therapy: hope beyond despair.* London: Whurr.

van Kalmthout, M. (1998). Personality change and the concept of the self. In B. Thorne and E. Lamberts (eds), *Person-Centred Therapy: a European perspective* (pp. 53–61). London: Sage.

van Kalmthout, M. (2002a). The farther reaches of person-centered psychotherapy. In J. Watson, R. Goldman and M. Warner (eds), *Client-centered and Experiential Psychotherapy in the Twenty-first Century: advances in theory, research and practice* (pp. 127–43). Ross-on-Wye: PCCS Books.

van Kalmthout, M. (2002b). The future of person-centered therapy: crisis and possibility. *Person-Centered and Experiential Psychotherapies*, 1(1 and 2), 132–43.

van Kalmthout, M. (2004). Person-centered psychotherapy as a modern system of meaning. *Person-Centered and Experiential Psychotherapies*, 3 (3), 192–206.

van Kalmthout, M. (2005). *Psychotherapie en de zin van het bestaan.* Utrecht: de Tijdstroom.

van Kalmthout, M. (2006). Person-centred therapy as a spiritual discipline. In J. Moore and C. Purton (eds), *Counseling and Spirituality: experiential and theoretical perspectives* (pp. 155–68) Ross-on- Wye: PCCS Books.

van Kessel, W. and Lietaer, G. (1998). Interpersonal processes. In L. Greenberg, J. Watson and G. Lietaer (eds), *Handbook of Experiential Psychotherapy* (pp. 155–77). New York: Guilford.

PART
III
Settings and Client Groups

Part III addresses the expansion of person-centred applications into more varied settings and with more diverse populations. During the early years of the development of person-centred psychotherapy and counselling, researchers and practitioners made few distinctions among different client populations. This absence was common in much of psychological literature. We know from descriptions of workshops, counselling tapes and the rich oral history of the person-centred approach that clinical studies did include persons of colour, of varying sexual and gender identities, and with diverse forms of problems, but for Rogers these aspects of his clients' reality were not his focus. He was interested in getting at what he thought were universals of psychological processes, and it was for succeeding generations to challenge the person-centred core hypotheses within wider and more particular sets of contexts. As the approach expanded into more areas of practice and with more varied demographic and problem groups, specialized approaches have developed to meet the particular needs of these diverse populations. As Lago's chapter in this section discusses, the past decades of research have revealed the limitations of a universalist stance and the significance of particular contextual realities such as race, sexuality and gender, class, physical ability, religion and national origin. At the same time, however, research within the person-centred community and beyond has revealed that person-centred theory and practices do indeed contain some universal threads that are applicable in many different settings (see Chapter 23, this volume).

Application of the approach has also expanded beyond the professional counselling dyad into consideration of familial, organizational, cultural and societal processes. Researchers and practitioners across the globe have tested the applicability of the core person-centred relational conditions in most of the arenas in which psychological knowledge is applied. A comprehensive catalogue of these multiple and varied ways of working would be beyond the scope of one handbook. In the following chapters we cover some of the principle contexts in which person-centred approaches can be found useful and hope to present the flavour of what person-centred approaches look like when applied to a range of clients and settings. Though applied in quite diverse situations and populations, what is most evident from the following chapters is the way in which a person-centred approach begins with the strengths and potentialities of its clients, whatever their challenges – whether facing death, crisis or severe mental disabilities – rather than their 'pathologies', 'disorders' or limitations. The section also addresses another important aspect of a person-centred approach – its effectiveness in addressing intervention in larger systems. Through a range of engaging and moving case studies, these chapters span the breadth of human experience, from those people in deeply withdrawn psychotic states, to work for social equality and justice, to organizational health, mutual-help and to art and creativity. The chapters separately and together provide a sense of some principles we now might consider as universal. Regardless of context, the core faith in people's abilities to reach their full potential, with appropriate encouragement and support, can facilitate a shift towards wholeness and higher levels of functioning in individuals and groups.

This section opens with Prouty and Van Werde's discussion of Pre-Therapy: that is, working with clients who are psychotically withdrawn, with mental impairment that renders them at the outset of therapy beyond the reach of therapeutic contact. It describes work with clients who are 'contact-impaired', in particular people diagnosed with schizophrenia and special needs. After a long period of development Pre-Therapy is one of the most rapidly expanding fields of person-centred practice and this chapter, written by founder Garry Prouty together with Dion Van Werde, the European representative of the Pre-Therapy Network, gives a concise and comprehensive introduction to this pioneering work.

This is followed by a chapter by Colin Lago, who addresses the issues raised when working with clients who have been seen by mainstream society as 'other'. In the past several years, Lago has written a number of seminal works in this area, including *Race, Culture and Counselling* (2005, Open University Press), and his chapter presents an in-depth, critical analysis of how issues of race, class, gender and other 'differences' have been addressed in the person-centred domain. More importantly perhaps, he presents some key recommendations for how the person-centred field can become more adept at working across boundaries of difference and more sensitive to the full range of needs and backgrounds that our clients might have.

Chapter 20 explores the application of person-centred therapy to work with couples and families. Written by family therapist Charles O'Leary from the United States, author of *Counseling Couples and Families: a person-centred approach* (Sage, 1999) and his colleague Martha Johns, this chapter introduces the literature in this area and addresses some of the questions and paradoxes needed to be an effective person-centred practitioner with families and couples.

In Chapter 21, Jobst Finke and Ludwig Teusch, two German psychiatrists closely involved with the person-centred movement, explore the issue of how person-centred therapy can be conducted in a medical framework in which diagnosis and positivistic assumptions predominate. Here they present an extended case example of a woman with panic disorder and agoraphobia, showing how the client's difficulties can be understood and interpreted from a person-centred standpoint, and how this can be used as the basis for 'treatment'. The authors attempt to strike a balance between the requirements of a medical setting and the more postmodern and relational assumptions of the person-centred worldview.

In the aftermath of such disasters as the Asian Tsunami in December 2004 and Hurricane Katrina in July 2005, as well as the countless private crises that occur every day, there is a growing awareness of the urgent need to develop approaches that are effective with people in crisis. This is explored by Lorna Carrick, who has specialized in this area for many years. Carrick shows how, from a person-centred perspective, even the greatest challenges in a person's life can be seen as an opportunity for growth and development.

The section concludes with a chapter that moves beyond the professional counselling and psychotherapy sphere. Its four contributing authors all worked with Carl Rogers personally, and collaborated with him to expand the application of person-centred principles beyond the therapeutic context and apply them to a range of personal, interpersonal and socio-political concerns and practices. Valerie Land Henderson from the United States (co-editor with Howard Kirschenbaum of *The Carl Rogers Reader* (1989, Houghton Mifflin)) describes moving work with groups of people who are facing terminal illness and impending death. Maureen O'Hara provides an introduction to person-centred work in organizational change. Gay Barfield describes a diverse array of initiatives for intergroup peace and reconciliation, including the Carl Rogers Peace Project which she co-directed with Rogers and for which Rogers was nominated for the Nobel Peace Prize. The section concludes with a concise and moving account of Person-Centred Expressive Arts developed by Rogers' daughter Natalie and now experiencing a period of rapid growth worldwide.

18

Pre-Therapy

Dion Van Werde and Garry Prouty

In this chapter, we will present Pre-Therapy and the concept of the pre-expressive self. These are the method and the rationale for working with pre-relational and pre-experiential functioning and for dealing with it in a psychotherapeutic way (Prouty, 1994; Prouty et al, 2002).

Besides the already well-documented applications in fields of care for people with special needs (see also Krietemeyer and Prouty, 2003; Pörtner, 2002, 2005; Peters, 1999) and psychotic people (see also Sommerbeck, 2003: 68–173), there is now a growing literature on the influence of Pre-Therapy in applications in varied fields: for example, home situations (Clarke, 2005: 16–17; McWilliams and Prouty, 1998), working with people who tend to dissociate and other trauma related functioning (Coffeng, 2005), in music therapy (Leijssen, 2000), nursing work in everyday care (Van Werde, 2000, 2004, 2005), remedial education (Ondracek, 2005: 391–4). The fields of autism and dementia are being studied also (Van Werde, 2002b; Van Werde and Morton, 1999; Dodds et al, 2004). Van Werde, coordinator of the Pre-Therapy International Network (dion.vanwerde@sint-camillus.be) and close associate of Prouty for many years, implemented Pre-Therapy in everyday practice in residential psychiatric care for people suffering psychotic functioning (Van Werde in Prouty et al, 2002: 61–120; Van Werde, 2002a, 2005). This represents a translation of Pre-Therapy into the creation of a multidisciplinary contact-milieu.

After Prouty's initial research efforts, and after Dinacci and associates' work with chronic psychotic people (Dinacci, 2000; Poli, 2005), a new wave of research is in progress on such issues as how the body is addressed in low level functioning (De Keyser) and working with people with dementias (Dodds).

Introduction

Pre-Therapy theoretically directly evolved from Rogers' (1957: 96) concept of psychological contact. As he described 'all that is intended by this first condition is to specify that the two people to some degree are in contact; that each makes some perceived difference in the experiential field of the other'. Prouty (1990) asserts that such a definition lacks theoretical conceptualization leading to treatment or quantitative developments. Pre-Therapy is a theory of psychological contact specifically designed to provide concepts of treatment and measurement. Rogers goes on to say 'this first condition of therapeutic change is such a simple one that perhaps it should be labelled an assumption or a *precondition*.' Prouty (1976, 1990) thus coined the term 'Pre-Therapy'. Pre-Therapy as psychological contact is a precondition for client-centred therapy as applied to persons who have schizophrenia, are mentally retarded and those with dementias.

The second author's concern with the concept of contact originates from his life history, coming as he did from a family background where different family members experienced different forms of contact-impaired functioning due to retardation and/or psychosis (Prouty et al, 2002: 3–4). It was only later, when he was studying and being supervised in his clinical practice by E.T. Gendlin, that 'Pre-Therapy' as such was born, at the crossroads of personal and professional experience. Seen in the framework of person-centred therapy, it represents an evolution in person-centred and experiential theory and practice (Prouty, 1994). Carl Rogers, listening to Garry Prouty's lecture at the celebration of the 15th anniversary of the Chicago Counselling Center in 1986, explicitly acknowledged his innovative and historically important professional work (Prouty et al, 2002: 8–9).

Psychological contact

Sanders and Wyatt (2002) present a history of contact within client-centred theory. Gestalt and psychoanalytic psychotherapies (Perls et al, 1969: 371–447; Perls, 1969; Havens, 1986) also present views of contact. Contact theory as presented in the work of Garry Prouty is structurally described as 1) contact reflections, 2) contact functions, and 3) contact behaviours (Prouty, 2003). *Contact reflections* are extraordinarily concrete and literal. They include situational, facial, word-for-word, bodily and reiterative therapist reflections. They are the therapist's 'work'. *Contact functions* are an expansion of Perls' (1969) concept of contact as an 'ego function'. They are reality, affective and communicative functions. *Contact behaviours* are the emergent social words and sentences of the client. They become the basis for measurement.

Contact reflections

Reflections were first introduced by Otto Rank (Rychlak, 1971: 410) to clar- ify cognitive content for both the therapist and the client. Carl Rogers (1966) evolved them to include both cognitive as well as affective content. Eugene Gendlin (1968) conceived reflections as facilitating the experiencing process. Pre-Therapy utilizes them for developing or restoring psychological contact. Contact reflections are a 'pointing at the concrete'. They point at the concreteness of schizophrenic and brain-damaged functioning (Arieti, 1955: 13; Gelb-Goldstein, 1966). The concreteness of the contact reflections is meant to 'meet' the concreteness of client-expression. Also it conveys the atti- tudes of unconditional positive regard and empathy (Prouty, 2001a, 2001b).

The following (Prouty, 1994, 2001a, 2001b: 42) is a treatment vignette that illustrates the development of contact functioning. By means of using contact- reflections, and in doing so addressing the surrounding reality (RR), the spoken words (WWR), body posture (BR) and facial expression (FR) (see further), real- ity, affective and communicative contact evolve into the client–therapist interac- tion. The client ('C'), diagnosed as 'chronic schizophrenic' is a hospitalized person in a long stay facility. The therapist ('T') is a student.

C: Come with me.
T: WWR Come with me.

The patient led me to the corner of the day-room. We stood there silently for what seemed to be a very long time. Since I couldn't communicate with her, I watched her body movements and closely reflected these.

C: [The patient put her hand on the wall.] Cold.
T: BR-WWR [I put my hand on the wall and repeated the word.] Cold.

[She had been holding my hand all along, but when I reflected her, she would tighten her grip. Dorothy would begin to mumble word fragments. I was careful to reflect only the words I could understand. What she was saying began to make sense.]

C: I don't know what this is anymore. [Touching the wall (REALITY CONTACT).] The walls and chairs don't mean anything anymore. [Existential autism.]
T: WWR-BR [Touching the wall.] You don't know what this is anymore. The chairs and walls don't mean anything to you anymore.
C: [The patient began to cry (AFFECTIVE CONTACT).]
C: [After a while she began to talk again. This time she spoke clearly (COMMU- NICATIVE CONTACT).] I don't like it here. I'm so tired ... so tired.
T: WWR [As I gently touched her arm, this time it was I who tightened my grip on her hand. I reflected] You're tired, so tired.
C: [The patient smiled and told me to sit in a chair directly in front of her and began to braid my hair.]

Clearly, this example shows the emergence of the contact functions in a therapeutic context.

Situational reflections (SR):

Being embedded in living concrete situations, environments or milieu constitutes our literal 'being in the world'. It implies awareness of people, places, events and things. Accordingly, situational reflections facilitate reality contact for the client. An example could be 'Mary pulls her hair'; other examples could be 'you're sitting on the floor'; 'a red floor'.

Facial reflections (FR):

The human face, described as the 'expressive organ', contains not yet formed, pre-expressive affect. Facial reflections facilitate the experiencing or expression of affect. They develop the client's affective contact. An example would be 'You look sad' or even more concretely 'There are tears in your eyes.'

Word-for-word reflections (WWR):

Many contact-impaired clients present symptoms of verbal incoherence. Such a flow of communication could be 'fire' (unintelligible), 'rat' (unintelligible) 'moon', and so on. Even though this makes no conventional sense, the social language would be reflected word for word: fire – rat – moon. Incoherent sounds are sometimes included. This approach develops communicative contact.

Body reflections (BR):

Many schizophrenic patients express bizarre body symptoms such as echopraxia (an involuntary repeating of other person's movements) and catatonia. There are two types. One is verbal 'Your arm is in the air'; the other is literal body duplications, such as holding your arm in the air when the client does. Prouty and Kubiak (1988) present a case study using body reflections with a catatonic client.

Reiterative reflections (RR):

Not specific techniques, reiterative reflections embody the principle of 're-contact'. If a particular reflection produces a response it should be repeated, thus sustaining the contact. 'Short term' reflections are immediate. For example: T: (SR) 'you touch the wall'; C: smiles; T: (FR) 'you smile'; T: (RR) 'you touched the wall and (FR) now you close your eyes'. 'Long term' reflections are at longer time intervals to 'revive' the contact. For example, T: (SR) 'you are holding your toy-duck in your lap'; (SR) 'you flip his head'; (RR) 'yesterday you were holding your duck and said it was your baby'.

A web of contact

After a period of consistent empathic application of the contact reflections, a 'web of contact' is developed between client and therapist which provides sufficient communication to enable therapy. A newer example of such work is described in Krietemeyer and Prouty (2003).

Contact reflections facilitate the contact functions resulting in the emergence of contact behaviours.

Contact functions

Merleau-Ponty describes human consciousness in terms of three polarities or 'concrete *a priori*' (Malin, 1979: 138): the 'world', the 'self' and the 'other' (Merleau-Ponty, 1962: 60). Prouty et al (2002: 12–13) state, 'I live with and consciously experience the world in all its immanent power. I live with and experience the self with all its psychological value. I live with others and all their significance.' These are the *structural priorities of involvement* for our daily conscious life.

Such a description can be translated into psychological terms by translating Perls' (1969: 139) concept of contact as an 'ego function' into three awareness function(s): reality (world), affect (self) and communication (other). These contact functions are the 'revelatory absolutes' of the phenomenal field through which concrete existents manifest themselves.

Reality contact

Reality contact (world) is defined as the awareness of people, places, things and events. If we describe the world as we concretely experience it we can see that we live with all types of things – door handles, shoes and so on. Our world is 'peopled'. They are on planes, buses, in houses, practically everywhere. Spatial loci or 'places' are a concrete part of our reality. We live in space. Things are in space: 'The ball is here, you are there.' Things, people and places have their temporal locus in events: 'I am here now, you are there now.' This tapestry of things, people and temporal-spatiality is the weave of our conscious reality.

Affective contact

Affective contact is the client's response to the world and the 'Other'. It is defined as the awareness of moods, feelings and emotions – each phenomenologically distinct. Mood is subtle and diffuse. It is a background sensing or a 'colouring' of current experience. I can be with friends, yet experience an anxiety or depression without realistic focus. Feeling is clearer in that it has a more specific locus, it is a response to the event itself as in 'I liked your smile' or 'the cat makes me angry'. Instead of being background it is foreground. Emotion is affect that is much more intense. It is sharp, clear and more filling of psychological space. It has the quality of being totally foreground: 'I am enraged if you slap my wife.'

Communicative contact

Communicative contact is defined as the symbolization of reality (world) and affect (self) to others. It is the meaningful expression of the client's perceived world and self. It reveals generally through social signs as words and sentences.

The development or restoration of the contact functions (reality, affect and communication) is the necessary precondition of psychotherapy and functions as the theoretical goal of Pre-Therapy (Prouty, 2002a).

Contact behaviours

Contact behaviours are the emergent behavioural changes that emerge from the application of Pre-Therapy. They are the operationalized aspect of psychological contact.

Reality contact is operationalized as the verbalization of people, places, things and events. Affective contact is operationalized as the bodily or facial expression of affect as well as the use of feeling words (e.g. sad, happy). Communicative contact is operationalized as the use of social words and sentences.

These dimensions of contact can be measured and such measurement reflects a shift in the client from a pre-expressive to an expressive state. We measure the client's contactful expression about the world, self and other.

Prouty (2002b) reviews empirical studies in Pre-Therapy. Hinterkopf et al (1979) found significant increases in gain scores in reality and communicative contact with chronic schizophrenics when compared with a control group receiving recreational therapy. The patients had an average hospitalization of 20 years. A single case pilot study (Prouty, 1990, 2002b) explored the effects of Pre-Therapy with a hospitalized special needs/psychotic client with a Stanford-Binet IQ of 17. Large increases of reality, affective and communicative contact were recorded. Prouty (1994: 45–6) in another single case study measured the inter-rater reliability of 'psychological contact'. The client was a young hospitalized woman diagnosed with schizophrenia and special needs who received Pre-Therapy. There were two sets of observations, one for a single day and another for a three-month period. For the single-day observations a correlation co-efficient of 0.9847 with a p-value of .0001 was found. The three-month observations yielded a correlation coefficient of 0.9966 with a p-value of .01, presenting strong evidence against the null hypothesis. In yet another pilot study, De Vre (1992) further confirmed inter-rater reliability and provided evidence for reliability. There were three clients. The first two were chronic schizophrenics with normal intelligence. The third was diagnosed as also having low intelligence scores. In other words, he was classified as 'special needs'. The initial rating produced kappa 0.39. The next two ratings with improved Flemish translations produced kappa 0.76 and kappa 0.87. The reliability measure was obtained using independent psychiatric nurses trained in the Pre-Therapy scale. Dinacci (Prouty, 2002b, 1994) produced a video study of clients receiving Pre-Therapy. This study involved

a single therapist, two experimental and two control clients. They were diagnosed with special needs/schizophrenia with hospitalization averaging 30
years. The experiment produced strong clinical and quantitative evidence for
marked communicative increases in the near-mute clients, using the evaluation criterion for the Pre-Therapy interview (ECPI) scale, which measures
verbal coherence and severe levels of disorganization.

In sum, Pre-Therapy (contact reflections) evolves from Rogers' conception
of 'psychological contact' as the first condition of a therapeutic relationship.
It describes psychological contact in terms of therapist method (contact reflections), client process (contact functions) and client measurable behaviours
(contact behaviours). Pilot studies provide suggestive evidence that warrant
further empirical investigation. It can also be said that the technique of using
Pre-Therapy reflections is easy, but the art is difficult.

Episodes of lucidity and the pre-expressive self

The pre-expressive self is a heuristic concept derived from personal experience, case histories and quantitative explorations of Pre-Therapy (Prouty,
2000). Prouty has long recognized the influence of his schizophrenic/retarded
brother on the development of Pre-Therapy. He says:

> One day when I was 11 or 12 years old, I invited a friend to visit my home.
> While we were talking I said 'I wonder if he (brother) understands what we are
> saying?' To my intense surprise my brother responded by saying 'You know I do
> Garry,' and then he relapsed back into his autistic-regressed state. This 'episode
> of lucidity' 'haunted' me for many years, often giving the feeling 'there was
> someone in there' (later to be understood as the pre-expressive self). It was
> several weeks *after* the publication of my first book (Prouty, 1994) that the
> meaning of that experience became clear. In the forward of the 1994 book, Luc
> Roelens, a Belgian psychiatrist, reported a similar case arguing against the
> medical understanding of psychotic states. He describes several cases of patients
> suddenly making contact. One case involves a woman with a severe, chronic and
> muted catatonia. When informed her husband had fallen of the roof of their
> home and broken his leg, she promptly replied by saying she would go home and
> take care of everything. There was no relapse. A four and ten-year follow-up
> revealed only a mild autism. Another 'episode of lucidity' involved a mute male
> schizophrenic who had been in a dementia-like state. He was drinking through
> a straw close by a nurse when he coughed and spat all over her. He immediately
> responded by saying: 'Excuse me, I did not mean to do that.' After that he
> relapsed into his isolation.
>   My brother and these cases express 'episodes of lucidity' which point to the
> presence of the 'pre-expressive self' embedded in autism, regression, psychosis,
> brain-damage, retardation and dementia and so on (Dodds et al, 2004). The
> 'episodes of lucidity' manifest the pre-expressive self.

The pre-expressive self is also revealed in other signs. First is the fact that all
case histories and quantitative studies illustrate movement from fragmented,
incomplete, bizarre, incoherent expression to fuller cogency and self-congruence – a movement from a pre-expressive state to an expressive state. Signs of

the pre-expressive self are also observed in the verbal process of psychotic expression. The semiotic structure of initial psychotic expression can be characterized in the following way. These pre-expressive forms have no general context to derive meaning from and they have no referent to complete their symbolic function. This means the expression lacks reality sense and appears to be void of a reality source. Hence their dismissal by psychiatry. For example, a young male catatonic expresses himself by saying 'Priests are devils' repeatedly. By carefully using 'word-for-word' reflections, this eventually processed into the reality of a homosexual overture by a local priest. The highly condensed metaphor contained 'latent-reality' content. The movement from a highly condensed metaphor to latent reality is called 'pre-expressive process'. Without understanding that latent reality is 'packaged' in a pre-expressive way, the therapeutic potential of psychotic expression is not envisioned.

Clinical vignette

On the person-centred ward where the first author works (see earlier references), the goal is to practise a multidisciplinary contact milieu that on the one hand matches the ideas and practice as expressed by Prouty about working with low-contact-level persons, and on the other hand fits the tasks and responsibilities of the medical context. Constantly, especially as a nurse, one has to bridge a more individual-focused and experientially oriented approach, with the everyday and more general concerns for housekeeping, motivating clients, receiving visitors, organizing leisure activities, administrating medication and so on. The following vignette dramatically illustrates a way of doing this in a crisis intervention situation in a manner that is in alignment with the formulated existential phenomenological approach. It represents the use of contact reflections in what we call 'nurses' contact work'.

Band-aid to prevent scars

Author's first person account

In the small room for physical care (for activities such as giving injections or measuring blood pressure) next to the nurses' office, a situation seems to be going out of control. A staff member comes to get me, the ward psychologist, since a crisis intervention is necessary. In the small room, on the adjustable table for medical examinations, a young man is sitting with his legs over the side and obviously very agitated about his right knee, which already has several pieces of band-aid stuck on it. A nurse who recently joined our team and who does not have a lot of professional experience – nor any formal training in Pre-Therapy yet – is with him in the room. She is clearly intimidated by his loud insistence on an extra band-aid. So far, she has given in to his demands to apply four of them to his knee, although she cannot understand why he wants them. She is not willing to give in to his demand that yet a fifth be applied. He wants them there to prevent scars, he has told her. The nurse can't see any wounds or scars, so his demand is clearly coming from how he pre-expressively lives his private world and tries to communicate about it, rather than from objective reality. The nurse hoped that he would be satisfied with one band-aid and would then be willing to join the others for lunch, but he has kept asking for more. When he now demands to have his knee shaved and to have a fifth band-aid applied, she has reached her limit. She is not prepared to go along with that. She thinks using a razor is too risky – besides being totally unnecessary – and after all, she wants to end this confrontation.

As I come in the room, the nurse steps aside and hands me the band-aid. I start doing contact work.

(In the transcription below, the words spoken by the client are in italics. See the earlier section on 'Contact reflections' for explanations of the abbreviations of the type of reflections used. The client, here called 'Chris', consented to publication of the interaction so long as we changed his name.)

(Starting with an ordinary question to estimate the level of functioning.)

T. Hi Chris, what seems to be the matter?

C. *I must have a pair of scissors.* (This seems like an answer to my question but at the same time it is a repetition of what he has been saying all the time. I estimate his level in between congruent and psychotic functioning and begin applying Pre-Therapy reflections.)

T. WWR You must have a pair or scissors. (SR) I see your pants on the floor, you sitting on the table, four band-aids on your knee.

C. *The band-aid must go here!* (commanding and looking at his knee)

C. *My hair must be removed!* (raising his voice)

T. WWR The hair should go off and the band-aid on.

C. *Stick on the band-aid!* (addressing me directly)

Here it seems that his level of contact has increased somewhat; I can understand him. I pick up the affective side of the communication and give a kind of summary of what has been happening, be it in a very concrete and brief mode.

T. Seems like something very important to you, the band-aid. I heard that you also asked the nurse to stick it there. (I point at the knee)

He seems to hear me. I consequently shift the level of communication further up and try a question:

T. Why the band-aid?

C. *It has to go!*

This again is an unclear communication, so I shift back to reflecting to match his pre-expressive level:

T. WWR, BR It has to go and you point to your knee.

C. *No scars.*

T. BR, WWR I see a red spot and you say 'no scars'.

C. *The hair is growing right through it.*

T. SR (again very concrete) I see four band-aids on your knee. I see a small red spot there, some redness there.

C. *It has to go.*

T. WWR ... that has to go (he starts smiling) (FR) and you smile.

T. RR, SR, RR You smile, you look into my eyes and smile.

C. (then very serious again) *It must go on it.*

T. SR I'm standing here with the band-aid in my hand and you want me to stick it on. I don't know exactly why, but hear that you want me to.

C. *And it needs salve properly spread on to it, otherwise it will melt and drip from underneath it. Put it on! No scars.*

Because he is describing the care he wants, I get the impression that his level is up again and I decide to take the risk of putting the 'shared' reality gently next to his 'private' reality of the scars and the care wanted. Crucial again is the need to stay very close to the concrete reality that is given. Still no interpretations, judgements, orders, taking over the process from my side. Meanwhile, his aggravation seems less. A bridge between different realities is beginning to form ...

T. SR Chris, I don't see scars. I do see some redness – like a small wound that is recovering.

C. *Hair grows through it and should be cut off.*

T. (I closely inspect the red dot and say in a conversational mode, SR) Oh yes, I do see little hairs growing in it ... (and then like a nurse that would present the realities of how to take care of a wound) ... looks like it's recovering. It doesn't need salve nor a band-aid. I'm sorry, I can't follow you on that.

C. (He looks at me again, seems speechless for a moment, than smiles and says) *Put it on* (in a less harsh tone).

I repeat and thus anchor him into the reality of a situation earlier that day. He had walked into the nurses' office with a tube of salve of his own, demanding the nurse to put some salve on his temple. Later I heard that he had also complained about his two knees lowering [sic]. ... Again keeping very close to what had happened and again formulating it in a very concrete way, I say:

T. RR Just a while ago, you came for salve on your temple and you and the junior nurse put it on together, here in the room, in front of the mirror ... (in saying so, not limiting my understanding to this specific situation).... seems like a lot of things going on, Chris.

C. (probably, he really feels understood and his affective contact deepens) *Yes, sure!* (this makes some psychological space and I present the reality of ward life)

T. By the way, have you had lunch yet? (SR) It is ten past twelve already ...

C. (he answers congruently, clearly reality contact as well as communicative contact is restored) *No, I haven't have lunch yet.*

T. Is it OK about the band-aid and can you go for lunch?

C. (He looks straight in my eyes again and says) *I don't want to look like a monster ...*

T. WWR You don't want to look like a monster, I hear you.

Afterwards, this seemed to me the crux of what had been going on. In his pre-expressive state, he had wanted everything done to prevent him from looking a monster! Than, making some space and a bridge to another moment to address these things, if he wants to, I say:

T. If you want to, we can talk about this later. (And again offering the reality of the meal) Is it OK for you to put your trousers on again, Chris, and go for lunch?

He steps down from the table, puts his trousers on and goes for lunch.

The vignette of the interaction illustrates that 'contact' is the precondition of any (psychotherapeutic) work. The situation had come to an unbearable intensity involving anger, screaming and potentially overt aggression. As hypothesized in Pre-Therapy, when contact increases, symptomatology – conceptualized as contact loss – decreases. Once Chris felt seen and heard, once he connected with the other person present and the surrounding reality, he was able to choose for himself to cross the bridge to the other and the shared reality again. He let go of his pre-expressive and psychotically expressed demands. He consequently connected with the structure of ward life again and went for lunch.

Obviously, there had been problematic pre-relational and pre-experiential functioning. Nevertheless – and it is important to realize and value this – this man had been (pre-expressively) addressing somebody else and had asked for help. It was only through the contact offer made that further escalation of 'unadjusted' behaviour was prevented. In the end, and by his own choice, he even fitted in with the structure. No violence had to be used, there was no need to take over his psychological process.

It is important to note that the significance of this rather complex example of crisis intervention isn't limited to working with people with low or borderline levels of psychotic functioning. One can easily transfer these kinds of situations to the care for people with special needs, to some extent to the care for persons with dementia, to people in a chronic situation, to people with dissociative functioning and so on.

CONCLUSION

Prouty – touched by the suffering of people due to troubled awareness of their material environment, frozen affective functioning and being deprived of proper social communication – formulated 'Pre-Therapy'. He defined 'psychological contact' as a precondition for any (psycho)therapeutic work and Pre-Therapy as a way of restoring contact whenever it was absent or still fragile.

Radical in its starting point of take symptomatic functioning and individual freedom seriously, and never forgetting 'that there is always somebody in there', this method has proved to be a centripetal evolution of person-centred/experiential thinking and practice.

REFERENCES

Arieti, S. (1955). *An Interpretation of Schizophrenia*. New York: Robert Brunner.

Clarke, C. (2005). A carer's experience of the mental health system. In S. Joseph and R. Worsley, *Person-Centred Psychopathology: a positive psychology of mental health* (pp. 9–20). Ross-on-Wye, PCCS Books.

Coffeng, T. (2005). The therapy of dissociation: its phases and problems. *Person-Centred and Experiential Psychotherapies*, 4, 90–105.

De Vre, R. (1992). Pre-Therapie. Masters thesis, Gent: rijksuniversiteit Gent, Belgium.

Dinacci, A. (2000). ECPI: Objective evaluation criteria for the Pre-Therapy interview. *Pre-Therapy International Review*, 1, 0, 31–42.

Dodds, P., Morton, I. and Prouty, G. (2004). Using Pre-Therapy techniques in dementia care. *Journal of Dementia Care*, 12(2), 25–8.

Gelb-Goldstein, K. (1966). Gelb-Goldstein's concept of 'concrete' and 'categorical' attitude and the phenomenology of ideation. In A. Gurswitch (ed.), *Studies in Phenomenology and Psychology* (pp.359–84). Evanston: Northwestern University Press.

Gendlin, E.T. (1968). The experiential response. In A. Hammer (ed.), *Use of Interpretation in Treatment* (pp. 208–28). New York: Grune and Stratton.

Havens, L. (1986). *Making Contact: uses of language in psychotherapy*. Cambridge: Harvard University Press.

Hinterkopf, E., Prouty, G. and Brunswick, L. (1979). A pilot study of Pre-Therapy method applied to chronic schizophrenics. *Psychosocial Rehabilitation Journal*, 3, 11–19.

Krietemeyer, B. and Prouty, G. (2003). The art of psychological contact: the psychotherapy of a mentally retarded psychotic client. *Person-Centred and Experiential Psychotherapies*, 2(3), 151–61.

Leijssen, S. (2000). Zorg die als muziek in je oren klinkt. Muziektherapie bij dementerende oudere mensen. *Praktijkboek kwaliteitszorg* (Praktijkvoorbeeld 12: 113–32), VVSG.

Malin, S.B. (1979). *Primordial Contact: Merleau-Ponty's philosophy*. New Haven Connecticut: Yale University Press.

McWilliams, K. and Prouty, G. (1998). Life enrichment of a profoundly retarded woman: an application of Pre-Therapy. *Person-Centered Journal*, 1, 29–35.

Merleau-Ponty, M. (1962). *The Phenomenology of Perception*. New York: Humanities Press.

Ondracek, P. (2005). Personzentriertheit. In H. Greving and P. Ondracek, *Handbuch Heilpädagogik* (pp. 382–400). Troisdorf: Bildungsverlag EINS.

Perls, F. (1969). *Ego, Hunger and Aggression: the beginning of Gestalt therapy.* New York: Vintage Books.

Perls, F., Hefferline R. and Goodman, A. (1969). *Gestalt Therapy: excitement and growth in the human personality.* New York: Julian Press.

Peters, H. (1999). Pre-Therapy: a client-centred experiential approach to mentally handicapped people. *Journal of Humanistic Psychology,* 45, 8–29.

Poli, E. (2005). Paolo: the rediscovery of contact and the world. *Pre-Therapy International Review,* 4(4), 11–12.

Pörtner, M. (2002). Psychotherapy for people with special needs: a challenge for client-centred psychotherapists. In J. Watson, R. Goldman and M. Warner (eds), *Client-Centred and Experiential Psychotherapy in the Twenty-first Century: advances in theory, research and practice* (pp. 380–6). Ross-on-Wye. PCCS Books.

Pörtner, M. (2005). Nine considerations concerning psychotherapy and care for people 'with special needs'. In S. Joseph and R. Worsley, *Person-Centred Psychopathology: a positive psychology of mental health* (pp. 242–59). Ross-on-Wye: PCCS Books.

Prouty, G. (1976). Pre-Therapy: a method of treating pre-expressive psychotic and retarded patients. *Psychotherapy: Theory, Research and Practice,* 13, 290–4.

Prouty, G. (1990). Pre-Therapy: a theoretical evolution in the person-centred/experiential psychotherapy of schizophrenia and retardation. In G. Lietaer, J. Rombauts and R. Van Balen (eds), *Client-Centred and Experiential Psychotherapy in the Nineties* (pp. 645–58). Leuven: Leuven University Press.

Prouty, G. (1994). *Theoretical Evolutions in Person-Centred/Experiential Psychotherapy: applications to schizophrenic and retarded psychoses.* Westport Connecticut: Praeger.

Prouty, G (2000). Pre-Therapy and the pre-expressive self. In T. Merry (ed.), *The BAPC Reader* (pp. 68–76). Ross-on-Wye: PCCS Books.

Prouty, G. (2001a). A new mode of empathy: empathic contact. In S. Haugh and T. Merry (eds), *Rogers' Therapeutic Conditions: evolution, theory and practice.* Volume 2. *Empathy* (pp.155–62). Ross-on-Wye: PCCS Books.

Prouty, G. (2001b). Unconditional positive regard and Pre-Therapy: an exploration. In J. Bozarth and P. Wilkins (eds), *Rogers' Therapeutic Conditions: evolution, theory and practice.* Volume 3. *Unconditional Positive Regard* (pp. 76–87). Ross-on-Wye: PCCS Books.

Prouty, G. (2002a). Pre-Therapy as a theoretical system. In G. Wyatt and P. Sanders (eds), *Rogers' Therapeutic Conditions: evolution, theory and practice.* Volume 4. *Contact and Perception* (pp.60–62). Ross-on Wye: PCCS Books.

Prouty, G. (2002b). Humanistic psychotherapy for people with schizophrenia. In D. Cain and J. Seeman (eds), *Humanistic Psychotherapies: handbook of research and practice* (pp. 579–601). Washington, D.C.: American Psychological Association.

Prouty, G. (2003). Pre-Therapy: a newer development in the psychotherapy of schizophrenia. *The Journal of the American Academy of Psychoanalysis and Dynamic Psychiatry*, 31, 1, 59–73.

Prouty, G. and Kubiak, M. (1988). The development of communicative contact with a catatonic schizophrenic. *Journal of Communication Therapy*, 4(1) 13–20.

Prouty, G., Van Werde, D. and Portner, M. (2002). *Pre-Therapy: reaching contact impaired clients*. Ross-on-Wye: PCCS Books.

Rogers, C. (1957). The necessary and sufficient conditions of therapeutic personality change. *Journal of Consulting Psychology*, 21(2), 95–102.

Rogers, C. (1966). Client-centered therapy. In S. Arieti (ed.), *American Handbook of Psychiatry*, Vol. 3 (pp. 183–200). New York: Basic Books.

Rychlak, J. (1971). *Introduction to Personality and Psychotherapy*. Boston: Houghton Mifflin.

Sanders, P. and Wyatt, G. (2002). The history of Conditions One and Six. In G. Wyatt and P. Sanders (eds), *Rogers' Therapeutic Conditions, Evolutions and Practice*. Volume 4. *Contact and Perception* (pp.1–24). Ross-on-Wye: PCCS Books.

Sommerbeck, L. (2003). *The Client-Centred Therapist in Psychiatric Contexts: a therapists' guide to the psychiatric landscape and its inhabitants*. Ross-on-Wye: PCCS Books.

Van Werde, D. (2000). Persoonsgerichte psychosezorg: de tegenstelling 'maatschappij' en 'proces' overstegen? *Tijdschrift cliëntgerichte psychotherapie*, 38, 4, 274–9.

Van Werde, D. (2002a). The falling man: Pre-Therapy applied to somatic hallucinating. *Person-Centred Practice*, 10(2), 101–7.

Van Werde, D. (2002b). Prouty's Pre-Therapy and contact-work with a broad range of persons' pre-expressive functioning. In G. Wyatt and P. Sanders (eds), *Rogers' Therapeutic Conditions: evolution, theory and practice*. Volume 4. *Contact and Perception* (pp. 168–81), Ross-on-Wye: PCCS Books.

Van Werde, D. (2004). Cliëntgericht werken met psychotisch functioneren. In M. Leijssen and N. Stinckens (eds), *Wijsheid in gesprekstherapie* (pp. 209–24). Leuven: Leuven University Press.

Van Werde, D. (2005). Facing psychotic functioning: person-centred contact work in residential psychiatric care. In : S. Joseph and R. Worsley (eds), *Person-Centred Psychopathology: a positive psychology of mental health* (pp. 158–68), Ross-on-Wye: PCCS Books.

Van Werde, D. and Morton, I. (1999). The relevance of Prouty's Pre-Therapy to dementia care. In: I. Morton (ed.), *Person-Centered Approaches to Dementia Care* (pp. 139–66). Bicester, Oxon: Winslow.

CHAPTER 19

Counselling Across Difference and Diversity

Colin Lago

It was 1977. I was 15. My local comprehensive school in the north-east was notorious for being rough. Being different in any way was far from cool. I was different. My family was part Jewish, part Catholic, and we were, as my mum kept telling us 'not raised to be sheep'. Oh and I was a lesbian, in love with my best friend. I only knew what a lesbian was because I had been called one at school by horrible boys.

(Bindel, 2004)

Introduction

Historically, the person-centred approach was conceived as a sufficient and satisfactory therapeutic form for all client populations. The approach offered a model that conceptualised a sensitive interpersonal therapeutic relationship and it was supported by good research evidence (Stubbs and Bozarth, 1994).

Little attention, however, was given to the particular and specific needs of persons/clients from minority populations. Encapsulated within this term 'minority' are a wide variety of client groups broadly deemed in contemporary parlance (both within the UK and North America) to be 'different' and 'diverse'. A substantial body of research evidence exists that demonstrates unequivocally that persons from these groups experience oppressive and discriminatory behaviour from the 'majority' society. These patterns of discrimination are, sadly, evident in every facet of socio-cultural life: education, employment, medicine, social work, policing, the judiciary and penal systems and so on (Harris, 2004; Mason, 2001; Halpern, 2004; Read, 2004; Willie et al, 1995; Pilkington, 2002).

What guarantee do we have, as a professional body of therapists, that we will not repeat these same patterns of discriminating behaviour in our therapeutic work with minority-group clients, when so many others in 'caring' services have been found wanting?

Counselling across difference and diversity demands that therapists enhance their awareness of their own identity development and attitudinal base as well as developing their knowledge of the specific minority client groups with whom they work. Implicit in this enhanced sensitivity and knowledge will be an understanding of the myriad of discriminatory mechanisms that pervade society (and thus individuals within it) and a commitment and willingness to seek new language/s and behaviours that are respectful and anti-discriminatory for all clients. To explore these issues, therapists, particularly those from 'majority' groups in society, may well have to face major challenges to their assumptions, views and preconceptions.

Attitudes are learned. But attitudes towards members of other groups are not determined so much by experience as by attitudes prevailing among older members of the group to which one belongs (Forgas and Williams, 2002).

Societally embedded concepts, attitudes and ideas concerning social and intergroup relations become, for the individual, his/her own concepts and ideas. They become part of the individual's personal identity, accepted, adopted, internalized, and introjected. Eventually these group based attitudes become so smoothly incorporated into the individual that they become owned, affirmed and an unquestioned part of the self (Althusser, 1971).

These then must become one of our targets for reflection, consideration and change in relation to working with those deemed as 'different' or 'diverse'. Not to address one's attitudes and prejudices to 'other' groups within society is to risk, however well intentioned one is to clients, repeating discriminatory practices within the therapeutic setting.

Towards a definition of difference and diversity

The terms 'difference' and 'diversity', surprisingly, have seldom been defined. In 2004 the Equality and Diversity Forum of the British Association for Counselling and Psychotherapy produced a working definition of the concepts and ventured a listing of those groups deemed to be privileged, 'different' and 'diverse' within society.

There are particular groups which are privileged in UK society. These groups represent the often-unexamined norm from which 'difference' is defined. For example:

Advantaged/Norm includes white people, heterosexual people, able-bodied people, men and people of working (income generating) age.

Disadvantaged/different includes black and minority ethnic people, lesbian, gay and bisexual people, disabled people, women, young people/older people/unemployed people ...

As may be seen from the above statements, there are a considerable number of categories of persons deemed 'different' or 'diverse'. Each group or category (e.g. gay and lesbian people, disabled people) will have their own 'languages', knowledge and models of being. Therapists will be at a considerable disadvantage if they do not possess some competence within these specific fields of application.

In addition, these group-specific ideas, principles, jargon, and specialized language are also part of a shifting dynamic phenomenon, i.e. descriptors and ideas held within minority groups and those who work with them change over time. These changes represent an inevitable movement in ideas and language, shifting towards greater accuracy of self-description and ascription, and towards addressing and confronting their relationship with the prevailing attitudes held by the dominant group. These shifts represent a minority group's aspirational movement towards seeking parity with dominant society, towards seeking respectful and socially just treatment, towards seeking an end to the pervasive, pernicious and damaging oppressive dynamics its members suffered over time.

Diversity and difference are relational

Meta research on counselling and psychotherapy has suggested that the relationship between client and therapist accounts for 30 per cent of the success outcome variables in therapy. (Lambert, 1992: Lambert, Shapiro and Bergin, 1986). By contrast, only 15 per cent of the success variables are accounted for by therapists' theoretical perspective and techniques.

The person-centred approach (PCA) is in the main a two-person theory of therapy that focuses to a great extent on relational factors. For the clients these are:

- an impulsion into therapy created by their sense of distress and incongruence
- that they and the therapist achieve psychological contact
- that they perceive the therapist as relationally responsive and attentive.

For the therapist, there are the attitudinal and behavioural perspectives of:

- acceptance of the client
- an empathic attitude towards the client
- a genuineness in relating to the client.

The approach is thus uniquely poised to equip therapists with a modus operandi for working with all clients from wherever they hail. Its great contribution is that it names in the above therapeutic conditions some of the component parts of the helping relationship.

However, where a therapist is working with a client of a different or diverse group, what the theory does not take into account is:

- The therapist's own comfort and competence in working with the particular client. For example, if the therapist has strong negative feelings towards the group from which the client hails, how might he/she offer warmth and acceptance? How might he/she manage to attain congruence/transparency in relation to the client?
- The client's previous experience of relating to and working with someone, either from the majority group or from outside the group to which he or she belongs.

Can a therapist coming from the 'majority' group within society truly and empathically indwell in a minority client's experiencing and views of the world, particularly if those views are alien to the therapist's? Can the therapist create a 'good enough' relationship with the client that they may work well enough together? Might the therapist, however inadvertently and unconsciously, repeat behaviours and views that have had negative impacts upon the client previously? These questions, and many more, have great consequences, in practice, for the outcomes for the client. There is a constant danger that clients will be exposed, yet again, to all the discriminatory mechanisms with which they may be so familiar and by which they have been deeply hurt. In short, the creation of a relationship that is trustworthy, therapeutic and non discriminatory between two persons of 'difference' is a profoundly important therapeutic aim and it may be riven by immense complexity in practice.

Whose is the difference anyway?

> What Jennifer was saying was that she accepted who she was, including the deaf part of herself. Her experience of disability came from expectations placed on her to conform to the common stereotype of deafened people and assumptions that her deafness must be the most important aspect of her life. She said later: 'I wouldn't experience being deaf at all if they allowed me to continue being who I am. Really, the deafness belongs to them.'
>
> (Corker in Lago and Smith, 2003: 45)

The above section introduced the very important concept of the relationship of difference and diversity to those not deemed different and diverse. The terms 'different' and 'diverse' exist only as descriptions for those who are not deemed as different or diverse! Inevitably, in meeting, both parties may become implicated in the co-construction of difference. The client from the 'minority' group may well adopt a form of 'proxy self' that is assumed when meeting members of the dominant group. Similarly therapists from the majority group may be so anxious about how they respond to the minority client that this anxiety then affects their self-presentation. Inevitably, these dynamics will impact upon the ensuing quality of the relationship.

Whilst acknowledging this effect of co-construction, between the minority-group client and the majority-group counsellor, I am keen, here, to focus the spotlight upon therapists and the nature of their attribution of 'difference' towards the 'other'. Seeing and naming the 'other' as different profoundly affects the comfort levels and manner in which therapists embark upon their work with clients.

The quote used above to introduce this section exemplifies this further. Disability in this case belongs to the perceiver not the perceived. Indeed, to transform the words of the old saying: 'beauty (and difference and diversity) is/are in the eye of the beholder'.

Difference and diversity are determined by the majority culture. Sadly for those named, measured and judged under such aspersions, they may suffer considerably and systematically, in the material, social and psychological realms due to various discriminatory behaviours (broadly defined as sexist, racist, disablist, ageist, homophobic, etc.). The power and dominance positions of society that are reflected in and evidenced by repeating patterns of discrimination and oppression are inevitably also present (though not necessarily always tangible) in the micro-meeting system of dominant-group therapist and minority-group client.

The person-centred approach: tensions and criticisms (in relation to difference and diversity)

Gillian Proctor has noted tensions between the person-centred approach, which aspires to enter into the unique world of each client, and the feminist approach that recognizes the particular situation of women within society (Proctor and Napier, 2004). This tension is one that must be borne in mind when counselling across the whole range of difference and diversity. At a most serious level, this distinction is a separating schism between the various approaches (including PCA) that respond to the individual and those approaches (woman-centred, anti-disablist, anti-oppressive, etc.) that respond to individuals in their environment.

The criticisms that have been levelled at the approach include the following:

- The assertion that the model is 'lily white'; in other words, that it was conceived in and borne out of mid-Western, white American male cultural experience (Holdstock, 1993).
- That the approach ignores both the client's and the therapist's contextual circumstances in society (Chaplin, 1988).
- The approach is not suitable for particular populations who would expect a more directive style from therapists (Laungani, 2004; Khoo et al, 2002).
- In a recent text, Carl Rogers' two demonstration interviews with an African-American client, recorded in the 1970s, have been scrutinized from a series of different theoretical and research-based perspectives. Most notably, Barbara Brodley, in her chapter, notes that Rogers was 'uncharacteristically directive' with this client compared with many of his other demonstration interviews (Brodley in Moodley et al, 2004).
- O'Hara (1996: 185) has noted the limitations she experienced in Carl Rogers' capacity to understand her particular, culturally different perspective: 'there were times that not even the empathic genius of Carl Rogers could bridge the gap and reconcile the fundamental differences in "world view" ... "construction of reality" ... "ways of knowing" ... between himself – a famous, powerful, successful, upper-middle class, white, American male – and myself – a young unknown immigrant, working-class, white English female.'
- Several authors in the text by Moodley et al (2004) also note that, despite Rogers' obvious empathic and therapeutic behaviours with this client, he is 'race avoidant'; that is, he hardly ever acknowledges the client's ethnic identity, even when the client makes frequent reference to it.

Thompson and Jenal (1994) in their research on white therapist/black client relationships found that 'race-avoidant' therapists had shorter and less successful therapeutic relationships than those who were able not only to openly acknowledge the differences between themselves and their clients, but to be comfortable with them. In a further corroborative piece of research conducted in the United States, it was discovered that therapy proved more successful when therapist and client were able to discuss the client's ethnic identity openly. Interestingly, the European American therapists consistently felt unable and/or uncomfortable with such conversations as compared with African-American therapists (Carter, 1995).

The criticisms in this section have been mainly derived from therapeutic endeavours as applied to cross-race/cross-ethnic encounters. In attempting to extrapolate from the above research in order to generalize our learning across other differences and diversities, it would seem that the therapist's comfort in recognizing and responding directly to the client's particular identity or circumstances is a key ingredient towards successful therapeutic outcome.

Identity development

Various models of 'ethnic' identity development have been being developed within the United States, since the late 1980s and early 1990s (Helms, 1990, 1994; Atkinson et al, 1989; Phinney and Alipuria, 1990; Cross, 1991). These models of identity development have been developed for a wide range of groups including ethnic and adolescent minorities, African- and Asian-Americans, Chicanos and white racial consciousness.

In essence, these psychological models posit five stages of identity development for those in society who hail from both 'majority' and 'minority' groups. The models strive to describe the process of increasing awareness (identity development) through which persons may proceed from an initial stage of unawareness of who they are (in relation to the contrasted group), moving through the stages until a later and comfortable state of awareness about themselves (in relation to those both from their group and from other groups) is reached. Notwithstanding a critique of these models – that they are 'stage' theories, and as such, do not account for the full complexity of human experiencing and fluidity – they do offer a conceptual framework from which thinking may be generated about identity in relation to others in society. One further critique of these models is that they do not, and indeed cannot, account for those who occupy a position of multiple oppressions, for example persons who are disabled and of minority ethnic origin and elderly.

Extensive research is provided by Carter (1995) to show that the levels of development of identity awareness within therapists can be critical to the outcome of the therapy process – where therapists are at the same stage or one stage or more of development ahead of their client, then it is more likely that there will be a more successful outcome to the therapy. As Carter has noted, it is not your ethnicity per se that matters (in therapy) but your psychological resolution to it that is critical.

Some modest research in the early 1990s pointed to possible effectiveness for therapist–client matching, but this work has been substantially surpassed by the recognition that what is of most importance is that the counsellor is 'culturally sensitive' to the client. These findings have recently been supported by evidence gathered by Dutch psychologists at Utrecht University (Knipscheer and Kleber, 2004). Various definitions of what constitutes 'cultural sensitivity' are elusive, though several authors (D'Ardenne and Mahtani, 1989; Sue et al, 1992; Lago, 2006; Ridley, 1995) elucidate desirable key elements of knowledge, skills and attitudes. A series of recommendations for sensitive practice are also included at the end of this chapter.

Again, in attempting to generalize from this specific set of findings (where race, ethnicity and culture have been the dynamics studied), it might be possible to hypothesise, in relation to any specific difference or diversity, that there is a greater likelihood of good therapeutic outcome when therapists are comfortable and aware of who they are, as persons within themselves and as subjects located within society. This comfort, awareness and acceptance of the therapists' self will facilitate their capacity to work with different and diverse clients. Their psychological resolution of these issues is a critical factor in their capacity to work sensitively with 'difference'.

The psychological impact of being labelled 'different' and 'diverse'

> My first experience of queerness centered not on sexuality or gender, but on disability. Early on, I understood my body to be irrevocably different from those of my neighbours, playmates, and siblings. Shaky; off-balance; speech hard to understand; a body that moved slow, wrists cocked at odd angles, muscles knotted with tremors. ... I heard: 'wrong, broken, in need of repair, unacceptably queer', every day, as my classmates called out cripple, retard, monkey; as people I met gawked at me; as strangers on the street asked, 'what's your defect?': as my own parents grew impatient with my slow clumsy ways.
>
> (Clare, 2001)

Clare (2001) goes on further to explain how he came to believe that his 'body was utterly wrong' to the extent that he wanted to cut off his right arm so that it would not shake. In similar circumstances I have known of clients who have attempted to scrub their dark skin white, or who have coped with their feared homosexual tendencies by completely removing themselves from any friendly or social contact with persons of either sex.

Inhabiting the position of being 'different' or 'diverse' may mean a life lived in fear, continually exposed to negative attitudes and behaviours from mainstream society and impoverished life opportunities. As suggested in the identity development models earlier in the chapter, persons from minority groups at the first stage of development have little awareness of these oppressive dynamics and will identify with the majority group in society and its attitudes. They will believe that they and persons like them either deserve these attributions or that society is fine and there is no problem.

However as people become sensitive to and aware of these societally embedded and reinforced 'slights' or 'put downs', they begin to recognize the negative, corrosive effect these have had upon their own personality structures. In addition, such negative attributions from others may become introjected into the 'diverse' person's psyche (as exemplified in the quote below) so that part of them also internalizes and identifies with society's negative attributions.

> The women I had met at the disco with David were either so butch they looked like they could donate to a sperm bank, or so feminine they appeared to be in drag, and congregated together at the bar while their butch girlfriends played pool together and fought with each other, drunk out of their minds. I now know it was a kind of self-protection – that lesbians experienced so much hatred from others that they internalised most of it, and tried to become invisible by aping heterosexual couples.
>
> (Bindel, 2004)

In extreme forms this may lead to self-hate or a wish to radically change that part of self which has attracted these negative assertions (as is evidenced by Eli Clare's statement above). Many who are defined as 'different and diverse' will have experienced teasing, exclusion and victimization. Frequently they may experience the further insult of feeling they are, and/or being blamed for being, 'victims'. This fundamental denial of responsibility by society further damages the victims, who subsequently internalize irresponsibility and self-blame. They are thus exposed to a three-level attack on their sense of self, an experience of triple jeopardy.

The journey from 'oppression' to 'liberation' for any client deemed 'different' and 'diverse' is potentially a long and frequently painful one. Hopefully, ultimately, this process may prove a deeply rewarding and life changing experience. This journey will inevitably heighten the person's sensitivity to all of society's attributions, both overt and implicit.

As was once said of a dear friend of mine: 'he could smell "racism" from a long way off'.

A recent handbook of research in social psychology (Forgas and Williams, 2002) conjectures that there are three aspects for the self:

- the individual self
- the interpersonal self (who one is in relation to friends/relatives)
- the social self (one's relationship to the wider world).

This delineation of different notions of self is not, of course, the same as Mearns' (1999) developmental ideas of configurations of self, but nevertheless this tripartite separation raises interesting ideas about the psychological interrelationship between these three domains.

Might, for example, a therapist from the majority culture classify (a) his/her individual self as one that is accepting of all others, (b) indeed have some friends who are 'different' and 'diverse', yet c) also hold negative views of particular minority groups in the world? This tripartite model of selves advanced by Forgas and Williams (2002) facilitates a method of understanding what are often complex contradictions in our own belief systems. At the three levels, different attitudes and beliefs may pertain.

Research by Dhillon-Stevens (2004) revealed that white therapists seldom examined their attitudes towards their own and others' ethnic identities within their training therapies (an aspect of the social self?), but rather focused on material from their individual and interpersonal selves. It is curious yet comprehensible within this three-fold conceptualization of selves, to appreciate that white therapists in training will pursue 'self-awareness' and self-exploration through their own therapy experience, yet may not touch at all upon their attitudes towards those who are 'different' and 'diverse'. This research by Dhillon-Stevens further substantiates the necessity for therapy training courses to address seriously these issues of diversity.

A good number of salutary research findings are proffered in the different chapters of *The Social Self* (Forgas and Williams, 2002). Quoted below are just a few of those findings that affect people who have been/are socially excluded.

- Medical research suggests that mortality from nearly all physical diseases is higher among people who are single and/or lack a network of close relationships than among people who have close relationships.
- Mental illness is likewise significantly higher among people who are alone.
- Suicide rates are higher among people who are alone than among those with a network of relationships, and suicide is especially likely among people who have recently lost close relationships.
- Being numb might be preferable to feeling pain, anxiety and sadness, and so people shut down quickly when confronted with the distressing experience of social rejection.

There are considerable implications in this last statement for (diverse) counselling trainees who have experienced exclusion and discrimination. The training process opens them up to their emotions, their own backgrounds, to other's views of themselves and the world. These intense personal and group dynamics can produce both certain volatility in and silent withdrawal from engagement in the training environment for those students who have been previously excluded/disenfranchized/discriminated against by society (Watson, 2006). Watson's doctoral research proves extremely depressing reading for those committed to providing quality training experiences for those who are different and diverse. Rather than learning through engagement with the training group, minority-group students tended to withdraw into silence for fear of further hurt and misunderstanding. Many end up, sadly, choosing the silent route to qualification.

In this we are faced with the sheer complexity of all individual change. To unfreeze attitudes that have become central constituents of the self, our sense of identity itself is attacked at a deep primary level. Matters of difference and diversity, when discussed in training environments, have the capacity to evoke considerable anxiety, fear and apprehension. It may only be at such times as this, or when faced with a client who is so challenging to you in his or her difference, that one is forced into the recognition that the person-centred approach, however attractive it is as a humanistically embodied theory, may not be sufficient in and of itself. Personal, social, societal and political awareness are all required in working optimally across difference and diversity.

On being part of the dominant majority

Many therapists hail from 'dominant' groups within society. In the Western world a considerable number will be classified ethnically as white. White, male, middle-class, heterosexual, able-bodied therapists occupy the dominant, societal power position (according to the BACP definition of diversity quoted earlier in the chapter). Though therapists are not predominantly male (83 per cent of the membership of BACP is female), there is a frequent assertion that most hail from white, upper and middle-class backgrounds. The costs incurred in counselling and psychotherapy training, where little or no other funding is available to trainees than personal finances, inevitably leads to a situation where those of impoverished means are less able and thus less likely to embark on a course of training.

To be part of a majority group that holds power is for many an experience of which they are completely unaware. For them, this is just how life is. It is the unquestioned norm. Consequently, being part of a majority has attracted little social scientific attention until recent decades. Richard Dyer sums up a component part of this apparent non-seeing of the obvious in his book *White* (1997). There he asserts that 'whiteness' has so long been assumed to be the position from which everything is judged, that it has set a norm.

> The invisibility of whiteness as a racial position in white (which is to say dominant) discourse is of a piece with its ubiquity. ... Research – into books, museums, the press, advertising, films, television, software – repeatedly shows that in western representation, whites are overwhelmingly and disproportionately predominant, have the central roles, and above all are placed as the norm, the ordinary, the standard ... there is no more powerful position than that of being 'just' human. The claim to power is the claim to speak for the commonality of humanity. Raced [different and diverse] people can't do that – they can only speak for their race. [Or their group of difference and diversity.]
>
> (Dyer, 1997: 2)

Penetrating this 'norm' is an extremely challenging task, for it is multi-layered, opaque and difficult to catch (see Lago, 2005). Nevertheless, in following the dictum 'know thyself', this chapter strongly urges 'majority group' therapists to explore the significance of their majority group status, particularly as it relates to those in various minority positions.

Key recommendations for person-centred therapists working across difference and diversity

> A (counselling) trainee who is a wheelchair user reported that he had to phone 35 therapists before he could arrange to meet one that was wheelchair accessible. His choice of therapist is reflected by his ability to find one that he can actually meet,

face to face and this impacts on his ability to make an informed choice in finding a therapist he feels he can work with.

(Dhillon-Stevens, 2004: 54)

This quotation above immediately grasps our attention. Working with clients from 'diverse' communities requires that we have to completely re-contextualize our therapeutic work, from the primary moment of contact through to completion.

- 'Retain a strong ideographic stance towards your client' (Ridley, 1995). In short, this means 'respect each client, each person's uniqueness and story'. (Despite the apparent crassness of this so obvious statement, given the nature of this complete text, there are sufficient evidences of practice that do not meet these criteria.)
- Remember that when your client is from a 'different and diverse' group from yourself, this may not be what that person is seeking counselling for.
- Explore your attitudes, prejudices and stereotypes about the many groups who are 'different'. Where did these perceptions come from? How operational are they now in your cultural life? How might these preconceptions manifest themselves in therapy with 'diverse' clients?
- Consult appropriate identity development models to aid your own awareness of where you might situate yourself and your development in relation to those in other groups.
- Strive to enhance your knowledge of current thinking in relation to diversities and modify your skills and language appropriately.
- Listen deeply to the experiences of those who have suffered because of their differences. Do not gainsay it, even when your experience runs counter to anything they claim. Strive to understand it. (The strong emphasis on empathic listening with the PCA is critical here theoretically, but the challenge to therapists practically, to maintain this stance when they feel they and/or their group is under criticism or attack, is very considerable indeed. Such episodes represent a schism between theoretical intention and clinical practice.)
- Monitor your humour and throwaway lines, your assumptions and your critical opinions. There may be important learning gained through self-reflection about your attitudes or your acculturation in these areas.
- Normative, general information about groups may be generally helpful but be guided by Jung's dictum: 'Learn your theories as well as you can, but leave them aside when it comes to meeting the miracle of the living soul.'
- Strive not to be avoidant of the difference and diversity the client represents. Recognize and acknowledge it. Meet it squarely when the client raises it.
- Some counsellors have found the process of 'associative identification' useful when establishing relationships with different and diverse clients. That is to say, they search for elements of similarity between themselves and the client to forge the therapeutic relationship.
- Use supervision extensively to explore your attitudes and therapeutic relationships with different and diverse clients.

- Actively seek to work with therapists and supervisors from 'different' groups.
- Consider the overall context within which you work:
  - Does your agency embody principles of equal opportunity?
  - Is your office easily accessible for those without private transport and for those who have mobility difficulties?
  - Do you have appropriate access and toilet facilities for all clients?
  - Does your agency work with a cross-section of clients that is similar to the cross-section of the local population you serve? If not why not? What could be done about it?
  - Is the internal environment of your agency sensitive and conducive to clients from 'diverse' origins?
  - Does your agency employ different communication forms to work with different and diverse clients? Examples include use of interpreters, written materials in other languages, signers, use of text messaging, telephones and other electronic forms to enhance communication, hearing loops and so on.
- In your training and in practice, systematically reflect upon the various facets of your identities (colour, ethnicity, class, ability, gender, sexual preference, age and others) and strive to understand these, particularly in relation to others who are different and diverse.
- 'Identity is always multiple, always complex, frequently conflicted and always changing' (Kettle, 2004). Remember that neither the client nor you are only the identity/ies you consider yourselves to be or the identity/ies others perceive you to be. Identity/ies is/are always more than you may perceive or intuit them to be. The client cannot and should not be reduced to his or her visible identity.
- Encourage your colleagues to regularly discuss the challenges presented by different and diverse clients.
- Support and encourage the training of therapists from different and diverse groups.
- Strive to understand where you are socially situated and how others may believe you are situated in relation to personal power, role power, and 'societal' (reference group) power.

I am only too aware, in writing much of this chapter, how apparently simple some of the suggestions and recommendations in the above sections may seem. However, it is my experience that each of these hypotheses for increased awareness and enhanced practice in relation to difference and diversity may expose therapists to pain, discomfort, shame and guilt. Considerable commitment to the notion of anti-oppressive/anti-discriminatory practice will be required for therapists to continue in their learning about themselves, about others and about society's multiple discriminatory practices.

The profound and far reaching contributions made by Rogers and his colleagues to the theory and practice of person-centred therapy cannot be underestimated. Rogers' ideographic stance, a deeply respectful, attentive, understanding-seeking approach serves as a profound theoretical and clinical platform upon which to base one's professional practice as a therapist. However, when it comes to working with 'diverse' and 'different' clients, then additional knowledge, attitudes and skills are required, as argued in this chapter.

REFERENCES

Althusser, L (1971). Ideology and ideological state apparatuses. In L. Althusser, *Lenin and Philosophy and Other Essays*. London: New Left Books.

Arce, C.A. (1981). A reconsideration of Chicano culture and identity. *Daedelus*, 110, 177–92.

Atkinson, D., Morten, G. and Sue, D.W. (1989). *Counselling American Minorities: a cross cultural perspective*. Dubuque, USA: William C. Brown.

Blindel, J. (2004). If we wanted to be straight, we would be. *Guardian*. Tuesday 14 December.

Brodley, B.T. (2004). Uncharacteristic directiveness: Rogers and the 'On anger and hurt' client. In R. Moodley, C. Lago and A. Talahite (eds), *Carl Rogers Counsels a Black Client: race and culture in person-centred counselling* (pp. 36–46). Ross-on-Wye: PCCS Books.

Carter, R.T. (1995). *The Influence of Race and Racial Identity in Psychotherapy: towards a racially inclusive model*. New York: Wiley.

Chaplin, J. (1988). *Feminist Counselling in Action*. London: Sage.

Clare, E. (2001). Stolen bodies, reclaimed bodies: disability and queerness. *Public Culture*, 13(3) 359–65.

Cross, W.E. (1991). *Shades of Black: diversity in African-American identity*. Philadelphia: Temple University Press.

D'Ardenne, P. and Mahtani, A. (1989). *Transcultural Counselling in Action*. London: Sage.

Dhillon-Stevens, H. (2004). Healing inside and outside: an examination of dialogic encounters in the area of anti-oppressive practice in counselling and psychotherapy. PhD thesis, Middlesex University.

Dyer, R. (1997). *White*. London: Routledge.

Forgas, J.P. and Williams, K.D. (2002). *The Social Self: cognitive, interpersonal and intergroup perspectives*. New York: Psychology Press.

Halpern, D. (2004). *Social Capital*. United States: Polity Press.

Harris, P. (2004). The paradox that divides Black America. *Observer*, 14 December, 21–22.

Helms, J.E. (ed.)(1990). *Black and White Racial Identity: therapy, research and practice*. Westport, Conn.: Greenwood Press.

Helms, J.E. (1994). Racial identity and social constructs. In E.J. Trickett, R. Watts and D. Birman (eds), *Human Diversity* (285–311). San Francisco: Jossey Bass.

Holdstock, L. (1993). Can client centered therapy transcend its monocultural roots? In G. Lietaer, J. Rombauts and R. Van Balden (eds), *Client-Centered*

Experiential Psychotherapy in the Nineties. Leuven: Leuven University Press.

Kettle, M. (2004). Identity. *Guardian.* 19 October: 24.

Khoo, P.L.S., Abu-Rasain, M.H. and Hornby, G. (2002). Counselling foreign students: a review of strategies. In S. Palmer, *Multicultural Counselling: a reader* (p. 107). London: Sage.

Kim, J. (1981). Process of Asian-American identity development: a study of Japanese American women's perceptions of their struggle to achieve positive identities. Unpublished doctoral dissertation, University of Massachusetts, Amherst.

Knipscheer, J.W. and Kleber, R.J. (2004). A need for ethnic similarity in the patient–therapist interaction? Mediterranean migrants in Dutch mental health care. *Journal of Clinical Psychology,* 60(6), 543–54.

Lago, C. (2005) You're a white therapist: have you noticed? *Counselling and Psychotherapy Journal,* 16(3), 35–7.

Lago, C. (2006). On being a white therapist: have you noticed? In C. Lago (ed.), *Race, Culture and Counselling: the ongoing challenge* (2nd edn). Maidenhead: McGraw-Hill and Open University Press.

Lago, C. and Smith, B. (2003). *Anti-Discriminatory Counselling Practice.* London; Sage.

Lago, C. and Thompson, J. (1996/2004). *Race, Culture and Counselling.* Buckingham: Open University Press.

Lago, C. and Thompson, J. (1997). The triangle with curved sides: sensitivity to issues of race and culture in supervision. In G. Shipton (ed.), *Supervision of Psychotherapy and Counselling.* Buckingham: Open University Press.

Lambert, M. (1992). Psychotherapy outcome research. In J.C. Norcross and M.R. Goldfried (eds), *Handbook of Psychotherapy Integration* (pp. 94–129). New York: Basic Books.

Lambert, M.J., Shapiro, D.A. and Bergin, A.E (1986). The effectiveness of psychotherapy. In S.L. Garfield and A.E Bergin (eds), *Handbook of Psychotherapy and Behavior Change* (pp. 157–212). New York: John Wiley.

Laungani, P. (2004). *Asian Perspectives in Counselling and Psychotherapy.* Hove: Brunner, Routledge.

Mason, M.A. (2001). *The Equality Trap.* United States: Transaction Publishers.

Mearns, D. (1999). Person-centred therapy with configurations of self. *Counselling.* 10(2), 125–30.

Mearns, D. and Thorne, B. (1999). *Person Centred Counselling in Action* (2nd edn). London: Sage.

Moodley, R., Lago, C. and Talahite, A. (2004). *Carl Rogers Counsels a Black Client: race and culture in person-centred counselling.* Ross-on-Wye: PCCS Books.

O'Hara, M. (1989). Person-Centered Approach as Conscientizao: the works of Carl Rogers and Paulo Freire. *Journal of Humanistic Psychology,* 29(1), Winter.

O'Hara, M. (1992). Relational Humanism: a psychology for a pluralistic world. *The Humanistic Psychologist*, 22(2 and 3), Summer and Autumn.

O'Hara, M. (1996). Feminist analysis of a session of psychotherapy between Carl Rogers and a female client 'Silver'. In B.A. Farber, P. Raskin and D. Brink. (eds), *Carl Rogers: casebook and critical perspectives*. New York: Guilford.

Phinney, J.S. and Alipuria, L. (1990). Ethnic identity in older adolescents from four ethnic groups. *Journal of Adolescence*, 13, 171–83.

Pilkington, A. (2002). *Racial Disadvantage and Ethnic Diversity in Britain*. London: Palgrave MacMillan.

Proctor, G. and Napier, M.B. (2004). *Encountering Feminism: intersections between feminism and the person-centred approach*. Ross-on-Wye: PCCS Books.

Read, J. (2004). Poverty, ethnicity and gender. In J. Read, R. Bentall and L. Mosher (eds), *Models of Madness: psychological, social and biological approaches to schizophrenia* (pp. 161–94) London: Brunner/Routledge.

Ridley, C.R. (1995). *Overcoming Unintentional Racism in Counselling and Therapy: a practitioner's guide to intentional intervention*. Thousand Oaks, Calif.: Sage.

Stubbs, J.P. and Bozarth, J.D. (1994). The dodo bird revisited: a qualitative study of psychotherapy efficacy research. *Journal of Applied and Preventive Psychology*, 3(2), 109–20.

Sue, D.W., Arrendo, P. and McDavis, R.J. (1992). Multicultural counseling competencies and standards; a call to the profession. *Journal of Counseling and Development*, 70, March/April: 477–86.

Thompson, C.E. and Jenal, S.T. (1994). Interracial and intraracial quasi-counseling interaction when counsellors avoid discussing race. *Journal of Counseling Psychology*, 41: 484–91

Usher, C.H. (1989). Recognizing cultural bias in counselling theory and practice: the case of Rogers. *Journal of Multicultural Counseling and Development*, 17(2), 62–71.

Watson, V. (2006). Key issues for black counselling practitioners in the UK with particular reference to their experience in training. In C. Lago (ed.), *Race, Culture and Counselling: the ongoing challenge* (2nd edn). Maidenhead: McGraw-Hill and Open University.

Willie, C.V., Perri Rieker, P., Kramer, B.M. and Brown, B.S. (1995). *Mental Health, Racism and Sexism*. Pittsburgh: University of Pittsburgh Press.

20

Couples and Families

Charles J. O'Leary and Martha B. Johns

Person-centred couple and family therapy has always existed as a possible application of the principles of the person-centred approach, although the field of couple and family therapy developed and flourished quite separately during the same period that the person-centred approach was evolving. Many core ideas from the person-centred approach, such as the importance of therapist non-directiveness (Butler and Bird, 2000: 156) and the primacy of empathy (Johnson, 1996) are dominant themes in contemporary couple and family therapy literature; while many person-centred therapists include work with families, and especially couples, as part of their practice. The goal of person-centred couple and family therapy is to create an atmosphere in which couples and families are safe to be congruent, able to listen and show each other empathy and acceptance, so that they can solve the problems that can be solved or recognize those predicaments that can only be understood and accepted. The successful practice of working with pairs or groups of intimately related people necessarily includes training, observation of and supervision by those who have worked in such a setting.

Helpful literature to consult

Many outstanding contributors to person-centred literature have written about couple and family therapy: Rogers (1961, 1972), Raskin and Van der Veen (1970), Warner (1983, 1989), Barrett-Lennard (1984, 1998), Guerney (1984), Levant (1984), Mearns and Thorne (1988, 1999), Anderson (1989a, 1989b), Cain (1989), Snyder (1989), Mearns (1994). The writing of Gaylin (1989, 1993, 2001), who was both a student of Rogers and, for decades, the director of a university marriage and family therapy graduate programme, has most consistently integrated the person-centred approach with couple and family therapy. Gaylin (1989) was the first to explicitly describe the applications of Rogers's six conditions (1957) to work with families.

A bridge between the person-centred approach and the mainstream of couple and family therapy is the work of Greenberg and Johnson on *Emotionally Focused Therapy for Couples* (1988) and Johnson (1996, 2003) This approach is closely allied to the spirit of the person-centred approach and is one of the two modalities of couples therapy showing the strongest research results (Johnson and LeBow, 2000: 25). Johnson's verbatim transcripts often seem as though Rogers himself was the therapist because of her painstaking and respectful effort to exactly track the emotional heart of all client utterances.

The person-centred therapist interested in serious couple and family work would be wise to consult the work of mainstream couple and family thera-pists, as found in *The Journal of Marriage and Family Therapy*, for example. Indispensable, in our view, is the exhaustive research of John Gottman (1999), who has studied couples for over 25 years through thousands of hours of videotaped interactions, physiological measurements under stressful conditions, and surveys of distressed and non-distressed couples followed over decades.

O'Leary in *Couples and Families: a person-centred approach* (1999) makes an explicit case for integrating the core ideas of the person-centred approach with the evolving development of couple and family therapy. It is this approach that we will present here, with the understanding that the readers will decide which elements of couple and family practice are compatible with their own understanding of the person-centred approach.

An internal and external job description for a person-centred couple and family therapist

1. Actively seek to understand and show acceptance of each person present

- At the beginning of the therapy, the therapist *welcomes each person sepa-rately and invites him/her to share reasons for being there*. He practices multi-directional partiality (Boszormenyi-Nagy et al, 1991: 222–5), that is: he does not take sides, but establishes his willingness to take all sides, understanding each as deeply as possible and acting as a trustworthy translator for all.
- Internally, the therapist *considers all participants*, silent or talkative, open with feelings or apparently guarded, *to be doing the best they can* in the situation. ('Eighty per cent of life is just showing up,' says comedian Woody Allen.)
- The therapist *actively reflects back what each person says*, especially in the early sessions, unless doing so would interfere with a couple's natural responses to one another.
- It will usually emerge that one client will invoke more natural sympathy in the therapist than another. The therapist's task is to *remain curious and*

open to the meanings of the client who is harder to understand. It is important that he does not view one client as the one with the greater emotional needs and therefore relegate a partner, parent or child to the role of supporter, adversary or bystander. For example, a wife who feels emotionally unsupported is not more the client than a husband who appears unresponsive or rigid; a child who feels criticized is not a more important client than a parent who is absorbed by disapproval and anxiety. This is one of many examples of multi-directional partiality in action: not preferring one way of being over another.

- A useful technique for the therapist is to *ask clients' permission* to understand each perspective without joining into implied or explicit disapproval of others. 'I am going to be listening to the parent side of this thing for a while. Do you understand that I will be listening, in a few minutes, to the kid side of this, too?'
- The therapist *shows the ability to understand and accept the couple or family as a whole.* Couples and families in therapy often feel shame or expect to be seen as foolish – 'How could a couple get into such a terrible situation?' – and are sensitive to any perceived judgements by the therapist and very relieved by the therapist's 'non-anxious presence' (Friedman, 1991) in the face of their dilemma. The therapist may sometimes describe both sides of a dilemma that both people suffer rather than cause: 'When Claire expresses her longing for more independence and time alone, Jonathan feels unwanted. Claire ends up feeling trapped while Jonathan feels pushed away, even though neither of you intends to control or distance the other.'

2. Provide structure for the sessions, paying particular attention to the first and final sessions in a course of therapy, as well as to the conditions of each session's beginning and ending

Couple or family therapy with an inactive therapist can be unhelpful, even harmful, and has no support in research on couples therapy (Gottman, 1999). Structure, however, does not mean 'directiveness (teaching, advice giving, interpreting)' (Butler and Bird, 2000) or taking a hierarchical position, but must always be in the service of each client's congruent and self-directed participation in dialogue. This apparent paradox must be resolved in partnership with each unique couple and family.

Structuring is essential for the following reasons:

1. Clients will be caught up in well-established reactions to one another rather than listening, in the moment, to the feelings that are at the core of the other's alienation.
2. Without structuring, the person most able to talk and express feelings will do so for most of the therapy hour, even while experiencing distress that her partner remains withdrawn and/or unreceptive.
3. Couples and families will rarely return to a counselling experience marked by chaos, confusion or unmediated rage.

- *The beginning of a course of therapy:*
  Clients are asked about their purpose in being there, and they have the opportunity to ask about what the therapist will do and not do. As is appropriate and necessary, the therapist may clarify expectations such as:
  – Each person will have a chance to have a say.
  – The therapist will sometimes interrupt in order to facilitate dialogue with others in the room.
  – Each person has the right to disagree, be angry, be disappointed or otherwise share negative feelings.
  – *However*, clients cannot insult or non-verbally show contempt.
  The managing of these expectations is a shared task of everyone in the room. In describing this structure, the therapist may invite all participants to comment if she seems to them too intrusive or gets in the way of their working on problems in their own way.
- *The beginning of each session:*
  The therapist will usually begin the session by asking all clients what they would like to focus on and facilitating a consensus about where to begin. He will also take responsibility for bringing up other subjects or, at end of session, acknowledging they were not addressed and marking them for the beginning of the next session if they remain a concern for the person who suggested them. If the therapist does not do this then one or more clients will, by default, find themselves in a dialogue not of their choosing. Unlike in small groups, little time is usually taken with this process.
- *The end of each session:*
  The therapist will wisely reserve the last five or ten minutes for her own use in summarizing the events of the session, checking that someone has not been left unexpectedly hurt or disempowered, acknowledging agreements reached and issues unresolved, and deciding if and when to schedule a next session. It is most important that the therapy hour end with the therapist's active facilitation of observation of the process rather than re-engagement in highly emotional issues that could leave the clients in a state of frustration or futility.
- *The last session of the therapy:*
  If possible (and sometimes clients leave therapy before this can happen), the therapist will use the last session to invite process-oriented discussion. What is different? What cannot be translated into change at home? What has been resolved? What remains unresolved? What change in each person do individual clients wish to be acknowledged? These questions make explicit Rogers' sixth condition that emphasizes the clients' experiencing of the presence or absence of facilitating elements in the therapy.

3. Ask for, clarify and refer back to each person's purpose in being in the session

Virginia Satir, the only female co-founder of family therapy, once built a day-long small workshop on her question to each participant: 'What do you want?' She followed with empathic reflection of both what was said and its meaning in relation to what others had said. This is the technique of techniques: making sense of what people want; returning to the question frequently; explicitly connecting events in the session to clients' stated goals.

- Whenever clients become anxious, argumentative or lost in a monologue, *reference to each person's stated reason for being there enables them to become present to the dialogue at hand.* For example, the therapist may ask: 'Is this it? Is this the kind of dreadful moment you were describing?'
- Frequently a teen or a reluctant partner will not be willing to answer the question explicitly. The therapist may *venture an empathic guess or reassurance* about their right in their own time to say what they want or simply *find a way to acknowledge her willingness to bring them into the conversation when they are ready.* For example a therapist may say to a teen who shows dramatic reluctance to participate: 'I will ask you questions from time to time, but you don't have to answer, OK? Let me also ask this: if you disagree with something that is said or have something to add, will you let me know?' By so doing, she may release a parent from forcing a child to participate along with the tension such an attempt would likely produce.
- The question: *'What do you want?'* or variations may be particularly helpful when, as is common, *anger is expressed* in the session. O'Leary (1999: 20) comments: 'The counselor's presence matters in the expression of anger. He puts it in context, punctuates it and makes sense out of it. It is not just anger expressed but anger, which is expressed in a counselor's office. This does not mean anger denied, forbidden or turned by clever wordplay into something more positive and thus misunderstood. The counselor dialogues with the angry person as well as with that person's partner. ... The counselor may ask what is the meaning of this anger. ... [He] models freedom not to accept anger as a given, but as a roadmap to learning and connection.' A therapist may ask: 'What do you really want to have understood right now?' 'What are you looking for from your partner when you feel so frustrated?' Or, if the person is unable to speak, may say: 'The feeling of anger is so strong right now that it is impossible to find words to say what it may be about,' which is a description that acknowledges a difficult but common state without the element of judgement.

4. Sustain the conviction that each person is attempting to actualize him/herself; do not try to change anyone

When couples and families find an atmosphere in which they can be both accepted and congruent, they often do find a solution which, although not what the therapist might have chosen, lets them move to the level of problem-solving or acceptance of an immutable predicament. The therapist acts as a respectful translator, being sure that each speaker feels the others are getting the important messages about their wishes as well as their frustrations.

He does not need to urge, force, pressure or otherwise talk anyone into change. If he looks for surprising forms of constructive change, he often finds them. The more experienced couple and family therapist learns that, given a setting in which they feel safe to be heard, most couples and families will find a way out of their difficulty that the therapist could never impose and might not even imagine. It is this conviction of the actualizing tendency in action that allows the therapist to be relaxed rather than feel like a teacher trying to get five-year-olds to sit still during a two-hour church service.

- The therapist *slows down the conversational tempo* so that clients can become observers of their own and their intimates' change in words as well as tone.
- She *asks questions of the speaker such as 'What are you most trying to get across right now?'* 'Is this close to what you are looking for in your partner?' 'Did we just get to what is the source of your loneliness in this relationship?'
- He also *addresses the listener(s) regarding their responses to the speaker*: 'You have been listening without moving for several minutes. Are you ready to share what is happening with you?'
- She 'does not need to supply motivation toward the positive' (Kirschenbaum and Henderson, 1990b: 59) but *calls attention to progress already present* in the clients' conversation.
- He *observes difference in clients between sessions and invites inquiry as to what created change* in words, non-verbal behaviour and felt atmosphere. 'Am I right to think that something different has occurred between you this week?' This kind of question, asked about negative as well as positive change, allows clients to pay close attention to their relationship as something evolving rather than a static, unchangeable entity.
- She *responds to any moments in the dialogue in which one or more persons says something that varies from a static position*. For example, a husband in a terrible impasse about the possibility of his marriage being at an end said: 'I asked you about that, but you hung up on me.' His wife said: 'I didn't hang up on you. I thought you hung up on me.' The therapist asks: 'Did I hear that correctly? Have both of you been living with the thought that the other hung up on you?'

5. Exercise a teaching function compatible with a non-directive approach

Relationship therapy is always affected by the objective situation that Martin Buber highlighted in his dialogue with Carl Rogers: 'not only he confronts you, the person, but also the situation' (Kirschenbaum and Henderson, 1990a: 51). The therapist needs to integrate her awareness of the many objective conditions impinging on a relationship while staying faithful to empathic reflection of each client's experience. Mentioning conditions that have a role in a predicament does not diminish the uniqueness of a client's experience but rather shows compassion for and acceptance of the reasonableness of his or her plight.

Ned Gaylin (1989) has commented that sometimes a guidance function is called for when objective developmental issues unnecessarily confuse a couple or family's dialogue. He uses the example of parents arguing about readiness for toilet training as though their opinions matter more than their child's developmental readiness. The therapist can take on a teaching role temporarily before returning to a therapeutic mode.

The following conditions, among many others, put pressure on members of a couple that can cause frustration, resentment and outright blame of the other person:

- financial change for better or, especially, for worse
- differences in families of origin
- different gender socialization
- unexpected illness
- ageing
- the birth of a child or children
- special needs in one or more children
- change in one person's sexual physiology
- homophobia.

The authors believe that it is impossible to do useful couple or family therapy without attention to these developmental issues: for example, the time after a baby is born is almost universally experienced as a time of difficulty and loss, even while a couple rejoices in the presence of an adored and wanted baby. The therapist does not interrupt client sharing, nor try to neutralize a client's strong feeling. She may, however, raise the possibility of mutual loss and unexpected disappointment as an alternative to the rigid accusations of selfishness and non-caring frequently expressed by new parents.

It is also sometimes necessary for the therapist to explain the attention to process that is the heart of the therapy. Clients who are confused by the therapist's unwillingness to tell people how to solve their problems or judge who is right or wrong have a right to a clarification of the rationale for this approach. (Not a wordy lecture, of course.) Facing confusion about the condition of their lives or relationships can't be avoided; confusion because of therapist withholding or presumptuousness can irritate the clients at best and disempower them at worst.

6. Practise consistent non-defensiveness, which allows you to work in a relaxed way for client goals and create the emotional ground for deeper client expression

- Moments when clients challenge the therapist or (more rarely) are upset with him can be seen as opportunities for client learning and growth. *When the therapist is not defensive in these moments, clients can feel safe to speak frankly* about what is most important to them. In so doing they may feel able to risk speaking openly and clearly to their loved ones.
- *Occasionally sharing information about one's own humanity can be useful; denying or concealing this humanity is always a barrier* to the goal of being helpful to clients in relationship. Every therapist is a person who has been a good and not good partner, friend, son or daughter, brother or sister, father or mother. Like others, he can get lost in fixed positions and call

them his true feelings. He can harden suddenly in stubbornness or in an exaggerated sense of being the injured party. A therapist can also know what it's like to soften and change if allowed a glimpse of openness or vulnerability in a loved one.

- In practising non-defensiveness, *the therapist notices his own tone and attitude as well as the clients' non- verbal responses.* 'I just noticed I was trying to talk you into listening to your wife more. Did it sound that way to you?' 'I think what I just said must sound very male to you and that I may have joined your husband without realizing it. What do you think?'
- The therapist *can sometimes bring humour into a situation without making light of anyone's words or actions except her own.* 'Do you think I am doing a very good job as facilitator right now?' may sometimes bring laughter into a situation that, moments before, seemed only hopeless.

Common problems of the novice person-centred couple and family therapist

- He allows one member of the family or couple to dominate, shout down or even verbally abuse other family members.
- She gets so absorbed in the feelings of one of the clients that she ignores the effects that person's language has on other family members.
- He allows the session to end with whatever theme and mood the time dictates, rather than using the last five minutes to make sense out of what the session was about. (Discouragement disables communication, and appears and reappears suddenly and fiercely throughout couple and family therapy.)
- She is so concentrated on the process of listening and humbly entering into the experience that her voice is unheard, and one or more members of a couple think her incompetent, frightened or uninformed about the way relationships work.

Common problems of the experienced person-centred couple and family therapist

- He talks far too much.
- Her reframing, summing up or just plain preaching becomes more important than her primary job of facilitating the preferred process of the clients present with her.
- He seems so experienced, so much the man who has heard, and indeed knows, everything, that he will appear to be someone's oily uncle, full of useless advice, rather than a person engaged in understanding the unique persons with whom he is meeting.

Case example: facilitating a dialogue (from O'Leary, 1999)

Bill and Tony came to me for counselling every two weeks for nine months, then returned for a series of four or five sessions once a year for three years.

Their relationship was at a turning point: would they remain partners or drift into polite and distant friendship? I was not seen as an expert on their relationship, but as a person who could faithfully translate each person's unique perspective and predicament. My efforts in empathically tracking and confirming each person's thought process was central to the counselling. The attitudes that seemed most important in the counselling were:

- *I would provide permission to suspend final decisions so that any possibility could be discussed without threat.* A third party who is calm in the middle of urgent competing views can facilitate dialogue about subjects that could otherwise provoke demands and counter-demands. For example, when Bill said it was really time for him to leave town and return to the mountains of Arizona even though Tony was intensely involved with a social service agency, my presence allowed them to engage in exploratory conversation rather than any rush toward either/or decision making. Bill, it turned out, needed to speak about his readiness to be back in the mountains where there was a chance for a complete change in work and where he could climb and otherwise live a simpler, more outdoor life. He wanted to pretend Tony was not in his life so that he could hear his own voice. Within the setting of counselling Tony was more receptive than expected. He was eager, in fact, to hear Bill talking more from his heart about what mattered to him. He didn't rule out the possibility that, if Bill wished him to move, the mountains might be a welcome relief from the stress of his current job. Though they did not move, it was important for each to feel safe in talking about his widest vision for himself without the other feeling threatened and defensive.

- *I would not see any problem as meaning that one of them was right and the other was wrong.* One issue dominating their attention was the great unevenness with which they worked at renovating their house. The counselling office could be full of Bill's frustration and resentment that he shouldered most of the work, about commitments not fulfilled, about feeling foolish in his seemingly one-sided devotion to what he had thought was a common project. Without denying Bill's experience, Tony could admit that he did not care as much about the house as Bill. He would much rather Bill would do less than have to live with Bill's unhappiness at working alone. In addition, Tony felt that he tried to make other contributions to their common enterprises than work on the house. Finally, Tony was, gradually, even becoming more naturally attached to undertaking skilled work on the house rather than acting as a grudging subordinate trying to improve his habits. It is an achievement of counselling that strong contradicting opinions can be laid side by side with neither one diminished nor refuted.

- *That I would not take on the job of facilitating equal justification for both partners.* Sometimes couples are very unequal in what they contribute and only the words 'I'm sorry' or 'I appreciate what you do' or 'What do I need to do to make up for it?' or other similarly non-defensive responses have any meaning. For example, only with an extra lifetime could Tony ever catch up with Bill in quantity (and especially quality) of work on their house. Frequently, a relational ledger cannot be balanced by action, but only by understanding and forgiveness. (See Boszormenyi-Nagy, 1991: 163–5 for his discussion of the family ledger.)

- *That I would provide safety for strong emotions to be expressed without becoming rigid positions.* I attempted to hear the full content and meaning of each person's words, making space for meanings to be thoroughly understood, rather than ground under the feet of heavy urgent attempts to persuade. Both of these men were good at active listening and at empathic connection with the other. At times of high emotionality, however, when, as with most couples, topics included sex, money, time spent together and other people in their lives, they were unable to hear the other's voice without feeling either a judgement or a demand. The counsellor was then a representative for the space in between: the time in which each person can hear one person's truth before it is driven out by the other's very different position. Coming to the counselling meant, in part, a choice in favour of that space and an acceptance that in some stages of the relationship it was not possible. Not every difficult subject was discussed in the counselling (only one was comfortable talking about their sex life in the sessions) but the counselling ended with the couple more committed, comfortable and close.

CONCLUSION

Person-centred couple and family therapy involves a dialectic between the essential principles of the core conditions and their expression in the context of intimates in dialogue. The therapist must offer more structure and be more active than is usual in individual therapy. At the same time, he or she must allow empathy and trust in the actualizing tendency to place the themes and direction of the process in the hands of the clients. While supervision and training with highly experienced couple and family therapists (even from other approaches) is necessary for work in this medium, the core conditions will remain the most valuable guide to facilitating therapeutic change.

REFERENCES

Anderson, H. (1997). *Conversation, Language and Possibilities: a postmodern approach to therapy*. New York: Basic Books.
Anderson, W.J. (1989a). Family therapy in the client-centered tradition: a legacy in the narrative mode. *Person Centered Review*, 4(3), 295–307.
Anderson, W.J. (1989b). Client-centered approaches to couple and family therapy: expanding theory and practice. *Person Centered Review*, 4(3), 425–7.
Barrett-Lennard, G.T. (1984). The world of family relationships: a person-centered systems view. In R.F. Levant and J.M. Schlien (eds), *Client-Centered Therapy and the Person-Centered Approach* (pp. 222–42). New York: Praeger.

Barrett-Lennard, G.T. (1998). *Carl Rogers' Helping System: journey and Substance.* London: Sage.

Boszormenyi-Nagy, I., Grunebaum, J. and Ulrich, D. (1991). Contextual therapy. In A.S. Gurman and D.P. Kniskern (eds), *Handbook of Family Therapy*, Volume 2 (pp. 200–39). New York: Brunner/Mazel.

Boszormenyi-Nagy, I. and Ulrich, D. (1991). Contextual family therapy. In A.S. Gurman and D.P. Kniskern (eds), *Handbook of Family Therapy*, Volume 1 (pp. 159–86). New York: Brunner/Mazel.

Bozarth, J.D. (1984). Beyond reflection: emergent modes of empathy. In R.F. Levant and J.M. Schlien (eds), *Client-Centered Therapy and the Person-Centered Approach* (pp. 222–42). New York: Praeger.

Brown, L.S. and Zimmer, D. (1986). An introduction to therapy issues of lesbian and gay male couples. In N.J. Jacobson and A.S. Gurman (eds), *Clinical Handbook of Marital Therapy* (pp. 451–71). New York: Guilford.

Butler, M.H. and Bird, M.H. (2000). Narrative and interactional process for preventing harmful struggle in therapy: an integrative empirical model. *Journal of Marital and Family Therapy*, 26(2), 123–43.

Cain, D.J. (1989). From the individual to the family. *Person Centered Review*, 4(3), 248–55.

Clark, W.M. and Serovich, J.M. (1997). Twenty years and still in the dark? Content analysis of articles pertaining to gay, lesbian and bi-sexual issues in marriage and family journals. *Journal of Marital and Family Therapy*, 3: 239–53.

Friedman, F. (1991). Bowen theory and therapy. In A.S. Gurman and D.P. Kniskern (eds), *Handbook of Family Therapy*, Volume 2 (pp. 134–71). New York: Brunner/ Mazel.

Gaylin, N.L. (1989). The necessary and sufficient conditions for change: individual versus family therapy. *Person Centered Review*, 4(3): 263–79.

Gaylin, N.L. (1993). Person-centred family therapy. In D. Brazier (ed.), *Beyond Carl Rogers* (pp. 181–201). London: Constable.

Gaylin, N.L. (2001). *Family, Self and Psychotherapy: a person-centred perspective.* Ross-on-Wye: PCCS Books.

Goolishian, H.A. and Anderson H. (1992). Strategy and intervention versus nonintervention: a matter of theory. *Journal of Marital and Family Therapy*, 18(1), 5–15.

Gottman, J.M. (1994a). An agenda for marital therapy. In S.M. Johnson and L.S. Greenberg (eds), *The Heart of the Matter: perspectives on emotion in marital therapy* (pp. 256–97). New York: Brunner/Mazel.

Gottman, J.M. (1994b). *Why Marriages Succeed and Fail ... and how you can make yours last.* New York: Simon and Schuster.

Gottman, J.M. (1999). *The Marriage Clinic.* New York: Norton.

Greenberg, L.S. and Johnson, S.M. (1988). *Emotionally Focused Therapy for Couples.* New York: Guilford.

Guerney, B.G. (1984). Contributions of client-centered therapy to filial, marital and family relationship enhancement therapies. In R.F. Levant and J.M. Schlien (eds), *Client-Centered Therapy and the Person-Centered Approach* (pp. 261–77). New York: Praeger.

Gurman, A.S. and Kniskern, D.P. (eds) (1981). *Handbook of Family Therapy*, Volume 1. New York: Brunner/ Mazel.

Johnson, S.M. and Greenberg, L.S. (1994). Emotion in intimate relationships: a synthesis. In S.M. Johnson and L.S. Greenberg (eds), *The Heart of the Matter: perspectives on emotion in marital therapy* (pp. 297–325). New York: Brunner/Mazel.

Johnson, S.M. (1996). *The Practice of Emotionally Focused Marital Therapy: creating connection*. Philadelphia, Pa.: Brunner/Mazell.

Johnson, S.M. (2003). The revolution in couple therapy: a practitioner-scientist perspective, *Journal of Marital and Family Therapy*, 29(3), 365–84.

Johnson, S.M. and LeBow, J. (2000). The 'coming of age' of couple therapy: a decade review. *Journal of Marital and Family Therapy*, 26(1), 23–38.

Kirschenbaum, H. and Henderson, V. (eds) (1990a). *Carl Rogers: dialogues*. London: Constable.

Kirschenbaum, H. and Henderson, V. (eds) (1990b). *The Carl Rogers Reader*. London: Constable.

Koerner, K. and Jacobson, N.S. (1994). Emotion and behavioral couple therapy. In S.M. Johnson and L.S. Greenberg (eds), *The Heart of the Matter: perspectives on emotion in marital therapy* (pp. 207–27). New York: Brunner/Mazel.

Levant, R.F. (1984). From person to system: two perspectives. In R.F. Levant and J.M. Schlien (eds), *Client-Centered Therapy and the Person-Centered Approach* (pp. 261–77). New York: Praeger.

Mearns, D. (1994). *Developing Person-Centred Counselling*. London: Sage.

Mearns, D. and Thorne, B. (1988). *Person-Centred Counselling in Action*. London: Sage.

Mearns, D. and Thorne, B. (1999). *Person-Centred Counselling in Action*. (2nd edn) London: Sage.

Mearns, D. and Thorne, B. (2000). *Person-Centred Therapy Today*. London: Sage.

O'Leary, C.J. (1989). The person-centred approach and family therapy: a dialogue between two traditions. *Person Centered Review*, 4(3), 308–23.

O'Leary, C.J. (1999). *Counseling Couples and Families: a person-centred approach*. London: Sage.

Raskin, N.J. and Van der Veen, F. (1970). Client-centered family therapy: some clinical and research perspectives. In J.T. Hart and T.M. Tomlimson (eds), *New Directions in Client-Centered Therapy* (pp. 387–406). New York: Houghton Mifflin.

Rogers, C.R. (1957). 'The necessary and sufficient conditions of therapeutic personality change', *Journal of Counseling Psychology*, 21(2), 95–103.

Rogers, C.R. (1961a). *On Becoming a Person: a therapist's view of psychotherapy*. Boston: Houghton Mifflin.

Rogers, C.R. (1961b). The implications of client-centered therapy for family life. In *On Becoming a Person: a therapist's view of psychotherapy* (pp. 314–29). Boston: Houghton Mifflin.

Rogers, C.R. (1972). *Becoming Partners: marriage and its alternatives*. New York: Delta.

Rogers, C.R. and Buber, M. (1990). Martin Buber. In H. Kirschenbaum and V. Henderson (eds), *Carl Rogers: dialogues* (pp. 41–64). London: Constable.

Snyder, M. (1989). The relationship enhancement model of couple therapy: an integration of Rogers and Bateson. *Person Centered Review*, 4(3), 358–84.

Warner, M. (1983). Soft meaning and sincerity in the family system. *Family Process*, 22, 522–35.

Warner, M. (1989). Empathy and strategy in the family system. *Person Centered Review*, 4(3), 324–44.

Wood, J.K. (1995). The person-centered approach: toward an understanding of its implications. *Person Centered Journal*, 2(2): 18–36.

Using a Person-Centred Approach within a Medical Framework

Jobst Finke and Ludwig Teusch

Medical science is framed in the logic of the natural sciences. When considering the application of person-centered therapy (PCT) within the medical framework, it is important to keep in mind that the epistemological foundation of the medical world is positivistic and objectivist. This position also implies an instrumentalist point of view. In psychotherapy, for instance, this leads to regarding the therapeutic relationship as nothing more than an instrument used to eliminate the clients' symptoms. Such a view contrasts greatly with a person-centred viewpoint, which goes beyond positivism and embraces a perspective that is more postmodern and relational. Despite the apparent clash of frames, we believe that PCT has a great deal to offer those working in the medical context. This chapter attempts to create a bridge and to reconcile the two frames of reference.

History and research

The medical framework (MF), presents a challenge for the person-centred psychotherapy because the MF is conceptually grounded in positivist scientific research logic that requires the therapists to take an 'arms-length' or objective point of view during the therapeutic process as well as during diagnosis. Furthermore, a schematic, diagnosis-specific application of predetermined treatment protocols that address specified target problems, as determined by the diagnosis, is required. If the person-centred approach (PCA) is to gain acceptance within this framework, then it cannot – and we will argue should not – totally reject these core aspects of the MF. In particular, when working within an MF it is not possible to entirely reject the importance of diagnosis and treatment planning in psychotherapy practice.

It can be argued that an analogous perspective to the MF has already been advanced by some early PCA proponents. Truax (1966), for instance, pointed out that Rogers was intuitively aware of the need for differential application of the core conditions at different stages of therapy. Rogers thus implicitly modified his manner of intervention on the basis of diagnostic criteria. Regarding the treatment criteria of self-disclosure and confrontation, for instance (Rogers et al, 1967; Carkhuff, 1969), it was shown that these are expressed to varying degrees depending on the client's diagnosis (Mitchell and Berenson, 1970). In this way, the therapeutic relationship was specifically focused on predetermined outcomes and modified for various client groups. This matching of specific intervention with diverse client needs requires identification of different client groups, and this in turn requires that some form of differential diagnostic record be made.

Many writers have explored the question of linking specific disorders with different therapeutic interventions, providing a rich literature supportive of an MF use of person-centred principles (Greenberg and Watson; 1998; Finke, 2004; Speierer, 1990; Swildens, 1990; Teusch and Böhme, 1999). There have also been attempts to conceptualize the therapeutic process such that there would be a relationship between specific aspects of a disorder and the recommended interventions (Teusch and Finke, 1995; Finke and Teusch, 1999). Developments along these lines are moving towards the creation of a PCT manual.

At the Essen University Clinic for Psychiatry, the effectiveness of a disorder-related (in-patient) PCT was examined with regard to different disorders. Examined in particular were anxiety disorders, depressive disorders, somatoform and personality disorders, as well as alcoholic addiction. We examined the changes in the level of symptoms such as anxiety and depression, and we examined these on the level of personality and process characteristics as well as subjective experience. In a randomized clinical study, PCT was highly effective with patients suffering from severe agoraphobia and panic. Both the agoraphobia and the panic symptoms were remarkably reduced. In a research project with add-on design, in the case of anxiety disorders, we compared 'pure' PCT (that is a person-centred therapeutic programme that did not include any additional elements of behavioural therapy) with a combination treatment consisting of PCT and behavioural exposure treatment. Many authors consider the latter treatment as the most effective form of psychotherapy in the case of anxiety disorders. In our examinations, the pure PCT was just as effective as the combination treatment, with regard to symptoms of agoraphobia and panic (Teusch et al, 1997).

Compared with the above-mentioned combination treatment, especially good results were achieved with the pure PCT, on the level of personality and subjective experience. The recovery from the sense of extreme responsibility and reduction of feelings of being under constant stress and suffering from bodily discomfort were significantly more pronounced with pure PCT than with the combination treatment. Not only were these therapeutic results sustained over the follow-up period of one year, but a slight subsequent improvement was also indicated. This additional subsequent improvement after ending the PCT has been described by Grawe (1976) for the outcome of a controlled study.

Process examinations of the Essen studies indicated that PCT-induced changes are achieved by means of factors (such as reducing of incongruence, improvement of self-regulation) that are different from those of the behavioural exposure treatment (Teusch and Böhme, 1999).

PCT is very successful in treating depressive disorders (Elliott et al, 1990; Greenberg and Watson, 1998). In a different series of studies, we examined the effectiveness of 'pure' PCT (i.e. a PCA-centred therapeutic programme without pharmaceutical therapy) compared with a combination of PCT with psycho-pharmaceutical therapy (predominantly with anti-depressants). Patients with depressive disorders (Teusch et al, 2003) as well as patients with personality disorders and depressive symptoms (Teusch et al, 2001) achieved equally good results in both treatment groups. Thus the additional pharmaceutical therapy did not improve upon the demonstrable effectiveness of the PCT alone. Concerning certain process variables, such as assimilation of problematic experiences (Stiles et al, 1990), patients treated with pure PCT achieved better results than patients treated with the combination treatment mentioned above. We interpreted this as indicating that the additional treatment with psycho-pharmaceuticals resulted in the patients having a more passive attitude towards their therapy.

Disorder-focused therapy

The following case study illustrates the procedure of disorder-focused PCT. The patient was suffering from a panic disorder with agoraphobia (*Diagnostic and Statistical Manual of Mental Disorders* (DSM IV): 300.21).

A 22-year-old female student of education was in a wallpaper store when she experienced her first panic attack with heart palpitations, sweating and dizziness. In the weeks thereafter, more of these attacks were experienced on busy streets and in stores. The student was in the process of moving from her parents' home and furnishing her own small apartment. She was a single child and very attached to her caring and dominant mother. Her mother was in the habit of organizing matters in her daughter's daily life. The father seemed to play only a minor role in the life of the patient. A general practitioner referred the student to the hospital psychotherapy unit. At this stage the student had already given up the idea of moving to her own apartment. She now felt that she would have to rely entirely on her mother's care. In her mother's company, these panic attacks were less frequent. The student was unable to continue her studies at the time when she started treatment.

The incongruence of panic and agoraphobia clients

Rogers described the phenomenon of fear in connection with incongruence – the discrepancy between self-conception and organismic experience. In the case of the above-mentioned client (also relevant for many clients with panic disorders) there is such a discrepancy. There is a feeling of general uncertainty (found in the self-concept), and a yearning for safety on the one hand, and the 'organismic' longing for independence, autonomy and expression of individual creativity, on the other. If this longing for independence and the wish for unlimited freedom emerges towards the end of a period of being taken care of, then as the feeling of safety is being endangered, the individual will react with fear (Rogers, 1959: 203):

> Anxiety is a state in which the incongruence between the concept of self and the total experience of the individual is approaching symbolization in awareness. When experience is obviously discrepant from the self-concept, a defensive response to threat becomes increasingly difficult. Anxiety is the response of the organism to the 'subception' that such discrepancy may enter awareness, thus forcing a change in the self-concept.
>
> (Rogers, 1959: 204)

Such incongruence could be the result of the influence of marginally congruent parents, who are ambivalent themselves. In the case of our client, this was largely due to the influence of the mother, who was overly protective, smothering and dominant on the one hand, and anxious and always warning of the dangers of life, on the other. Our client was strongly attached to her, but was also ambivalent. It is quite typical to be ambivalent towards a person who is so important. These clients are seeking security on one hand and unlimited freedom on the other. Frequently, however, this yearning is not clearly recognized, is symbolized incompletely or is distorted.

In agoraphobic clients, anxiety symptoms are often triggered by separation, which can be real or imagined. The fantasy separation conforms to the (unconscious) longing for independence. Yet this wish is linked to the idea of separation, and can be full of anxiety, the fear of being left behind. Thus there is also anxiety in situations of leaving and being independent, such as moving from an apartment or going on a trip. This was the case with our client. The symptoms appeared when she actually began to make the move from her parents' home. Therefore the fear of physical destruction may be seen as a 'distorted symbolization' (Rogers, 1959) of fear of loneliness. Loneliness is the opposite of freedom and independence.

Key topics common for clients with panic disorders

The conceptualization of the disorder described and explicated in the *Diagnostic and Statistical Manual of Mental Disorders* (DSM IV) or in the *International Classification of Diseases* (ICD 10), the client's biographical anamnesis (case history) and the reflections on the specific incongruence indicate certain key themes which are important for her (or his) experiencing of the disorder. The key themes of a disorder (see Table 21.1) are characteristic of the problematic disorder as well as of the problem profile of the specific personality. These themes will appear during the therapeutic process. Therapists must be aware of them and be able to differentiate among them when offering their understanding of the client's meanings.

Table 21.1 Key themes associated with anxiety disorders

Fear of physical destruction
Fear of body failure
Death panic
Fear of shame
Fear of being seen as a malingerer
Fear of losing control
Fear of being left alone
Fear of helplessness
Fear of loneliness
Disappointment in closely connected persons
Fear of dependence
Fear of losing oneself
Longing for independence
Fear of guilt

Fear of physical destruction

The anxiety attacks experienced by the client when she is in a busy department store, are associated with strong bodily sensations. There is a feeling of immediate fear, namely of the entire loss of bodily control. This is the central subject or theme at the beginning of the treatment.

Fear of body failure

This fear is understandable. Clients with this disorder experience heart palpitations, dizziness and sweating. This bodily experience is quite real and just as strong as, or even stronger than, the feeling of anxiety. Here the client misidentifies the source of the body feelings, identifying them not as fear – separation anxiety – but as a bodily malfunction. S/he interprets this bodily malfunction as the primary cause of the fear. In order to be trusted by the client, this subjective truth has to be acknowledged by the therapist, initially, and this subjective concept has to be explicitly defined.

On the level of empathic understanding, the therapist could say, for instance:

T: This is a terrible fear. You feel that your heart could stop at any time.
T: When you get that feeling of total destruction, do you lose trust in your body?

The task lies in empathy and understanding. This means helping the client become precisely aware of the bodily sensation connected to the anxiety and to point out that the meaning given to the symptoms is a misinterpretation.

In the sense of self-transparency, that is to say self-disclosure (Carkhuff, 1969: section 3), and the expression of empathy and care (Finke, 2004), the therapist will make clear that s/he understands the client's desire for certainty and avoidance of anxiety. In the case of an anxiety-driven client, the therapist should also try to actually calm down the client, for example by reassuring the client that her heart palpitations are not a sign of physical illness. Anxiety clients often need to be calmed down through expressions of solidarity from the therapist and to be encouraged to feel a greater sense of security.

T: I believe this must be terrible – this feeling of losing control. But I am sure that nothing can happen to you.

The balance here is delicate. If support is too intense and forceful, this can cause the client to become attached to the therapist and thus to intensify his/her avoidance of separation. Furthermore, if too much attention is focused on the client's bodily functioning, this may be an expression of denial of awareness of relationship conflicts. This in turn often requires careful treatment of this denial (Finke, 2004) by addressing the negative consequences of such a denial.

T: The anxiety regarding your health now takes up all your time and you no longer seem to have room for other questions?

Death panic

This is often a very central feeling during strong anxiety attacks. Initially, it is important to understand the fantasies the client has regarding death and dying, and what role other people play here – whether they are close or distant.

T: The idea of dying – for you this is connected to the feeling of having been left behind.

Fear of shame

Fear of shame often plays a central role in clients with anxiety attacks. If the therapist is aware of this, and also addresses this carefully and empathically, it may quickly result in access to the internal frame of reference, that is, to the self-conception of the patient. Feelings of shame can be a reason for the defence processes of the client – defence against accepting the concept of illness, for example. When these feelings are clarified, this can also be seen as a form of treatment of the defence system.

Fear of being seen as a malingerer

This may be based on a sense of difficulty in communicating how bad the illness is despite the lack of a physical pathological diagnosis. These clients are of the opinion that others might believe they are pretending to be ill. Initially, many clients fear that the therapist might secretly share this opinion. It is therefore necessary to intervene in order to clarify the relationship, by using immediacy (Carkhuff, 1969).

T: You are almost ashamed that you do not have a physical illness, which would make it all a lot easier.

P: I would not say I was ashamed, but this is all hard for me to understand. One could easily call me a malingerer or the like.

T: Maybe you are afraid I secretly think you are a malingerer?

Fear of losing control

This is often connected to an intense feeling that one could lose control of one's body, that one might for instance experience intense dizziness or even faint right in front of other people, and be horribly embarrassed. It is not infrequent for clients to talk about a fearful fantasy of 'flipping out' and going mad, which is also a source of embarrassment.

Fear of being left alone

For anxiety patients, the fear of being/having been left alone is known as separation fear and is a key topic in all forms of the disorder. When patients become aware of these central fears, their 'inner world' becomes more open and they get in touch with the fundamental experience pattern of their illness and of their personality problems.

T: In this threatening situation your experience is that you need a person who will take care of you.

Fear of helplessness

This occurs when the client feels exposed to anxiety attacks due to the apparent failure of all capacities for control and coping. In this case it is important to stabilize the client and to offer support – by supporting self-esteem and by encouraging the client with therapist self-transparency (that is, self-disclosure).

T: You have accomplished a great deal. If I were you, I would be just a little bit proud of myself.

Fear of loneliness

This may be based on the client's strong desire for safety and protection. A desire for a feeling of absolute safety is also characteristic of the student described above. This should be understood with reference to her family history where she constantly experienced insecurity.

Disappointment in closely connected persons

Disappointment arises when the client does not experience attention from significant others to the degree she expected, or when attention is given only along with a demand for subordination. When dealing with the latter, the client is able to become more clearly aware of the longing for independence, which may not have been fully symbolized until now.

T: Are you currently experiencing your relationship to your mother as being harmonious?

P: I would say yes.

T: Then you are very satisfied with the situation.

P: Well yes, it gets on my nerves at times, when I always have to act according to my mother's wishes.

T: Then you feel very limited where your desires and plans are concerned.

P: That's right. I then wish I could be more myself.

Fear of dependence

The fear of losing oneself

This is the experience of fearing that, while one depends on others, one's own needs will not be fulfilled. The client needs to become very intensely aware of her needs.

Longing for independence

When the client more intensely and more exactly symbolizes her own needs, she can then become increasingly able to recognize and express her own longing for independence.

Fear of guilt

Many different aspects of the self-concept might make it difficult for the client to precisely symbolize her longing for independence. In the case of our student the difficulty is connected to the fear of guilt. She was constrained by a conceptual construction (which was only vaguely symbolized) to present herself to her mother as a child that needs care, and thus to provide her mother with the feeling that she is needed. The student's longing to be independent (initially this was not clearly symbolized) made her feel guilty because she was depriving her mother of the central meaning of her life. When, with empathic understanding, the therapist picked up this fear of guilt as a central theme, the client was increasingly able to move away from this limiting self-conception and to modify it appropriately. At the conclusion of the therapy process the student had no more anxiety symptoms and she was happy to resume her studies.

Relationship concepts

The PCA is understood to be a 'relationship therapy' in which the therapeutic relationship itself is seen as central. We now need to consider how two specific relational forms may be characterized in the PCA.

The alter-ego-relationship and the dialogue-relationship

Early on, while discussing the process of empathic understanding, Rogers (1951) mentioned the therapeutic role of the alter ego of the client. He suggested at that time that the therapist should attempt to step aside, away from the regular form of interaction, and should try to take on the perspective of the client and look at the client's world with the client's eyes. The therapist's task, in this view, is to encourage the client's inner dialogue with him/herself. In a way, this relationship is a monologue, consisting only of the client in conversation with him/herself (Rogers, 1951). In making empathic responses, the therapist only voices what s/he interprets as the ego aspects of the client. Later on, Rogers added to this 'inner conversation' view of the therapist–client engagements a concept of a dialogue relationship (Schmid, 2006). Rogers was led to this dialogical view while working with heavily disordered patients, especially schizophrenics (Rogers et al, 1967), and also through discussions with Otto Rank (Pfeiffer, 1990) and Martin Buber (Kirschenbaum and Henderson, 1989). He emphasized the fundamental criterion of congruence/genuineness (Rogers, 1957). He insisted on the importance of the real presence of the therapist and that the therapist should be transparent. This view leads to the idea of the therapy meeting as an existential encounter: a contact that is 'person to person'. Thus the therapist should be a real person who is a partner in a real dialogue. In this view, the frame of reference of the therapist should not remain detached but be brought into meeting (Rogers, 1961). Carkhuff (1969) used the term self-disclosure for this.

These are two distinct, divergent relationship concepts – the alter ego relationship and the dialogical relationship. In therapy, neither of these concepts excludes the other. They are complementary. They have various meanings with different clients, themes and therapeutic situations. The therapist should ask him/herself in each therapeutic situation which type of therapeutic relationship s/he will use to intervene (Finke, 2004).

The observer relationship and the participant relationship

A client (or any other person) can be viewed through different epistemological points of view. One viewpoint is from a perspective of modern science and another is through an original and primary communication, which might be considered a postmodern perspective. In our view, to be of the most aid to the client, PCA should attempt to reconcile these two points of view, excluding neither.

Modern science is associated with a particular model of relationship – as in the case of the relationship between researcher and his or her object. This relationship is determined by an ideal of objectivity. Any indirect spontaneous movement, reply or participation is to be excluded from this relationship in order to avoid any influence on the objective judgement or bias of the observer. Rogers rejected this form of relationship during interaction with the client. In his view, the therapist-to-client relationship should not be one of observing the client from an emotional distance and judging the client objectively. The

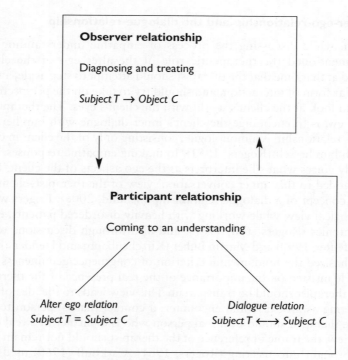

Figure 21.1 Concept of the therapeutic relationship

therapist should not be a distant spectator but should instead be a partner, participating in and co-creating the interaction, where the essence lies in communication rather than in recognizing and influencing. Thus we have two contrasting concepts of relationship: the observer relationship, which is important to MF, and the participant relationship. The participant relationship may be expressed in either of the above mentioned alter-ego or dialogical forms. We propose that both relational forms are appropriate in the therapeutic context (Finke, 2004, 2005) (see Figure 21.1).

The modern and the postmodern position in the PCA

In psychotherapy, Rogers takes a radical position that offers a critique of the observer relationship. By implication this also means that Rogers (1961) rejects a therapeutic stance that requires an objective monitoring and categorization within the therapeutic process. As person-centred therapists we share the postmodern reluctance to accept unreservedly the modernist modes of thought that privilege predictability, control and instrumentalism (O'Hara, 1998). Like Rogers, we regard this post-positivist and non-instrumental position as a core aspect of the PCA (as one aspect of what we today call postmodernism). Yet we are reluctant to totally reject modern forms of thinking in psychotherapy. In our view, such an extreme would represent a one-sided position, when expressed as 'problem-centred is not person-centred' for instance (Mearns, 2004). We are of the opinion that psychotherapy must acknowledge certain aspects of the observer relationship, particularly when it is a part of a modernist healing method. We also believe that PCA as a field must do this if it is to remain acceptable in reviews of modern psychotherapy and not be marginalized in the health care system (Eckert et al, 2003). We propose that the person-centred approach needs to be able to apply both modernist and postmodern epistemologies, moving between the two views as relevant and as required by the medical context. This means that the therapist will take the position of an observer at times. S/he will then be able to utilize the MF (diagnostics, subject-focused treatment plan, concepts for handling, therapeutic techniques). With regard to the therapeutic process this means that the therapist will oscillate between viewpoints and will take turns being an observer and a participant. S/he will take turns in being a spontaneous actor and participant, as well as performing diagnostics, being critical about his or her own participation with the client.

Future trends

Today, PCA takes many forms (Keil and Stumm, 2002). This is a sign of the vitality of the approach. Among these multiple forms, there are two basic positions that often seem hopelessly opposed. On the one hand we have the 'postmodern' position, where therapy is considered only as the direct person-to-person encounter. This encounter is not seen as being directed towards a particular function or outcome. Modernist scientific logic is rejected. In this view, the essence of the therapeutic encounter is a non-specifiable emergent process that is inconsistent with diagnostics, treatment plans and operational guidelines. From this point of view, no problem-centred or disorder-centred approach can be considered person-centred (Brodley and Brody, 1996; Schmid, 2004; Mearns, 2004). On the other hand, we have those positions wherein therapy is regarded as a target-oriented process. The therapist, an expert, is responsible for appropriately influencing the process towards specific outcomes. In this view, it is the techniques of therapy and diagnostics that are consistent with the PCA. The debate between the two positions was a feature at the 2003 gathering of person-centred therapists in Egmond, the Netherlands, reported in the journal *Person-Centered and Experimental Psychotherapies* (2004, Vol. 3, 1 and 2), where these two divergent orientations appeared irreconcilable.

We support the instrumentalist position, yet we do not want to support it in a one-sided or fundamentalist way. We accept and appreciate certain aspects of the 'postmodern' position. We are of the opinion that there should be a synthesis of both positions in PCT – a synthesis of the modern and the postmodern, the observer perspective and the participant perspective – and believe that both positions have a place within the PCA school. We take this position both theoretically, as we hope we have shown in this chapter, and as a matter of professional pragmatics. In these days of fierce competition among schools of psychotherapy, the versatility and scope of PCA is an important resource that needs to be acknowledged for its versatility and effectiveness. We propose that the ongoing dialogue between the postmodernist and modernist positions is fruitful and can only strengthen Rogers' important legacy.

REFERENCES

Brodley, B. and Brody, A. (1996). Can one use techniques and still be client-centered? In R. Hutterer, G. Pawlowsky, P.F. Schmid and R. Stipsits (eds), *Client-Centred and Experiential Psychotherapy: a paradigm in motion* (pp. 369–74). Frankfurt, Lang.

Carkhuff, R.R. (1969). *Helping and Human Relations: a primer for lay and professional helpers.* Volume 1. *Selection and Training.* Volume 2. *Practice and Research.* New York, Chicago, San Francisco, Atlanta, Dallas, Montreal, Toronto, London, Sydney: Holt, Rinehart and Winston.

Carkhuff, R.R. and Berenson, B.G. (1967). *Beyond Counseling and Therapy.* New York, Chicago, San Francisco, Atlanta, Dallas, Montreal, Toronto, London: Holt, Rinehart and Winston.

Eckert, J., Höger, D. and Schwab, R. (2003). Development and current state of the research on client-centered therapy in the German language region. *Person-Centered and Experiential Psychotherapies,* 1, 3–18.

Elliott, R., Clark, C., Kemeny, V., Wexler, M.M., Mack, C. and Brinkerhoff, J. (1990). The impact of experiential therapy on depression: the first ten cases. In G. Lietaer, J. Rombauts and R. van Balen (eds), *Client-Centered and Experiential Psychotherapy in the Nineties,* 549–77. Leuven, Belgium: Leuven University Press.

Finke, J. (2004) *Gesprächspsychotherapie: Grundlagen und spezifische Anwendungen* [Client-Centred Therapy: Basic positions and applications]. Stuttgart: Thieme.

Finke, J. (2005). Beziehung und Technik: Beziehungskonzepte und störungsbezogene Behandlungspraxis der Personzentrierten Psychotherapie [Relationships and technique: concepts of therapeutic relationship and disorder-centred concepts of treatment in person-centred psychotherapy]. *PERSON,* 1, 51–64.

Finke, J. and Teusch, L. (1999). Entwurf zu einer manualgeleiteten Gesprächspsychotherapie der Depression [Outlines of a manual-directed client-centred therapy of depressive disorders]. *Psychotherapeut,* 44, 101–7.

Greenberg, L.S. and Watson, J.C. (1998). Experiential therapy of depression: differential effects of client-centered relationship conditions and process experiential interventions. (York I) *Psychotherapy Research,* 8, 210–24.

Grawe, K. (1976). *Differentielle Psychotherapie.* I. Bern: Huber.

Keil, W. and Stumm, G. (eds) (2002). *Die vielen Gesichter der Personzentrierten Psychotherapie* [The multiple faces of person-centred psychotherapy]. Vienna, New York: Springer.

Kirschenbaum, H. and Henderson, V.L. (eds) (1989). *Carl Rogers: dialogues.* Boston, Houghton Mifflin.

Mearns, D. (2004). Problem-centred is not person-centred. *Person-Centered and Experiential Psychotherapies,* 2, 88–101.

Mitchell, K.M. and Berenson, B.G. (1970). Differential use of confrontation by high and low facilitative therapists. *The Journal of Nervous and Mental Disease*, 37, 437–42.

O'Hara, M. (1998). Personzentrierte und experientielle Psychotherapie in einem kulturellen Übergangszeitalter [Person-centred and experiential psychotherapy in a cultural interim age]. *PERSON*, 1, 5–14.

Pfeiffer, W.M. (1990). Otto Rank und die klientenzentrierte Psychotherapie [Otto Rank and client-centred psychotherapy]. In M. Behr, U. Esser, F. Petermann and W.M. Pfeiffer (eds), *Jahrbuch für personzentrierte Psychologie und Psychotherapie*, Bd. 2 (pp. 8–21). Salzburg: Müller.

Rogers, C.R. (1951). *Client-Centered Therapy*. Boston, Houghton Mifflin.

Rogers, C.R. (1957). The necessary and sufficient conditions of therapeutic personality change. *Journal of Consulting Psychology*, 21(2), 95–103.

Rogers, C.R. (1959). A theory of therapy, personality, and interpersonal relationships, as development in the client-centred framework. In S. Koch (ed.), *Psychology: a study of a science. Study 1: conceptual and systemic.* Volume 3. *Formulation of the Person and the Social Context*. New York, Toronto, London: McGraw-Hill.

Rogers C.R. (1961). *On Becoming a Person: a therapist's view of psychotherapy*. Boston, Houghton Mifflin.

Rogers, C.R., Gendlin, E.T., Kiesler, D. and Truax, C.B. (1967). *The Therapeutic Relationship and its Impact: a study of psychotherapy with schizophrenics*. Madison: University of Wisconsin Press.

Schmid, P.F. (2004). Back to the client: a phenomenological approach to the process of understanding and diagnosis. *Person-Centered and Experiential Psychotherapies*, 1, 36–51.

Schmid, P.F. (2006). The challenge of the Other: towards dialogical person-centered psychotherapy and counseling. *Person-Centered and Experiential Psychotherapies*, 4, 240–54.

Speierer, G.W. (1990). Toward a specific illness concept of client-centered psychotherapy. In G. Lietaer, J. Rombauts and R. van Balen (eds), *Client-centered and Experiential Psychotherapy in the Nineties*, (pp. 337–59). Leuven, Belgium: Leuven University Press.

Stiles, W.B, Elliot, R., Liewelyn, S.P., Firth-Cozens, J.A., Margison, F.A., Shapiro, D.A. and Hardy, G. (1990). Assimilation of problematic experiences by clients in psychotherapy. *Psychotherapy*, 27, 411–20.

Swildens, H. (1990). Client-centered psychotherapy for patients with borderline symptoms. In G. Lietaer, J. Rombauts and R. van Balen (eds), *Client-Centered and Experiential Psychotherapy in the Nineties* (pp. 623–35). Leuven, Belgium: Leuven University Press.

Teusch, L. and Böhme, H. (1999). Is the exposure principle really crucial in agoraphobia? The Influence of client-centered 'nonprescriptive' treatment on exposure. *Psychotherapy Research*, 9(1), 115–23.

Teusch, L., Böhme, H., Finke, J. and Gastpar, M. (2001). Effects on client-centered psychotherapy for personality disorders alone and in combination with psychopharmacological treatment: an empirical follow-up study. *Psychotherapy and Psychosomatics*, 70, 328–36.

Teusch, L., Böhme, H., Finke, J., Gastpar, M. and Skerra, B. (2003). Antidepressant medication and the assimilation of problematic experiences in psychotherapy. *Psychotherapy Research*, 13, 307–22.

Teusch, L., Böhme, H. and Gastpar, M. (1997). The benefit of an insight oriented and experiential approach on panic and agoraphobia symptoms: results of a controlled comparison of client-centred therapy and a combination with behavioural exposure. *Psychotherapy and Psychosomatics*, 66, 293–301.

Teusch, L. and Finke, J. (1995). Grundlagen eines Manuals für die gesprächs-spsychotherapeutische Behandlung von Panik und Agoraphobie [Fundamental principles of a manual for client-centred therapy of panic and agoraphobia]. *Psychotherapeut*, 40, 88–95.

Truax, C.B. (1966). Reinforcement and nonreinforcement in Rogerian psychotherapy. *Journal of Abnormal Psychotherapy*, 71, 1–9.

CHAPTER 22

Crisis Intervention

Lorna Carrick

Introduction

The Chinese symbol for 'crisis' captures its essential elements, with its combination of pictographs for danger and opportunity. Clients entering therapy in a state of crisis or reaching a point of crisis during therapy present the therapist with the challenge and the opportunity to work at a pivotal point between maladaptive regression and positive change. Crisis is a widely used term in the helping professions and in society. In this chapter I propose to define the term from a person-centred perspective and to look closely at how the person-centred approach works with the client in crisis. There is a fairly widely held perception that person-centred therapy is not the 'treatment of choice' to work with clients in crisis. This perception predominantly comes from within a health system where crisis is seen as a problem rather than an opportunity and where management of risk and symptom reduction takes precedence over psychological reconfiguration and longer-term personality change.

> Definition of Crisis: 1a: a decisive moment, b: a time of danger or great difficulty;
> 2: the turning point.
>
> (*Oxford English Dictionary*)

A crisis may be defined as an acute state of distress wherein one's usual coping mechanisms have failed in the face of a perceived challenge or threat and some degree of functional impairment is caused. For some clients a crisis is an event which will only occur rarely and will involve extreme events such as a violent attack, an accident, rape or the death of someone close to them. For other clients crisis will occur more frequently, provoked by less extreme events such as difficulties at work, relationship problems and threats to their self-esteem. Past experiences and the ability to cope in challenging situations affect whether an event is perceived or subceived as threatening by clients. From a person-centred perspective, crisis can only really be defined from a phenomenological standpoint, in terms of how the individual experiences and understands events. Crisis can be seen as the individual's response to a perceived risk or threat, whether real or imagined, involving what Mearns (2005) describes in terms of 'dissonance' within the client. The dissonance may occur when experience or perception of reality is affected by crisis so that the concept of self or 'life picture' is threatened.

When Rogers (1959) expanded his theory of personality and therapy with the introduction of his concept of the self-structure, he provided the basis for under-standing crisis from the person-centred perspective. He went on to assert that experiences which are incongruent with the self-structure are subceived as threatening, and therefore that clients will avoid accurate symbolization of the threatening experience. A typical response from a client might be: 'I can't believe this is happening to me.' Or 'I can't believe he is gone.' Rogers (1959: 201) described the process of breakdown and disorganization of the self-structure in which 'an experience is perceived or anticipated (subceived) as incongruent with the structure of the self' and that 'psychological maladjustment exists when the organism denies to awareness significant experiences'. A client experiencing a crisis would seem to present an extreme case of breakdown and disorganization. This often presents as a de-configuration of the self, where the client seems very disintegrated and confused. In an attempt to hold the dissonance between self-concept and experience the client will talk from different parts of the self. For example: 'part of me knows I need to get over this, but there's the other bigger bit that just feels so hopeless and scared, I can't even think about it'. When accurate symbolization occurs, re-configuration and integration can take place. Van der Kolk et al emphasize the importance of conceptual processes in the contain-ment of affect. 'When the mind is able to create symbolic representations of these past experiences, there seems to be a taming of the terror, and a related desomatization of the experience' (1994: 727).

Historical development

Crisis intervention began its development at the beginning of the twentieth century. Historically 'crisis theory has developed from diverse sources, the most important contributions having derived from Social Psychiatry, Ego Psychology and Learning Theory' (Hobbs, 1984: 24). Everly and Mitchell (1999) chart the major milestones in the development and practice of crisis intervention and critical incident debriefing. They pay particular attention to the work of Caplan and others (Caplan, 1964) on the creation of a commu-nity mental health programme. Caplan and his colleagues at the Harvard School of Public Health made significant contributions to the development of theory based on the concept of emotional homeostasis. He conceived of the individual striving to live in a state of emotional equilibrium, and crisis as destabilizing that equilibrium. In 1963 President John Kennedy called for 'a bold new approach' to the delivery of mental health services. The result was the establishment of community mental health initiatives and the expansion of crisis intervention programmes leading to a change in the delivery of psychiatric services across the world.

Erikson (1965) constructed a model of the life-cycle of the individual, involving a series of psychosocial tasks, described as the 'eight stages of man'. He defines developmental tasks which must be accomplished. In each stage there is the possibility of making an adaptive response, and also the possibility that the social environment will positively affect or inhibit the individual's response. At each stage there is the possibility of a crisis. Erickson thus defined transitional or maturational crisis. Hobbs (1984) made the distinction between developmental and accidental crisis. The former refers to inevitable life transitions such as adolescence, childbirth, menopause and retirement. There is a developmental task to achieve at each stage, and failure to do so would equate to a developmental crisis; the likelihood of the individual achieving the task may be affected by the 'adaptive resources of the individual and the encouragement of his social milieu' (1984: 26). Hobbs defines an accidental crisis as one which involves 'accidental hazards' which have evolved from 'non-developmental life-events' (1984: 26). Examples include the physical, social or biological environment.

Everly and Mitchell (1999: 7) describe the period which followed in the 1960s and 1970s as the 'heyday of fundamental crisis intervention services'. The primary interventions employed at this time were non-directive client-centred counselling, and basic problem-solving and conflict-resolution techniques. Significantly, in 1980, post-traumatic stress disorder (PTSD) was recognized in the third edition of *The Diagnostic and Statistical Manual of Mental Disorders*. Recognition legitimized the development and provision of services in response to crisis, specifically the development of trained crisis intervention teams. Critical incident stress management was born.

Historically there has been little written on crisis from a person-centred perspective. That which does exist focuses on the treatment of PTSD (Joseph, 2005). Other existing studies, which refer to using the person-centred approach as crisis intervention, have used the term in the broadest sense, as is the case in numerous studies into the use of pastoral care as crisis intervention.

The person-centred approach to crisis intervention

A key concept in assessing the appropriateness of the person-centred approach in relation to crisis intervention lies in how we define and view crisis. In the past, the medical model has responded mainly to the danger in crisis and been less in tune with the opportunity for change. As such there has been a tendency to look to therapeutic models which offer symptom reduction and cognitive re-framing. The person-centred approach works from a potentiality model, believing that the self-curing abilities of the client are a formidable resource (Taylor, 1983). Central to this approach is the belief that the actualizing tendency (Rogers, 1959) will bring about psychological re-adjustment, and that if the client is offered a relationship in which the basic core conditions of person-centred therapy are present at optimal levels, this adjustment is likely to be adaptive, even at the point of breakdown. Faith in the client's self-righting capacity as an expression of an inherent actualizing tendency means that there is no need for the therapist to lead the client or direct him or her towards solutions. The person-centred approach to working with crisis involves the therapist in following the client cognitively and emotionally, facilitating the accurate symbolization of both realms of experience. Mearns and Thorne (1988: 104) state: 'the very activity of empathic understanding often has the effect of diffusing a crisis, of slowing it down and relieving to some extent the crippling effect of anxiety and dread which the client may be undergoing'.

Case illustration

Prior to the onset of crisis, Alice described herself as a busy, confident and successful professional woman with a responsible job as an auditor and a stable marriage. Alice was referred for 'bereavement and relationship issues'. Crisis was not mentioned. On opening the door at our first meeting she stumbled in and immediately fell to the floor sobbing. She rocked herself in a foetal position for some time as I sat beside her on the floor. I noticed a series of cuts on her legs and bruising on her hands and face. Much later she said how important it was to simply be met in that place. In no way did I attempt to take her into the source of her distress; it was by simply attending empathically to her in the moment that she was able to become calm enough to begin to hold the dissonance she was experiencing.

First session

Alice: I really can't cope since my mum died I just feel torn in pieces. You have to help me I'm really falling apart. It's like it's all my fault, she was never happy.

LC: You really feel in bits and that it's your fault that she wasn't happy. I feel a real sense of how desperate this is for you.

Alice: Yes, oh yes! I feel like everything is pressing down on me, I must be a really bad person. You know every thing tells me that ... I am bad. Peter [her husband] is leaving me, I've always tried to be a good wife and to look after him I'm going to have his baby and I'm so, so scared that I won't be a good Mum.

LC: You've tried hard and now he's leaving you feel you must be a bad person and so scared that you won't be a good mum.

Alice: Yes my father says I'm useless and it's my fault that Peter is leaving, because I need too much from him, the way I needed too much attention from my Mum. When I was little I used to want them to notice me, they were always arguing and if Dad was in a mood Mum would be so upset. Gary [her brother] was always so good, top marks in school ... better than me at everything. {Sobbing} I had to be good and work hard. No one ever seemed to notice though, except when I got sick. Then I'd get medicine and there were lots of times when that felt good.

LC: So you really tried to be good and do well and seemed to be standing in his shadow and to get noticed you had to be sick ... and as you say that, you are looking so sad.

Alice: I hadn't realized that I was crying, it's like I see that small person and I'm really sad for her. I don't want my baby to feel like that.

Alice's crisis began with the death of her mother and was exacerbated by her husband's decision to leave her. Her mother's death brought about an initial crisis which forced her to question her role in life and to confront her fears of annihilation of her experiences by her father. Her husband's decision to leave her brought her whole self-concept into question. Alice's family life had helped to create a rigid self-concept with many introjections and conditions of worth. She was only acceptable to her father when she achieved, and she was expected to bolster his ego. In order to receive any attention at all she had to put the needs of others first and deny her own feelings.

Alice: I always feel that it's my job to make things better, if Dad was happy then he didn't upset my Mum, if I could make him happy then maybe Mum would notice me.

At an early stage in our work she identified 'sick sad me' as part of her self-concept. Later Alice identified a part of herself which she both liked and mourned for. She described this as the part of her inner child-self that was joyous and high-spirited and rebellious.

Alice: {sigh} I've felt sad and sick for so long, he [father] didn't like me unless I was doing what he wanted, he didn't like the dancing, naughty little girl who painted her face and would pretend to be a fabulous superstar. 'Only quiet and good little girls get to go to grandma's house.' That little person needed a friend {cries} I would have liked her as a friend.

LC: There is sadness for the part of you that was dancing and naughty and you like her.

Alice: Oh yes I do like her she's fun and it's so sad that he made her go away!

This configuration of self had to be suppressed to conform to the needs of the family. 'A "configuration" is a hypothetical construct denoting a coherent pattern of feelings, thoughts and preferred behavioral responses symbolized or pre-symbolized by the person as reflective of a dimension of existence within the self' (Mearns and Thorne, 2000: 102).

This part of her self began to re-emerge in therapy, initiating the reconfiguration within her self-concept.

At the initial point of crisis she could not cope with the challenge to her view of herself. She began self-harming as way of dealing with the pain of the dissonance she was experiencing. Previously she saw herself as a person who coped in life and as someone who was always 'there' for others. Her self-concept was under threat and she felt bad and unacceptable. Her father's judgement of her confirmed that to have needs was bad. She feared annihilation. This resulted in functional impairment.

Alice: I'm so scared, I can't go to work I feel like they are all judging me I can't see where to go from here. Sometimes I just pull the blanket over my head and want to die.

LC: You are feeling so bad about being judged that you just want to die. Do you think you might harm yourself when you feel like that?

Alice: That's when I hurt myself it {shows small cuts} helps to deal with the pain inside. I don't know who I am. I can make no connection with what I thought was real, everything has changed overnight. It's like dropping a stitch in some knitting and unravelling the whole piece. I am completely pulled apart.

LC: Your whole sense of yourself has unravelled like the knitting and you're left in bits. I get a sense of you needing to be held together whilst you try to make sense of it all.

Alice: Oh! that's exactly it {sobbing} ...

LC: So how would it be to take some time now to think about how you might be helped to hold together between our sessions?

Throughout the process of therapy I realized the importance of empathically tuning in to the felt-sense and meaning of Alice's experience (Gendlin, 1996). She described the effect of being understood in this way as liberating and challenging. There was so much of her experience which had to be denied, that she would temporarily reach a pre-verbal stage. Then it was necessary to work with body reflections and contact reflections (Prouty et al, 2002).

LC: Alice sits in the chair rocking ... you have a sad face.

Alice: {looking up after a long time} I feel really small and sad.

We often spent time in sessions working on how she might find ways to 'hold' herself in crisis. Sometimes this would be 'clearing a space', as in focusing. Gradually she began to develop a new more fluid sense of self which was more open to her own vulnerability.

Alice: You know it's actually right to be sad for myself, I was just a little person trying to be good and I didn't have the grown-up me to rely on.

LC: You can let yourself be sad and know that your grown-up self would understand about that.

Alice moved beyond her pre-crisis self to a more congruent self-structure which became open to and in touch with her experience. The process involved the exploration and discovery of the many parts of herself. Alice conceived of the parts as a 'team'.

Alice: My team has a 'center forward' now who makes sure all the parts of the team get a place in the game.

Important themes emerged from my work with crisis, which inform my practice. The quality of the initial contact is crucial. An important difference in the way that person-centred therapy engages at the point of crisis is that the therapist in no way seeks to change the crisis. The therapist does not engage in symptom reduction in the medical sense. However, a discussion of how clients might deal with suicidal thoughts, self-harm or feeling overwhelmed between the sessions can lead to a self-assessment of risk which truly puts the client's experience at the centre of the therapy. It is vital that we pay attention to the risk element of crisis, and in early sessions the level of therapeutic engagement necessary for the client should be assessed, should be explored. Alice said clearly that to begin with she needed sessions more than once a week. Bi-weekly sessions for the first month achieved exponential movement and the beginnings of stabilization. Alice reported feeling that her experience had been 'held', she felt attended to and understood. She said that this made her want to come for therapy. I believe that this feeling also helped her to hold the dissonance she was experiencing between the sessions.

She later talked of how important was the sense of empathic connection with her 'here and now' experiences which helped her to begin to feel safe enough to revisit the sources of crisis. This she did in her own time and pace. The importance of the client leading the way in is underlined by Rothchild (2005) in relation to work with clients recovering from trauma. She describes how highly competent colleagues, working in theoretically sound modalities (e.g. psychodynamic psychotherapy, EMDR – eye movement desensitization and reprocessing – body psychotherapy and cognitive-behavioural) have experienced 'clinical mishaps' in their work. She identifies the notion of the traumatic material being addressed before the client is equipped to handle it and suggests a strategy to 'Put the brakes on'. In person-centred therapy we would not direct the client to the traumatic material. Initial understanding of the client's frame of reference and following the client's process is essential. This differs from the process of critical incident debriefing, which directs the client to process the crisis experience and aims to prevent the development of post-traumatic stress disorder. Rose et al (2006: 1) report that 'No evidence has been found that this procedure is effective.' The report goes on to say that 'there is some suggestion that it may increase the risk of PTSD and depression.'

Application of the person-centred approach

Working with clients in crisis presents the therapist with a unique challenge and opportunity. There is an opportunity to meet the clients where the usual defence structures have failed and they are both vulnerable and wide open to change. Alice's rigid self-structure prior to the crisis made it almost impossible for her to change. The strength of conditions of worth placed on her made it a priority for her to maintain the self-concept she had developed 'at all costs'. Only when evidence from the external environment presented a profound challenge did the coping mechanisms of denial and distortion break down to create the opportunity for change. What makes the experience of working with clients in crisis unique for person-centred therapists is the therapist's 'differential response' to the client (Purton, 2004: 254). My experience is that therapists describe engaging with heightened levels of energy with clients, and are prepared to extend the therapeutic context to offer sufficient 'holding' and safety to crisis clients. They describe themselves as doing more assessment, giving information to clients and using their own experiences of crisis to engage fully in the work (Carrick, 2006).

Not all clients in crisis will have been in a highly incongruent state prior to the crisis, even though at the point of crisis clients describe a sense of threat and destabilization. Mearns says that 'Disorder is caused when the person becomes chronically stuck within his own process such that the homeostatic balance cannot reconfigure to respond to changing circumstances' (Mearns and Thorne, 2000: 184). At the point of crisis the powerful forces of the actualizing tendency and the biological need for homeostasis appear to temporarily shift in their relationship to each other, in that the loss of homeostasis removes the normal resistance to change. This creates the opportunity for growth or destruction.

The person-centred approach aims to facilitate the changing process, by closely following the client as the various parts of the self-structure re-configure to 'a different point of homeostasis, a different balancing point' (Mearns, 2005: 17). Issues of client safety and therapeutic context need to be considered alongside the demands placed on the person of the therapist. Assessment is a term often avoided in the person-centred approach (Wilkins, 2005). However, in person-centred crisis intervention it is necessary to assess from a phenomenological standpoint the sufficiency of the context in which the work takes place. Does the client require a wider contract? Mearns states:

> It is important that person-centered counselors who are choosing to work with more demanding clientele and involving more therapeutic contracts are able to be flexible in the way they work whilst they are in full control of the work. Contextual considerations such as frequency of sessions, the possibility of 'crisis call outs' and working in settings that are safe for the client, are all aspects which may be varied by the experienced and well supported counselor.
>
> (Mearns, 2003: 47)

Good supervision is essential. Potential over- or under-involvement is a critical factor in crisis intervention. A counsellor who feels overwhelmed by the depth or nature of the client's crisis may choose not to engage with the client and be under-involved. Over-involvement may lead to trying to 'fix' the client – using techniques or interventions from other approaches, becoming directive, or attempting to 'rescue' – or the infringement of boundaries, with disastrous results for the already vulnerable client.

Inter-disciplinary team working can afford a wider context of support, which may become part of the contract with the client. In some circumstances, for example where the therapist feels that the client is at risk of serious harm or suicide, or is unable to function because s/he has lost the ability to stay in psychological contact, then it may be necessary to offer more help from the wider team. In private practice the therapist's ethical responsibility to the client is the same, to ensure that the therapeutic context is sufficient and that the rights and autonomy of the client are respected. Where possible this should be done with the client's involvement, bearing in mind the importance of avoiding disempowering clients or sending the message that their crisis is too much to handle.

In some extreme cases the dissonance may be so great that the client arrives in a state of dissociation. In this state the client has multiple 'selves' which may or may not be aware of each other's existence (Warner, 2000). In such instances the client has developed fragmented constellations of parts of the self, which operate to hold the dissonance which the crisis has provoked. These constellations may have formed in response to an earlier crisis, such as abuse, and be reconfigured or reinstated in the face of a new crisis. Warner emphasizes the importance of working with all aspects of the self. Crisis may also provoke a psychotic state in which psychological contact is impaired (Van Werde in Mearns, 2003). In such cases the skills and competencies of the therapist dictate whether it is safe and ethical to engage in the work.

A principal task of therapy is to assist clients to accurately symbolize their experience. '[U]nless the experience is accurately symbolized, unless suitably accurate differentiations are made, the individual mistakes regressive behavior for self-enhancing behavior' (Rogers, 1951: 491). Crisis intervention involves ensuring more accurate symbolization at a point where the client seems closer to his or her own existence and open to change. Clients will often say 'I just want to get back to normal' even when normal was a maladaptive way of being. Human beings seek familiarity and homeostasis. It seems that nothing is more threatening than inconsistency and destabilization of the self-concept. What crisis does is to create such a tension between the self-concept and experience that the individual senses or subceives the need for change. Assisting accurate symbolization and helping the client to 'hold' that experience in awareness at this critical point facilitates the development of a more congruent self-structure.

What are the elements of the person-centred approach which hold and facilitate this process of change? Emotion-focused therapists (Greenberg et al, 1993: 271) emphasize the importance of empathy and 'its role in a specific task, that of providing empathic affirmation of the vulnerable self'. The role of empathic understanding of the client's frame of reference in facilitating accurate symbolization of experience cannot be overstated. It is through such understanding that the dissonance between self and experience is reduced and psychological tension decreased.

The notion that empathic connection and attunement to the client facilitate the process in therapy fits well with the importance of the relationship with the client in the person-centred approach. The client in crisis requires to be held, metaphorically, in his or her experience, by the therapist whilst in such a vulnerable state. The closeness and connectedness of this relationship can often lead to moments when client and therapist meet at what Mearns (1996) describes as 'relational depth' very early in the therapeutic process. The working alliance between client and therapist is essential. Clients describe these moments in terms such as 'feeling really seen', 'feeling as if you [the therapist] are part of me'.

Alice: I feel as if you are a safe extension of my thinking and feeling space. When I am between sessions I remember how I feel 'connected' to you and it really helps me to survive until the next session.

Crisis intervention, then, demands a great deal of the therapist. Caplan (1964: 291) and the Harvard team observed that 'Whether a person emerges stronger or weaker is not necessarily determined by his "character" or his "inner strength" but by the quality of help he gets during the trouble.' Caplan states that the 'only way to survive a crisis is to be aware of it, the only way of forgetting is through remembering' (1964: 192). Caplan's research indicated that those who survive crisis do so because they face the dangers and confront them. Caplan (1964) discovered that mothers who talked about their fears of losing their child, who examined their worries and questioned doctors about the likely outcomes coped better and developed less anxiety and depressive symptoms than those who did not. More recent studies indicate that there is a danger in assuming that all clients are ready or need to talk about the crisis event. What is helpful within the person-centred approach is that the client leads the way and the therapist is actively engaged in the pursuit of accurate symbolization of the here-and-now experience. This is not about directing or getting in the client's way. It is about attending to catching all the subtle nuances and felt meanings the client is expressing. The therapist must be able to grasp aspects of the client's experience which are conscious, and those at the edge of awareness. To support this work therapists must pay attention to their own ongoing personal development. One of the principal places where this can occur is in supervision.

In crisis intervention, engaging fully with the client may involve tapping one's own personal depths of experience, including one's personal experience of crisis. In doing so we may touch aspects of self-experience that have brought us close to the sense of our own existence. Mearns (Mearns and Cooper, 2005: Chapter 8) refers to these self-experiences which we may draw on in the therapeutic encounter as 'existential touchstones'. These touchstones are experiences that form the milestones in the development of each of us: coping with puberty, facing the death of someone we love, coping with embarrassment or experiencing powerlessness. In using my own personal touchstones too I may get a deeper sense of their experience, and in doing so there is a sense of going beyond tracking and understanding the client. Touching one's own experience of crisis may seem particularly dangerous if there is a fear of being overwhelmed. It is therefore particularly important, as part of the therapist's developmental agenda, that these touchstones are fully explored in supervision, experiential workshops and in contexts which help us to learn to use them therapeutically.

REFERENCES

Caplan, G. (1964). *Principles of Preventative Psychiatry*. London: Tavistock.
Carrick, L. (2006). Client-centered therapists experiences of working with

clients in crisis. Paper delivered at the WAPCEPC Conference, Potsdam, Germany.

Elliot, R., Watson, J.C., Goldman, R.N. and Greenberg, L.S. (2004). *Learning Emotion-Focused Therapy: the process experiential approach to change*. Washington DC: American Psychological Association.

Erikson, E. (1965). *Childhood and Society*. London: Penguin.

Everly, J.R. and Mitchell, J.T. (1999). *Critical Incident Stress Management: a new era and standard of care in crisis intervention*. Ellicott City: Chevron.

Gendlin, E.T. (1996). *Experiencing the Creation of Meaning* (2nd edn). Evanston, Il.: Northwestern University Press.

Greenberg, L.S., Rice, L.N. and Elliot, R. (1993). *Facilitating Emotional Change: the moment-by moment process*. New York: Guilford.

Hobbs, M. (1984). Crisis intervention in theory and practice: a selective review. *British Journal of Medical Psychology*, 57, 23–4.

Joseph, S. (2005). Understanding post-traumatic stress from the person-centred perspective. In S. Joseph and R. Wordsley (eds), *Person-Centred Psychopathology: a positive psychology of mental health* (190–201). Ross-On-Wye: PCCS Books.

Mearns, D. (1996). Working at relational depth with clients in person-centred theapy. *Counselling*, 4, 3006–11.

Mearns, D. (2003). *Developing Person-Centred Counselling*. London: Sage.

Mearns, D. (2005). Personal communication, taped interview.

Mearns, D. and Cooper, M. (2005). *Working at Relational Depth in Counselling and Psychotherapy*. London: Sage.

Mearns, D. and Thorne, B. (1988). *Person-Centred Counselling in Action*. London: Sage.

Mearns, D. and Thorne, B. (2000). Person-centred therapy today. In D. Mearns and B. Thorne, *New Frontiers in Theory and Practice*. London: Sage.

Prouty, G., Van Werde, D. and Portner, M. (2002). *Pre-Therapy: reaching contact-impaired clients*. Ross-on-Wye: PCCS Books.

Purton, C. (2004). Differential response, diagnosis and the philosophy of the implicit. *Person-Centred and Experiential Psychotherapies*. Ross-on-Wye: PCCS Books.

Rogers, C. (1951). *Client-Centred Therapy*. Boston: Houghton Mifflin.

Rogers, C. (1959). A theory of therapy, personality and interpersonal relationships as developed in the client-centred framework. In S. Koch (ed.), *Psychology: a study of a science*. Volume 3. *Formulations of the Person and the Social contract* (pp. 184–256.). New York: McGraw-Hill.

Rose, S., Bisson, J., Churchhill, R. and Wessely, S. (2006). Psychological debriefing for preventing post traumatic stress disorder (PTSD). *The Cochrane Database of Systematic Reviews*, 4.

Rothchild, B. (2005). Applying the brakes. *Counselling and Psychotherapy Journal*, 16, 12–16.

Taylor, S. (1983). Adjustment to threatening events. *American Psychologist*. 38, 1161–73.

Van der Kolk, B.A., Hostetler, A., Herron, N. and Fisler, R.E. (1994). Trauma and the development of borderline personality disorder. *Psychiatric Clinics of North America*, 17(4).

Van Werde, D. (2003). Dealing with the possibility of psychotic content in a seemingly congruent communication. In W. Dryden (ed.), *Developing Person-Centred Counselling*. London: Sage.

Warner, M. (2000). Client-centered therapy at the difficult edge: work with fragile and dissociated process. In D. Mearns and B. Thorne (eds), *Person-Centred Therapy Today: new frontiers in theory and practice*. Thousand Oaks: Sage.

Wilkins, P. (2005). Person-centred theory and 'mental illness'. In S. Joseph and R. Worsley (eds), *Person-Centred Psychopathology: a positive psychology of mental health*. Ross-on Wye: PCCS Books.

23

Applications Beyond the
Therapeutic Context

Valerie Land Henderson, Maureen O'Hara,
Gay Leah Barfield and Natalie Rogers

Though the emphasis in this volume is on person-centred approaches to counselling and psychotherapy, it is important to acknowledge the wider ramifica-
tions of person-centred efforts, which have been part of the client-centred story
since the outset. Carl Rogers was a man with widely varied interests. Even as a
22-year-old, these included science, religion, agriculture and Asian culture
(Kirschenbaum, 1979). He was in the world as a learner and he was an activist.
Wherever he saw a problem in the world that touched his heart, he considered
how his knowledge could be brought to bear on finding solutions. Sometimes
that was by conducting empirical research in diverse contexts (Rogers, 1942;
Rogers and Dymond, 1954) and later it was in action projects, where he and
his colleagues sought to apply the basic client-centred and person-centred ideas
in new venues. Over the years many people whose interests extend beyond therapeutic contexts have embraced the core relational principles that PCA encompasses and have sought ways to base their practice on them. Included in this
chapter are discussions of four such arenas in which person-centred ideas and
practice have been successfully applied: the arts and creativity, social action,
organizational change and support for the dying. All four authors worked with
Rogers directly over many years, three of them (Barfield, Henderson and
O'Hara) at the Center for Studies of the Person, in La Jolla, California, and
Natalie Rogers was both his daughter and his colleague.

Person-centred approaches to work with life-threatened people

Valerie Land Henderson

For the purposes of this section the term 'life-threatened' refers to people who have received such a diagnosis from their physician. There is a sense, of course, in which we are all life-threatened.

The application of Rogers' client-centred methods in the care of dying and seriously ill people has been very much in evidence in the pastoral care movement since the 1950s (Holifield, 1983; Fuller, 1984). In the 1970s, death and dying pioneer Elizabeth Kübler Ross freely acknowledged her debt to Carl Rogers in the development of her approach to caring for dying children (2005, personal communication from Maureen O'Hara). Since then the foundational person-centred values and communication skills have come to provide the background for much end-of-life care, patient peer support groups, non-directive listening and an emphasis on honesty characterizing the core philosophy of the 'wellness' movement. Recently palliative nursing care has stressed the use of basic aspects of the person-centred approach in addressing the nursing needs of patients facing terminal diagnosis (White, 1997; Boerum, 1999; Steinhauser et al, 2000; Egbert and Parrot, 2003). Here I will focus on the work of psychiatrist Gerald Jampolsky, pioneer in working with dying children and founder of the Center for Attitudinal Healing.

In 1975, while making rounds in a hospital, Jampolsky overheard a life-threatened child ask his physician, 'What is it like to die?' The physician evaded the question without really responding. It made Jampolsky realize there was a need for such children to be able to talk about their feelings and questions around the experience of dying. He started a programme for these young patients, in which they joined together in a group where they were encouraged to explore these issues with one another. Though a facilitator was provided, there was to be no 'expert' providing answers. The primary skill required for facilitation was the ability to be truly present and to listen. As it turned out, there were experts present, but these were the children. The group was a place where no subject was off limits and where *listening* had a high priority. Eventually, other family members – parents, siblings – expressed a need for the same kind of group, one focused on their own specific issues. Out of those rather small beginnings, the Center for Attitudinal Healing was born and now offers to the community a variety of peer-support groups at no charge to the participants. Research studies have consistently reported that peer-support meetings provide a context whereby patients facing end-of-life circumstances may successfully address the existential challenges and complete the psychologically important processes incumbent on dying. (For a recent review of such studies, see Steinhauser et al, 2000.)

Although not described formally as client-centred or person-centred psychotherapy, the principles that frame the methods employed at the Center for Attitudinal Healing are essentially similar to the therapeutic conditions described by Rogers. Inherent to the person-centred approach of Rogers and to attitudinal healing is the belief that individuals are capable of finding their own best answers and are able to make constructive choices if given an authentically supportive environment and certain relational conditions (Rogers, 1957).

The goal of the attitudinal healing process is that individuals facing serious challenges – whether the prospect of an imminent death, loss of a loved one, or other painful events – should achieve inner peace; perhaps a sense of completion, and a state of mind that is neither judgemental nor defensive. In an attitudinal healing peer-support group there is no 'expert', but rather a group of others facing similar challenges wherein an attitude of equality and authenticity is established. A facilitator is present to make certain every person has the opportunity to be heard. The facilitator is usually a trained volunteer rather than a professional counsellor. Much of the facilitation is done by other group members. In groups with participants who are dealing with life-threatening illness, it is especially necessary that group members can explore what it is they are feeling in response to their illness and its effect on their families. Solutions are not offered. Advice is not given. Sharing medical information is discouraged within the group, but is strongly encouraged elsewhere. It is felt that group time is too precious to be used for the exchange of data. Time for the exploration of the personal is a rare opportunity and a vital need.

The stated principles which provide the therapeutic conditions include:

- Creating a relational context of equality and authenticity – or genuineness – where professional roles are suspended, facades are dropped, power hierarchies are flattened and people meet as equals to find common experiences.
- Offering unconditional positive regard in the form of love and support, wherein each person is valued and accepted as they are. Here is no requirement that people behave in any particular way or live up to anyone else's expectations in order to earn acceptance and love.
- Providing empathy and non-judgemental listening, wherein all participants do what they can to be present to another, giving them undivided attention: to enter the experience of the others, to see things through their eyes and to feel the feelings they are having. Offering empathy in this way allows all participants to have the psychological room to fully experience their own feelings and to freely examine their choices and to find their best answers.
- Trust in the emergent process.

When the above conditions are present, psychological safety is created. In such a relationship people are willing to listen to themselves, to take risks, to be more self-accepting and to forgive their mistakes, to find their own answers and to believe in their own intrinsic worth. Nothing additional needs to be added beyond trusting that when these conditions are present, people who are facing the most extreme situations can move towards healing and growth (Jampolsky and Cirincione, 1991; Jampolsky, 2000).

When these conditions are present, the group becomes a sacred circle wherein its members are free to rage against fate, weep for the unfairness of it all, externalize all problems – whatever is true for the person – and know that no one will try to talk them out of their feelings or try to give them advice about ways to 'get over it'. It often happens that a shift occurs when a person is given the freedom to ventilate pain and fear, and understands at a profound level that he or she has been truly heard and accepted.

The experience of being life-threatened does not automatically ennoble. Often it illuminates to the person how emotionally unready they are to face their death and how little thought they had previously given to it. Initially, there may be panic, bitterness, anger, blaming. These feelings need to be expressed if the individual is to be able to move beyond them. It can be a gift to hear one's own voice expressing the reaction to having been given a diagnosis of limited time. For some it is the first time in their lives that they have listened or attended to their inner voice. And, more significantly, confronted their own mortality.

William, a 13-year-old boy, was diagnosed with a malignant brain tumour and came to the group with some hesitation and a lot of denial, but a willingness to be present. He soon recognized that there were other children in the group who were younger than he who were even more fearful. Since he was older than most of the others, William gradually became a caregiver to the others. The more he helped create a safe and caring environment for the other children, the more comfortable he became with his own situation. His cancer went into remission for a time, but he continued to come to the group and to encourage the others. Unfortunately, his cancer recurred. His anxiety did not though, and he still was a beacon of love and good humour. One of his favourite jokes was, 'I think I have a brain tumour, but the doc says it's all in my head.' His life and his personality are not lost to those of us who knew him. They continue on and on.

A middle-aged woman came to the adult group having been diagnosed with lung cancer. She had been given six months to live. After she had attended the group for about three years, the doctors told her, 'We don't know what you're doing, but keep doing it.' Her belief was that being in the group with other persons who were dealing with the same kind of issues had allowed her to open to life in a new and expanded way. She became ready to really live and, as a result, also to die. I do not suggest that being in the group will extend a person's life. However, a shift in attitude and becoming peaceful with what is, has been shown to affect all aspects of one's experience.

It is not my intention to state that all life-threatened persons who attend a group with others who are life-threatened automatically become heroic (though, in my experience, that has been the case more often than not). Nevertheless, the evidence has shown that being given a climate that is authentic, caring and understanding can cause great shifts in a person's attitude, whatever the external realities. So many times I have heard group members refer to their diagnosis as a 'gift'. Participating in the group somehow frees them to explore and examine the meaning of their lives and they tell me it has allowed them to 'really live' the life they'd been missing. They had achieved the quality of life they desired, whatever the quantity. A question that suggests itself might be, 'Do I need to receive a life-threatening diagnosis in order to allow myself to lead the life I most truly want?'

Person-centred approaches at work

Maureen O'Hara

History

In the first major expression of his ideas, the classic work *Counseling and Psychotherapy*, Rogers (1942) proposed applications of client-centred counselling approaches in the workplace. In 1947 he described managerial approaches for dealing with workplace group tensions, and individual dissatisfactions (Rogers, 1947). At a time when advice giving, directive, hierarchical, command and control management, and manipulation by behavioural engineers were the orders of the day, Rogers' discoveries offered nothing less than a new ethics for human relationships (Farson, 1975). These humanistic ideas were eagerly embraced by a post-war generation seeking to participate in new and empowered ways in every aspect of their lives.

Like many social scientists of his day, Rogers was strongly influenced by the famous Hawthorne Works studies at the Western Electric Company in the 1920s and 1930s, in which it was learned that workers were motivated to become more productive when they experienced acceptance and good communication with their co-workers, and when they felt their ideas and experience were respected (Roethlisberger and Dickson, 1939). Rogers recognized that these were essentially the same conditions that seemed to be emerging in his own research as facilitative of effective counselling and psychotherapy. When the *Harvard Business Review* selected its top 15 most influential business articles in 1998, it included a 1952 article by Rogers (co-authored with Fritz Roethlisberger, one of the authors of the Hawthorne studies). In his commentary on the 1952 article in 1991, Gabarro reflected that 40 years later these straightforward but hard-to-practice relational rules had contributed to a sea-change in workplace culture (Rogers and Roethlisberger, 1952, 1991) that led to the worker empowerment movement, the development of more participatory management approaches, and increasing emphasis on the 'soft skills' (of effective human relationships) in the board room, in management, on the shop floor, in sales and in customer service. Whereas theorists such as Bion, Lewin and Likert pioneered the theory of organizational functioning as whole systems, it was Rogers who gave organizational practitioners their focus on the experience of the individual employee (Alban and Scherer, 2005).

After a flurry of enthusiasm in the 1950s and 1960s, research literature that explicitly refers to PCA in organizations has been scarce. Much basic Rogerian thinking and practice, however, has been incorporated by generations of organizational theorists and practitioners. *Process Consulting* by Edgar Schein (1987), *The Seven Habits of Highly Effective People* by Steven Covey (1989), *The Fifth Discipline* by Peter Senge (1990), *On Becoming a Leader*, by Warren Bennis (1989), *Working with Emotional Intelligence* by Daniel Goleman (1998), *Dialogue: the art of thinking together*, by William Isaacs (1999), *Management of the Absurd*, by Richard Farson (1996) and many more classic works on organizations all take the core person-centred relational conditions as givens, though only Bennis and Farson fully acknowledge their debt to Rogers. They also concur that what contributes to success in work settings is more a function of who one is – the level of personal development achieved – than what one knows or does. In the 1970s, Thomas Gordon (1977) codified the core principles into a series of discrete skills which he offered as *Leader Effectiveness Training*. According to the Gordon website, http://www.gordontraining.com/, over 1.2 million people have been through LET training.

PCA at work

Person-centred work in organizations today falls into three major categories:

- personal growth and capacity development for individuals
- communication and teamwork enhancement for small groups such as work teams, committees and governing boards
- systems interventions for organizations and divisions within organizations.

Though operationally quite varied, what makes such practices person-centred is the attitudinal stance of the practitioner. Unlike many intervention approaches, the person-centred practitioner holds a faith that individuals, groups and organizations have within them vast resources for self-direction, and in the right relational climate – where certain core conditions are present, namely genuineness and congruence, acceptance and respect, and empathy and understanding – these resources can be mobilized to solve challenges at hand.

Personal development of individuals

Employee communications

Robert Tannenbaum is reported to have made early in the history of organizational development a distinction between 'training' – where the desired outcome is to have everyone learn some similar predetermined set of skills – and 'education', where the desired outcome is for people to realize ever higher levels of human potential. Rogers agreed with this distinction and resisted skill-focused applications of client-centred principles or codification of the core principles into a behavioural technology. That said, the most widespread workplace application of person-centred ideas today is in the area of employee training that focuses on fundamental communication skills, and is aimed at improving interpersonal relationships among workers and between managers and those whom they supervise. Much of this work is conducted using some version of the small group, where participants use the group setting to learn active listening, non-evaluative communication and no-lose conflict resolution, to trust themselves to be authentic in their relationships, and to experience the creative power of distributed leadership.

Norman Chambers and Robert Lee were early innovators in diversity education. They and other colleagues from the Center for Studies of the

Person in La Jolla, California, were among the first to conduct multicultural person-centred encounter groups with the US military, police forces, city government and educational institutions, after laws outlawing discrimination based on race and gender necessitated relationships in the workplace based on respect, mutual understanding and cross-group empathy. Since then diversity training has become an integral part of corporate life, and much of it tacitly, if not explicitly, reflects an essentially person-centred stance.

In the late 1960s Rogers participated in T-Groups and leadership development programmes for executives at the National Training Laboratory. He acknowledged the contributions of early pioneers in organizational psychology such as Argyris, Bennis, Schein, Bradford, Benne and Gibb (Rogers, 1970: 14). The La Jolla Program, in which Rogers participated for many years, drew managers and administrators in search of personal development. Since then other practitioners, including this author, have applied person-centred principles in these and additional areas, such as training in constructive feedback skills, conflict resolution, customer service, basic interviewing skills and sexual harassment prevention.

Individual executive and management coaching, and leadership development

It is generally recognized that today's workplaces place intense psychological demands on employees, especially leaders (O'Hara, in press). Companies are increasingly realizing the importance of providing support services to their best people to help them cope with the complexity of conditions in the emerging global society and develop higher levels of personal effectiveness, but do not want these services to be provided in the public setting of the group. In the last decade a new profession has emerged – coaching – that provides services to individual managers and executives to help them succeed in the psychological dimensions of their work. Based squarely in the person-centred tradition, at its core coaching is personal counselling and mentoring about work issues. Coaching's non-pathological frame makes it much more palatable to high-functioning individuals who resist the dysfunctional image connoted by the concept of counselling. The best coaches use an essentially person-centred relational stance and engage with their clients in a process of mutual appreciative inquiry (Cooperrider and Whitney, 2000) and personal discovery to expand awareness and responsibility, and provide clients with authentic feedback within a relationship of support (Bergquist et al, 1999). Closely related to coaching, person-centred leadership development includes (but is not limited to) a focus on development of the necessary higher-order psychological capacities to succeed in leadership roles in today's uncertain times (Bennis, 1989).

Team building

As the structure of work has changed, many tasks are now completed by teams. Effective teams are those in which relationships among members exhibit mutual agreement as to task, open communication, mutual trust and acceptance, mutual support and open exchange across difference (Burke, 1982). The facilitative skills necessary to establish these conditions closely parallel those identified as required for an effective person-centred group (Rogers, 1970; O'Hara and Wood, 1984). These days, the basic small group process is likely to be embellished with a whole spectrum of creative team building techniques. This may help speed up team learning, but more likely reflects a decline in the level of cultural acceptance of unstructured and emotionally intense experiences at work. Arguably, however, this undermines the power of the small group to effect personal development, because it is precisely the conditions of ambiguity and vulnerability common in small unstructured groups with which leaders need to become comfortable in times of rapid change. For a contemporary discussion see Embleton Tudor et al (2004).

Person-centred management and administration

Given the extraordinary success in fostering effective human relationships on a small scale, it was natural that attempts would be made to apply person-centred attitudes and methods to management. Such efforts have not been particularly effective. Rogers himself was surprisingly ignorant about organizational dynamics and had no organizational theory. Though he had been successful in leading the Counseling Center at the University of Chicago in a non-hierarchical manner consistent with person-centred principles, he encountered far less success in other organizations in which he participated and which attempted to base their governance and management principles on his ideas. In thinking about organizations he extrapolated from his personal experience in counselling, encounter groups and short-term communities, where his knowledge was well grounded both theoretically and empirically, to the management of systems, where he was less knowledgeable, often with disappointing outcomes (Farson, 2005, personal communication). William Rogers describes his experience with person-centred administration in the context of higher education, in particular two Quaker colleges in the United States. He points out that the stress on collegiality, flattened organizational structures and an emphasis on the personhood of individuals in the educational environment 'tend to be more compatible with ... Theory Z institutional styles' (Ouichi, 1981). Recently there has been renewed interest in non-hierarchical forms of management that focus on the interpersonal capacities. Fairtlough for instance, has revisited the notion of heterarchical organizations (whose members share common goals and the same horizontal position of power and authority) and suggests that what makes such organizations effective are 'interpersonal process skills, the special skills for dialogue, teamwork and mutual respect' (2005: 63).

Systems-wide organizational development consulting

Consultants working on systems-wide interventions generally combine basic person-centred dialogical philosophy with some other methodology designed for systems interventions. William Coulson has made a public speaking career of condemning the impact of the organizational intervention he, Rogers and others made at the Immaculate Heart of Mary (IHM) College in 1967, which Coulson maintains resulted in the destruction of the order and the loss of spiritual vocation for hundreds of Sisters (Coulson, 1994). Kugelman (2005) argues however, that when the Rogers team arrived the IHM order was already in considerable conflict with the Archbishop of Los Angeles, who was attempting to crack down on the religious women's increasing activism and, encounter groups or no encounter groups, nuns were already leaving the Catholic Church in droves. Nevertheless, it does seem that by today's standards of organizational development practice, the intervention was naïve. My own experience as a member of the Center for Studies of the Person also suggests that despite Rogers' fascination with groups, his impatience with conversations or analysis of group-level dynamics – such as leadership, hidden power hierarchies, gender bias or inclusion/exclusion dynamics other than at the level of individual feelings – created a myopia that kept organizationally corrosive issues invisible.

Today no responsible consultants would enter an organizational system with only one string to their bow. Though an essentially person-centred perspective still tacitly underpins most organizational consulting, effective organizational consulting is complex and multilayered and requires consultants to have a range of diagnostic and technical skills with which to help their clients achieve their goals. Anyone considering exploring this territory will find Rothwell and Sullivan's text (2005) a good place to begin.

Current and future trends

This is actually a very good time for the person-centred organizational consultant. It is becoming increasingly obvious to business management that the most important resources of any organization are its people, and they are increasingly willing to invest in programmes to help their people increase their capacity to deal with the complex, uncertain human situations that characterize today's work settings. For work with individuals, teams and whole-organization change management, the simple but revolutionary relationship ethics at the core of all person-centred efforts increasingly resonate with the human development challenges of today's workplaces.

Person-centred approaches to peace and reducing political tension

Gay Leah Barfield

Introduction and history

Carl Rogers' keen interest in the bigger issues, especially peace, began in the earliest days of his career (Rogers, 1944b; Rogers and Wallen, 1946; Rogers and Russell, 2002) and continued throughout his life, as he took up the conflicts of each era and examined how the client-centred approach (CCT) and the person-centred approach (PCA) could be applied to these larger issues at each new level of the evolution of the theory and practice. This interest was a productive and ongoing focus of his work throughout his career. At the time of his death in 1987 he was nominated for the Nobel Prize as a result of his life-long concerns and his collective body of work for peace.

Theoretical underpinnings

The theoretical principles that form the foundations of Rogers' ideas about the applications of person-centred principles in intergroup conflict resolution and peace making are its now famous fundamental conditions or attitudes. The combination of empathy, respect and prizing (unconditional positive regard) and congruence and faith in the formative or actualizing tendency which trans-lates into faith in the capacity of human systems to self-organize – provide a relational sanctuary and safe haven, as well as the co-creative raw materials of growth and change. From these simple and elegant theoretical premises, Rogers tested his hypothesis in practice in many diverse contexts and was able to show that no matter what the frame or perspective or context from which or within which one operates, whether in private therapy or in tense political dialogue, if that context is imbued with these fundamental attitudes and ways of being, then it will nurture, accommodate and catalyze positive change, even with people who are in conflict and where suspicion and hostility might be high.

Earliest indications of Rogers' social and political concerns

Rogers' own concerns for social justice appear in his earliest writings and formulations of his approach. His political interest was a consistent theoretical thread throughout his professional life in every decade from 1940 to his death in 1987. As early as 1944, he was writing about his work with returning servicemen from the Second World War (Rogers, 1944a; Rogers and Wallen, 1946). A 1952 presentation, which later became a chapter in *On Becoming a Person*, 'Dealing with breakdowns in communication: inter-personal and inter-group' discussed the Soviet-US conflict (Rogers and Roethlisberger, 1991). His paper 'A therapist's view of personal goals' (1960) which later appeared as 'Social implications' (Kirschenbaum and Henderson, 1989) discussed America's attitudes and roles in the world. In *Freedom to Learn* (Rogers, 1969, 1988) he explored the issues of power and politics in education and in 1972 he wrote about the Viet Nam war. Throughout the 1970s the application of PCA to ease political and intergroup tensions and work towards peace was a constant theme in his work (Rogers, 1975, 1977a, 1977b, 1982a). In *A Way of Being* (1980) he criticized the first Bush administration nuclear policy. His preoccupations with nuclear disarmament were a constant theme in his work until his death. An article 'Dealing with psychological tensions', which appeared in the *Journal of Applied Behavioral Sciences* in 1965, addressed the threats of the nuclear arms race worldwide, as did the forceful statement, 'One alternative to nuclear planetary suicide'. Just prior to his death, his final publications expressed a continuing concern for these wider international issues. He described working with groups in the then Soviet Union in 'Inside the world of the Soviet professional' (1987) and a multi-nation encounter process held in Rust, Austria, with high-level diplomats aimed at reducing tensions towards ending a bloody war then raging in Nicaragua (Rogers, 1986). Personal letters, notes and several oral presentations address a breakthrough series of dialogues in South Africa between blacks and whites, which he co-facilitated with Ruth Sanford. These remain unpublished, with one exception (Rogers and Sanford, 1987).

Reading statements made over decades reveals the evolution of his social and political theory. One of the best and most important formulations of his thought in this arena is to be found in his statement, 'My politics' (Rogers, 1982b) which was given during a ten-day cross-cultural encounter in 1978 at El Escorial, Spain, attended by 175 people from 26 nations. In this short and pointed work he summarized his political values as they aligned with PCA principles. Running through this and all his other writing on peace and politics is a stress on the importance of mutual respect, a capacity for empathy across differences, egalitarian engagement and collaborative decision making.

Theory and practice

Throughout the 1970s and 1980s, to test and apply his theory to larger political arenas, Rogers accepted invitations to convene workshops in Poland 'behind the Iron Curtain' and to lead encounter groups and lecture in Northern Ireland, El Escorial, Spain, South Africa and Russia, with uncommon combinations of participants who sometimes risked their lives and safety to participate in cross-cultural, cross-racial and cross-political events.

In 1984, he established the Carl Rogers Institute for Peace at the Center for Studies of the Person with this author as co-director. The Peace Project convened the first international peace workshop on 'The Central America Challenge' in 1985 in Rust, Austria, with high-level US and international diplomats and lay leaders from 17 countries in attendance. A second follow-up workshop was held in Costa Rica, again with the support of the University for Peace of the United Nations, and of Presidents Oscar Arias and Rodrigo Carazo of Costa Rica, and other US and international diplomats who chose to gather posthumously in Carl's name and principles to continue the search for peace in that region. Also out of the Peace Project grew programmes on urban diversity, dialogues with diversity, and cross-border dialogues. This large body of work was recognized in 1987, when Rogers received a posthumous nomination for the Nobel Peace Prize.

Current applications and future directions

Currently some very original applications of the PCA to peace making are embodied around the world by new generations of practitioners. In England, Lago offers PCA-informed training workshops in diversity and multi-cultural practices around power and oppression (see Chapter 19, this volume). Jane Hoffman applies PCA to 'citizens' juries' in Scotland and advises local government authorities on difficult community issues (2005, personal communication from Colin Lago). Natalie Rogers for many years has offered international workshops and training in expressive art therapy as a means of finding inner and outer peace (see her section in this chapter). In Italy, Pierpaolo Patrizi and Alberto Zucconi and colleagues currently carry on peace projects through their PCA institutes to reduce 'mobbing' (bullying) among students and employees, and work in Ecuador with Amazonian Indians (2005, personal communication from Alberto Zucconi). Dee Aker, Deputy Director of the Joan B. Kroc Institute for Peace and Justice at the University of San Diego (IPJ) and former staff member of the Carl Rogers Institute for Peace is a conflict resolution specialist, particularly interested in developing gender-sensitive grassroots and political leaders participation in peace and reconciliation efforts. She is the founder of WorldLink – Connecting Youth to Global Affairs and currently heads the Women PeaceMakers Program and the Nepal Peace Project.

Steve Olweean directs the Common Bond Institute, organizing conferences, professional training programmes, relief efforts and professional exchanges internationally, and actively providing networking and coordination support to assist newly emerging human service and civil society organizations in developing countries. This year marks Common Bond's 14th Annual International Conference on Conflict Resolution together with the Harmony Institute in St Petersburg, Russia, and in October 2006 Common Bond and the Harmony Institute convened a conference entitled 'Engaging the other' in Michigan, United States, which featured dialogue projects between warring factions from around the world. Gay Leah Barfield, Maureen O'Hara and California State Senator John Vasconcellos, all founding members of the Carl Rogers Peace Project, were representative of one successful example of person-centred processes in the services of political healing.

Conclusion

The person-centred approach has shown in both its theory and in the practice of its core principles that it has both the framework and the means to provide a model for expressing diversity of ideas, respectful intellectual dialogue and ways of disagreeing with or exploring opposing perspectives. This dialogic container can provide contexts and attitudes to widen the horizons and enlarge the visions of possibilities for understanding and peace. There is plenty of reason to believe that, in the future, research on the outcomes of the application of the approach to large socio-political issues will ensure that the vibrant, hopeful and evolutionary energy that is fundamental to the PCA world view will continue to encourage women and men to trust their own power to change the world for the better.

Person-centred expressive arts therapy

Natalie Rogers

The psychotherapeutic process helps awaken creative life-force energy. Thus, creativity and therapy overlap. What is creative is frequently therapeutic. What is therapeutic is frequently a creative process. I integrate the creative arts into my therapeutic practice and use the term person-centred expressive arts therapy to include dance, art and music therapies, as well as journal writing, poetry, imagery, meditation and improvizational drama in a supportive, client-centred setting.

In humanistic therapies, the term expressive therapy usually means non-verbal and/or metaphoric expression. Humanistic expressive arts therapy differs from the analytic or medical model of art therapy, where art is used to diagnose and analyse. Rather, expressive arts therapists believe individuals find appropriate self-direction if the psychological climate is empathic, honest and caring, without outside interpretation. Our tradition draws from many humanistic psychologists – notably Carl Rogers (1951), Abraham Maslow (1962), Rollo May (1975), Clark Moustakas (1956), Arthur Combs (1982) and Sidney Jourard (1971). These pioneers defied the authoritarian medical model and created a relationship model of personal growth in which the therapist respects the client's dignity, worth and inherent capacity for self-direction.

Humanistic expressive art is a relatively new field. Shaun McNiff, a key figure, writes extensively on art as a healing process for individuals and groups. In his book, *The Arts and Psychotherapy* (1981), he stresses the unity of many forms of expression and evolves a theory of art as part of the psychotherapeutic process. His books, *Art Based Research* (1998) and *Art as Medicine* (1992), advanced the concept that artistic expression can be a powerful means of personal transformation and emotional and spiritual healing. Janie Rhyne's *The Gestalt Art Experience* (1973) also pioneered the notion that the creative process should be a part of psychotherapy and group process. Lucia Capacchione's many books give hands-on methods for using quick art forms to release feelings and gain insight. Her *Creative Journal: the art of finding yourself* (1979) and *Recovery of Your Inner Child* (1991) explain easy-to-use art processes.

There is a broad range of topics in this field including movement therapy, voice and sound therapy, journaling, music therapy, psychodrama and visual art therapy. Here I focus on those who use an intermodal approach, meaning that movement, art, sound, journal writing and psychodrama are used in combination. In *The Creative Connection: expressive arts as healing* (1993), I brought attention to the dramatic results of the intermodal approach. Daria Halprin's *The Expressive Body in Life, Art and Therapy* (2003) describes the body as the container of one's life experience, and movement and art as vehicles for release and understanding. Steven K. Levine and Ellen G. Levine edited *Foundations of Expressive Art Therapy* (1999), which includes a chapter by Paolo Knill, another noted proponent of intermodal work.

Expressively using art means having little or no concern about the beauty of the art, the grammar and style of the writing, or the harmonic flow of the sounds. Although interesting and sometimes dramatic products emerge, we leave the aesthetics and the craftsmanship to those who wish to pursue the arts professionally or for their own sake. This intermodal approach is for self-insight.

My term, 'creative connection®', describes a process in which one art form stimulates and fosters creativity in another, eventually linking all of the arts in the process of discovering and deepening experience of one's essential nature. Combining my client-centred training with training in movement and art therapy, I made some personal discoveries. My feelings and perceptions shifted dramatically when I danced my sadness or anger in the presence of an empathic, non-judgemental witness. And when I drew the images that arose after moving, the art became spontaneous, expressive and revealing. If I followed the drawing with free writing, I plunged further into awareness of guarded feelings and thoughts. This was when I fully realized that the empathic witness to art, movement and journal writing is similar to the client-centred therapist. The client allows the therapist entry to his/her private world of imagery and imagination because of the therapist's great respect and empathy. I discovered in my own personal work and work with clients that using the different art-forms in sequence evokes inner truths which often reveal themselves with new depth and meaning.

The verbal process of giving meaning to emotions and the cognitive aspects of psychotherapy will always be important. However, feelings and thoughts can be expressed also through colour, form, movement, sound or poetry. To use the arts expressively means going into our inner realms to discover feelings and to express them. Any art form coming from deep emotions communicates visually. Therefore, art is a language, too – an alternate path for intuitive, imaginative abilities supplementing traditional logical, linear thought. Like verbal therapy, the expressive arts move the client into emotions yet add a further dimension, release of the 'free-spirit'. Expressive arts therapy can include joyful, lively learning on many levels: sensory, kinaesthetic, conceptual, emotional and mythic. Although I listen to understand meaning in the client's words, I have an even greater understanding as I view the client's creation or exploration through movement and hear his or her own interpretations. Clients report that the expressive arts help them go beyond their problems to a new sense of soul or spirit that takes constructive action.

The person-centred expressive arts process

At what point does a therapist offer an art process? When a client is expressing strong emotion, the therapist may ask, 'Would you like to explore that in colour or movement as well?' The client may say, 'No, I need to talk some more,' which is fine and even strengthens the client's sense of self-determination. If, instead, the client agrees, the therapist then asks, 'Would you like to draw, or move, or make sounds?' It is important to follow the client's lead. If a client chooses visual art, the therapist witnesses in empathic silence until the process is finished and then asks, 'What was your experience as you created this piece?' The therapist and client look at it together and the therapist encourages the client to describe it and give it any meaning. The client who wants to move or dance the picture takes the journey even further. The therapist constantly checks: 'Does this feel right to you? Do you wish to explore more? Am I understanding you correctly? Do I get your real meaning here?'

One might ask, 'Is offering expressive arts a distraction from the purpose of therapy?' Quite the contrary. However, the expressive arts should be used cautiously by the therapist and only after training because the client may quickly plunge into his/her unconscious. The revelation of carefully hidden memories requires therapeutic skill on the part of the therapist.

The applications of this work are successful with many populations. Psychotherapists, social workers and self-help groups use expressive arts to help people explore feelings and change behaviours. Some people in 12-step recovery programmes use expressive arts to add depth to their personal growth as they go through each step. Many alcohol treatment centres utilize the expressive arts as an opportunity to go beyond recovery, to reawaken creativity and find hopeful images for the future (Adelman and Castricone, 1986). Expressive arts helps uncover buried wounds of sexual abuse as well as facilitate in their healing. When one is mourning, often there are no words for the pain. Colour and imagery are outlets for sorrow and anger. Hospice workers and grief counsellors find these non-verbal methods particularly rewarding, especially with children. Children use art freely until someone judges, grades or misunderstands their art. Then they may stop using their creative abilities until they enter an accepting, non-judgemental environment. Play therapy has always incorporated expressive arts as a language the child can use (Schaefer, 1988; Levine, 1999).

Research

Research in this field is just beginning. In 'A content analysis of person-centred expressive therapy outcomes', Drs Charles Merrill and Svend Anderson created a follow-up study of 32 former participants of my intensive training programme. 'Results revealed important learnings and shifts of self-perceptions towards greater self-awareness, improved self-confidence, risk-taking, deeper self-exploration and appreciation for the process involved in the creative act (1993: 354).' Mukti Khanna (1989) created her doctoral dissertation, 'A phenomenological investigation of creativity in person-centred expressive therapy' by interviewing 18 participants in depth in a person-centred expressive arts training programme. She found a major theme in the reported connection between creativity and spirituality. Presently, students at Saybrook Graduate School are developing new research in the effectivness of expressive arts in therapy (Rogers, 2004–5).

Future directions

Incorporating the arts as an integral part of psychological healing is the wave of the future.

The person-centred philosophy of my father, Carl Rogers (1951), is my foundation. I have deep faith in each person's innate capacity to reach toward full potential if given the person-centred environment. Just as Rogers veered away from psychoanalysis and interpretation, I, too, reject the analytical model which values the interpretations of the therapist over those of clients. In methodology, I follow the clients' lead, making art processes available as they wish. The creative process itself is a powerful integrative force and the creative connection, with its variety of art forms, has been shown to be a highly effective therapeutic tool in many settings (McNiff, 1981). Expressive arts enhance the therapeutic relationship in the clients' identification, exploration, discovery, release of negative feelings and the ultimate embrace of their personhood. When the client shares his or her personal art he/she is opening a window to the soul.

REFERENCES

Adelman, E. and Castricone, L. (1986). An expressive arts model for substance abuse group training and treatment. *Arts in Psychotherapy*, 13(1) spring, 53–9.

Aker, D. (2005). Personal communication.

Alban, B.T. and Scherer, J.J. (2005). On the shoulders of giants: the origins of OD. In W.J. Rothwell and R. Sullivan (eds), *Practicing Organization Development*, 2nd edn (pp. 81–105). San Francisco, John Wiley.

Barfield, G.L.S. (1987). When personal and political processes meet: the Rust workshop. *Journal of Humanistic Psychology*, 27(3) summer, 309–32.

Bennis, W. (1989). *On Becoming a Leader*. Reading, Mass., Addison-Wesley.

Bergquist, W., Merritt, K. et al (1999). *Executive Coaching: an appreciative approach*. Sacramento, Calif., Pacific Soundings Press.

Boerum, S. (1999). AIDS: an unconventional perspective. *Journal of Social Distress and the Homeless*, 7(1), 1–27.

Burke, W.W. (1982). *Organization Development: principles and practices*. New York: Scott, Forseman and Company.

Capacchione, L. (1979). *The Creative Journal: the art of finding yourself*. Athens, Ohio: Swallow Press.

Capacchione, L. (1991). *Recovery of Your Inner Child*. New York: Simon and Schuster.

Combs, A.W. (1982). *A Personal Approach to Teaching: beliefs that make a difference*. Boston: Allyn and Bacon.

Cooperrider, D. and Whitney, D. (2000). *Collaborating for Change: appreciative inquiry*. San Francisco: Berrett-Koehler.

Coulson, W. (1994). Repentant psychologist: how I wrecked the Immaculate Heart of Mary Nuns. *The Latin Mass: The Journal of Catholic Culture and Tradition* (Winter).

Covey, S.R. (1989). *The Seven Habits of Highly Effective People: restoring the character ethic*. New York: Simon and Shuster.

Embleton Tudor, L., Keemar, K., Tudor, K., Valentine, J. and Worrall, M. (2004). *Person-Centred Approach: a contemporary introduction*. London: Palgrave MacMillan.

Egbert, N. and Parrot, R. (2003). 'Empathy and social support for the terminally ill: implications for recruiting and retaining hospice and hospital volunteers.' *Communication Studies*, 54(1), 18–33.

Fairtlough, G. (2005). *Three Ways of Getting Things Done: hierarchy, heterarchy and responsible autonomy in organizations*. Bridport, Dorset: Triarchy Press.

Farson, R. (1975). Carl Rogers, quiet revolutionary. In R.I. Evans (ed.), *Carl Rogers: the man and his ideas* (pp. xxviii–xliii). New York: E.P. Dutton.

Farson, R. (1996). *Management of the Absurd: paradoxes in leadership*. New York: Simon and Shuster

Fuller, R.C. (1984). Rogers' impact on pastoral counseling and contemporary religious reflection. In R.E. Levant and J.M. Shlien (eds), *Client-centered Therapy and the Person-Centered Approach: new directions in theory, research, and practice* (pp. 352–69). New York: Praeger.

Goleman, D. (1998). *Working with Emotional Intelligence*. New York: Bantam Books.

Gordon, T. (1977). *Leadership Effectiveness Training LET: the no-lose way to release the productive potential of people*. New York: Wyden.

Halprin, D. (2003). *The Expressive Body in Life, Art and Therapy: working with movement, metaphor and meaning*. London: Jessica Kingsley.

Holifield, E.B. (1983). *A History of Pastoral Care in America: from salvation to self-realization*. Nashville: Abingdon Press.

Isaacs, W. (1999). *Dialogue: the art of thinking together*. New York: Doubleday/Currency.

Jampolsky, G.G. (2000). *Teach Only Love: the twelve principles of attitudinal healing*. Hillsborough, Oregon, Beyond Words Publishing.

Jampolsky, G.G. and Cirincione, D.V. (1991). *Love is the Answer*. New York: Bantam Books.

Jourard, S.M. (1971). *The Transparent Self*. New York: Van Nostrand Reinhold.

Khanna, M. (1989). A phenomenological investigation of creativity in person-centered expressive therapy. Unpublished doctoral dissertation, University of Tennessee.

Kirschenbaum, H. (1979). *On Becoming Carl Rogers*. New York: Dell.

Knill, P. (1999). Soul nourishment, or the intermodal language of imagination. In S.K. Levine and E.G. Levine (eds), *Foundations of Expressive Art Therapy* (pp. 37–52). London: Jessica Kingsley.

Kugelman, R. (2005). An encounter between psychology and religion: humanistic psychology and the Immaculate Heart of Mary nuns. *Journal of the History of the Behavioral Sciences*, 41(4).

Lago, C. (2005). Personal communication.

Levine, S.K. and Levine, E.G. (eds) (1999). *Foundations of Expressive Art Therapy*. London: Jessica Kingsley.

Maslow, A.H. (1962). *Toward a Psychology of Being*. Princeton, N.J.: Van Nostrand.

May, R. (1975). *The Courage to Create*. New York: Bantam.

McNiff, S. (1981). *The Arts and Psychotherapy*. Springfield, Il.: Charles C. Thomas.

McNiff, S. (1992). *Art as Medicine: creating a therapy of the imagination*. Boston: Shambhala.

McNiff, S. (1998). *Art Based Research*. London: Jessica Kingsley.

Merrill, C. and Anderson, S. (1993). A content analysis of person-centered expressive therapy outcomes. *The Humanistic Psychologist*, 21, 354–63.

Moustakas, C.E. (1956). *The Self: explorations in personal growth.* New York: Harper and Brothers.

O'Hara, M. (In press). The challenge for education in uncertain times. *Journal of Transformational Education.*

O'Hara, M. and Wood, J.K. (1984). Patterns of awareness: consciousness and the group mind. *The Gestalt Journal,* 6(2), 103–16.

Ouichi, W.G. (1981). *Theory Z.* Reading, Mass., Addison-Wesley.

Rhyne, J. (1973). *The Gestalt Art Experience.* Monterey, Calif.: Brooks/Cole.

Roethlisberger, F.J. and Dickson, W.J. (1939). *Management and the Worker.* Cambridge, Mass.: Harvard University Press.

Rogers, C.R. (1942). *Counseling and Psychotherapy: newer concepts in practice.* New York: Houghton Mifflin.

Rogers, C.R. (1944a). Psychological adjustments of discharged service personnel. *Psychological Bulletin,* 41(10), 689–96.

Rogers, C.R. (1944b). Wartime issues in family counseling. *Journal of Home Economics,* 36(7), 390–3

Rogers, C.R. (1947). Effective principles for dealing with individuals and group tensions and dissatisfactions. Executive Seminar in Industrial Relations, Session 10, Chicago, IL., University of Chicago Press.

Rogers, C.R. (1951). *Client-Centered Therapy: its current practices, implications, and theory.* New York: Houghton Mifflin.

Rogers, C.R. (1952). Communication: its blocking and its facilitation. *Northwestern University Information* 20(25), 9–15. Published again as C.R. Rogers and F.J. Roethlisberger (1952). Barriers and gateways to communication. *Harvard Business Review,* 1952 July/August, 28–34, and 1988, 19–25.

Rogers, C.R. (1957). The necessary and sufficient conditions for therapeutic personality change. *Journal of Consulting Psychology,* 21, 95–103.

Rogers, C.R. (1960). A therapist's view of personal goals. Pendle Hill Pamphlet no. 108. Wallford, Pa. p.30. Also published as Social implications, in H. Kirschenbaum and V. L. Henderson (eds), *The Carl Rogers Reader* (pp. 436–8). Boston: Houghton Mifflin, 1989.

Rogers, C.R. (1961). Dealing with breakdowns in communication: interpersonal and intergroup. In *On Becoming a Person* (pp. 329–37). Boston: Houghton Mifflin.

Rogers, C.R. (1965). Dealing with psychological tensions. *Journal of Applied Behavioral Science,* 1, no. 1, pp 6–24.

Rogers, C.R. (1969/1988). The politics of education. In Charles E. Merrill (ed.), *Freedom to Learn and Freedom to Learn for the 1980s* (pp. 185–94). Columbus, Ohio.

Rogers, C.R. (1970). *Carl Rogers on Encounter Groups.* New York: Harper and Row.

Rogers, C.R. (1972). Some social issues which concern me. *Journal of Humanistic Psychology,* 12(2), 45–60.

Rogers, C R. (1975). A person-centered approach to intergroup tensions. AHP conference, Cuernavaca, Mexico, December 19.

Rogers, C.R. (1977a). The person-centered approach and the oppressed. In

On Personal Power: inner strength and its revolutionary impact (pp. 105–14). New York: Delacorte.

Rogers, C.R. (1977b). Resolving intercultural tensions: a beginning. In *Carl Rogers on Personal Power: inner strength and its revolutionary impact* (pp. 115–40). New York: Delacorte.

Rogers, C.R. (1979). My politics. Oral presentation, El Escorial, Spain.

Rogers, C.R. (1980). The world of tomorrow and the person of tomorrow. In *A Way of Being* (pp. 335–56). Boston: Houghton Mifflin.

Rogers, C.R. (1982a). A psychologist looks at nuclear war: its threat, its possible prevention. *Journal of Humanistic Psychology*, 22(4), fall, 9–20.

Rogers, C.R. (1982b). My politics. *The Journey*, 1(6), 8. La Jolla: Center for Studies of the Person.

Rogers, C.R. (1986). The Rust workshop: a personal overview. *Journal of Humanistic Psychology*, 26(3) summer, 23–45. Also published in H. Kirschenbaum and V. L. Henderson (eds), *The Carl Rogers Reader* (pp. 457–77). Boston: Houghton Mifflin.

Rogers, C.R. (1987). Inside the world of the Soviet professional. *Journal of Humanistic Psychology*, 27(3), 277–304. Also published in H. Kirschenbaum and V.L. Henderson (eds), *The Carl Rogers Reader* (pp. 478–501). Boston: Houghton Mifflin, 1989.

Rogers, C.R. and Dymond, R.F. (eds) (1954). *Psychotherapy and Personality Change: co-ordinated research studies in the client-centered approach*. Chicago: University of Chicago Press.

Rogers, C.R. and Roethlisberger, F.J. (1952). Barriers and gateways to communication. *Harvard Business Review*, July/August, 28–34.

Rogers, C.R. and Roethlisberger, F.J. (1991). Barriers and gateways to communication. *Harvard Business Review*, November/December, 12–18.

Rogers, C.R. and Russell, D.E. (2002). *Carl Rogers the Quiet Revolutionary: an oral history* (pp 129, 147–9). Roseville, Calif.: Penmarin Books.

Rogers, C.R. and Ryback, D. (1984). One alternative to nuclear planetary suicide. *The Counseling Psychologist*, 12(2), 3–12. Also published in Ronald F. Levant and John Shlien (eds), *Client-Centered Therapy and the Person-Centred Approach: new directions in theory, research, and practice*. New York: Praeger, 1984.

Rogers, C.R. and Sanford, R. (1987). Reflections on our South African experience. *Counseling and values*, 32(1), 17–20.

Rogers, C.R. and Wallen, J.L (1946). *Counseling with Returned Servicemen*. New York: McGraw-Hill.

Rogers, N. (1993). *The Creative Connection: expressive arts as healing*. Palo Alto, Calif.: Science and Behavior Books.

Rogers, N. (2004–05). Expressive art for healing and social change: a person-centered approach. Class manual for credential programme at Saybrook Graduate School and Research Center, San Francisco, CA.

Rothwell, W.J. and Sullivan, R. (2005). *Practicing Organizational Development: a guide for consultants* (2nd edn). San Francisco, Pfeiffer (an imprint of Wiley).

Schaefer, C.A. (ed.). (1988). *Innovative Interventions in Child and Adolescent Therapy*. New York: Wiley.

Schein, E.H. (1987). *Process Consultation*. Volume 2. *Lessons for Managers and Consultants*. Addison-Wesley.

Senge, P.M. (1990). *The Fifth Discipline: the art and practice of the learning organization*. New York: Doubleday.

Solomon, L. (1987). International tension reduction through the person-centred approach. *Journal of Humanistic Psychology*, 27(3), Summer, 337–47.

Steinhauser, K.E., Christakis, N.A. et al (2000). Factors considered important at the end of life by patients, family, physicians and other care providers. *Journal of the American Medical Association*, 284, 2476–82.

Villas Boas Bowen, M.(1987). Special characteristics of the Rust workshop and their influence on my facilitation process. *Journal of Humanistic Psychology*, 27(3), 348–63.

White, S.J. (1997). Empathy: a literature review and concept analysis. *Journal of Clinical Nursing*, 6(4), 253–7.

Zucconi, Alberto (2005). Personal communication.

IV

Professional Issues

Part IV considers a range of issues of particular significance to professional practitioners and to those beginning to enter this field.

It begins with an issue of critical contemporary importance: the relationship between person-centred therapy and empirical counselling and psychotherapy research. Robert Elliott, author of this chapter, is well known for his profound and creative approaches to psychotherapy research and is closely aligned with the field of process-experiential therapy. In this chapter, he specifically considers the evidence in support of a person-centred way of working, presenting a uniquely systematic and state-of-the-art review of the effectiveness and efficacy of person-centred therapy. In this chapter, Elliott also discusses those research methodologies that are most compatible with a person-centred worldview.

In the second chapter in this part of the book, Richard Worsley, author of *Process Work in Person-Centred Therapy* (2001, Palgrave), outlines a range of important concerns for novice therapists to consider when setting up in practice, such as contracting, assessment and boundaries. Another key issue for both novice and experienced practitioners to consider is that of ethics, and this is examined in detail in Chapter 26. Here, co-authors Gillian Proctor (author of *The Dynamics of Power in Counselling and Psychotherapy*, 2002, PCCS Books) and Suzanne Keys (editor of *Idiosyncratic Person-Centred Therapy*, 2003, PCCS Books), outline the nature of a specifically person-centred ethics emphasizing, in particular, the relational nature that such an ethics takes.

Closely related to these issues of setting up in practice and ethics is that of supervision, and the following chapter by Elke Lambers, who has written several chapters in this area, addresses this topic in depth. Lambers reviews person-centred writings on supervision and highlights the particular qualities that differentiate it from a more generic approach: in particular, the emphasis is on the therapist's experiences (as distinct from the client's) and the development of relational depth within the supervisory relationship itself.

This part of the book concludes with a chapter by Keith Tudor, co-author

of the seminal *The Person-Centred Approach: a contemporary introduction*
(2004, Palgrave) on training in person-centred therapy. Here, Tudor looks at
the application of person-centred principles to the training of person-centred
therapists, and considers the role that person-centred trainers – and their
organizations – need to take in this endeavour.

Person-Centred Approaches to Research

24

Robert Elliott

Is person-centred research possible? In the early 1960s Carl Rogers gave up both academia and the practice of scientific research and spent the rest of his life engaging in action-oriented pursuits. In retrospect, some (e.g. Lietaer, 1990) have argued that this was a mistake of historical proportions, and accounts in large part for the current beleaguered status of person-centred therapy. Regardless, sometime about 1990, person-centred therapists, and therapists in closely related parts of our tradition, woke up to the fact that they were being system-atically and progressively excluded from training and health-care venues throughout the world and needed to do something. Re-engaging in research was put forward as a key proposed solution, especially by those working in Europe or in the process-experiential part of the tradition (e.g. Elliott, 2002; Greenberg, Elliott and Lietaer, 1994; Lietaer, 1990; Sachse, 2004).

In fact, a veritable profusion of research on person-centred and closely related therapies has occurred over the past 15 years, paralleled by the rapid emergence and acceptance of qualitative research during the same time period. Elliott et al (2004) reported that fully half of the available research on the outcome of person-centred and related therapies has been published since 1990.

However, in this rush forward, the issue of the consistency of the emerging research literature with person-centred principles has often been overlooked. Much of the recent spate of research has been quantitative and positivistic in nature (i.e. based on objective data and seeking definitive knowledge), in some cases using the randomized clinical trial design, typically viewed as the epitome of rigid scientism by person-centred followers, postmodernists and humanists in general (Bohart, O'Hara and Lietner, 1998). In fact, the body of so-called positivistic therapy research has been surprisingly supportive of person-centred and related approaches, in spite of the deck being stacked against them in multiple ways. Nevertheless, the ethical-philosophical issue remains: is it acceptable for political purposes to make use of research whose principles are antithetical to person-centred therapy, in order to fend off unfair attacks? More fundamentally, what is it about positivist research that might be anti-person-centred? Is a science based on person-centred principles possible? And, if so, what might it look like? These are some of the questions I will try to answer in this chapter.

What does positivist outcome research tell us about person-centred therapy?

Ironically, systematic, quantitative outcome has a person-centred pedigree: the first controlled study of the outcome of psychotherapy was reported by Rogers and Dymond (1954), although the features of modern randomized clinical trial design evolved later: psychiatric diagnosis, standardized symptom measures, placebo control groups, treatment manuals, complex statistical analyses and so on. (By contrast, the Rogers and Dymond study relied heavily on individualized and projective measures, used a general outpatient sample, was not completely randomized, and used primitive statistics.)

General effects of humanistic/experiential therapies

Over the past 50-plus years, person-centred therapy and related therapies have been the subject of at least 112 studies reporting pre-to-post-therapy results, including some 37 controlled studies comparing one of these therapies to an untreated control group, and 55 studies comparing one of these therapies to some other kind of therapy (Elliott et al, 2004; see also Elliott, 2001). My colleagues and I used meta-analysis methods to statistically combine the results of these studies, from which the following conclusions can be drawn (Elliott, 2001; Elliott et al, 2004):

- Clients who participate in person-centred therapy and related therapies show large amounts of change over time, with an average effect size of .99 standard deviation (sd) units (a standard metric used in meta-analyses, corresponding to a large effect).
- Post-therapy gains in person-centred therapy and related therapies are stable: they are maintained over early and late follow-up periods.
- In randomized clinical trials against untreated control groups, clients who participate in person-centred therapy and related therapies typically show substantially more change than comparable untreated clients (mean difference of .89 sd).
- In randomized clinical trials comparing active treatments, clients in person-centred therapy and related therapies show gains that are equivalent to those in clients seen in the other therapies, including cognitive-behavioural treatments (mean overall difference of +.04).

Slightly less than half of these results (52 studies), however, come from research in which pure person-centred therapy was studied. The rest consist of a mixed bag consisting of (a) so-called 'non-directive' therapies with minor directive elements added (usually these were control groups for studies done by cognitive-behavioural therapists: 11 studies); (b) process-experiential, gestalt or emotion-focused therapies (including couples therapy: 38); and (c) encounter groups or other therapies (16). Although interpretations of what counts as person-centred differ and are gradually liberalizing to include process-guiding approaches such as process-experiential therapy, person-centred therapy purists will consider these 'not person-centred enough'. So, let us take a look at the sub-sample of pure person-centred therapy studies.

Effects of person-centred therapy

As Table 25.1 indicates, the results of a more focused analysis of the 52 studies of pure person-centred therapy are generally very comparable to those reported for the larger meta-analysis. First, the overall pre-to-post effect is also quite large and of the same order (mean effect size [ES:] .91). Second, the effects are similar across time, from immediate post-therapy (mean ES: .84)

Table 25.1 Summary of overall pre-post change, controlled and comparative effect sizes for person-centred outcome research[1]

	n	m	sd
Pre-Post Change ES (mean d)			
By assessment point:			
Post	45	.84	.52
Early follow-up (1–11 mos.)	17	1.14	.76
Late Follow-up (12+ mos)	21	.94	.56
Overall (mES):	52	.91	.54
Controlled ES (vs. untreated clients)[2]			
Mean difference	11	.78	.63
Experiential mean pre-post ES	11	.84	.51
Control mean pre-post ES	11	.06	.57
Comparative ES (vs. nonexperiential treatments)[2]			
Unweighted mean difference	28	−.04	.50
PCT mean pre-post ES	28	.92	.68
Comparative treatment mean			
Pre-post ES	28	.96	.74

Notes:
1 Unweighted Hedge's d used; n is the number of studies in the analysis; m is the mean; sd is the standard deviation.
2 Mean difference in change ESs for conditions compared, except where these are unavailable; positive values indicate pro-PCT results.

through early follow-up (less that a year: mean ES: 1.14), to late follow-up (a year or longer: mean ES: .94). Indeed, as was the case for the larger analysis, if anything, the effects are slightly larger at follow-up. Third, in 11 studies comparing person-centred therapy to clients receiving no treatment, the effects were again large and comparable to the larger study (mean difference in pre–post ES between treated and untreated groups: .78). Fourth, in 28 studies comparing clients seen in person-centred therapy with clients receiving non-experiential therapies, there was essentially no difference (mean difference in pre–post ES: −.04).

Moreover, by applying a new statistical method called 'equivalence analysis', as in the larger study, it is possible to show that the average difference of −.04 indicates that person-centred therapies and non-experiential therapies are statistically equivalent: that is, not significantly different from zero, but significantly smaller than a recommended test value of .4 sd (see Table 25.2). This last is a bit tricky and bears some explaining. It is based on the assumption that in clinical research, differences that amount to less than .4 standard deviations are not interesting or useful. The value of .4 was picked because it is partway between what are considered to be small and medium effects in psychological research; so what we want to say is that the difference in the amount of pre-post change is less

Table 25.2 Equivalence analysis comparisons between PCT and non-experiential therapies[1]

	n	MES	sdES	t(0)	t(|.4|)	Result
PCT vs. non-experiential therapies	28	−.04	.50	−.44	3.79[3]	Equivalent
PCT vs. CB	20	−.19	.44	−1.94+	2.15[2]	Trivially different
Allegiance-controlled comparisons						
PCT vs. other (non-experiential) therapies	28	.01	.45	.09	4.60[3]	Equivalent
PCT vs. CB	20	−.03	.43	−.32	3.89[3]	Equivalent

Notes:
1   MES: mean comparative effect size (difference between therapies); sdES: standard deviation for the comparative effect sizes; t(0): usual one-group t value against a zero-difference null hypothesis; t(\|.4\|): equivalence t value against a ±.4 sd difference null hypothesis. The 'Result' column refers to the interpretation of the results of the equivalence testing: 'Equivalent': significantly less than ±.4 sd criterion, but not significantly greater than zero; 'Trivially different': both significantly different from zero and significantly less than ±.4 sd criterion.
2   p < .05
3   p < .01

than a value that is already clearly less than a medium effect (Elliott, Stiles and Shapiro, 1993). All this is a roundabout way of saying that we can trust that the difference in the effectiveness of person-centred therapy and non-experiential therapies is too small to worry about!

However, we are not yet done with the story, because in the current academic and health care situation, it is commonly believed that cognitive-behavioural therapies are more effective than person-centred therapy, as witnessed by their continuing to be the treatment of choice among cognitive-behavioural therapy researchers seeking a convenient straw person to make their favoured approaches look good (e.g. Beck et al, 1992; Kolko et al, 2000). It is therefore necessary to look more closely at the 20 studies involving direct comparisons of person-centred therapy with cognitive-behavioural therapy. As Table 25.2 indicates, the average difference in the amount of pre–post change in these studies is −.19 sd, a small effect, but one which is significantly different from both zero and −.4. This pattern of results means that there is a difference, but that it can be regarded as trivial for clinical purposes. In other words, over large numbers of people there appears to be a slight difference, but for any given situation, the characteristics of the client and therapist and their emerging relationship will greatly overshadow any residual difference.

Nevertheless, in an era of large-scale managed care, it is still possible that decision makers will look at this trivial difference and argue that, when taken across large numbers of people, even such small differences are important. In response to this rather bureaucratic position, there is yet one more argument: so far, the role of researcher allegiance has not been taken into consideration. This is the well-established finding that researchers comparing active therapies tend to find results that accord with their theoretical beliefs (e.g. Luborsky et al, 1999). In the larger meta-analysis from which the person-centred therapy vs. cognitive-behavioural therapy studies are drawn, there was a strong and statistically significant allegiance effect, in the form of a correlation of .59, indicating that researchers of either persuasion tend to find what they expect. Unfortunately, only one of the 20 person-centred therapy vs. cognitive-behavioural therapy studies was carried out by a supporter of person-centred therapy (Teusch, Böhme, and Gastpar, 1997), while ten were carried out by cognitive-behavioural therapy advocates and nine by neutral parties. In this breakdown, the cognitive-behavioural therapy-allegiance studies show a strong effect (mean ES: −.39) in favour of cognitive-behavioural therapy over person-centred therapy, while the neutral-allegiance studies show no difference (mean ES: .04). Thus, it is likely that the weakly supported negative overall finding favouring cognitive-behavioural therapy can be entirely accounted for by researcher allegiance. Indeed, when the effect of researcher allegiance is statistically removed, the effect disappears completely (see Table 25.2).

As might be expected, however, this is not the end of the story, because some cognitive behaviour therapists (e.g. Hunsley and Di Giulio, 2002) have made the opposite argument: that researcher allegiance effects derive from the effectiveness of their therapies, rather than the other way around. While the debate continues, important cognitive-behavioural therapy researchers like Hollon and Beck (2003) now concede that research allegiance plays a key role in cognitive-behavioural therapy outcome research. To conclude, one obvious moral that might be drawn is that person-centred therapy researchers should do more head-to-head comparisons with cognitive behaviour therapies, in order to even the score!

Anatomy of a number: a deconstruction of positivist therapy research

But what does a number like −.04 mean? Where does it come from? What does this have to do with the client's lived experience? In positivist therapy research, it all starts with the client sitting down to fill out a standardized, quantitative psychological measurement instrument, such as the Symptom Checklist-90–R (SCL90R), a widely used measure of client symptoms (Derogatis, 1983). In completing this instrument, our client (who let us say has been moderately depressed for the past month) is asked to rate a series of 90 descriptions of troubling symptoms for 'how much it has bothered you in the past week', using a standard 5-point scale, ranging from 0 ('not at all distressed') to 4 ('extremely distressed'). For example, when clients come to the item, 'Feeling low in energy or slowed down', they must then decide if this description captures the quality of their depression, and how distressed in general they have felt about it over the past week. Suppose they choose 3 ('greatly distressed'). Then they must rate the other 89 items on the SCL90R. Often there are two to six different instruments rating things like interpersonal problems, how they feel about themselves, how much in touch with their inner experiences they are, and so on. Then, perhaps four months later, at the end of 16 sessions of, say, person-centred therapy, the client is asked to complete these same questionnaires again. Let us say that the client is feeling much better, and this second time gives a 1 ('slightly distressed') for feeling low in energy or slowed down.

From a positivist point of view, these responses are just observable behaviours that psychometric research has shown to be related to other responses on the same and different instruments in certain ways. For example, the low-energy item tends to go up and down together with most of the rest of the items on the same instrument ('inter-item reliability'), and, in the absence of treatment, tends to be relatively consistent over a few weeks or a month ('test-retest reliability'). It also correlates to some degree with similar measures, like the Beck Depression Inventory ('convergent validity'), and does not correlate too much with nuisance variables like reading ability or a tendency to tell people what you think they want to hear ('discriminant validity'). In addition, the SCL90R has high measure utility, because it is easy to give to clients to complete in their own time, thus being perfect for bureaucratic purposes. (It also serves to maintain the controlling status of the researcher as expert, which could be termed 'political validity'.)

Because these conditions are reasonably met for the SCL90R, researchers believe they can confidently relate this item (along with others like it) to abstract psychological concepts like clinical symptom severity. Thus, the client's ratings of all 90 items are averaged together at time 1 (pre-therapy), say, for a mean score of 1.46, which indicates a moderate level of clinical distress, and also at time 2 (post-therapy), say, for a mean score of .62, which indicates only minor or subclinical distress, amounting to what is considered to be a substantial and statistically reliable improvement (in this case, .84).

Next, the researcher averages together the scores of the whole collection of clients receiving person-centred therapy at pre-therapy and at post-therapy, and calculates a mean and standard deviation for each set, obtaining, for example, a pre-therapy mean of 1.47 (standard deviation: .39) and a corresponding post-therapy value of .68 (sd: .61). In order to determine how much this amounts to, the researcher then finds the difference between pre and post-therapy group means (here, .79) and then converts this difference score into a common metric by dividing it by the 'pooled standard deviation' (a special kind of average of the two standard deviations, in this case, .51); the resulting value is referred to as a pre-post effect size (here, 1.56 sd units, a very large value). The same process is followed for all five outcome measures, resulting in an average pre-post effect size of, say, 1.13 sd units (in our example, some of the other instruments, like the self-esteem measure, have much smaller effects than the SCL90R).

Because this is a comparative treatment randomized clinical trial conducted by a cognitive-behavioural therapy advocate, there is also another group of clients who have been given 16 sessions of, say, cognitive-behavioural therapy focused on depression. For a variety of reasons, these clients show somewhat larger pre-post effects across the five outcome measures, say 1.52 sd. These reasons are likely to include: cognitive-behavioural therapy is easier to learn; the therapists are more closely and competently supervised; the cognitive-behavioural therapists are more comfortable with the treatment they are asked to carry out, and therefore make better relationships with their clients, who also like the structure; and the therapists 'teach to the test', signalling implicitly to their clients how they are expected to respond at post-therapy. The comparative effect size in our example is thus −.39 in favour of cognitive-behavioural therapy, exactly the value reported earlier in the meta-analysis of person-centred therapy vs. cognitive-behavioural therapy research, for studies carried out by cognitive-behavioural therapy adherents. When combined with the other 27 comparative treatment studies, however, the overall comparative effect size is −.04 sd: that is, the person-centred therapy and other therapies are statistically equivalent.

But, again, what does this mean? −.04 is an extremely abstract number, from which all specific references − such as characteristics of client and therapist or the way in which person-centred therapy or the other therapy were carried out, or the type of outcome measure − have been removed. In other words, all but the most general meaning has been stripped from this number. It has virtually nothing to do with the client's lived experience any more; the client's inner valuing process is ignored; and there is no way of determining its authenticity. In other words, it fails the fundamental person-centred therapy principles of contact, empathy, acceptance and genuineness.

On the other hand, it is politically a very useful number, because it can be used to persuade professional bodies and government officials that person-centred therapy is a valid and effective treatment, so that they will allow person-centred therapy training to continue and perhaps even mandate insurance or government health-service payments for person-centred therapy. Such numbers are therefore valuable, and probably even essential, for person-centred therapy to continue to survive. (This is another example of 'political validity'.) But there is nothing person-centred about this number; in fact, it fundamentally violates person-centredness. So what is to be done about the necessity of such numbers? If we remain ideologically pure, we risk passing out of existence, thus depriving clients of a unique way of working with them. But if these kinds of numbers and the ends-justify-the-means logic that go with them are all that we aim to achieve as researchers, then we will have totally sold out ourselves and our clients for a positivist golden calf.

Mixed model person-centred therapy research: render unto Caesar

It seems to me that there is really only one sensible way forward: to simultaneously carry out both political-positivist and person-centred research, to render politically expedient quantitative data to the government and professional bodies ('Caesar'), while at the same time carrying out (even in the same study) research that completely honours the client and person-centred principles (Elliott, 2002).

Several writers, including Mearns and McLeod (1984) and Barrineau and Bozarth (1989), have begun to spell out what this kind of research looks like, by applying basic person-centred principles to the conduct of therapy research:

- The person-centred therapy researcher focuses on understanding, from the inside, the client's lived experiencing.
- The person-centred therapy researcher accepts and even prizes the client's experiencing, and does not judge it.
- The person-centred therapy researcher tries to be an authentic and equal partner with the client, treating the client as a co-researcher and allowing the client to see the researcher as a fellow human being.
- The person-centred therapy researcher creatively and flexibly adapts research methods to the research topic and questions at hand.

These precepts have inevitably led person-centred therapy researchers to qualitative methods, especially empirical phenomenology (the Duquesne approach; e.g. Wertz, 1983), grounded theory analysis (GTA; Strauss and Corbin, 1998), along with variants such as heuristic research (Moustakas, 1990), consensual qualitative research (CQR; Hill, Thompson and Williams, 1977), and co-operative inquiry/participatory inquiry (Heron, 1996; Reason and Rowan, 1981). These classical qualitative methods, while they differ in important ways, share many common interests with each other and with person-centred therapy, including the central place accorded empathy, attention to issues of meaning, suspension of the natural attitude of having to arbitrate the nature of reality, and valuing empowerment as a goal and process in research (Mearns and McLeod, 1984). In addition, they draw on a common body of qualitative research strategies, including (Elliott and Timulak, 2005):

- negotiating with the informant-client in a transparent, collaborative manner over the nature of the participation
- carrying out the interview in a careful, intentional manner, helping the informants to stay focused and clarifying their meanings as they attempt to put them into words
- transcribing the recording of the interview at the appropriate level of detail and accuracy
- preparing the data record by breaking it into meaning units and dropping irrelevant material
- constructing categories or themes to describe each meaning unit
- putting meaning units into existing categories, where these apply
- clustering or connecting categories or themes with one another in order to develop a model or story of the phenomenon.

Methods such as these can be used to study just about any human experience, from being criminally victimized (Wertz, 1983) to loneliness (e.g. Moustakas, 1990). Furthermore, these are the more traditional forms of qualitative inquiry; other forms, such as autoethnography, e.g. Reed-Danahay, 1997, are constantly emerging.

What are the possibilities for person-centred therapy research?

Given the considerations reviewed so far in this chapter, I think that there are many questions open for person-centred therapy research.

What are the general effects of person-centred therapy with specific client populations?

Both traditional group design and randomized clinical trials studies continue to be very much needed, both for commonly studied populations such as depression and especially for little-studied populations such as health problems (e.g. coping with cancer) and severe problems (e.g. schizophrenia). It would also be a very good idea for researchers in our tradition to study anxiety problems, instead of leaving this topic entirely to cognitive-behaviour therapists! (For more suggestions, see Elliott et al, 2004.)

What are the specific effects of person-centred therapy with specific clients?

An alternative to positivist therapy research of the sort just described is the systematic case study design, in which a single client's treatment is studied carefully and in detail in order to draw inferences about (a) whether the client changed substantially, (b) whether therapy contributed substantially to those changes, and (c) how the changes came about (Elliott, 2002). Elliott and Zucconi (2005) describe a research protocol suitable for this sort of research, including a combination of qualitative and quantitative data collection formats.

What are the effects of the facilitative conditions on the outcome of person-centred therapy?

In a recent meta-analysis of process-outcome research on therapist empathy (Bohart et al, 2002), we found only six studies of experiential-humanistic therapies in which this relationship had been studied! Thus, Rogers' key theoretical claim has only rarely been applied to his own therapy. This sort of research question is highly appropriate for naturalistic samples of person-centred therapy, in which empathy is measured by client, therapist and/or observers during therapy and used to predict the amount of pre–post client change. (See Bohart et al, 2002, for more suggestions for research on therapist empathy.)

What are the immediate in-session effects of therapist facilitative responses on depth of client processing?

The relationship between specific therapy responses and productive client responses within person-centred therapy sessions has been studied extensively by Sachse (see Sachse and Elliott, 2002, for a summary), but most of Sachse's somewhat controversial findings, which suggest a high degree of therapist influence on client process, have not yet been replicated by others, making this a prime topic for further person-centred therapy research.

What do clients experience as most helpful in person-centred therapy?

If the preceding research topics seem too positivistic, a purely phenomenological strategy can be used, in which clients are asked to describe in their own words what they found most helpful, either in particular sessions, using the 'Helpful aspects of therapy' (HAT) form (Llewelyn, 1988), or overall looking back over their therapy, using the 'Change interview' (Elliott, Slatick and Urman, 2001). These accounts can then be analysed using grounded theory analysis (GTA) or a similar method (for more information, e.g. Elliott and Timulak, 2005).

What are the characteristics of transformative moments in therapy?

Finally, the idea that there are special moments of insight, awareness, relief or other forms of personal healing in therapy is a key theme in the person-centred therapy literature, dating back to Rogers' writings on the therapy process (e.g. Rogers, 1961). Using the 'Helpful aspects of therapy' form or the more intensive 'Brief structured recall' method (Elliott and Shapiro, 1988), person-centred therapy researchers can identify important moments from clients' perspectives and then investigate them further in order to unpack the process of change, including the momentary qualities of the client's experience and the accompanying discourse.

Other research questions and investigative strategies are possible; these are simply the ones with which I am most familiar. Other promising strategies, such as participatory research (Whyte, 1991) and narrative research (McLeod, 2001) are also possible.

CONCLUSION

Promoting research on person-centred therapies

As an example of the kind of research efforts that are possible for person-centred therapists interested in becoming involved in research, Elliott and Zucconi (2005) describe a research framework for an International Project on the Effectiveness of Psychotherapy and Psychotherapy Training (IPEPPT). The general goal of this project is to improve psychotherapy and psychotherapy training in a broad range of theoretical approaches, by encouraging systematic research in therapy training institutes and university-based training clinics. More a loose network than a specific study, IPEPPT consists of a network of web-based virtual communities to support research, including a fairly elaborate site for research into person-centred and experiential therapies and a collection of interested research teams working in several countries, including the UK, Belgium, the United States, Canada, Slovakia, Ireland and Italy. The research framework offers a set of concepts for guiding the research and a range of research protocols for various purposes. Although the project as a whole cuts across different theoretical orientations, person-centred therapy has been a key player in this work from its inception, and it is important that person-centred therapists continue to play an important role in such developments. I conclude with a list of ways that readers of this chapter can contribute to these sorts of efforts, beyond the suggestions already made earlier for mounting their own separate studies (see Elliott and Zucconi, 2005, for more details):

- Person-centred therapists can contribute to dialogues on how to measure therapy and training outcomes within person-centred psychotherapies.
- They can join a virtual community or discussion group and contribute to the discussions and collections of resource materials there (e.g. www.communityzero.com/pcepirp).
- They can begin using simple research tools with their own clients and in their own training setting, including, for example, brief quantitative measures of client problem distress and therapeutic alliance, with systematic collection of background information about client and therapist.
- If they are located in a non-English speaking country, they can help with translations of key research instruments; or if they work with a special

client population they can help develop the research protocol for that population (e.g. people living with schizophrenia).

- They can contribute to psychometric research aimed at improving existing instruments and at equating different instruments for similar constructs.
- They can take part in more formal collaborations with similarly inclined training centres to generate data for pooling.

Clearly, many possibilities exist for person-centred therapists to reclaim their scientific heritage, building on recent advances and continually emerging new resources and support for practical, humanizing research. After all, research is one of the purest expressions of the actualizing tendency!

REFERENCES

Barrineau, P. and Bozarth, J. D. (1989). A person-centered research model. *Person-Centered Review.* 4, 465–74.

Beck, A.T., Sokol, L., Clark, D.A., Berchick, R., and Wright, F. (1992). A crossover study of focused cognitive therapy for panic disorder. *American Journal of Psychiatry*, 149, 778–83.

Bohart, A.C., Elliott, R., Greenberg, L.S., Watson, J.C. (2002). Empathy. In J. Norcross, *Psychotherapy Relationships that Work* (pp. 89–108). New York: Oxford University Press.

Bohart, A.C., O'Hara, M. and Leitner, L.M. (1998). Empirically violated treatments: Disenfranchisement of humanistic and other psychotherapies. *Psychotherapy Research*, 8, 141–57.

Derogatis, L. R. (1983). *SCL-90-R manual.* Minneapolis, Minn.: NCS Assessments.

Elliott, R. (2001). Research on the effectiveness of humanistic therapies: a meta-analysis. In D. Cain and J. Seeman (eds), *Humanistic Psychotherapies: handbook of research and practice* (pp. 57–81). Washington, D.C.: APA.

Elliott, R. (2002). Render unto Caesar: quantitative and qualitative knowing in person-centered/experiential therapy research. *Person-Centered and Experiential Psychotherapy*, 1, 102-117.

Elliott, R., Greenberg, L.S. and Lietaer, G. (2004). Research on experiential psychotherapies. In M.J. Lambert (ed.), *Bergin and Garfield's Handbook of Psychotherapy and Behavior Change* (5th edn) (pp. 493–539), New York: Wiley.

Elliott, R. and Shapiro, D. A. (1988). Brief structured recall: a more efficient method for identifying and describing significant therapy events. *British Journal of Medical Psychology*, 61, 141–53.

Elliott, R., Slatick, E. and Urman, M. (2001). Qualitative change process research on psychotherapy: alternative strategies. In: J. Frommer and D.L. Rennie (eds), *Qualitative Psychotherapy Research: methods and methodology* (pp. 69–111). Lengerich, Germany: Pabst Science Publishers.

Elliott, R., Stiles, W.B. and Shapiro, D.A. (1993). Are some psychotherapies more equivalent than others? In T.R. Giles (ed.) *Handbook of Effective Psychotherapy* (pp. 455–79). New York: Plenum.

Elliott, R. and Timulak, L. (2005). Descriptive and interpretive approaches to qualitative research. In J. Miles and P. Gilbert (eds), *A Handbook of Research Methods in Clinical and Health Psychology* (147–59). Oxford, UK: Oxford University Press.

Elliott, R. and Zucconi, A. (2005). *Doing Research on the Effectiveness of Psychotherapy and Psychotherapy Training: a person-centered/experiential perspective.* Unpublished manuscript, University of Toledo, Toledo, Ohio.

Greenberg, L.S., Elliott, R. and Lietaer, G. (1994). Research on humanistic and experiential psychotherapies. In A.E. Bergin and S.L. Garfield (eds) *Handbook of Psychotherapy and Behavior Change* (4th edn) (pp. 509–39). New York: Wiley.

Heron, J. (1996). *Co-Operative Inquiry: research into the human condition.* London: Sage.

Hill, C.E., Thompson, B.J. and Williams, E.N. (1997). A guide to conducting consensual qualitative research. *The Counseling Psychologist, 25,* 517–72.

Hollon, S.D. and Beck A.T. (2003). Cognitive and cognitive behavioral therapies. In M.J. Lambert (ed.), *Bergin and Garfield's Handbook of Psychotherapy and Behavior Change* (5th edn) (pp. 447–92), New York: Wiley.

Hunsley, J. and Di Giulio, G. (2002). Dodo bird, phoenix, or urban legend? The question of psychotherapy equivalence. *The Scientific Review of Mental Health Practice, 1(1).* On-line journal accessed at: www.srmhp.org/0101/psychotherapy-equivalence.html.

Kolko, D.J., Brent, D.A., Baugher, M., Bridge, J. and Birmaher, B. (2000). Cognitive and family therapies for adolescent depression: treatment specificity, mediation, and moderation. *Journal of Consulting and Clinical Psychology, 68,* 603–14.

Lietaer, G. (1990). The client-centered approach after the Wisconsin Project: a personal view on its evolution. In G. Lietaer, J. Rombauts and R. Van Balen (eds), *Client-Centered and Experiential Psychotherapy in the Nineties* (19–45). Leuven, Belgium: Leuven University Press.

Llewelyn, S. (1988). Psychological therapy as viewed by clients and therapists. *British Journal of Clinical Psychology, 27,* 223–38.

Luborsky, L., Diguer, L., Seligman, D.A., Rosenthal, R., Krause, E.D., Johnson, S., Halperin, G., Bishop, M., Berman, J.S. and Schweizer, E. (1999). The researcher's own therapy allegiances: A 'wild card' in comparisons of treatment efficacy. *Clinical Psychology,: Science and Practice, 6,* 95–106.

McLeod, J. (2001). *Qualitative Research in Counselling and Psychotherapy.* London: Sage.

Mearns, D. and McLeod, J. (1984). A person-centred approach to research. In R. F. Levant and J. M. Shlein (eds), *Client Centred Therapy and the Person-Centred Approach: new directions in theory, research and practice* (pp. 370–89). Eastbourne: Praeger.

Moustakas, C. (1990). *Heuristic Research: DESIGN, methodology, and applications*. Bevery Hills, Calif.: Sage.

Reed-Danahay, D.E. (ed.) (1997). *Auto/ethnography: rewriting the self and the social*. New York: Berg.

Reason, P. and Rowan, J. (eds) (1981). *Human Inquiry: a sourcebook of new paradigm research*. Chichester: Wiley.

Rogers, C.R. (1961). *On Becoming a Person*. Boston: Houghton Mifflin.

Rogers, C.R. and Dymond, R.F. (eds) (1954). *Psychotherapy and Personality Change*. Chicago: University of Chicago Press.

Sachse, R. (2004). From client-centered to clarification-oriented psychotherapy. *Person-Centered and Experiential Psychotherapies, 3*, 19–35.

Sachse, R. and Elliott, R. (2002). Process-outcome research in client-centered and experiential therapies. In D. Cain and J. Seeman (eds), *Humanistic Psychotherapies: handbook of research and practice* (pp. 83–115). Washington, D.C.: APA.

Strauss, A. and Corbin, J. (1998). *Basics of Qualitative Research: techniques and procedures for developing grounded theory* (2nd edn). Thousand Oaks, Calif.: Sage.

Teusch, L., Böhme, H. and Gastpar, M. (1997). The benefit of an insight-oriented and experiential approach on panic and agoraphobia symptoms. *Psychotherapy and Psychosomatics, 66*, 293–301.

Wertz, F.J. (1983). From everyday to psychological description: analyzing the moments of a qualitative data analysis. *Journal of Phenomenological Psychology, 14*, 197–241.

Whyte, W.F. (ed.) (1991). *Participatory Action Research*. Newbury Park, Calif.: Sage.

CHAPTER 25

Setting up Practice and the Therapeutic Framework

Richard Worsley

There can be no doubt that every therapist, even when he has resolved many of his own difficulties in a therapeutic relationship, still has troubling conflicts, tendencies to project, or unrealistic attitudes on certain matters.

(Rogers, 1951: 42)

Entering therapeutic practice

Good therapy depends crucially upon the personal development of the therapist. For mature therapists the tasks of personal and professional development are important enough, but for the beginning therapist the task is indeed challenging. At the very time when shifts within the personality are taking place both through training and through client contact, it is necessary to find a personal stability upon which the therapeutic framework can be built together with the client.

This chapter explores a number of tensions which characterize the work of the beginning therapist. It is written mainly for the new therapist, but is also relevant to trainers, supervisors and more experienced colleagues. The more experienced therapist may feel exempt from these dynamics. Is this really the case? When the service in which I work is under the pressure of a long waiting list, I can feel myself circling through some of this material once more. The purpose of the chapter is to bring to light some of the processes which mark out personal development during the early days of practice, and which are specific to beginning work as a therapist. The new therapist needs to become consciously aware of both the pressures inherent to her situation and her own responses to them. She strives to be a reflective practitioner, who can engage openly and honestly both within herself and with others to integrate into her attitudes and her way of being her personal reactions to her meeting with clients (Schön, 1987).

Until the beginning of client work, learning about counselling and psychotherapy will have been stretching enough. We face the ghosts of earlier learning processes; we struggle to relate theory to our own growth and experiencing; we encounter the growth and the pain of our fellow-students in group work and in practicum. Yet, until the first client, all is preliminary. On many courses, finding a practice opportunity proves difficult, frustrating, a source of fear of failure. Most students of therapy will have to struggle against internal constrictions in order to find freedom to practise.

The focus of this chapter is the need to deal at a conscious level with unfamiliar pressures from within and from without. The therapeutic framework requires competence in a number of practical skills. I make brief reference to these in the next section. However, these can be a distraction from the development of inner stability, and in any case form the core to professional development modules of diploma and degree courses. At the heart of moving from the role of novice to that of sound practitioner is the capacity of the therapist to be free and available to provide psychological containment for the client.

Practical considerations

Good, brief guidelines for beginning practice already exist (Dryden et al, 1995; Mearns, 1997). These do not need to be repeated here. Mearns (1997: 69–70), summarizing Dryden et al (1995), notes the following as needing understanding in particular:

- selecting and contracting with a supervisor
- the practical and ethical issues of recording counselling sessions
- personal safety and security for the counsellor
- writing case notes
- record keeping, confidentiality and the law
- writing letters to clients
- developing a resource network
- making referrals
- introduction to the relevant professional code of ethics
- ethical decision making and problem solving
- advertising
- dealing with client fees
- insurance
- setting up and working with an organization
- monitoring and evaluating one's competence
- evaluation of client work
- using research reports
- issues of accreditation or registration
- understanding national and international issues in therapy
- the nature and purpose of supervision

- stress and burn-out
- professional development and further training.

All of these matter, but all depend upon the new therapist finding reflective stability.

Freedom to practise

Carl Rogers' theories of therapy (1957) and of human personality (1959) state that, as people experience acceptance, empathy and congruence, they will be able to take back into themselves the responsibility for evaluating life experience. This change involves a clearer, less conditioned and less conflicted relationship between their self-concept and their experiencing of the world around them. This is not just true for the client who seeks to reduce distress. It is basic to all human growth, and hence to activities as diverse as counsellor supervision (Tudor and Worrall, 2004) and schooling (Rogers, 1969). This freedom is a freedom from others' judgement. It is a freedom to move into fluency of self-experience. Hence, for therapists, it is a freedom to practise.

The image I have developed for the freedom to practise is that of a raised platform on which the therapist dances with the client. Only a small portion of the surface of the platform is near the edge. We need to know where the edge is, and what shape it is. If we do not, one or both may fall off. However, if we are dominated by fear of the edge, we will never dance freely. Let us then consider the edginess of early practice, so that, in freer self-awareness, the dance of psychotherapy may commence.

The early pressures

There is a fundamental paradox of beginning practice. All practitioners are responsible for acting within their competence. Yet trainees bear this responsibility when their competence might be most fragile and when their ability to assess both their own abilities and their clients' needs is immature. Beginning practice brings external pressures that in turn interact with the trainee's internal dynamics. This complex interaction is difficult for even the well-supported new therapist to manage. Reflective practice is at a premium.

Trainees are themselves in process of growth – some with vigour and freedom, and others with fear and hesitancy. My experience as a teacher was that a group of nurses could learn about conditions of worth in half an hour, so long as the idea did not occur to them that Rogers' understanding of the personality might disrupt their own self-concept. By contrast, professional-level therapy students have to wrestle with their own conditions of worth and incongruence. This is painful and disruptive. The fear of failure and other manifestations of conditionality, both conscious and unconscious, are often prevalent at exactly the time that the first client enters the scene.

Courses and tutors can make matters worse. In the first term of a professional training course, I became aware that there was a suspicion that the tutors could not do what they were expecting others to do. (This is a common enough group defence against learning.) However, one session of demonstration later led to the so-called halo effect – the idealization of the tutors as another defence against the anxiety of learning. The tutors, it turns out, are not totally incompetent. In fact they are not bad. The trainees are now intimidated and thrust down into their own sense of inadequacy. Occasionally, trainers can aggravate the situation. Recent supervision debate has identified a tendency for some tutors who are rigid or dogmatic in the face of their own underlying fears to produce stress, suspicion and mistrust in students (Tudor and Worrall, 2004). In a number of ways, the processes of training, competent and incompetent alike, can add to trainees' burdens.

One or two trainees in any year will have a poor experience of supervision. I recall in particular watching one young woman sculpt her supervisory relationship. She placed her supervisor standing on a table behind her, facing away. The client was curled up, foetus-like, in a ball at her feet. I terminated the placement, but the harm to confidence was already done. It felt to me as if the foetus-figure was not only the client but part of the counsellor.

The beginning therapist finds herself in a network of trainers, supervisors, agency managers and clients. At a point of vulnerability, it is crucial for the trainee to distinguish accurately his or her internal dynamics from genuinely difficult, even aggressive and attacking external dynamics. Fear, concealment and some paranoiac feelings are to be expected. Supervisors and trainers have to strive hard to accord the trainee the freedom to recognize and process the so-called negative. This general dynamic is rooted in specific issues.

Facing the issues

The good enough client – or will my needs be met?

Therapists provide boundaries or containment for clients, as well as accompanying clients on their journey. To hark back to my metaphor, therapists delineate the ring, the sacred space of meeting, and then move with the client within it. Both the containment and the dance constitute the necessary safety – good enough safety – to facilitate change. In order to provide containment, therapists must be congruent about their own needs.

The beginning therapist can be open both to the fear that her needs will not be met and to the fear of acknowledging this hunger. Peggy Natiello observes: 'Collaborative systems depend on open, full participation of each member. Persons who hold themselves back out of fear of taking over often inhibit the success of the experience' (2001: 70).

For example, the new counsellor needs practice hours to complete the qualification. It is so easy to feel that the client who fails to attend the session is letting her down. It becomes a source of irritation instead of an aspect of the therapeutic process. Yet, the counsellor feels she owes the client unconditional, positive regard. The irritation cannot be admitted. The relationship can slip into incongruence. Concealed anger and frustration with the client produces in the therapist a rigid and unresponsive, self-judging and fearful presence. Acceptant self-awareness can only be achieved through recognition of both this process and of the legitimacy of the needs of the new therapist, although not at the client's cost.

Again, some beginning therapists 'require' their clients to express feelings. This satisfies their need to be empathic. Sometimes this comes from within, sometimes from the trainer who exalts empathy to the be-all and end-all of therapy. As a supervisor, I have heard, from time to time, new therapists disapproving of clients who endlessly re-tell their story, devoid of overt emotion – as if this were somehow invalid. The fears and requirements of the new therapist distort her listening to the client and so prevent the dance of psychotherapy.

Containing – beginnings and endings

When the first client walks into the room, it is a moot point as to who is the more anxious – client or therapist. Even as an experienced therapist, I still feel nervous at times. I meet the fantasy of my limitations and feel a drive to 'do well'. Meanwhile clients may be very unsure about what counselling and psychotherapy are, what they will be expected to do, and whether therapy will not just be another failure in their lives. The underlying anxiety of the therapist can manifest in a number of ways: will the client talk? Will I be liked? Will I 'get to' what the client feels? There is a paradox in play here. The anxiety is understandable enough. Yet the job is not to do well, not even to 'do it right'.

There are indeed things to think through about contracting:

- Do the clients understand the limits to confidentiality?
- Do the clients have some sense that they will not be 'done to' as they might be by their doctor, for example?
- Do the clients feel safe enough?
- What are the time limits if any?
- When will the work be reviewed?

The beginning and the ending are present together from the word go. All these practical things matter. However, the paradox is that they must not matter too much. Dave Mearns and Brian Thorne (2000) describe their own contracting style as 'sloppy'! This is not irresponsible, but a question of good balance. I take it from some personal knowledge of the undoubted competence of both Mearns and Thorne that 'sloppy' here encodes a potential criticism they fear from the up-tight, but also a willed decision in the face of this to relax and welcome the client. 'Sloppy' signals exactly that which is precise and balanced: clients can explore in contracting whatever safety issues they feel, while counsellors can take the risk of not being 'on guard' against imagined hazards. It is easier for either Mearns or Thorne than for the beginning counsellor to provide this level of containment.

The idea of containment is often associated with psychodynamic thinking. Yet, it is and has been at the heart of person-centred practice from the beginning. Patrick Casement describes the client's needs thus:

> In more human terms, what is needed is a form of holding, such as a mother gives to her distressed child. ... And it can be crucial for a patient to be thus held in order to recover, or to discover maybe for the first time, a capacity for managing life and life's difficulties without continued avoidance and suppression.
>
> (Casement, 1985: 133)

Rogers (1951) had described the containing process in terms of the therapist's addressing the client's fear and consequent dependency, through providing safety and openness sufficient to facilitate the exploration of painful or denied material.

Clients are often afraid of what they feel, or of the sense that this may spill out everywhere, or even of the belief that they ought to spill it out straight away. A warm but calm contracting, brief maybe, relaxed, checking for informed consent with respect, can help the client experience the possibility from the very beginning that the process of therapy is not a spilling out but a gentle receiving.

Assessing and relating

By now the reader may have a sense that beginning work as a therapist is about facing one's own self through a number of paradoxes. Some of these are about the anxiety inherent in being inexperienced. Others are inherent in the person-centred paradigm itself. Beginning work with any given client is first and foremost to enter into relating. Yet therapists are ethically bound to work within their competence and to be able to monitor and demonstrate this. The beginning therapist in any approach is most likely to need to consider referring on, on the grounds of competence, and yet will be under-experienced in assessing competence. Indeed it is understandable that beginning practitioners often fail to appreciate the power of the person-centred approach across a wide range of presenting mental health issues (Joseph and Worsley, 2005). It is tempting to say: 'I do not know about trauma,' or 'I have never worked with people who are anorexic' (Worsley, 2005).

We are obliged to assess our clients, and yet we work within an approach that has been thought to scorn assessment as being 'too expert'. For those who espouse the role of expert, assessment can be a complex and time-consuming technical exercise (Palmer and McMahon, 1997). Some within the person-centred and experiential field who incline to a more experiential or focusing orientation will also rely upon psychodiagnosis (see, for example, Greenberg et al, 1993, and Purton, 2004). Yet the classical, client-centred practitioner, along with others, will be chary of the notion of diagnosis.

In this there is a complex debate to be had (Cain, 2002: 385–414). Tony Merry (1999: 65) has set out crisply and accessibly the main objections to diagnosis:

- Diagnostic labels are often meaningless and poorly defined.
- Labels can become self-fulfilling prophecies.
- Diagnosis leads to the stereotyping of clients.

- It focuses on history rather than current states and attitudes.
- A preoccupation with pathology can lead a therapist to underestimate a client's strengths.
- Diagnostic categories tend to be biased according to gender and race.
- Diagnosis puts the therapist into an expert role, a role for which she is likely to have received inadequate training.
- Diagnostic labels can be beguilingly scientific, and can skew the therapeutic attitude.

Yet to reject the idea of assessment completely is a misunderstanding, and an ethically dangerous one at that. Paul Wilkins (2005) and Wilkins and Gill (2003) have explored what is meant by person-centred assessment. What is to be avoided is recourse to the medical model to label and hence, in mental health contexts, dehumanize the client (Sanders, 2005). It is not just an ethical issue but a technical one too. Each person is unique. People are unique in their processing, their ways of functioning and their life patterns. It is only when I let go of mental health stereotypes that I can see the true potential for growth in each client. However, assessment need not be about this classificatory nonsense.

Assessment happens *in relating itself*. It has at its heart the question: can this person and I enter into a therapeutic relationship? Is there psychological contact between us? It is both useful and reassuring to be able to recognize something of those parts of client process that are contact-impaired (Prouty et al, 2002). Yet, difficult clients must be taken to supervision. The ability to work with challenging client groups comes with experience.

Assessment is then an ongoing, therapy-long process. The skill is to listen to the client from two places. With most of my attention, I strive to accompany the client, but with a small part of my attention I seek to know what might get in the way of this contact. The beginning therapist is often working with senior colleagues whose model involves thorough, formal and sometimes paper-bound assessments in agencies that are increasingly risk-averse. It takes personal stability to maintain a practical commitment to person-centred assessment.

Intimacy and boundaries: or why what I feel is not open to judgement either

It is the quality of our presence that matters. There is a growing amount of research into what constitutes good therapeutic presence (Geller and Greenberg, 2002). Brian Thorne (2004) has explored in some depth the notion that tenderness is at the heart of person-centred therapy. He does not put it forward as what one might call a fourth therapeutic condition, but rather as a way of encapsulating the whole enterprise of person-centred therapy. It is Thorne's experience that tenderness given and received liberates us into a wholeness in which the other person is no longer the feared Other but a welcome and beloved companion.

Jan Hawkins (2002b) has argued fluently from her experience of working with those who have been sexually abused that for the client, remaining with the distress feels paradoxically safer than moving into new and therefore feared territory. Tenderness, intimacy is an essential quality in that it provides just enough safety for the frightened client. Similarly, clients whose fear leads them into challenging behaviour need the safety of intimacy before they can find a more functional pattern of relating to others (Hawkins, 2002a: 101–36).

Person-centred therapists are called to be available for intimacy with others. (Those of us who are shy can find this a strain at times; sometimes it is easier to be intimate with clients than the rest of humanity!) Intimacy requires that boundaries be thoroughly in place. It is not, I think, enough, to know that it is unethical to have sex with a client. Do you know why you would not have sex with a client? How do you relate to that part of you that keeps that boundary in place? If you see it as a necessary but tedious old puritan, how safe are you? How do you relate to that part of you that wants to have sex with a client? Do you deny it? Are you, or do you pretend to be, appalled by it? Perhaps it too needs your love and acceptance. It can be telling you something useful. If we aim at intimacy, it is not enough to know what is ethical.

Intimacy is that condition in which, while professional boundaries remain in place, tenderness, a sense of affection and even love (*agapé*) can be felt and appropriately expressed. Intimacy subsists in a respect for the hiddenness of others within themselves, and hence for the deep preciousness of their self-disclosure. Intimacy can encompass feelings and even fantasies of friendship and of the erotic, but always directed to the wholeness of the other. It is a powerful affirmation of the ability of the other person to enter into deep relating, into what Buber (1958) has termed the I–Thou relationship.

In order to be intimate with another person, I must know and accept all that I feel. Beginning therapists are sometimes afraid of the intensity of positive, and in particular erotic, feelings. They are also afraid of strong, negative feelings, mistaking them for a lack of unconditional positive regard. I do not want to be misheard here. It is perhaps rarely appropriate to disclose strong feelings without careful reflection. If I am going to work with strong feelings towards a client I would normally opt to work them through in supervision, and above all ask the perplexing question: why would my feelings be therapeutic for the client?

So why do strong feelings matter? I fancy my client. I can't stand her. I fear her. I feel huge affection for her. Beginning supervisees often betray a sense of guilt at such feelings even when they get around to expressing them. Yet my feelings too are not open to judgement. They are valid because they exist. They may be 'my stuff' or they may be of greater significance.

Strong, personal feelings of liking or disliking can, I believe, function in two separate ways. They can be informative. I recall a client whom I found very attractive – increasingly so, in fact. I noted this. My supervisor would not let me escape it, but nor was I to blame for it. After a number of sessions, my client recognized in herself that she used her sexuality habitually – and usually outside of her own awareness – as a bargaining power in order to cover up her radical lack of self-esteem (Cashdan, 1988: 72–3, 98–109). My erotic feelings – at least in part – were very informative. They mirrored how my client normally influenced men: a potentially destructive pattern.

Yet this view of my feelings as useful has limits. It can feel to me rather instrumental. My feelings about the client are not there to inform me, but to be part of me as I accompany another human being on her journey. My feelings are me. All of my feelings are me. I bring to any relationship even – perhaps especially – those feelings which are so readily seen as politically incorrect. I need to know and accept, albeit critically, all that I feel. Encounter, which is at the heart of therapy, involves two people learning to be willing to bring to each other their whole selves as fully as is warranted (Schmid, 1998).

The question of facing all that I feel is just one case of the need for therapists to face what they meet in their clients. Person-centred therapy has an existential dimension to it (Worsley, 2002: 145–77; Cooper, 2003). We meet all that makes up human existence. In others we will meet our sexuality, our mortality, our guilt, our shame, our joy – and so the list could go on. Unless we have acceptingly befriended our fears and hopes in our own existing, we will simply fail to hear as fully as we might our clients' experiencing.

Idealizing the client – or how to misunderstand the core conditions

The new practitioner is often prone to feel defensive towards the process of supervision. If the supervisor notes a feeling in the counsellor that the latter cannot accept in herself, then the observation will be experienced as judgement, condemnation. (And, indeed, some supervisors recycle their own insecurity as judgementalism!) Therapeutic practice often begins before the counsellor experiences a high level of self-acceptance through the personal development elements of training. Thus, as noted above, the new practitioner will often condemn or reject her own feelings towards the client.

In parallel to this, the client is often idealized. It is thought that empathy must involve not only a warm accompanying, but also a rejection of all negative feelings towards the client. Unconditional positive regard then becomes a requirement to disregard negative feelings. This is clearly a misunderstanding of the core conditions of therapy. Campbell Purton (1998) has argued cogently that all attempts to offer unconditional acceptance will flounder either upon the client's shortcomings or the counsellor's. True acceptance is not, Purton claims, an empirical opinion about the client, but rather is a stance in principle. It is to believe from the depths of one's being that humans deserve acceptance and love without reservation. For Purton, this is rooted in Buddhist philosophy, while for me it is an aspect of Christian faith. Each person-centred practitioner needs to locate the philosophical roots of their acceptance of others.

These roots should not be idealistic, in the sense that they function as just another 'ought'. In fact, they should call the practitioner away from an idealization of the client. When acceptance is absolute, transcendental, then our feelings, however messy, can co-exist with our acceptance.

I remember all too easily a client with whom I worked some eight years ago. He was objectionable, not because he was immoral or cruel, not because he was attacking or aggressive, but because he whined incessantly with self-pity. I did not like him. But then neither his wife nor his mother liked him. I pitied him. My desire to be a 'good' counsellor stopped me from being congruent. I was unable to express my dislike, for fear of being judgemental. In this I robbed him of the one thing that I could have given him: the knowledge that others' reactions to him were rooted in his way of presenting himself and his needs. His needs were legitimate enough. He needed to discover that he had choice in how to present them.

When the feelings that might get in the way of empathy and acceptance are allowed into full awareness, then congruence flourishes. In the end, I will be able to work through in supervision how and in what way – if at all – my negative feelings can appear in the therapy room in a way that is truly therapeutic. The offering of the core conditions should not lead to an idealization of the client or the relationship but should open up the fact that really good relationships can indeed be quite messy.

CONCLUSION

Each therapist begins work as a person with unique gifts and equally unique and valid personal needs. What binds each new practitioner with every other one is the need to do therapy with a reflective insight that links practice with personal awareness. Whether we feel exultant or fearful of our task, we can fool no one more treacherously than fooling ourselves.

REFERENCES

Buber, M. (1958). *I and Thou*. Edinburgh: T. and T. Clark.
Cain, D. (ed.) (2002). *Classics in the Person-Centred Approach*. Ross-on-Wye: PCCS Books.
Casement, P. (1985). *On Learning from the Patient*. London: Routledge.
Cashdan, S. (1988). *Object Relations Therapy: using the relationship*. New York: W.W. Norton.
Cooper, M. (2003). *Existential Therapies*. London: Sage.
Dryden, W., Horton, I. and Mearns, D. (1995). Client work. In W. Dryden, I. Horton and D. Mearns. *Issues in Professional Counsellor Training*. London: Cassell.
Geller, S. and Greenberg, L. (2002). Therapeutic presence: therapists' experience of presence in the psychotherapy encounter. *PCEP*, 1(1 and 2), winter, 71–86. Ross-on-Wye: PCCS Books.
Greenberg, L.S., Rice, L.N. and Elliott, R. (1993). *Facilitating Emotional Change: the moment by moment process*. New York: Guilford.
Hawkins, J. (2002a). *Voices of the Voiceless: person-centred approaches and people with learning difficulties*. Ross-on-Wye: PCCS Books.
Hawkins, J. (2002b). Paradoxical safety: barriers to the actualizing tendency,

and beyond. *Person-Centred Practice*, 10(1), spring, 21–6. Ross-on-Wye: PCCS Books.

Joseph and Worsley (2005). *Person-Centred Psychopathology: a positive psychology of mental health*. Ross-on-Wye: PCCS Books.

Mearns, D. (1997). *Person-Centred Counselling Training*. London: Sage.

Mearns, D. and Thorne, B. (1999). *Person-Centred Counselling in Action* (2nd edn). London: Sage.

Mearns, D. and Thorne, B. (2000). *Person-Centred Therapy Today: new frontiers in theory and practice*. London: Sage.

Merry, T. (1999). *Learning and Being in Person-Centred Counselling*. Ross-on-Wye: PCCS Books.

Natiello, P. (2001). *The Person-Centred Approach: a passionate presence*. Ross-on-Wye: PCCS Books.

Palmer, S and McMahon, G. (eds) (1997). *Client Assessment*. London: Sage.

Prouty, G., Van Werde, D. and Pörtner, M. (2002). *Pre-Therapy: reaching contact-impaired clients*. Ross-on-Wye: PCCS Books.

Purton, C. (1998). Unconditional positive regard and its spiritual implications. In B. Thorne and E. Lambers (eds), *Person-Centred Therapy: a European perspective* (pp. 23–37). London: Sage.

Purton, C. (2004). Differential response, diagnosis and the philosophy of the implicit. *PCEP*, 3(4), winter, 245–55. Ross-on-Wye: PCCS Books.

Rogers, C.R. (1951). *Client-Centered Therapy*. London: Constable.

Rogers, C.R. (1957). The necessary and sufficient conditions of therapeutic personality change. In *Journal of Consulting Psychology*, 21(2), 95–103.

Rogers, C.R. (1959). A theory of therapy, personality and interpersonal relationships, as developed in the client-centred framework. In S. Koch (ed.), *Psychology: a study of a science*. Volume 3. *Formulations of the Person and the Social Context* (pp. 184–256). New York: McGraw-Hill.

Rogers, C.R. (1969). *Freedom to Learn*. Columbus, Ohio: Charles E. Merrill.

Sanders, P. (2005). Principled and strategic opposition to the medicalization of distress and all of its apparatus. In S. Joseph and R. Worsley (eds), *Person-Centred Psychopathology: a positive psychology of mental health* (pp. 21–42). Ross-on-Wye: PCCS Books.

Schmid, P. (1998). 'Face-to-face': the art of encounter. In B. Thorne and E. Lambers (eds), *Person-Centred Therapy: a European perspective* (pp. 74–90). London: Sage.

Schön, D. (1987). *Educating the Reflective Practitioner*. San Francisco: Jossey-Bass.

Thorne, B. (2004). *The Quality of Tenderness*. Norwich: Norwich Centre.

Tudor, K. and Worrall, M. (2004). *Freedom to Practice: person-centred approaches to supervision*. Ross-on-Wye: PCCS Books.

Wilkins, P. (2005). Assessment and 'diagnosis' in person-centred therapy. In S. Joseph and R. Worsley (eds), *Person-Centred Psychopathology: a positive psychology of mental health* (pp. 128–45). Ross-on-Wye: PCCS Books.

Wilkins, P. and Gill, M. (2003). Assessment in person-centred therapy. *PCEP*, 2(3), Autumn, 172–87. Ross-on-Wye: PCCS Books.

Worsley, R.J. (2002). *Process Work in Person-Centred Therapy: phenomenological and existential perspectives*. Basingstoke: Palgrave MacMillan.

Worsley, R.J. (2005). Small-scale research as personal development for mental health professionals. In S. Joseph and R. Worsley (eds), *Psychopathology and the Person-Centred Approach* (pp. 337–47). Ross-on-Wye: PCCS Books.

Ethics in Practice in Person-Centred Therapy

26

Suzanne Keys and Gillian Proctor

Introduction

Ethics is a fluid, internalized and vital part of our everyday lives, where the personal and professional are intertwined. It is about how we act in the world on the basis of what we value and believe. Ethical decisions are triggered by the fact that we exist in relationships, not only with others but also with ourselves and our environments. The complexity of ethics stems both from the multiplicity of our relationships and from the influences of a cocktail of morals, values, principles and beliefs; which themselves come from a range of cultural, social, political, spiritual and personal sources. Moreover, we make our ethical decisions based on a range of ways of knowing, including rationality, emotion, bodily sense and intuition.

Given this complexity, it is hardly surprising that the area of ethics is one where questions often have no single answer and fixed rules cannot be made to fit every situation. Nevertheless, ethics does involve making decisions, which inevitably entail assessments, judgements and choices about what is 'right' and 'wrong'. In the writing of this chapter we have been challenged by our tendency to be prescriptive and write how we think a person-centred therapist should be. This is the tension inherent in ethics: how to balance what feels right for me as an individual with what may be right for the other or the common good. How do we navigate between the 'soggy sands of relativism' and the 'cold rocks of dogmatism' (Blackburn, 2000: 26)? We suggest by being as aware as we can be of the struggles inherent in the ethical decision-making process, by being open to the range of influences on the process, by being prepared to be challenged and change and by trying to articulate the process as clearly as we can.

Accountability, risk-management and regulation are terms from a culture where external standards, conformity and suspicion prevail over uniqueness, humaneness and trust. They are nevertheless crucial issues to address in terms of our ethical practice as therapists. To be accountable is to be able to articulate our ethics in a meaningful way to others, to be able to communicate what we are thinking, feeling, sensing and intuiting about issues and how we use this to make decisions. Risk-management involves being aware of the inevitable risks of being in relationship with another person and being open and honest about our fears and responsibilities. Regulation entails openness to the ongoing self and peer assessment emphasized in person-centred training and practice.

Our aim in this chapter is to open up the territory of ethics in the practice of person-centred therapy and to encourage practitioners to find their own ethical path based on their own and others' experiences and learnings. We have connected our thinking with other writers familiar to us in the person-centred therapy field but we are aware that ethics is implicit in most writing within the approach. Ethics comes alive through articulation, discussion and dialogue. It is our hope that this chapter stimulates such engagement and exploration.

We begin by looking at ethics in the context of therapy, then focus on some specific moral principles from the perspective of person-centred theory. We then explore how we might know we are practising ethically and finish with an example of ethics in practice, which brings together some of the issues we've highlighted.

Ethics in therapy

As therapy has become increasingly professionalized it has tended towards enshrining ethics in rules or codes of practice within regulatory bodies involving quasi-judicial complaints procedures. The claim for this process is that it protects the client. In fact, research and experience have not shown that it diminishes the amount of abuse or harm caused by professionals (House and Totton, 1997; Bates and House, 2003). The danger with rules-governed ethics is that a therapist can become so concerned with an external locus of evaluation and fearful of censure that she loses touch with a sense of her own internal ability to evaluate and make decisions. Strict adherence to codes takes responsibility for the relationship away from the two people involved, which leads to unthinking, unaware and therefore unethical practice. On the other hand collective frameworks and guidelines can be vital as a point of reference for therapists in their decision-making processes. Any collective engagement with ethics needs to be congruent with the values of therapy. These include openness to process, reflection and enquiry; all of which require the acknowledgement of mistakes and conflicting view points, and a commitment to hearing and responding to a range of perspectives. An example of an organization working in this way is the Independent Practitioners Network (IPN; www.i-p-n.org). The IPN offers not only a non-hierarchical framework for practitioners to self- and peer-assess but also a mechanism for processing complaints through mediation and conflict resolution. It is also useful to see how personal and professional ethics fit in with international ethical statements such as the Universal Declaration of Human Rights (www.udhr.org; Keys, 2000) and The Earth Charter (www.earthcharter.org).

Ethics in therapy has traditionally been based on a primary ethic of autonomy, one of the four principles forming the traditional approach to moral philosophy and biomedical ethics known as the ethics of justice (Beauchamp and Childress, 1994 in Bond, 2000; Banks, 1995). Bond, a key writer and thinker in the field of professional therapy ethics in the UK, has considered the significance of a recent shift to a primary ethic of 'relational trust' in therapy. This move parallels the feminist critique of the ethics of justice as being focused on individuals and not concerned with humans as social and relational beings (Banks, 1995). Bond suggests that an ethic of relational trust requires 'the quality of the relationship to be sufficient to withstand the major ethical challenges of therapy, which arise from inequality, difference, uncertainty and risk' (Bond, 2004a: 3). It involves constant awareness and monitoring of the idiosyncrasies of each changing relationship.

In what follows, we consider the four principles of the ethics of justice (i.e. respect for autonomy, beneficence, non-maleficence and justice) alongside ethics of anti-oppressive practice and relational trust in the context of person-centred practice and theory. In order to illuminate the complexities of decision making from different ethical principles we mention a few of the possible issues which may arise in therapy situations. These examples are not intended to be in any way exhaustive or conclusive. They are the kinds of dilemmas that might be discussed in supervision with a trusted therapist where empathy, unconditional regard and congruence are present, where each situation can be explored in its uniqueness, where vulnerability can be revealed and mistakes challenged. This is a vital component of ethical practice.

Ethics of justice: principle of respect for autonomy

Rogers' focus on the autonomy of the client, embedded as it is in a phenomenological approach to therapy, was, and is, challenging to those who want to see the therapist as the expert who will diagnose and 'cure' clients. In person-centred theory it is the clients who are the experts in their world, the clients who lead the process of therapy and who have the resources and capacity to grow constructively and fulfil their potential, given the right conditions. At work here is an underlying belief in a potentiality rather than a deficiency model of human nature (Mearns and Thorne, 2000: 33) and in the organism's tendency to actualize towards autonomy (Rogers, 1959: 196; Tudor and Worrall, 2006: 51). It is a biological force and thus 'an amoral concept' (Mearns and Thorne, 2000: 181). This belief leads to the central, and vigorously debated, principle in person-centred therapy of non-directivity. Grant sees non-directivity in clear ethical terms, as being about 'the morally best way of doing therapy'. Principled, as opposed to instrumental, non-directivity honours a primary ethic of autonomy, 'essentially an expression of respect' with no preconceived idea about outcome (Grant, 2002).

A focus on the primary ethic of autonomy in person-centred therapy has led to criticisms about it being an individualistic approach (e.g. Proctor and Napier, 2004) which does not consider the consequences of actions on others, does not acknowledge the relationship and obscures awareness of the wider social and political contexts.

Consider a scenario where a client does not attend a therapy session and does not contact the therapist. If autonomy is prioritized, the therapist may decide not to contact the client. However, such strict prioritizing does not take into account the relational aspects of the therapy, including the quality of the relationship, the level of trust, the importance of the therapist demonstrating his or her caring of the client and an awareness of the power dynamics. These considerations may lead to the therapist contacting the client.

Ethics of justice: principle of doing good or beneficence

Beneficence is a commitment to doing good. It is often explained as promoting the client's well-being or acting in the best interests of the client based on professional assessment (BACP, 2002). It is seen as particularly important if the client's capacity for autonomy is limited. In consideration of ethical dilemmas in therapy, the principles of autonomy and of doing good are often presented as being in conflict: the first based on trusting the client, the second based on trusting the therapist to know best.

In person-centred therapy, what is understood to be doing good is to respect the client's autonomy such that the principles of autonomy and beneficence are in accordance. An inability to establish psychological contact – one of the pre-requisites for therapy to happen – could be seen as a threat to the client's capacity for autonomy within the relationship. Pre-Therapy (Prouty et al, 2002) is a way of working to establish contact with those who might be seen, for example, as 'psychotic' or 'dissociated' or as having 'severe learning disabilities'. This way of working aims to maximize the chances for a client to make the best autonomous decisions possible. In a situation where there is a risk of harm to self or others then all aspects of the relationship and context need to be taken into consideration, including the therapist's responsibilities towards the client, herself and society.

Consider a scenario where a client is feeling suicidal and the therapist, despite exploring the issues during the session, is left concerned for the client's safety after the end of an appointment. Does she contact the client or another person such as a doctor or family member or does she wait until the next appointment? Does she trust and prioritize the client's autonomy or does beneficence here mean 'life at all costs' even the cost of the breakdown of relational trust? Personal values and beliefs about life and death play a part, as do the limits of the therapist herself, knowing what she can and cannot live with. Her assessment of the quality of the relationship, her empathic understanding and acceptance of the range of the client and also of any systemic or institutional context will all come into play in this decision.

Ethics of justice: principle of doing no harm or non-maleficence

Non-maleficence is a commitment to avoid harm and is often referred to as avoiding exploitation in therapy. Bond suggests that 'professional ethics are particularly, but not exclusively, concerned with the moral challenges arising from the power imbalance between the service provider and the recipient' (2004b: 4). It is therapists' responsibility to be aware of the ways in which they could use 'power-over' (Proctor, 2002: 94) the client and to avoid doing so.

By prioritizing the principle of respect for autonomy in order to ensure therapy meets the client's and not the therapist's needs, person-centred therapy takes the principle of avoiding exploitation very seriously. However, Proctor (2002) suggests that in emphasizing the person-to-person equality of the therapy relationship, person-centred therapists are in danger of minimizing or obscuring the power still inherent in the roles of therapist and client. To ensure potential for harm is noticed and taken seriously, it is important that person-centred therapists do not emphasize the agency of individuals at the expense of appreciating the impact of structures of power on our lives.

For example, a therapist may want to respect the client's autonomy by answering a client's question about what the therapist would do in a given situation. However the therapist may be wise to also consider how much authority the client invests in the role of the therapist. Although trying not to behave as an expert, the therapist may still need to check whether the client perceives the therapist's response as the 'right' thing to do.

On the other hand, fear of doing harm to a client can lead to risk-averse practice, particularly in increasingly litigious societies. Therapists can become paralysed by fears of harming clients or of doing 'the wrong thing' and of being sued. This can lead them to withdraw, disengage and adopt rigid boundaries in a bid to stay 'safe' and keep the client 'safe'. This under-involvement (Mearns and Thorne, 2000; Proctor, 2004) is harmful to both therapist and client as it denies the opportunity for person-to-person relating, which lies at the heart of person-centred therapy. It is vital to listen, read and learn from clients' experiences of therapy, particularly those who have felt harmed and abused in their therapy relationships (e.g. Heyward, 1994; Ironside, 2003; Bates, 2006). Themes which emerge from such accounts are the clients' desires for a demystifying of therapy; for more co-operative, collaborative and co-creative relationships; for more recognition of the complexities of the interdependent nature of therapy; and for more human contact and warmth. Abuse, according to Heyward, 'is not simply a matter of touching people wrongly. It is, as basically, a failure to make right-relation, a refusal to touch people rightly' (Heyward, 1994: 10).

Ethics of justice: principle of justice

The principle of justice refers to treating all people equally and can be applied as the fair and impartial treatment of all clients and the provision of adequate services (BACP, 2002). This concept may conflict with a phenomenological approach where each therapy relationship is unique. Person-centred therapy cannot be said to be 'applied equally'. Similarly, the notion of 'impartiality' and the principle of justice has been critiqued by feminists as being based on a rational idea of ethics, which does not account for the emotional links or attachments between people in relationships (Banks, 1995). However, it may be useful to interpret the principle of justice as saying that, within the awareness that each relationship will be different, the person-centred therapist has a responsibility to be equally open to a therapeutic relationship with each client.

This principle also indicates a responsibility for person-centred therapists to be aware of issues of access to their services and to allocate services without discrimination or judgement. This requires an awareness of discrimination in society and how this may affect access; people are not all equal in their situations. For example, have therapists considered access to therapy for people who use wheelchairs, who are visually impaired or who require interpreters? This awareness changes an interpretation of the principle of justice to suggest that situated knowledge rather than impartiality is necessary for just or fair treatment of people. This is the basis of an ethic of anti-oppressive practice.

Ethic of anti-oppressive practice

To act from this ethic a therapist needs to be continually aware of how, for example, the social, cultural and religious environments of both therapist and client create a complex interplay of power dynamics within the relationship. Here is where person-centred therapists need to acknowledge the power of their role as therapists, in addition to other structural positions of power they may hold. The key consideration is about being aware of how this power may become oppressive to the client and trying to ensure this does not happen. This demands an openness on the therapists' part to exploring their outer as well as their inner worlds, to hearing feedback as to how they are perceived by others, to being honest and challenging their fears, assumptions and prejudices, to acknowledging their powerfulness and powerlessness and to being ready to change.

An able-bodied, white, Christian therapist working in the UK with a person who is physically impaired and from a minority culture and religion, for example, needs to be aware of how they might each experience power in relationships differently and how this may be enacted in their relationship. Any ideas of what empowerment means must come from the client rather than any preconceived ideas of the therapist. Therapists' continual mindfulness of their own prejudices and assumptions is important, as is the ability to engage pro-actively with the client on these issues (Keys, 2006).

Ethic of relational trust

Relational trust, according to Bond, is 'situational' and:

requires continual ethical mindfulness, active responsibility and accountability as situations arise. ... Ethical education and awareness are paramount rather than excessive reliance on rules. ... The quality of relationship is foregrounded for active reflection in the therapeutic process and is a basis for client's innovations in feeling, thinking and acting.

(Bond, 2004a: 3)

Meta-analyses in psychotherapy research consistently indicate that, regardless of theoretical approach, it is the quality of the relationship which is usually the key healing agent (Mearns and Cooper, 2005), pointing to the importance of an ethic of relational trust. One of the relational factors which has been found to be 'probably effective' is the 'willingness and ability to repair breakdowns'. This is very significant in the context of ethics because it underlines the importance of the engagement of both therapist and client in facing difficult and challenging dilemmas in their relationship. An ethic of relational trust leads to an emphasis on mediation and dialogue in cases of relationship breakdowns. Totton (2001) suggests most complaints would be avoided if we focused on how to repair breakdowns through acknowledgement of hurt and dialogue.

Recently, person-centred theorists have focused on the relationship rather than on the therapist or client individually. Tudor and Worral (2006) write of the organism's tendency towards homonomy or belonging as well as autonomy. Schmid (2001) sees the core of person-centred therapy in ethical terms: a response to the call of the other, an act of solidarity and response-ability. He points out that a 'person' is not just an individual, but is also defined in relation to others. Barrett-Lennard (2005) writes about 'client-centred relational psychotherapy' and Mearns and Cooper (2005) about 'two-person-centred therapy'. This relationship-centred therapy leads to ethical developments where interdependence and interconnectedness are acknowledged and valued (e.g. Thorne, 2002). Relational and social factors are given more weight and therapy moves beyond the private and the individual, becoming not only an ethical but also a political, spiritual and existential activity.

If we look at Rogers' 1959 conditions for a therapeutic process, contact and perception (Wyatt and Sanders, 2002) are as important as the often overemphasized 'core conditions' of therapist congruence, empathy and unconditional positive regard. They give the context for the conditions as relational concepts or principles. Congruence, empathy and unconditional positive regard within an ethic of relational trust are seen as more than attitudes held by the therapist towards the client but as the very fabric of what makes a relationship safe, trustworthy, healing and therapeutic. They come alive through reciprocation and a working together of therapist and client. Thus, an ethical person-centred therapist no longer sees herself as offering the conditions but as being continually mindful of the quality of the relationship being co-created between herself and the client.

The ethics of congruence arise from the tensions inherent in the interplay of the therapist's openness to self and her ability to acknowledge and articulate this meaningfully in relationship. She needs a commitment to challenging what may be denied, distorted or subceived within herself, but also to being in tune with how congruent the relationship is with the client and how truthfully she is being perceived by the client, and whether and how to verbalise any of this. This suggests that self-awareness, courage, openness, honesty, truthfulness and integrity are important values to the person-centred practitioner. I am working ethically when I am in 'right' or congruent relationship with my self and the other in all our fullness and complexity. This can have a political aspect for those who see the person-centred approach as a way of being. Every aspect of living is seen as needing to be congruent with core values and principles. This may lead to political activism as in, for example, Rogers' work for peace and reconciliation, which led to him being nominated for a Nobel Peace Prize. Likewise, incongruent practice and living can be seen as unethical. For Embleton Tudor et al 'the higher the level of congruence between an individual practitioner's personal values and the values that underpin the approach to which she subscribes, the more effective a practitioner she will be' (2004: 20).

The ethics of empathy in the context of relational trust in therapy requires a therapist to be able to be congruent, self-empathic and self-accepting whilst also being able to be in the world of another person. There is tension here between self-awareness and self-forgetfulness: being present to oneself and to the other. Being empathic to different worlds extends to the range of external and internal environments both therapist and client occupy. Some of the values implied in the ethics of empathy are those associated with unconditional positive regard: care, respect and humility.

The tension inherent in the ethics of unconditional positive regard lies in the paradox that change happens through acceptance. It is a radical ethic in terms of relationship in that it requires a therapist to accept all parts of a client equally, even the client's 'not for growth' parts (Mearns and Thorne, 2000) and to see everyone as worthy of the utmost respect or, as Thorne (2003) puts it from a spiritual perspective, as 'infinitely beloved'. This is equally true of the therapist's attitude to herself and, in fact, it could be seen as an ethical imperative for the therapist to work on her self-love as much as on the nature of her love for her client (Thorne, 2002: 23).

A theoretical development of unconditional positive regard which puts it firmly in the context of an ethic of relational trust is the notion that as human beings, alongside our 'universal', 'pervasive and persistent' need (Rogers, 1959: 223) for unconditional positive regard, there is also a basic need to express unconditional positive regard to others (Brazier, 1993; Thorne, 2002) and to have that received. This highlights the significance of a therapist respecting and responding to a client's need to express their caring or loving within the therapy relationship. This challenges some of the long-standing 'ethical' rules in the psychotherapy world, which, for example, consider receiving gifts from a client as always transgressing professional boundaries.

Mutuality is a characteristic of an ethic of relational trust. It is the process whereby both therapist and client are open to being changed in the relationship (Jordan et al, 2004: 3). It implies 'some reciprocity in the relationship between therapist and client ... as regards understanding, power and humanity' (Tudor and Merry, 2002: 86) although it does not deny the asymmetrical nature of the therapy relationship (Aron, 1996: xi). Proctor (2004, 2007) emphasizes the practitioner's awareness of her own needs and limitations in an ethic of mutuality. In this context, a therapist is aware of her limitations as a basis for her boundaries and can acknowledge these to the client whilst at the same time being able to negotiate co-created boundaries specific to the relationship that are open to re-negotiation.

The therapist aims to respond honestly and with care to the needs of clients whilst being aware and also prioritizing her own needs. Can she be flexible and dynamic in arrangements with clients and open to reconsidering any decision made concerning a therapy contract, in terms of timing of sessions or any other factors? Therapists do have restrictions on how much they can offer clients, perhaps due to the services they work within and due to personal limitations: emotional, practical and financial. However, the key here is for therapists to be honest about these limitations, and to work with the client to negotiate between each of their needs. So, for example, if a client wants more frequent or longer sessions a therapist is clear about why she can or can't do that. Equally, if she is unsure about what she feels in the moment she can express this and take time to think about or discuss her response with her supervisor.

How do I know I'm an ethical practitioner?

To keep asking this question is in itself an indication of ethical practice. It is in the ongoing openness to others through questioning and exploration – with clients, in supervision and in personal and professional development – that we can trust that we are practising ethically. This questioning and reflecting on practice is not the same as self-doubt and self-criticism, which can be undermining and disabling. Likewise, living with the tension between striving for clarity and the acceptance of ambiguity need not be the same as crippling indecision. For a reflective practitioner the emphasis is on growing self-awareness, ongoing openness to challenge and learning and a willingness to embody theory idiosyncratically. A key question to ask is how in touch we are with what may be on the edge of our awareness and those areas of our lives where we deny, distort and subceive experiences. An example of this is sexuality, an area where the conditionality of many societies and cultures means that there are often incongruencies between our organismic experiencing and what we allow into awareness. It is essential that as therapists we are aware of the sexual component in our therapy relationships and are open to discussing this in supervision. If it is denied then the resulting incongruence is unethical and we become untrustworthy as practitioners (Schmid, 1996).

A charge levelled against person-centred therapists might be that in trusting ourselves and the client and in valuing idiosyncratic practice (Keys, 2003) we practise an 'anything goes approach' where the individual's unique understanding outweighs any external codes or constraints. This makes no sense in the context of relationship and the definition we have given of ethics in this chapter, as decisions are never taken from a purely individualistic point of view. In person-centred theory the organismic valuing process 'describes an ongoing process in which values are never fixed or rigid, but experiences are being accurately symbolized and continually and freshly valued in terms of the satisfactions organismically experienced' (Rogers, 1959: 210). These 'satisfactions' must be seen in a context where there is social mediation of the actualizing tendency (Mearns and Thorne, 2000) which takes into account the constraints of external factors and social realities (Tudor and Worrall, 2006). Therefore, to be ethical as a person-centred therapist demands that a high degree of self-awareness is grounded in an awareness of context. The awareness, for example, of the power differential inherent in the therapy relationship and the prioritizing of a client's needs would suggest that behaving sexually with a client is never likely to be therapeutic. An awareness of the institutional or systemic contexts we work in also informs how we make ethical decisions with clients.

An example of ethics in practice

A long-term client is very distressed during a session and talks particularly about how alone she feels. At the end of the session, the therapist wants to reach out to touch the client. In the moment she may touch the client or let her know that she'd like to do it either verbally or non-verbally. What are the possible ethical considerations when reflecting on such a decision-making process?

From a primary ethic of autonomy, the therapist would consider that it is important that the client must decide whether she wants to be touched or not. Consideration of this principle alone would suggest that the therapist should not touch the client unless this touch is initiated by the client.

From an ethic of anti-oppressive practice, however, the therapist is aware of the dynamics of power in the therapy relationship. The client has let the therapist know that she finds it difficult to trust anyone, having had much previous experience of being judged and treated with no respect. The therapist is aware that the client feels unable to ask for anything in most of her relationships, feeling unworthy of care, and feels guilty using the therapist's time, so it is unlikely that she would feel able to ask for physical comfort even if she wanted this. She is also aware that the client's experiences of belonging to oppressed groups make it even more unlikely for her to ask for care.

From an ethic of relational trust, the therapist considers her decision in the context of their relationship. What is happening in the immediacy of the relationship on that day? What has gone before? What is the quality of the relationship? Can they talk about what is happening in the relationship? Would the relationship withstand it if the therapist's touch is inappropriate? Would not touching be a denial of the quality of the relationship? What is the sexual dynamic in the relationship? Could the touch be misinterpreted as a sexual advance?

The therapist considers her own emotional responses within the relationship. Given the level of the client's distress does she herself want some kind of comfort in this situation? She is aware of where her own views on physical touch come from in terms of her history and experiences and the value she places on touch. Is she responding to the client's emotional need which she is aware of through her empathic experiencing of the client both on this occasion and previously? Are there conditions attached to her touch?

To assess these questions and the risks involved, the therapist relies on her own self-awareness in the context of her relationship with her client (congruence) and her unconditional positive regard and empathic understanding of the client, her self and the relationship. She considers external factors to further evaluate her decision. What would her supervisor's response be? If she is a member of a professional body what can their ethical framework add to her considerations? Her ethical processing continues after the session as she writes up her notes and discusses it with her supervisor.

She remains open to the fact that in another session at another time with the same client her response may well be different. This experience does not therefore become a rule or a generality; thereby allowing for the fluidity of the person, the relationship and the process.

CONCLUSION

This chapter has begun to explore ethics as a dynamic, complex and evolving process of making decisions about how to be and act in person-centred therapy relationships. Ethics in therapy is particularly important because the role of the therapist comes with a position of power and with this power comes responsibility and accountability. We have considered different ethical principles from a person-centred perspective and explored a possible shift from a primary ethic of autonomy to one of relational trust, whilst not negating the importance of autonomy as one of the key principles in person-centred therapy. We have also highlighted the importance of a consideration of an ethic of anti-oppressive practice. We suggest that a considered approach of moral pluralism, an ability to live with ambiguity, fear and risk, an acknowledgement of limitations and failures and a commitment to continually analyse our therapy relationships from an ethical perspective will provide the foundation for becoming ethically mindful, reflective, responsible practitioners.

REFERENCES

Aron, L. (1996). *A Meeting of Minds: mutuality in psychoanalysis*. Hillsdale: Analytic Press.

BACP (British Association for Counselling and Psychotherapy) (2002) *Ethical Framework for Good Practice in Counselling and Psychotherapy*. Rugby, England: BAPC. Available online at www.bacp.co.uk/ethical_framework/.

Banks, S. (1995). *Ethics and Values in Social Work*. London: Macmillan.

Barrett-Lennard, G.T. (2005) *Relationship at the Centre: healing in a troubled world*. London: Whurr.

Bates, Y. (ed.) (2006). *Shouldn't I Be Feeling Better By Now? Client views of therapy*. Basingstoke: Palgrave Macmillan.

Bates, Y. and House, R. (2003). *Ethically Challenged Professions: enabling innovation and diversity in psychotherapy and counselling*. Ross-on-Wye: PCCS Books.

Blackburn, S. (2000). *Ethics: a very short introduction*. Oxford: Oxford University Press.

Bond, T. (1993/2000). *Standards and Ethics for Counselling in Action*. London: Sage.

Bond, T. (2004a). *Professional ethics: creating a secure base*. Handout from lecture at AUCC conference.

Bond, T. (2004b). An introduction to the ethical guidelines for counselling and psychotherapy. *Counselling and Psychotherapy Research*, 4(2): 4–9.

Brazier, D. (1993). The necessary condition is love: going beyond self in the person-centred approach. In D. Brazier (ed.), *Beyond Carl Rogers* (pp.72–91). London: Constable.

Embleton Tudor, L., Keemar, K., Tudor, K., Valentine, J. and Worrall, W. (2004). *The Person-Centred Approach: a contemporary introduction*. Houndmills: Palgrave Macmillan.

Grant, B. (1990/2002). Principled and instrumental non-directiveness in person-centred and client-centred therapy. In D.J. Cain (ed.), *Classics in the Person-Centred Approach* (pp. 371–7). Ross-on-Wye: PCCS Books.

Heyward, C. (1994). *When Boundaries Betray Us: beyond illusions of what is ethical in therapy and in life*. New York: HarperCollins.

House, R. and Totton, N. (eds) (1997). *Implausible Professions: arguments for pluralism and autonomy in psychotherapy and counselling*. Ross-on-Wye: PCCS Books.

Ironside, V. (2003). Experiences of therapy. *Ipnosis* (an independent journal for practitioners) (11), 4–7, and (12), 4–6.

Jordan, J.V., Walker, M. and Hartline, L.M. (eds) (2004). *The Complexity of Connection: writings from the Stone Center's Jean Baker Miller Training Institute*. New York: Guilford.

Keys, S. (2000). The person-centred counsellor as an agent of human rights. In T. Merry (ed.), *The BAPCA Reader*. Ross-on-Wye: PCCS Books.

Keys, S. (ed.) (2003). *Idiosyncratic Person-Centred Therapy: from the personal to the universal*. Ross-on-Wye: PCCS Books.

Keys, S. (2006). Disability, multi-dimensionality and love: the politics of a counselling relationship in further education. In Proctor et al (eds), *Politicizing the Person-Centred Approach: an agenda for social change*. Ross-on-Wye: PCCS Books.

Mearns, D. and Cooper, M. (2005). *Working at Relational Depth in Counselling Psychotherapy*. London: Sage.

Mearns, D. and Thorne, B. (2000). *Person-Centred Therapy Today: new frontiers in theory and practice*. London: Sage.

Proctor, G. (2002). *The Dynamics of Power in Counselling and Psychotherapy: ethics, practice and politics*. Ross-on-Wye: PCCS Books.

Proctor, G. (2004). Disordered boundaries? In G. Proctor and C. Shaw (eds), *Asylum Magazine for Democratic Psychiatry*, 14(3), 24–5.

Proctor, G. (2007). Disordered boundaries?: a critique of borderline personality disorder. In H. Spandler and .S Warner (eds), *Beyond Fear and Control: working with young people who self harm: a 42nd Street reader*. Ross-on-Wye: PCCS books.

Proctor, G., Cooper, M., Sanders, P., Malcolm, B. (eds) (2006). *Politicizing the Person-Centred Approach: an agenda for social change*. Ross-on-Wye: PCCS Books.

Proctor, G. and Napier, M.B. (eds) (2004). *Encountering Feminism: intersections between feminism and the person-centred approach*. Ross-on-Wye: PCCS Books.

Prouty, G., Portner, M. and Van Werde, D. (2002). *Pre-Therapy: reaching contact impaired clients*. Ross-on-Wye: PCCS Books.

Rogers, C.R. (1959). A theory of therapy, personality, and interpersonal relationships as developed in the client-centred framework. In S. Koch (ed.), *Psychology: a study of science*. Volume 3. *Formulations of the person and the social context* (pp. 184–256). New York: McGraw Hill.

Schmid, P. (2001). Acknowledgement: the art of responding: dialogical and ethical perspectives on the challenge of unconditional relationships in therapy and beyond. In J.D. Bozarth and P. Wilkins (eds), *UPR* (pp. 49–64). Ross-on-Wye: PCCS Books.

Thorne, B. (2002). *The Mystical Power of Person-Centred Therapy: hope beyond despair*. London: Whurr Publishers.

Thorne, B. (2003). *Infinitely Beloved*. London: Darton, Longman, Todd.

Totton, N. (2001). Scapegoats and sacred cows: towards good enough conflict resolution. In R Casemore (ed.), *Surviving Complaints against Counselors and Psychotherapists* (pp. 99–110). Ross-on-Wye: PCCS Books.

Tudor, K. and Merry, T. (2002). *Dictionary of Person-Centred Psychology*. London: Whurr.

Tudor, K and Worrall, M. (2006). *Person-Centred Therapy: a clinical philosophy*. London: Routledge.

Wyatt, G. and Sanders, P. (eds) (2002). *Contact and Perception*. Ross-on-Wye: PCCS Books.

27

A Person-Centred Perspective on Supervision

Elke Lambers

This chapter explores supervision as a facilitative relationship focused on the development and maintenance of the counsellor's ability to relate congruently and at depth to clients.

Supervision as a professional activity: generic models of supervision

Most person-centred counsellors have experience of being in supervision. For many, supervision is a compulsory requirement only during training, but in some countries, counsellors are required to have supervision throughout their working lives as an ethical requirement and as a condition for professional accreditation or legal registration. For instance, in the United States supervision is an integral element of counselling training programmes, but there is no formal requirement for ongoing supervision after the training period; in Austria, where counselling and psychotherapy are regulated, being in continuing supervision is a legal requirement for registration. In the UK, therapists who are members of national counselling and psychotherapy associations are required to have regular supervision while practising.

Much of the literature and research about supervision for counselling and psychotherapy is written from a generic perspective, seeking to define the purpose, function and practice of supervision in terms of models which are applicable to supervision across different therapeutic orientations. There is an emphasis on developing an overarching framework for understanding and describing the supervision process and the supervision relationship, encouraging a movement away from 'approach specific' supervision which would only be of use to the 'purist' therapist (Page and Wosket, 2001: 31). Carroll (1996) suggests that supervision requires a theoretical understanding in its own right and that supervision demands different skills from counselling. He wants to 'move individuals away from counselling bound models of supervision [ie. ones in which supervision is closely allied to the counselling orientation of the supervisor] to developmental and social role models of supervision [which start with the learning situation of the supervisee]' (Carroll, 1996: 4).

While the generic literature on supervision generally accepts the importance of supervision for self-development and as support for the therapist, the primary focus is on the work with the client, 'to maintain adequate standards of counselling' (BACP, 2004) or to 'enhance the therapeutic value of the counselling process' (Page and Wosket, 2001: 41). Here, the growth of the therapeutic competence of the supervisee is the secondary purpose. The supervisor has a responsibility to monitor the work of the supervisee, and Carroll goes even further when he states that the client should be 'at the centre of supervision' and that 'counselling bound models of supervision can often stress aspects of the counselling work that ignore the client and concentrate on what is happening to the supervisee' (Carroll, 1996: 42).

Perspectives on person-centred supervision

A central feature in all writing about supervision from a person-centred perspective is the focus *on the experience of the therapist* and on the development of the therapeutic ability of the supervisee through the *supervision relationship*. In contrast to the generic approaches, there is a strong emphasis on the importance of congruence between the theoretical orientation of supervisor and supervisee (Hackney and Goodyear, 1984; Schmid, 1997). 'The supervisor needs to be aware of the person-centred approach at practical and theoretical depth' (Mearns, 1997: 84), or as Patterson states even more strongly: 'supervisor and supervisee need to be committed to the same theory' (1983: 21). In order to support in the supervisee the development and integration of the therapeutic qualities of empathy, acceptance and congruence, these same qualities need to be present in the supervision relationship. In that sense, supervision provides a model for the supervisee's practice: not by teaching the supervisor's way of doing therapy but, consistent with the theory of person-centred therapy, by offering a 'growth promoting environment that will enable the supervisee to find his or her own style' (Villas-Bowen, 1986: 296). Villas-Bowen distinguishes this approach to supervision, which puts an emphasis on the development of the supervisee's locus of evaluation, from 'form-oriented supervision', where the supervisor has a commitment to a particular form of person-centred therapy and discourages styles of expression that do not fit that model. Such an approach, in its concern with the preservation of a 'pure form' of person-centred therapy, is fundamentally inconsistent with a basic philosophical principle of the person-centred approach: the trust in the capacity for self-direction and self-determination (1986: 293).

Much of the early writing on person-centred supervision, particularly in the United States, is centred on supervision with trainee therapists and students (Rogers, 1942, 1951; Patterson, 1964, 1983; Rice, 1980). The supervisor frequently also takes on the role of trainer, and the challenge for the person-centred supervisor is to integrate developmental, facilitative elements with teaching and evaluative responsibilities in the supervision relationship.

Rogers was very aware of the importance of supervision; it was an integral part of his work with students. Writing about the training of therapists, he states that by providing the supervisee with an accepting, empathic and genuine atmosphere, the supervisor creates a climate in which the supervisee can explore feelings, blocks and difficulties that come up while learning to be a therapist (Rogers, 1951). His focus in supervision is firmly on the supervisee: 'to help the therapist grow in self-confidence and to grow in understanding of himself or herself, and to grow in understanding of the therapeutic process' (Hackney and Goodyear, 1984: 283). Patterson takes a similar view: emphasizing the importance of the basic conditions of empathic understanding, respect, genuineness and concreteness in the supervision relationship, his view of supervision is that it is concerned with the 'development of sensitivity in the student, of understanding of therapeutic attitudes' (Patterson, 1983: 25). He describes supervision as being concerned with the 'actual relationship between the supervisee and the client, and not concerned with diagnosis or conceptualization of the internal dynamics of the client' (1983: 24). His focus is on the experience of the supervisee, rather than on technique or on the learning of specific responses to clients.

Rice (1980) also writes about supervision in the context of training therapists. She conceptualises the supervision process as a balance between supporting the supervisee's experience in the genuine human relationship with the client and supporting his or her understanding of therapy as a process that can be learned. She distinguishes two groups of attitudes, related to the therapist's ability to implement the client-centred conditions, that can be worked with in supervision: attitudes about human nature and the nature of change, and attitudes towards self (in the therapist) (1980: 138). However, her emphasis appears to be slightly different from that of Rogers and Patterson. As one of the founding theorists of the process-experiential approach, her focus is more on the theory of the client's process and on the therapist's style of participation in that process (and less on the supervisee's self-experience in the relationship with the client or on the relationship in supervision). A focus on supervision with trainee therapists is also at the core of Barrett-Lennard's (1998: 333–8) overview of person-centred writing on supervision. He too attempts to capture the essence of supervision when he describes it as 'growth-learning', supporting an 'evolution of consciousness, not only in respect to self, but in span of receptivity toward the experiencing of others' (1998: 336). As one of Rogers' ex-students, and with first hand experience of supervision with him, he describes Rogers' movement from a evaluative, guiding style of supervision in the early 1940s to the much more student-centred and facilitative style after 1951.

More recent writing on person-centred supervision continues to explore the nature of the supervision relationship, the relevance and applicability of the core conditions in supervision, and the purpose of supervision not only for trainees but also as part of the ongoing development of the therapist. Lambers defines supervision as 'facilitating congruence' (2000: 196). She explores the meaning of the therapeutic core conditions in the supervision relationship, and looks at the challenge for person-centred supervision in the context of current professional and ethical thinking. The theme of developing the therapist's congruence is also present in the writing of Schmid (1997, 2000), who extends the concept of 'encounter' to the meeting in supervision.

Merry integrates the core conditions in his concept of supervision as a process of 'collaborative enquiry': 'an open, empathic and non-judgemental environment that is simultaneously questioning and supportive, promoting congruence and an internal locus of evaluation in the supervisee' (Merry, 2001: 183; 1999; Bryant-Jefferies, 2005). His concept of supervision as a kind of 'personal research project' fits well with the spirit of Rogers' view of person-centred therapy as a process of testing the central hypothesis of the approach. In what may be the first book completely focused on person-centred supervision, Tudor and Worrall (2004) develop a theory of person-centred supervision based on Rogers' theory of therapy and personality change. As well as exploring the relevance of the six core conditions in supervision, they apply Rogers' process conception of psychotherapy (Rogers, 1967) to the process of development in the supervisee. Through the experience of being fully received in the supervision relationship, supervisees are enabled to become more fluid and open to both their own and their client's experience and to communicate more openly and freely. Worrall further defines empathy as a central dimension in the therapeutic process and therefore the primary task of supervision is 'facilitating the supervisee's capacity to offer empathic understanding' (Worrall, 2001). The supervisor's congruent empathic stance in relation to the supervisee in turn fosters the supervisee's ability for congruent empathic understanding of the client.

An experiential perspective is represented by Baljon (2002), illustrating how supervision can be used to 'teach congruence' to supervisees, using Gendlin's (1981) focusing concepts. Madison (2004) also explores how attending to supervisees' experiential processes can help them to develop their reflective ability and to become more deeply in touch with their responses and reactions in relation to the client.

The dynamic of the supervision relationship is a relatively unexplored area. The term 'supervision' in itself is sometimes criticized as having implications of 'control' and 'overseeing', implying a power imbalance and authority relationship which is fundamentally incompatible with the philosophy of relationship in the person-centred approach. Mearns (1991) acknowledges the importance of being aware of the 'unspoken relationship' between supervisor and supervisee and the need for a commitment to make time to examine the unspoken norms and expectations that may have developed in the relationship. He defines a 'healthy supervision relationship' as one characterized by the supervisor's commitment, congruence, empathy and consistent valuing of the supervisee. In such a relationship the supervisor can be a 'supportive challenger' – someone who will offer the challenge of another perspective, but in a context where the supervisee feels respected, both personally and professionally. This theme of challenge is explored in some detail by Kilborn (1999). Her study shows that challenge in a trusting supervision relationship can be experienced as stimulating and valuing. A similar positive welcome to challenges is found in the work of Auckenthaler (1995), a German psychotherapist, who sees supervision as a place for critical exploration and dialogue in a supportive relationship. The combination of critical and 'benevolent' attitude creates an 'error friendly' ('fehlerfreundliche') context where both supervisor and supervisee can acknowledge errors, welcome their exploration, take responsibility and learn from them.

Relatively little is written about the direct experience of the supervision relationship, either from the perspective of the supervisor or that of the supervisee. Those new to supervision may be interested to hear the experience of students of person-centred therapy, in particular with developing an understanding of the purpose of supervision and managing the relationship dynamic in the supervision (Buchanan and Hughes, 1999). Moore (1991) and Gibson (2004) give an account of their experience as supervisees, each confirming the value of the experience of being deeply heard and being supported and encouraged to find their own style as therapists, and describing their experience of the core conditions in the supervision relationship. A unique and courageous three-way perspective (supervisee, supervisor and client) is offered by Jacobs (1996). His experience illustrates powerfully how the therapist's greater awareness of himself, facilitated by the supervisor's attention to his experience in relation to the client, made it possible for both client and therapist to become more congruent with each other and to express some of their unspoken relationship.

Focus on the therapist's experience

A consistent theme in the above-mentioned literature is that the purpose of person-centred supervision is defined in terms of the development of the therapist's ability to be congruent, integrated and fully present in the therapeutic relationship. Central in supervision is the experience of the therapist and the reflection on the relationship between client and therapist, rather than the exploration of a client 'case' (Patterson, 1983; Mearns, 1997; Lambers, 2000). Rogers writes about supervision as offering 'primarily a listening, facilitative understanding, helping the therapist to become clearly aware of their own feelings in the therapeutic sessions so he can be more adequately come to be himself in the relationship' (Rogers, 1957: 86). Particularly relevant in his view of supervision is his wish to avoid 'imitative modelling' (Villas-Bowen, 1986: 296), and of guiding or coaching the supervisee to respond according to the supervisor's model (Rogers, 1957). The supervision relationship offers a context where the therapist can bring into awareness experiences and processes emerging in her in the relationship with the client, and where she can explore the relationship qualities necessary for her therapeutic work. She may explore a wide range of experiences: strong feelings of attraction or repulsion, sadness, anger, powerlessness, love, fear, hopelessness. She may bring barely symbolized sensations on the edge of her awareness – a shivery feeling, a whiff of dread, a sensation of tiredness. She may bring experiences that she is familiar with, but equally she may discover something completely new in the course of the supervision session. In this view of supervision the supervisor's intention is to facilitate and support the development of the therapist's ability to be open to her experience, to be fully engaged and present with her clients, and of her ability to relate at depth.

However, this does not mean that the focus in supervision is exclusively on the therapist's feelings. There is a common misconception that person-centred work favours a focus on the exploration of feeling and on relating in the affective realm of experience (Lambers, 2000: 201). The imposition of such a narrow focus, both in therapy and supervision, may in effect create a condition of worth: 'to be accepted I must talk about feelings, or even better, show feelings.' Relating to the 'whole person' involves relating to the person in all aspects of their experience and their existence. In supervision, 'focusing on

Table 27.1 An illustration of the breadth of focus in supervision

A supervision session may consist of some (or all) of the following:

- Encouraging reflection and expression of the therapist's experience in relation to clients.
- Exploring understanding of the client's perspective and experience of the therapy relationship; unspoken relationship.
- Exploring the therapist's presence, congruence and relational depth.
- Integrating the therapeutic conditions in the therapist.
- Thinking about different ways of responding to the client.
- Listening to an audio-tape or watching a videotape of a therapy session.
- Exploring theoretical understanding in support of the work with a specific client.
- Understanding the client in the context of his or her culture; awareness of impact of cultural difference on the therapy relationship.
- Challenge of working with clients who are very different from the therapist.
- Understanding 'difficult client process'.
- Professional issues: ethical framework, multi-disciplinary teamwork, communication with other professionals.
- Reflecting on social context of therapy.
- Attention to 'self' of the therapist: personal development, competence, current functioning, workload.
- Impact of current life events on therapist's relationship with clients.
- Acknowledging and exploring stress, burnout, fitness to practice.
- Identify needs for training and development of therapist.
- New writing in PCE approaches, relevant to therapist's work.
- Supervision relationship; unspoken relationship and power dynamic in the supervision relationship.
- Ending with a client; impact of holidays and breaks in therapy.
- Learning from a conference or training event.
- Plans for research.
- Exploring ways of 'expanding imagination'.

- Add your own ....

the supervisee's experience' means being open to affective, cognitive, physical and spiritual dimensions, as well as to the exploration of professional and ethical questions (see Table 27.1).

The table shows some of the possible topics that can be worked with in supervision. To support such explorations a variety of methods can be used. Personal dialogue and theoretical discussion, the therapist's reflective notes or diary, role play, audio or videotapes of sessions with clients, all bring variety and creativity into the sessions. Supervisees may also find it useful to develop a checklist of questions that can assist them in their reflection (Mearns, 1997).

In the early writing on supervision, frequent reference is made to the use of tapes of actual counselling sessions – a practice pioneered by Rogers in the early 1940s and continued to this day (Mearns, 1997). Rogers (1942) writes with enthusiasm about the learning through listening together with students and colleagues to recordings of therapy sessions. Consistent with her approach to supervision, Rice (1980) uses taped material to facilitate reflection on the therapy process. Patterson (1983) describes the use of tapes both for teaching purposes (in group settings) and in individual sessions, to facilitate reflection on the supervisee's experience. Bringing the actual interaction between client and therapist into the supervision session has many benefits. It allows the therapist to relive his or her experience, offers opportunities for systematic exploration of the process of a session and it is the only way in which the client, and the therapist's interaction with the client, can be directly represented in the supervision session (Mearns, 1997).

Responsibility and ethics

Working so closely with the therapist's experience and process, and sometimes on the powerfully felt edge of the experience of humanity, the person-centred approach to supervision is sometimes accused of mainly reinforcing a theoretical tradition or even worse: of being unethical through its focus on the supervisee 'at the expense of client welfare' (Davenport, 1992; Feltham and Lawton, 2000). Underlying this judgement is, as well as a profound misunderstanding of person-centred practice, a view that supervision should and can ensure the welfare of the client, and that this should be done through assessment and evaluation of the supervisee's therapeutic ability, through monitoring of the supervisee's practice and through clinical discussion of the client's diagnosis, motives and needs.

Therapeutic practice can be viewed from two perspectives: from inside the approach of the therapist and from outside, representing a societal or professional perspective. The outside perspective represents the frame of reference of the profession, of society and of the culture in which the therapist and the supervisor operate. This view represents a moral and legal view of the activity of therapy and defines ethics in term of moral and legal standards (Lambers, 2000). Therapists from all orientations have a responsibility to work within this framework. Person-centred supervisors aim to offer a context where both frameworks are present and can be explored, and where supervisees can evaluate their practice from the perspective both of professional ethics and of their understanding of person-centred therapy.

Within the perspective of person-centred therapy, ethical practice is to maintain a consistent offer of authentic relating to the Other (Schmid, 2001), based on an attitude of deep respect for the uniqueness and psychological freedom of the other person (Grant, 2004). When there are specific concerns about the supervisee's practice from this ethical person-centred perspective, the challenge to the supervisor is to offer a consistent, accepting relationship through which the supervisee can explore his/her functioning as a therapist and move towards greater congruence and authenticity in relation to the client. In doing so, the supervisor acts ethically and supports the supervisee to act ethically.

> The supervisor who is able to see from both perspectives, who can function confidently within both frameworks and who offers the supervisee congruent acceptance, creates in the supervision relationship an excellent basis for support, challenge and for open, respectful exploration and dialogue about both therapeutic and ethical issues.
>
> (Lambers, 2000: 210)

Relationship qualities in supervision

It would seem obvious that in order to make it possible for the therapist to explore the depth of her experience with the client, the supervisor in turn needs to be prepared to offer a high level of engagement and presence in the relationship with the supervisee. As in therapy, empathy, acceptance and congruence are important relationship qualities, supporting and facilitating a climate of mutual trust and respect. In supervision these qualities help to create a relationship where supervisor and supervisee can work together creatively towards a genuine dialogue, in a spirit of 'collaborative enquiry' (Merry, 2001). In such a climate the supervisee is secure and free to give expression to thoughts, feelings and concerns that are in her awareness, to focus on not yet symbolized experiences in relation to her clients, or to bring questions and issues related to external factors that have an impact on the therapy relationship.

The supervisor's empathic presence facilitates the supervisee's process of 'tuning in' to whatever is around in her experiential process. Supervisees sometimes have only a vague sense of what is going on for them, there may be just a feeling of something on the edge of awareness; on those occasions a 'focusing' response, making space for the experience, may be particularly helpful. As said earlier in this chapter, empathy should be extended to all of the supervisee's experiences and concerns, not only to emotions.

The supervisor's acceptance, the willingness to respect and value the supervisee as a person of worth, communicates trust in the supervisee to find his or her own unique way of relating to their client. The experience of the supervisor's acceptance may enable the supervisee to allow into awareness experiences which are unacceptable or a threat to his or her own self-concept (both personal and/or as a therapist) and may offer support towards a greater openness in their exploration of the therapeutic relationship. Supervision is not about monitoring or assessing practice, nor is it about ensuring that the supervisee works in a recognized, approved 'person-centred' way. The function of supervision is to support the supervisee in 'finding her or his own style of being a therapist' (Villas-Bowen, 1986: 293). Against the background of this non-judgemental position the supervisor's contribution to the supervisee's exploration can be experienced as challenging, but nonetheless as 'stimulating and enriching' (Kilborn, 1999). This challenge does not come from criticism, authority or judgement, but from a congruent, consistent acceptance that invites the supervisee to enter into an open, non-defensive reflection and to take responsibility for his or her own congruent self-exploration.

Congruence is an essential condition in the supervision relationship. To acknowledge fully the experience of being, or striving to be, in relationship with a client may leave the supervisee feeling exposed and vulnerable. In those moments, there may a conflict between the wish to be open to experience and the need for self-protection, and the supervisee may struggle with being congruent. The supervisor's full engagement with the process of the supervisee is only possible if she is open to her own experience – congruent expression of empathy and acceptance gives depth and meaning to the relationship. It helps the supervisee to become more present and congruent; it also provides a model for their own practice (Lambers, 2000). Transparent self-reflection and communication are important ingredients in the development of a collaborative relationship in supervision. Congruence in the supervisor facilitates self-reflection in the supervisee and strengthens that person's internal locus of evaluation (Merry, 2001).

Supervision or therapy?

All approaches to counselling and psychotherapy subscribe to the view that it is important that therapists are open to personal exploration of unresolved issues, arising either out of their past or current life experiences or in the relationship with a client, which may constitute 'blocks' or 'blind spots' in the therapeutic relationship or interfere with the therapeutic process. Supervision offers an opportunity to bring such vulnerabilities and unresolved issues into awareness, to consider their impact on the therapist's functioning and on the therapy relationship, and to reflect on the best course of action (Lambers, 1993). Because of the emphasis on the relationship and on the therapist's self-development, person-centred supervision is sometimes viewed with some suspicion, as though it confuses therapy with supervision. In fact, in most of the writing mentioned above, some space is given to the discussion of the difference between supervision and therapy, and without exception all agree that while supervision can touch deeply personal aspects of the supervisee's experience, supervision is not therapy – although it can be therapeutic (Patterson, 1964, 1983; Rice, 1980; Hackney and Goodyear, 1984; Mearns, 1997).

The supervision relationship can be conceptualised as parallel to the therapy relationship, but there is an important difference in focus: in therapy the client has absolute freedom to talk about any aspect of his or her experience, but in supervision the primary focus is on the therapist's experience as it emerges in the relationship with the client (Villas-Bowen, 1986; Patterson, 1964). It is important that supervisor and supervisee remain clear about the purpose of the supervision relationship, particularly when issues emerge (either in the relationship with the client or in the supervision relationship) that expose important areas of conflict or unresolved personal issues, problematic patterns of relating or vulnerability. Some exploration of such difficulties in supervision may be necessary and indeed of great value, but both supervisor and supervisee need to take responsibility for maintaining and managing the boundaries of the relationship, and it may be necessary to explore other arenas for exploration of severe or persistent difficulties.

The supervisor too may experience personal challenge or discover areas for personal learning through the relationship with the supervisee, both through the in-the-moment relationship in supervision and through the shared exploration of therapeutic work. Many supervisors, myself included, report that they find working as a supervisor of enormous benefit to their therapy work and to their own personal and professional development.

Relational depth in supervision

In modern thinking about person-centred therapy increasing emphasis is placed on *the centrality of the relationship*. In this relationship, both client and therapist are touched by the experience of each other's presence – what Schmid (2002) refers to as the person-to-person encounter. Mearns re-emphasizes the importance of relationship in person-centred therapy as follows:

> not just 'relationship' at the superficial level of the 'therapeutic alliance' – my emphasis is on the creation of a particular depth of relationship between client and therapist – a depth of relationship which allows the client to feel an extraordinary safety, such that they can go to particular depths within their own experiencing.
>
> (Mearns, 2005)

Mearns and Cooper define this concept of 'relational depth' as: 'A state of profound contact and engagement between two people, in which each person is fully real with the other, and able to understand and value the Other's experiences at a high level' (2005: xii). The therapist who is willing to engage fully with the client at the deepest level of their being will feel the impact of that experience. Such encounter offers both client and therapist the potential for a new experience of Self, and a powerful experience of Self in relation to another person. To be able to offer such depth of relating the therapist needs to be integrated, fully present, and free to respond to the total person of the client (Mearns and Thorne, 2000). The challenge for the person-centred therapist is to become able to offer that depth of relating to every client (Mearns and Cooper, 2005). Initial training can only prepare the counsellor for this challenge; after training the development of the ability to meet every client at depth is part of the ongoing developmental agenda of the therapist.

In particular, supervision provides an excellent forum for exploration of 'existential touchstones': 'events and self-experiences from which we draw considerable strength and which help to ground us in relationships as well as making us more open to and comfortable with a diversity of relationships' (Mearns and Cooper, 2005: 137). They add: 'The therapist draws strength from their sense of what has been fundamental to their own existence as they engage with the client at relational depth.'

To be able to support the supervisee in the development of their ability to relate at depth, to be fully open to the experience of being 'our own person' and to be authentically present (Schmid, 2001) in the relationship with clients requires a high degree of presence and authenticity on the part of the supervisor. Paraphrasing the definition above, relational depth in supervision is:

> a high level of contact and engagement in which both persons are contributing to a real dialogue around their shared experience in the moment – both of the supervisee's experience of self in relation to the client and of the relationship between supervisee and supervisor.

Not only may this enable supervisees to become more aware and integrated in their therapeutic work, but the experience of 'meeting and being met' is enriching, both personally and professionally, for both supervisees and supervisors.

REFERENCES

Auckenthaler, A. (1995). *Supervision psychotherapeutischer Praxis. Organization- Standards- Wirklichkeit*. Stuttgart: Kohlhammer.

Baljon, M. (2002). Focusing in client-centred psychotherapy supervision: teaching congruence. In J.C. Watson, R.N. Goldman and M.S. Warner (eds), *Client-Centred and Experiential Psychotherapy in the Twenty-first Century: advances in theory, research and practice* (pp. 315–24). Ross-On-Wye: PCCS Books.

Barrett-Lennard, G. (1998). *Carl Rogers' Helping System: journey and substance*. London: Sage.

British Association for Counselling and Psychotherapy (BACP) (2004). What is supervision? (Information sheet 2.) Rugby: British Association for Counselling and Psychotherapy.

Bryant-Jefferies, R. (2005). *Person-Centred Counselling Supervision: personal and professional*. Oxford: Radcliffe.

Buchanan, L. and Hughes, R. (1999). *Experiences of Person-Centred Counselling Training: a compendium of case studies to assist prospective applicants*. Ross-on-Wye: PCCS Books.

Carroll, M. (1996). *Counselling Supervision: theory, skills and practice*. London: Cassell.

Davenport, D.S. (1992). Ethical and legal problems with client-centred supervision. *Counselor Education and Supervision*, 31, 227–31.

Feltham, C. and Lawton, B. (eds) (2000). *Taking Supervision Forward: enquiries and trends in counselling and psychotherapy*. London: Sage.

Gendlin, E. (1981). *Focusing* (2nd edn). New York: Bantam Books.

Gibson, D. (2004). On being received: a supervisee's view of being supervised. In Tudor, K. and Worrall, M. (eds), *Freedom to Practise: person-centred approaches to supervision* (pp. 31–42). Ross-on-Wye: PCCS Books.

Grant, B. (2004). The imperative of ethical justification in psychotherapy: the special case of client-centred therapy. In *Person-Centred and Experiential Psychotherapies*, 3(3), 152–65.

Hackney, H. and Goodyear, R.K. (1984). Carl Rogers' client-centred approach to supervision. In R.F. Levant and J.M. Shlien (eds), *Client-Centered Therapy and the Person-Centred Approach* (pp. 278–96). New York: Praeger.

Jacobs, M. (1996). Review and response. In M. Jacobs (ed.), *In Search of Supervision* (pp. 135–76). Buckingham: Open University Press.

Kilborn, M. (1999). Challenge and person-centred supervision: are they compatible? *Person-Centred Practice*, 7(2), 83–91.

Lambers, E. (1993). When the counsellor shares the client's problem. In W. Dryden (ed.). *Questions and Answers for Counselling in Action* (pp. 68–72). London: Sage.

Lambers, E. (2000). Supervision in person-centred therapy: facilitating congruence. In D. Mearns and B. Thorne (eds), *Person-Centred Therapy Today: new frontiers in theory and practice* (pp.196–211). London: Sage.

Madison, G. (2004). Focusing-oriented supervision. In K. Tudor and M. Worrall (eds), *Freedom to Practise: person-centred approaches to supervision* (pp. 133–51). Ross-on-Wye: PCCS Books.

Mearns, D. (1991). On being a supervisor. In W. Dryden and C. Feltham (eds), *Training and Supervision for Counselling in Action* (pp. 116–28). London: Sage.

Mearns, D. (1997). *Person-Centred Counselling Training*. London: Sage.

Mearns, D. (2005). *How I Work as a Person-Centred Therapist*. Public lecture at Kansai Counseling Center, Osaka, Japan (April).

Mearns, D. and Cooper, M. (2005). *Working at Relational Depth in Counselling and Psychotherapy*. London: Sage.

Mearns, D. and Thorne, B. (2000). *Person-Centred Therapy Today: new frontiers in theory and practice*. London: Sage.

Merry, T. (1999). *Learning and Being in Person-Centred Counselling*. Ross-on-Wye: PCCS Books.

Merry, T. (2001). Congruence and the supervision of client-centred therapists. In G. Wyatt (ed.). *Congruence: Rogers' Therapeutic Conditions: evolution, theory and practice* (pp. 174–83). Ross-on-Wye: PCCS Books.

Merry, T. (2004). Supervision as heuristic research enquiry. In K. Tudor and M.Worrall (eds), *Freedom to Practise: person-centred approaches to supervision* (pp. 189–99). Ross-on-Wye: PCCS Books.

Moore, J. (1991). On being a supervisee. In W. Dryden and C. Feltham (eds), *Training and Supervision for Counselling in Action* (pp. 129–42). London: Sage.

Page, S. and Wosket, V. (2001). *Supervising the Counsellor: a cyclical model* (2nd edn). Hove: Brunner-Routledge.

Patterson, C.H. (1964). Supervising students in the counselling practicum. *Journal of Counseling Psychology*, 11, 47–53.

Patterson, C.H. (1983). A client-centred approach to supervision. *The Counseling Psychologist*, 11(1), 21–5.

Rice, L.N. (1980). A client-centred approach to the supervision of psychotherapy. In A.K. Hess (ed.), *Psychotherapy Supervision: theory, research and practice* (pp. 136–47). New York: Wiley.

Rogers, C.R. (1942). The use of electronically recorded interviews in improving psychotherapeutic techniques. *American Journal of Orthopsychiatry*, 12, 429–34.

Rogers, C.R. (1951). *Client-Centered Therapy*. Boston: Houghton Mifflin.

Rogers, C.R. (1957). Training individuals to engage in the therapeutic process. In C.R. Strother (ed.), *Psychology and Mental Health* (pp. 76–92). Washington D.C.: American Psychological Association.

Rogers, C.R. (1967). A process conception of therapy. In *C.R. Rogers: On Becoming a Person: a therapist's view of psychotherapy* (pp. 125–59). London: Constable.

Schmid, P.F. (1997). Förderung von Kompetenz durch Förderung von Kongruenz. Inhaltliche und berufspolitische Aspekte personzentrierter Supervision. *Person*, 2, 144–54.

Schmid, P.F. (2000). Begegnung und Reflexion. Personzentrierte Supervision als Förderung der Person im Spannungsfeld zwischen persönlichkeitsentwicklung und Organization. *Person*, 4(2), 15–27.

Schmid, P.F. (2001). Authenticity: the person as his or her own author. Dialogical and ethical perspectives on therapy as an encounter relationship. And beyond. In G. Wyatt (ed.). *Rogers' Therapeutic Conditions: evolution, theory and practice* (pp. 213– 228). Ross-on-Wye: PCCS Books.

Schmid, P.F. (2002). Knowledge or acknowledgement: psychotherapy as the art of not- knowing: prospects on further development of a revolutionary paradigm. *Person-Centred and Experiential Psychotherapies*, 1(1–2), 56–70.

Tudor, K. and Worrall, M. (eds) (2004). *Freedom to Practise: person-centred approaches to supervision*. Ross-on-Wye: PCCS Books

Villas-Bowen, M. (1986). Personality differences and person-centred supervision. *Person-Centred Review*, 1(3), 291–309.

Worrall, M. (2001). Supervision and empathic understanding. In S. Haugh and T. Merry (eds), *Empathy. Rogers' Therapeutic Conditions: evolution, theory and practice* (pp. 206–17). Ross-on-Wye: PCCS Books.

Training in the Person-Centred Approach

Keith Tudor

Person-centred therapy is one of the few theoretical orientations to therapy which also has a distinct approach to education. Carl Rogers' own contribution to the field of education emphasizes a student-centred approach to learning and training. This provides the basis for educators and trainers who believe in the principles and practice of the person-centred approach to embody them in all aspects of their training, and to offer, maintain and enhance the constituent elements – or, as Rogers (1969) puts it, the 'climate of freedom' – of any training in a way which is congruent with the philosophy and principles of the approach (see Tudor and Lewin, 2006).

Taking its inspiration from Rogers' groundbreaking book *Freedom to Learn* (originally published in 1969, revised in 1983, and further revised and published posthumously in 1994), and drawing on some of the extensive literature on person-centred approaches to education and training, this chapter examines the implications of these approaches for the education and training of therapists. I use the plural 'approaches' to acknowledge the different tribes within the person-centred 'nation' (see Warner, 2000).

Arguably, person-centred approaches to therapy have never been more popular, especially in Europe, Japan and some countries in South America. However, this is a mixed blessing. The more popular it has become, the more it is seen as superficial and insufficient. Its profound implications for personality, personal, social and political change are commonly misunderstood and misrepresented, both from outside the approach and by those who espouse the approach. With rare exceptions, this is true of the person-centred education and training of therapists. Apart from the lack of philosophical and theoretical integrity this represents, it is confusing for students: on the one hand they may be introduced to the principles of the person-centred approach, such as the human organism's tendency to actualize and to develop an internal valuing process and self-direction, whilst on the other hand, they may be told what to think, what to do and, often, when to do it, and even what to write. In Rowan's (2005) terms this represents a confusion between a relational/authentic way of training, and an instrumental one.

In this chapter I examine the relationship between philosophy, practice and theory in a way which seeks to support and enhance the person-centred education and training of person-centred therapists. In the first part I consider the requirements of a freedom to learn, especially from the student's perspective; in the second part I consider the role and tasks of the educator/trainer in fostering this freedom. The aim of the chapter is to offer current and potential students, as well as educators and trainers, an opportunity to reflect on their experiences of learning and training, including issues concerning course requirements, syllabus, style of training, and external 'requirements' of professional and academic bodies. Following Rogers' example, I set these discussions about the education and training of therapists in the broader context of current debates about education.

Freedom to learn

In his original and ground-breaking work Rogers (1969) describes various examples of freedom – and the lack of freedom – in education. Amongst other things, he outlines his views about learning and its facilitation, deconstructs implicit and explicit assumptions in graduate education, and emphasizes the philosophical and value base of person-centred education. Re-reading Rogers' book as background for writing this chapter I am again struck by the clarity and radicalism of his writing and ideas, and recommend it to all person-centred trainers and students, whom it may help give voice to their expression, creativity, curiosity and questioning.

In this work Rogers identifies two types of learning, on 'a continuum of meaning' (1969: 3) from a meaningless 'learning', driven by syllabi, to 'significant, meaningful, experiential learning' (1969: 4). His critique is well made and, half a generation later, still relevant with regard to the school and education system in general, and to the education and training of therapists in particular. Rogers was and is not alone in his criticisms of traditional approaches. He cites both A.S. Neill, who founded Summerhill School in Devon, and Paolo Freire, the Brazilian educationalist and revolutionary. Table 28.1 represents some of the differences between the traditional, conventional approach to education and student-centred alternatives.

The student-centred approach to learning is based on a view of the person as a human organism with an inherent tendency to actualize (see Rogers, 1959; Barrett-Lennard, 1998; Tudor and Worrall, 2006). The importance of this for the student – and for her or his educator – is that, as Rogers (1969: 251) puts it: 'There is an organismic base for an organized valuing process within the human individual.' It is important, therefore, that students are supported and facilitated to know their own values and how they come to

Table 28.1 A comparison of the traditional, conventional approach to education and student-centered alternatives

Traditional, conventional approach to education	Student-centered approach to education
Prescribed curriculum	Student-led and process-led curriculum, mindful of but not subservient to the standards and requirements of external accrediting or validating bodies.
Same assignments for all students	Student-directed assignments e.g. choosing her or his essay title.
Lecturing and tutorials	Facilitated and self-directed learning through experiential learning, large and small group discussion, some didactic presentations, demonstrations and personal development groups.
Standard tests by which all students are externally evaluated	A variety of evaluative schema, consistent with an internal locus of evaluation and negotiated and agreed learning outcomes.
Teacher-assessed grades	Self, peer and tutor assessment and grades awarded by a combination of parties to assessment, again, in the context of the requirements of external validating bodies.

them (see Combs, 1988/2002). Thus, with regard to the practice component of a training course, after a student has practised as a therapist, say, with another student (usually in triads with another student as observer), it is important that she or he takes some time to reflect on the experience. Commonly, in this situation, the practising therapist gets 'feedback' from the observer – and, ironically, given the client-centred nature of the activity, often no feedback from the client. By definition, feedback from an observer represents an external locus of evaluation, and thus discourages and discounts the development of the student's own internal valuing process. Of course, from the basis of approaches which value relationship, engagement and dialogue, knowing how we are experienced by others is also an important aspect of self-development. In a training setting, the developing therapist has a unique opportunity to get feedback from the client with the help of the third party who, in this scenario, becomes more of a facilitator of the dialogue between therapist and client, and who, thereby, also develops these skills.

If the student is encouraged to develop this inner freedom, then she or he can, of course, process feedback from the environment. After all, the organism cannot be understood outside of its environment. This encompasses an awareness of realities, such as course requirements, and the further external requirements of course accreditation and validation. In *Freedom to Learn*, Rogers reports on an experiment in person-centred learning, observing that, amongst other things, the pupils were not only aware of the (external) realities, but came up with creative solutions through group problem-solving, such as contracts for grades. 'The point is,' Rogers (1969: 24) reflects, 'that when freedom and self-direction are given to a group, it is also easier for the members to accept the constraints and obligations which surround the psychological area in which they are free.' Children and adult learners can thus be mindful of external requirements; be encouraged to question their necessity; and be facilitated to come up with creative solutions for those which they and the institution have to accept. I say 'question', partly in the spirit of what is a reflective, inquiring approach, and because what are often understood and presented as 'require-ments' are sometimes not. On one course, the students challenged the tutors about giving them set essay titles. The tutors responded by saying that it was a requirement of the university which had validated the course. On further inves-tigation it turned out that this was not the case, with the result that both students and tutors were liberated – and challenged – by this particular freedom.

Person-centred approaches encourage the person, in this case the student, to (re)claim her or his own 'authority within'. Elsewhere, Rogers (1980) talks about the 'person of tomorrow' as, amongst other qualities, being anti-institutional. As they sow self-direction, fluidity (as distinct from fixity), creativity, personal power, non-conformity and dissent, so person-centred approaches to education reap students' natural anxiety and tension, and what Rogers (1969: 115) refers to as 'living the uncertainty of discovery'. It is clearly incompatible with person-centred approaches to tell students what to think or what to do. Of course, this means that there are fewer apparent certainties, for instance, about the issue of whether or not to touch a client (see Tudor and Worrall, 2004). What person-centred approaches do offer students are means whereby they become clearer about what they think and believe – and why (see Combs, 1988/2002). This process is, of course, personal and involves a high degree of personal development (see below).

These approaches and these strategies support the student's internal valuing process, which is effective in achieving self-enhancement, according to Rogers (1969: 251) 'to the degree that the individual is open to the experiencing which is going on within himself'. Thus, a person-centred education needs to offer an environment which supports the student's openness to such inner experiencing. The emphasis on the environmental conditions, necessary, sufficient or other-wise, is one of the hallmarks of person-centred approaches and, in the educa-tional field, provides the theoretical basis for experiential learning. In practice this includes the following:

- *Learning through experience*, including the experience of therapeutic prac-tice, both on or within and outside the course, on placements and in inde-pendent, private practice. Indeed, Rogers (1951: 433) argues 'that the prac-tice of therapy should be a part of the training experience from the earliest practicable moment'. Experiential learning demands a quality of personal involvement, including reflecting on and thinking about all aspects of ther-apeutic practice. Whilst this process – and ensuing discussions – may take longer, students who have experienced this are more likely to 'own' their own thinking and consequent decisions.

- *Learning through personal development.* Person-centred approaches to training therapists place more emphasis than most other therapeutic training approaches on students' personal development taking place as an integrated part of the training experience in groups such as year groups, whole course groups or community groups. This is because of the importance given to the development of the personal attitudes, qualities and responsiveness of the therapist. Mearns (1997) is particularly eloquent about the importance of personal development. Whilst Rogers (1951: 437) acknowledges that 'the experience of personal therapy ... is a valuable experience for the student', Mearns (1994: 35) is sceptical of its value, arguing that 'Personal development for professional working is so crucial to the person-centred approach that it cannot be left to the vagaries of individual therapy.'

  Significantly, in its statement of principles or guidelines for person-centred and experiential training, the Network of the European Associations for Person-Centred and Experiential Psychotherapy and Counselling (NEAPCEPC) (2001) states that person-centred training is understood as 'the facilitation of personalisation', by which it means the development of the personality of the trainee. In another contribution to this debate Keil (1996) advocates 'training therapy' and views the motivation and goals of personal therapy during training as primarily didactic rather than therapeutic. This is a particularly important point in the light of the requirements of many national and international accrediting and regulatory bodies for training therapists to undertake personal therapy. Apart from the debate about the relative value of personal therapy and personal development, there is also the issue of compulsion and compliance. From a person-centred perspective, there is a strong argument against requiring students to have personal therapy.

  My own view is that personal therapy is so important that it shouldn't be a requirement. From a perspective which values and promotes organismic direction and self-responsibility, it makes sense to distinguish between – and important that trainers make explicit – the different requirements of professional bodies and, in some countries, of government regulation, and those of a particular training course or institute, and not to confuse or conflate the two.
- *Learning through relationship.* Rogers places a high value on the relationship between teacher and student, and their ability to negotiate most elements of learning. This is as challenging now as it was when Rogers originally formulated and developed his ideas. As two of his colleagues (Aspy and Roebuck, 1988/2002: 246) put it: 'Rogers asked teachers to shift from being the center of attention to a relationship that recognized students as coseekers of learning.' Training courses which are congruent with the principles of the person-centred approach to education, namely in embracing student-directed and process-led learning, tend to have a fluid and flexible curriculum which, in any case, is more rather than less negotiated.
- *Learning through self-directed work, assignments and self-assessment.* Clearly it is consistent with person-centred approaches that a training course encourages student to explore their interest in practice and in

theory. Far from being an easy option, most students acknowledge that, for example, it's much harder to choose their own essay title ('There's so much choice!') than to write to a set, and often unchanging title. Furthermore, as Rogers (1969: 142) argues: 'The evaluation of one's own learning is one of the major means by which self-initiated learning becomes also responsible learning.' Over the years, a number of courses have experimented with variations on this theme, notably, in Britain, in the early days of counselling training, the South West London College counselling courses (see Blomfield, 1997). Of course, the logic of self-assessment is that students are also involved in awarding their grades; in establishing the criteria which form the basis of assessment and grading (see Klug, 1977); and, ultimately, in self- and peer-accreditation and regulation (see House, 1997).

Freedom to train

With regard to the training of therapists, Rogers writes a chapter on the subject in *Client-Centred Therapy* (Rogers, 1951), in which he emphasizes learning from experience. Others since have applied and developed his ideas:

- With regard to training in academic settings, Thomas discusses an experimental model of person-centred education he used in a particular college course which based its curriculum on the fullest possible development of the individual. For an education that prioritizes personal learning and learning through reflection on the person, he asserts (1988/2002: 264): 'the persistent encouragement of authenticity as the first priority is perhaps the best policy I know.' Natiello (1998) reports on a person-centred training programme which decided to remain independent rather than accept the constraints which would have accrued with external accreditation. This stands as an inspiring example for educators, trainers and students today of a critical and principled resistance to increasing pressures for external loci of evaluation, a pressure which is experienced throughout the education industry in the UK and other countries (see Embleton Tudor et al, 2004).

- With regard to training counsellors and psychotherapists, Combs (1986/2002) critiques certain traditional, behavioural assumptions of counsellor training programmes, and offers his own person-centred assumptions for an education based on, amongst other things, a focus on the students' beliefs and need for knowledge, as well as their commitment to the learning process. Mearns (1997), in the first book on the subject, applies person-centred principles and theories to the training of counsellors. In 2001 the NEAPCEPC agreed a document which makes a number of points about person-centred and experiential training, including that it is an enterprise which involves both process and experience; which aims 'to foster creativity and to acknowledge personal and cultural diversity'; which is committed to 'a self-guided way of learning', to clearly defined ethical standards, and to research; and which comprises four elements of self-development, theory, the concrete application of Rogers' conditions, and supervised practice. More recently, Embleton Tudor et al (2004) offer a critical view of schooling as a background to their discussion of person-centred training in the context of lifelong learning; and Tudor and Lewin (2006) explore the importance of the congruence or 'fit' between the philosophy and principles on which a training course is based and the organization and administration of that training and of the training organization itself.

- With regard to research on the effects of a person-centred approach to training, Rogers' own work (1969, 1983) contains a number of original research studies; Aspy and Roebuck (1988/2002) report on research which showed positive results from their evaluation of teachers' levels of congruence, unconditional positive regard and empathic understanding; and Barrett-Lennard (1998) discusses student–teacher relationship studies, some of which suggest some correlation between the therapeutic conditions and pupil outcomes in education.

In the introduction I suggest that the educator/trainer embodies his or her person-centred approach. I use this word deliberately as it is echoes something of the visceral nature of the human organism and represents a holistic approach to education on the part of the educator. In this second part of the chapter I consider ways in which the trainer can facilitate students in a manner and method which is consistent with and, indeed, based on person-centred principles.

These require the trainer/facilitator:

- firstly, to be mindful that she or he is educating rather than schooling the adult learner
- secondly, not to get in the way of students' learning
- thirdly, to be the best facilitator she or he can be.

There is a clear distinction between education and schooling. For the educator it is the difference between educating the learner in the spirit of a freedom to learn, to practise, to enquire, to reflect, and so on, and schooling the student in a particular school of thought. Rogers (1951: 432) says that 'no student can or should be trained to become a client-centred therapist.' For Rogers (1951: 432–3), 'It is far more important that [the student] be true to his experience than that he should coincide with any known therapeutic orientation.' This was a radical statement 50 years ago, and stands as such today when the organization of training is predominantly along 'school' lines of theoretical orientation.

The point about not getting in the way of students' learning represents a principled non-directive attitude which follows from a trust in the learning human organism. As D.H. Lawrence put it, writing in 1918: 'How to begin to educate a child. First rule, leave him alone. Second rule, leave him alone. Third rule, leave him alone. That is the whole beginning.' Given the current UK government's lack of trust in pupils, students and teachers, and its highly interventionist policies on education, Lawrence's 'rules' are a topical reminder of the value of a non-directive approach to the education of children and adults.

There is a lot written in the person-centred literature about being a facilitator (see Rogers, 1969, 1978, 1983), a term mostly used in the context of facilitating groups and learning. Some of the characteristics of an effective facilitator are:

- an *attitude* of being genuinely free of a desire to control the outcome of a group or a course
- a *belief* in the capacity of the individual or group to deal with her, his or its own problems
- a *commitment* to the philosophical principles of the person-centred approach
- a *knowledge* of the philosophical and theoretical roots and framework of the approach
- the *skilled capacity* to maintain contact, congruence, positive regard and empathic understanding, and to help individuals within a group to express themselves.

With specific regard to education, the person-centred facilitator holds a number of considerations which, of course, may be shared, and are certainly observed by students:

- That s/he trusts the human organism and its tendency to actualize, in this context, in the service of individual and group learning. Rogers (1970/1973) and others (e.g. Wood, 1982) view the group as an organism. This makes a difference in terms of group-centred group process and decision making and, in person-centred training/learning groups, can involve a lot of discussion, negotiation – and frustration! This is something which students, new to the approach, often find strange and not a little disconcerting, but ultimately rewarding.
- That the freedom to learn is by no means a given. Most adult learners will have had some previous experience of education and for many, if not most, this has been at best traditional and hierarchical and, at worst, damaging and abusive. Much person-centred education involves helping students first to deconstruct their previous experiences in order to be open to different ways of learning and teaching. One effect of this is that groups in person-centred learning/training can spend some time in silence (and often more time than people are used to) – although this is not compulsory! Again, students may initially be a little disconcerted about this and angry with the facilitator. In working with silences in groups, I find Lynch's (1997) distinction between the 'silence of oppression' and the 'silence of the limits' (that is, the recognition that spoken language is inevitably limited) useful.
- That s/he makes and maintains contact with the students. Rogers (1969: 101) approvingly cites Buber as saying that: 'Contact is the primary word of education.'
- That, initially, s/he is primarily responsible for establishing the space for learning, including the geography of the classroom or learning environment, and for setting the mood of climate of the group.
- That, following this, the relationship between facilitator and student/s – and, for that matter, between fellow students – is the most important factor in the facilitation of learning (see Rogers, 1969, 1983; Aspy and Roebuck, 1988/2002; Barrett-Lennard, 1998).

- That, of all the qualities, attitudes or conditions, in the educational context, congruence or genuineness is the greatest or most important (see Rogers, 1969). In the context of training therapists I translate this as 'non-defensiveness'. A good trainer/facilitator is one who is open to 'co-seeking' students and to their ideas. Moreover, students can spot the trainer who is defending his or her position or simply, as some people put it, 'wearing my person-centred hat' (with the implication that she can take it off). Unfortunately, too many so-called person-centred training courses, especially those at an introductory level, are taught by trainers who are neither steeped in nor committed to person-centred principles, practice, theory or organization.
- That the facilitator is primarily facilitating learning, and often not 'teaching' or lecturing as such. Such facilitation may include: eliciting and clarifying the student's purpose and intention in training and learning; providing a range of resources for learning, which, in turn, may involve ascertaining different learning styles and needs in the learning group; being acceptant of differences, including different expressions; and being understanding of different internal frames of reference. Of course, there are times for the 'chalk and talk' or PowerPoint presentation of a lecture or seminar but, in terms of a person-centred training course, these are better coming out of the process when appropriate.
- That the facilitator, too, is 'living the uncertainty of discovery' and that to facilitate learning in this way requires her/him to be prepared to be prepared – and prepared to be surprised. In practical terms this means, as a facilitator, having more material 'up your sleeve' and being willing not to use it. This can cause the facilitator some anxiety both before and during the course, but often leads to students having a more personal and participative experience of learning than the more traditional and conservative approach to training and teaching.
- That the facilitator is also responsible for holding any curriculum or other external requirements in such a way that students can be aware of but not oppressed by them. Elsewhere, Rogers talks about wanting to free the client from the threat of external evaluation. However, whilst we may help people feel less threatened, it is unrealistic to think that we can remove all external evaluation, especially in the context of a professional training involving a number of stakeholders. The best the facilitator – and administrator – can do is to help students engage with the relevant external evaluations that are in the field. Through finding, giving and processing information about the requirements of external bodies, both trainers and students can take more personal power over decisions to meet such requirements – or not – and develop a critical, responsive and creative practice in all aspects of education and training.

In Hindu mythology, Lord Ganesha is the god of knowledge and is also called Vighneshwer, the god who removes obstacles. In this way, the best facilitator is one who not only actively facilitates but equally actively helps removes obstacles from the students' path, including, at times, her or himself. Discussing the role of the facilitator in 1983, Rogers cites the Chinese philosopher Lao-tse who says (I paraphrase) that the best leader is one where the people, in this case, students, barely know he exists and at the end say 'We did it'. Here Rogers is challenging the culture of narcissism and, specifically, the cult of the individual in the classroom or training institute, whereby students go away thinking that the teacher is marvellous, but having learnt little or nothing.

As is evident from the argument in this chapter, person-centred approaches to the education of therapists are challenging. One of the themes which emerges in response to this challenge is that of balancing, on the one hand, an acceptance of certain external conditions which have an impact on training, regarding, for instance, the validation of courses, and the accreditation and registration of therapists, with, on the other hand, the courage of our convictions to challenge, critique and change – and, as St Francis of Assisi puts it, the wisdom to know the difference.

REFERENCES

Aspy, N. and Roebuck, F.N. (2002). Carl Rogers' contribution to education. In D. Cain (ed.), *Classics in the Person-Centred Approach* (pp. 245–9). Llangarron: PCCS Books. (Original work published 1988.)

Barrett-Lennard, G.T. (1998). *Carl Rogers' Helping System: journey and substance*. London: Sage.

Blomfield, V. (1997). Practitioner development through self-direction: the South West London College counselling courses. In R. House and N. Totton (eds), *Implausible Professions: arguments for pluralism and autonomy in psychotherapy and counselling* (pp. 255–70). Llangarron: PCCS Books.

Combs, A.W. (2002). Is there a future for humanistic or person-centred education? In D. Cain (ed.), *Classics in the Person-Centred Approach* (pp. 255–9). Llangarron: PCCS Books. (Original work published 1988.)

Combs, A.W. (2002). Person-centred assumptions for counsellor education. In D. Cain (ed.), *Classics in the Person-Centred Approach* (pp. 269–75). Llangarron: PCCS Books. (Original work published 1986.)

Embleton Tudor, L., Keemar, K., Tudor, K., Valentine, J. and Worrall, M. (2004). *The Person-Centred Approach: a contemporary introduction*. Basingstoke: Palgrave MacMillan.

House, R. (1997). Participatory ethics in a self-generating practitioner community. In R. House and N. Totton (eds), *Implausible Professions: arguments for pluralism and autonomy in psychotherapy and counselling* (pp. 321–34). Llangarron: PCCS Books.

Keil, W.W. (1996). Training therapy in the client-centred approach. In R. Hutterer, G. Pawlowsky, P.F. Schmid and R. Stipsits (eds), *Client-Centred and Experiential Psychotherapy: a paradigm in motion* (pp. 413–25). Frankfurt-am-Main: Peter Lang.

Klug, B. (1977). *The Grading Game*. London: NUS Publications.

Lynch, G. (1997). Words and silence: counselling after Wittgenstein. *Counselling*, 8(2), 126–8.

Mearns, D. (1994). *Developing Person-Centred Counselling*. London: Sage.

Mearns, D. (1997). *Person-Centred Counselling Training*. London: Sage.

Natiello, P. (1998). A person-centred training programme. *Person-Centered Journal*, 5(1), 39–47.

Network of the European Associations for Person-Centred and Experiential Psychotherapy and Counselling (NEAPCEPC) (2001). *Principles for Person-Centred and Experiential Training and Further Training in Psychotherapy and Counselling*. Available online at www.pce-europe.org/ntraining.htm.

Rogers, C.R. (1951). *Client-Centred Therapy*. London: Constable.

Rogers, C.R. (1959). A theory of therapy, personality and interpersonal relationships, as developed in the client-centred framework. In S. Koch (ed.), *Psychology: a study of a science*. Volume 3. *Formulation of the Person and the Social Context* (pp. 184–256). New York: McGraw-Hill.

Rogers, C.R. (1969). *Freedom to Learn*. Columbus, Ohio: Charles E. Merrill.

Rogers, C.R. (1973). *Carl Rogers on Encounter Groups*. Harmondsworth: Penguin. (Original work published 1970.)

Rogers, C.R. (1978). *Carl Rogers on Personal Power*. London: Constable.

Rogers C.R. (1980). The world of tomorrow, and the person of tomorrow. In C.R. Rogers *A Way of Being* (pp. 339–56). Boston: Houghton Mifflin.

Rogers, C.R. (1983). *Freedom to Learn for the 80s*. Columbus, Ohio: Charles E. Merrill.

Rogers, C.R. and Freiberg, H.J. (1994). *Freedom to Learn* (3rd edn). New York: Merrill.

Rowan, J. (2005). *The Future of Training in Psychotherapy and Counselling*. London: Routledge.

Thomas, H.F. (2002). Keeping person-centred education alive in academic settings. In D. Cain (ed.), *Classics in the Person-Centred Approach* (pp. 260–8). Llangarron: PCCS Books. (Original work published 1988.)

Tudor, K. and Lewin, P. (2006). Fit for purpose: the organisation of psychotherapy training. *Self and Society*, 34(1), 33–40.

Tudor, K. and Worrall, M. (2004). Introduction. In K. Tudor and M. Worrall (eds), *Freedom to Practise: person-centred approaches to supervision* (pp.1–8). Llangarron: PCCS Books.

Tudor, K. and Worrall, M. (2006). *Person-Centred Therapy: a clinical philosophy*. London: Routledge.

Warner, M.S. (2000). Person-centred psychotherapy: one nation, many tribes. *The Person-Centered Journal*, 7(1), 28–39.

Wood, J.K. (1982). Person-centred group therapy. In G. Gazda (ed.), *Basic Approaches to Group Psychotherapy and Group Counseling*. Springfield, Il.: Charles Thomas.

Resources

Roelf J. Takens

This chapter can be dipped into and used as a source of information, and does not need to be read sequentially from beginning to end. Website addresses are given in the final part of this chapter.

National organizations

Around 200 national organizations and training centres around the world are dedicated to researching and applying the principles developed by Rogers and the person-centred approach (Kirschenbaum and Jourdan, 2005). Examples of some of the key national organizations listed by these authors are presented in Table R.1. The size of these organizations vary considerably, from a handful of members in the case of training institutes (e.g. PCA Institut Praha and PCAI-F in France) to several thousand in national associations directed at professional interests, like the GwG in Germany (more than 4000 members), BAPCA in Britain (over 1000 members) and the VCgP in the Netherlands (about 850 members). Noticeably, in the United States, the ADPCA counts only a few hundred members, pointing at a diminishing interest in the person-centred approach in that country over the past decades.

International cooperation

International cooperation between professionals and researchers is more common nowadays than ever before. However, in humanistic and person-centred circles, networking is not as intense as it seems to be in other orientations. This may be because of the emphasis on personal freedom and the

Table R.1 Examples of person-centred organizations around the world

Country	Organization	
Argentina	AEDECeP	Asociación para el estudio y desarrollo del Enfoque Centrado en la Persona
Austria	PCA	Person-Centered Association in Austria
Belgium	AFPC	Association Francophone de Psychothérapie Centrée-sur-la-Personne et Expérientielle
	VVCgP	Vlaamse Vereniging voor cliëntgerichte psychotherapie (Flemish-speaking society)
Brazil	CEP/RS	Cento de Estudos da Pessoa
Canada	CRAM	Centre de Relation d'Aide de Montréal
Czech Republic	PCA	Institut Praha
France	PCAI-F	Person-Centered Approach Institute
Germany	GwG	Gesellschaft für wissenschaftliche Gesprächspsychotherapie
Greece	PCA	Hellenic Association of Person-Centered Approach
Hungary	HAPCCPM	Hungarian Association for Person-Centered Psychotherapy and Mental Health
Italy	IACP	Istituto dell'Approccio Centrato sulla Persona
The Netherlands	VCgP	Vereniging voor Cliëntgerichte Psychotherapie
Portugal	APPCPC	Associação Portuguesa de Psicoterapia Centrada na Pessoa e de Counselling
Scotland	PCT	Person Centred Therapy
South Africa	APCASA	Association for the Person-Centered Approach South Africa
Switzerland	SGGT-SPCP	Swiss Association for Person-centered Psychotherapy and Counseling
United Kingdom	BAPCA	British Association for the Person-Centred Approach
United States	ADPCA	Association for the Development of the Person-Centered Approach

autonomy of the individual. It is known that Rogers, himself, hated bureaucracy and institutionalization. For instance, he showed great reluctance when he was asked to lend his name to associations like the Vereniging voor Rogeriaanse Therapie in the Netherlands (founded in 1962). He was worried that it would foster a personality cult and lead to rigidity with respect to further developments of the approach. Rogers' death in 1987 freed up a great deal of energy and initiative by person-centred theorists, researchers and practitioners around the world, making the person-centred approach more of a broad-based, international movement than it ever was during Rogers's lifetime (Kirschenbaum and Jourdan, 2005).

Networks

The most important international networks in the field of the person-centred approach are:

- The World Association for Person-Centred and Experiential Psychotherapy and Counseling (WAPCEPC)
- The European Network of Associations for Person-Centred and Experiential Psychotherapy and Counseling (NEAPCEPC)
- The Association for the Development of the Person-Centred Approach (ADPCA).

In the United States, the Center for Studies of the Person (CSP), co-founded by Rogers in 1968, is still functioning, gathering people from all over the world. However, the organization no longer holds the leading position that it had in the days of Rogers.

WAPCEPC

The World Association for Person-Centered and Experiential Psychotherapy and Counseling was founded in 1997 during the 4th International Conference on Client-Centered and Experiential Psychotherapy in Lisbon, Portugal. The statutes were confirmed at the next international conference in Chicago in 2000. Since that time, WAPCEPC has come to be seen as the most important umbrella organization, connecting person-centred therapists and counsellors worldwide. According to its statutes, the aim of the WAPCEPC is to provide a global forum for those professionals in science and practice who:

- have a commitment to the primary importance of the relationship between client and therapist in psychotherapy and counselling
- hold as central to the therapeutic endeavour the client's actualizing process and phenomenological world
- embody in their work those conditions and attitudes conducive to therapeutic movement first postulated by Carl Rogers
- have a commitment to an understanding of both clients and therapists as persons who are at the same time individuals and in relationship with others and their diverse environments and cultures
- have an openness to the development and elaboration of person-centred and experiential theory in light of current and future practice and research.

This forum function is realized in different ways:

- by publishing a journal (*Person-Centred and Experiential Psychotherapies*)
- by (co-)organizing international conferences (the first to be organized under the auspices of the WAPCPEC was the 6th International Conference on Client-Centered and Experiential Psychotherapy and Counseling at Egmond aan Zee, the Netherlands, in 2003; followed by conferences in Postdam, 2006, and Norwich, 2008)
- by supporting people in their joint efforts to conduct research in the field of person-centred/experiential psychotherapy (e.g. the Network for Research on Experiential Psychotherapies).

Members of WAPCPEC include individuals as well as organizations, such as institutes and associations.

In 2006 the association consisted of approximately 400 individual members and 20 organizational members.

NEAPCEPC

The history of the Network of the European Associations for Person-Centered Counseling and Psychotherapy (NEAPCEPC) goes further back than that of the WAPCEPC, to the year 1989. Then, representatives of national associations from a range of European countries met in Salzburg to talk about political issues and developments regarding their profession: the position of the person-centred approaches in their countries in particular. This round-table discussion was a continuance of the yearly meetings of the boards of the German-speaking countries (Austria, Germany and Switzerland). Locations of subsequent gatherings can be seen in Table R.2.

The NEAPCEPC network was officially founded in 1998. Its general purpose was to support client-centred/person-centred organizations throughout Europe and to ensure the presence of the approach on the European level. It adheres to the same principles as the WAPCEPC (see above). It also has liaisons with the European Association for Psychotherapy (EAP) and the European Association for Counselling (EAC).

According to its website (www.europsyche.org), the EAP represents 128 organizations (including 24 national umbrella associations and 17 European-wide associations for psychotherapy) from 41 European countries, representing more than 120,000 psychotherapists. Membership is also open to individual practitioners.

Table R.2 Location of European network gatherings

1990	Bonn
1991	Zürich
1992	Vienna
1993	Amsterdam
1994	Gmunden
1995	Aachen
1996	Zürich
1997	Kasterlee
1998	Luxemburg
1999	Athens
2000	Budapest
2001	Brussels
2002	Vienna
2003	Egmond aan Zee
2004	Dijon
2005	Lisbon
2006	Potsdam

Based on the 'Strasbourg Declaration on Psychotherapy of 1990', the EAP opts for high training standards for a scientifically based approach and stands for a free and independent practice of psychotherapy in Europe. In an attempt to establish mutual recognition and consistent conduct of psychotherapy in this part of the world, it has established a European Certificate for Psychotherapy (see further under Training and Certification). The EAP has also developed ethical guidelines for the protection of clients, which are mandatory for its members.

ADPCA

The Association for the Development of the Person-Centred Approach (ADPCA), founded in 1986 in Chicago, welcomes the participation of educators, therapists, psychologists, psychiatrists, nurses, social workers, health service providers, pastoral counsellors, organization development specialists and all people who are interested in the field of human relations and personal and interpersonal development. The association sponsors an annual conference, a distinctive feature of which is large community group meetings, and disseminates information about other person-centred activities and organizations throughout the world. It publishes a newsletter, a journal and an annual membership directory.

Journals and bibliographies

Since its inception in 2002, the journal of the WAPCEPC: *Person-Centred and Experiential Psychotherapies* (PCEP) has been the most important international journal. The mission of this peer-reviewed journal, which is published four times per year, is: to create dialogue among different parts of the person-centred and experiential tradition; to support, inform, and challenge fellow practitioners and theorists; to stimulate creativity; and to influence the broader professional, scientific and political context.

Since, 1994 the ADPCA has also published the *Person-Centred Review*. Currently, one volume of this journal is produced per year.

Finally, the international journal *PERSON*, founded in 1997 and published by the major associations of all German-speaking countries, serves as the academic journal for the German language.

Alongside these there exist some other international journals like *The Folio* (journal of the Focusing Institute) and the *International Pre-Therapy Review*, which are directed at more specific branches of the Person-Centred family.

National journals in the person-centred field with an international relevance include:

- *Person Centred Quarterly* (newsletter of the BAPCA)
- *Gesprächspsychotherapie und Personzentrierte Beratung*, journal of the GwG (Germany)
- *Tijdschrift Cliëntgerichte Psychotherapie* (journal of the Dutch and Flemish associations).

Bibliographies in the person-centred field are manifold. The two most well-known are those of Germain Lietaer (Leuven University), regularly published throughout the years 1970–2000; and the German and English language-oriented reviews by Peter F. Schmid (from 1940 to the present) (see Internet addresses below). Professor Schmid has also compiled complete reviews of Rogers' publications (*Person-Centred and Experiential Psychotherapies*, 4(3–4), 2005). See Internet addresses below for further listings in a range of languages.

Empirical research

Although research on person-centred and experiential therapies is flourishing again in all continents (see Chapter 24, this volume, and Elliott et al, 2004), not much international cooperation is going on. An exception to this is the International Project on the Effectiveness of Psychotherapy and Psychotherapy Training (IPEPPT). The goal of this international project is to improve psychotherapy and psychotherapy training in a broad range of theoretical approaches by encouraging systematic research in therapy training institutes and university-based training clinics. More specifically, it aims at constructing an agreed-upon common core protocol for evaluating therapy (training) outcome, utilizing practice-based research methods. Further, it aims to carry out an international collaborative study of therapy (training) outcome in training institutes and clinics. Although this international collaboration is not restricted to person-centred and experiential trainings, some of the initiators and leading figures of the project are from this orientation (including Robert Elliott from Scotland and Alberto Zucconi from Italy).

Robert Elliott is also one of the initiators of the Network for Research on Experiential Psychotherapies (NREP), a website devoted to the purpose of stimulating research on experiential/humanistic psychotherapies. It has been founded to provide an overview of the whole range of experiential therapy research, including research on:

- client-centred/person-centred therapy
- gestalt therapy
- focusing-oriented psychotherapy
- process-experiential psychotherapy
- psychodrama
- existential psychotherapy
- emotion-focused therapy
- expressive/arts therapies
- basic experiential/phenomenological research on particular problems of living (e.g. depression, trauma) which might help experiential therapists better understand their clients.

Students as well as experienced researchers can download instruments and protocols from the Network's website (www.experiential-researchers.org/index.html) and use them in dissertations and other studies.

Training and accreditation in European countries

With the unification of Europe, there is a desire to make university courses more comparable, compatible and exchangeable within the European countries. From this perspective, the NEAPCEPC has, already in 1990, formulated a statement on mutual recognition of (parts of) training of person-centred therapists by its members:

> In case of a change of residence, completed [training courses] or individual components of [training courses] in person-centred psychotherapy will be recognized reciprocally if:
> – the conditions for participation of the training as recognized by the association of the new country of residence are met and
> – the entire training or individual components of [training courses] are compatible with the training curriculum of the association in the new country.

The representatives of the boards of the associations further stated that: 'the conditions of participation, the structures, the components and the content of their training curricula of person-centred psychotherapy are compatible to a large extent.' A decade or so later, in 2001, a further step towards unification was set by agreeing upon common basic principles for person-centred and experiential training courses and further training in psychotherapy and counselling (see Box R.1). These principles meet the requirements of the EAP psychotherapy training conditions (see Box R.2) and underscore the 'Strasbourg declaration of 1999', which states that:

> In accordance with the aims of the World Health Organization (WHO), the non-discrimination accord valid within the framework of the European Union (EU) and intended for the European Economic Area (EEA), and the principle of freedom of movement of persons and services, the undersigned agree on the following points:
> – Psychotherapy is an independent scientific discipline, the practice of which represents an independent and free profession.
> – Training in psychotherapy takes place at an advanced, qualified and scientific level.
> – The multiplicity of psychotherapeutic methods is assured and guaranteed.
> – A full psychotherapeutic training covers theory, self-experience, and practice under supervision. Adequate knowledge of various psychotherapeutic processes is acquired.
> – Access to training is through various preliminary qualifications, in particular human and social sciences.

According to the EAP, on 11 February 2004, the European Parliament voted to implement the harmonization of the profession of psychotherapy across the European Union. This decision should enable psychotherapists in future to work with the national diploma in all European Union countries. The training will be based upon the guidelines of the European Certificate for Psychotherapy. As the NEAPCEPC has been approved by the EAP as a European-Wide Organization (EWO) and European-Wide Accrediting Organization (EWAO), membership of NEAPCEPC is an attractive option for organizations and institutes in the field of person-centred/experiential psychotherapy.

Box RI

Principles for person-centred and experiential training and further training in psychotherapy and counselling as formulated by the NEAPCPEC (2001)

- Person-centred/experiential training and further training in psychotherapy and counselling is understood as the facilitation of personalization, i.e. the development of the personality of the trainee, by a person-centred/experiential relationship and encounter between the trainers and the trainees aiming at the personal and professional abilities required to offer, establish, maintain and develop person-centred/experiential relationships with clients.
- It is an enterprise both orientated towards the process and experience as well as committed to a profound theoretical reflection of experiences.
- It consists of:
  - experience in self-development in different settings (e.g. training groups, personal development groups, group therapy or counselling, individual therapy or counselling, etc.)
  - dealing with the theoretical works of Carl Rogers and other person-centred and experiential theoreticians as well as the continuous development of the trainee's own theoretical stances
  - the concrete application of the conditions
  - supervised practice of person-centred/experiential relationships with clients.

Among other elements the theoretical learning consists of: anthropological, philosophical and ethical foundations, theory of personality and relationship development, both in general and regarding processes of different persons and groups in different situations, theory of psychopathology and therapy, contextual (legal, medical, economic, etc.) necessary knowledge.

- It is carried out in relationships with different facilitators/psychotherapists/counsellors/teachers and in various settings in order to profit from diverse learning possibilities, to foster creativity and to acknowledge personal and cultural diversity.
- It is committed to a self-guided way of learning on the basis of empowerment and the 'freedom to learn' as postulated by Carl Rogers and to self-evaluation while meeting the requirements within the respective given legal and institutional frames.

Institutions and persons providing training are committed to clearly defined ethical standards, a continuous scientific development of theory and practice of the person-centred/experiential approaches, to scientific research and to working together with similar institutions and persons on national and international levels.

Box R2

EAP psychotherapy training conditions

1. The total duration of the training will not be less than 3200 hours, spread over a minimum of seven years, with the first three years being the equivalent of a university degree. The later four years must be in a training specific to psychotherapy.
2. The training includes the following elements:
2.1. Personal Psychotherapeutic Experience, or equivalent. This should be taken to include training analysis, self-experience, and other methods involving elements of self-reflection, therapy, and personal experience (not less than 250 hours). No single term is agreed by all psychotherapy methods. Any training shall include arrangements to ensure that the trainees can identify and appropriately manage their involvement in and contributions to the processes of the psychotherapies that they practice in accordance with their specific methods.
2.2. Theoretical Study. There will be a general component of university or professional training and a component which is specific to psychotherapy. University or professional courses leading to a first university degree or its equivalent professional qualification in subjects relevant to psychotherapy may be allowed as a part of, or the whole of, the general part of psychotherapy theory, but cannot contribute towards the four years of specific psychotherapy training. Theoretical study during the four years of training specific to psychotherapy should include the following elements:
    - theories of human development throughout the life-cycle
    - an understanding of other psychotherapeutic approaches
    - a theory of change
    - an understanding of social and cultural issues in relation to psychotherapy
    - theories of psychopathology
    - theories of assessment and intervention.
3. Practical Training. This will include sufficient practice under continuous supervision appropriate to the psychotherapeutic modality and will be at least two years in duration.
4. Placement in a mental health setting, or equivalent professional experience. The placement must provide adequate experience of psychosocial crisis and of collaboration with other specialists in the mental health field.

Internet addresses

National organizations

For an almost complete and up to date listing of organizations, see: www.pca-online.net.

International organizations and networks

- World Association for Person-Centered and Experiential Psychotherapy and Counseling (WAPCEPC): www.pce-world.org.
- European Network of Associations for Person-Centered and Experiential Psychotherapy and Counseling (NEAPCEPC): www.pce-europe.org.
- Association for the Development of the Person Centered Approach (ADPCA): www.adpca.org.
- Center for Studies of the Person (CSP): www.centerfortheperson.org.
- Center for the Study of Experiential Psychotherapy (CSEP, Toledo, USA): www.experiential-researchers.org/methodology/csepsumm.html.
- Emotion-focused therapy: www.emotionfocusedtherapy.org (York University, Toronto, Canada).
- The Focusing Institute (New York, USA): www.focusing.org.
- Pre-Therapy International Network: www.pretherapy.com.
- Network for Research on Experiential Psychotherapies (NREP): www.experiential-researchers.org/index.html.
- International Project on the Effectiveness of Psychotherapy and Psychotherapy Training (IPEPPT): ww.communityzero.com/openforum.

Publications

The PCA-online website (www.pca-online.net) gives an extensive overview of all national and international journals, newsletters and bibliographies.

Bibliographies

- The Carl Rogers Bibliography Online (by Peter F. Schmid): www.pca-online.net/rogers.htm.
- The Carl Rogers Collection/Archive (University of California at Santa Barbara): www.oac.cdlib.org/dynaweb/ead/ucsb/rogers.
- Primary Bibliography of Eugene T. Gendlin (by Frans Depestele): www.focusing.org/bibliography.html.
- The Person-Centered and Experiential Bibliography Online (by Peter F. Schmid): www.pca-online.net/pce-bibliography.htm.
- Client-Centered/Experiential Psychotherapy and Counseling Bibliographical Survey (until 2000) (by Germain Lietaer): www.pce-world.org/biblios.htm#lietaer (See also: http://www.pce-world.org/idxbiblios.htm).

Journals

- *Person Centered and Experiential Psychotherapies* (WAPCEPC): www.pce-world.org/idxjournal.htm.
- *The Person-Centered Journal* (ADPCA): www.adpca.org/Journal/journalindex.htm.
- *PERSON* (German): www.personzentriert.at.
- *The Folio* (Focusing Institute): http://www.focusing.org/folio.html.
- *International Pre-Therapy Review*: www.pretherapy.com.
- *Person Centred Practice* (BAPCA): http://www.bapca.org.uk.
- *Gesprächspsychotherapie und Personzentrierte Beratung* (GwG) (German): www.gwg-ev.org/verlag/#GwG-Zeitschrift.
- *Tijdschrift Cliëntgerichte Psychotherapie* (VCgP and VVCgP) (Dutch): www.vcgp.nl/tijdschrift.html.

Listings of publications in ...

- English (by Paul Wilkins): www.pce-world.org/biblioenglfrom2000.doc.
- German and English (by Peter F. Schmid): www.pfs-online.at/pce-bibliography.htm.
- Dutch (by Roelf J. Takens): www.vcgp.nl/mainindex.php?page=01publications_intro
- French (by Jean Marc Priels): www.pce-world.org/bibliofranfrom2000.doc
- Spanish and Portugese (by Alberto Segrara): under construction
- Italian (by Valeria Vaccari): www.pce-world.org/biblioitalfrom2000.doc

REFERENCES

Elliott, R., Greenberg, L.S., and Lietaer, G. (2004). Research on experiential therapies. In M.J. Lambert (ed.), *Bergin and Garfield's Handbook of Psychotherapy and Behavior Change* (5th edn) (pp. 493–539). Chicago: John Wiley.

Kirschenbaum, H., and Jourdan, A. (2005). The current status of Carl Rogers and the person-centred approach. *Psychotherapy: Theory, Research, Practice, Training*, 42(1), 37–51.

Index of Persons

Note: this index details all persons mentioned in the text, except names cited only in references or in lists of sources. While most entries are exhaustive, that for Carl Rogers is necessarily selective. Chapters by contributors are not specifically listed, although notes on contributors are indexed when (and only when) the individual is otherwise referred to in the text. Co-authors of works discussed are indexed even when not named in the text.

A
Aker, Dee, 316
Allen, Frederick, 21
Anderson, Svend, 319
Angyal, A., 70
Aquinas, Thomas, 35
Aristotle, 32
Aspy, N., 383, 385
Auckenthaler, A., 370
Augustine, St, 35
Aykroyd, M., 149

B
Baldwin, M., 172
Baljon, M., 369
Barfield, Gay Leah, xiv, 316
Barrett-Lennard, Godfrey T., xiv, 33, 34, 40, 56, 112, 359, 368, 385
  Carl Rogers' Helping System (1998), 23, 26, 78
  developmental issues, 85, 87, 87
  student of Rogers, 27

Barrineau, P., 334
Bateson, G., 33
Beck, A. T., 198, 332
Beebe, J. III, 58
Bergin, A. E., 58
Best, K. M., 59
Biermann-Ratjen, E.-M., 33, 83–4, 158
Binder, J., 33
Binder, U., 33
Blindel, J., 251
Boëthius, 34
Bohart, Arthur C., xiv, 32, 41, 53, 58, 59, 71
Bohm, David, 98
Bond, T., 355, 358–9
Bowen, 32
Bown, Oliver, 183
Bozarth, Jerold D., xiv–xv, 32, 111–12, 175, 184–5, 197, 198, 334
  recollections of client, 187–8
Brodley, Barbara T., 32, 74, 111–12, 176, 186, 199, 255
Brunswick, L., 242
Bryant-Jeffries, Richard, 157, 161
Buber, Martin, 32, 33, 36, 37, 38, 40, 112, 196, 287, 348, 386
Bugental, James, 31
Butler, John, 163

C
Cain, D. J., 134–5
Cameron, Rose, 144, 147, 148, 149
Capacchione, Lucia, 317
Caplan, G., 294, 302
Carkhuff, R. R., 195, 287

Subject index